Ireland

Ireland has rarely been out of the news during the past thirty years. Whether as a war zone in which Catholic nationalists and Protestant Unionists struggled for supremacy, a case study in conflict resolution or an economy that for a time promised to make the Irish among the wealthiest people on the planet, the two Irelands have truly captured the world's imagination. Yet single-volume histories of Ireland are rare. Here, Thomas Bartlett, one of the country's leading historians, sets out a fascinating new history that ranges from prehistory to the present. Integrating politics, society and culture, he offers an authoritative historical road map that shows exactly how – and why – Ireland, north and south, arrived at where it is today. This is an indispensable guide both to the legacies of the past for Ireland's present and to the problems confronting north and south in the contemporary world.

THOMAS BARTLETT is Professor of Irish History at the School of Divinity, History and Philosophy, University of Aberdeen. His previous publications include *The Fall and Rise of the Irish Nation: the Catholic Question, 1690–1830* (1992), *A Military History of Ireland* (1996, with Keith Jeffery) and *Revolutionary Dublin: the Letters of Francis Higgins to Dublin Castle, 1795–1801* (2004).

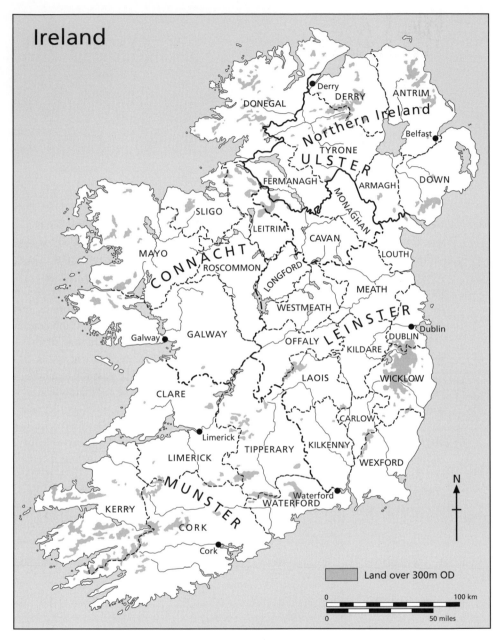

Map 1 Map of Ireland, showing major towns and political divisions

IRELAND

A History

THOMAS BARTLETT

Professor of Irish History,
University of Aberdeen

 CAMBRIDGE
UNIVERSITY PRESS

CAMBRIDGE UNIVERSITY PRESS
Cambridge, New York, Melbourne, Madrid, Cape Town, Singapore,
São Paulo, Delhi, Dubai, Tokyo, Mexico City

Cambridge University Press
The Edinburgh Building, Cambridge CB2 8RU, UK

Published in the United States of America by Cambridge University Press, New York

www.cambridge.org
Information on this title: www.cambridge.org/9780521197205

First published 2010
Reprinted 2010

Printed in the United Kingdom at the University Press, Cambridge

A catalogue record for this publication is available from the British Library

Library of Congress Cataloguing in Publication data
Bartlett, Thomas.
Ireland : a history / Thomas Bartlett.
   p.   cm.
Includes bibliographical references and index.
ISBN 978-0-521-19720-5 (hbk.)
1. Ireland – History.   I. Title.
DA910.B375   2010
941.7 – dc22   2010006631

ISBN 978-0-521-19720-5 Hardback

CONTENTS

MAPS

ILLUSTRATIONS

PREFACE

This book has been long in the writing and I have incurred many debts and obligations along the way. Technically I began work on it in 2002 when I was Parnell Fellow in Irish Studies at Magdalene College, Cambridge. I continued with it when back in University College Dublin, brought it with me to the University of Aberdeen and put the finishing touches to it at Boston College where I am Burns Library Fellow in Irish Studies, 2009–10. However, the book has been in gestation for much longer than these years and while it would be rash to claim that I have been thinking about writing a history of Ireland for my entire academic career, it would not be entirely fanciful.

I began the serious study of Irish history when I was at school in Belfast – St Mary's Christian Brothers' School on the Falls Road – in the early 1960s, where I was fortunate to be taught by Frank Thompson, who encouraged me to read widely. His encouragement would have been pointless without the existence nearby of a great Belfast institution – the Central Library, with its specialist Irish collections. I was indulged by a number of reference librarians who saw no problem in allowing a schoolboy to borrow some books for a few days. Later at Queen's University I was taught by a remarkably talented group of historians – Michael Roberts, J. C. Beckett and Peter Jupp were particularly influential and indeed Jupp was to supervise my doctoral thesis. After Queen's I spent a year at the University of Michigan, Ann Arbor, where I was entrusted to the leading American colonial historian John W. Shy, who not only taught me colonial history but also impressed me with the need to pay attention to style in communicating ideas. I also benefited from a period spent school-teaching at the Royal Belfast Academical Institution in the mid-1970s, where I learned – the hard way – how to teach. At University College Galway, where I achieved my first university position, then at University College Dublin and latterly at the University of Aberdeen, I have been lucky enough to encounter gifted historians who were happy to share ideas and discuss issues (and to gossip). At Galway I have to mention particularly Nicholas Canny (who read and commented on sections of this book),

Daibhí Ó Cróinín (likewise), Gearóid Ó Tuathaigh, Caitriona Clear, Steven Ellis and Niall Ó Ciosáin. At University College Dublin I learned much from my colleagues in Irish history – notably Tadhg Ó hAnnracháin, Michael Laffan and Tim O'Neill – and from colleagues outside the Irish history department – Ronan Fanning, Michael Staunton, Tom Garvin and Cormac Ó Gráda. A special debt is due to Michael Laffan for his good humour in reading and commenting on successive chapters of this book. At the University of Aberdeen my colleagues Alistair MacDonald and Andrew MacKillop reminded me of the importance of the Scottish dimension in Irish history.

It will be seen that my formation as a historian has taken place in a variety of institutions, in a number of countries and during what has been a remarkable, even tumultuous forty years in Irish history. This book bears the marks of this scholarly journey, and those mentioned above helped shape it in ways that they might not recognise or possibly approve. For all that, the book remains my sole responsibility; in so far as it has merit, then that should go to those scholars whose work I have relied on and to those who have lent me scholarly support over the decades.

I owe a special debt of gratitude to a number of individuals and institutions. At Cambridge, Eamon Duffy encouraged me to take on the book; at Trinity College Dublin, Jane Ohlmeyer and Mícheal Ó Siochrú discussed with me the 1641 rebellion, and Frank Barry guided me through the literature on the Celtic Tiger. The University of Aberdeen helped defray the cost of the illustrations, and Dáire Keogh, St Patrick's College, and Kevin Whelan, Notre Dame University, advised on them. Matthew Stout drew the maps. Christopher J. Woods read and commented on the nineteenth-century sections as did Professor Alvin Jackson of the University of Edinburgh. For their assistance with illustrations, my thanks to the staff of the Irish Photographic Archive, to Siobhan Fitzpatrick, Royal Irish Academy, to Trevor Parkhill and Michelle Ashmore, Ulster Museum, to Lar Joye, Michael Kenny and Finbarr Connolly, National Museum of Ireland and to Mary Broderick at the National Library of Ireland. My publishers at Cambridge University Press – Michael Watson and Helen Waterhouse – have shown great patience with me, for which many thanks.

My thanks to my family, and especially to Rebecca, for putting up with me while this book was written. This book is for my grandson, Roc Bartlett McDonnell (b. 2008), in the hope that his Ireland will be both peaceful and prosperous.

1 EARLY IRELAND, AD 431–1169

Origins

May I begin in the year AD 431? It is the first authentic date in Irish history and provides a reassuringly firm vantage point from which to survey the next sixteen hundred years or so. Ireland, and Irish history, are of course much older than that. The oldest rock in Ireland – Inishtrahull, off the north coast of county Donegal – is reckoned by geologists to be some 17,000 million years old and archaeologists tell us that Ireland was first inhabited some 10,000 years ago – very recent in European terms; but for some 8,000 of those years we know next to nothing. True, the inhabitants of the island during those eight millennia (we may call them for convenience the pre-Celts) did leave behind them elaborately designed and precisely calibrated passage-tombs, some decorated with spirals and whorls, such as those at Newgrange, Knowth and Dowth, which command the bend of the River Boyne; but of the builders of these architectural treasures – their hopes, their desires, their religion, their language and their society – we know little, and can only wonder. At Newgrange the tomb, built *c.* 3,800 BC, is the oldest known astronomically designed structure in the world; the rifle-shot of sunlight that penetrates deep into the burial chamber during the winter solstice (21 December) has proved particularly fruitful in setting the imagination racing.

That we know little of these early inhabitants of Ireland has by no means prevented the creation or fabrication of origin legends, which, over the centuries, have sought to give historic legitimacy to contemporary institutions and to validate contemporary political stances. A manuscript *History of Ireland* compiled in *c.* 1819, but based on seventeenth-century compositions (which in their turn borrowed from the twelfth-century compilation, *The Book of Invasions*, the core of which can be dated to the seventh century), states baldly, 'The first [inhabitants] that landed upon this island were three Spanish fishermen drove upon the coast by a storm'. Happily, after some discussion of how the wives and families of Capa, Laighne and Luasat arrived, the anonymous scribe had a moment of doubt and confessed: 'Note, this landing of the fishermen is deemed fabulous'.

Fable or not, the legend of a Spanish origin, and the story of successive waves of invaders each of whom were assimilated to the 'native' stock, proved enduring. The Irish admiration for the writings of the seventh-century Isodore of Seville was one benign aspect of this; but in the late sixteenth century, when Hugh O'Neill, the Gaelic chief then in revolt against English rule, was soliciting Spanish military aid, he made much of a shared ancestry between the Irish and the Spanish, boasting that a thousand years before the birth of Christ 'a king called Milesius sent his sons with a fleet of sixty ships which sailed from the port of La Corunna to conquer and populate Ireland'. In the 1930s those (on both sides) in favour of Irish intervention in the Spanish Civil War cited the legend of *Míl Espáinne*, or common Milesian ancestry, in their favour.[1] Similarly, by 1800 the notion of Gaelic antiquity had been appropriated by various contending groups on the island who sought to nail their contemporary anxieties by anchoring themselves to a prehistoric past and a splendid pre-Christian civilisation. Nor by that time had the legends of invasions and of *Míl* run their course, for in the nineteenth century older notions of race and romance were added to the cocktail of national identity to produce the stereotype of the feckless, fun-loving, if improvident, Celt, a standing rebuke to the equally stereotypical, hard-headed, sober and dull Saxon.

The archaeological and historical evidence for pre-Christian Ireland unfortunately does not enable us confidently to discern fable from fact. It seems that around 700 BC the *Keltoi* or Celts, migrating or, very probably, fleeing from northern Europe in the face of Roman and Germanic expansion, moved into Ireland, and by the first century AD their language and culture had been firmly established; but quite how, and precisely when, all this was done remains a mystery. It cannot be emphasised strongly enough that there are no archaeological findings to support the later literature of full-scale invasions and pitched battles; and in the absence of these most modern scholars have inclined towards a more benign, assimilative and absorptive contact between the Celtic newcomers and the neolithic natives. And yet it seems perverse to dismiss entirely the view that the incoming Gaels – the last of the Celtic peoples to arrive – treated the existing population any differently from other invaders in other lands, or indeed at other times. That they were a small but powerful band of warriors, early *conquistadores*, seems incontrovertible, for there is no evidence of large-scale settlement. The discovered material remains of the Celts in Ireland would hardly fill a wheelbarrow and, significantly, most of what the archaeologists have found has to do with weaponry. The likely scenario is that the invading Celts killed some of those who opposed them, dispossessed others and exacted tribute from the rest. Minority or not, by the first century AD the Gaels, their language, laws and culture were supreme, and their royal forts at Tara, Eamhain Macha and Dún Ailinne (and others likewise probably taken over from their predecessors) bore testimony to their power, if not to their unity, for rivalry, division and disputed successions were endemic among their numerous kings. But to return to 431 . . .

Palladius and Patrick

In the contemporary *Chronicle* of Prosper of Aquitaine under the year 431 we read: 'To the Irish believing in Christ, Palladius having been ordained by Pope Celestine, is sent as first bishop' (*Ad Scottos in Christum credentes a papa Caelestino Palladius primus episcopus mittitur*). Prosper has an earlier reference to Palladius in 429 which shows him as an enemy of the Pelagian heresy. Unfortunately that is the extent of the historical record concerning Palladius and Ireland. The later Irish annals make no mention of him and, apart from the two one-line entries in Prosper's *Chronicle*, we are entirely in the dark concerning what Palladius did or where he went in Ireland (or indeed if he ever went there). Admittedly a much later source does cite a tradition that Palladius was martyred by the Irish soon after his arrival, but this is unreliable by virtue of its distance from the period and in any case very unlikely, for the early Irish church was so entirely bereft of martyrs that one so illustrious would surely have attracted many notices. None the less the mention of Palladius' mission is of the greatest significance for it reveals clearly that there were Christians in Ireland in 431; that they were sufficiently numerous to warrant a bishop; and finally that Palladius was to be the first.[2]

These early Christians in Ireland, it has been surmised, may have come from Britain as migrants, or as prisoners captured on raids, and the earlier reference to Palladius and heresy may indicate that he was dispatched to Ireland because of concerns that heresy was gaining a hold among the small number of Christians there. But it was not Palladius who was to become the 'Apostle of Ireland', but a Briton, Patrick, who, according to a seventh-century source, arrived in Ireland in 432 AD, suspiciously close to the date of Palladius' mission. The coincidence of the two dates – 431 for Palladius and reputedly 432 for Patrick, and perhaps also the approximation of the two names (Palladius/Patricius) – led to confusion between the two men, argument as to the order in which they arrived in Ireland and even conjecture about the existence of two or more Patricks. Given Patrick's modern status as the patron saint of the Irish, and icon of Ireland, this latter speculation, when published in the 1940s, was denounced as something akin to national sabotage. And yet the blame for this unsatisfactory state of affairs lies not with the historians but with Patrick's hagiographers from the seventh century and later, who were so determined to inflate Patrick's reputation, airbrush from the record any rivals and boost Armagh's claims to precedence in the Irish church, that they excised all mention of Palladius from the record and sought to have only 'Holy Patrick, our Papa' as the sole instrument of conversion. In fairness Patrick himself may have colluded in the spin, for in his writings, two unique documents incontestably by him, he too makes no mention of Palladius. And yet while Patrick's *Confessio* and his *Letter against the soldiers of Coroticus* ignore his presumed predecessor, they do tell us something about Patrick and much about fifth-century Ireland.[3]

The context within which the *Confessio* was written, possibly in the late 470s, need not detain us. Patrick was apparently betrayed by a close friend, who had revealed some 'sin' that Patrick had committed in his youth, and which possibly called into question his fitness as a bishop. In his defence Patrick composed a *Confessio* or declaration. In this document he divulges a few details of his own history: he gives his name, his father's name (Calpurnius) and his grandfather's name (Potitus). He tells us that his father was a minor Roman official who had a small estate, and that he, Patrick, was brought up in relatively comfortable circumstances – the family had servants – near Bannaven Taberniae, possibly present-day Carlisle on the Anglo-Scottish border. On this estate Patrick, along with many others, was seized by Irish raiders, and carried back with them into slavery. After six years working as a shepherd 'beside the western sea', during which time his faith in Christ was strengthened, Patrick managed to escape back to Britain on board a ship. However, after some years in his parents' home he received a vision in which he was begged to return to Ireland to preach the gospel there, which he duly did. There he baptised 'many thousands of people', with the result that

> it came about in Ireland that people who had no acquaintance with God, but who up to now always had cults or idols and abominations, are recently – by this dispensation – made a people of the lord, and are known as children of God. Sons of the *Scotti* [=Irish raiders] and daughters of the chiefs are openly monks and virgins of Christ.

These details are infuriatingly vague. Beginning the well-known Irish tradition of 'whatever-you-say-say-nothing', Patrick notoriously gives no date for any of his adventures; he omits the names of all of those who were enslaved with him; he says nothing about the people he met, or who helped him escape; and out of all the places that he visited, travelled to or was confined in, he names only two – neither of which has been satisfactorily identified. In exasperation one Irish historian has exclaimed that 'Patrick could hardly have told us less if he had not bothered to write at all'.[4] Nor is the second document by Patrick any more revealing. His blistering *Letter against the soldiers of Coroticus* was prompted by their 'unspeakably horrible crime', an attack on newly baptised Christians, some of whom they slew, others hauled off into slavery and – for the women – into whoredom ('they have distributed young Christian girls as prizes'). Patrick understandably excoriates Coroticus' thugs as 'allies of the *Scotti* and the apostate Picts . . . bloodthirsty men embrued in the blood of innocent Christians', but as before, he gives no details about the date or location of the outrage. While Coroticus might have been the first (though assuredly not the last) recorded British commander whose soldiers massacred people in Ireland, he remains a shadowy figure and his identity is unclear. He has tentatively been linked with a British king of Dumbarton of the same name, but it is by no means certain that they are one and the same. And yet, for all their vagueness and imprecision these documents – incontestably composed by Patrick in the fifth century – shed light on the Ireland to which he was dragged as a slave and to which he returned as a missionary.

St Patrick's Ireland

We may begin with the prevalence of slavery. Patrick's fate was clearly not uncommon. As the Roman empire in Britain began to crumble in the early decades of the fifth century, attacks by *Scotti* became more daring and more devastating – Patrick tells us that many thousands were seized along with himself. Historians have suggested that Patrick used the term 'thousands' simply to signify 'many'; but his Latin was precise, even if his dates and place names were not. He may well have meant that thousands were in fact seized and it may be that these captives were the main way in which Christianity came to Ireland, for it is clear that Palladius and, initially, Patrick set out to minister to existing Christian communities. Equally, these captives may suggest how Roman influence spread in Ireland. Famously, no Roman legionnaire ever set foot in Ireland, and in later centuries the fact that Ireland had lain outside the Roman empire was held to explain irremediable Irish barbarism. However, with the collapse of Roman rule in Britain in the early 400s, of which the increasingly daring raids of the *Scotti*, and the proliferation of Irish settlements in what is now Wales were both cause and symptom, a process which may be called the romanisation of Irish culture began. Not the least of the many ironies in the history of Ireland is that 'Rome', its language, literature and its religion, came to Ireland in the period when Rome itself was succumbing to the barbarian onslaught.

From Patrick's writings we also learn that he worked as a shepherd in the far west and this highlights the obvious point that fifth-century Ireland was a wholly rural society in which cattle and sheep-rearing were all important. In later centuries land would be the key indicator of a person's social and political standing and authority; but in Patrick's time, livestock counted for everything; many of the Irish law tracts that survive (admittedly, dating from the late sixth century) have to do with livestock. However, dead stock too were valuable: Patrick tells us that, on his escape from captivity, he and the sailors killed some pigs and ate their flesh. Again, the fact that forests figure prominently in Patrick's narratives indicates just how much of Ireland was wooded at that time; but from archaeological evidence, it is clear that arable farming was also practised – wheat and oats were planted, and barley and flax too. Bee-keeping would have been carried on during Patrick's time, though he makes no mention of it. Patrick also writes that he escaped on board a ship and this detail reveals the nexus of trading, settling and preying that connected the sister islands of Ireland and Britain.

Patrick's writings also shed some light on the position of women in early Ireland. In his *Confessio* he tells us that 'there was a certain blessed noblewoman, of Scottic [=Irish] origin, mature and beautiful whom I baptised', and who had been commanded by an angel of God to be a 'virgin of Christ'. And in his *Letter against Coroticus* he writes that he could not count the number of 'daughters of chiefs' who had done likewise and become nuns. He also reveals that, on occasion, these 'religious women . . . would spontaneously offer me gifts or throw some of their personal ornaments on the altar', but that he declined, for fear of scandal, to accept them. Again, he claimed that he had baptised slave women, and he admitted that both sets of women, the well-born and the slaves, had to withstand 'harassment and false accusations' and 'continual fears and threats' from their parents and masters in order to draw nearer to the Lord.

These are significant details. Early Irish heroic literature may be full of warrior women, such as Queen Medb, powerful and sexually voracious, but the reality was rather different. In the early Irish law tracts women were defined as 'legally incompetent, senseless' and on a par with slaves, children and the insane. However, this bleak assessment is not entirely borne out by the individual laws that have come down to us. Women, especially propertied women, and widows had certain protections; and in the matter of marriage and divorce, Irish women were probably 'ahead' of their sisters in continental Europe. For example, the Irish law tracts set out nine types of sexual union, with the first type ('union of joint property') down to the sixth and seventh types (union through willing abduction) being allowed, but with the eighth (union through rape) and the ninth (union between two insane persons) being forbidden. The matter was further complicated by the widespread practice among the very well-to-do of polygamy, in which the concubine was apparently valued less – in the eyes of the law – than the 'chief wife'. Divorce too was common, though while a man had any number of reasons to divorce his wife (among them infertility, abortion, infidelity, child-killing or even for being a slattern about the house), the wife had relatively few, among them if her husband were impotent, homosexual, violent or was given to blabbing about what happened 'under the blankets'. In such cases the divorced woman might receive compensation and might have her 'bride price' returned. We may compare this with the situation under Burgundian law where a woman attempting divorce was to be drowned in a cesspit. And, as noted, Irish women were free to dispose of their own jewellery as they saw fit – something which, notwithstanding Patrick's doubts, the church was quick to welcome. Significantly, Patrick encouraged his female converts, his virgins of Christ, to flout social conventions and it might be argued that in doing so he was very daring, even quietly revolutionary.

Lastly, in an aside, Patrick discloses that when he sought to flee Ireland on the ship, he entered into terms with the sailors, but that he 'refused, for fear of God, to suck their nipples'. This startling remark – given matter of factly – has been a cause of some embarrassment to Patrician enthusiasts, but it has to be seen in the context of Patrick's detestation of 'cults or idols and abominations' which he had dedicated his life to overthrowing. What Patrick was doing was pointing to the prevalence of pagan practices – sucking nipples was a way to pledge loyalty – and in doing so he was making the obvious point that the Ireland in which he had been a slave was largely pagan.

Like so much else, the nature of Irish paganism remains obscure. None of the pagan teaching was committed to writing, and the first Christian writers were so determined to obliterate all record of pre-Christian beliefs and practices that they deliberately drew a veil over them and, with a shudder of revulsion, moved on. Modern scholars have resisted too precise a definition of pagan beliefs on the grounds that since pagans evidently drew little distinction between what might be called the supernatural and the natural, nor should we. From Patrick's writings we learn that sun-worship was a central tenet of the pagans among whom he ministered, though given the Irish climate, devotion must have been sporadic rather than constant. Undoubtedly some woods, rivers and wells held sacred significance too. Later traditions have Patrick doing battle with a priestly caste of druids, and it is likely that the *filid* or poets, and brehons or judges, also exercised priestly powers. What is clear is that Christianity in Ireland, as elsewhere in continental Europe, adopted and adapted pagan practices and heathen ceremonies to its own purposes. Thus 'patterns' (festivals held in honour of a local saint), *turasanna* (local pilgrimages) and the great harvest festival of

Lughnasa (1 August), still celebrated to an extent in Ireland, all probably trace their origins to pagan practices.

Consider the history of Tara, county Meath.[5] For a thousand years before Patrick, Tara had been a vital pagan site (their Babylon, according to one seventh-century writer) in which kings had been inaugurated following the Feast of Tara or *Feis Temro*, a primitive fertility rite. Tara was also the royal fortress in which Patrick had overcome, according to later tradition, the heathen high-king, Lóegaire mac Néill (their 'Nabuchodonosor') and his druids (but note that Patrick in his writings does not mention Tara). Notwithstanding these powerful pagan associations (indeed, because of them) in later centuries the site was colonised for Christianity and synods of bishops were held there; and it was also the power-centre of the Ó Néill dynasty, sometimes described as high-kings of Tara, until the early middle ages. The potent resonances of this pagan place persisted: archaeological evidence suggests that in the year 800 Tara was little more than 'a series of undulations in the grass', but a thousand years later the Meath rebels of 1798 used it as a rallying and assembly point; and in 1843 Daniel O'Connell, the Liberator, was canny enough to stage one of his 'monster meetings' on its slopes. In 1850 the discovery of the 'Tara' brooch – a bronze clasp overlaid with gold, amber and glass (figure 1.1) – served to anoint the site as the *fons et origo* of Celtic art and design, and the brooch itself quickly joined the harp, the colour green and the shamrock as emblems of essential and authentic Irish identity.

The find confirmed Tara's pre-eminence as a place sacred to the Irish, and belonging to them alone; threats from outsiders were seen off in a robust fashion. In 1902 a group of British Israelites, believing that the Ark of the Covenant lay under Tara, to the fury of the Irish started illegal excavations at the site. This 'desecration' was speedily ended through pressure from an unlikely alliance of W. B. Yeats, Arthur Griffith, Douglas Hyde and George Moore.[6] Similarly, when in 1915 Ishbel, Lady Aberdeen, the then viceroy's wife and a headlong enthusiast for all things Irish, sought to have Tara added to her title, she faced popular clamour at her temerity. Mere enthusiasm for things Irish emphatically did not bring membership of the 'Celtic' race. The tactless Lady Aberdeen and her husband had no option but to compromise, and instead they made do with Aberdeen and Temair, the latter word an approximation of the Gaelic version of Tara, and thus curiously less open to objection. In 2008, a battle royal raged over a proposed motorway route which threatened to wreck the integrity of the Tara site.[7]

During her time at Dublin Castle, Lady Ishbel Aberdeen had involved herself in various projects to help the Irish poor and she promoted the products of Irish cottage industries, particularly Irish lace. She also hosted many Irish nights at

1.1 Tara brooch. Probably made in the eighth century and found on a beach near Drogheda in 1850, the Tara brooch, along with the Ardagh chalice, also eighth century, was highly prized by cultural revivalists in late nineteenth-century Ireland as proof of early Ireland's superiority in material civilisation. National Museum of Ireland.

the castle, most notably perhaps a St Patrick's night ball on the eve of the Great War, when guests danced Irish jigs and were then given a special treat – songs in Irish 'heard in the Castle for the first time'. Just as the memory, the mystery and the romance of pagan and royal Tara had survived long after Tara itself was 'in grass', so too had the fugitive, though real, Patrick of history been transformed by the laying on of legends over the centuries to become the fictitious St Patrick, patron saint of the Irish whose feast day, 17 March, would be commemorated wherever there were Irish.

This astonishing outcome could not have been predicted in the fifth century. If we know little about Ireland in the two centuries before Patrick, we know even less about the island (and Patrick) in the two centuries after him. His name is not mentioned in any extant record or annal for well over a hundred years after his death (variously given as 461 or 493), and it was another hundred years before any attempt at a biography was made. The first effort at Patrick's story was essayed by Muirchú, who placed him firmly in Armagh and portrayed him as a superhero from the early Irish sagas rather than as the modest, all too human (though still quite remarkable) individual revealed in his writings. Muirchú also established the cheering tradition that on Judgement Day Patrick would sit alongside Jesus when the fate of the Irish was to be determined; less-favoured nations would have no one to intercede for them. Intriguingly, Muirchú also appears to have incorporated details from Palladius' life into Patrick's. His confused work, not surprisingly, has been dismissed as revealing 'an unconquerable bias towards inaccuracy'.[8]

Muirchú's efforts were supplemented by one Tírechán, whose overriding motive in writing about Patrick was likewise to establish the primacy of Armagh in the Irish church, and who therefore needed to establish (fabricate if need be) a Patrician connection to Armagh by claiming that Patrick built his church and was buried there. These two seventh-century hagiographers in effect launched the legend of Patrick, and later medieval scribes enthusiastically embellished it. Secular rulers too soon realised the potency of Patrick: the Ó Néill dynasty had already used Patrick to legitimise their ascendancy from the seventh to the tenth centuries and when, in the late twelfth century, the newly arrived in Ireland soldier of fortune, John de Courcy, attempted to conquer the kingdom of Ulster (present-day Antrim and Down) he aligned himself with Patrick by striking coins with his own name on one side and Patricius on the other. He also promoted the cult of Patrick, doubtless believing that this would give his land-grab some domestic and historic validation.

And so it continued: by the end of the seventeenth century, the fable of Patrick's banishment of the snakes from Ireland had been added to the literature (a Roman writer had noted the absence of snakes from Ireland over two hundred years before Patrick's arrival); and by the early eighteenth century, Patrick's creative use of the shamrock had also been established – 'by this three-leaved grass, he emblematically set forth to them [the Irish] the mystery of the Trinity'. As for St Patrick's day, it had long been a 'national' day for the Irish, marked by Irish monks as early as the eighth and ninth centuries, and by the end of the seventeenth century (and probably before) it was exhibiting its twenty-first-century characteristic as a day when the Irish 'wet their seamar-oge [=shamrock] and often commit excess in liquor'.[9]

Ireland after St Patrick

The cult of St Patrick (see figure 1.2) stemmed entirely from the power and conviction of his fifth-century writings; Palladius left only scraps and hence faded from view. The extraordinary personality of Patrick shines through his writings, and though he declares himself to be *stoltus* (a blockhead), he was anything but, for his works exhibit a sophistication in their structure that is only now being fully appreciated. Without the *Confessio* and the *Letter against the soldiers of Coroticus* there would have been no saint and no cult. The unmistakable presence of piety and passion in his writings determined that Patrick would be acknowledged as the 'Apostle of Ireland', while the lack of names, the absence of dates, the failure to identify places and, especially, his silence about what exactly he did (unlike his admirers, Patrick never claims to have converted all or even most of the Irish) made necessary the provision of appropriate legends. What the legends do not, and cannot, do, is cast any light on what remains one striking feature of Patrick's legacy. We know that he left behind him a Christian church organised in a diocesan pattern with small communities governed by their own bishop along recognisably British and continental lines; and yet, a hundred years after his death, when the veil lifts, this diocesan/episcopal organisation was in full retreat before, and within a further hundred years would almost entirely surrender to, a monastic system in which dispersed foundations were linked in federations (*paruchiae*) to a mother-house where the primary authority resided with the abbot not the bishop. There were, of course, still bishops and some of them were also abbots; but by the seventh century the balance of power had swung decisively towards the abbots and their monasteries.

This church organisation centred on the abbot and his monastery was markedly different from the British and continental models, where bishops and dioceses were the norm. Nor was the difference of the Irish church confined to its administrative organisation. In liturgical and ritual matters such as the dating of Easter (the most important feast in the Christian calendar), or the proper

1.2 Shrine of St Patrick's hand, county Down; gilt silver; fourteenth–fifteenth century. Ulster Museum.

tonsure of a monk (a matter of no small moment), the Irish church pursued an independent line. As early as the seventh century Irish aberrations were drawing censure from outsiders, and by the twelfth century Irish deviance in these matters would be seen not just as abnormal but as savage, and to require firm intervention. In the sixteenth century, by contrast, the early Irish Christian church was esteemed for its lack of corruption, i.e. its perceived lack of overt Roman links and, according to James Ussher, the antiquarian researcher and archbishop of Armagh, this pre-twelfth-century church was the true forerunner of the (Protestant) Church of Ireland. As in the secular arena, so in the sacred: validation of a contemporary aspiration, position or institution was sought by reference to early Ireland, and this has continued to be the case. Early Ireland was somehow authentic, though largely unknown; contemporary Ireland – of whatever period – was somehow bogus, and everyone knew it.

The reasons for this drastic shift away from the customary diocesan organisation at the time of Patrick have conventionally been ascribed to the fact that Ireland had never been part of the Roman empire, and hence had never been carved up administratively like Britain and much of continental Europe. Without a Roman administrative structure, so the argument goes, it would have been very difficult to build a Roman religious structure on Irish soil. Irish monasticism to an extent was a reflection of the prevailing Irish social and political structure. The argument is persuasive, but it should not be carried to extremes. We are dealing with the early church, not that of the nineteenth century, when the jurisdiction of bishop and abbot was carefully demarcated, and when the distinction between a monastery and a diocese was precisely drawn. In the sixth and seventh centuries the uniformity of Roman religious organisation was more aspirational than real, for there were many bishops in continental Europe whose background was monastic, and whose authority was originally abbatial. On occasion we find bishops who were kings and abbots and members of the local power group. That said, it is undeniable both that abbots had achieved primacy over bishops by the mid-seventh century and that monasticism was the distinguishing feature, the central characteristic, of the early Irish church. In this it may well have mirrored Irish society.

In 1954 Daniel A. Binchy, the doyen of early Irish historians, famously described early Irish society as 'tribal, rural, hierarchical and familiar'.[10] Ever since his words have inspired or tormented generations of university students, variously required to confirm, refute or illustrate his *ex cathedra* pronouncements. Fifty years on Binchy's *obiter dicta* look uncomfortably like a *cri de cœur* for the sort of society he would have been at home with in twentieth-century Ireland – not at all like the 'unitary, urbanised, egalitarian and individualist society' in which he actually found himself marooned. To repeat, early Ireland, and

Map 2 Early Christian Ireland

early Irish society, has ever been a screen on to which contemporary anxieties could be projected.

That said, Binchy's preoccupation with the lack of unity – or even the prospects for united authority – within Ireland from the seventh to the tenth centuries mirrored that of earlier historians and to an extent still does. By the current reckoning, early Christian Ireland (map 2) had a population of around half a million dispersed among some 185 *tuatha* or petty 'kingdoms', each with its own king (and very often its resident scholar and poet). In the early seventh century such *tuatha* appear to have corresponded to the diocese of a 'bishop' – Patrick allegedly appointed nearly three hundred such bishops – each of whom would have had his own church. What seems clear is that these kings cannot be considered as of equal importance, and nor were they necessarily more important than the resident poet or scholar or bishop. This is a point of some importance, for it marked social organisation in Ireland off from that of England where, by the year 800, there was already a steady advance towards a single unitary monarchy. In Ireland, by contrast, power and authority were dispersed not just among kings but among other high-status professions – clergy, poets, scholars, lawyers/judges – and the settlement pattern on the island reflected this, for there were few Irish living in village communities and even fewer in towns.

Reserved for those of the highest social class was the *crannóg*, or artificial lake-dwelling, built on wooden and sometimes stone foundations some distance from shore; around two thousand of these have been identified. But far and away the most common type of settlement was the large farmstead encircled by dry stone or earthen walls roughly two metres high. These raths (Gaelic: *ráith*) are also called ringforts, though the suffix 'fort' may give a misleading impression, for while they were generally located on higher ground they were not in any real military sense defensible. Within each rath or ringfort resided an extended family, complete with foster-children, servants, dependants, slaves, animals and, on occasion, armed retinue; but these were not stand-alone nuclear families. On the contrary, because these compounds were generally thrown up in close proximity to each other, it is likely that clusters of them formed cooperative networks within defined areas, and that social interdependency was customary. Some sixty thousand of these ringforts dating from the eighth and ninth centuries (not a single one has been dated post-1000) have been plotted on maps, showing that while there were concentrations in the west of Ireland they were to be found everywhere in profusion.

The ringfort varied in size from 30 to 110 square metres, almost certainly depending on the social standing of the families residing therein; in the largest ringforts, the products of luxury craftsmen – enamelled jewellery, bronze artefacts and the like (figure 1.3) – have been found. However, it should be stressed that while the size and intricacy of a ringfort reflected the owner's status, in early Irish society the wealth that underpinned that status was measured not in 'bricks and mortar' but by the size of his cattle herd.[11]

What early Irish society lacked in political, or indeed racial, unity, it more than compensated for in cultural cohesion, for this was a society that was, above all, culturally homogeneous. A common, dialect-free Gaelic language, known

1.3 The Ardagh chalice. Made of silver, bronze and gold and standing six inches high, the chalice is generally regarded as one of the leading treasures of early Ireland. Eighth century. National Museum of Ireland.

to scholars as Old Irish, was spoken throughout an Ireland that itself was a unitary whole, though divided into five provinces or 'fifths'. In addition, and astonishingly, Old Irish was also written down (figure 1.4), initially in the fifth century in the form of ogham inscriptions on stone memorials, but then by the seventh century to produce the first vernacular literature in western Europe, a literature unparalleled in quantity and variety. Thus it was that the epic tales of Irish heroic literature – the cattle-raid of Cooley, or the stories of the Fenian cycle (both destined to have enormous influence on those early twentieth-century anti-modernists, the poet W. B. Yeats and the revolutionary Patrick Pearse) came to be written down and passed on to subsequent generations.

Among the other glories of this Old Irish literature is the series of seventy-seven law tracts detailing the legal pronouncements of earlier generations that have come down to us from the eighth century.[12] These tracts do not constitute anything like a code of law, and there is no indication that they were ever publicly issued, and to that extent they are in marked contrast to the formal systems of

1.4 Detail of writing tablet found on Springmount bog, county Antrim.
National Museum of Ireland.

Roman jurisprudence. Nor can these tracts be described as royal, for in contrast to the few legal tracts that have come down to us from early medieval England, the role of the king in the enforcement of early Irish law is very circumscribed. That said, these early Irish legal tracts are unique in early medieval Europe in terms of their quantity, originality and sophistication. Unconcerned with crime and punishment, but very much taken up with compensation for wrongs suffered or injuries received, these legal pronouncements were produced by what was in essence a mandarin caste of legal specialists. Crucially, early Irish law was 'national', standing above all local or regional customs, and in the scope of its jurisdiction it was an exceptionally powerful bond of unity.

The writing, though not necessarily the composition, of the vernacular – in stories, poems, legal statements and religious works – was essentially a monastic invention and it was to remain exclusively monastic until the twelfth century. Remarkably, and uniquely in western Europe, the monks in the *scriptoria* in the monasteries drew on the earlier, pre-Christian knowledge of the *filid*, the learned classes of Gaelic Ireland, who were the custodians of an oral culture that had been islandwide. The monks' fusion of the oral and the written enabled the transmission to posterity of those pagan or pre-Christian stories, histories and sagas that elsewhere were cast into oblivion as something unworthy, shameful or godless. One scholar of Old Irish literature has written that 'this enduring interaction of the oral and the written is a crucial fact of Irish literary history'. Equally distinctive was the 'Irish hand' in which the earliest Irish manuscripts were written. There was a standard continental hand, 'uncial' for important works, 'cursive' for routine items. For whatever reason, however, the Irish scribes spurned these, and instead devised their own 'half-uncial' script, which quickly gained acceptance in Ireland and the neighbouring island – hence its customary designation as 'insular' script, which even today still dazzles the eye by its beauty.

Irish missionaries

The monasteries were the power-houses of Irish culture from the early seventh century on. While the rest of Europe was being torn apart in the fall-out from the collapse of the Roman empire, Ireland remained a beacon of light in what have traditionally been described as the Dark Ages. The reputation of the Irish monks for piety, manuscript production (figures 1.5, 1.6, 1.7) and Latin scholarship was unsurpassed. Indeed, so exuberant was the Irish delight in Latin learning (a language that had to be learnt in Ireland, as there were few Latin speakers there, unlike in Britain or Gaul) that the monks won a reputation for punning and double meaning in that language. One Latin text, *Hisperica famina*, has been translated into English as 'Latinacious Speakifications', which conveys something of the dexterity and nimbleness of the monkish wordsmith. As well as in Latin the monks wrote in Irish, very often and, valuably for later scholars, glossing Latin words, phrases and texts in that language. The monks loved Irish, boasting that the language was made up of the best bits from all the other languages after the fall of the Tower of Babel, and regarding it as a language that, in tandem with Latin, was well suited to spiritual, literary and intellectual pursuits. Unlike other societies where Latin displaced the vernacular, in early Ireland Latin proved the salvation of Irish.

Not surprisingly, as the output of the monastic *scriptoria* grew, and as the fame of the Irish monastic training grew, students began to flock to them. It seems that a seventh-century version of the late twentieth-century Erasmus scheme for student exchange set up by the European Union was soon operating informally. Bede in his *Historia Ecclesiastica* describes approvingly how foreign students

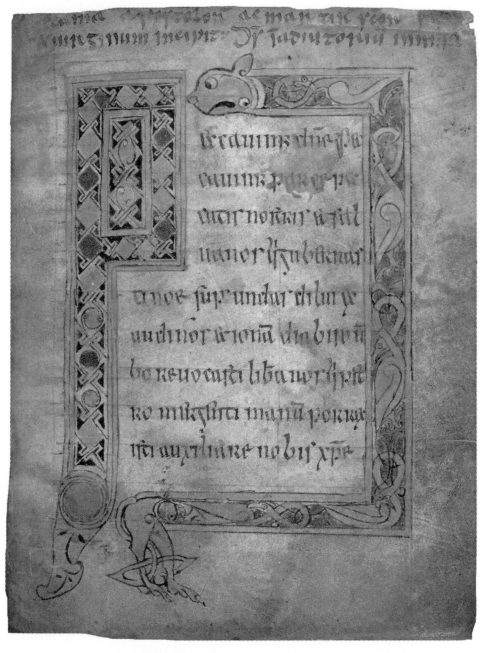

1.5 Stowe Missal. Dating from the late eighth or early ninth century, the missal was discovered hidden in the wall of Lackeen castle, county Tipperary in 1735. Royal Irish Academy.

1.6 The decorated opening page of the Stowe Missal. Royal Irish Academy.

came to the Irish monasteries where 'the Irish welcomed them gladly, gave them their daily food and also provided them with books to read and with instruction, without asking any payment'.[13] It was not, however, all one-way traffic: another key feature of the seventh century was the movement of Irish monks to Britain and to continental Europe (map 3). There they founded monasteries and

1.7 Possibly the oldest Irish manuscript, the Cathach or psalter of St Colum Cille (Columba) has been dated to the late sixth century and is a masterpiece of early Irish calligraphy. Royal Irish Academy.

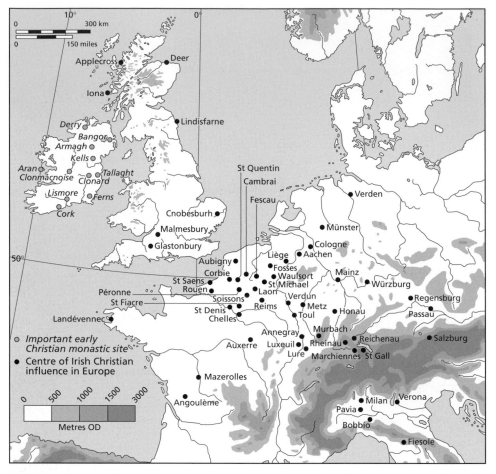

Map 3 Irish missionaries abroad

promoted learning and further enhanced the reputation of the Irish for piety and scholarship wherever they went.

Already in 563 AD, Colum Cille (figure 1.8) (Latin, Columba) had sailed to Iona in the Hebrides where he set up a monastic foundation which proved to be a bridgehead for the conversion of Pictland (roughly present-day Scotland). Writing (an unkind critic might say inventing) Colum Cille's biography some one hundred years after his death in 597, his biographer Adomnán depicted him as the very model of the abbot/saint who, as the head of a community of monks, would lead them to heaven. According to Adomnán's *Life*, Colum Cille could foretell the future, perform miracles of power and – irrefutable evidence of sainthood – was able to see angels. Analysis of this text and of a praise-poem in his honour, the *Amra* or eulogy, the oldest copy of which dates from the

1.8 Late nineteenth-century representations of Ireland's patron saints.
National Library of Ireland.

eleventh century, but which from internal evidence was written shortly after his death, reveals something about the historical figure of Colum Cille and about his mission.

We may note, for example, that while Colum Cille journeyed to Iona in the Hebrides to set up a monastery, this should not be seen as a self-imposed exile or *peregrinatio* to a remote area of the world. In the seventh century the Irish sea should be viewed as a bridge between the territory of the Dál Ríata, which extended from Antrim to Argyll, and for centuries after that it was used as a corridor between north-east Ireland and Scotland. (The Scottish settlement in east Ulster in the seventeenth century was both logical and predictable.) For this reason, therefore, movement to Iona could hardly mean the end of Colum Cille's interest in Ireland, and it appears that not only did he visit the country several times after his exile, but that he founded the famous monasteries at Durrow and Derry after he had moved to Iona. In addition Colum Cille's royal pedigree has been noted. As a well-connected member of a subordinate branch of the northern Ó Néill – then moving into prominence throughout Ireland, but with ambitions also in the west of Scotland – Colum Cille was unusually well placed to deploy his political influence to further his mission. He was also well positioned to use his monastic foundations to promote the wider secular claims of the Ó Néill dynasty. Certainly study of the available evidence for Colum Cille's life and achievement leads inexorably to the conclusion that its main historical importance was to have revealed how cooperation between church and state could be to the advantage of both in terms of missionary endeavour. In Ireland the secular and the sacred would not easily be prised apart, and it is clear that the government of Colum Cille's monastic foundations, for example, was based on secular models in which overlordship, kinship and inheritance were of central importance. It has been suggested that it was in the manner of an Irish *Ard Rí*, or high-king, that Colum Cille exercised supreme jurisdiction over the family of monasteries that he founded in Ireland and Scotland.

None of this, of course, is in any way to downplay Colum Cille's role as a Christian monk and ascetic, who undertook in Pictland the conversion work for which Patrick is celebrated in Ireland. Moreover, Iona's influence did not cease at what we might anachronistically call the Scottish border. Twenty years after Colum Cille's death, one of the monks of Iona, Aidan, founded a monastery at Lindisfarne off the coast of north-east England which was to be of signal importance in the conversion of the English kingdoms. The clockwise conversion of the British Isles – the Briton Patrick to Ireland, Colum Cille to Pictland, Aidan to England and then missionaries from continental Europe, some of whom were trained by Columbanus of Bangor, into Kent – was proceeding apace.

Colum Cille's influence was, by and large, confined to Britain; however, his near contemporary, Columbanus, through his journeys, his monastic foundations and his writings – letters, monastic rules, poems and sermons – was to enjoy a huge European reputation. In 590 or 591 Columbanus, then a monk at Bangor, on the southern shores of Belfast Lough, and already an internal exile from his birthplace in Leinster, sought permission from his abbot to undertake a *peregrinatio*, a 'white martyrdom', made by those 'who separate for the sake of God from everything [they love]', and embrace a life of permanent exile abroad. Such a commitment was much more severe than that of a pilgrimage to a holy place, for there the assumption was always that the pilgrim would return; but for Columbanus his exile was predetermined to be permanent. (In parenthesis we may note that the later Irish record of return migration from the nineteenth century on was among the lowest in the whole of Europe.) In pursuit of his monastic goal of rigorous asceticism, no half measures were permitted. Columbanus' journeys took him to continental Europe, where, in the Vosges region of the Frankish kingdom, he set up monasteries at Annegray, Luxeuil and Fontaine. Running into opposition from the local bishops he journeyed on, arriving in north Italy where he founded a monastery at Bobbio and where he died in 615 AD.

Columbanus had many gifts: he was a complete master of Latin, for whom grammar, biblical exegesis and even computus (the study of the ecclesiastical calendar) were part of a seamless learning. His letters in Latin (of which six are extant) were masterpieces of the stylist's art. Consider his Rhine boatman's song, addressed to those toiling at the oars of his vessel:

> Stand firm in soul and spurn the foul fiend's tricks and seek defence in virtue's armoury – you men, remember Christ with mind still resounding [deep breath] 'heave'

> Firm faith will conquer all and blessed zeal and the old friend yielding breaks at last his darts – you men, remember Christ with mind still sounding [deep breath] 'heave'

He was not, however, an easy man to get along with. He bore his authority like a banner, around which his monks were expected to rally, and with which his opponents could be bludgeoned. There were many of these latter, for in addition to vows of poverty, mortification and fasting, Columbanus appears to have sworn never to walk away from a dispute. He fought with the local bishops in the Frankish lands and he had the temerity to remind Pope Boniface IV that 'we, all the Irish, dwellers at the ends of the earth' had never been ruled by Rome – a piece of effrontery on a par with the the *Skibbereen Eagle*, a nineteenth-century Cork newspaper, memorably warning the Tsar of Russia that it had its eye on him, and to watch his step.

Columbanus' monastic rule was one of unmitigated severity: vows of poverty, obedience and fasting were strictly adhered to ('let him [the monk] be forced to rise while his sleep is not yet finished'), while minor transgressions by the monks (coughing while chanting, for example, or over-eating) were to be punished by a rain of blows to the head, or (less painfully?) by a diet of bread and water for a week. Moreover, while Columbanus self-consciously sought physical exile far away from Ireland, he was not at all prepared to leave behind him those Irish religious traditions which were by the early seventh century out of kilter with religious practices found elsewhere in Europe. 'It is clear', he wrote, 'that we are in our native land so long as we accept no rules of these Franks.' In other words, Columbanus could get out of Ireland, but he could not get Ireland out of him; in this respect he was not alone, then or later.

And yet, however Columbanus despised them, the rules of 'these Franks', on various church matters, but crucially on the dating of Easter (loosely stated, a nineteen-year cycle) were now those of the Roman church and were backed by papal authority. By contrast Irish tradition adhered to the older eighty-four year cycle, and this was stoutly defended by Irish missionaries in Britain and on the continent, and maintained by large elements within the church in Ireland. Ironically it was the very success of Irish missionaries such as Colum Cille, Aidan, Columbanus and their followers that forced the resolution of the issue, for their travels abroad brought them into contact with continental practice, and it was evident that a single uniform date for Easter was needed to avoid grave scandal.

In 664 AD, at the Council of Whitby, in the north-east of England, the Roman dating prevailed: Bishop Wilfrid, an ardent pro-Romanist and one eager to 'sift out the poisonous weeds planted by the Irish', enforced not just the Roman Easter but also introduced Roman script, Roman architecture and the rule of St Benedict (in place of that of Colum Cille and Columbanus) into the monasteries. It was to be another fifty or more years before the Roman conquest of the 'Celtic' church was complete. It was not until 716 AD that Colum Cille's foundation at Iona finally adopted the Roman Easter; but the decision at Whitby marked the end of a special era of Irish religious particularism.

It did not, however, mark the end of the *peregrinatio* of Irish monks, and for the next three hundred years, 'contemptuous of the dangers of the ocean', they continued to export themselves and their learning in literature, grammar and computing to the heartlands of Europe. Witness the two Irish monks who gained entry to the court of Charlemagne in the late eighth century by offering to sell their 'wisdom'. Their immodesty paid off. Charlemagne's biographer tells us that they indeed proved to be 'unrivalled in their knowledge of sacred and profane letters', and that Charlemagne found positions for them. Consider also the three others who blagged their way into the court of King Alfred, claiming, like Oscar Wilde, that they had nothing to declare but their genius. In an act of supreme confidence the 'three Gaels' (as the *Anglo-Saxon Chronicle* describes them) had set out from Ireland 'in a boat without any oars' and after seven days drifting had made landfall in Cornwall. Other *peregrini* can be glimpsed through the chance survival of stray letters: a manuscript at Leyden contains letters written by ninth-century Irish wandering scholars and pilgrims in Liège, a staging-post on the road to Rome. And the survival of manuscripts by Irish scribes in European libraries bears witness to their endeavours. Only ten manuscripts dating from the period up to 1000 AD survive in Ireland, but fifty survive abroad.

At least two of the wandering scholars were genuinely world-class intellectuals: Sedulius Scottus and Johannes Eriugena (John the Irish-born). The first was based in Liège, where he composed an astonishingly rich variety of literature: light verse, biblical commentary, treatises on Latin grammar and, notably, manuscripts of the four gospels in Greek with interlinear Latin translations. The second enjoyed – and continues to enjoy – a huge reputation as a theologian, philosopher and Greek scholar. Snobby contemporaries marvelled at how 'that barbarian living at the ends of the earth' (Johannes Eriugena) could display such a complete mastery of Greek. Unfortunately, we know next to nothing about either man – no vital dates, not even their Irish names; in this respect, they both resemble Patrick in their reticence.

Sedulius Scottus and Johannes Eriugena were working in the ninth century, and their departure from the scene has generally been taken as the *terminus ad quem* for the flowering of Hiberno-Latin scholarship in Europe. There were Irish scholars in Europe after them, of course, but increasingly there was little that was distinctive about their learning or their methods. From the eleventh century on Irish learning to a large extent focused on the Irish language and became detached from European influences.

Vikings

One of the reasons for this sustained exodus of Irish monks to Europe from the eighth century on, and indeed for the re-orienting of Irish scholarship in the ninth and tenth centuries, may have been the Viking onslaught on Ireland. Beginning in 795 with the sack of Rechru (probably Rathlin Island, off the north Antrim coast), over the next thirty years the Vikings launched almost annual attacks on selected coastal areas of Ireland, England and Scotland. Then in the 830s these attacks became more sustained, with the deployment of larger numbers, and the penetration of inland areas via the Rivers Boyne, Shannon, Liffey and Erne. The success of these lengthy expeditions encouraged more permanent settlements in Ireland, and from the mid-ninth century through to the early tenth century, *longphorts* (defensible sea-bases) were founded at Dublin, Cork and Annagassan (county Louth), and later at Waterford, Wexford and Limerick. Throughout the tenth century the Vikings were key players in Irish power politics, and they also intervened forcefully in Northumbria and in York (which they 'twinned' with Dublin); but by the early eleventh century their power had waned and their scope (and appetite) for independent action had much diminished. In 967 the *longphort* at Limerick had fallen to the Dál Cáis dynasty of Munster, and the battle of Clontarf (1014), north of Dublin, was another defeat, though hardly a decisive one. However, by the end of the eleventh century, Viking power in Ireland, to all intents and purposes, was at an end.

This short narrative reveals three salient points about the Vikings in Irish history (map 4). First, the Viking era lasted nearly three hundred years; second, throughout this period, the Vikings viewed Ireland and Britain, and the islands about them, as a single sphere of operations; and third, the Vikings themselves underwent several metamorphoses during these centuries, from raiders to settlers to traders to dynastic power-brokers. Any attempt at a single all-embracing assessment of the Viking experience in Ireland is, therefore, doomed to failure. For Christian churchmen and monastic chroniclers, however, such cautious reserve would have appeared astounding, and given that the monasteries (because of their wealth) bore the brunt of the initial Viking onslaught such protests are understandable. When one's throat is being cut, it is difficult, even for a Christian priest, to fully appreciate the entrepreneurial skills and building talents of the Viking attackers (for a Viking Sword see figure 1.9).

It is not clear what ignited the Viking onslaught on the western isles of Europe. Historians have suggested population pressure in Scandinavia, pointed to technological advances in sailing and cited the aggressive territorial expansion of the (Christian) Frankish kingdom into Scandinavia as causes of (pagan) Norse aggression. All of these explanations have merit: but it might also be claimed that the Norsemen came initially because these islands were ripe for the plucking. That the Vikings first launched raids on the monastic foundations at Lindisfarne and Iona is suggestive, and surely indicates that they were well aware of the wealth in gold and silver religious artefacts housed in these establishments. 'The ravaging of heathen men miserably destroyed God's church in Lindisfarne' mournfully noted the monk-chronicler in 793 AD; and Iona was sacked in 802 AD and again in 806 AD, when sixty-eight monks were put to the sword. In 821 AD a foundation north of Dublin at Howth was sacked and the attackers made off with a large number of women captives, possibly nuns. In 823 AD, Columbanus' monastery at Bangor, county Down, was attacked and the relics of Comgall, its founder, were tipped out of their reliquary. In the same year the rocky outcrop of Sceilg Mhichíl, off the coast of Kerry, was raided by the Vikings, who kidnapped the abbot. Two years later the abbot of Iona, the saintly Blathmacc mac Flaind, was tortured to death for refusing to reveal the hiding place of Colum Cille's sacred relics.

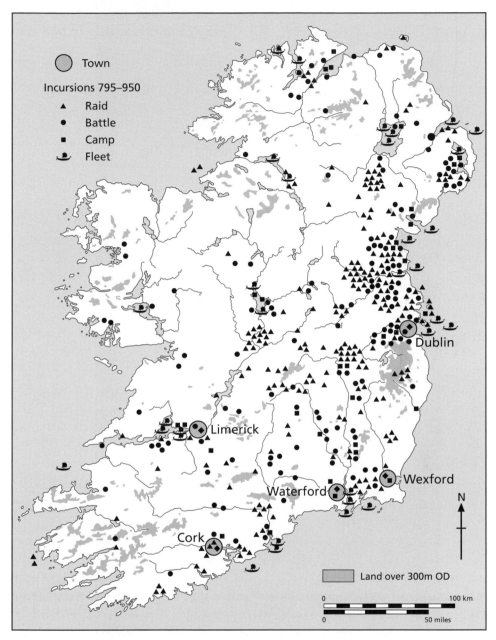

Map 4 Vikings

Not surprisingly in the face of such repeated onslaughts, the monks on Iona admitted defeat, and removed themselves to Kells, county Meath, far away from the coast. And, of course, because of these hideous raids, the annalists in the monasteries thereafter never had a good word to say about the Vikings or, as they variously termed them, the heathens or pagans. Equally, it was almost certainly

1.9 Viking sword found in Ballinderry *crannóg*, county Westmeath and dated to the ninth century. National Museum of Ireland.

fear of the Vikings that lay behind the large exodus of monks to the continent in the ninth and tenth centuries. From a landlocked monastery probably in present-day Switzerland, one monk mused on a stormy night:

> The bitter wind is high tonight
> It lifts the white locks of the sea
> In such wild winter storm no fright
> of savage Viking troubles me

Such whistling in the dark testifies to the sheer terror which the Viking raids in the early ninth century engendered, even in those far removed from the action, a terror which cannot be argued away by any amount of special pleading for Viking virtues one thousand years on.

That said, we must remember that the Vikings did not introduce the sword into an Irish rural idyll. Coroticus' men, as we have seen, had carried out the first historically recorded massacre of civilians hundreds of years before the Vikings; and during the ninth century, Viking raids on monastic settlements were punctuated by Christian raids, every bit as ferocious, on the same targets. In 833 AD the monastery at Clonmacnois was sacked by the Munster king (and keen monastic reformer), Feidlimid mac Crimthainn, and so too was that at Durrow. In 835 AD it was the turn of the Vikings to loot and burn what remained of Clonmacnois. When one's throat is being cut is it a consolation to know that the perpetrator is a Christian?

Against this picture of relentless violence as depicted by the annalists (and Professor Binchy), there is the archaeological evidence which is rather more muted. Excavations at Iona, 'sacked' by the Vikings in AD 795, 802, 805 and 806, confirm that the many Celtic crosses, and other items of Christian sculpture, famous features of the site, were left standing; but curiously that some stones were smashed soon after carving. We cannot say that the Vikings did it. Moreover, excavations of the Viking settlements of Dublin and York show – as one would expect – much evidence of military hardware such as swords, shield bosses, axeheads and the like; but they also reveal regular house structures, coins (the Danes struck the first Irish coins in 995 AD (figure 1.10)), boat-building, drainage schemes and, above all, much evidence of trading. The Irish goods that have been excavated in Norway in the last fifty years are possibly the product of trade rather than plunder. Moreover, by the eleventh century there is plentiful evidence of intermarriage between the Vikings and the local Irish, though few were quite as broadminded as Gormlaith, daughter of a king of Leinster, who married first a Viking king of Dublin, then a high-king of the Ó Néill and lastly none other than Brian Boru, victor at Clontarf in 1014. The christianisation of the Scandinavians was also continuing apace (some of their coins by the 990s bore the sign of the

1.10 Viking coins struck in Dublin *c.* 995–*c.* 1140s revealing the deterioration in Viking power over that period of time. National Museum of Ireland.

cross) and this, along with intermarriage, fostering of children and trading, was bringing about a progressive assimilation.

Meanwhile Danish power in England was on the wane. In 865 AD the Danes had invaded East Anglia with a 'great army' and remained there for ten years, raiding and pillaging. The Danes certainly considered the British isles as a single maritime zone of operations, but England took precedence over the other theatres; and it may be suggested that Ireland's role, and to an extent that of Scotland and the Isle of Man, was to act as a bridgehead to the lusher territories of the south. England was wealthier than Ireland, had a network of towns (which Ireland lacked), was much more populous and hence altogether more enticing for conquest and settlement. Moreover, in terms of the distribution of Scandinavian place names there is a clear distinction between Ireland and Britain, for while these place names are confined to isolated towns around the Irish coast they are very plentiful throughout eastern England. This variation may in turn reflect the differing impacts of the Viking incursions on the two countries.

In a famous lecture delivered in 1959 entitled 'The passing of the old order', Professor Binchy put forward the case for a Viking armageddon, shattering the existing social order, destroying native Irish institutions and instructing the native Irish in (and accustoming them to) total warfare. Few historians would now accept such an apocalyptic assessment of the Viking impact. With the triumph of Christianity, the 'old order' had passed already by the end of the seventh century; native Irish institutions remained intact after the Vikings and, as we have seen, the native Irish themselves needed few lessons in carrying out massacres and engaging in plundering and looting. That said, the memory of the Vikings – Danes or Norse – as pitiless warriors, endured: in 1690, the arrival of William of Orange with, among others, contingents of Danish troops, sparked off great alarm among their Irish opponents; and the minor battle of Clontarf (1014) was duly celebrated in the nineteenth century as one in which the merciless foreigners had received their come-uppance at the hand of the pious Brian Boru and the Irish.

Such folk memories may have been deceptive. The evidence, archaeological, if not literary, points to a much less devastating Viking impact on Ireland than on, say, England or Scotland. If subsequent research bears this out, then it may be further suggested that the altogether more intrusive attacks in England (and Scotland) forced the pace in those countries for the creation of a national monarchy capable of leading the struggle against the Vikings. We may conclude that the 'milder', less intrusive onslaught of the Scandinavians (at least after the first few decades of the ninth century) was not devastating enough to force a comparable united response within Ireland. By contrast, towards the end of the tenth century the kingdom of the West Saxons had emerged as *the* English monarchy, leading the opposition to Danish control of eastern England. For the most part the Vikings in Ireland were content to be yet another power group within a divided Irish polity, allying with one dynasty, then with another, but never attempting the wider conquest that they embarked on in England. The consequences of this omission become clear when, in the fullness of time, the new invaders of England, the Normans, victors in the climactic battle of Hastings (1066) turned their attention to Ireland a hundred years later.

2 FROM LORDSHIP TO KINGDOM: IRELAND, 1169–1541

The English invasion of Ireland

There are at least two puzzles concerning events in Ireland between 1169 and 1171: what happened, and who was involved. Happily, these two puzzles can be easily solved, though most historians of medieval Ireland have, with misplaced tact, managed to avoid doing so. First, what happened was an invasion, followed by a conquest of a large portion of the island; all attempts to portray the invaders as if they were guests of an Irish king, or medieval tourists who simply fetched up in Ireland, fail to recognise the determination of the invaders or the formidable degree of violence they deployed against those who stood in their way. They also ignore the fact that the invaders proudly described their action as a conquest (*expugnatio*) for centuries thereafter. Second, it was an English invasion and partial conquest: all talk of the 'Normans' or the 'Anglo-Normans', or 'Anglo-French', or even the 'Cambro-Normans' coming to Ireland is simply ahistorical. The invaders called themselves English (*Engleis, Angli*), were called Saxain (=English) or *Gaill* (=foreigner) by the Irish, and for the next seven hundred years were designated as English in the historical literature. Contemporaries never described them as Norman, Anglo-Norman or much less Cambro-Norman. Only in the late nineteenth century, and largely on grounds of political sensitivity, was the identity of the English invaders fudged by these non-historical terms. This is not merely a matter of semantics, for the cultural identity, if not always the national origins, of the invaders was indisputably English. Moreover, their confident Englishness, their conviction that Englishness and, for want of a better word, Irishness, were incompatible and, later, their growing anxiety lest the despised Irish ways prove beguiling to English settlers, were all to play a vital role in the unfolding story of the English colony in Ireland, and its relationship with the other people on the island.

There is, however, a third puzzle which is not so simply resolved: why was the English invasion of Ireland so long delayed? After all, Duke William of

Normandy and his band of French adventurers and assorted mercenaries had conquered the kingdom of England a century earlier and, after ruthlessly wiping out the Anglo-Saxon ruling class, by 1100 had made huge inroads into Wales and begun to intervene in Scotland. Surely Ireland must have been the next target for this restless, acquisitive, warrior aristocracy? In the event, more than sixty years were to elapse before the English, as the Normans had become within two generations of the descent on England, made their move.

One reason for the delay was undoubtedly the stern opposition that Henry I (1100–35) encountered in Wales; more ambitious schemes for territorial expansion had to be postponed until this resistance was put down. Again, the political distractions of the reign of King Stephen (1135–54), sometimes erroneously referred to as a civil war or 'anarchy' were, none the less, sufficiently serious to rule out any intervention in Ireland. If anything, during these decades, the English monarchy looked set to lose its grip on Wales, and even to shed some of its continental territories; and Henry II (1154–89), Stephen's successor, had as his first ambition to recover and consolidate, rather than expand, his Angevin empire, so called after his birth-place, Anjou, in France. None of this is to suggest that the Normans of 1066, and the English of the 1140s, had Ireland and its conquest as a constant preoccupation in the hundred years after the battle of Hastings, and that their aims in that respect were frustrated by events. Certainly, there is evidence that Duke William and Henry I were aware of Ireland, and of opportunities there; there was substantial trade between Dublin and Wales, and the west country, in the century after 1066; and English clergy, especially those connected to Canterbury, which had a long-standing claim of jurisdiction, had in 1155 brought the pressing problems – as they saw them – of the Irish church to Henry II's attention. Rather, what might be suggested is that on any reading of the relentless Norman advance in the eleventh and twelfth centuries, not just from France to England, Wales and Scotland, but much further afield to Italy, Sicily, Spain, southern France and North Africa, there was a certain inevitablity to their English successors' armed intervention in Ireland; only the timing of the onslaught was uncertain.[1]

The immediate background to Henry II's invasion of Ireland may be quickly sketched in. In 1165 Diarmait Mac Murchadha, king of Leinster, having been worsted in his struggles with Tigernan ua Ruairc, king of Breifne and with Ruadhrí Ó Conchobair, king of Connacht, for control of Dublin and south-east Ireland, sailed for Bristol and the court of Henry II to seek military assistance. Mac Murchadha eventually caught up with the frenetic Henry in Aquitaine. Henry was sympathetic to Mac Murchadha's request, but he was unable at that time to offer him direct military assistance. Instead Henry permitted Mac Murchadha to recruit mercenaries from within his empire to support the Irish

king's renewed contest with his rivals. Henry well understood that such a permission gave him a major stake in the enterprise. In Wales Mac Murchadha's
offer of lands and money in return for military service was taken up not so
much by the usual riff-raff that constituted the ranks of mercenaries but by none
other than Richard Fitzgilbert, earl of Pembroke. Strongbow, as Fitzgilbert was
better known, now pledged assistance in return for the hand in marriage of Mac
Murchadha's daughter, Aoife and, sensationally – for it was in flat defiance of
custom and kin – he demanded to succeed Mac Murchadha as king of Leinster. Leading members of the important Fitzgerald family also threw in their lot
with Mac Murchadha, and were promised the town of Wexford and adjacent
territories.

These English barons had come under pressure in Wales. Welsh lands had
proved less lucrative than anticipated, while Welsh resistance had proved more
obdurate. Many of Mac Murchadha's new partners had incurred King Henry's
wrath over earlier succession squabbles, and could hope for little favour from
that quarter. Moreover, as was common with aristocratic families everywhere
in Europe, for whom inheritance was governed by the rules of primogeniture,
making provision for younger sons was a perennial headache, especially in a
period of shrinking domestic opportunities. Mac Murchadha's offer of 'land or
pence, horses, armour or chargers, gold and silver . . . very ample pay . . . sod or
soil', proved all too tempting a lure to a warrior caste 'at the bottom of Fortune's
wheel' (as the contemporary chronicler, Gerald of Wales, put it), but yet mindful
of its glorious past, anxious about the current silted-up avenues of promotion
and eager for new adventures.[2]

The arrival in Ireland in May 1169 of these English invaders, with their
mounted knights and their archers – no more than a few hundred all told –
triggered few alarm bells. Even the landing of Strongbow with a much larger
force a year later aroused little comment. The Irish annals are largely silent on the
subject, and when they do advert to Mac Murchadha, they portray the English as
simply his mercenaries, through whose efforts he hoped to recover his kingdom.
Nor was this perception either naive or unrealistic. On the island of Ireland,
with its endemic low-intensity warfare, there were many mercenary forces and
the addition of what appeared to be further bands of English mercenaries was
not that remarkable; mercenaries were, after all, just that, soldiers of fortune
who fought merely for money without long-term dynastic ambitions. Indeed, as
if to confirm this point, one recently arrived English band of mercenaries would
quickly change sides and go off to fight for Mac Murchadha's enemy. Three
factors changed matters dramatically. First was the overwhelming success of the
Mac Murchadha/English campaigns – Wexford, Waterford and then Dublin,
fell to their forces. Then, following the fall of Waterford in August 1170, Mac

Murchadha, as agreed, gave his daughter, Aoife, in marriage to Strongbow. Finally, on Mac Murchadha's death in May 1171 his son-in-law Strongbow, as promised, succeeded to the kingship. These striking events electrified Ireland; they also galvanised Henry II into action. He had envisaged down-on-their-luck English freelances or desperadoes – younger sons perhaps – signing up for Mac Murchadha's invasion force; instead, no less a figure than the earl of Pembroke, Strongbow, had joined the Irish challenger, carved out a sizeable stretch of territory for himself by his sword, married his master's daughter and had now succeeded him as *king of Leinster.*

Throughout his thirty-five year reign Henry II would leave his French territories only in an emergency; Strongbow's land-grab in Ireland, which strategically placed him on both sides of the Irish Sea, and, especially, his newly acquired 'kingly' title, a challenge to Henry's own status, constituted just that. What had begun as an attempt by Mac Murchadha to reverse a battlefield decision with the help of English allies became a full-scale invasion once Henry determined to involve himself personally. Henry's decision to leave France was also hastened by news that papal legates were on their way seeking an explanation for the murder of the archbishop of Canterbury, Thomas Becket, in December 1170.

Spurred on by news from Ireland, and from Rome, Henry prepared a major expedition for Ireland and in October 1171, accompanied by 500 knights and 4,000 foot-soldiers, including a large body of archers, he landed near Waterford. He also brought with him siegecraft with which to attack, if necessary, any towns or forts that refused to yield to him, and nearly 1,000 lb of wax for lighting purposes and, presumably, for sealing charters. He had also had carried over to Ireland a large amount of exotic food (almonds by the hundredweight and supplies of crane), for word had reached Henry that the Irish diet – a conservative mix of grain, dairy products and meat – might not be to his liking.

Henry stayed in Ireland for six months during which time many of the native Irish kings – though not Ruadhrí Ó Conchobair, king of Connacht – pledged homage to him. They were content to do so because they believed that Henry had come to protect them from the depredations of his English barons. Henry kept Dublin, Wexford, Waterford and their hinterlands as his royal demesne, but divided up the adjacent territories among his barons, to be held by the feudal tenure of knight service. In addition, as a counterweight to Strongbow, whom he confirmed as lord of Leinster, Henry awarded 'the land of Meath', a large territory much bigger than the present-day county, and containing within it the Hill of Tara, to Hugh de Lacy, a close confidant.

As a series of postscripts to Henry's intervention in Ireland we may note that in 1175 the treaty of Windsor was agreed between Henry and Ó Conchobair's representatives, by which something akin to spheres of influence were accorded to both sides. Such an arrangement was well-nigh unenforceable and speedily proved a dead letter: Ó Conchobair could not rein in the aggression of his children, or keep other Irish provincial kings in order, and Henry could not control his barons at long distance. His failure in this respect was revealed all too clearly in 1177 when John de Courcy, described as 'pauperum et mendicum', with a small body of knights and archers, broke out of Leinster, invaded present-day Antrim and Down and, after a series of ferocious battles, captured and held Downpatrick. The collapse of the treaty of Windsor and, perhaps, de Courcy's unchecked rampaging in the north-east of Ireland, appear to have convinced Henry that a fresh approach to Ireland was required. Hence in 1177 he had his council at Oxford declare Ireland to be a separate lordship under his youngest son, John, then aged ten. It seems clear that Henry's ultimate objective was to have all Ireland as a separate kingdom, with John as its king. To that end, he applied to the pope to recognise Ireland as a kingdom for his son and for a royal crown for him. The pope duly obliged, sending a crown of peacock feathers for John.

Henry would dispatch his son John to Ireland in 1185, presumably to prepare the ground for his regal elevation. However, the seventeen-year-old John lacked experience and gravitas, and his frivolity, and fondness for games and gaming did not inspire confidence. He also alienated potential Irish supporters by mocking their long beards, and he angered alleged English supporters – notably de Lacy – by his attempts to curb their expansionist plans. The expedition was not a success and, after eight months, John returned to England; Henry's plan for John to be king of Ireland was shelved. However, John's interest in Ireland remained undimmed. In 1192 he granted Dublin its most important early charter which defined its limits, and detailed the privileges its citizens were to enjoy. Almost certainly it was John who gave the order in 1204 for the building of Dublin Castle, the seat of English government in Ireland for the next seven hundred years. And in 1210, as King John, he returned to Ireland to deal with troublesome English barons and to win the confidence of his Irish subjects.

Long regarded as the coping-stone to the first phase of the English invasion of Ireland, John's expedition has generally been accounted a great success, in so far as both of its aims were largely achieved. Native Irish rulers and English barons hastened to submit to him. Moreover, he established an administrative structure for the whole lordship with a justiciar, or chief governor, at its apex; he created a judicial system with English common law as its basis; and, importantly, he reiterated his father's declaration that English and Irish were to have access to this law. He also found time to establish St Patrick's cathedral in Dublin. When he departed after only nine weeks in Ireland, he might well have felt pleased with himself; but his satisfaction with his Irish achievements was not to last.

Why was the English invasion a success?

The success of the English invasion of Ireland has traditionally been ascribed first, to the military superiority of the invaders, and second, to Irish disunion. The main sources for the invasion, the contemporary writings of Gerald of Wales (Giraldus Cambrensis), and the anonymous and somewhat later 'Song of Dermot and the earl' are compelling (and downright gleeful) on this point. The English were heavily armed, deploying a variety of weapons – lances, long straight-bladed swords or maces (spiked clubs) – and carrying the familiar kite-shaped shield. Crucially, they were mounted on powerful warhorses – destriers, the tanks of the medieval period. Additional and highly lethal firepower was provided by their archers. In sharp contrast, their Irish opponents, we are told, appeared 'naked' or in 'shirts of thin satin' before them, made little use of horses, possessed few, if any, archers and instead relied on short spears and slingshots. Such an apparently unevenly matched contest – as one-sided as that of Cortez against the Incas, or German panzers against Polish cavalry – could have only one outcome. Gerald of Wales again: the Irish, he reported, were 'paralysed and panic-stricken' by the overwhelming firepower of the English and, time and time again, were bested by the resolute, though numerically inferior, invader.

Compelling though it may be, it would be unwise to take Gerald's commentary at face value. His analysis of Irish military deficiencies was a central part of his overall thesis concerning Irish primitiveness, Irish backwardness and, ultimately, Irish barbarism. Irish military inferiority was of a piece with barbarous Irish social practices; these failings in turn were replicated in the religious sphere, and the presence of all three was designed to explain and, above all, justify, England's invasion and conquest. In purely military affairs we may note that the Irish annalists saw no contrast – in scale or in techniques – between English and Irish warfare; that there were always many Irish combatants on both sides; that Irish bogs and woods, covering large swathes of the country, were ill suited to heavily mounted cavalry; that the conquest was far from complete; that other evidence shows the Irish wearing helmets and metal breastplates; and finally, that despite the apparent one-sidedness of the conflict, there were a few Irish successes – at Kilkenny in 1173, at Thurles in 1174 and at Slane, whose castle fell to the Irish, in 1176. Even Gerald, in explaining the incomplete conquest, concedes that the Irish proved very adept pupils of the supposed new style of war – hardly likely if they were so irremediably backward, and so irredeemably primitive, as he had earlier claimed.[3]

Perhaps more attention might be paid to Irish disunion? As already noted, there were always Irish in the English invasion forces – they had a distressing habit of beheading prisoners, a dead giveaway; and the struggle was never the simple Irish–English one that Gerald of Wales so insouciantly describes. But what is striking is that, when the novel outcome of the partial English conquest was revealed – colonisation through an influx of English and Welsh settlers – there was no general, widespread, resistance. The localism and disunion of the Irish, which had been evident for hundreds of years, may in fact have been increased by the English invasion, opening up, as it did, the possibility of further multiple and transient alliances.

The arrival of many thousands of English and Welsh settlers in the years after 1169 sets the invasion of Ireland decisively apart from other Norman incursions in southern Italy, Sicily or Gascony. It also distinguishes it from the earlier Norman conquest of England, for that had merely seen the obliteration of the Anglo-Saxon ruling class, and its replacement with another. There had been little movement of settlers from France to England and, as we have seen, the Norman invaders of England, within two generations saw themselves as English, wrote themselves into the mythical histories of ancient Britain and by the twelfth century had found a role for themselves in Anglo-Saxon history. With Ireland, however, it was all to be very different, and the difference was to be decisive in determining the shape of Irish history for the next millennium. The English who invaded Ireland, and those who settled there in their wake, would never – apart from the occasional rogue element – describe themselves as Irish; indeed they would go to considerable and sometimes extraordinary lengths – linguistic, legal and legislative – to prevent any such assimilation or, as they called it, degeneracy. Why the Normans who conquered England were happy to call themselves English within two generations of their arrival, while the English conquerors of two-thirds of Ireland, barely a generation later, were just as determined to reinforce and ringfence their English identity, by any means possible, is one of the key questions in all Irish history.

One answer to this question, and possibly the main one, lies in the time lapse between 1066 and 1169. At the period of the Norman conquest of England, Ireland was still *insula sanctorum*, whose leading saints, Patrick, Brigid and Colum Cille, enjoyed cult status among English Christians, while England and Ireland generally shared many bonds of a common Christian heritage. Less positive features of Irish society were the endemic warfare that revolved around cattle-raiding and slave-taking, as it had done since time immemorial, and the organisation of the Irish church on a monastic basis, which set Ireland apart from the rest of western Christendom. Some of these features were criticised as variously improper, archaic or even abhorrent; but what is noticeable in the century after the Norman conquest of England is how the language employed to denounce Irish practices increased in vehemence and violence. Predictably, English churchmen (and some Irish too) were to the fore in the rising tide of unrestrained denunciation of Irish practices, and in the strident demands for reform. What had been improper, irregular or even illegal, in 1050 – married clergy, hereditary bishops, unreformed liturgies and the like – would, a hundred years on, be condemned as an abomination, as bestial, as pagan and as abuses that had to be eliminated by outside, armed intervention.

Irish warfare too for those who observed it, was equally an affront.[4] The recent continental emphasis on the chivalric conduct of war – which seems to have meant in practice ransoming high-born captives, not beheading them, as was the Irish wont – along with a new-found English repugnance at carrying off prisoners into slavery and a growing contempt for war-as-cattle-raid came together to isolate as archaic and regressive these prominent features of Irish life. Irish dynastic disputes – frequently murderous – also seemed to push Irish society decisively beyond what a later generation would call the Pale. The *insula sanctorum* had become *insula barbarorum*: a seismic shift in designation and concurrent attitudes. Once this notion of Irish barbarism was grasped, there was no shortage of additional evidence to support it: the backward state of the Irish economy; the lack of towns; the conservative nature of Irish diet; Irish male and female costume and haircut; Irish horse-riding styles and so on, were all entered into the negative column on the index of civilisation. (Only Irish music, but not Irish musicians, appears to have escaped censure.)

Equally rapidly, the lurid, the prurient, the depraved and the fantastic, tumbled into the picture: Irish mating habits, the prevalence of bestiality and Ireland as a gateway to the otherworld, a place of magic, all began to feature prominently in English writings on Ireland. Ireland was different, inferior, outlandish; a country rich in flora and fauna, whose inhabitants lived filthily and who, instead of hunting and hawking, appeared to prefer war as recreation. Irish customs were depraved, Irish society was primitive and Irish church organisation and practices were an affront to God and man and the pope and Henry II (and presumably Archbishop Becket had Henry not (allegedly) had him murdered in 1170). And because this was the case Ireland was not really a Christian country: it was a pagan land, a barbaric island, even a deranged state of mind, that was the antithesis of Englishness and invasion, conquest and colonisation of this formerly Christian country, now agreed by all to have decayed into barbarism, were therefore imperative in order to impose change.

Bolstered by this vision of a new crusade against the infidel, not in the Middle East, but in an adjacent island, emboldened by their military prowess (a bench-mark of their superiority) and fired by the prospect of loot, the English con-querors of Ireland, like imperialist adventurers everywhere (and since), defined their struggles in terms of the triumph of true religion over paganism, modernity over primitivism and civilisation over barbarism. When these goals were not speedily achieved, or even if 'progress' in some areas was reported, but not in quite the way envisioned – clearly incomplete and with galling signs of delinquency and backsliding – then frustration and self-doubt soon set in, which in their turn led to furious denunciation of Irish ingrates and recidivists and to shrill calls for ever-sterner measures of repression. Perhaps worst of all – and, again, they were not unique in this – the settlers would come to the speedy realisation, like an ice splinter in the heart, that the 'primitive', 'depraved' and even 'bestial' ways of the Irish might not only prove difficult to eradicate, they might even hold undoubted attractions for increasing numbers of their group. Degeneracy, and the struggle to stem it, would be a preoccupation of the English settlers in Ireland throughout the medieval, early modern period and beyond.

Lastly, English settlers in Ireland, along with a consciousness of failure in their stated mission and a gnawing anxiety about the superiority of English ways, would have to endure the condescension and incomprehension of the home government – a denial of metropolitan recognition that was the lot of all colonial groups everywhere. Gerald of Wales chillingly revealed the dilemma of the invaders: there was no point in the small invasion force seeking further military aid from England in their contest against the Irish, he wrote, for 'just as we are English as far as the Irish are concerned, likewise to the English we are Irish, and the inhabitants of this island and the other [England] assail us with an equal degree of hatred'. In this revelation may be seen the seeds of the colony's decline and the origins of Anglo-Irish conflict.

The doubtful progress of the English colony

It might have been expected that the success of King John's visit would have prompted a sustained royal involvement in the affairs of the Irish lordship. The lords of Ireland, whether Irish or Anglo-Irish (as we must now describe those English barons who settled in Ireland), responded extremely well to the royal presence, vying with each other to submit and to offer homage and fealty. As it turned out John's expedition, with that of his father thirty years earlier, constituted something of an aberration. After John's return to England in 1210 it was not until 1394 that another king of England, Richard II, deemed Ireland worthy of the royal presence. To some extent, this near two-hundred-year gap in regal visits can be seen as an accident: kings such as Henry III, in 1233, and again in 1241, and Edward III in 1332, had planned military expeditions to Ireland only to call them off at the last moment; and the wretched Edward II had tried to flee to Ireland in 1326, but contrary winds had forced him back to Wales, and his famed encounter with the business end of a hot poker. No doubt other

English kings from time to time had toyed with the idea of an Irish excursion; and Edward III's appointment of his third son, Lionel, duke of Clarence and earl of Ulster, as lieutenant (chief governor) there (1361–6) surely showed his keen interest in the lordship.

None the less the fact remains that no king found the time to undertake the relatively short voyage in person; and even if all those who had professed an interest in coming to Ireland had in fact ventured there, royal expeditions would still have been few and far between. (We may note in passing that after Richard II's second expedition in 1399, it was not until 1689 – if we exclude 'King' Oliver Cromwell's devastating campaign of 1649–50 – that another English king, a most reluctant James II, arrived in Ireland (pursued a year later by an equally reluctant William III); and a further one hundred and thirty years were to elapse before George IV disembarked at Dunleary (renamed Kingstown in his honour.) Given this six-hundred-year perspective, the three royal visits by Henry II and John in a forty-year period marked the highpoint and, in effect, the end of sustained royal intervention in Ireland for many centuries.

This lack of royal expeditions is curious: Ireland was not difficult of access, for the Irish Sea was a medieval motorway between Ireland and England, nor did English kings dislike leaving England, for they were prepared to campaign in Scotland and Wales, and wage war in France, the Low Countries and the Holy Land when opportunity offered. The stark fact was that they did not come to Ireland because in comparison with other overseas territories – notably Gascony and Guienne in France, but also Scotland and Wales – Ireland simply did not count. The contrast in royal travels to Ireland and Scotland is particularly striking: all three Edwards, and Henry IV, 'honoured' Scotland with (most unwelcome) expeditions during the medieval period; but none came to Ireland. In general royal attention throughout the medieval period was fixed, first, on France (in Edward III's estimation 'a fairer marke to shoot at than Ireland, and could better reward the conqueror') and then on Scotland and Wales. Ireland, by and large, could be left to its own devices; and while the country constituted a very useful source of men and money – during the reign of Edward I, we are told, 'three several armies were raised of the king's subjects in Ireland . . . and several aides [taxes] were levied there for the setting forth of those armies' – that was no compelling reason for direct royal intervention. This inescapable conclusion explains a further puzzle concerning 'the conquest of Ireland by the English' (as contemporaries described it). Why had it remained incomplete?

Four hundred years after King John's expedition an apparently comprehensive answer to this question was given by Sir John Davies, a former Irish attorney general, in his book *A Discovery of the True Causes why Ireland was never entirely Subdued and brought under obedience of the crown of England* (London,

1612). In Davies's view the chief 'true cause' was the lack of royal interest in the colony, as evidenced by the notorious failure to mount royal expeditions there. Happily, however, at the time of writing, Davies was able to declare that the conquest begun in the late twelfth century had now at last been completed in the late sixteenth century. Against Davies, however, we may note that, even if there had been an ambition to conquer Ireland entirely – and there is no evidence of this – such an undertaking would probably have been beyond the reach of any of the medieval English kings, even if they had not had continental commitments and distractions and wider British ambitions.

The reality was that Ireland was not at all like England in 1066, when the Norman adventurer Duke William was able to take over a monarchy, a unified state and its administrative apparatus, in one fell swoop. In 1200 Ireland was more an idea than a country, a place where sovereignty was fragmented ('there are as many kings in Ireland as there are counts elsewhere', noted one observer), kin-group loyalties predominated and political authority was fractured. In addition, Ireland with its bogs and woods (20 per cent wooded in 1200 and over 20 per cent in bogland), like Russia with its steppes, was a physical deterrent to all but the most foolhardy, until the time of the Tudors. And yet the deplorable incompleteness of the medieval conquest – as later English commentators saw it – meant that assimilation, if desired, had never been possible, for the colony would always be too uneasy in its situation, and the colonists always too uncertain in their identity, to allow any coming together with the native inhabitants of the island. The piecemeal medieval conquest also meant that when the conquest was in fact completed under the Tudors it would be too late for any such fusion; only the chance of subjugation, not integration, would be on offer.

Assimilation?

In contemplating the English colony in Ireland, from the invasion down to 1541, and its interaction with existing and emerging Gaelic lordships, historians have customarily pointed to the early fourteenth century as marking its highpoint in terms of land under English control (perhaps 75 per cent of the island by the death of Edward I in 1307). Then, having described what we might call the crescendo of the English lordship's development since the late twelfth century, they have gone on to depict its diminuendo over the next two hundred and fifty years, a process of decay that became so advanced that Elizabeth I was apparently left with no choice but to abandon Ireland or complete the conquest. This thesis of the rise and decline of the English lordship, followed by a renewed and, this time, triumphant English conquest of Ireland has a satisfying symmetry to it; but as an interpretative framework for the history of Ireland, rather than merely the history of the English lordship of Ireland, it is inherently flawed and based on unspoken assumptions.

The first of these was that the fortunes of the English colony were central to the historical narrative, while those of the fifty or so Gaelic lordships were, somehow, peripheral. The second was that only the English lordship could expand and contract, while the Gaelic lordships, it was argued, remained largely unchanged from the time of the arrival of the English, if not earlier, to the end of the sixteenth century. As a corollary, therefore, lay the assumption that the Gaelic lords could only react, not act. The third assumption was that the rise and decline of the English lordship was a matter of prime concern, a major preoccupation, of the Gaelic lords themselves. None of these assumptions will survive scrutiny: because we know what happened does not mean that the path of Irish history was pre-ordained; the Gaelic lords, or some of them, were advanced enough to introduce into thirteenth-century Ireland the single most innovative, if destructive, force in the medieval period – the Gallowglass or Scottish mercenaries (heavily armed and hardy foot-soldiers). And they were always more alert to personal rivals and territorial threats from within Gaeldom than to the fortunes of the English colony.

This is not to say that the history of the English lordship ought not properly to command the major portion of our attention. On grounds of the bulk of the evidence alone, such a proposition would be absurd. Nor can we say that only scores of narratives – one for each of the Gaelic lordships – will suffice for any history of Ireland, for this would hide or disguise the very many points of contact, and interpenetration, between the Gaelic and the English worlds and obliterate the no-man's-lands that rapidly grew up between them. The frontiers of Gaelic Ireland and Anglo-Ireland were remarkably porous because people, as opposed to governments, wished them to be so. However, the borderlands were also scatterzones of conflict, seedbeds of that degeneracy which commentators had early identified as a dagger pointed at the heart of the first English colony. The task for the historian of medieval (and modern) Ireland is to identify where, and why, peaceful contact became deadly friction; to balance the local with the provincial, national and international perspectives; and to present a narrative that reflects contemporary realities, rather than the preoccupations of later generations.

The twelfth-century English invasion of Ireland, unfinished though it was, transformed the shape and appearance of the Irish landscapes. The importation of thousands of English and Welsh settlers was quickly launched and the settlers soon made their presence visible in south-east Ireland, and in the hinterland of Dublin.[5] By 1300 Gowran, county Kilkenny, was home to between two and four thousand settlers. Attracted to Ireland by the promise of cheaper land than in

England, but also lured by the prospect of a rise in status from unfree villein, or peasant, to the coveted rank of farmer, the settlers quickly introduced field patterns, house types and agricultural practices in the English fashion. Often overlooked in the historiography of medieval Ireland – possibly because they never staged a peasants' revolt, unlike their cousins in England – they gave the colony 'demographic depth' and, through all the vicissitudes of the next few hundred years, they ensured its survival. (We may note in passing that where new lords were not accompanied by settlers, as in Connacht, then the venture did not take root.)

The English farmers' masters too, the English and Welsh warriors and courtiers who received lands in Ireland from their king, also made their presence felt. Under the feudal patterns of tenure which they imported with them, they swore homage and fealty to the king as their feudal overlord, undertook to provide armed men for his army and, in return, held their lands from him under military tenure. As if following a manual on feudal tenures, they immediately embarked on a complex process of infeudation, and sub-infeudation, by which Irish lands were divided up in terms of knights' fees. However, such theoretical vertical ties to the king meant little in practice for, in the absence of the king, his barons quickly became accustomed to doing more or less as they pleased. Moreover, the military tenure by which they held their land enabled them, from an early date, to maintain those private armies that were to be such a scourge to the colony in the years to come.

Along with feudal tenure went castles and, from an early date, an extensive programme of castle-building (c. 750 moated sites remain) was initiated. Initially, these castles were of the motte-and-bailey kind (wooden forts built on mounds of earth) but by 1300 dressed stone was the preferred building material and castles had become ever more elaborate – those at Trim, county Meath, and Carrickfergus, county Antrim, for example rival any in Britain. From whom were these castles intended to offer protection? Obviously, they afforded some form of security from the uprooted Gaelic Irish, deemed unworthy of being retained as farmers on the land, and cast now as helots or simply ejected. They also provided a defence against those Gaelic lords for whom making war (i.e. cattle-raiding) was a sport to be played as often as possible. Increasingly, however, they offered protection from fellow English magnates who, ruthless in their desire to see off rivals and quick to avenge insults, were all too ready to make mayhem in the Irish marches. Hugh de Lacy was in open rebellion in the 1220s but that did not stop him succeeding to the earldom of Meath in 1226; and he may have been implicated in the murder of Richard Marshall in 1234. The 1290s witnessed the first *inter-Anglos* baronial civil war between the de Burghs and the FitzGeralds. By then it was evident that the civilising mission to Ireland, launched a hundred years earlier, had had its day.

Warfare between recently arrived English barons or the descendants of those who had come over to Ireland in the first wave, the Anglo-Irish, should not distract us from the more positive contributions of the first hundred years of the English presence. Perhaps surprisingly, the moral pretext for the invasion of Ireland – the elimination of barbarous practices, and the imposition of church reform – was not forgotten in the aftermath of the conquest. However, the problem here was that despite the clamour of English (and some Irish) clerics, it is not altogether clear that Irish religious practices were, in fact, all that benighted or backward. For example, a proper diocesan structure had been worked out thirty years before the initial conquest; continental religious orders such as the Cistercians were already in Ireland; and it might be suggested that, if left alone, the 'new model christianity' espoused by the colonists might have been introduced in its own time. That said, by the end of the thirteenth century a parochial system had been created to complement the diocesan structure, and further continental religious orders such as the Dominicans, Franciscans, Carmelites and Augustinians had arrived in Ireland. In addition, the new rulers proved keen benefactors of religious houses: by the 1230s, of the 200 religious houses in Ireland, 80 had been founded by the English in the previous sixty years. Even a rogue warrior such as John de Courcy founded six religious houses in Ireland (perhaps in compensation for those he had burned down).

We have already noted the creation of Dublin Castle as the administrative headquarters of the English colony, the appointment of a chief governor or justiciar, the establishment of courts of law and the introduction of English common law. By 1250 an Irish chancery and exchequer – complete with appropriate administrative practices – had been set up. Moreover, by the end of the thirteenth century, an Irish Parliament, albeit with a very restricted membership and no fixed place of assembly (Dublin, Drogheda and Kilkenny were the usual venues), had begun to meet, largely for the purpose of voting supplies to the justiciar and his administration, and for promulgating English laws. This Parliament assembled only fitfully in the thirteenth century (as did its counterpart in England): it first met (possibly) in 1264, with another meeting in 1278, and three more in 1289–91 and a final one in 1297, and it did not become a permanent feature of the Irish political landscape until the late seventeenth century. However, its medieval origins were vital to the establishment of a parliamentary tradition that has persisted to this day in both parts of contemporary Ireland. Moreover, the existence of a Parliament for Ireland, however impermanent it appeared, along with a separate Irish administration, however restricted its functions, showed clearly that, despite superficial similarities, Ireland was not regarded as an English borderland, or indeed as an English possession on the model of Gascony or the Channel Islands. Ireland's distinctiveness in this respect was shown by the promulgation of a decree in 1254 claiming that the land of Ireland could never be alienated from the English crown.

By the end of the thirteenth century, the Irish Parliament was drawing representatives from the Irish shires or counties. This process of shiring had begun before 1200 with the separation of Dublin City from the county. By the mid-1230s Cork, Waterford, Louth, Kerry, Limerick and Tipperary had been marked out, with most of Connacht being divided up in the 1240s. Only Gaelic Ulster, and the south-west, and far west, of Ireland, remained firmly beyond the administrative reach of Dublin Castle. The Irish Parliament, like its English counterpart, also drew members from a range of boroughs or towns and these, too, were largely an English import. Before the English invasion, the major towns in Ireland – Dublin, Cork, Limerick – were of Viking origin; but by 1300, some 225 boroughs (some based on pre-conquest Gaelic power-centres or monastic sites) had been granted royal charters and the urbanisation of Ireland, along with its encastellation, was under way. Some of these boroughs were not destined to survive, but most did and, with their regular markets (map 5), they became foci for commercial development as well as strongholds of Englishness – this latter feature perhaps explaining suspicions in modern Ireland of urbanisation, regarded as somehow inauthentic.

For a warrior aristocracy, these were not inconsiderable achievements; but there were a number of negative aspects to these developments that threatened to undo all of them. First, from the beginning, an evident spirit of petulant defiance was evinced by the English lords towards Dublin Castle and the king's administration in Ireland. Their attitude stemmed from the circumstances of the invasion, and manifested itself periodically in open, armed action. As we have seen, Henry II and his son John had attempted to reassert control over their barons in Ireland; but once they had departed, their barons' waywardness had quickly re-emerged – and their private armies gave them the means to act as they saw fit. The problem here was that given the incomplete and still-contested nature of the English conquest of Ireland, the freebooting activities of a John de Courcy, a Hugh de Lacy or a Peter de Bermingham could not be entirely disavowed by the authorities. De Courcy had waged war without royal authorisation, not only in north-east Ulster, but also in Connacht. De Lacy had been out of control in the early 1220s, but that had not prevented his promotion in the peerage. In 1305 de Bermingham would be the prime mover in the massacre of the O'Connors, after inviting them to a banquet. He subsequently had the corpses decapitated and the heads sold for reward. Not for the last time in its history, Dublin Castle reluctantly had to concede that while such men and their armed retinues, to put it plainly, might have been right bastards, 'they were our bastards', and in the absence of a substantial royal army they formed an essential defence of the colony against the king's 'Irish enemies' and, hence, were in effect beyond the law.

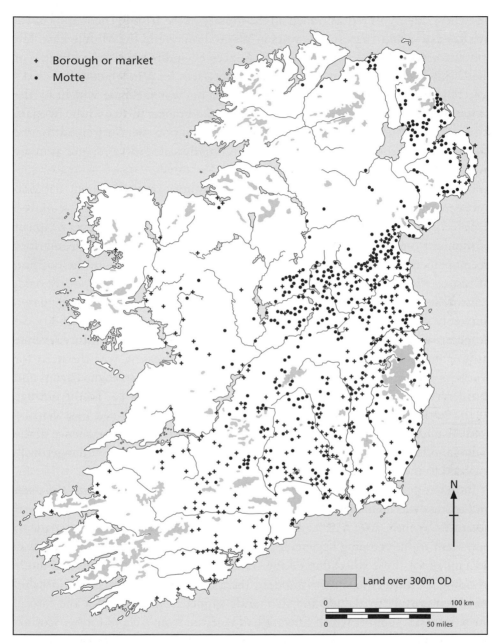

Map 5 Medieval settlement

Second, the entirely predatory attitude of English kings towards Irish treasure, men and matériel through much of the thirteenth and fourteenth centuries may have encouraged such lawlessness among the barons. From an early date it was clear that the strategic vision of the English kings for the Irish lordship extended no further than what they could extract from it for their military adventures elsewhere. Henry III requisitioned all the monies of the Irish exchequer in 1230, 1238, 1242–4 and 1247 for his wars in Wales, France and the Middle East. His son Edward I followed his father's lead. Supremely indifferent to the fortunes of the Irish lordship, except in so far as a farmer cares for a milch cow, Edward's sole object was to obtain money and men for his war machine which, by the 1290s, was grinding away in Scotland, Wales and France. In 1295 John Wogan, Edward's current justiciar, was ordered to raise 10,000 men in Ireland for the king's army in Scotland. Over 3,000 men eventually sailed in 1296, and as many more in the early 1300s.

Edward and his agents bled the lordship white, extracting some £40,000 between 1278 and 1306, and setting in train the process by which it moved decisively from being a contributor to the royal exchequer to being a net recipient of monies from England. Major financial, administrative and legal irregularities accompanied these demands for the wherewithal for war. Because the position of justiciar was such a thankless one, not least because it was so poorly paid, Edward appointed no fewer than eleven in eighteen years (his father had had two in twenty years), and such a turnover, on its own, was a recipe for instability. So desperate was the king's need for money that it became routine for future revenue to be pawned against an immediate return, and so pressing was the need for warriors and men abroad that pardons were often extended to rogue barons and murderers on condition of their embarking on overseas service. To the outrage of the settlers scarce food supplies were frequently requisitioned (=stolen) by soldiers under the custom of purveyance. And, of course, the consequence of the removal of so many soldiers overseas was that the lordship was left dangerously exposed to the king's 'Irish enemies', and lawlessness thrived.

In the 1297 Parliament the colonists' grievances were brought into the open and redress was demanded. There were earnest pleas for the apparent territorial advances by the Gaelic Irish to be turned back, and strident calls were made to put a halt to the creeping degeneracy of the English of Ireland. Punishment was demanded for those who adopted the Gaelic language, dress, haircut and mode of riding. Edward I died in 1307 and, by then, the administration of the lordship had been gravely weakened and its morale sapped. Ominously for the future, the substantial support which Edward had received from Ireland for his Scottish wars had had the effect of directing Scottish attention towards Ireland. In later centuries Spanish and French governments would mount expeditions to Ireland as a way of damaging England's capacity to wage war; but it was the Scots who, in the early fourteenth century, first recognised the potential for wounding England through Ireland's side.

There was a final weakness at the heart of the English lordship of Ireland which, on its own, guaranteed it a contested presence and a conflicted future. This was the narrow spirit of exclusion and racial antipathy towards the Gaelic Irish that was its prevailing ethos. Such discrimination against the Gaelic Irish was emphatically not royal policy. Henry II and John had had no wish to exclude the Gaelic Irish from the benefits of English rule and, especially, English law; John, we are told, specifically 'caused English laws and customs to be established there'; but his wishes were ignored. The consequences were dire, for the exclusion of the Gaelic Irish from English law gave rise to the idea of a natural enmity, an immemorial hostility, between English and Irish that was to prove remarkably enduring. The English invasion of Ireland can be set in the context of a wider European expansionary movement in the eleventh and twelfth centuries, and to that extent normalised. But it was in Ireland, not in Spain where Christian and Moor collided, or in the lands east of the Elbe where German and Slav were locked in combat, that the most extreme form of legal discrimination against a colonised (and fellow-Christian) people was to be found. Until 1541, and then in very different circumstances, the principle of *una et eadem lex* for all subjects in Ireland was comprehensively ignored.

Rejection?

The three bases for the exclusion of the Gaelic Irish were language, customs and law. From an early date we find Gaelic speakers the object of suspicion and discrimination, for they were widely regarded as the king's enemies and, very often, viewed as spies among the English. In the 1270s the citizens of Cork objected to the appointment of a Gaelic Irishman as collector of customs; in 1285 the Dominicans and Franciscans were denounced for 'making much of the Irish tongue', and as we have seen, in the Parliament of 1297 there were protests at the growing use of Irish among the English of Ireland. Frequent efforts were made to have bishops enforce preaching in English only, and to have them exclude Irish clerics from cathedral churches; and, depressingly, the religious houses themselves could be hotbeds of ethnic and linguistic hatred. In 1291 a dispute between Gaelic Irish and English friars over control of their monastery left sixteen dead.

Inevitably, Irish customs came under sustained fire: Irish costume, horse-riding style and haircut, in particular, all drew harsh criticism. In this latter regard it was not until the 1790s, when sporting a 'cropped' haircut revealed one's French sympathies, that so much anxious attention was again paid to a hairstyle, in this case the *cúlan*, or flowing back-cut hair, a distinguishing mark of the Gaelic Irish in the medieval period. It was, however, in the area of law that the most virulent hostility manifested itself. Throughout Europe, parallel legal systems were often tolerated. In Wales, for example, Welsh law and English law coexisted; but this was not to be the case in Ireland. So far as Edward I was concerned, Irish laws, with their blood-feud compensation and elaborate system of sureties and hereditary jurors, were 'detestable to God and so contrary to all laws that they ought not to be called laws', and there could be no question of allowing Irish laws as an alternative within the lordship. Where an Irish lord, say, an O'Neill, was in undisputed territorial control, then (reluctantly) Irish law could be allowed to operate; but if an Irishman lived in the lordship, and by 1300 this in theory covered three-quarters of the island, then he was *hibernicus*, deemed unfree and denied access to the king's courts. It was therefore a serious slander to call someone Irish, for that ruled him out of the protection of the law, and if it was shown that a plaintiff was Irish his case collapsed. In an extreme case – and there were a few of these – the murder of an Irishman by an Englishman was not considered a felony, for the victim was merely *hibernicus et non de libero sanguine*. Similarly, Irish widows were denied dower rights and the Gaelic Irish could not make wills.

Later generations affected outrage at these exclusions, and in truth there was much to be indignant about. After all, the English invasion of Ireland had given itself the lofty aim of ending barbarism, but it was evident that the reality had turned out to be quite different. Most of those who had been free 'before the conquest', if they resided in the lordship now found themselves excluded from the law of the conqueror, and legally much worse off. That said, there were exceptions: the 'five bloods', as the five main Gaelic families were known – the Ó Néill of Ulster, the Mael Shechnaill of Meath, the Ó Conchobair of Connacht, Mac Murchadha of Leinster and the Ó Briain of Munster – were allowed access to the king's courts, presumably for reasons of diplomacy, and so too were Gaelic Irish bishops and prelates. And investigation of the private legal affairs of the FitzGerald (Kildare) and Butler (Ormond) families shows that these great Anglo-Irish families were prepared to use Irish or English law when it suited. However, these were the exceptions: for most Gaelic Irish men and women, their studied and persistent exclusion from the common law courts was a harsh reality. In their Remonstrance of 1317 to the pope complaining of their treatment, the Gaelic Irish identified this exclusion as an oppression; and three hundred years later, Sir John Davies concurred, citing the denial of access to the courts as a key reason why the Gaelic Irish had never been entirely subdued. Moreover, in the decades after 1300, as the colony felt itself under severe pressure from the Gaelic 'rally', there was even less interest in according legal recognition to those dubbed the 'king's enemies'.

There was no single Gaelic reaction to what amounted to the transformation of Ireland, or at least of those parts that were under English control. Gaelic Ireland remained a collection of lordships which stretched from one end of Ireland to the other, with links across the Irish Sea to Scotland; and the rivalries, enmities and shifting alliances, of the O'Connors, O'Neills, O'Donnells, O'Briens, MacCarthaighs and others precluded any concerted response. The conventional wisdom has been that these Gaelic lords were immune to outside ideas and impervious to the new developments that were quickly altering the political and physical landscape of Ireland. Certainly, they showed no enthusiasm for any sustained and concerted action against the English lordship, and as before, pursued with unabated enthusiasm their wars against each other and against the Anglo-Irish lords. They also were quite happy to league with disaffected Anglo-Irish lords against joint enemies; and on occasion they journeyed abroad to fight for English kings – Henry III brought a contingent of Gaelic soldiers to Wales, and Edward III had Gaelic soldiers at Calais in 1347.

Gaelic poems, usually composed in honour of the Gaelic lords, and the annals, mostly monastic records of their exploits, are our principal source for Gaelic Ireland. These offer a picture of a world filled with little more than battles, murders, mutilations and cattle-raids, almost always described without context, analysis or explanation. Thus, Cathal Croderg O'Connor, king of Connacht, was hailed in the annals as a king who had 'most blinded, killed and mutilated rebellious and disaffected subjects' – hardly an encomium that would qualify him as a moderniser. In most cases these wars, murders and ambushes were linked to bloody succession struggles, for it was notorious that in Gaelic Ireland, unlike in England, the eldest son did not succeed the father but, rather, the royal successor emerged from within a four-generational common descent group. Such a system meant that conflict was inescapable. Almost any male within the extended royal family (including illegitimate male children) was eligible to succeed and, if successful, frequently had to contend with violent opposition from those worsted in the game. (A comparable procedure is utilised nowadays in the appointment of professors in Irish universities.) Of the thirteen kings of Connacht between 1274 and 1315, no fewer than nine were killed by brothers or cousins in succession struggles. It is understandable that the unending recitation of the witless martial exploits of the Gaelic lords, hacking their way to the throne, seeing off rivals and devastating (to unqualified applause) neighbouring territories, Gaelic or English, has been pronounced 'suffocatingly tedious' by one historian, and taken as evidence of a primitive, and regressive, social organisation.[6]

And yet it would be unwise to dismiss the social structure of Gaelic Ireland as mired in a world that had had its day. It still possessed its strong points. It is impressive, for example, how many of the prominent Gaelic Irish families, for all their internecine warfare, survived from the seventh century to the close of the sixteenth century; and note also how many leading English families such as the de

Lacys, de Courcys, Marshalls and others, went under in the hundred years after the invasion of Ireland through their failure to produce the necessary male heir, generation after generation. We may also note how adept the Gaelic Irish were in copying the battle tactics and weaponry of the English invaders, and in putting the lordship under severe military pressure by the early fourteenth century. Again, the single most innovative, if destructive, development in medieval warfare in Ireland – the introduction of Gallowglass – was undertaken by the O'Donnells of Ulster in the late thirteenth century. Lastly, we may also note that by 1300 the rise of the Ó Néill dynasty of central Ulster, but with linkages to other Gaelic families in the west and south, was well underway and, in time, was to pose the greatest threat to English control of Ireland. As the fourteenth and fifteenth centuries were to show, Gaelic Ireland was well capable of a resurgence and, as the colonists never tired of proclaiming, the king's Irish enemies were far from beaten. In the event, however, it was to be the king's Scottish enemies, between the years 1315 and 1318, who did most to bring the English lordship to its knees.

The Bruce invasion

In May 1315 Edward Bruce, a brother of Robert, king of Scotland, invaded Ireland with an army of some six thousand men and, a year later, near Dundalk, was crowned king of Ireland. Robert was fully behind his brother's invasion. It would, at the very least, divert the attention of Edward II from Scotland where he had continued to wage war since his accession in 1307. A large Scottish army in Ireland would also prevent vital military supplies from Ireland reaching the English king's forces in Scotland. Lastly, and no small matter, an invasion would give the restless Edward Bruce something to do, and – who could tell? – he might just pull it off.

Citing the 'same national ancestry' and 'common language', the Bruce brothers attempted to depict their invasion as a Scottish-Irish crusade against the common enemy, the English, and a document was drawn up, the so-called Remonstrance of 1317, in which some Gaelic lords, notably the Ó Néills, the O'Cahans and the MacCartans, justified their support for Bruce because of English oppression. But many Gaelic lords stayed aloof, rightly suspecting that the Ó Néills' backing for Bruce was merely a ploy by that family to use the Scots against their rivals. Nothing came of the proposed pan-Gaelic front and nothing more was heard of it. Significantly, the Declaration of Arbroath (1320), a ringing statement of Scottish national identity, was entirely silent on any Irish dimension. (In fairness, there is some suggestion that the Irish Remonstrance was a silent model for the Scottish Declaration – a very insincere form of flattery!)

Edward Bruce's invasion was soon in dire trouble. For a start his timing had been far from propitious. In 1315 Ireland, like most of Europe, was in the grip of a devastating famine. Torrential rains had wrecked the spring and autumn sowings, the winter was to see very large falls of snow, and food everywhere was in short supply. At any time Bruce would have faced massive difficulty in feeding his men but in a famine-stricken land his problems were magnified. His army's solution, looting what it needed and burning the rest, was hardly calculated to win Irish hearts and minds and when, after a series of militarily futile, but massively destructive, campaigns to the gates of Dublin and as far south as Tipperary, Bruce met his death at the battle of Faughart, outside Dundalk (1318), there was rejoicing on all sides. With pardonable exaggeration *The Annals of Lough Cé* described the death of that 'destroyer of all Erin, both Gael and English', Edward Bruce, as the best thing that had happened 'since the beginning of the world'.

The Bruce invasion had huge effects on the English lordship in Ireland. It set in train a process of economic decline and territorial recension, and it contributed to a 'general malaise' besetting the lordship that was to continue over the next hundred years and more. Admittedly the signs of decay had been there before the Bruce invasion: falling revenue, increasing lawlessness, endemic war and concerns over degeneracy (probably exaggerated) were clear indications that the English lordship was in deep trouble. Moreover, the damage wrought by the Bruce campaigns was followed in the 1320s by cattle plague, influenza epidemics and outbreaks of smallpox and crop failure, all of which set back recovery.

Gaelic revival/English decline?

In August 1348 the Black Death arrived in Ireland, having reached England from continental Europe a month earlier. This killer disease was seen as falling disproportionately on the colonists, for those who lived in towns (mostly English) rather than those who lived in the countryside (mostly Irish) were apparently at the greater risk of death. Friar John Clyn, stoically chronicling the course of the plague in Kilkenny (and 'awaiting death among the dead' – prophetically, for he seems to have fallen victim himself), described how 'hardly in any one house did one only die but commonly man and wife with their children and household'. Mortality soared: perhaps 14,000 dead in the first few months, and in the decades before the infection had run its course between 35 and 50 per cent of the population may have perished. Depopulation on such a sustained scale was, of course, catastrophic for the colony.

As the Black Death was no less deadly in England, there was no longer any prospect of attracting new settlers to Ireland from across the water. Worse, from the point of view of the English in Ireland, massive population loss in England freed up landholdings there and made that country an attractive place for those whose fathers and grandfathers had settled in Ireland and who were now disillusioned by royal neglect, worn down by endless fiscal demands and wearied by persistent Gaelic Irish attacks. In short, the demographic surge which had underpinned the English invasion of Ireland from the twelfth century on, and had sustained the English lordship there ever since, shuddered to a halt in the late fourteenth century. It was not to be renewed until the late sixteenth century. It is crucial to understand that all talk of the English lordship's decline in the fourteenth and fifteenth centuries and, equally, all claims that there was a Gaelic revival, rally or resurgence during this period have to be set against this key demographic fact.

In the wake of this demographic disaster, crown revenue, already falling in the early decades of the fourteenth century, plummeted further: it had been £6,300 per annum in the 1280s; by the 1380s it was £2,500 and falling. As one consequence of this growing financial crisis, the position of justiciar (governor) proved very difficult to fill (four were appointed between 1346 and 1357), for there were rarely sufficient funds to pay the holder, and bitter experience had shown that promises of assistance from England could rarely be relied on. Already in 1337, with the onset of what would become the Hundred Years' War with France, English interest in Ireland, never great, had diminished further. The lawless, predatory Gaelic Irish, or rebellious Anglo-Irish neighbours, became more brazen. For example, conscious that he was, in effect, above and beyond the law, Maurice Fitzthomas, first earl of Desmond, marauded with impunity for over two decades (1319–46), blinding, mutilating and murdering any, English or Irish, who got in his way. He may even have had aspirations to be king of Ireland, and he appears to have called on the kings of France and Spain, and on the pope to help him in this object. It was a telling comment on the weakness of English government in Ireland that, far from being brought to book for his outrages, Desmond ended his days in 1356 as the king's justiciar of Ireland.

As colonial control faltered, the frontiers of English Ireland began to contract, and the concept of a Pale, the 'land of peace', as opposed to the 'land of war', began to emerge, decades before the word itself. In Ulster, following the murder of the 'brown' earl of Ulster (apparently by his own men) in 1333, English advances into the region stopped and were not to be resumed until the late sixteenth century. Ominously for the future, in the absence of a substantial English power in east Ulster, stronger ties, both military and dynastic, were forged between the *Gaeil* on both sides of the North Channel. In the 1340s Connacht fell entirely outside government control, and the whole region was convulsed by a series of wars between the O'Connors, MacDermotts and O'Kellys.

By the 1350s a number of areas in Kildare, Tipperary and Kilkenny that had been English dominated, came under Irish control, while during these years the Irish of Wexford and Waterford were reported to be in continuous insurrection. In the face of this apparent Gaelic resurgence, some Anglo-Irish lords – the earl of Kildare in 1318 or Ormond in 1336 – took the pragmatic option and cut a deal with the local Gaelic families. In return for a nominal overlordship, they would accept an Irish reoccupation of landholdings. However, numbers of settlers, clearly dismayed by what appeared to be the impending collapse of the English lordship, sold out and returned to England; others, wealthier, opted to become absentee landowners, though very often their land in Ireland fell under Gaelic control.

And yet, for all this catalogue of disasters, the lordship did not collapse, and the tenacity of those who remained, known variously as the English-born-in-Ireland or the English-by-blood, and by historians as the Anglo-Irish, commands our attention. In choosing to remain in Ireland, they consciously fashioned a new identity for themselves, one that was, of course, in opposition to the Irish of Ireland, but one that also put some distance between them and the English-born-in-England, a people with whom they had less and less in common. Then (and perhaps now), it was a truism that neither the Gaelic Irish, nor the English-by-birth, much liked the English-by-blood and yet it was to be this group, the middle nation, that emerged intact from the severe trials of the fourteenth century. They had endured the ceaseless hostility of the Gaelic Irish, and they had known neglect, exploitation and incompetence at the hands of successive kings and their agents in Ireland. But, from the period of the Bruce invasion, they would reveal those characteristics of sturdy independence, self-reliance and self-assertion, that would make them a power in the land in the centuries to come. When, in the face of incompetence or, worse, treachery, it looked as if Dublin might fall to Bruce in 1316, it had been the citizens of that city who of their own accord had thrown up defences against his forces, and he had been deterred from attacking. It was too local levies of Anglo-Irish settlers who had defeated Bruce's army at Faughart, for despite a promise of a thousand Genoese mercenaries, no military assistance had been forthcoming from England. Moreover, in the decades after the Bruce invasion, the English-by-blood were vocal in their criticisms of inept, corrupt and poverty-stricken justiciars, who knew nothing of Ireland or the Anglo-Irish and who, starved of funding from England, resorted to extortion in Ireland in order to raise money. English policies aimed at reserving certain Irish positions for the English-born-in-England were also condemned unreservedly. In the same vein absentee landowners were denounced: they weakened the colony militarily, encouraged the Irish and disheartened those who remained. Lastly, these Anglo-Irish settlers were savage in their denunciation of those errant colonists who succumbed to the temptations of Gaelic life, culture and customs; and at the Parliament held in Kilkenny in 1366 they gave full vent to their fury at such degeneracy.

The Statutes of Kilkenny

In 1360 Edward III, responding to bitter complaints from the colonists that they were oppressed by the Anglo-Irish magnates, and left defenceless against the resurgent Gaelic Irish, had decided not to lead an expedition there himself but to do the next best thing: his third son, Lionel, would go to Ireland as lieutenant or chief governor in command of an army. In the event Lionel's expedition was not a military success. The 'great army' promised by Edward did not materialise and, quite predictably, the small force of around two thousand men that Lionel commanded proved capable of little more than limited police or garrison duties. In any case, what Lionel described as 'divers dissensions and debates' between the Anglo-Irish and the English as to how these soldiers should be deployed rendered joint campaigns against the Gaelic Irish very difficult. However, in 1366, he summoned a Parliament at Kilkenny at which a comprehensive attempt to solve the problems of the colony by legislative means would be undertaken. The result was the Statutes of Kilkenny.

The preamble to the Statutes was quite clear in its analysis of the colony's troubles. 'At the conquest of the land of Ireland', it began, all had gone well, for 'the English of the said land used the English language, dress and manner of riding, and... were governed by English law.' But now, 'many English... forsaking the English language, fashion, manner of riding, laws and usages, live and govern themselves by the manners, fashion, and language of the Irish enemies', and the result was, that the land and people 'are put in subjection and decayed', while the Irish enemies 'are raised up'. In order to put an end to this wholly undesirable state of affairs, some thirty-six clauses forbade all contact between English and Irish (whether by blood or by birth). Uniquely in Christendom, marriage alliances between the members of two Christian communities were outlawed. 'Sexual liaisons', concubinage between Irish and English, acting as godparents for each other and mutual fostering of children were also, for the future, taboo. Henceforth, all the clergy of the colony were to be of English stock. Irish customs, dress, riding-style and haircuts were to be entirely abandoned by the English. The Irish language came in for particular denunciation: it was seen as a hallmark of degeneracy, and therefore the English must speak English, not Irish, and must bear English names, not Irish ones. Those Irish who resided in the colony had to forsake the Irish language and converse in English. Again, because Irish musicians were commonly believed to act as spies they were to be barred from English lands.

There was little, we have been assured, that was new in the Statutes of Kilkenny. Even the strictures on the Irish language had been anticipated nearly a hundred years earlier. And as we have seen, in the Parliament of 1297 severe criticism had been levelled at those colonists whose 'Englishness' had slipped. Since then the hostility of the colonists to those who chose to embrace barbarous Irish ways had, if anything, become more pronounced. In 1329 the shocking (and still mysterious) massacre by Dundalk townsfolk of John de Bermingham, earl of Ulster, and over 150 of his household at Braganstown, county Louth, may have had as much to do with his perceived degeneracy as with the depredations of his men. It was surely significant that some twenty Irish musicians – 'spies' according to the Statutes of Kilkenny – and a similar number of 'kerne' (Irish foot-soldiers) in the earl's retinue perished in the massacre. Again, as recently as 1351, ordinances had been issued from Dublin Castle prohibiting alliances between English and Irish, and forbidding the use of brehon law.

The Statutes of Kilkenny, then, to a large extent were a codification and consolidation of what had gone before. But there is still a case for arguing that, in their comprehensiveness, they broke new ground and that they were unparalleled in Europe. The Statutes, in effect, signalled *finis* to any possibility of assimilation or integration between English and Irish, and they drew a circle around the notion of Englishness, defining its essence as that which was not marked as Irish. Tellingly, the punishment for those English who transgressed the code was to be regarded as Irish, i.e. not just treated as inferior but held to be disloyal. The Statutes of Kilkenny aspired to hold the line against resurgent Irishness and to ensure that English areas remained English. However, those behind the Statutes could only hope to do so by avoiding eye-contact with reality, for the rot had set in, so to speak, long before 1366, and 'degeneracy' would always be the worm at the heart of every colonial project. The Statutes of Kilkenny were less a bugle-call to arms, more the declaration of a siege, and their enthusiastic confirmation in subsequent Parliaments down to 1494 and beyond could not but place conflict and contestation at the heart of relations on the island. So far as peaceful accommodation was concerned Ireland had become a never-never-never land.

The Statutes of Kilkenny changed nothing: Lionel returned to England, and a new lieutenant, William of Windsor, was appointed. Before long there arose from Ireland the by-now familiar chorus of complaints concerning the imposition of penal taxes, the iniquities of purveyance and the failure to deal effectively with the resurgent Gaelic Irish. Windsor was removed, then reappointed, then succeeded by Ormond, who in his turn was succeeded by Edmund Mortimer, earl of March, a popular choice among the colonists. However, Mortimer died in 1381, and it proved very difficult to find a replacement. Eventually, Mortimer's son, a boy aged seven, was appointed lieutenant, and although his uncle was deputed to carry out the duties, the situation was profoundly unsatisfactory. Increasingly, the English lordship appeared to be drifting to disaster. In desperation the colonists called for Richard II himself to come to Ireland and put matters right. Fortunately for them, with peace in France and Scotland in the 1390s, Richard was in a position to do so. In October 1394, accompanied by a truly formidable army of 8,000–10,000 soldiers and, including, for the first time in Ireland, an artillery train, he landed at Waterford; his mission was, 'the punishment and correction of our rebels there, and to establish good government, and just rule over our faithful lieges'.

For those dreaming of military glory and a completed conquest of Ireland the resulting campaign was a huge anti-climax. With an army comparable in size and composition to those that had been attempting to conquer France, Richard opted instead to receive peaceful submissions from the Gaelic lords rather than winning military victories. Admittedly, attacks were launched on the rebellious Irish of Leinster, principally on Art Mór Mac Murchadha, whose ancestor had been Diarmait Mac Murchadha of 1169 fame (or infamy), and on 'our rebels who call themselves captains and kings of Munster and Connacht'. Mac Murchadha quickly submitted and he was followed in a few months by around eighty other Gaelic lords, including, notably, the two Niall Ó Néills, grandson and great-grandson of Domhnal Ó Néill who had backed Edward Bruce, and whose territory in Ulster had expanded greatly since the brown earl's murder sixty years earlier. These latter were persuaded, as Richard II put it, 'to surrender to us, submit, recognise their offences, and receive for them whatever we will devise'. They promised fidelity and service for the future, and they also pledged themselves to abandon Irish habits of horse-riding, apparel and cuisine.

Richard appears to have had an imaginative plan of settlement in view, involving land transfers and the enlistment of the Gaelic Irish of Leinster as elements in the royal army, with the object of making Ireland secure for England and re-establishing the lordship as a source of profit to the crown. For such a scheme to work, however, the king's presence, a firm hand and a large army were necessary, at least in the short term. None of these was available. Richard returned to England in May 1395 taking most of his army with him, and leaving the youthful and impetuous Roger Mortimer, earl of March, behind him as chief governor. Renewed disturbances broke out almost immediately. It has been customary to accuse the Gaelic Irish of bad faith in triggering this renewed war. Some two centuries later, Sir John Davies wrote that Richard was 'no sooner returned into England, but those [Gaelic] Irish lords laide aside their maskes of humility, and scorning the weake forces which the king had left behinde him beganne to infest the borders'.

However, March and other Anglo-Irish lords were by no means blameless in these conflicts. March, in particular, had been engaged for years in a power struggle with the Ó Néill of Ulster and, with Richard gone, he had quickly taken the offensive, raiding into south Ulster and burning Armagh. A warrior rather than a conciliator he was killed two years later in Carlow fighting against the O'Byrnes. Richard II returned to Ireland in 1399 with another army but, before he could make an impact, news came that his English rival, Henry Bolingbroke, had raised his standard against him. Richard was forced to return immediately to England, but the journey was to be his undoing: as Davies put it, 'shortly after, hee ended both his raigne and his life'. In the end Richard's two expeditions to Ireland (and we may note that he was the only English monarch before Victoria to visit Ireland twice), for all the exaggerated claims made at the time, had achieved nothing, except perhaps to confirm that an exclusively English Leinster was militarily impossible.

Matters did not improve for the colony in the new century. War in Wales, along with domestic disturbances in England, meant that from an early date there was no attempt made to build on Richard's efforts in Ireland. The resumption of war with France in 1415 pushed Ireland further down the English government's military and financial priorities. When Ormond was made lieutenant of Ireland in 1442 he was allowed a derisory three hundred archers for his retinue, and allocated a paltry stipend of £2,000; by contrast, when John, earl of Huntingdon, was appointed lieutenant of Guienne in 1439 he was given three hundred men-at-arms, three thousand archers, and payments totalling £36,000. Even the governors of the Channel Islands were much better supported and remunerated than those of Ireland. With pardonable exaggeration, Ormond would claim that if what was spent in France in one year was diverted to Ireland, the problems of the colony could be solved for all time. With the drying up of English subsidies and with no improvement in Irish income (running at a very low £1,000 per annum), English power in Ireland diminished proportionately. Even the literary energies of the lordship seem to have faded: not a single original work in English can be shown to have been written in Ireland during the fifteenth century; by contrast, a considerable number of Gaelic manuscripts have been dated to this period.

An empty treasury in Dublin meant that candidates from England were reluctant to take on the poorly paid and largely thankless task of lieutenant. By and by it became routine to seek a chief governor among the Anglo-Irish themselves, and it was made explicit that they should find their stipend within Ireland. By the end of the fifteenth century, the FitzGeralds, earls of Kildare, had almost monopolised the post of lieutenant. However, raising up one man and one family at the expense of others over time fuelled poisonous rivalries among the magnates and added to the Anglo-Irish sense of detachment, where England's, or indeed the king's interests, were concerned. Lastly, reduced income meant that the small English garrison in Ireland frequently found their pay in arrears and, as soldiers did everywhere when not paid, they had resorted to 'free-quarters'. This oppressive practice had previously been a much criticised feature of Gaelic society, but in the early decades of the fifteenth century, and now dubbed 'coign and livery', it became widespread in the English lordship.

Coign was derived from the Gaelic custom of 'guesting', while livery came from the English practice of offering straw and corn. Brought together (by the devil, claimed Davies), 'coign and livery' meant the seizure 'for nought, without any peny paying therefor' of food, shelter, fuel, forage and even money from hapless husbandmen encountered by unpaid and ravenous soldiers on campaign. This yoking together of Gaelic and English customs came to symbolise the erosion of distinctions between the king's 'Irish enemies' and the king's 'English rebels', and to encapsulate that degeneracy of the Anglo-Irish magnates which the Statutes of Kilkenny, reconfirmed in 1406, had sought to prevent.

Gaelic Ireland in the fifteenth century

The great Anglo-Irish families – the Burkes, Talbots, Butlers, FitzGeralds and Fitzmaurices – had developed by the mid-fifteenth century a hybrid lifestyle in which they were borrowing freely from their Gaelic counterparts. (Figures 2.1 and 2.2 illustrate some Gaelic artefacts of the period.) Not only in quartering soldiers among the farming community, but also in such matters as fostering their children, composing Gaelic poetry, adopting Gaelic naming practices and, on occasion, utilising brehon law, the Anglo-Irish lords appeared to be blurring the distinction between themselves and their Gaelic rivals (who, in their turn, were not above 'anglicising' themselves for their own advantage). However, it was the Anglo-Irish lords who caught the eye. Constant murderous feuding (Butler–Talbot in the early part of the century, FitzGerald–Butler towards the end), frequently in association with Gaelic allies, and even with Scottish Gallowglass, led some historians to conclude that a rapid process of Gaelicisation was underway among the Anglo-Irish lords in the fifteenth century.

Such a conclusion is, however, largely unwarranted. The Anglo-Irish certainly adopted Gaelic customs and laws, as they saw fit (the English in Wales did something similar), but such borrowings did not in any way diminish their profound sense of English identity and nationality. They described themselves proudly as 'the English of the land of Ireland'. Nor did their relentless warring

2.1 Iron helmet with bronze mounts from Lough Henney, county Down.
Fourteenth–fifteenth century. Ulster Museum.

2.2 Iron carpenter's axehead on original woodhaft. Clonteevy, county Tyrone; twelfth–fourteenth century. Ulster Museum.

between themselves identify them as Gaelic: the contemporaneous Neville–Percy feud in the north of England was little different from that between the Butlers and the Talbots in the south of Ireland. That said, it is evident that the authorities in England had their own view of the English colonists in Ireland. Increasingly, they regarded both the English-of-Ireland, and the Gaelic Irish, as simply *Hiberniores* and they refused to draw a distinction between them. For the first half of the fifteenth century, the English-of-Ireland living in England were officially classed as aliens there and a number of proclamations were issued ordering them back to Ireland. Such discrimination can only have increased Anglo-Irish disenchantment with the mother country, but it would be an exaggeration to view their rejection by England as impelling them into Gaelic ways.

As English influence diminished in the first decades of the fifteenth century, so too did the territory under the control of the Dublin administration. By the 1420s an area known as 'the land of peace' consisting, more or less, of present-day Dublin, Louth, Meath and Kildare, was being treated separately from other English districts and, by the 1470s, the term 'the Pale' had been deployed to designate the English area of Ireland (map 6). In 1488 when its dimensions were fixed by statute it stretched from Carlingford, fifty miles north of Dublin, curved inland to Mullingar at the widest point, then plunged south to Carlow before swinging into the coast in north Wicklow. Beyond the Pale were the marcher lands occupied by Anglo-Irish magnates, whose large palatinate jurisdictions were in effect independent lordships. Beyond these lay the porous and shifting frontiers of Gaelic Ireland, a huge swathe of territory north and west of a line running from Carrickfergus to Galway, but also in south-west Ireland.

Conditions in the Pale and in the coastal towns would undoubtedly have appeared familiar to an observer from the north of England or the lowlands of Scotland. However, Gaelic Ireland, notwithstanding four hundred years of the English presence on the island and an ostensibly shared religion and church organisation, would have appeared exotic and outlandish: a society outside the range of ordinary European mores, as one historian has described it. Outwardly, little had altered in Gaelic Ireland since the English invasion. The complex succession system in force in Gaelic Ireland for hundreds of years, by which the 'king' was drawn from a large pool of contenders, was substantially unchanged. As a result, bloody succession struggles were as common in the fifteenth century as they had been in the tenth century and earlier. Similarly, the professional learned classes of brehon (judge), poets, historians, musicians and physicians remained largely intact (figures 2.3–5). To this list of hereditary occupations should be added that of cleric, for despite frequent strictures, married clergy were common, and so too was the passing on of parishes and bishoprics from father to son.

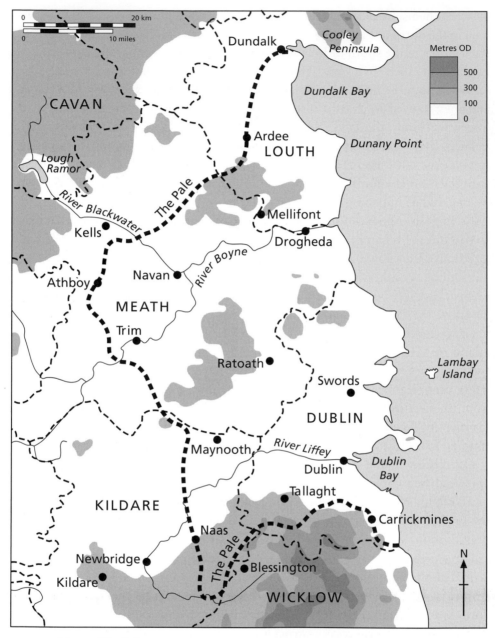

Map 6 The Pale

In Gaelic Ireland, while corn and other cereals were grown – probably more than allowed for by historians – the economy was overwhelmingly pastoral, with large herds of cattle and horses being driven by herdsmen over wide tracts of waste. This dominance of pastoral over tillage meant that there was a strong nomadic element to Gaelic life, for cattle had to be moved to summer grazing

2.3 Page from the Book of the O'Lees, probably compiled c. 1438 and containing an Irish translation of the Islamic physician, Ibn Jazlah's (d. 1100) medical treatise. Royal Irish Academy.

2.4 Opening page from a sixteenth-century introductory tract on bardic teaching. Royal Irish Academy.

on mountain slopes (booleying). The importance of cattle also determined the pattern of Gaelic warfare, for in many cases this was little more than cattle-raiding for prestige and sport. And Gaelic diet too could not but be based on meat and dairy products, in sharp contrast to cereal and beer-consuming societies. English and continental observers identified the lack of bread made

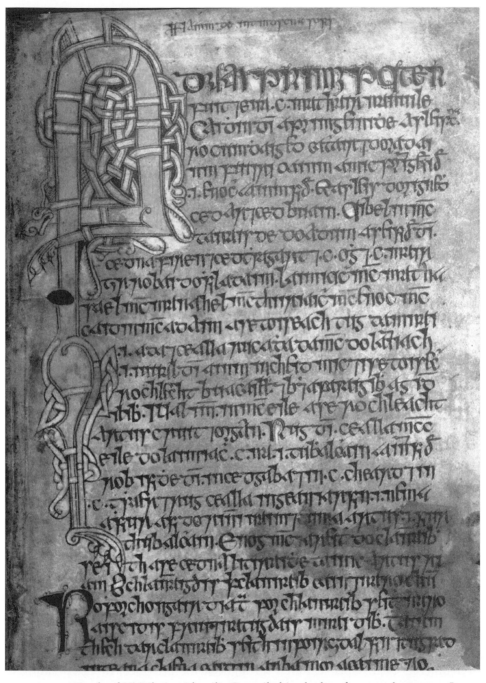

2.5 Book of Uí Mhaine (detail). Compiled in the late fourteenth century. Its scribe may have had access to books from outside the Irish tradition. Royal Irish Academy.

from wheat as a mark of primitiveness, and were horrified at the large amounts of butter, beef, pork and horsemeat consumed, washed down with milk (hot, sour or mixed with animal blood) and whiskey (first mentioned in 1405, but assuredly around for much longer).

Irish costume, or the lack of it, also attracted a good deal of attention. The pilgrim, Raymond de Perelhos, *en route* to St Patrick's purgatory in 1397, was astonished at the lack of modesty of the women in Ó Néill's camp where he had stayed for a time. Everyone, he wrote, went barefooted and barelegged but, to his astonishment, the women made no attempt to cover their private parts, but rather 'showed all they had with as little shame as they show their faces'. Gaelic Irishmen, by contrast, drew censure for the opposite reason for failing to reveal their countenances. By the 1450s a Gaelic Irishman would typically sport a large moustache and espouse the 'glib' – a style of haircut in which the back of the head was shaven and the hair on top combed forward over the eyes. Such adornments were denounced, for they made it, as one hostile observer put it, 'very hard to discern [an Irishman's] thievish countenance'. For similar reasons, the Irish mantle, a woollen cloak worn by men, likewise provoked much criticism from English observers. This enveloping, weatherproof garment was certainly practical for the Irish climate. Some observers conceded as much, and English soldiers on campaign in the 1590s in Ireland were quick to appreciate its qualities against foul weather; but its voluminous folds led to the mantle being viewed as something altogether more sinister – 'a fit house for an out-law, a meet bed for a rebel, and an apt cloke for a thief'. On the face of it, then, a certain timelessness seemed to have enveloped Gaelic Ireland over the previous five hundred years. Politics remained resolutely focused on the local; low-intensity wars, revolving around cattle-raiding and disputed successions, abounded; and political authority remained fragmented. And yet, beyond the clamour of constant war within Gaelic Ireland, certain changes, ominous for the future of the English lordship in Ireland, can be discerned.

The first of these was the near complete withdrawal of royal authority from Ulster. After 1468, apart from the castle at Carrickfergus, the fishery on the River Bann and a coastal strip at Lecale (county Down), royal or English government was non-existent in that large area. Second, from the 1450s, and under the leadership of Enrí Ó Néill (1455–83), the Ó Néill dynasty of Tír Eoghain had begun to emerge as the main power in central Ulster, and to assert its supremacy over other Ó Néill septs scattered throughout the province. In 1463 Tadhg Ó Briain of Thomond acknowledged Enrí's claim to the high-kingship. In addition, the Ó Domhnalls in west Ulster, ably led by Aodh Rua, king of Tír Conaill (1461–1505), were also consolidating their lordship and intervening militarily in Connacht. The Ó Domhnalls had allied with the Mac Sweeneys in the 1460s and this brought them additional military strength, for the MacSweeneys were a leading Gallowglass connection. The first recorded use of firearms in Ireland was by Aodh Rua's soldiers in 1487, and it seems clear that the military potential of Gaelic Ulster, fully revealed only in the sixteenth century, was slowly awakening. On the surface, the rivalry between the various Ó Néill septs, and between the Ó Néills and the Ó Domhnalls, would persist throughout the fifteenth century, and English commentators could take comfort from this. 'God... setting continuall dissension amongst them and continuall warre', claimed one observer in 1490, had ensured that the Gaelic Irish could never cooperate effectively. In Ulster, however, in the late fifteenth century, the way was being cleared for just such a coming together of the leading septs, backed by the formidable Gallowglass, with their armour, battle-axes and six-foot swords, and equipped with the latest weaponry.

The rise and fall of the house of Kildare

The appointment in 1447 of Richard, duke of York, as lieutenant appeared to be the answer to the colonists' prayers. They had long sought a 'great man' as chief governor, and Richard, heir apparent to Henry VI, certainly fitted the bill. Like his namesake from the 1390s, Richard, on his arrival in 1449, immediately set about bringing his ostensible Gaelic vassals to submission, and when he had assembled a formidable force and marched against them, they were quick to yield. Enri Ó Néill, soon to be king of Tír Eoghain, submitted at Drogheda, signed an indenture agreeing to return all lands and castles seized from the English in the past hundred years, and in general, promised to conduct himself loyally in the future. He was followed by what amounted to a rollcall of Gaelic Ireland. However, when the duke of York failed to follow up his military exertions, these submissions were soon shown to be worthless. The allegiances of Gaelic lords – to each other as well as to an English ruler – were purely personal, and always transient, never institutional.

In the 1450s dynastic turmoil, not unlike that which frequently wracked Gaelic Ireland, broke out in England as a result of Henry VI's insanity and led to York's withdrawal from Ireland. The crisis of the lordship deepened.

Despite his failure in Ireland, York remained a favourite there (the start of an Irish love affair with heirs to the English throne) and, when he fled to Ireland in 1459 as a fugitive from the Wars of the Roses, he was welcomed as 'another Messiah' by the English of Ireland. York was quickly accused of treason for making war on Henry VI and his return to England to face trial (and certain execution) was ordered. His robust response to this challenge was to summon a

Parliament in Ireland which passed legislation confirming him as chief governor, extended the treason law to cover his person and, sensationally, declared that 'the land of Ireland is and at all times has been corporate of itself'. In effect, this legislation stated that English laws and writs did not run in Ireland without the Irish Parliament's agreement. To give an edge to this striking assertion of legislative independence, the unfortunate messengers who had brought over to Ireland the writs of treason against York were themselves promptly seized and executed.

Historians have on occasion tended to view this legislation as tantamount to a declaration of 'Home Rule' on the part of the Anglo-Irish, or else dismissed it as a mere tactical device designed to protect York from the consequences of finding himself, for the time being, on the losing side in the dynastic wars of the 1450s. In fact the legislation may have had both objects in view. Certainly, the 'Messiah' had to be protected; but the Irish claim to legislative autonomy had no substance to it, for English laws had been applied for a century in Ireland without any need for re-enactment in the Irish Parliament. None the less the choice of words was striking, the concept of Ireland as corporate of itself was novel, and the declaration would be quoted down the centuries by those who wished the Irish Parliament to be separate from, and equal to, the English Parliament. After 1460 legislative independence was on the Irish political agenda, though over three hundred years were to elapse before something approaching it was achieved.

A year after summoning the Irish Parliament in 1460 the duke of York was killed at the battle of Wakefield while seeking to overthrow Henry VI; but his death was not in vain, for his son took the throne as Edward IV. This, however, did not settle matters, for further struggles ensued between Yorkists and Lancastrians, in which Ireland, firmly Yorkist, became embroiled. It was not until the late 1470s that dynastic distractions eased in England and, with the consolidation of Edward's rule in England, came the emergence of Gerald, eighth earl of Kildare, as deputy in Ireland. For the first time in decades, a 'great man' had been appointed who was unburdened by foreign distractions, who resided in the Pale, and who had the financial resources, military muscle and political shrewdness to manage the lordship. He also proved adept in handing on the deputyship to his son, also called Gerald, so that the FitzGeralds more or less monopolised the job down to the 1530s.

From an English point of view a Kildare ascendancy was not at all the perfect solution to England's Irish problem, but it was a pragmatic one. Edward IV might well have preferred a more forward policy, even a direct intervention in Ireland, but the money for this was simply not available. He could appoint an English deputy – and had done so by naming Sir John Tiptoft in 1467 – but without massive support from England such appointees tended either to be little more than pageants of state or, worse, reckless individuals who failed to recognise the limits of their power. Within five months of his arrival Tiptoft had attainted the earls of Desmond and Kildare, and then had Desmond put to death – an action that shocked the colony and left the powerful Desmond family disaffected from royal government for the next hundred years. Tiptoft himself was soon recalled and subsequently executed; Kildare, father of Gerald, was appointed governor in his place and was succeeded by Gerald in 1479.

The last twenty years of the fifteenth century, in so far as these things can be measured, witnessed an upswing in the fortunes of the lordship under the guiding hand of 'the great earl' of Kildare. The doomsayers fell silent as Kildare, with his home base in the Pale secure, recruited Gallowglass and kerne and pushed back the frontiers of the English areas in Kildare, Wicklow and Carlow. Customs revenue also improved dramatically during this period. All of this, however, came with a price, which was that Kildare should be permitted freedom of action to further his own interests, as well as those of his royal master. He was not the last royal governor who conveniently saw no conflict between his own fortune and that of the king. It was perhaps inevitable that, as he grew accustomed to power in the 1480s, Kildare should overreach himself; but that his fall (a temporary one) would result from further dynastic squabbles in England could hardly have been foreseen.

Edward IV had died in 1483, and after the Gaelic fashion, his sons had been murdered, and Edward had been succeeded by Richard III (of York), the probable murderer. This usurpation was not unfavourable to Kildare's interest because he had hitched his wagon to the Yorkist cause since the 1460s. However, Richard's swift overthrow and death, at the hands of Henry Tudor in 1485, came as a most unwelcome bolt out of the blue. Understandably, Kildare chose to regard Henry VII as not destined to remain long on the throne. This seems to be the main explanation for why the normally prudent Kildare allowed himself to be drawn into the plot by Lambert Simnel, masquerading as the earl of Warwick, to oust Henry as king of England.

Simnel's expedition was mounted from Ireland, though with support from continental mercenaries, but it came to a disastrous end at the battle of Stoke in 1487, and Henry VII survived the challenge. Kildare was suspected of close involvement in the plot, but for the time being Henry did nothing. However, when another impostor, Perkin Warbeck, claiming to be the murdered son of Richard III, fetched up in Ireland late in 1491 and, once again, received support and countenance from the Anglo-Irish, including Kildare, Henry's patience was exhausted, and he was forced to take decisive action. Kildare was replaced as governor in 1494, and summoned to London. His successor was Sir Edward Poynings, whose period in office was chiefly memorable for the passing of the law that bore his name, and which was designed to curb the independence of governors, such as Kildare. Sir Edward would have been astonished to learn that 'Poynings' law' was still in force over three hundred years later, and that it was much appreciated by London, because it restricted the powers, not of the governor, but of the Irish Parliament.

Given the extent of Kildare's involvement in Yorkist affairs, and in the plots of Simnel and Warbeck, it comes as something of a surprise to learn that, so far from paying for his treachery (or foolishness) with his life, Kildare was restored as deputy in 1496, and reappointed on even more favourable terms than he had enjoyed previously. The explanation for this unexpected outcome appears to lie in two areas, the personal and the political. Put simply, against all the odds, Henry and Kildare got on well together, for both had a black sense of humour. Henry had installed Lambert Simnel as a servant in his kitchens, so that he would wait on the table of his erstwhile Irish supporters when they came to court, to their evident discomfort (and the king's glee); and Kildare had, apparently, won over Henry who had accused him of burning down Cashel cathedral; Kildare explained patiently that he had only done so because he believed the archbishop was inside. One rogue recognised another: Kildare's attainder was lifted and Henry permitted Kildare to marry his kinswoman.

On a deeper level, however, Henry's restoration of Kildare was a recognition that he had no realistic alternative, for financial restraints ruled out a forward policy, and however much Henry VII might muse on the possibility of a self-financing conquest of Ireland, he was wise enough to realise that this was a pipe-dream. He had really little option but to back Kildare, and Kildare, duly chastened by his experience in London, stayed loyal to Henry until the latter's death in 1509. The 'great earl' died in September 1513, and was succeeded as deputy by his son, Gerald, ninth earl of Kildare. On the surface, the transition of power from one generation to the next, both in Ireland and England, had proceeded smoothly; but appearances were deceptive. Fatally, the new king, Henry VIII, was a genuine intellectual in a job that required very modest attainments, and he quickly revealed himself to be a restless individual, given to bursts of reforming energy followed rapidly by periods of lethargy, and always anxious to make a splash in the world. It was inconceivable that he would be content to let matters remain indefinitely as they were in Ireland; but at the same time, a galling lack of money enjoined for a time a certain prudence on him.

In 1519 Kildare was summoned to court in London. He would not fare as fortunately as his father had done, for his detention in England was ordered, and he was replaced as deputy by the earl of Surrey, a military commander. The choice was significant, for Henry was known to be mulling over the classic English problem since the time of the incomplete conquest: 'how Ireland may be reduced, and restored to good order and obedience'. Quite what Surrey's military expedition to Ireland was supposed to accomplish was never made clear. Surrey took the conventional view that the Gaelic Irish were incorrigible, that only military conquest would suffice to bring Ireland to good order and that English settlers should be brought in to colonise Gaelic areas. For his part Henry VIII famously maintained that Ireland could be brought to civility by 'sober ways, politic drifts, and amiable persuasions, founded in law and reason'. The distinction between the two approaches has probably been exaggerated: Henry VIII might have preferred mild measures, but implicit in his remarks was the threat of stunning violence should these be rejected.

At the same time it is clear that Henry was already turning over in his mind some of the key issues to do with Ireland. He was especially affronted by the denial of legal protection to the vast majority of the Gaelic Irish. In Henry's view, there were only 'disobeisant subjects', English and Irish, in Ireland, and he rejected the long-standing distinctions between 'Irish enemies' and 'English rebels', especially where these involved discriminatory treatment before the law. He was prepared to introduce a legal system which drew on both traditions in the hope of drawing the Gaelic Irish from their barbaric ways and he was prepared to facilitate an exchange by giving up his title to Gaelic territories provided the Gaelic Irish restored lands to which the crown had title.

In the event nothing came as yet of these ruminations, for Surrey's expedition was a complete failure. An attempt to govern through Ormond also collapsed, largely because of mischief-making by Kildare's allies, especially Desmond. There was, it seemed, nothing for it but to reappoint Kildare, like his father before him, and this was done in 1524. But Henry was uneasy at this 'solution', and it could only be seen as temporary. Within two years, Kildare was replaced, and summoned to England, where he was, once again, detained in the Tower. His enemy, Lord Ossory, a Butler, took over as deputy but, as before, this proved a recipe for disaster. Ossory was dismissed in 1530 and the aged William 'Gunner' Skeffington, a man with much experience of campaigning in Ireland, took over. Kildare was freed and allowed to return to Ireland in the expectation, never very likely, that he would facilitate Skeffington's deputyship.

Emboldened by a belief that he was indispensable to the smooth running of English government in Ireland, Kildare continued to run huge risks in his dealings with London. But the times were turning against him. During the early 1530s Henry VIII was facing the diplomatic, dynastic and political fall-out of his messy divorce from Catherine of Aragon and his subsequent wedding to Anne Boleyn. Simultaneously, he was also engaged in severing religious links between England and Rome. He was in no mood to be indulgent toward over-mighty subjects in Ireland (or elsewhere). And yet, for all that, Kildare's strategy appeared vindicated: despite adverse reports of his scheming against Skeffington, he was appointed deputy in succession to him in 1532. Complaints against him mounted, particularly from John Alen, clerk of the Irish council and a close confidant of Thomas Cromwell, Henry's principal adviser, to the effect that Kildare had been moving armaments from Dublin Castle into his own strongholds. More serious charges concerning making private peace treaties with the king's enemies followed; and in 1533 Kildare was summoned, once again, to England to answer them.

On his arrival there, early in 1534, he was imprisoned for the third time in the Tower, dying of natural causes some months later. Before then, however, in reaction to his father's arrest, 'Silken Thomas', Lord Offaly, Kildare's heir, had risen in rebellion in June 1534, denounced Henry as a heretic, appealed to the pope, sought aid from Charles V, seized and murdered Archbishop Alen (the cousin of his father's chief accuser) and laid siege to Dublin Castle. A Kildare had finally thrown all his toys out of the pram; how would Henry VIII respond?

The precedents were both uniform and compelling: as before, the crown would surely back off before such an exhibition of power and enter into face-saving terms. Accordingly, Palesmen flocked to Silken Thomas, many of the Gaelic Irish chiefs rowed in behind him and a substantial number of priests supported him by preaching against the heretic king of England. All things considered, the tenth earl of Kildare seemed certain to be restored to power, with little more than a rap on the knuckles. He would succeed in his aim of demonstrating that, if the Kildares were not in control, no one else would be. For a time it appeared that Kildare's ploy had paid off, for Henry sent out peace feelers and sought to ascertain Kildare's terms for coming in from the cold. Henry, however, was insincere in these moves: he was determined to punish Kildare, for his rebellious Irish subject had undermined his authority in England and, no less serious, made a show of him in the eyes of the emperor, Charles V. Thomas Cromwell was ordered to assemble a large army and in October, under the command of the elderly and rather infirm 'Gunner' Skeffington, a force of 2,500 sailed for Ireland. Contrary to precedent, Henry would not negotiate with the rebels, he would crush them.

The consequences of this display of military force were immediate. The Palesmen, now threatened with treason, began to step back from their exposed positions in support of Silken Thomas. Increasingly, it appeared that Kildare's main support lay in Gaelic Ireland, and Kildare himself withdrew to his castle at Maynooth. The fall of the castle in March 1535, and the massacre of the garrison after it had laid down its weapons (a pointer to the Tudor definition of surrender on terms), marked the effective end of the rebellion. In August, outgunned and shorn of the anticipated foreign support, Kildare surrendered on being promised his life and was duly dispatched to the Tower of London.

Henry VIII was undoubtedly bent on destroying the family, but he had to move cautiously: allegations of a breach of trust might follow too precipitate an act of vengeance and Kildare's Gaelic allies might seek retaliation. Sixteen months of a miserable confinement in the Tower followed and then, in February 1537, the tenth earl of Kildare, accompanied by his five uncles, who had been imprisoned with him, 'were draune from the Tower into Tyborne, and there alle hongyd and hedded and quartered, save the Lord Thomas [Kildare] for he was but hongyd and hedded'. The fall of the house of Kildare was complete.

It is tempting to see the crushing of the Kildare rebellion, and of the Kildare family, as the fulfilment of a wider plan drawn up by Henry VIII and his adviser Cromwell. In the 1530s over-mighty subjects who dared defy Henry, not just in Ireland, but also in the north of England, were cut down to size and this stern policy was accompanied by a new drive to achieve national consolidation. In 1536 Wales was united to England, and granted representation in the London Parliament. The administration of the English outpost in Calais was reformed and it, too, was granted a few seats at Westminster. Events in Ireland appeared to be part of this pattern of reform and consolidation. After the fall of the Kildares, royal authority, delegated to Lord Leonard Gray, the king's deputy, and backed up by a standing army, was established as the new power in Ireland. A determined effort was made to incorporate the Gaelic lordships into a new kingdom of Ireland: the Gaelic chiefs were to hold their lands by royal title; in return they would receive a peerage, and the crown would give up unenforceable claims to Gaelic lands. In addition, the Gaelic chiefs, now substantial landowners in their own right, and with fancy titles to boot, would accept royal government and justice, adopt English customs and language and manage their lands on the English model by building houses, paying rent and promoting tillage.

In June 1541, as the coping-stone to this policy, Henry's royal title was changed by the Irish Parliament from lord of Ireland to king of Ireland. Potentially, this was a change with far-reaching, even revolutionary, implications; but at the time it represented an aspiration rather than an achievement, and unless resolutely followed up might make little practical difference. It was obvious that the elimination of the Kildare dynasty had created a power vacuum in Ireland, and Henry, whether as lord or king of Ireland, had no option but to remain involved in Irish affairs. But where that involvement might lead him had yet to be determined, and nor were the precedents encouraging in that regard. For centuries the English crown had, for the most part, ignored Ireland, and Henry's new-found interest might well prove transient once the cost of any forward policy hit home. There was always a good chance that religious, domestic or foreign distractions might arise. Significantly, Henry had rebuked those who had presented him with the new title of king of Ireland on the grounds that the revenues of Ireland were not sufficient to support such an honour. The execution of Thomas Cromwell (and Lord Leonard Gray) in the same month as the passing of the Kingship Act would do nothing for continuity of policy. While many Gaelic chiefs had shown great interest, at times amounting to enthusiasm, for the so-called 'surrender and regrant' strategy, this could be no guarantee of their continued loyalty.

That said, the lordship of Ireland created in 1171 was ended and the kingdom of Ireland inaugurated. Centuries-old distinctions between loyal subjects, and aliens (or 'Irish enemies'), were to be done away with. Henceforth, there would only be subjects (or rebels). Again, a title based on some nebulous papal grant, doubtless doubly offensive to Henry, was replaced by one derived from conquest. However, the conquest was far from complete, nor was it by any means clear that the English state had the resources or the commitment to complete it. And if the English state did have the men, the money and the will to finish the conquest of Ireland begun in 1169, it remained to be seen whether 'sober ways, politic drifts, and amiable persuasions' would be the effective instruments. The severed heads, limbs and privy members of the Kildare dynasty were hardly reassuring on this count.

3 THE MAKING OF PROTESTANT IRELAND, 1541–1691

Themes

The one hundred and fifty years between the establishment by parliamentary statute of the kingdom of Ireland (1541) and the confirmation by military victory at the Boyne (1690) and Aughrim (1691) that that kingdom would be a Protestant one are the most momentous in the history of Ireland between the English invasion of the late twelfth century and the setting up of the two Irish states in the twentieth. During this century and a half the English conquest of Ireland, begun in 1169 and since then pursued only fitfully, if even that, was completed under the later Tudors, and an intensive process of colonisation was started, with the stated view of making Ireland both English and Protestant. By processes that alternated for long periods between creative and destructive, persuasive and coercive, but which concluded with a comprehensive military victory, a united Ireland under the crown became a reality.

However, while a genuine united kingdom of Ireland had been achieved, and Protestants installed as its governing elite, cultural, ethnic, linguistic and, above all, religious unity would prove impossible. It is only fair to point out that in 1541 none of these outcomes could have been foreseen, would have seemed possible or even, perhaps, deemed desirable. Equally, we may note that the elements of contingency, accident and the unforeseen that govern present-day interpretations of sixteenth- and seventeenth-century Irish history would have bemused earlier generations of historians who saw in these decades the inexorable progress of those twin juggernauts, conquest and colonisation. On the other hand, earlier historians would surely not be surprised by the emphasis currently placed on situating Irish history in this period, first, within a three-kingdom model of Ireland, England and Scotland, second, within a wider continental model embracing the rivalries of Spain and France and, lastly, within a still broader Atlantic context which situates colonisation in Ireland within the context of other colonial endeavours in the New World.

Ireland after Kildare

The destruction of the house of Kildare on the scaffold of Tyburn brought to an end the long-standing English policy of relying on an Anglo-Irish magnate to conduct affairs in Ireland. Kildare had reckoned that his network of alliances with other magnates, both Anglo-Irish and Gaelic, rendered him and his family irreplaceable to English government in Ireland, and that therefore he could, in effect, rebel with impunity. The first of these calculations was largely correct; and nearly a hundred years were to elapse before a chief governor arrived – Thomas Wentworth, earl of Strafford – who could emulate the firm control exercised by the earls of Kildare. But the second calculation proved disastrously wrong; Henry VIII, and his chief minister, Thomas Cromwell, had no time for over-mighty subjects whether in the north of England, or Wales or Ireland, and the heads of Kildare and his uncles duly ended up in the wickerwork basket. However, the conundrum remained: how to replace the 'irreplaceable' Kildares? Resolving this problem, or reformulating it, was to preoccupy English rulers and government ministers for the remainder of the century.

The Kingship Act of 1541 did not offer much assistance. True, it appeared to mark a decisive shift in the medieval view of Ireland as divided on ethnic grounds; after 1541, in theory, there were to be no distinctions between the king's subjects in Ireland based on ethnic origins; the sole difference between the inhabitants of the island was to be that between the loyal subject and the rebel. However, hundreds of years of ethnic categorisation and discrimination could not be undone by the stroke of a pen and, as noted, the thrust of the 1541 Act was as much aspirational as descriptive. It did, however, commit the English government to a policy of reform and innovation; the trouble was that, those best equipped to carry out this new strategy, the remaining members of the Kildare dynasty, were currently and for the foreseeable future *hors de combat*. There was nothing for it but to appoint a chief governor from England to implement the new reform policy that was implicit, if not explicit, in the 1541 Act. The question now was whether such a blow-in governor would have the power to carry out new policies in Ireland. Could such an *arriviste* put together a coalition of the willing to assist him in his task? Would he receive unflinching support – moral, material and financial – from London? On their own, these knotty problems had the capacity to wreck the career of any Tudor governor in Ireland; but there were at least three further complicating factors which rendered highly suspect the entire reform enterprise, as envisaged with such careless aplomb in the 1540s.

The first of these, as ever, was finance. Intervention in medieval Ireland had proved costly, and modest, let alone extravagant, plans had nearly always foundered on the rock of financial exigency. Tudor resources, while greater, were not overwhelmingly so, and certainly not limitless. The suppression of the Kildare rebellion had cost a heart-stopping £40,000 (about forty times the revenue derived from Ireland per annum), and it was evident that the success of even minor reform policies was dependent on the procurement of a standing army for the English chief governor; without the sword, persuasion might fall on deaf ears.

Where was the money to come from? And who was to pay? And what if there was resistance? In theory, Irish reform should be underpinned by Irish resources but what if this was not possible? How long would the English exchequer continue to bail out Tudor governors, and underwrite Tudor programmes in Ireland? And behind these questions, lay that long-standing puzzle, so pithily articulated by Fynes Morrison, secretary to a chief governor in the early seventeenth century: why was it, he mused, that 'so rich a kingdom [Ireland] should be so great a burden to the state of England?'

A further complication was that Ireland's geopolitical and strategic importance was changing with the 'discovery' of the New World. It was formerly one of the most remote outposts of a Europe whose economic centre was the Mediterranean; but with Columbus's landfall in 1492 in the West Indies (as they later became), the European continent was re-oriented westwards. In time the Atlantic world would displace the Mediterranean as the economic powerhouse of the continent, and Ireland's geopolitical importance would thereby be transformed; hitherto the western *ultima Thule* of the known world, Ireland could now conceivably be a bridgehead to the New World and to its fabled riches.

This is not to say that Ireland had, hitherto, been of little interest to either France or Spain. Irish soldiers had fought in various campaigns in France in the middle ages, where they were highly regarded because of their hardiness and where they also enjoyed an unhappy reputation for savagery. Spanish pilgrims had also ventured to Ireland, and recorded their (unflattering) observations of the country, and its people (particularly the women), and there had been, for hundreds of years, a relatively constant, if small-scale, religious and commercial intercourse between all three countries.

None the less it is significant that beginning in the 1520s, the French and later the Spanish courts were targeted by successive Irish malcontents who sought military assistance, and that equally France and Spain could see sound strategic reasons for involvement in Ireland's affairs. Ireland, formerly *étrange et sauvage*, where France and Spain were concerned, and an object of almost complete indifference to both, from the early sixteenth to the early nineteenth centuries would become a major diplomatic and strategic object, with many expeditions being mounted, large quantities of arms shipped and tens of thousands of Irishmen recruited for French and Spanish armies. Ironically, Ireland's new strategic importance to England may first have been unwittingly signalled to the French and Spanish courts in the early sixteenth century by the high level of concern exhibited in London at the attempts by Gerald FitzGerald, a refugee from the massacre of his senior relatives in 1536, to raise French support for his cause after his flight to the continent in 1540. London's acute anxiety at these efforts offered the clearest proof to the French that in his search for continental allies, FitzGerald had touched a nerve.

For an Irish chief governor in the sixteenth century, these new diplomatic and strategic complications made his job all the more challenging. In the fourteenth and fifteenth centuries Ireland had posed a potential dynastic threat within the British archipelago; but especially in the late sixteenth century, with probable allies in Catholic France (already interfering in Scotland) and in Catholic Spain, it conceivably constituted part of an international coalition that might first surround and then overwhelm Protestant England. Thus, while Ireland might cost a fortune to govern and garrison, and while that country could ruin reputations and armies and would become synonymous with war, rebellion and repeated failure, there could be no question of withdrawal, for such a course without doubt would mean handing the country over to the French or Spanish. This could never be permitted, not least for the geopolitical reasons already mentioned, but also because both countries were aggressively Catholic powers apparently committed to the destruction of Protestant England. Thus to the geopolitical factors enjoining England's commitment to its Irish possessions, from the 1530s on equally vital geo-religious considerations have to be added.

Henry VIII's marital problems in the early 1530s led him directly to repudiate the authority of the pope in 1531 and to establish himself as Supreme Head of the Church of England, and in 1536 of the Church of Ireland. For the most part these innovations were accepted with equanimity in Ireland; unlike in England, no one was martyred in Ireland until the 1570s. Nor indeed did the dissolution of the monasteries in Ireland (1537) produce any protest movement, again unlike in England, where the Pilgrimage of Grace (1539) resulted in the deaths of thousands. A specially convened, all-Ireland Parliament put the necessary instruments through with a minimum of fuss, again unlike the reaction in England. The reality was, we are told, that Irish monasteries had become so secularised in their habits that many of those well disposed towards the monastic ideal viewed monastic lands as a huge hindrance to the realisation of the monastic mission. Their loss, therefore, was a good riddance. Confiscated monastic lands in Ireland were sold off to favoured English administrators, new arrivals and to a small number of the descendants of the medieval settlers, soon to be dubbed the Old

English. Very few Gaelic Irish, however, were invited to share in the sell-off, an exclusion that was to become of some importance during the Confederation of Kilkenny, a hundred years later.[1]

It was in the mid-1530s that the line was drawn. Institutional change could be accepted, new titles approved for Henry VIII and the windfall of monastic lands could even be viewed as providential; but doctrinal change would meet with determined resistance from both the Old English and the Gaelic Irish. Already by the mid-1540s there were cries (albeit muted) of 'heretic!' voiced by those who sought to justify their opposition to crown government in Ireland. However, the accession of Elizabeth as queen (1558) and soon after as Supreme Governor of the Church of England (1560), and the confirmation of England as a Protestant state, was greeted with outright hostility by much of Ireland, whether Old English or Gaelic Irish. The promulgation of the papal bull *Regnans in Excelsis* against Elizabeth in 1570, in effect a declaration of war – for she was not just excommunicated but deposed – both sharpened the conflict and internationalised it. Gaelic rebels and Old English malcontents could henceforth look to the Catholic powers of Europe for military assistance in their Irish contests. By the 1570s loyal and disloyal had become equated with Protestant and Catholic, a division in no way foreseen in the 1540s, but one that was to persist, by and large, for the next five hundred years.

Quite why the bulk of the Gaelic Irish and the Old English should so resolutely have resisted the new dispensation in church and state has, since the sixteenth century, exercised the minds of Irish and other historians. Catholic historians for long celebrated what they saw as the innate fidelity of the Irish to the Roman church, while Protestant historians, for their part, were given to berating the Irish for their addiction to superstitious ways. Recent scholarship has emphasised that Ireland could have gone either way (as indeed could England) in the religious wars of the mid-sixteenth century. True, there was no tradition of heresy in Ireland, no Irish Lollards to pave the way, and nor was there a university churning out Protestant preachers to challenge Catholic doctrine or promote the new religious teaching (crucially, the Protestant seminary of Trinity College Dublin did not open its doors until as late as 1592); and all of this was in contrast to the situation in England. But against that, ignorance about Catholic teachings and practice was widespread and profound, even (especially?) among the clergy. Married priests or those with concubines were commonplace, hereditary bishoprics routine and pre-Christian (pagan) observances were everywhere. In short Ireland posed a huge challenge to both sets of reformers, whether the extreme Protestants of Jean Calvin or the equally extreme Jesuits of Ignatius Loyola. The eventual outcome – a supposedly 'Catholic' people in a skeletal 'Protestant' state – could never have been foreseen in the 1540s.

In explaining why the Reformation failed in Ireland it may be significant that the Observant Friars (monks pledged to a strict rule), both Dominicans and Franciscans, had maintained an active presence among the Gaelic Irish from the 1490s, and that the Society of Jesus (the Jesuits) had dispatched its first mission to the English of the Pale as early as 1542. Neither had encountered much opposition from Protestant preachers in their efforts to promote Catholic teaching and to stiffen resistance to the doctrinal changes proposed after 1560. The arrival of these stalwarts of the Counter-Reformation long pre-dated that of the clergy of the reformed church and, in effect, constituted a pre-emptive strike against the reformed religion. That said, given the absence of indigenous popular support, neither the Protestant Reformation in Ireland nor the more secular reconstruction of Ireland could be other than extraneous, top-down, state-sponsored affairs.

And yet, since English governors, with their proclamations, their military retinues and their fondness for martial law, would necessarily be the drivers of Protestant evangelisation (how could it be otherwise?), surely this ought to have given cause for concern? Was it possible that such worldly and unworthy instruments could really achieve godly ends? Soldiers, it has to be admitted, almost never make good missionaries. Moreover, on a more practical level, since the Tudor apparatus of government in Ireland was weak and its reach limited, is it surprising that, as the designated engine for the dissemination of Protestantism, it failed to bed down the new religion? In the end it may be suggested that because the Reformation was perceived as an English import, it attracted opposition from those resolutely opposed to the more secular reforms proposed in church and state. The prime promoters of both kinds of reform in Ireland were newly arrived English administrators, soldiers or clergy, most of whom appeared to be down on their luck, and thus unconvincing and unlikely exponents of *une mission religieuse*. Whether pursued through conciliatory or coercive methods, reform, both religious and secular, derived wholly from England and that was why both were resisted.

Conquest and colonisation

Curiously, it appears that it was only in the 1570s, when the failure of the various Tudor reform policies, plans and programmes had been all too clearly revealed,[2] that attention turned to what was seen as the stiff-necked adherence of the bulk of the population to Catholicism. It was then that sombre conclusions were drawn regarding Irish recalcitrance, the failure of persuasion in matters of reform and the necessity for compulsion which, by this time, meant military conquest followed by colonisation. What had begun in the 1530s as a humanist-inspired programme of reform that had as its initial object the extension of English institutions and administration to the Pale, and then the further application of the rule of law to the entire lordship, had become by the 1570s nothing less than the completion of the conquest of Ireland begun in 1169. This military solution, expressly disavowed in the 1530s on grounds of finance and morality, was in the 1570s positively embraced as the necessary prelude to the great work of making Ireland English and Protestant. 'Lenity and gentleness' had clearly not worked, and the Irish, whether Old English or native Irish, had remained mired in their criminal, ungodly and bestial ways. Therefore, for reform to succeed, there was no alternative; as one exasperated commentator wrote: 'it must be fire and sword, the rod of God's vengeance that must make these stubborn and cankered hearts to yield for fear'. Where had it all gone wrong?

There is no single answer to this question and no single reason why affairs in Ireland turned out so drastically at odds with the cheery forecasts of the early decades of the sixteenth century. It was not that there were no reform plans: there were any number and they agreed on the essentials. Whoever was appointed English governor must be powerful enough to command authority; he must have an army substantial enough to give him independence; and he must concentrate his attention, in the first instance, on the English Pale. In that area, roughly a 50-mile radius around Dublin, he would establish, or re-establish, the cultural, legal, social and linguistic norms that existed throughout England and then, confident that the problems of the Irish lordship were similar to those which had beset England in earlier centuries, and for which proven remedies had been found, he would turn his attention to the lordship at large. He would move immediately to outlaw 'coign and livery', that network of criminality and extortion that oppressed the populace and underpinned the private armies (and, hence public lawlessness) of the great Anglo-Irish magnates. So far as the Gaelic Irish were concerned, they would be won over from their primitive ways by 'surrender and regrant'. By this procedure, Gaelic chieftains would 'surrender' their Gaelic titles, receive box-fresh, replacement English ones (albeit encumbered with fiscal and military duties owed to the king), and would be permitted to pass on their lands and title to a designated heir rather than relying on the outcome of a violent succession struggle. All of these policies were based on an easy assumption of cultural superiority, and on a conviction that their very reasonableness and attractiveness in English eyes would overcome all opposition. Little thought was given to the likelihood, or even the probability, of resistance. That said, buried somewhere and soon to surface in the reform mission lay the conviction that its opponents should expect coercion. As with colonisers everywhere, if the natives would not freely embrace civilisation, then they must be compelled to do so.

The twenty years following the fall of the house of Kildare were dominated by Lord Leonard Gray, governor from 1536 to 1540, and by Sir Anthony St Leger, governor for most of the period between 1540 and 1556. Both came armed with plans and programmes and, while both made valiant attempts to implement them, neither made much headway. In Gray's case this was scarcely his fault: he was a protégé of Thomas Cromwell, the new power behind the throne of Henry VIII; and when Cromwell was disgraced in 1540, 'his' man was duly recalled and, absurdly, executed for treason. Gray's tenure of office was so brief and his fall so unrelated to Irish affairs that no overall conclusion can be drawn on his period in Ireland. His fate, however, did reveal the necessity of cultivating friends in the king's court in order to protect one's back (or neck) while in Dublin, a lesson that was not lost on future chief governors, such as Wentworth in the 1630s, or Ormond in the 1660s; nor indeed was the lesson lost on those in opposition to them.

Judged by conventional standards, Gray's successor, St Leger, achieved much. He persuaded the Irish Parliament, complete with, for the first time, Gaelic representatives, to agree to the key elements in the Henrician Reformation, the royal headship of the church and the dissolution of the monasteries; and he managed to put through the Kingship Act of 1541 (in English and in Gaelic) which (apparently) dramatically changed Ireland's constitutional position. Moreover, as a resident governor sent from England, St Leger was quick to recognise that he needed his own network of connections to support him in Ireland and he proved quite successful in creating a resident 'king's party' among the Anglo-Irish. (We may note in parenthesis that some two hundred years later, another would-be-resident chief governor sent from England, Lord Townshend (1767–72) and, like St Leger, embarked on yet another, though less bloody, attempt at direct rule, similarly saw the need to create a 'king's party' or 'Castle party', in order to assure himself of consistent support; in Anglo-Irish relations, certain problems of governance have a habit of recurring.)

More immediately St Leger was active in promoting the policy of 'surrender and regrant' among the Gaelic Irish. None other than the mighty Conn O'Neill, head of the O'Neill dynasty in west Ulster, surrendered his Gaelic title in 1542 and with great pomp and ceremony was created earl of Tyrone – a major propaganda coup. A year later, Ulick MacWilliam Burke of Connacht was, in a similar fashion, created earl of Clanricard and Murrough O'Brien of Munster was made earl of Thomond. By 1541 a clear majority of the Gaelic Irish chiefs had swapped their Irish title for a royal one, and so loyal had the Gaelic Irish apparently become that St Leger was able to dispatch an Irish contingent to the English army besieging Boulogne in 1544. In the end, however, St Leger's 'successes' proved more illusory than real. He proved unable to control Shane

O'Neill, self-appointed heir to the earl of Tyrone, though he was not his father's declared successor. Until his death in 1567 (in possibly the first contract killing in Irish history), the furious Shane led the English authorities in Ireland a merry dance over large areas of south Ulster and the Pale.

The achievement with which St Leger is most associated, and for which he has been most praised, surrender and regrant, could not but destabilise Gaelic Irish society. Gaelic chiefs, for the most part, held their title for life only; but surrender and regrant sought to turn a temporary chief into a permanent dynast. Of course, many Gaelic chiefs could see real advantages for themselves and their sons in these royal titles; but their excluded relatives, such as Shane O'Neill, saw few or no gains for themselves. The net result was to arouse opposition to other reform policies and to increase dramatically the risk of all-out war. In retrospect St Leger's deputyship was not a golden age of humanist reform policies carried out in a conciliatory way, but rather marked the start of a campaign to destroy Gaelic Ireland and then the initiation of a new policy of colonisation which segued imperceptibly into the full conquest of Ireland.

It was in the 1530s that St Leger, infuriated at the constant raiding by the O'Mores and O'Connors into the Pale, first mooted colonisation as a solution to endemic Irish resistance. There could be no security, he wrote to a correspondent, until Leix and Offaly, the territories at that time most disturbed, 'be peopled with others than be there already'. This idea, that a submissive population in a district was vital to security and that, if one did not exist, it ought to be imported and the existing one expelled or pushed aside, was newish at the time; but it took hold, and by the end of the sixteenth century, suitably expanded, elaborated and justified, it was to be the preferred solution to England's Irish problem.

The immediate response to St Leger's suggestion was muted: surrender and regrant remained the cornerstone of official policy for dealing with Gaelic rebels and, in any case, dynastic uncertainty in England, the ebb and flow of religious change there and, inevitably, exchequer objections, ruled out major initiatives where Ireland was concerned. However, the concept of colonisation did not go away and it was in 1556 during the reign of Queen Mary, the last Catholic queen of England, that an elaborate plan was drawn up for the confiscation of the land, dispossession of the natives and resettlement by 'English subjects', of what were, henceforth, to be known as Queen's county (nowadays Laois) and King's county (now Offaly).

According to this plan the Irish were not to be entirely expelled; rather it was envisaged that they would be removed and confined to the area furthest from the Pale, and their share of the confiscated land would be less than one-third. English settlers were to be awarded individual tracts of land of some 360 acres in extent and they were to maintain armed men who could defend the plantation – the preferred official and benign term for colony. Not surprisingly, progress was slow, for the O'Mores and the O'Connors proved understandably hostile and settlers from England – or elsewhere in Ireland – were hard to find and retain. None the less, two fortified settlements, Philipstown and Maryborough (present-day Dangan and Port Laoise), and a small plantation of perhaps five hundred settlers, were established and proved just about sustainable. No doubt the treacherous massacre in 1577 of some forty members of the O'Mores and O'Connors at Mullaghmast (they had been summoned there for 'discussions' with royal officials) had helped secure the settlers' fingerhold in the confiscated districts by eliminating 'troublemakers', actual or potential.

The plantation of Leix and Offaly was the first in what was to become a lengthy list and a process was begun that was to culminate in the Williamite confiscations of the 1690s. By that time well over two-thirds of the island of Ireland had changed hands, around a hundred thousand British (English and Scottish) settlers had been introduced and Catholic landowning outside Connacht had largely become a memory. The landscape of Ireland, if not the people, would be made English, with hedgerows, markets, manorial courts, towns, parkland, field patterns, stone houses and apparel, all on the English model, to be found everywhere. The English language, in decline in the fifteenth and sixteenth centuries, would undergo a resurgence, coming to dominate as never before public and official space, and leaving the Irish language to the private and the domestic. In short by the 1690s, as a result of the policy of plantation, Irish Protestants – its main beneficiaries, for the masses remained wedded to the mass, and were therefore excluded – could congratulate themselves that finally Ireland looked and sounded like England. We may note, however, that English visitors were not so persuaded, a sneer rather than a cheer being their usual response to a sojourn in Ireland.

What is striking is how plantations quickly came to be seen as the preferred solution to the Irish question. Certainly, the progress of the plantation of Leix–Offaly offered little encouragement in this respect, for it barely survived; and the experience of colonising in Ulster was to prove even less rewarding. In the early 1570s Elizabeth I had awarded grants to two favourites, Sir Thomas Smith and the earl of Essex, authorising them to conquer and to plant lands in Strangford (present-day county Down) and in north Antrim. Both enterprises ended in complete failure: Smith's men deserted him, his son was killed by locals and his body was fed to dogs (1573). Essex, dubbed by one historian 'a chivalrous but unthinking knight', had a similarly unrewarding time. In his efforts to drive out the Scots whom he found on his lands, he embraced the Spanish notion of colonisation by massacre, and ordered Sir Francis Drake and his men to slay some six hundred Scots women and children on Rathlin Island, off the coast of present-day county Antrim. Then, mercifully, he gave up in frustration, and died in 1576. And yet, despite these futile endeavours and bloody reverses, plantations were resolutely endorsed as the way forward. Why was this?

The primary attraction of plantations was that in theory they offered royal officials a way to achieve both of those hitherto elusive goals – security and profit. Previously, ambitious policies to make Ireland secure had had to be abandoned on grounds of cost. However, it was unthinkable to give up Ireland, for it would undoubtedly fall into the hands of foreign (or domestic) enemies. Plantations offered security on the cheap: it was envisaged that ex-soldiers or, at least, those trained in arms, on the Roman model of military colonies, would be attracted to the country as settlers and that, therefore, they could keep the natives under control without recourse to a large standing army.

Equally important, plantations meant profit: there was money to be made through 'antiquarian buccaneering' (investigation of ancient land titles), and there was extensive territory to be acquired by unscrupulous royal officials, adventurers and even the monarch. Enthusiasts for plantations, some of them Irish born, for many Old English (Catholics) reckoned them an excellent bridle on the native Irish (Catholics) (hence their horror when they later found themselves deemed fit for plantation), chirped that once the recalcitrant Gaelic Irish had had models of civilised living displayed before their eyes, they would abandon their filthy and lawless ways. They would then seek to emulate the newly arrived colonists and, in a short period, begin to live like the English, or indeed like the Old English. Furthermore, plantations had a important social purpose: they offered an outlet for England's, and Scotland's, surplus population, for the damage done by the Black Death in the fourteenth century had been overcome, and there was now, so it was claimed on rather uncertain authority, a demographic bulge. Mid-Tudor panics about numerous masterless men and a proliferation of sturdy beggars could, in theory, be defused by the removal of these paupers to a sparsely populated Ireland, or further afield. Indeed, by the 1580s Ireland looked a more promising destination than the colonial outposts in British north America.

In short, by the last decades of the sixteenth century, Ireland was a magnet for those down on their luck, younger sons without fortune, soldiers without a war or for those who had long-term ambitions further afield. Plantations in Ireland could be a stepping-stone to similar endeavours in the New World, a career trajectory, so to speak, attested to by the (bloody) presence in Ireland from the 1570s on of those later New World celebrity colonisers, Francis Drake, Humphrey Gilbert and Walter Raleigh. Then again, the very fact that the Spanish and the Portuguese, arch-enemies of Elizabeth's England, were busy in the New World setting up colonies well-nigh guaranteed that pride (and prudence) would prompt

Protestant Englishmen to emulate or surpass such foreign Catholic enterprises, whether in the New World or the old.

Lastly, there was a vital religious dimension to the plantation project, one that cannot be dismissed as mere hypocrisy or the inescapable cant of conversion. By the 1570s it was evident that the Protestant Reformation was having little impact on the mass of the Irish people – whether Gaelic Irish or Old English. Such obduracy in the face of truth and such obstinacy in adhering to Romish superstition, it was held, could only be overcome by a thorough-going plantation, not just of the Gaelic lordships, but of those lands in the possession of the Catholic Old English as well. Only by dispossessing the current owners and bringing in new settlers could Ireland be made both English and Protestant. It was surely no accident that those most committed to a policy of plantation in Ireland – Lords Deputy Sussex (1556–62), Sidney (1565–75), Sir John Perrot (1584–88) and even Essex, the adventurer – were to be found in the ranks of those extreme Protestants who saw plantations as the key way to spread Protestantism. Colonisation and evangelisation were two sides of the one coin, and it was only by creating a civil environment that Protestantism could flourish.

All of this was, it is worth reminding ourselves, a far cry from what was proposed when the 'reform of Ireland' was first embarked upon some fifty years earlier in the reign of Henry VIII. Then, persuasion and conciliation had been much trumpeted as the chosen instruments, not conquest and colonisation. Yet by the early 1580s only the latter were thought serviceable, and an entire literature had been composed which, in effect, justified and celebrated massacre, treachery and expropriation – if the objectives were indisputably and ultimately moral.

Perhaps it had been inevitable that persuasion would fail to produce that reform deemed necessary; previously, reform of any kind had not succeeded in Ireland unless accompanied by overwhelming force. The early Tudors, however, had ruled out such martial means on grounds of expense. As a result, in the yawning gap between vaulting ambition and inadequate resources, disillusion, resentment and anger were nourished. As successive projects, programmes and plans ran aground or foundered on the rocks of English ineptitude, Irish perfidy or the usual financial shortfalls, the temptation to lash out proved irresistible; hence the massacres of Mullaghmast, Smerwick, Rathlin and elsewhere. Moreover, as in decade after decade failure followed failure, the official mood grew darker and the possibility of any reform in Ireland without a comprehensive military victory came to be viewed with deep scepticism, and then ruled out. The rediscovery of the twelfth-century Gerald of Wales's views of the barbarous and bestial nature of the Irish, a verdict which their rejection of the reformed religion copperfastened, scarcely helped matters.

The conviction that the original medieval settlers, the Old English, had so far degenerated from their original role as bearers of civilisation in Ireland as to be almost, if not actually, irreformable, led ineluctably to deeply pessimistic conclusions about the possibility of any successful reform in an Irish context. That the Old English clung to Catholicism and, worse, that they actually were prepared to solicit military assistance from Philip of Spain, the anti-Christ's warrior, made it all the more acceptable to brush aside the (very few) ethical constraints that surrounded sixteenth-century warfare, which sought to prevent indiscriminate slaughter of non-combatants. It was easy to conclude that only military conquest, by any means, followed by a thorough-going plantation would serve the cause of Christian reform. This was indeed a harsh prescription, for colonisation was always, and has ever been, inseparable from carnage; but the stubborn loyalty of the Gaelic Irish to Catholicism had offered fresh proof of their barbarism, while the similar adherence of the Old English to the old religion had confirmed their degeneracy. On grounds of security and profitability, then, but also because of the requirement to evangelise, plantations from the 1560s on were determined upon as the way forward in Ireland. St Leger's persuasion had given way to coercion; but perhaps extreme violence had always been implicit in the reform agendas of early modern governments?

These aspirations, motives, objectives, fears and anxieties lay behind the plantation of Munster, an undertaking that encompassed about half a million acres in Cork, Kerry and Waterford. This was a scheme that dwarfed anything hitherto attempted and one that in some senses had been flagged since the 1530s. In that decade the idea of setting up a provincial presidency, a type of military government which had proved effective in troubled areas of Wales and England, was suggested for Connacht and Munster. Eventually in 1569 a presidency was established in Connacht under Sir Edward Fitton and, a year later, one was established in Munster. In Connacht a series of tough-minded, i.e. ruthless, military governors imposed peace and order of a sort, but in Munster there was resistance.

This was because since the 1550s, tentative probings, deemed preparatory to an extensive colonisation, had been launched into land titles there. By the 1560s a plantation, or at least military colonies with forts, was being promoted for Munster. From the outset it was stressed that there was no intention of driving off the existing inhabitants. However, James Fitzmaurice FitzGerald, a cousin of the earl of Desmond, interpreted these vexatious inquiries, and the installation of a president, as a prelude to a conquest and he determined on opposition. His rebellion in 1569 may not, in fact, have been entirely unwelcome to Dublin Castle, since defiance of the royal will inevitably produced traitors who, of course, forfeited their land and thus in a direct way facilitated colonisation.

What set FitzGerald's protest in arms apart from earlier uprisings was his appeal, as fellow Catholics, to the Spanish for assistance against the heretics in power in England and in Ireland. His rebellion was also distinguished by the ferocious methods used by royal officials to bring the disturbed areas of Munster into a semblance of obedience. FitzGerald soon fled to Spain, where he spent years trying to persuade Philip II to send an army to Ireland. However, Philip had worries of his own, for the rebellious Dutch in the Netherlands, backed by the English, were proving more than a handful. When in 1579 FitzGerald returned to Ireland to raise once again the standard of rebellion, he brought only a small number of men with him. None the less, in association with his cousin Desmond, he unfurled the papal banner and a new religious war was proclaimed. The rebels drew some encouragement from the arrival at Smerwick, near Dingle, county Kerry, of a small force of some six hundred Spanish and Italian mercenaries under the command of Sebastiano de San Giuseppi (a self-styled colonel who, despite claims to the contrary, had a mandate from neither Philip nor the pope). Rebel hopes were also further boosted by the open support for Desmond's treason and rebellion from among the ranks of the hitherto unimpeachably loyal Old English of the Pale.

The explanation for this new and, for Dublin Castle, ominous development lay in the fact that by the late 1570s many Palesmen had become altogether alienated from royal government in Ireland. Their disaffection had been provoked in part by the increasingly oppressive financial exactions levied by successive governors since the 1550s. Dubbed 'cess' by the Palesmen on whom it principally fell, this tax had been levied in order to recruit and pay for a standing army of some seven thousand men; by the 1570s, many of the great – and not so great – Pale families, because of these oppressive taxes, were facing financial ruin. As Lord Deputy Sidney noted complacently, 'soldiers be no Angels', and their predatory habits as they helped themselves to whatever took their fancy helped heap material misery on to financial woes. As a further insult, lucrative administrative posts were progressively being denied to members of the Old English because of their suspect religious affiliation and, instead, reserved for those recently arrived from England who were firmly Protestant.

As Elizabeth committed herself irrevocably to a Protestant settlement in England and Ireland, and was denounced for it by Pope Gregory (and Philip of Spain), a number of Old English families argued that resistance to royal government in Ireland was a religious, even a sacred, duty. Desmond's proclamation of a holy war, therefore, for many reasons, found an echo among some prominent Old English families in the Pale. A number of scions of these houses had received their university education abroad in Catholic seminaries where they had imbibed the ideology and the rhetoric of the Counter-Reformation. The rebellion of Viscount Baltinglass, and the Nugent conspiracy, both adjuncts to Desmond's rebellion, and both failures, can in large measure be traced to these continental religious influences.

The earl of Desmond's rebellion of 1579 to 1583 can be compared to the 1798 rebellion in that, like the later rebellion, it lacked coherence from the outset and, instead, proceeded in fits and starts over a long time period in Munster, Connacht and in parts of Ulster and Leinster. The utter lack of coordination among the rebels in south Ulster, east Leinster and south Munster, in 1579, as in 1798, gave Dublin Castle its opportunity to strike first at one rebel centre then at another. And of course, the absence of significant foreign military assistance in both rebellions was to prove decisive in their failure. The six hundred French and Italian mercenaries, allegedly dispatched by the pope, who came ashore at Smerwick in 1579, can be compared with the thousand or so French soldiers under the command of General Jean Humbert who would land at Killala, county Mayo, in August 1798. Neither force could make much difference to the final outcome but, happily, Humbert's men were allowed to return home, while those at Smerwick were, after surrender, every one knocked on the head and flung into the sea.

This grim end to the continental adventurers at Smerwick was a grisly reprise of the frightfulness that had distinguished the previous repression of rebellion in Munster in the early 1570s. In the new contest the killing soon resumed in earnest. In 1579 there was a massacre of those unable, or unwilling, to flee Desmond's lands – 'blind and feeble men, women, boys, and girls, sick persons, idiots, and old people', as one account had it. Such butchery was accompanied by the routine execution, under martial law, of many hundreds of able-bodied men, and by the promotion of man-made famine in the Munster area. The resulting devastation was scarifyingly described by the poet Edmund Spenser, at that time secretary to the pitiless and implacable chief governor, Lord Grey de Wilton. As famine and disease took hold, wrote Spenser, 'from glens and woods ... came creeping forth upon their hands ... anatomies of death ... like ghosts crying out of their graves'. With the death of Desmond himself in November 1583 (his head was sent to London to adorn Tower Bridge, by now very crowded with other skulls), the rebellion was finally over, for the Nugent and Baltinglass affairs had earlier been quashed.

The famine, devastation and depopulation that accompanied the Desmond rebellion proved very useful in promoting colonisation, for it was now unarguable that, for the sake of Munster's recovery, repopulation had to come from England. The work of reconstruction was begun. Desmond, and over a hundred of his followers, most of whom had been killed during the rebellion, were attainted and their property seized. An estimated half a million acres was now available for plantation, for the rebels' individual claims to own all surrounding territory, claims hitherto resisted by royal officials, were now, with their deaths, willingly accepted (a precedent later applied in Ulster).

The resulting plantation of Munster was supervised at the very highest level in England, an indication of the hopes that were vested in its success. Queen Elizabeth and her ministers decided that there was no point in substituting a number of English magnates to replace the fallen Irish chiefs. What was needed was not a new ruling class, but rather, large numbers of English colonists. Hence, English 'undertakers' were to be given parcels of land, in extent between 4,000 to 12,000 acres, on condition that they 'undertook' to bring in up to ninety English families, including a number of horsemen and footmen assigned to each holding, for the purpose of defence. They also agreed not to intermarry with, or lease land to, the native Irish. Eventually, about thirty-five 'undertakers', a mixture of soldiers, courtiers, royal officials, merchants and country gentlemen, were allocated land and they set about attracting English settlers to Ireland.

It was at this point that things began to go awry. The confiscated lands were not themselves in tidy parcels, contiguous to one another: very often their extent and location were unclear, and their title was disputed by locals and even by other settlers. Such problems produced legal challenges and led to delays in settling the holdings. Then the Old English, along with Desmond's old enemy, the earl of Ormond, were allowed to bid for the confiscated lands. However, neither had much interest in bringing in English tenants, though both had every interest in maximising profits and this meant, in effect, ignoring the prohibition on Gaelic Irish tenants. These latter were now recruited and because they were prepared to pay higher rents were much sought after. English would-be colonisers quickly saw what was happening and followed suit. As profit was prioritised over security, the aspirations surrounding the Munster plantation faded from view. In all, up to 1598, only about four thousand English settlers arrived and in addition to being too few, they were, most agreed, the 'wrong' sort. Skilled tradesmen and husbandmen were what was needed: those who actually arrived were the flotsam and jetsam of late Elizabethan England. Some had fled England to escape authority, others were, as a contemporary observer put it, 'traitors, murderers, thieves, coseners, conycatchers, shifting mates, runners away with other men's wives, some having two or three wives, persons divorced living loosely, bankrupts, carnal gospellers, Papists, Puritans and Brownists'. All in all, the settlers who did arrive hardly constituted promising material, either for a garrison or for a godly mission.[3]

In the event, the plantation was almost entirely swept aside in the rebellion of 1598, and it was only with the collapse of Gaelic resistance, following the battle of Kinsale (1601), that rebuilding could recommence. However, there was now a significant shift in personnel, for the New English, the label attached to those who had arrived in Ireland in the 1590s, and who had generally been ignored in the share-out of confiscated lands, at this point moved into a position of dominance. During the extremely disturbed 1590s previously confiscated land was available for sale at a discount and New English adventurers – prominent among them Richard Boyle, later earl of Cork – were swift to take advantage of the availability of cheap land. They were also prepared to run the risks involved in investing in Irish land, at a time when a return to England might have seemed the more prudent option. With the repression of the Munster revolt in 1601, the plantation resumed and, over the decades down to 1641, it flourished.

Since the 1570s the attention of the various royal governors sent to Ireland had been focused on events in Munster, and to an extent, in Connacht. In the latter province, as noted earlier, a presidency was set up and a series of military governors – Sir Thomas Fitton, Sir Nicholas Malby and Sir Richard Bingham – were installed. By the ruthless implementation of martial law, which led to the execution of hundreds, the pretensions of the over-mighty earls of Thomond and Clanricard were curbed and the Gaelic chiefs brought under control. However, with rebellion and resistance apparently crushed in Leinster, Munster and Connacht, Ulster, the last Gaelic stronghold, was by the 1580s left dangerously exposed. It was not that Ulster had been consciously ignored by the Dublin government; there had been some talk of establishing a presidency there but it had come to nothing. Rather, the long struggle with the will-o-the-wisp Shane O'Neill had proved so costly in blood, treasure and reputation that when his death at the hands of Scots bounty-hunters in 1567 brought a respite there was little enthusiasm on the part of royal officials to renew the war. Accordingly, it was accepted that any reform of Gaelic Ulster had to proceed slowly, cheaply and, in so far as was possible, with the agreement of the leading players among the Gaelic Irish. By the early 1580s there were encouraging signs that this strategy might succeed.

The new power among the O'Neills, Hugh, baron of Dungannon, and then earl of Tyrone, had spent time in his youth both in the Pale and in England, and had since given every appearance of loyalty to the crown. He regularly sent forces to assist in campaigns against fractious clansmen in south and west Ulster; he acted as a restraint on Scottish expansion into east Ulster; and he was ferocious in his treatment of the Spanish survivors who struggled ashore on to his territory from the wrecked armada ships in 1588. For Dublin Castle, so far so reassuring; however, a number of circumstances outside O'Neill's control, as well as some within, conspired in 1594 to bring about the hitherto unthinkable – a full-scale rebellion in Ulster, conducted by Hugh O'Neill, earl of Tyrone, against the crown. It was to be a rebellion which would see the previously divided Gaelic clans, along with their Scots and Spanish allies, pitted against Elizabeth's best generals and soldiers in a conflict altogether more formidable and on a greater scale than anything seen in Ireland since the Bruce invasion in the thirteenth century. At stake was nothing less than England's hold on Ireland.

Given the encouraging, and apparently unambiguous, signs of harmony between successive lords deputy and Tyrone, quite why a full-scale war should have broken out by the mid-1590s has long puzzled historians. We may discount the view soon put about that Tyrone, later dubbed the 'arch-rebel' or the 'grand traitor', had long planned treason and rebellion, and that all indications to the contrary were simply the customary dissembling, deceit and deception natural to the Gaelic Irish. It is true that Tyrone devoted much time and energy to increasing and training his forces in Ulster; but he was moved to do so by the threats to his position from the Scots to the east, and from the O'Donnells to the west. There is no evidence that his military build-up in the 1580s was preparatory to an onslaught on crown rule. If Tyrone was to be an intermediary between Gaelic Ulster and royal government, and there is evidence that this was a role he sought to play, he simply had to have a military capacity to give him political credibility. In Gaelic, as in English strategy, the sword had to accompany the word.

On the other hand, was Tyrone's preferred position of cultural and military mediator sustainable in the long run? The increasing militarisation of Ulster throughout the sixteenth century, a product of the large-scale recruitment of Gallowglass, and a process to which Tyrone himself contributed through his mobilisation of his own tenantry for military service (*bonnacht*) was, on its own, destabilising, for it is axiomatic that societies organised for war must have war to survive. In addition, and notwithstanding the fair words of successive lords deputy, it was inconceivable, on religious, and perhaps cultural, grounds that Gaelic Ulster could remain indefinitely outside the orbit of English government in Ireland. Tyrone, with his background in the Pale, with his English wife, Mabel Bagenal, daughter of Sir Henry Bagenal, and with his understanding of the thrust of English policy in Ireland, must surely have recognised this. He could be either 'The O'Neill', Gaelic chieftain, or he could be the earl of Tyrone, English courtier, but he could not be both; and in the early 1590s, when Hugh O'Donnell, earl of Tyrconnell, joined forces with the Maguires of Fermanagh, in outright opposition to royal government, the earl of Tyrone/The O'Neill had to choose. That he opted to put himself at the head of the resistance could not have been predicted and there were many signs that he was a reluctant rebel, constantly striving to keep open lines of communication to royal officials. But reluctant or not, he proved an extremely forceful adversary, with a gift for command and a talent for ambush and for battle that brought him victory at Clontibret

(1595) and, famously, at the Yellow Ford (1598), where an English army under his father-in-law, Sir Henry Bagenal, was cut to pieces and Bagenal himself slain.

Success, however, was to prove Tyrone's undoing, for, emboldened by victory, he and his allies solicited military assistance from Philip of Spain, reminding him of the 'Spanish' origins of the Irish, and calling on him to join with them in defeating the heretical English, the 'enemies of Christ'. They even offered the kingdom of Ireland to Philip and, if he declined, suggested that Cardinal Archduke Albert, governor of the Spanish Netherlands, would be a suitable substitute. Necessarily drawing a veil over Tyrone's slaughter of those Spanish armada survivors who had come his way, Philip decided to send both a military force and munitions to the Irish rebels who, by the late 1590s, had drawn areas of Munster and Leinster into rebellion. No doubt his calculation was that he might yet make Ireland England's Netherlands, for the English over forty years had backed the Dutch rebels there in a war against Spain. In Spanish eyes supplying men and munitions to Irish rebels was, in a real sense, payment in kind for English interventions in the Netherlands. In the event, the Ulster rebels' hubris in seeking foreign intervention was to bring about their nemesis, for the English government, as in the 1790s at the time of a threatened French landing, would spare no effort, whether in blood or treasure, to see off these domestic and continental challenges. The successes, military and diplomatic, of O'Neill, O'Donnell and their allies throughout Ireland, meant that their rebellion had become a threat to the integrity of the Tudor state, and it therefore had to be crushed at all costs.

Lord Mountjoy travelled to Ireland with an army of some 20,000 men and began what amounted to a scorched-earth policy. The arrival of a Spanish army at Kinsale in 1601 brought no respite for the rebels, for Mountjoy quickly blockaded them in the port, and when Tyrone and Tyrconnell marched the length of Ireland to their assistance, they were defeated with heavy losses at the battle of Kinsale in December 1601. The war was to drag on for just over a year; but after Kinsale, the result was no longer in doubt. In March 1603 by which time the back of resistance had been broken in Ulster by famine, disease and military defeat Tyrone surrendered to Mountjoy.

It was a measure of the relief with which Tyrone's surrender was viewed that Mountjoy was authorised to offer him generous terms. Tyrone received a pardon and retained his title and his lands; but such concessions were surely just a stay of execution. There could be no disguising the fact that the king's writ now ran thoughout Gaelic Ulster and from one end of Ireland to the other. Tyrone's surrender marked the end of an era, and this stark truth had been brought home to Tyrone in the closing months of the war by the smashing of the centuries-old stone inauguration chair of the O'Neills at Tullahoge, county Tyrone. Henceforth, English law and county divisions, English language and dress, English mortgages and tenurial arrangements, perhaps even the English religion, would now permeate into the former Gaelic bastion. The old order had passed, never to return. O'Neill may have been the greatest of the Gaelic lords, but he was also destined to be the last.

Did he recognise some, or any, of this? Certainly, he knew that his surrender and the lenient terms he had received had been greeted with fury by those who had demanded condign punishment for his transgressions, up to and including his head and his lands. Equally, he was assured that his enemies in Dublin Castle would not rest until he had received a traitor's death. After 1603, as Gaelic practices were outlawed and the anglicisation of Gaelic Ulster proceeded apace, he found his world more and more constricted. In 1606 a Commission for Defective Titles was set up and, as its name suggests, was designed to challenge his claim to ownership of his lands. As a result, when his former allies, O'Donnell and Maguire, decided that the future held nothing for them and determined on exile abroad with a view to seeking further military assistance, O'Neill had in reality no other option but to go along with them. Had he stayed, he would almost certainly have been treated as privy to their conspiracy.

In the event, the 'flight of the earls' in September 1607, as the departure of O'Neill, O'Donnell and their respective retinues was described, was taken as proof of treasonable intent, and their lands, to the widest extent of their claims, were declared confiscate to the crown. To contemporaries, this event, more than anything, marked the completion of the English conquest of Ireland which in their eyes had first been embarked upon in 1169. It also brought down the curtain on a civilisation that had existed for well over a millennium, that had created a literature of rare quality and originality, and that had fashioned an artistic output of similarly rare beauty. True, a united kingdom of Ireland, an objective long sought for but equally long despaired of by the Gaelic poets, had finally been achieved. However, it had not come about by succession, election or agreement. It was rather a product of war and its handmaidens, famine, plague and disease. Elizabeth's reign would never be a glorious one in Irish popular memory; nearly two hundred years later, a primitive agrarian secret society, active in south Ulster, the Defenders, had as one of its mottos or passwords, 'Elishamorta' (Elizabeth of the dead), a grim comment indeed on the last of the Tudors.

Elizabeth died in 1603 and her successor was James Stuart, already James VI of Scotland. The Gaelic literati found much to celebrate in his accession. The collapse of Gaelic Ulster had, for the first time, brought about the political unification of the island and there was now a real chance of the emergence of a high-king of all Ireland. James, as a Scot and a Stuart, was technically eligible for that near mythic position. However, James was also, simultaneously, king of Scotland and of England, and he was a Protestant. Political unity had been accomplished, but ethnic, cultural, linguistic and, especially, religious unity, as ever, would prove elusive.

The Ulster plantation

It was inevitable that the departure of Tyrone and Tyrconnell, and their associates, would open the door to a major plantation of the earls' lands, now adjudged to include the whole of Ulster except for the north-east counties of Antrim and Down, and the southern county of Monaghan. The terms to be offered to those native Irish who remained had yet to be determined, though promises of fair treatment were made. In this latter respect, however, the quixotic and abortive rebellion of the diehard, Sir Cahir O'Doherty, who seized and burned Derry in April 1608, had far-reaching consquences. His rebellion was speedily put down but, in what amounted to collective punishment, and in clear violation of earlier assurances, the conditions offered to the native Irish in the plantation areas were made noticeably harsher.

Those officials charged with planning the plantation of Ulster sought to draw appropriate lessons from previous attempts at colonisation elsewhere in Ireland. Fortunately for them the long-held view that no sustainable plantation was attainable until, so to speak, the site had been cleared of its Gaelic architecture, its Gaelic social infrastructure and its Gaelic leadership cadre, had to an extent been achieved. Shorn of leaders, forced to go soldiering abroad or, if remaining, kept in line by the rigours of martial law, the native Irish of Ulster appeared to offer little threat and a thorough-going plantation could proceed apace. The chief lesson that had been learned from previous efforts at colonisation was that the provision of capital was crucial to success. In so far as the Leix–Offaly plantation and that of Munster had clear weaknesses, these were attributed to inadequate financial provision which had hindered the flow of settlers and prevented the creation of a civil environment. The plantation of Ulster, it was determined, would be different and, as it was axiomatic that the royal coffers were inadequate to fund such a major undertaking, from an early date pressure was exerted on the merchant companies of the city of London to enter into what would later be called a public–private partnership. These city companies – the drapers, salters, ironmongers, haberdashers and so on – were more or less compelled to take part in the enterprise and by 1610 the appropriate plans had been devised.

There were two aspects to the proposed plantation: the territorial arrangement for the new settlers, and the conditions imposed on them. Several categories of grantee can be identified. First, there were the London companies which were offered, at a low rent, large tracts of land, centred on Derry in the north-west. These merchant companies were to build and fortify towns in the north-west of Ulster, to bring in large numbers of Protestant settlers and to exploit the area commercially. In their honour, Derry, which they were expected to rebuild after the O'Doherty revolt, was soon renamed Londonderry, and the former county of Coleraine was enlarged with a piece of Tyrone and designated county Londonderry. Large parcels of land were also to be awarded to the established church; it had long been evident that an impoverished, underendowed, church could not fulfil its mission, either in the religious or educational sphere.

A further category of grantee was that of 'undertaker' (individuals with significant resources, or royal connections); these were awarded large parcels of land of between a thousand and two thousand acres, and were expected to set up self-sufficient colonies, peopled entirely with British Protestants. The third type of grantee was the 'servitors' – former English soldiers or military officials – who were to be granted manageable portions of land. The thinking here was that because of their military background and experience they would be especially valuable in Ulster where the natives might still prove hostile. In addition, by removing themselves to Ireland, these demobbed ex-soldiers would no longer pose a law-and-order problem in England. Perhaps surprisingly, the final category of grantee was that of deserving Irish. Many of them had acted as the eyes and ears, and the bone and sinew, of the English armies sent against O'Neill and O'Donnell, and they had played a key role in their defeat. Dismayed at the lenient terms offered to the earls in 1603 which had placed them, their native Irish opponents, in great peril, they had cheered O'Neill's and O'Donnell's departure in 1607. These 'loyal' native Irish were to be awarded some 20 per cent of the land made available for plantation.

Initially, it appears that the land awarded to the native Irish was little different in quality from that of other grantees. Maps and surveys of the plantation acres were primitive or non-existent and it would not have been always possible to distinguish good quality land from indifferent. Within thirty years, however, the quantity of land held by the deserving native Irish had sharply shrunk, while its quality had noticeably deteriorated. The explanation for this significant development, to a large extent, lies in the fact that those native Irish who got into financial difficulties were not allowed to sell their holdings to fellow Irish, but instead were forced to sell it to English and Scottish settlers. Similarly, those settlers who began to flounder, and there were many, had to sell their holdings to other settlers. The net result of this requirement was a large increase in the land held by the newcomers, and a corresponding decline in Gaelic Irish landowning. By 1640 Gaelic Irish settlement was concentrated above the 150-metre contour line and away from the more prosperous river valleys – with political consequences that were soon to be revealed.

The conditions imposed on the grantees varied according to their status. The city of London companies and the other 'undertakers' were forbidden to retain native Irish tenants, were required to bring in British settlers at a rate of twenty-four per 1,000 acres, and were instructed to improve their lands by constructing defensible towns, establishing markets and anglicising the physical environment. By contrast, the terms demanded of both the servitors and the native Irish were much less onerous. The former army officers were ordered to build defensible homes but were permitted to retain native Irish tenants, the reasoning here being that they would be well able for them should trouble erupt. Those native Irish awarded lands were, of course, allowed to retain native Irish tenants, but they were required to adhere to English ways.

Alongside this official, crown-sponsored plantation (see map 7) in Ulster, a narrower, private-enterprise, colony was making progress in counties Antrim and Down in east Ulster. This area had long been coveted by the Scots, whether the Catholic MacDonnells of the islands or Protestant lowlanders, and their movements into it had been, for some years, a cause of anxiety to English officials. Scottish settlement in the north-east was viewed by Queen Elizabeth as an attempt at a dedicated Scottish colony on 'English' territory, and, therefore, was not to be supported. Moreover, English suspicion of the Scots' motives was sharpened by the close political connection, for most of the sixteenth century, between Scotland and Catholic France. Hence, Dublin Castle's tacit recognition of the value of a strong O'Neill military presence in mid-Ulster in order to keep the Scots corralled along the coast. However, with the collapse of Gaelic power in Ulster, and with the accession of the Scottish king, James VI and I, Scottish expansion into east Ulster – and into the plantation proper – was now to be encouraged, though with results that were not always comforting to Dublin Castle.

During the years 1610 to 1640 Ulster was transformed under the impact of extensive settlement by both English and Scottish, or, as the new term had it, British, settlers. In this period, perhaps ten thousand Scots moved into Antrim and Down, with another thirty thousand British settling in the official plantation areas. These were substantial numbers of men and women and their movement to Ulster compares favourably with the figures for those choosing to emigrate to the new colonies of Virginia and Massachusetts, then just being settled. However, the scale of transformation in material culture and the built environment can be exaggerated. Scottish agriculture was scarcely, if at all, more advanced than

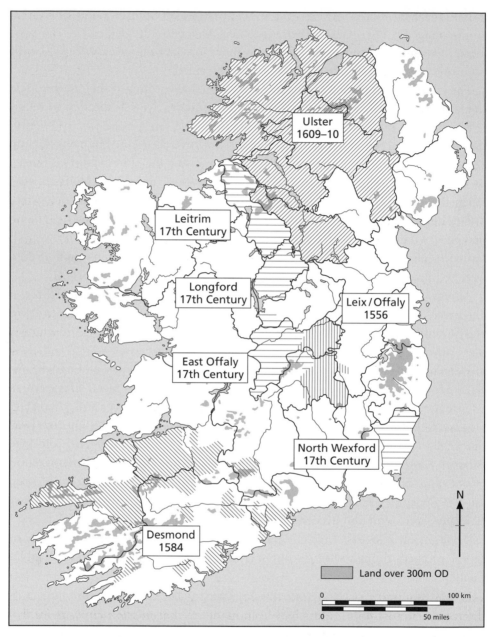

Map 7 Tudor and Stuart plantations

Irish, and hence the new settlers had little to teach the native population; indeed there are indications that primitive Irish practices, such as ploughing by the tail (much reprobated as barbarous), were quickly adopted by the newcomers. Again, there had been fortified towns in O'Neill's Ulster – Sir Arthur Chichester, lord deputy from 1605–16, chose as his reward O'Neill's own castle of Dungannon, county Tyrone; and while the newcomers did construct new defensible settlements, the more successful or long-lasting tended to be located on pre-existing Gaelic centres of population. Nor was commercial farming entirely foreign to the rural economy of Gaelic Ulster. That said, the felling of woods for building purposes, for commercial gain and to deny shelter to diehard woodkerne was immediately undertaken by the settlers, and quickly, and literally, opened up Ulster to radical change. County divisions were enforced, assize courts set in train and English law replaced all others. There is no need to claim that the settlers brought the 'market economy' with them, that mortgages, leases and debts, were in their baggage on their arrival, and that none of these had been known in Gaelic Ireland. However, these aspects of modern economic life assuredly did flourish in plantation Ulster, and those who could not cope with them, mostly native Irish, though some settlers too, went to the wall in the decades before 1640 – a development that might help explain the great Ulster rebellion of 1641.

And yet, for all that the modern observer sees change, innovation and transformation in the colonisation of east Ulster and the plantation counties, contemporaries were more critical, and the predominant notes for most of the 1620s and 1630s were ones of failure, disappointment and, especially, anger at the non-fulfilment of the pledges that the original grantees had agreed. Much of this criticism was misplaced. It is true that a series of inquiries into the progress of the plantation found that the original conditions attached to the land grants had been widely flouted. Far from clearing native Irish tenants from their land, the undertakers had positively embraced them, valuing their pledges to pay high rents and, equally perhaps, appreciating their lack of assertiveness, a trait all too evident in those unruly settlers brought in from England. In 1622 the undertakers in Tyrone had 866 British families on their estates; but they also had 1,199 Irish families, though there were supposed to be none.

Moreover, in flat defiance of solemn agreements, many towns had still not been made defensible. Not only had plantation in Ireland not fulfilled its promise of paying for English government in Ireland, but a subsidy of £50,000 per annum was still required from England to keep the whole enterprise afloat. Equally damaging, almost no progress had been made on that *mission civilisatrice* that had provided the moral basis for expropriation and colonisation. However, if there were notable failures in the plantation enterprise, then the explanation may well lie in the stark fact that the terms imposed at the outset had always been quite impossible of fulfilment. We also need to be wary of the conclusions of politically inspired investigations deliberately designed to find failure as a pretext to levy fines. Given the resources available, even those at the disposal of the merchant companies, it would have taken generations to have effected that transformation prescribed in the plantation covenants; in the circumstances, the wonder was that so much was in fact accomplished.

How did the native Irish react to the Ulster plantation? As we have seen, quite a large proportion of land was reserved for deserving natives, and this must have assuaged some anger. In addition, for many of the native Irish in Ulster, including many O'Neills from rival septs, Hugh O'Neill was as much a usurper as those who replaced him and his departure for the continent was accordingly welcomed. Moreover, the numbers of native Irish who were displaced appear to have been relatively few; ownership certainly changed, but not occupancy. Indeed those historians who have investigated the native response to colonisation have, in general, concluded that assimilation, integration and fusion were widespread in the plantation areas. They point to the adoption of Gaelic fostering practices, the prevalence of intermarriage and the existence of a population which in plain contradiction to the segregation laid down by the original planners in fact clearly lived 'promiscuously', native with newcomer, throughout the plantation area.

Perhaps this rosy picture of communal harmony has been too readily accepted? The evidence from Gaelic sources is fragmentary and difficult to interpret, but there is enough to point to a visceral hatred, on religious, ethnic and social grounds, of the new settlers, even if there was some regard shown for the new owners (so long as they lived nobly and generously). And, against the picture of plantation Ulster in the early decades of the seventeenth century resembling a land of harmony in which native and newcomer engaged in cheery cooperation, must be placed the persistence of martial law, and the use of military force, both of which appear to have been regarded as normal aspects of English government throughout Ireland. We have also to record the beginnings of a pattern of segregation of British and Irish settlements, based on land quality and distance from market centres, that has persisted to this day. We may also note that the new regime in Dublin Castle headed by Sir Arthur Chichester (lord deputy, 1605–15), was manned by anti-Catholic zealots who made no attempt to conceal their determination to rid Ireland of Catholicism. A notable prize for them was the execution in 1611 of the Catholic bishop of Down and Connor, Cornelius O'Devany.

An all-out assault on Catholicism, however, had to be deferred for financial reasons; but there was no mistaking the ultimate intentions of those in command in Dublin Castle towards both native Irish and Old English Catholics. It is possible that Gaelic reaction to the plantation was relatively muted, until the early 1620s, because the threatened or promised numbers of settlers failed to materialise, and because the new owners, in many instances, proved indulgent towards the old occupiers. But sustained migration in the 1620s and, especially, the progressive marginalisation, in all senses and at all levels, of the Gaelic Irish bred up a murderous hatred for the new settlers which was to have its day in 1641.

Like so much else in early modern Ireland, the plantation of Ulster, embarked upon in 1610 with such high hopes, nearly foundered on the rocks of Irish reality. Settlers were hard to attract, harder to keep and occasionally subject to poaching by others involved in colonial enterprises in the New World. As in previous attempts at colonisation, security all too often took second place to profit, and the native Irish were kept on as tenants almost everywhere. Still, there was a substantial and growing British presence in Ulster in the first three decades of the seventeenth century, and the presence of so many British armed men was a source of reassurance to Dublin Castle, even if their dispersal among the natives was considered militarily unsound.

As noted above, prominent among these British settlers was a substantial contingent of Scots and while, on the face of it, this ought to have been an added boost to the new colony's security, in reality, the Scottish presence was to prove a cause of concern to Dublin Castle. For the most part, Scottish settlers had little time for the established church and, instead, professed a raw Presbyterianism which distinguished itself by an aversion to bishops, a total reliance on the Bible and a contempt for what they saw as the crypto-Catholic, bishop-ridden, state-established, Church of Ireland. These Scots frequently sprang from an impoverished background and their growing presence was to prove, on ethnic, social and religious grounds, a hugely complicating factor in an already complex situation. Frequently the central theme of seventeenth-century Irish history is taken as the struggle between Catholic and Protestant, Irish and English, for mastery in Ireland. The large numbers of Scottish Presbyterians, however, who were concentrated in north-eastern Ireland, and who espoused a distinctive politico-cultural outlook, maintained cross-channel alliances and harboured colonial ambitions in greater Ulster, renders such a simple, bipolar, theme untenable.

So far attention has focused on the effects of the Ulster plantation on the economy, the landscape and the people directly affected. However, it might be argued that the greatest impact of the Ulster plantation was on those descendants of the medieval settlers, the Old English of the Pale, who had persisted in adhering to Catholicism, while loudly protesting their loyalty to the crown. On the face of it, this seems absurd, for the Old English as a body had been opposed to O'Neill and O'Donnell, and had applauded their downfall. Nor had the resulting plantation affected their lands. Moreover, they had been enthusiastic proponents of plantation elsewhere in Ireland, their main complaint being that they had been largely ignored in the distribution of the confiscated lands. And yet the very fact of an Ulster plantation was an unmistakable signal that the Old English were no longer to be trusted with a governing, let alone a garrison, role in Ireland. With the renewal of a programme of plantation it was clear beyond question that their claims of political reliability, protestations of loyalty and assurances of military competence were not to be accepted. The burden of securing Ireland would rest on the shoulders of new men – British settlers, or royal officials – who would combine loyalty with Protestantism. For the time being, the government of James I would have to temporise with the Old English: but their claim that Catholicism and loyalty were compatible would never be accepted, and the future would lie with the New English. The plantation that was consequent on the destruction of Gaelic power in Ulster brought home forcibly to the Old English that they would not be a part of that future.

The conclusion that Catholicism and loyalty must be at odds and that, therefore, there could be no long-term role for the Old English in the government of Ireland, was not one that they would or could accept; and until they joined in rebellion with the native Irish in 1641, and even after, it was one that they aspired to reverse. In this endeavour to prove their loyalty and their worth they could point to the experience over many generations which they had of Irish government, and to the influence that they wielded at court in London, for many of them had connections there, both familial and political. Their substantial economic and financial resources meant that impoverished royal officials, even the king himself, would hesitate before pushing them too far, and might even seek to tap into their wealth. The Old English possessed at least one-third of the best land in Ireland and, through their hold on the towns outside Ulster, controlled much of the trade and manufacturing. Again, among the ranks of the Old English was a substantial body of lawyers and their legal expertise might prove invaluable should the government seek to enact and, especially, to enforce, exclusionary and religious penal laws against them. Lastly, in seeking to persuade the king that loyalty and Catholicism were not impossible bedfellows, the Old English could draw on their considerable political power, for they constituted a majority in the Irish Parliament. Any action against them on grounds of religion would have to be approved in that assembly, and they were quietly confident that their political power and political experience would be sufficient to see off, or at least dilute, any overt challenge to their age-old status as the English garrison of Ireland.

In marked contrast, the New English – the settlers and their landlords, plus those army officers, royal officials and Protestant clergy who had come into Ireland since the 1580s, perhaps three thousand in number – welcomed the firm declaration of intent, implicit in the Ulster plantation, that the future would lie with them and, in the years to come, they would be strenuous advocates for ever sterner measures against the Old English. Old and New English can be distinguished from one another by social origins, political outlook, date of arrival in Ireland, even attitude towards England, but at the heart of the matter was religion. The New English were not merely Protestant on the model of Queen Elizabeth's middle way; they espoused a more Calvinist type of Protestantism that was based on the notion of a division between the elect and the non-elect, the regenerate and the unregenerate. In this worldview, Catholicism was not merely in error, it was the faith of the anti-Christ, and those, like the Old English, who professed it and who persisted in so doing in the face of all persuasion, were no better than devils themselves and might very well be beyond redemption. Into this theological, zero-sum world two further calculations intruded. One was that the armies of the Counter-Reformation were clearly gaining the upper hand against Protestantism in Europe, that England was a prime target of those forces and that Catholic Ireland might be a bridgehead for an invasion of England. Hence, there could be no question of permitting Catholics to play any role in the defence or even in the government of Ireland. The second was that, on grounds of public security, as well as private gain, the Old English, because of their evident degeneracy and incipient disloyalty, both of which were proved by their stubborn adherence to Catholicism, ought themselves to be dispossessed and have their lands subject to plantation.

In making the case for a tough, even ruthless, policy against the Old English and for themselves alone to be entrusted with the government and the defence of Ireland, the New English had to confront at least three weaknesses in their position. One was that many of them were men of no fortune, who had come to the Irish wars with an eye wholly fixed on the main chance. A few had succeeded: Richard Boyle, later earl of Cork, by 1620 the richest man in Ireland and possibly in the three kingdoms, had landed in Ireland as a penniless, younger son from an impoverished English gentry family. Another problem was that most of the New English had fought in Ireland but, as noted above, ex-soldiers are rarely convincing as agents for the spread of civilisation, and the recent military origins of many of the New English told against them in that respect. So too did the way they had accumulated their wealth, for they had not scrupled to cut corners, and the occasional throat, to expand their estates. It was notorious that church lands had regularly been invaded by New English magnates, and Richard Boyle was prominent in these semi-legal thefts. A final weakness lay in their overall numbers: at most three thousand, though increasing annually, they were still a tiny minority of the one million or so on the island in the early 1600s, and any demands that government offices and all the loaves and fishes of patronage should go to them alone would, if agreed to, simply render Ireland ungovernable and might even reignite rebellion. And yet these weaknesses were cast aside because in the one area that mattered, religion, the New English were indisputably Protestant and, hence, incontestably loyal. The Old English might have resources with which to promote their case, and this might induce a certain prudence so far as a forward policy against them was concerned – there was certainly a concern not to drive them into revolt – but in London's eyes the New English were the future of English government in Ireland, and as the decades passed the hollowness of the Old English position was progressively revealed.

When the Irish Parliament was summoned to meet in 1613 the much-vaunted political power of the Old English was soon shown to have its limits. At this date the Irish Parliament had not yet become an institution, with a regular round of meetings; instead, it was more of a special event, called whenever parliamentary approval was required or deemed desirable for a course of action. The primary task of the 1613 Parliament was to tie up loose ends relating to the plantation of Ulster, and the attainder of O'Neill and his alleged fellow conspirators. Ordinarily, the Old English could be assured of a comfortable majority. However, to their horror, James I created a large number of new constituencies, mostly in the area of the Ulster plantation, though with some in the Pale, all of which would unquestionably return Protestant Members of Parliament. In effect, at the stroke of a pen, the parliamentary majority of the Old English had vanished. The Irish Parliament duly met and, while the Old English successfully challenged James's actions on procedural grounds, and thus delayed the full impact of the creation of the new constituencies, it was clear that in future Parliaments their New English rivals would be in a majority.

From the 1620s on it was the financial muscle of the Old English rather than their political clout that was targeted. King James was dismayed at the continued annual subsidy to Ireland of around £50,000 and he sought to recoup some of the money by exploiting existing Irish revenues. Soon the Old English were complaining loudly at the oppressive payments imposed on them by the Court of Wards in lieu of their feudal obligations, and protesting at the heavy fines levied for failing to attend Protestant church service (or, alternatively, at the bribes paid to officials to have them turn a blind eye to their non-attendance at religious ceremonies). Even more worrying, there was serious talk of a plantation of Old English land in Connacht based on the flimsy nature of land titles in that province. Few Old English families could rest easy if land titles anywhere in Ireland were to be inquired into. Hence, when an offer came in 1626 from King Charles, James's successor, that in return for payment of three annual subsidies of around £30,000, Old English grievances such as land titles in Connacht, the Court of Wards and recusancy fines, would be resolved, it was accepted with alacrity. However, in what amounted to sleight of hand, the subsidies, levied exclusively on the Old English of the Pale, were paid over promptly to royal officials but there was to be no sign of the 'Graces' (as the concessions were known). Understandably, Old English insecurity and anger increased. It was clear that they were valued for their money, not for their loyalty. Nor did their mood lighten with the naming as lord deputy of Thomas Wentworth in 1631.

Wentworth in Ireland

Wentworth had formerly been a critic of Charles I's government, but in the late 1620s he had become a supporter, if not an admirer, of the king. A stint as president of the Council of the North (of England) enabled him to display his managerial talents, political skills and utter ruthlessness to great effect. By the time he was sent to Ireland he had wrecked the independent fiefdoms that had long been a feature of the north of England, and he had established Charles's interests there as paramount. His attempts to do the same in his new post would quickly lead to his being denounced as 'the most accursed man to all Ireland'.

On his arrival in Ireland in July 1633 Wentworth learned that his personal baggage had been stolen by pirates in Dublin Bay; it was an inauspicious start, though the note of criminality thus introduced was to be predominant throughout his deputyship. Essentially, what Wentworth wished to establish beyond any doubt was that the crown had no friends in Ireland, only interests, and that those interests in the shape of lands, rents, fees and dues had been systematically and illegally, stolen, concealed, plundered or diverted for decades. He set to work with a will. The New English were the first to come under scrutiny. Charles and his father before him had always been highly suspicious of so-called 'rags to riches' stories in colonial Ireland, and had believed that such rapid elevations could only have been at the crown's expense. Wentworth's initial target was the earl of Cork, far and away the wealthiest *arriviste* coloniser. Investigations were launched into his landholdings in Munster, and inevitably – for such inquiries were not disinterested – evidence of land-grabbing, especially of church lands, was uncovered. Cork was threatened with imprisonment, heavily fined and, to rub salt into the wound, was forced to dismantle his wife's tomb which he had erected in a prominent position in St Patrick's cathedral in Dublin. In matters large or petty Wentworth would tolerate no opposition. Other members of the New English were also made to smart. One, Lord Mountnorris, was court-martialled for dereliction of duty – he thought he had held merely a ceremonial military position – and sentenced to death, a sentence which was commuted on payment of a large money fine. More elevated and certainly more dangerous opponents lay in the merchant companies of the city of London but Wentworth did not flinch from investigating how they had managed (i.e. neglected) their plantation lands in Ulster. A fine of £70,000 was levied on them for their failure to adhere to their agreements.

With the New English brought to heel, Wentworth turned his attention to the Old English. He quickly reopened talks on the 'Graces', and he successfully persuaded the Old English of the Pale to offer further subsidies in order to secure their enactment. The money was paid but, as before, the promised concessions were not forthcoming. Not surprisingly, to the Old English, Wentworth was no better than a 'mountebank'. Moreover, the powerlessness of the Old English to resist Wentworth, or to make an effective protest (beyond name-calling) was revealed in the Parliament of 1635–6, for it was now that the Old English found themselves in a definite minority. Their political power, crumbling since 1613, had now gone and at a time when Wentworth's grand plan was finally revealed. It now became clear that since his arrival in Ireland Wentworth had been determined on a plantation of Old English lands in Connacht and elsewhere. In 1635–6 juries in Galway, Sligo and Roscommon were browbeaten into finding for the king's title to these counties, an action clearly preparatory to a thorough-going plantation. No longer a punishment reserved for the rebellious native Irish, plantation was to be visited on those who had remained Catholic, even if, like the earl of Clanricard in Galway, they had stayed loyal. The Old English were staring into the abyss.

Nor did the native Irish, and the Scots in Ulster, have any more cause to celebrate Wentworth's government. Native Irish lands in county Wicklow, the so-called Byrne's country, were subjected to a land-grab by Wentworth himself, with a view to enlarging his personal fortune, while the Scots in Ulster, after decades of relative toleration, were progressively harassed over their religious practices. Wentworth was temperamentally hostile to Presbyterians as potential enemies of lawful authority, and he was not prepared to leave them alone. An ecclesiastical court of high commission was set up to enforce uniformity and a number of church ministers were dismissed from their livings for, among other misdemeanours, refusing to bow at communion. In 1639, when Wentworth sought to force the Presbyterians to take an oath, soon branded the 'Black oath', which in effect meant them renouncing their Presbyterianism, many refused to do so, preferring instead to flee to Scotland rather than subscribe. There, they added their voice and their weight to the growing opposition to the attempted imposition of Laudianism, i.e. in their eyes, popery by another name, in that country. By the end of the 1630s Wentworth appeared to be supreme in Ireland, with all dissent quashed and the king's interests established as paramount. Elsewhere in the Stuarts' multiple kingdom, however, matters were beginning to unravel for both Wentworth and Charles, and in a manner neither could have foreseen.

The objective of Wentworth's rule in Ireland was of a piece with the whole centralising thrust of Charles's policies in his other kingdoms. Charles was determined to live 'off his own': he was not prepared to go cap in hand to the English Parliament for subsidies, nor was he prepared to accept parliamentary scrutiny of his actions or countenance parliamentary involvement in policy-making. Charles answered to God, not mortals. Equally, he was determined to impose a uniformity of religion throughout his three kingdoms and he had given a free hand to the archbishop of Canterbury, William Laud (whence 'Laudianism') to implement this religious policy. Wentworth had proved a key ally of Laud in Ireland, active in recovering church lands and harassing Presbyterians and Catholics. None of these actions was entirely disinterested. In return for Wentworth's energetic promotion of religious orthodoxy, Laud had defended Wentworth at court from his critics, offering him, for example, crucial backing over the affair of Cork's wife's tomb.

The depth of the opposition generated by Laud's religious policy cannot be wholly understood until it is realised that what was commonly called Laudianism, or Arminianism, was in fact perceived, quite incorrectly, as out-and-out Catholicism. Opponents of Laud believed that the whole point of his policies and those of his master King Charles was to re-Catholicise England and Scotland and enlist those countries into the ranks of the Counter-Reformation. It mattered not that Charles and Laud were both pious Protestants: to those who viewed with dismay the evident retreat of Protestantism throughout Europe, they were both the agents of the anti-Christ. The presence of a Catholic coterie surrounding Charles's Catholic wife, Henrietta Maria, gave added weight to this paranoid analysis.

Thus, when Laud sought to enforce uniformity in Presbyterian Scotland, the reaction was immediate and ferocious. In February 1638 a Scottish national covenant was drawn up, pledging each signatory to resist by arms if necessary innovation in religion, i.e. popery; and an army was mobilised in Scotland to give teeth to this declaration. An impetuous attempt by Charles to coerce the Scots failed dismally when the army, dispatched for that purpose, disintegrated on its march northwards and Charles was forced to sign a truce with the Scots in June 1639. In these circumstances Charles had no option but to approach the hitherto ignored and despised English Parliament in order to seek funding for a military campaign. To manage that Parliament he turned to Wentworth, who had displayed his parliamentary skills in Ireland, and he summoned him to London. However, those English parliamentarians who were convinced, however bizarrely, that Charles's policies in Scotland, Ireland and England were indisputably a popish plot designed to destroy Protestantism in the three kingdoms were not about to be browbeaten by the king's most able minister. Wentworth was fixed upon as the evil counsellor, whose removal might bring Charles to see reason. Accordingly, evidence was sought in Ireland of Wentworth's wrongdoing and, predictably, much was found, notably that which related to his recruitment of Irish Catholics into a 9,000 strong army destined for the Scottish war (or, as was darkly hinted, to intimidate the English Parliament). Less predictably, perhaps, representatives of the Old English and New English communities had cooperated with each other to – so to speak – dish the dirt on Wentworth.

While preparations for Wentworth's trial were proceeding apace an army of Scottish covenanters invaded the north of England in August 1640, forcing Charles yet again to appeal to Parliament to authorise those financial subsidies needed to conduct the war against the Scots. Unknown to Charles, however, some covenanting leaders had been in discussion with the more disaffected of Charles's subjects, notably the fiery John Pym, who had informed his fellow Members of Parliament that Charles's object was to seek to 'prepare us for poperie', and his Ulster-based brother-in-law, John Clotworthy, a Presbyterian sympathiser, also involved financially in the city of London's plantation in Ulster. On religious, financial and political grounds, therefore, Clotworthy was no friend to Wentworth. There can be no doubt that Pym, Clotworthy and their supporters secretly encouraged the Scots to invade England in order to keep the pressure on Charles.[4] They were also determined to have Wentworth's head, for he was the one man who conceivably might have managed the crisis to Charles's advantage. In May 1641, despite Charles's assurances that he would never sacrifice him, Wentworth was found guilty of treason and executed. As Charles's authority took a sustained battering in two of his three kingdoms, his Irish subjects looked on, and sought to draw lessons from the clear Scottish triumph and what appeared to be the incipient collapse of Stuart government. Wentworth's death, like that of the earl of Kildare over a hundred years earlier, had opened up a power vacuum in Ireland; who would be tempted to fill it?

The Ulster Rebellion

The events unfolding in England in the summer of 1641 were viewed with grave misgivings by the Old English and by the native Irish leaders in Ulster (figure 3.1).[5] In England, the 'puritan' or 'malignant party', as the king's opponents were dubbed by Irish Catholics, appeared to be in the ascendant. These parliamentarians sought by a thorough reform in church and state to bring about that godly commonwealth which, since the adoption in the 1560s of Elizabeth's despised middle way in religion, had proved elusive. Central to their demands was an unswerving crown commitment to a vigorously anti-Catholic policy throughout Charles's kingdoms, and especially in Ireland, where anti-Catholic legislation was to be enforced and Wentworth's 'popish' army was to be dispersed.

3.1 Much more to the taste of later Irish nationalists was this heroic image dating from 1900 of Owen Roe O'Neill wearing Spanish armour and leading his troops to victory at Benburb, county Tyrone in 1646. National Library of Ireland.

Too late Irish Catholic leaders realised that, however harshly they had been treated by Charles and Wentworth, they could expect much worse should the English parliamentarians succeed in their struggle with Charles I.

The decisive response of the Scots when faced with (in their eyes) the destruction of their religion, seemed to offer the native Irish leaders a credible course of action. The Scots, confronted with a wholly unpalatable *diktat* from London, had bound themselves together under oath to resist it, had defeated the king's army sent to enforce it and had even invaded the north of England, causing Charles to pay them monies to advance no further. By any standards the Scots had achieved a brilliant success. They had demonstrated that they were not to be trifled with, Charles had been forced to concede to their demands and the offending religious policy was abandoned. Was there a lesson in any of this for those native Irish leaders who, as the English Parliament gained the upper hand over the king, gloomily contemplated the likely implementation of a rigorous, anti-Catholic, policy in Ireland? After all the native Irish were not entirely devoid of military muscle. They could point to the presence of many native Irish commanders, as well as thousands of native Irish soldiers in the Spanish and French services. In theory, these constituted an Irish Catholic standing army abroad. Could it be deployed in aid of their co-religionists at home? While Wentworth's Catholic army of some nine thousand men raised for the Scottish wars had been stood down at parliamentary insistence, the men had not yet been dispersed and might speedily be reassembled. Military calculations of this sort, as well as gnawing fears for the future should Parliament triumph over Charles, undoubtedly lay behind the conspiracy hatched in the summer of 1641. Clearly based on the Scottish model for successful resistance and designed to demonstrate that the native Irish Catholics still retained a capacity to command attention, the plot drew in native Irish leaders such as Sir Phelim O'Neill and Lord Maguire in Ulster, exiles such as Owen Roe O'Neill in Spanish Flanders, foreign sympathisers such as Cardinal Richelieu in France and some kindred spirits among the Old English.

The plans of the conspirators included the seizure of Dublin Castle but they failed to achieve this because word of their intentions had been divulged to the authorities who were therefore able to take precautions. Meanwhile, throughout west and south Ulster from 23 October on, groups of native Irish seized control of a large number of towns, castles and forts. Within a few weeks, as native Irish bands of soldiers marched south and as they inflicted a key defeat at Julianstown, county Louth, on forces loyal to Dublin Castle, leading members of the Old English of the Pale, alarmed by growing restlessness among their tenantry and reassured by the rebels' repeated declarations of loyalty to Charles I, moved to join them and to take control of their protest. They were, however, too late: the damage had been done, for while in its conception the rebellion was to have been an armed demonstration on the Scottish model, in its execution it had immediately become a genuine people's uprising – the first in Irish history – with, as its principal feature, a pitiless onslaught by the native Irish on the settler population and their possessions. The rebellion plunged Ireland into a twenty-year nightmare of massacre and mayhem, involving total war, man-made famine and wholesale confiscation, and it quickly pitched the three kingdoms into multiple civil wars with frequent and bewildering changes of line-up in each conflict. Ever after, the rebellion was called upon to justify all manner of revenge, retribution and retaliation on the Irish. Indeed, it is arguable that Protestant–Catholic relations in Ireland have never wholly recovered from the Ulster explosion of October 1641.

An early headline in an English fly-sheet set the tone (figure 3.2). Dated 1 December 1641, it screamed '**BLOUDY NEWES** from **IRELAND**, or, The barbarous Crueltie BY the Papists used in that KINGDOME', and went on to describe

> the putting men to the sword, deflowring of women, and dragging them up and downe the streets, and cruelly murdering them, and thrusting their speers through their little infants before their eyes and carrying them up and down on pike-points in great reproach, and hanging mens' quarters on their gates in the streets at Armagh, Logall [Loughgall].

Reports were received of wholesale massacres, of thousands, tens of thousands and even hundreds of thousands of Protestants tortured, drowned, mutilated, robbed, slain in cold blood and cast out on the roadside, stark naked and forced to make their own way to shelter. It mattered not that the casualty figures cited were, by a factor of ten, in excess of the probable settler population for the reality was frightful enough; perhaps four thousand died and another six thousand settlers perished of exposure. Nor were readers spared the grisly details of atrocities or denied the woodcut scenes (almost all lifted from illustrations of atrocities committed elsewhere in Europe) that brought home the full horror of the rebellion.

From the beginning, many in England held – and this is surely a measure of how far all trust had broken down between king and Parliament – that Charles I was, in some way, complicit in the rebellion. The Ulster rebels had announced that they were fighting to help the king maintain his position against the puritans, had claimed that they were in rebellion on his behalf and had even furnished themselves with a (forged) royal commission authorising their actions. In addition, at least in the early days, those in arms frequently made a point of not harming Scottish settlers and this, too, was seen as highly suspicious, for Charles was at that time negotiating with the Scots and a massacre of Scottish

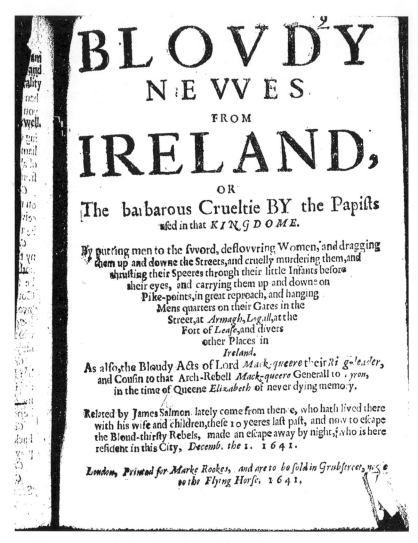

3.2 News reports in London of the Irish rebellion. Sensational reports of massacre and cruelty would later justify exceptional severity against all those believed to be rebels. © British Library Board.

settlers in Ulster, by those claiming to act on his behalf, would not have been helpful. There had been repeated rumours throughout 1641 that the devious Charles had been seeking to make use of the Irish army recruited by Wentworth (just as Clotworthy and Pym had sought to profit from the presence of a Scottish army in the north of England). Under these circumstances of plot upon plot there could be no question of entrusting the suppression of the rebellion to the king, for his name and authority had been invoked by those in arms, and he was as likely to turn his army against his English subjects as against his Irish rebels

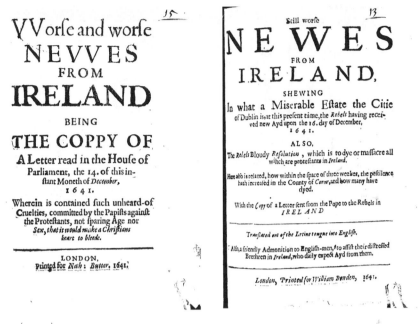

3.2 (cont.)

(or friends). Eventually, in 1642, separate Scottish, parliamentary and royalist armies, were dispatched to Ireland.

What lay behind the frightfulness (figure 3.3) inflicted on the settlers in the popular uprising of 1641? An indiscriminate onslaught on them was neither planned nor sought by those behind the conspiracy. The likes of Sir Phelim O'Neill, Sir Philip O'Reilly and Rory Maguire had plotted a demonstration that would force the king and Parliament to back off from interfering in Ireland; murder and massacre were the last things they wanted. Perhaps it was a measure of how far they had grown apart from their followers that they too were taken by surprise by the eruption of sectarian fury which engulfed the Ulster plantation. O'Neill, O'Reilly and Maguire can be classed as 'deserving natives' who had done well out of the plantation of Ulster. All three were Members of Parliament and had apparently integrated well into the new, post-flight-of-the-earls dispensation. They made no demand for the destruction of the plantation: why should they, when they had profited from it? Maguire even held land taken from the great O'Neill. Admittedly, they were all of them deep in debt but they were motivated primarily by a well-grounded fear that a parliamentary triumph would bring total disaster, and by an overwhelming urge to hold on to what they had. There is little evidence of a burning desire to avenge wrongs.

With their followers, however, it was all very different. They had suffered under the plantation, had been subjected to harsh laws and had been

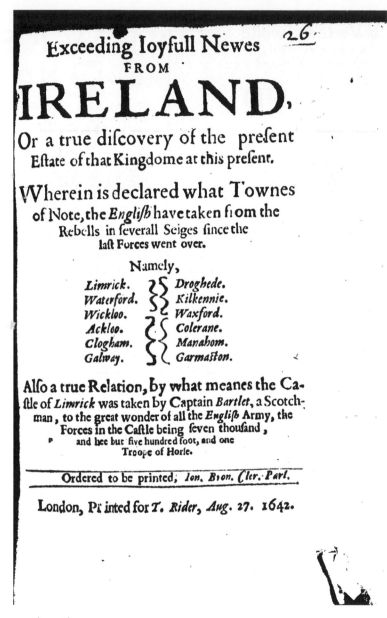

Exceeding Ioyfull Newes FROM

IRELAND,

Or a true difcovery of the prefent Eftate of that Kingdome at this prefent.

Wherein is declared what Townes of Note, the *Englifh* have taken from the Rebells in feverall Seiges fince the laft Forces went over.

Namely,

Limrick.	Droghede.
Waterford.	Kilkennie.
Wickloo.	Waxford.
Ackloo.	Colerane.
Clogham.	Manahom.
Galway.	Garmafton.

Alfo a true Relation, by what meanes the Caftle of *Limrick* was taken by Captain *Bartlet*, a Scotchman, to the great wonder of all the *Englifh* Army, the Forces in the Caftle being feven thoufand, and hee but five hundred foot, and one Troope of Horfe.

Ordered to be printed, *Ion. Bion. Cler. Parl.*

London, Printed for *T. Rider, Aug.* 27. 1642.

3.2 (*cont.*)

progressively marginalised ever since the conquest. High rents had meant that that little was left over for creature comforts, which might explain the high incidence of stealing garments and other items from the settlers in the first weeks of the rebellion. Again, as the years had passed, the amount of land held by the native Irish had declined sharply, as had the quality of that land retained in their

3.3 Lurid images of rebel atrocities in Ireland, almost all taken from continental publications, leave little to the imagination. Cambridge University Library.

3.3 (cont.)

English Protestantes striped naked & turned
into the mountaines, in the frost, & snowe, whe:
reof many hundreds are perished to death,
& many liynge dead in diches & Sauages
upbraided them saynge now are ye wilde
Irish as well as wee,

3.3 (cont.)

possession, both of which sharpened resentment and bred rancour. And who is to deny the impact of the technicolour Counter-Reformation rhetoric of the Franciscans and Dominicans who were active in the plantation areas? Everywhere in the Europe of the Thirty Years' War, 'heretics', whether Protestant or Catholic (or Jewish), were denounced as pollutants who had to be cleansed from the community in order to render it healthy. Economic resentment, religious frenzy and visceral hatred of all things English and Scottish came together to produce the popular explosion in Ulster in October 1641. A comet had appeared in the night sky over Ulster, one that would reappear at intervals over the next four hundred years.

Confederate Ireland

In June 1642, at clerical instigation, the leaders of the Ulster rebellion agreed to take an oath of confederation (modelled on the Scottish covenant) with the Old English, and to bind themselves jointly to pursue common ends.[6] They also agreed to locate their headquarters in Kilkenny, far away from turbulent Ulster where the rebellion had broken out. The two groups had much in common, including a shared Catholicism, a naive trust in the king's promises and a dread of what might lie in store should the English Parliament carry the day against Charles. However, these were not, on their own, sufficient for a confederation to be formed. The reality was that the Old English had little option but to throw in their lot with the native Irish. Their lands had already been listed for plantation by Wentworth and since Dublin Castle had quickly blamed *all* Irish Catholics for the rebellion, the Old English had already been pronounced guilty and, therefore, could expect no mercy. In addition, and no small consideration, the Ulster Irish were sweeping into the Pale and destabilising the region. Faced with a choice of joining in or being swept aside, it made sense for the Old English to form a confederation, situate its headquarters deep in their territory, draw up its objectives and thereby seek to control the direction in which it would move.

The Confederation of Kilkenny met for the first time in Kilkenny in October 1642, and it remained in existence until the fall of Kilkenny to Oliver Cromwell and his army in March 1650. However, the execution of Charles I in January 1649 is probably a better *terminus ad quem*, for the king's death deprived the Confederation of its main *raison d'être*. Modelled on the Irish Parliament, with a supreme council consisting of six members from each province and acting as an executive, and with a general assembly drawn from pre-existing parliamentary constituencies and functioning as a legislative body, the Confederation as a whole constituted both the last Home Rule parliament and independent government in Ireland until the 1920s. During its existence the Confederation raised taxes, recruited armies, maintained a navy, held prolonged negotiations with Charles's agents, conducted diplomatic relations with the chief Catholic powers in Europe and hosted that controversial figure, the papal nuncio, Archbishop Giovanni Battista Rinuccini. While the Confederation was eventually to succumb to internal rivalries and external attack, its existence for nearly eight years was a notable achievement and it represents, along with the later 'Patriot Parliament' of 1689, yet another of those quasi-legal representative assemblies that maintained, against all odds, the continuity of the parliamentary tradition in Ireland.

As the countdown to rebellion in October 1641 had shown, events in Ireland could not be understood without reference to developments in Scotland and, especially, in England, and this remained the case for the next sixty years. The *wars* of the three kingdoms began with the Scottish or Bishops' war of 1638, continued with the Irish rebellion of 1641 and finally engulfed England when Charles raised his standard at York in August 1642. These wars of many fronts, we may say, lasted until the final submission of the Irish confederates in 1653. There was, however, also a parallel crisis of the three kingdoms which was not so easily resolved, for it had long pre-dated the outbreak of the Bishops' war and it would continue until the creation of an English Protestant fiscal-military state in the 1690s. It was a crisis that was not susceptible to a simple military solution, for it had multiple political, financial and religious origins. Was the English Parliament to be an event or an institution? How could the evident military incapacity of the Stuart state be remedied without recourse to absolutism? Was England to be a genuine Protestant power, rather than a sham one? What was Ireland's position to be in the multiple Stuart monarchy? The outcome of the wars of the three kingdoms would determine whether the multiple Stuart kingdom would survive; but the final resolution of the crisis that provoked the wars would take many decades.

The progress of the war in Ireland in the 1640s can be explained in a number of ways. One key to understanding is that provided by the ebb and flow of royal power in England in the 1640s. Between 1642 and 1645 the confederates devoted much time and effort to negotiations with Charles I, each side seeking to advance their cause. Charles sought a speedy cessation of hostilities, followed by a permanent peace in order to permit the royalist army in Ireland to return to England to engage his parliamentary foes. For their part, the confederates sought assurances from Charles on land titles, estates and on the position of the Catholic church. A cessation for one year was quickly agreed in September 1643, and subsequently extended, but a final peace proved elusive and by the time one was concluded in the summer of 1646 it was too late to make much of a difference, for Charles's military position in England was, by then, untenable.

The slow pace of the negotiations conducted by Charles's chief agent, the earl of Ormond, with the confederates over the years 1642 to 1645, can only be explained by the fact that Charles reckoned his initial position in England to be a strong one, and that therefore he need not offer much by way of concession to Irish papists. He also had to weigh up military advantage against adverse publicity in England, for any hint of an alliance with those who had allegedly perpetrated the wholesale massacre of Irish Protestants in 1641 would have been fatal to his cause in England. However, by 1645 Charles's cause was seemingly desperate: the entry of the Scots into the English Civil War on Parliament's side (September 1643), and the ensuing heavy royalist defeats at Marston Moor (July 1644) and Naseby (June 1645), persuaded him that only an Irish army acting on his behalf could turn the tide. His long-time negotiator, Ormond, had proved adept at prolonging discussions with the confederates while steadfastly avoiding commitments that might offer a propaganda victory to the parliamentary forces. Ormond's tactics were now redundant and he was to be sidelined. Charles dispatched his own man, the earl of Glamorgan, who in effect offered whatever the confederates wanted in return for an army to fight for the king in England. The sad reality was that the Glamorgan mission to the confederates was a measure of Charles's desperation rather than a change of heart; when he was in a position to offer much, in the early years of the war, he preferred to stonewall, but after Naseby, when he was in no position to offer anything, much less deliver on his promises, he authorised everything to be put on the table. Embarassingly, when news leaked out of the terms Glamorgan had offered, especially those offering considerable improvement in the position of the Catholic church in Ireland, there was uproar in England and Charles was forced to repudiate him.

Another key to understanding developments in Ireland in the 1640s is that the dilemma of the Old English had by no means been resolved by the outbreak of hostilities. They had spent over forty years arguing that loyalty and Catholicism were compatible, and they had claimed to be loyal subjects of the king. Yet now they found themselves in rebellion with those whom they had long regarded as 'the king's Irish enemies'. They were very reluctant rebels, deeply uneasy at their alliance with the native Irish, and unhappy at not being able to fight openly for Charles. The shared Catholicism between the Old English and the native Irish was little more than skin deep, for the native Irish had clung to older practices – married clergy and the like – that had generally been purged from the more advanced 'Roman' Catholicism practised in the Pale.

In any case, there was ample scope for conflict between the two groups over monastic lands (of which the Old English, though not the native Irish, had been major beneficiaries), and indeed over the history of the past five hundred years. The Old English had, after all, grown great on the confiscation of native Irish lands and that had neither been forgotten nor forgiven. Moreover, while the Old English sought to win binding concessions from Charles, they well understood that delays in concluding a deal might render their military assistance ineffective, especially once the Scots added their firepower to that of Parliament. They also knew that Charles simply could not be trusted: as God's anointed one, he could lie, cheat and betray with impunity; his promises were meaningless – as Wentworth had learned to his cost. In short, the Old English dilemma of how to square loyalty and Catholicism, how to reconcile supporting the king's cause with opposing his wishes, so far from being resolved by the setting up of the Confederation of Kilkenny was in fact considerably sharpened.

Happily for the Old English, matters were no less complicated on the Protestant side, for the outbreak of the English Civil War in August 1642 had divided Protestant Ireland no less than Protestant England, and this division offers yet another key to understanding the events of the 1640s. Those Irish Protestants who adhered to the royalist side – Ormond was the most notable – could not but deplore the king's desire to conclude a deal with the confederates, and they would have their loyalty sorely tested by his attempt to recruit Irish Catholics for his armies in England and Scotland. In the event, when it came to the test, their loyalty quickly proved to lie with Protestant Ireland rather than with the king.

Rather than yield Dublin to Irish Catholic confederates who had concluded an alliance with his king, Ormond surrendered it in June 1647 to parliamentary forces under the command of Michael Jones.

Those Irish Protestants, mostly new English officials and settlers, who supported the parliamentary side had far fewer dilemmas to resolve. Their enemy was, in theory, the confederate Catholics, but any Catholic would do, for they were all presumed guilty and within a few days of the rebellion, volunteer forces commanded by Sir Robert Stewart in the Laggan area of Ulster, and Morrogh O'Brien (a fervent Protestant despite his native Irish origins), pledged themselves to Parliament and set out to roll back the rebels' territorial gains. In warfare that harked back to the darkest days of the wars of Elizabeth indiscriminate massacres of non-combatants, priests, prisoners and rebel soldiers were celebrated and scorched-earth tactics were adopted.

Early newssheets on the rebellion had clamorously announced disaster after disaster but, within months, the tide had begun to turn, and the message was now 'Exceeding Ioyfull Newes from **IRELAND** . . . wherein is declared what townes of note the English have taken from the rebells'. Moreover, the truce signed between Ormond and the confederates was entirely disregarded by those loyal to Parliament; indeed, any cessation of hostilities with papist rebels must surely have confirmed Parliament's suspicions that Charles was ready to deal with the devil, and it immediately issued orders that any Irish soldiers captured on English soil were to be promptly executed.

So far as those Irish Protestants who supported Parliament were concerned the chief cause for anxiety was the presence in north-east Ulster of a Scottish army of some ten thousand men commanded by Major-General Robert Munro. Admittedly, this force had been dispatched from Scotland, with the approval of the English Parliament, but once in Ulster it showed no disposition to move beyond the borders of that province, and there was rarely any cooperation between the settler-led Laggan army and the Scots under Munro. It was known that the Scots had long regarded all of eastern Ulster as theirs, and that they had designs on other adjacent areas. The static nature of Munro's campaigning throughout 1642 fuelled suspicions that the strengthening and consolidation of Scottish interests in Ulster took priority over both the punishment of Irish rebels and the amelioration of the plight of Irish Protestants.

The native Irish who had begun the rebellion had been quickly reinforced by the return to Ireland of thousands of swordsmen who had earlier fled Ireland to fight in Spanish regiments in the army of Flanders. At their head was Owen Roe O'Neill who had served for nearly forty years in the Spanish army, and who had recently defended Arras against the French. He was by far the most able military commander on the confederate side, and was to win an important victory over Munro at Benburb, county Tyrone, in June 1646. His experience of war on the continent and his Counter-Reformation perspective led him almost immediately into the camp of the papal nuncio, Rinuccini, who arrived from Rome in October 1645 and who saw the Irish conflict as an episode in the continuing struggle between Reformation and Counter-Reformation. Rinuccini was, therefore, deeply suspicious of Old English eagerness to conclude a peace with the heretic king of England. He was equally distrustful of that other heretic, Charles's negotiator, Ormond. Rinuccini forcefully reminded the confederates that they had sworn an oath of association which included a vow to restore the Catholic church to the status it enjoyed in the reign of Henry VIII. To his horror he saw that the Old English were quite prepared to abandon their oath if they could cut a deal with Charles, but he was resolved to keep them up to the mark, threatening with excommunication any who broke their undertakings. Owen Roe O'Neill sided with Rinuccini in this struggle, using his victory over Munro at Benburb to boost the nuncio's standing in Kilkenny. However, by this stage, matters were unravelling fast in England: even before Benburb, Charles had surrendered to the Scots, and, within a few months he was in the hands of English parliamentary forces. With Charles a prisoner, and the first civil war over, Parliament could turn its attention to Ireland.

Cromwell in Ireland

In June 1647 the Irish-born parliamentary commander, Michael Jones, with an army of two thousand men landed at Dublin.[7] Within a matter of weeks he had inflicted a crushing defeat at Dungan's Hill, near Dublin, on the Confederation's Leinster army commanded by Thomas Preston. For the next two years, until Cromwell arrived with his Ironsides in August 1649, matters in Ireland defy coherent description. In December 1647 Charles escaped to the Scots, concluded an agreement by which he would introduce Presbyterianism throughout his kingdoms (ten years earlier he had tried to introduce Laudianism throughout his kingdoms) and promptly ignited the second civil war, this time with the Scots on his side. Meanwhile, relations between Rinuccini and the supreme council at Kilkenny had so far deteriorated that he had excommunicated its members for signing up to various truces with 'heretics'. With the defeat of the Scots by Cromwell, the capture of Charles, once again by parliamentary forces, and the announcement that he was to be put on trial for his life, it was clear that endgame had been reached. In February 1649, some weeks after Charles was executed, Rinuccini left for Rome, still bitter at the duplicitous Irish (Catholic and Protestant), and no doubt pleased that Charles had been vanquished; a Protestant king killed by fellow Protestants would surely scandalise all Europe. He left behind him a scene of military and political chaos. Highly improbable local alliances, grounded on the well-known maxim of *sauve qui peut*, were frequently concluded between erstwhile foes – for example, that at Derry between Owen Roe O'Neill, champion of the Ulster Irish, and Sir Charles Coote, hero of the Ulster settlers.

Cromwell's arrival at the head of some twenty thousand Ironsides in August 1649 and his ensuing swift campaign put a bloody end to all overt resistance. The storming of Drogheda and Wexford by his army and the ensuing massacres of their garrisons (including many English royalist soldiers) and of townspeople (mostly Irish Catholic), to the number of nearly five thousand altogether, were exulted in by Cromwell as fit punishment for the atrocities of 1641 (even though neither town had been involved in the rebellion). In accordance with the loose laws of war then in existence (and but poorly adhered to in the period), Cromwell was within his rights in ordering the garrison at Drogheda to be put to the sword if they refused to surrender. At Wexford, however, if not Drogheda, negotiations were still continuing when the Cromwellian soldiers ran amok. However, a 'no quarter' order was far from mandatory and, in any case, the killing of civilians – clerical and lay – was generally reprobated (though in the Thirty Years' War examples abounded where this prohibition was ignored). Even in the supposedly 'civil' English Civil War, excesses could occur: following the fall of the town of Bolton in 1644, the royalist attackers slew the defenders and as many as seven hundred civilians. Cromwell and his army might have been determined on exemplary violence *pour décourager les autres* (as Ludlow, one of his commanders, claimed), but they were also stoked up by a lust for vengeance, a desire fuelled by the grotesque pamphlet literature on the massacres that had appeared since 1641.

Cromwell's actions at Drogheda and Wexford have subsequently guaranteed his place in that Irish pantheon reserved for those sent out from England to inflict military massacre on Irish civilians (Coroticus was the first to be installed). When Cromwell left Ireland in May 1650 he left behind a devastated country in which famine and disease, including bubonic plague, were rife. The eleven years of conflict had taken their toll: in the 1650s the economic writer, William Petty, making no distinction between the wars of Cromwell and those of the confederates, estimated that over 600,000 had died out of a population of about 1.5 million. Modern historians, more conservative, have estimated that between 20 and 40 per cent of the population perished during the years 1641 to 1651 (compared with casualty figures of 3.7 per cent for England and 6.0 per cent for Scotland). Perhaps a contemporary Gaelic poet summed it up best when he wrote simply, 'this was the war that finished Ireland'. With the end of overt and organised resistance, the Cromwellians were now free to devise and implement whatever policies they chose for, as one of them put it, Ireland now lay like a 'white paper' before them. What would they write on that sheet of paper?

Cromwellian Ireland

'Cromwellian Ireland', the decade of the 1650s, during which Oliver Cromwell and his associates sought to govern Ireland has – to put it mildly – had a bad press, being synonymous in Catholic popular imagination with religious persecution, political outlawry, legal dispossession and forced transplantation of population.[8] Nor were Irish Protestants all that enamoured of the Cromwellians, for their fiscal policies proved onerous, their attempt at military rule by blow-in English captains was resented and their initial onslaught on the established church for complicity-through-negligence in the 1641 rebellion was resented. Admittedly, a legislative union between England and Ireland had quickly been declared, with a handful of Irish Members of Parliament going off to Westminster (and thus Cromwell could accurately be described as the first unionist); but his responsibility for the execution of Charles meant that he also possessed impeccable republican credentials; unsurprisingly, in modern Ireland neither Unionist nor republican has seen fit to acknowledge a debt to the Lord Protector, as he was to be titled in 1654.

Central to understanding the policies of Cromwell and the Cromwellians in Ireland is their experience of the civil wars of the 1640s, and the lessons that they drew from the favourable outcome to those conflicts. Cromwell, and the men in his army, were not mercenaries but rather ideological warriors who rejoiced in their Englishness and for whom, in their eyes, the victory vouchsafed to them by God was proof positive that they were on the side of godliness. Their triumph in Ireland, England and Scotland imposed a heavy burden on them to reconfigure church, state and society in these countries in strict accordance with God's plans, as revealed to them through prayer and biblical study. They must not rest on their laurels with military victory won; they had to go on to build that new Jerusalem, that city upon a hill which would act like a beacon to the ungodly, dazzling them, yet attracting them to the light.

In this scheme of things Ireland held a special place, both as challenge, given its perceived rooted papist culture, as exemplified by the horrid crimes of 1641, and as opportunity, given its clear lack of established or vested interests that might impede, as in England, the imposition of godly rule. Indeed the problems that the Cromwellians would encounter in England in the 1650s, and the corrosive disillusion that these gave rise to, made Ireland all the more important for the implementation of godly policies. Ireland, following the devastation of the 1640s, it was claimed, was available for godly experiment in a way that England was not, for vested interests remained thick on the ground and, as the Cromwellians saw it, were determined to stifle any perceived moves towards religious, let alone, social and political reform.

For these reasons, the energy, and the urgency, which the Cromwellians initially brought to their policies in Ireland, and the vision that lay behind them, have led commentators to claim that their actions were altogether new and unprecedented. In fact there was little that was novel about their policies, though the determination with which they were pursued, marked off Cromwellian plans from earlier reform programmes, save perhaps those of Wentworth, barely ten years earlier. As before, the English government, having crushed rebellion in Ireland, now turned its attention to preventing a future one and this meant deploying those by-now familiar instruments of anglicisation – extensive colonisation, population transfers, religious change and the promotion of English language, customs, costume and law. And as had happened before to earlier reform packages for Ireland, announced to a roll of drums and a flourish of trumpets, the Cromwellian programme fell far short of success, not just for the familiar reasons of lack of money, the perennial dilemma of choice between coercion and persuasion, and ultimately a lack of will, but also because, contrary to official belief, Ireland was not, in fact, a 'white paper' on which anything could be written. Once again, those English governors determined to remake Ireland as England-in-a-minor-key quickly discovered that English aspirations sat ill with Irish realities.

Land, as ever, proved the touchstone. It was inevitable that military victory would be followed by an extensive confiscation of the lands of the 'guilty', whether royalists or rebels. The debts owed by Parliament, not including arrears of pay due to some 35,000 soldiers, exceeded £3 million, and Irish lands had been pledged throughout the 1640s as the way to clear those debts. Indeed, within months of the outbreak of the Irish rebellion, Charles had signed into law the Adventurers' Act (1642), which had authorised a massive confiscation of Irish lands to reimburse and reward those who would 'adventure' their money to suppress the rebellion, and Parliament had added further legislation to similar effect. By the 1650s all that remained for the Cromwellians to do was to determine who would forfeit all, or part of, their estates, and who would receive them.

In theory, by the Act of Settlement (1652), and Act of Satisfaction (1653), Catholic landowning east of the Shannon was almost entirely brought to an end. It has been estimated that some eighty thousand Catholics – and some Protestants, of whom the royalist marquis of Ormond was the most notable – were comprehended in these Acts, and were to lose everything, up to and including their lives. Even those Catholic landowners who had shown 'constant good affection' during the wars of the 1640s were ordered to to remove themselves and their dependants to Connacht and to give up their lands in Munster or Leinster in exchange for much smaller estates in counties Galway, Roscommon, Mayo and Clare. A demand that all Catholics be corralled in Connacht was entertained for a time but, in a significant flexing of political muscle by the pre-1641 settlers, now dubbed the Old Protestants, this proposal was abandoned, largely on economic grounds. Catholic landowning was to be concentrated in Connacht, not because that was the poorest province (that distinction went to Ulster), but because it was the most Catholic, because plantation there had been deferred from Wentworth's time and because it was the furthest from the European mainland. A further security in this latter respect was provided by an enactment that those Catholics transplanted to Connacht were not permitted to reside within four miles of the coast in order to minimise the risk of foreign interventions. With Cromwellian thoroughness a new survey of the confiscated lands was undertaken so as to avoid both the exaggerations and understatements in acreage that had bedevilled earlier forfeitures. William Petty, the foremost political economist of his age, was deputed to undertake the task, and the resulting 'Down survey' of 1654–9 achieved, for the first time, a very high degree of cartographical accuracy. Indeed, Petty's maps were not generally superseded until the advent of the Ordnance Survey maps in the mid-nineteenth century.

Petty's survey had not begun when the order came for Catholic landowners, and their dependants, to remove themselves to Connacht. The original deadline of May 1654 was then put back to March 1655, and in May 1657 it was announced that the transplantation to Connacht had been completed. Inevitably, the results fell far short of what had been planned. Perhaps 1,900, mostly Old English, did in fact go to Connacht but as many again simply refused to move, and many of those who did travel west of the Shannon returned once times had become quieter. Religious settlement patterns in Wexford, for example, despite a precipitous drop in Catholic land titles in the 1650s, reveal a strong continuity between the 1640s and the 1790s: former owners, as had happened before, had simply become occupiers. The distribution of estates within Connacht, to Catholic landowners from elsewhere, was a shambles. Some did obtain the promised equivalence but a number received nothing, or much less than they were entitled to, and some who had been exempted by name from any compensation – the earl of Westmeath is a good example – ended up with over 11,000 acres. None the less, flawed as the distribution of estates was to prove, the overall conclusion was stark: the Cromwellians had achieved a revolutionary turnaround in landownership, with the Catholic share of the island of Ireland falling from around 60 per cent in 1640 to just 20 per cent in 1660. The transplantation to Connacht (however incomplete it was) was to enter Catholic popular memory as a banishment of biblical proportions and, when elaborated and exaggerated in the nineteenth century, was held to be a crime that could be expiated only by the ending of landlordism itself.

The Cromwellians had hoped that, as with earlier plantation projects, new settlers would come to Ireland to avail themselves of the opportunities opened up by Catholic dispossession and internal exile and thus promote anglicisation; but few newcomers arrived. At most 15,000 out of the anticipated 35,000, divided between ex-soldiers and adventurers, took up the lands allocated to them. The speculators quickly merged their interests with the Old Protestants, while the servitors, surprisingly, soon revealed a marked propensity to wed Irish papists. No distinctive Cromwellian interest ever formed, and in the end, it was to be the pre-1641 Protestant settler population that proved to be the major beneficiary of the Cromwellian confiscations.

It was the existing Protestant population too that derived most advantage from the Cromwellian onslaught on Catholic power in the towns and boroughs, and on the Catholic religion itself. Cromwell had already announced that he would not permit the saying of the mass, and a vigorous persecution of Catholic clergy, especially Jesuits and friars, was undertaken. Earlier laws against them were revived, and there were many executions, expulsions to the continent and transportations to the West Indies. In theory, this ought to have left the way open for a concerted campaign of conversion, but in practice this did not happen. Lack of money, divisions among Protestants themselves as to the 'redeemability' of Irish papists, or indeed about the desirability of converting them at all, along with a lack of qualified preachers, all meant that no sustained conversion impulse emanated from the Cromwellians. By contrast, there was a firm determination to destroy Catholic economic and political authority.

In pursuit of these objectives Catholics were ordered out of the towns and barred from the corporations and the trade guilds, on the grounds that they posed a threat to security. This policy was enforced. Cork Catholics probably fared worst, for they had already been expelled from their city, once before, in 1646; this time the expulsion was done with greater severity. Over the coming years, Catholics were to filter back into the towns, but it is from the 1650s that urban Ireland, and especially Dublin and Cork, became a Protestant bastion, and it was to remain so until the 1840s. Other towns in which Catholics had held a commanding interest, such as Galway and Waterford, went into prolonged decline with the collapse of Catholic economic clout.

The expulsion of Catholics from the towns and boroughs and the destruction of their economic power had important political consequences. The Irish Parliament, with its members drawn disproportionately from the boroughs, now passed completely into Protestant hands. In 1660 only one Catholic – Geoffrey Browne of Tuam, county Galway – was elected, but he did not take his seat. He was to be the last Catholic elected to a regular Parliament until Daniel O'Connell's triumph in the Clare election in 1828. In the literature, both historical and creative, as well as lurid and sensational, that purports to describe the iniquities of Cromwellian rule in Ireland, the themes of persecution, confiscation and transplantation bulk large; but arguably of more transcending significance for the future was the emergence of the Irish Parliament as a wholly Protestant institution. Irish Protestants' monopoly of political power, a direct product of their domination of urban life and of their ownership of over 80 per cent of the land of Ireland, was to be the central foundation of their ascendancy for nearly two hundred years.

With the death of Oliver Cromwell in 1658 Cromwellian rule began to unravel, first in England and then in Ireland. There was a real danger of a further civil war in 1659, as rival army commanders manoeuvred for position, but this prospect was averted, at least for the time being, with the return of Charles II as king. In retrospect the Cromwellians, for all their ringing declarations of reform and their determination that only the godly would rule, fitted into a well-established pattern of English government in Ireland, in which high-flying aspirations were brought crashing down to earth by Irish realities. The Old Protestants had been able to shape the settlement of Ireland in ways that suited their interests, for Ireland, despite the destruction of the Cromwellian war, and contrary to Cromwellian forecasts, lay open to reform. The zealously reforming government of Charles Fleetwood, ultimately gave way after 1655 to the more pragmatic, less programmatic, administration of Henry Cromwell, Oliver's son. Persecution of Catholic clerics slackened off, military government was scaled down and grandiose plans for large-scale population transfers were shelved. The Old Protestants took back Dublin Castle and took control of the Irish Parliament. Whether they would retain their gains on the return of Charles II had yet to be determined.

Restoration Ireland

In April 1660, in an obvious propaganda exercise, Charles II issued the Declaration of Breda to his soon-to-be subjects in the three kingdoms.[9] In effect, he promised that, on his return to his kingdoms, he would behave himself. Retribution would be minimal, pardon would be given to those who had backed the parliamentary cause and, famously, liberty would be offered to those of tender consciences. On 29 May 1660 Charles made his triumphant formal entry into London; two weeks earlier, however, to the cheers of his Protestant subjects, he had been proclaimed king in Dublin.

The affairs of Ireland were not a priority with the restored king, but he well knew that hopes and fears for the future were no less acute in Ireland than elsewhere, and he quickly attempted both to reassure those who had profited by the upheavals since 1641 and to comfort those who had lost out. Such an even-handed approach, of course, satisfied no one. The Old Protestants, who had enthusiastically cheered Charles's proclamation as king, sought confirmation that he would uphold the revolution in land, politics and social authority that had occurred since the outbreak of the Irish rebellion, and of which they were, by and large, the major beneficiaries. Catholics, for their part, aspired to recover what they had lost. These conflicting ambitions fuelled the tensions that were to beset Restoration Ireland. Land, inevitably, proved the battleground, so to speak.

In November 1660 Charles issued a declaration on the land question in Ireland. Cromwellian soldiers and adventurers were to keep their land, except where 'innocent papists' could establish a good title. If these soldiers and adventurers had to give up some of their land, they would receive compensation elsewhere. In addition, soldiers who had fought for Charles's father were to receive land, while a number of named individuals whose land had been confiscated under Cromwell (Ormond was the most prominent) were to be restored to their estates. Underpinning this plan was a belief that there was plenty of land in Ireland to satisfy all parties. But this was emphatically not the case: true, estates given to the regicides in the 1650s were available for redistribution, and this was helpful, but beyond that there was scarcely an acre of land whose owner was not persuaded that he – or she – satisfied the terms of Charles's declaration.

Over the next ten years, in an increasingly fraught atmosphere, separate Acts of Settlement (1662) and of Explanation (1665) were passed, and these sought to give effect to Charles's sweeping assurances. In the end, through the operation of two separate courts of claims which issued certificates of innocence (and hence eligibility for the recovery of at least a proportion of one's estate), there was a significant redistribution of land, particularly in the province of Leinster. Altogether it is estimated that from a low of around 10 per cent of the land of Ireland in 1660, Catholic landownership had risen to nearly 20 per cent by 1680. Protestant Ireland, however reluctantly, was prepared to accept this increase, provided that the land question was now definitively closed. Catholics, however, saw matters entirely differently. In 1641 they had owned nearly 60 per cent of Irish land and, therefore, the increase in landowning under the Restoration, while welcome, could never be regarded as a final settlement of their claims; instead, it was seen as a first instalment. Moreover, Catholic confidence in this respect was constantly buoyed by their realisation that James, duke of York, the king's brother, and an avowed Catholic, would ascend the throne after Charles's death.

In 1685 James duly became king, and immediately began to bring in measures designed to promote, and benefit, Catholics in England and Ireland. In Ireland a number of Catholics were given senior judicial posts and appointed as county sheriffs. The position of sheriff gave its holder a major say in parliamentary elections, and it was feared that a political resurgence of Irish Catholics might be on the cards. However, far more disturbing for Irish Protestants was the appointment in 1686 of Richard, 'Fighting Dick', Talbot, earl of Tyrconnell, a champion of Catholic land claims (and a noted duellist), as head of the entire Irish army. He quickly set about re-Catholicising his army by dismissing Protestant officers and commissioning only Catholics. A year later there was further consternation when he was made lord deputy and announced his intention of reopening the land question. So far so bad for Irish Protestants; and yet for all these alarms, they could console themselves that James could not live for ever, and that the next in line to the throne was his (Protestant) daughter Mary, whose husband, William of Orange, was a Protestant hero because of his continued opposition to the ambitions of Louis XIV of France.

Undoubtedly the speed with which James moved and the urgency of his actions were prompted by his desire to leave his fellow Catholics in a much stronger position than when he had ascended the throne. Fears that he intended to roll back the Reformation and bring his three kingdoms into the Catholic camp were almost certainly baseless. However, when Mary of Modena, James's wife, defied her troubled medical history and gave birth to a son in June 1688 the picture changed instantly. A Catholic king might possibly be endured by his Protestant subjects, but a Catholic dynasty? Never. Within weeks, William of Orange had been invited to invade England by disaffected elements within the English ruling elite, and in November 1688 he landed in Devon with a large force. James's army melted away in the face of the mixed Dutch and English force confronting it and in December James himself fled friendless to France.

In Ireland, among Protestants, there was huge enthusiasm and prompt endorsement for this revolutionary change.[10] In December the Protestant apprentices of Derry denied entry to forces loyal to James and, at opposite ends of the country, Sligo and Bandon, declared for William. Meanwhile, in Dublin Tyrconnell mulled over what action to take. In the event, after some dithering, he declared for James who, at French prompting, arrived in Ireland in March 1689. The French, undoubtedly, hoped that Williamite forces would become bogged down in a lengthy struggle in Ireland and thus would be unable to intervene as effectively as they had hitherto in the Low Countries. They may even have expected

James's forces to triumph. Either outcome would serve as a victory for French strategic objectives.

For his part, William had no desire to come to Ireland, nor indeed had he much interest in staying in England, for his sole focus was on combating the French menace on the continent. The arrival of James with a French force in Ireland was, therefore, hugely unwelcome to him, for it meant that a Williamite army had to come to Ireland to see off this challenge to his newly established rule. While this force was being assembled, Protestant Ireland was not content to bide its time and a number of hastily recruited local forces – the Enniskilleners were the most successful – engaged the Jacobite soldiers loyal to James. Derry finally closed its gates to James in April 1689 and was immediately subjected to probably the most inept siege in the history of modern warfare. Despite the incompetence revealed on both sides, the short siege (barely three months) was subsequently imbued with an epic quality and, ever since, has been both an enduring inspiration and a defining motif for Irish Protestants generally and for Ulster Unionists in particular. Elsewhere, there were a number of battles – Beleek, Newtownbutler, Dromore, Bandon – with the honours evenly shared between Williamite and Jacobite.

Against this background of military campaigns in the countryside, significant political developments were taking place in Dublin. In May 1689 James summoned an Irish Parliament and, although the proper procedures were not complied with, this cannot be dismissed as an illegal assembly. (For a coin struck by James in Ireland in August 1689 see figure 3.4.) This 'Patriot Parliament', as nineteenth-century nationalists termed it, swiftly launched an attack on the operation of Poynings' law and on the entire Restoration land settlement. James would not permit any change to Poynings' law, but the land 'settlement' of the Restoration period was now scrapped. Some 2,400 landowners, almost all Protestant, were attainted for disloyalty to James, and their estates declared confiscate. Later, when Jacobite hopes had been dashed by crushing military defeats, the actions of this Parliament would be used to justify equally stern punishment for those who had espoused the 'wrong' cause.

A Williamite army under Marshal Schomberg landed in Ireland in August 1689, and was later joined by Danish mercenaries hired by William. As noted earlier, the latter's arrival allegedly struck terror among the Irish, mindful of the reputation of their Viking ancestors. The winter passed in desultory campaigning and it was only with the arrival of William himself, near Carrickfergus in June 1690, that matters moved towards a conclusion. Battle between William and James and their respective forces was duly joined at the Boyne (figure 3.5) on 1 July 1690 (12 July new style) and, though no decisive military victory was gained, James chose to regard his cause as lost. The war would continue for over

3.4 A coin struck by James II in Ireland. As if he had a premonition of disaster, James chose to date his coins by both month and year. National Museum of Ireland.

a year, but there was no longer any question as to who would be king of England, Scotland and Ireland. James's flight from the battlefield was so precipitate – reportedly, he himself was the first to bring the news of his own defeat to Dublin – that it earned him the reputation of a poltroon and caused him to be derided by the Gaelic wordsmiths as *Seamas a Chaca* (James the Shit). From Dublin James hastened to Kinsale and, with his unhappy adventure at a humiliating end, he took ship to France and permanent exile.

William, no less anxious to leave Ireland than James (for a Williamite reverse see figure 3.6), none the less stayed on in hopes of putting an end to all Jacobite resistance. However, the failure of sieges at Athlone and Limerick in July and August 1690 brought him the realisation that the war in Ireland would drag on for at least another year and he returned to England in September. Hostilities resumed in the new year, with the Williamite forces, now commanded by Ginkel, laying siege to Athlone. The fall of Athlone presaged the end of the Jacobite cause and the decisive battle was fought at Aughrim, county Galway, on 12 July 1691. Many thousands of Jacobites fell in the battle, including their French

3.5 A highly stylised and non-contemporary representation of the battle of the Boyne, 12 July (new style) 1690. This is essentially the image that has passed into Irish Protestant consciousness. National Library of Ireland.

commander, St Ruth, his head taken off by an unlucky cannonball. In quick succession, Galway and Athlone surrendered to the Williamites and a truce was called between the besiegers and the defenders at Limerick. On 3 October, two sets of articles, civil and military, were concluded, and, with this so-called treaty of Limerick, the war was finally over.

Late seventeenth-century Ireland

One hundred and fifty years before the treaty of Limerick, Henry VIII had been declared king of Ireland and he, and his ministers, had embarked on a programme of reform for that country. Initially, they appeared to have assumed that the Irish could be relatively easily brought to adopt superior English manners, customs and even the 'English' religion, and the methods to be deployed were persuasion and example rather than coercion or threats. But that assumption had been quickly shown to be mistaken, and more robust means had been resolved upon.

3.6 Another exciting image for Irish nationalists was this early nineteenth-century one of Patrick Sarsfield's successful attack on King William's artillery train at Ballyneety, county Limerick. National Library of Ireland.

Eventually, by the 1590s, so far had lenient methods been abandoned in favour of sterner ones, that it might seem to an onlooker as if the Irish, and Ireland, might have to be destroyed in order to be, so to speak, saved. By 1603 Ireland had finally been conquered, and the promise (or threat) implicit in the 1541 Kingship Act had been fulfilled; Ireland was now incontestably an English dominion. However, the question of the identity of the governing elite in the kingdom of Ireland had yet to be resolved – New English Protestants or Old English Catholics? It was that matter that had rumbled, and occasionally exploded, down through the seventeenth century until it had been settled once and for all, it was hoped, at the battles of the Boyne and, especially, Aughrim. A governing elite had been entirely overthrown and had been replaced by another deemed more reliable by the parent country. For the future, Ireland would not only be an English kingdom, but a Protestant one, governed by the Protestant minority, who would have a near monopoly of land as well as of political power.

The profound upheavals in this one-hundred-and-fifty-year period were unparalleled in contemporary Europe and marked off Irish history decisively from that of other countries. Inevitably, this political and religious transformation was accompanied by huge shifts in social and economic affairs. The very appearance of Ireland was to change drastically over this period as the dense woods, so prominent a feature of the Irish landscape since early times, were progressively cleared. To an extent their disappearance had been brought about by a large increase in cattle-rearing at the expense of tillage. In the tumultuous conditions of the sixteenth, and much of the seventeenth, centuries, cattle production rose because animals could be moved quickly in the face of imminent threat. By contrast, grain stores were largely immobile and, hence, more vulnerable to seizure or destruction. Mostly, however, the destruction of the woods was undertaken by the settlers eager for a quick return on their investment (Irish wood was especially valued for barrel-making) and anxious, on security grounds, to remove the natural habitat of the Irish rapparee, or outlaw. Either way, Ireland was rapidly being opened up to anglicisation.

By the early seventeenth century, thoroughout Ireland, county divisions, which had existed on paper for decades, had become a reality and these would remain largely untouched until the present day. These counties – there were thirty-two of them – would constitute two-member parliamentary constituencies until the reforms of the nineteenth century; they would also from an early date form recruitment units for the armed forces of the crown. If the division of Ireland into counties was a recent development, the reverse was the case with the subdivision of counties into townlands of varying sizes, for these traced their origins to pre-Christian times. Townlands were adopted as the essential unit for land valuation and taxation and they were to remain in use for these purposes until the later nineteenth century. A final division was that made through the fencing and hedging of fields. Gaelic agriculture had made little use of enclosure, preferring to move cattle around but by 1690 hedges or stone walls were everywhere and the Irish countryside had taken on the appearance that it would retain until recent times.

Moreover by the end of the seventeenth century, the countryside was becoming the preserve of a crop largely unknown a hundred years earlier, for potato cultivation was everywhere and a revolution in Irish diet among the lower classes was occurring. Cereals would remain important, together with milk, butter and cheese, and these were occasionally supplemented by some fish (herring), or a portion of jellied blood drawn out of live cattle (a foodstuff repellent to English tastes). But the conquest of Ireland by the potato was well under way, and by the early 1700s the potato was a near staple among the lower sections of the population. Easy to grow, and high yielding per acre, the highly nutritious potato was to have profound consequences on Irish demographic history, both by reducing mortality (people were healthier on a potato diet), and by improving fertility, for healthier mothers carried more babies to term and were better able to feed them in infancy. A population estimated at around 2 million in 1700 would increase to 5 million at the end of the eighteenth century, and this demographic depth could be a major economic asset. Alternatively, population growth would put pressure on existing resources, igniting new conflicts over access to land and food, and ultimately leading to greater immiseration. The conquest and colonisation carried out over the previous one hundred and fifty years, and their legacy of religious rancour and ethnic hatred, might not prove the best bases for meeting the coming challenges.

By the end of the seventeenth century a pattern of landholding had been established that would remain, by and large, until the late nineteenth century. A small number of large estates, perhaps two thousand in number, owned by a landlord, who was usually Irish born (and proud of it), but of English origins, and almost always a member of the Church of Ireland, would be worked by leaseholding tenants, who were usually Catholic (or Presbyterian in east Ulster). The ethnic and religious split between those who owned the land, and those who worked the land, was replicated only in the countries of eastern Europe and distinguished Ireland from its nearer neighbours.

It would, however, be premature to see in this separation, between owner and occupier, the basis for endless civil or religious wars. Later generations had their own reasons (chief among them, the need to justify the dispossession of the possessor) for playing up the inevitability of conflict. Nineteenth-century campaigners against Irish landlords made a doubly compelling case, first to highlight the profoundly unsatisfactory state of the current Irish land system, with its notorious features of starvation, eviction and rack-rent, as well as other iniquities, and then to trace the origins of this malign state of affairs to the confiscations (theft) of Irish land in the seventeenth century. And yet, the evidence, at least for much of the eighteenth century, and beyond, does not support the theme of timeless struggle between an English-speaking, Protestant, landlord class of foreign origin, and a Gaelic-speaking, Irish Catholic tenantry. Rivalry, often bloody, between tenants of differing socio-economic status, rather than anti-landlord hostility, is more noticeable up to the 1840s. That said, it was undoubtedly true that, as long as religion continued to bar nearly 75 per cent of the Irish population from access to the state (the corresponding figure for Britain was 5 per cent), conflict could be confidently predicted; but all would depend on how the newly confirmed Irish Protestant governing elite would conduct itself in the coming decades.

The Irish economy had also, by 1690, taken on the shape that it would retain until the nineteenth century. As a result of continuous wars and rebellion, there was relatively little Irish manufacturing. True, from early times, linen had been a staple export and a valuable one (occasionally, bundles of linen were even used in place of currency), but Irish linen was generally of poor quality, and weaving was looked down upon as a trade for the poor. The arrival of French Hugenot (=Protestant) refugees, many of them skilled linen-workers, into Ireland in the 1690s, led to a dramatic improvement in both the quality – and quantity – of linen. Belfast, a town barely on the map in 1650, would become one of the top Irish ports by 1700, largely on the back of linen exports, and by 1800 it rivalled Dublin.

For most of the seventeenth century the major Irish export had been live cattle, almost entirely to England. In response to English protests, this livestock trade had been shut down in the 1670s. These Cattle Acts were the first of a number of English initiatives aimed at rendering the Irish economy complementary, rather than competitive, to the English one. In response, Irish cattle dealers had turned their hand, with some considerable success, to the export of 'dead-stock' (salted beef, tallow and hides), and to butter and salted fish exports once again to England but also to France and to the British colonies in north America and the West Indies. This export trade in provisions was to grow substantially in the eighteenth century, and would bring considerable prosperity to the cattle-rearing areas, chiefly Cork and its hinterland. The major Irish import in medieval, as well as more recent, times, had been wine from Spain and France almost entirely consumed by the better-off classes, and this continued to be the case throughout the eighteenth century. None of these activities permitted Ireland to escape from dependency on the English market, and with a population of under 2 million in 1700 it was poorly positioned to take advantage of more settled conditions post-1690 and achieve take-off into sustained economic growth.

Nor were matters, in this respect, helped by the passage of a series of anti-Catholic legislative enactments, usually styled the Penal Laws, the chief of which were put through the Irish Parliament between 1692 and 1705. Irish poverty, much commented on in the eighteenth century, was usually blamed on English restrictive legislation, or on the simple fact that the mass of the people were Catholic, and therefore naturally lazy, valuing leisure over labour; but the Penal Laws, by denying Catholics ambition, and by keeping Catholic money out of the land market, made their own contribution to keeping 'poor Ireland poor'.

How the ordinary Irish man or woman viewed these extraordinary changes is by no means clear. Given the central role of religion at all levels of society in Ireland (and in England), we can be certain that the 'winners' claimed to owe all to God's favour, while the 'losers' resignedly attributed their ill fortune to divine displeasure. In order to probe this question further, Gaelic Irish poetry, in the absence of other less elevated Irish-language material, has been interrogated for evidence of reaction at elite and popular level; but here the response is mixed. Some settlers were hated, and derided as heretics, churls and knaves, but equally some 'blown-in' landlords were admired and feted. Again, it seems clear that those Irish who adopted English ways, English speech and English dress were scorned and ridiculed; but such resentment may have been caused by rage at a perceived inferior moving ahead. Interestingly, there is less evidence that Irish Catholic converts to Protestantism incurred any particular opprobrium – at least from Catholics, though Protestants remained suspicious of their motives. Perhaps the central question is whether the brutal reality of conquest and colonisation broke through the pervasive localism or provincialism of Gaelic political culture to forge an encompassing Irishness. The evidence from the poetry is suggestive, but inconclusive. It can be argued that, under the impact of dispossession and colonisation, there did emerge a new way of thinking among the Gaelic Irish, a way that prioritised the national at the expense of the tribal or local. And certainly the 1641 rebels, with their forged seal from Charles I, and with their acute appreciation of the danger to their position posed by the rise of parliamentary power in London, showed no lack of political sophistication.

It was, however, among the Irish exiles training in the seminaries of Catholic Europe, or serving in the armies of the Habsburgs in the Netherlands, that the experience of exile and dispossession produced a new all-embracing Irishness. Derided abroad by the taunt that they had no national history and therefore scarcely numbered among the family of nations, the clerics and the soldiers reacted by producing a suitably heroic origin legend that supplied an appropriate genealogy for the Irish race. It was in the early seventeenth-century that the Gaelic word *Éireannach* or Irishman, a word that had been coined in the thirteenth century, took on a fresh meaning. It now denoted all those Irish – not just native Irish or Old English – who were Catholic. The cataclysm of conquest and dispossession had combined ethnicity and religion at the centre of Irish identity. Henceforth to be Irish was to be Catholic, and to be Catholic was to be Irish. The events of the period 1690 to 1840 did nothing to alter this fusion.

4 IRELAND'S LONG EIGHTEENTH CENTURY, 1691–1830

Introduction

The period 1691 to 1830, Ireland's 'long' eighteenth century, has traditionally posed a challenge to those historians who have sought first to establish and then to elaborate the main themes that make most sense of it. Relatively benign developments – at least until the 1770s – of vibrant political activity, impressive economic advance and splendid flowering in art and architecture have jostled uncomfortably, especially for the later decades with, in the debit column, the much more malign notes of political failure, bloody insurrection, savage repression, rampant sectarian conflict and, in the early nineteenth century, increasing immiseration. Where is the balance to be struck between such apparently opposed viewpoints? And what is the connection between the splendour and the squalor, the poise and the poverty, and the self-assurance and the self-doubt, all of which seem in equal measure to characterise what has been styled both a 'golden age' and a 'penal era'?[1] We may begin our examination of these questions with the creation and dissolution of the Irish political structure, and in particular with the rise and fall of the Irish Parliament.

I: ASCENDANCY, 1690–1790

The Irish Parliament

As we have seen, the Irish Parliament traced its origins back to medieval times, but its existence since then had been fitful rather than continuous: in the seventeenth century, for example, only four parliaments had met by 1692, and when, in that year, William III summoned one, it was the first such assembly since 1665. From 1692 on, however, the Irish Parliament began to meet regularly, usually once every two years until 1785, and then once a year thereafter. The eighteenth century was to be the century of the Irish Parliament; but when the curtain fell on that century, at midnight on 31 December 1800, the Irish Parliament closed its doors forever. Quite why the Irish Parliament, a vibrant institution with, by 1800, a lengthy tradition, should have agreed to vote itself out of existence at the end of the century has remained a key question in Irish political history.

The main reason for the Irish Parliament's continuous existence in the eighteenth century lay in its power of voting the 'additional duties' which were vital to the financial survival of the Irish administration. In earlier times the Hereditary Revenue, consisting of crown rents, hearth money, various customs and excise duties and licences for the sale of ale, beer and spirits, had proved sufficient to meet the expenses of administration and had generally been voted to the monarch for his or her lifetime. In 1692, however, as a result of spiralling costs, the Hereditary Revenue was found to be inadequate and additional duties had to be voted to make up the shortfall between income and expenditure. By this date the Irish Parliament had learnt that it was unwise to be too generous with lifetime grants, and the additional duties were only voted for a two-year period, thus making necessary a biennial parliamentary session.

These additional duties, passed by a Money bill, quickly became indispensable and, as it was felt that the consent of the Irish Parliament was necessary before they could be raised, it began for the first time to meet regularly. By 1735 the Irish Parliament appeared to have achieved a permanent position in the Irish Constitution. This status was most obviously revealed by its meeting place, for in 1731 it had taken possession of a new Parliament building, a splendid edifice designed by Sir Edward Lovett Pearce in the newly fashionable Italian classical style. But more than this, by the 1730s it had become both the focus of the political aspirations of the Protestant nation and a symbol of its burgeoning self-confidence. It was around this time that its books and journals (but not yet its debates) began to be published on a regular basis.

What was the Irish Parliament in the eighteenth century?[2] At first glance it appeared to be a model of the Westminster Parliament. The Irish Parliament, like the British, consisted of a House of Lords and a House of Commons, and the government of Ireland was by 'King, Lords and Commons in Parliament assembled'. Again, the general routine of the Irish Parliament, and even the very procedures for putting through legislation, seemed similar to those at Westminster. Certainly, the handful of Irish and British politicians who made the crossing from one assembly to the other during the eighteenth century were not noticeably disoriented in their new surroundings. The electoral systems of both countries were quite similar. They were weighted in favour of property and the established church, and they both exhibited numerous anomalies and curiosities

concerning eligibility to vote, qualifications for the franchise and size of constituencies. Again, both systems were regarded with self-satisfied approval by
the political elites on both sides of the Irish Sea at least until the 1780s. Lastly,
there was undoubtedly a common Anglo-Irish political arena, one in which the
leading politicians were acquainted with one another, on occasion corresponded
with one another, sometimes married into one another's families and clearly
understood each other's patronage structure (and sought to profit from it). Such
links helped foster a common political culture in which fear of Catholicism,
defence of Protestantism, pride in Britain's overseas empire and a standard civil
libertarian rhetoric were central elements uniting the political worlds of Britain
and Ireland.

At the same time such similarities as these between the Irish and British political
institutions masked vital differences in role, power and function which cumula-
tively rendered the Westminster model inappropriate to the Irish situation. The
300 members who sat in the Irish House of Commons were clearly less representative than their English counterparts: Catholics, at least three-quarters of an
Irish population of around four million, had been excluded since the 1660s from
the political process, although it was only in 1728 that they finally lost the right
to vote. Irish Presbyterians, the next most numerous group, were also hugely
underrepresented. Irish Presbyterians were predominantly tenants or traders,
with few large landowners in their ranks and, as a result, they could not do well
in a political system that privileged landed property as conferring both social
and political authority. Additionally, the sacramental test (the requirement to
take communion in the Church of Ireland), imposed in 1704 on all those who
sought public office, effectively eliminated the Presbyterians as a political force.
The result of these exclusionary policies was that Irish Members of Parliament
were drawn almost totally from the ranks of the Church of Ireland and as such
represented a minority of the Protestants on the island. Unlike the British Parliament, the Irish Parliament thus could not at all be considered a microcosm of the
nation. Hence, the important British concept (best expounded by the Irish-born,
English politician Edmund Burke) of virtual representation – the idea that while
every section or interest might not have been directly or actually represented
at Westminster, they were all virtually so – was meaningless in Ireland. Unless
and until the Irish Parliament could enlist the support – active, preferably, but
tacit would do – of the other peoples on the island then surely it would store up
trouble for the future.

In addition, the Irish Parliament, despite its impressive ceremonial and its
medieval origins, had not kept pace with the English (after 1707 British) Parliament, either in actual powers or in constitutional developments. The Irish
Parliament had no power to consider foreign policy and any attempt it made

to debate overseas affairs was steadfastly resisted by the British government. Similarly, a lack of control over the Irish armed forces (paid for by Ireland, but controlled from London, and legalised solely by the British Mutiny Act) meant that even if the Irish Parliament could find a role in foreign policy, its power to influence events abroad, much less have a say in the deployment of 'Irish' troops, would be negligible. On a wider scale, the development of the British constitutional concept of sovereignty residing in the king-in-Parliament – a legacy of the upheavals of the seventeenth century – had not been paralleled in Ireland, and the result was a massive divergence in constitutional theory between the two countries. Irish constitutional thought not only rejected the British Parliament's claim to legislate for Ireland, but also adhered to an increasingly outdated idea of having some direct connection with the monarch in his role as king of Ireland.

Nor, again unlike the British Parliament, did the Irish Parliament have any role in the creation of an Irish government or executive. The Irish executive was appointed by and was answerable to the British government that selected it. It was to be a fundamental weakness of the Irish executive that at no time during the eighteenth century was it any more than a subordinate branch of the current British government. How the English-appointed government in Dublin Castle could be brought to work in harmony with the Irish-elected Parliament remained a pressing question in Irish politics for the entire eighteenth century.

One solution to this problem, at least until the 1770s, was government by 'undertakers' – Irish politicians with influence who would undertake to get the king's business through the Irish House of Commons in return for a large measure of control of government patronage. Another solution was direct rule by a resident lord lieutenant who would conduct the king's affairs in the Irish Parliament by means of a 'Castle party' of lord lieutenant's 'friends'. The third, and final, solution was, however, a legislative union that would put an end to the Irish Parliament and transfer Irish politicians to the Westminister legislature. All in all there could be no denying that the Irish Parliament, outward appearances notwithstanding, in its internal economy bore little resemblance to Westminster.

Some attempts have been made to compare the Irish Parliament with colonial assemblies in the new world, but such efforts ironically have served rather to highlight the contrasts between the institutions concerned. Ireland, after all, was constitutionally a kingdom, with its own Parliament, and no other colony in the West Indies or on mainland America could boast as much. This is not to say, however, that the Irish Parliament was more powerful than the various colonial assemblies in British north America: as we shall see, the Irish Parliament was subject to a humiliating series of formal and informal controls from Britain and had much less freedom of action than other representative institutions in the British empire. Moreover, the lords lieutenant of Ireland (or chief governors) were generally noblemen of the first rank, or near it, while the royal governors of the British colonies in the new world were rarely distinguished. An Irish lord lieutenant had much more power (should he choose to exercise it) than any colonial governor. In any case, Ireland's status as a colony was disputed. Irish politicians understandably preferred Ireland to be regarded by England as a 'sister kingdom' rather than, as Jonathan Swift put it, as something akin to 'one of the colonies of outcasts in America'.

Perhaps a more appropriate comparison with the eighteenth-century Irish Parliament lies closer at hand, in the various quasi-representative institutions of *ancien régime* Europe, especially those of France. Certainly, the Irish Parliament, like the French *parlements*, saw itself at times as a 'defender of the nation against predatory governments' and, again like its French counterparts, it was vigilant in its defence of established laws, customs and liberties. The composition of those *parlements*, with their membership drawn from a narrow range of families, their strong hereditary element and their religious uniformity was not all that different from that of the Irish Parliament. Nor were their limited powers – effectively, the *parlements*' role in the legislative process was restricted to refusing to register royal edicts, suspending all, or part, of them or issuing lengthy remonstrances – in theory much removed from those of the Irish Parliament. Similarly, the eighteenth century witnessed a determined effort on the part of successive French monarchs, and their provincial *intendants* to curb the pretensions of these *parlements*, an assault that was observed with considerable interest in Ireland, with the appropriate parallels being drawn. Moreover, it is surely no coincidence that the Irish Parliament did not survive the passing of the *ancien régime* in Europe.

At this point, however, the similarities end: the *parlements* were first and foremost sovereign courts of justice, any representative function was purely notional and they were too provincial in outlook to rival the Irish Parliament with its wider concerns, its (albeit, heavily flawed) electoral basis and its uniquely national outlook. Crucially, a large majority of the French people were, at least nominally, Catholic, and the *parlements* reflected this in their membership. The Irish Parliament for its part distinguished itself from all other representative assemblies by expressly severing all connection with the majority population. What we can say with confidence is that the Irish Parliament was a subordinate Parliament, and that its subordination, both formal and informal, to the metropolitan legislature in London fitted into a pattern that was common in the Europe of the *ancien régime*.

The formal subordination of the Irish Parliament was enshrined first in an Irish Act, the celebrated Poynings' law (1495). This short Act, little more than a paragraph in length, in theory curtailed the Irish Parliament's ability to introduce bills during a session, for it required that all matters marked for legislation be certified in advance by the lord lieutenant for the approval of the English privy council meeting in London. It had also become a convention that among the 'causes and considerations' given for holding a Parliament in Ireland there should be at least one Money bill. Poynings' law had been slightly modified in the 1580s to make it more flexible, but it remained on the statute books, and it meant that the Irish Parliament could not lay claim to the initiative where legislation was concerned. Since the early 1660s Irish politicians had devised a cumbersome procedure by which they could circumvent the restrictions imposed by Poynings' law. During a parliamentary session, they began to introduce what were known as 'Heads of Bills', legislative proposals which, if agreed to by the Irish Commons and Lords, were sent on to the lord lieutenant and the Irish privy council and, if accepted by them, then became regular bills. In this convoluted way, Irish politicians had gained an important, though limited, say in passing laws. Despite this, however, Poynings' law continued to rankle with Irish parliamentarians and it was resented as a symbol of Irish legislative inferiority. In British eyes, by contrast, its longevity had won it the status of a fundamental law, and any perceived threat to it was taken with the utmost seriousness. The severe amendment of Poynings' law in 1782 has been represented as the defining triumph of the Irish Protestant political nation.

The second Act which formally bound the Irish Parliament was a much more recent British one, the so-called 'Sixth of George I' or Declaratory Act of 1720. This Act was declaratory of the British Parliament's claim to legislate for Ireland 'in all cases whatsoever'; and at the same time it removed the status of the Irish House of Lords as the final Court of Appeal for Irish cases. If this Declaratory Act had been fully exercised there would have been no need for an Irish Parliament. In the event the claim of British legislative superiority, although it was invoked on occasion, was more important in theory than in practice, and was always used with the utmost discretion. There was never the slightest hint of voting the Irish additional duties (the Money bill) by a British Act of Parliament, and nor was the British Parliament tempted to override the prejudices of the Irish Parliament by railroading through an Act, say, repealing the sacramental test against Irish Dissenters, or ending some of the Penal Laws against Irish Catholics. The Declaratory Act, together with Poynings' law, established the legal, or formal, legislative subordination of the Irish Parliament but, arguably, it was the informal control, usually known as parliamentary management and exercised by the lord lieutenant, his chief secretary or their agents, which effectively kept the Irish Parliament in a subordinate position.

Parliamentary management by the executive was common everywhere before the rise of political parties, but in Ireland the normal difficulties of management were sharpened by the separation of the executive from the legislature. The executive, referred to as 'the government', 'Dublin Castle' or 'the administration', consisted of the lord lieutenant, his chief secretary, various legal figures (the lord chancellor, the attorney and solicitor generals) and a handful of under-secretaries. The archbishop of Armagh (always an Englishman from the 1660s to the 1860s) should also be counted as a sort of *ex officio* member of the executive. This executive was only nominally 'Irish', for it was appointed by, received its instructions from and was answerable to the British Cabinet in London; none of its members depended for their political survival on the approval of the Irish Parliament. As a consequence of this drastic separation of powers, a means had to be found whereby the English-appointed executive could control the Irish-elected Parliament. In the early years of the century this problem had been solved to a large extent by the emergence in Ireland of party politics based on English political divisions. In Ireland, as in England, 'court' and 'country' parties in the 1690s, and Whigs and Tories in the first two decades of the eighteenth century, had battled for dominance within the framework of parliamentary politics. In general members of the court faction in Ireland tended to be hostile to the Irish Parliament's claims for equality with the English Parliament, and they feared more from a resurgent Presbyterianism than from a humbled Catholicism. Country Members, on the other hand, were loud in their demands for redress of Ireland's constitutional and economic grievances (increasingly these were becoming one and the same), and they wanted a greater commitment from the government on anti-popery laws. The Tory and Whig parties, for the most part, followed the same pattern.

In one sense the rise of these political parties in Ireland had been a worrying development, for they had revealed acute divisions within the Irish body politic; but given that the Irish Parliament had to be managed by the Irish executive, party divisions did serve an important purpose, for they enabled a lord lieutenant, whether a Whig, such as Wharton, or a Tory, such as Ormond, to employ a ready-made band of supporters to undertake the king's business in Parliament. However, the establishment of the Hanoverian dynasty in 1714 had spelled defeat for the English Tory party and its Irish allies. With the accession of George I, the earlier Whig–Tory configuration of Irish politics became largely devoid of meaning, and an incoming lord lieutenant found himself confronting an institution in which nearly everyone professed to adhere to Whig or Revolution principles.

The problem of management arose afresh and it was further exacerbated by the prevailing custom that a lord lieutenant resided in Ireland only while the Irish Parliament was in session, a period of roughly eight months every two years. In his absence three lords justice were appointed to look after routine administrative matters. An English lord lieutenant, frequently without any connection or knowledge of Ireland, and arriving on the eve of a parliamentary session, could hardly be expected to be well briefed on the personalities and issues that he would soon encounter. Even if an English chief governor had wanted to inform himself on the workings of Irish politics, the unfamiliar party structure of the Irish Parliament – essentially a complex network of competing families and interests – was a powerful deterrent. In the event, few lords lieutenant showed any inclination to take more than a passing interest in Irish politics, much less immerse themselves in them. The humiliating reality was that English politicians rarely regarded Ireland as an attractive posting: frequently, the lord lieutenancy was bestowed in order to be rid of a rival and sometimes it was accepted in order to repair a shattered fortune. In such circumstances, the easiest thing for an incoming lord lieutenant to do was to apply to the principal Irish politicians for that majority needed to ensure that everything went quietly in Parliament, and that the Money bills, in particular, were passed with minimum fuss. In Irish political history, the years 1735 to 1770 have been described as the 'age of the undertakers', for these were the years of the political dominance of the three greatest undertakers, Henry Boyle, Archbishop George Stone and John Ponsonby.

Henry Boyle, speaker of the Irish House of Commons from 1733 to 1756, and later first earl of Shannon, was the leading political figure in Ireland until his death in 1764. More than any other he personified the undertaker system of parliamentary management. In the 1720s he built up a considerable electoral base in county Cork, and in 1733 he was elected speaker of the Irish House of Commons, an office of great importance in the Irish political world. The holder was essentially a political broker who mediated between the Irish House of Commons and Dublin Castle, explaining the concerns, aspirations and anxieties of each to the other. Within a short period of time Boyle made himself indispensable and, until the 1750s, it was accepted by most lords lieutenant that a smooth parliamentary session was contingent on a good relationship with Boyle. He served as a lord justice, one of three substitutes appointed in the absence of the lord lieutenant, no fewer than nineteen times between 1734 and 1764. All in all, most Irish Members of Parliament seemed to be content with this state of affairs and were reassured that the interests of Ireland, which they identified as synonymous with those of the Protestant nation, were safe in Boyle's hands.

In contrast to Boyle's lengthy political apprenticeship, the rise to power of George Stone, archbishop of Armagh, had been rapid. The speed of his elevation can be almost entirely accounted for by his English connections – his brother, Andrew, was the duke of Newcastle's private secretary, and Stone was personally known to both Newcastle and Pelham, both of whom were at the heart of British government in the 1740s and 1750s. His first Irish church living, however, the deanship of Derry, was obtained for him in 1734 through the good offices of the then lord lieutenant, the duke of Dorset, whom he had accompanied to Ireland as chaplain. Seventeen years later, Dorset's reappointment to the governorship of Ireland would give Stone his chance to make his bid for power.

It was under the leadership of Brabazon Ponsonby, later earl of Bessborough, that the Ponsonby family rose to prominence. He had managed to put together a powerful parliamentary group in the 1720s and later, during the viceroyalty of the duke of Devonshire (1737–45), he had married off two sons to two of Devonshire's daughters, thus allying himself to the powerful Cavendish connection in England. John Ponsonby, Brabazon's son, was the leader of the party. He had entered Parliament in 1739, was quickly appointed secretary to the Irish Revenue Board and in 1743 succeeded his father as first, or chief, commissioner. Unlike Boyle's, the Ponsonby connection had no territorial basis and, as descendants of a Cromwellian soldier, the Ponsonbys had nothing like the Boyle pedigree; but Ponsonby's control of the Irish Revenue Board and, especially, his disposal of the hundreds of small, and not-so-small, employments (such as those of tidewaiters and gaugers) in the harbours and coves dotted around Ireland enabled him to consolidate a formidable parliamentary following and to establish a network of influence throughout the country.

Until the early 1750s, these three men, and their connections, were largely responsible for the relatively uneventful course of Irish parliamentary politics. In fact, the lack of controversy – much less crisis – in Irish politics between 1720 and 1750 has led some commentators to dismiss these years as ones in which 'Ireland was without a history', or as 'an era of political placidity', a period when 'politics centred very largely on a manoeuvring for position by rival political groups'. Admittedly, in comparison to what was to come later in the century, with impassioned debates on the Catholic question, parliamentary reform and legislative independence in the 1780s, there would appear to be strong support for those who regard the politics of those years as an issueless scramble.

At the same time it would be unwise to be too dismissive. Already in 1699 the English Woollen Act, designed to shut down the export of Irish cloth, had aroused Irish opposition and, more importantly, had prompted William Molyneux to write his *The Case of Ireland . . . stated* in which he categorically refuted the English Parliament's claim to legislative superiority over Ireland. And between 1722 and 1725 a major controversy had ensued over the issue of a patent to William Wood, an English entrepreneur, to manufacture halfpennies for Ireland. Popular hostility against the grant was supported by opposition within the Irish Parliament and eventually drew in Jonathan Swift, then languishing in St Patrick's deanery in Dublin. He took up his pen in support of the protest, and, in a brilliant series of *Drapier's Letters*, he denounced the patent as a gigantic scam which would be the ruination of Ireland. The withdrawal of Wood's patent saw the end of the protest, and the controversy, like the earlier one over the Woollen Act, quickly petered out. In the end, the two disputes may have been significant only for Swift's, and Molyneux's, intervention.

There existed an Anglo-Irish, even, perhaps, an imperial consensus that made the management skills of the likes of Boyle, Stone and Ponsonby quietly effective.[3] Politicians in Ireland and in England, by and large, saw eye to eye on the necessity of strengthening the Protestant interest in Ireland. Likewise, there was a common and deep-rooted suspicion of French and Spanish designs. Politicians on both sides of the Irish Sea took considerable pride in the success of British arms abroad and in the growth of the overseas empire. British politicians, too, were aware of Irish sensitivities on Poynings' law, trade restrictions and legislative subordination, and generally avoided raising such matters. Walpole's government in the 1730s, for example, may have been keen to have the sacramental test removed from Irish Presbyterians but in the face of determined resistance (led by Henry Boyle) it was forced to back off. Similarly, in the early 1730s an attempt was made by friends of Boyle to 'represent the disadvantages it [Ireland] lies under on acc[oun]t of the several restrictions on its trade', but this time the British government saw off the challenge.

Nor were Irish Protestants and the British government at one on the threat posed by the enlistment of Irish Catholics into foreign, principally French, armies. Irish Catholics were barred from enlisting in the British army, and to an extent in reaction to this prohibition, but also motivated by a certain loyalty to the deposed Stuarts, around a thousand Irish Catholics a year for the first forty years of the eighteenth century made the journey to France to join one of that nation's Irish regiments. The British government, with wider diplomatic considerations in view – France was Britain's ally in the 1720s, for example – preferred to turn a blind eye to this exodus of the 'Wild Geese' into French service. The Irish government, under political pressure from Irish Protestants, was resolved not to countenance it, and a tacit compromise was reached whereby the Irish authorities would occasionally arrest those suspected of recruiting for the French service, while the lord lieutenant reserved to himself the right to confirm or suspend the sentences of those convicted. Lastly, the British government and the Irish Parliament did not always agree on the need for more stringent Penal Laws. In 1719 an Irish proposal to castrate Catholic priests (the normal branding on the cheek was considered an insufficient deterrent) was thrown out, and further severe Penal Laws were likewise headed off by the lord lieutenant and by the privy councils of both countries. In other words, although there was ample scope for disagreement between London and Dublin, confrontation tended to be avoided by prudent circumspection on both sides. This relative calm was not, however, to last: throughout the 1740s and 1750s the Anglo-Irish governing consensus was progressively undermined by the rise of Irish Protestant patriotism, by increasing personal and political rivalries between the three chief undertakers and, momentously, by the re-emergence of the Catholic question.

Protestant patriotism

The patriotism that so distinguished the outlook and attitudes of Irish Protestants in the years up to 1750, and that proved disruptive to Anglo-Irish political consensus, can be seen as a product in about equal measure of Protestant resentment and self-confidence. The reasons for this resentment are not hard to discover. From an early date – the Irish Parliament of 1692 hardly lasted a month before it was peremptorily shut down by the chief governor in the face of loud protests over favouritism of William's Dutch friends – Irish Protestants were convinced that there was a settled policy of discrimination against them where the more lucrative crown appointments in the Church of Ireland, in the army or in the Irish administration were concerned. That this policy probably owed more to the voracious appetite for patronage of the English political system than to any general hostility to Irish candidates is beside the point; what mattered was the fact of discrimination. During the first decades of the eighteenth century, 'Irish' representation on the bench of bishops, in the higher reaches of the law and in the more important revenue or military appointments diminished substantially. Taking the eighteenth century as a whole, a majority of episcopal appointments and promotions went to English-born applicants; and it was a similar story with legal appointments and with the top positions on the Irish Revenue Board. This perceived policy of exclusion caused anger and frustration among the Protestants of Ireland, for it struck at both their prospects for advancement and their self-esteem. There was resentment too at what was seen as the flagrant abuse by the British government of the Irish pension list to cater for the financial needs of indigent foreigners, aged royal mistresses and English political hacks. And there was further disquiet at the cavalier, not to say contemptuous, way the Irish peerage was treated. George I (1714–1727), for example, clearly regarded the lowest English mark of rank (a knighthood) as worthier than any Irish title; and for most of the century Irish peerages were scattered about with scant regard for Irish sensitivities. By 1800 around one quarter of Irish titles (60 out of 230) were held by people who had no connection with Ireland.

Lastly, there was resentment at English restrictions on Irish commerce and at English interventions in Irish affairs, such as the Woollen Act of 1699 and the Wood's halfpence grant. Essentially, Protestant Ireland was livid at being treated as if Ireland were an English colony or conquered province. In the eyes of

Irish Protestants Ireland shared a monarch with England and it was, therefore, a kingdom co-equal in every respect with the kingdom of England. But, more than this, in the settled conditions of the period 1690 to 1750 the Protestants of Ireland, like settler populations everywhere in the Atlantic world, had begun to develope a strong local patriotism, an acute sense of place that would lead them to regard Ireland as their home and to regard themselves as forming, as Swift would put it, 'the whole People of Ireland'.

Protestant confidence stemmed from the legacy of the seventeenth century. So far as Irish Protestants were concerned the disasters that had nearly befallen them in the Catholic uprising of 1641, again in 1685 with the accession of James II and the deliverance that had been extended to them by the timely intervention of William of Orange in 1688, could scarcely be interpreted in any way other than providential. Twice in less than fifty years, in 1641 and in 1688, Irish Protestants had been brought to the edge of destruction and their escape on each occasion could only be interpreted as 'almost...a miracle', as 'next to miraculous'. Moreover, the apparent totality of the 'shipwreck' of the Catholic Irish at the Boyne (1690) and, especially, at Aughrim (1691), and the settlement of the dynastic question forever on Protestant terms, seemed to preclude any prospect of Catholic revival. Throughout the eighteenth century these historical events were kept constantly before later generations through the reprinting of key texts – by the 1720s Sir John Temple's *The Irish Rebellion* (first published in 1646) and Archbishop William King's *State of the Protestants of Ireland* (first published in 1691) were being sold in a single one-volume edition – and by the mandatory sermon, delivered every 23 October, by Protestant ministers to commemorate the 1641 massacres. Inspired, consoled and instructed by these tracts and speeches that bore witness to their extraordinary history, Protestants in Ireland faced the future with confidence.

This Protestant confidence manifested itself in several ways. Most obviously, there was a rash of house-building among the gentry, and tree-planting and estate improvement became fashionable. Whereas military security had tended to determine the domestic architecture and landscape gardening of the seventeenth century, in the decades after 1690 aesthetics, comfort and fashion derived from foreign example took priority. These splendid 'big' houses – Carton, Castleward, Castletown are perhaps the best known – proclaimed in an unmistakable way that Irish Protestants were there to stay, that Ireland was their home. As one Irish Protestant reminded the new lord lieutenant, the earl of Halifax, in 1762:

> Of this be assured, that now we are thoroughly naturalised [in Ireland] we are as warmly attached and bigotted to this little island as the best of yourselves are to old England...our bilberries and our potatoes are in

our mouths as delicious and high-flavoured as the best grapes and melons
in the mouth of an Italian or Frenchman, nor should we endure the man
who would propose an exchange.

Resentment at England's ungenerous treatment of, and condescending attitude
towards, them, along with a firm confidence that they knew best how to run
Ireland, constituted the most obvious strands in the patriotism of the Protestant
people of Ireland in the eighteenth century. But, running through the ensuing
mixture were deep-seated anxieties that muted Protestant protest and, at least
until the 1770s, determined that Protestant assertiveness would be hedged by
more than a little circumspection.

Most obviously, Protestant anxieties stemmed from the large number of
Catholics in Ireland, and from what was seen as the peculiar obduracy of that
religion. Like other colonial elites in the Atlantic world, the Anglo-Irish had
all along legitimised their position in Ireland by reference to their 'mission',
i.e. the need to anglicise and protestantise both Ireland and Irish Catholics. By
the 1730s, however, it was clear that Ireland had not been, and would not be,
either evangelised or anglicised, and this failure troubled many Irish Protestants
deeply, for its unavoidable consequence was that they would thereafter constitute a permanent minority on the island of Ireland. Equally, Protestant anxiety
was fuelled by the perceived expansionist tendencies of the Irish Presbyterians
and by the threat they posed to the established church. Admittedly, by the 1730s
that danger had appeared to recede as Irish Presbyterianism began to splinter
and fragment, and the emigration of whole Presbyterian communities to the New
World further helped divert Presbyterian energies. None the less the challenge
posed by the large Dissenter communities in the north of Ireland remained. No
doubt too, the dizzy changes of fortune in the seventeenth century had bred into
Irish Protestants an unwillingness to accept that matters would always remain
comfortable to them. Providence may have vouchsafed them victory in 1691; but
prudence would be necessary in order to retain the fruits of that triumph. More
important than any of these, however, in inducing Protestant anxiety was the
realisation that the English, so far from seeing them as partners in, and co-equal
beneficiaries of, the 'Glorious Revolution', viewed them as a subject people.

From the 1690s on it became clear that there was an enormous discrepancy
between the English view of the Anglo-Irish nexus and the Irish view. Molyneux's
claim of Irish constitutional equality was dismissed in England with a firm declaration of the stark realities of the Protestant position in Ireland. The English
were the protectors of Irish Protestants; a price had to be paid for that protection,
and if that price was restrictions on Irish trade, or constitutional subordination,
then Irish Protestants should accept these and not complain. To the English

Ireland was a colony whose primary purpose was to benefit England, and it was inconceivable that anyone should think otherwise. Irish Protestants, however, for the most part refused to accept that Ireland was a colony, with all the attendant attributes of inferiority and subordination. To them, the proper relationship between Ireland and England was that of 'sister' or 'brother' kingdom. They could never be brought to embrace the parent–child metaphor deployed by English writers as a valid description of the ties between Ireland and England, for this posited a profoundly unequal relationship between the two countries. Despite Irish protests, however, this parent–child metaphor continued to dominate English perceptions of the relationship between Ireland and England. As late as 1799, when William Pitt, the British prime minister, was arguing the case in favour of a legislative union with Ireland, he could blithely refer to that supreme example of Protestant assertion, the 'Constitution of 1782' as 'the childish measure of the independence of the Parliament of Ireland'.

From this parent–child paradigm two consequences flowed. First, if Ireland was a child-colony then it followed that the Protestants of Ireland were in fact colonists; but such a designation conjured up in English (and Irish) eyes an image of outcasts and deviants, the socially inept and culturally mimetic. This was, of course, most unflattering to a people who, whatever their origins, were now certain that 'Ireland [was] their home and they look[ed] upon themselves as principals'. Moreover, it was not long before the English ignored the English origins of these 'colonists' and began to endow them with those very traits and characteristics – excessive drinking, lavish hospitality, rapacity for patronage, a propensity for violence and a way with words (and horses) – that had hitherto been inseparable from the 'natives' of Ireland. In English eyes, then, not only were the Protestants of Ireland colonists, but they were Irish to boot – a double slight, that doubly rankled.

So far as Irish Protestants were concerned the problem was that the English had not woken up to the fact that, as one of them put it, since 1690 the Irish 'scene is rather changed from what it was... now almost all the lands of Ireland are in the possession of the descendants of British Protestants linked in the strongest manner... in the fortunes of Great Britain', and that, therefore, traditional attitudes had to be abandoned. Such pleas were to no avail. Perhaps, as another wrote, England's hostility to Ireland stemmed from the fact that

> this kingdom still bears the name of Ireland, and the Protestant inhabitants the denomination of Irish, with old ideas annexed to them of opposition to the interest of England and... these ideas are so strongly associated, like Sprights and Darkness, that many generous Britons find it difficult on the plainest conviction to separate them.

This inability or unwillingness of the English to alter their traditional perspective on Ireland was reinforced rather than diminished by their adherence to the parent–child model. Ireland was duly allocated its place in the world as a child-colony. However, if Ireland were a 'child', then it followed that it would, one day, become an adult and set up for itself. In other words, implicit in the parent–child paradigm was the threat of Irish independence and this threat was present no matter who was the leading interest in Ireland. As the British prime minister Sir Robert Walpole declared in the 1720s, and his words would be echoed throughout the century, the Irish 'both friend and foe' wished to 'shake off' their 'dependency' on England.

Irish Protestants were conscious of the English fear that one day Ireland would set up on its own as a direct rival to England. Some even argued that this fear was the real motive behind English restrictions on Irish trade; to keep Ireland poor and, hence, unable to contemplate any role other than that of dependence on England. Others observed that the English government viewed opposition to its policies in Ireland with a degree of anger that, at times, seemed to border on hatred for Ireland. In the 1730s and 1740s a number of pamphlet-writers even found it necessary to argue against 'the universally received opinion that it were better for England if Ireland were no more'; 'that it were well for England if (the people of Ireland being saved) the island were sunk under water'; 'that England is no friend to Ireland'.

It is entirely possible that the frequent accusation or suspicion that Irish Protestants 'dayly endeavour gradually to fling off their allegiance' may, in fact, have encouraged them in such fanciful notions. What is certain is that the English rejection of Irish Protestants' claim to be accorded the rights of Englishmen, or to be treated as English, and the English refusal to recognise their achievements, or admit them to partnership or value their presence in Ireland, deeply wounded Irish Protestants and stung them to make their protest. Such protests would take on a more embittered tone by the 1750s and, of course, would reinforce English suspicions that Protestants were 'foolishly and seditiously . . . aiming at independency'.

In turn English hostility, and English rejection, drove the Protestants of Ireland to fashion a new identity for themselves. If the English insisted on treating them like the Irish, then Irish is what they would become, and soon they were speaking and acting as if they were the Irish nation. In 1712 Alan Brodrick, later lord chancellor of Ireland, bemoaned the fact that, if he went to England, 'I shall be thought . . . (what of all things I would least chuse to be) an Irishman'. And even as late as 1726 Swift could complain that 'all persons born in Ireland are called and treated as Irishmen, although their fathers and grandfathers were born in England'. By 1753, however, so far had Protestants come to think of themselves as Irish that one of the main criticisms directed against that great bishop-politician, George Stone, was that 'he would have us in every instance consider ourselves as Englishmen', and it was reported in the same year that 'the cry thro' the country is "Ireland for ever" and sometimes with the addition of "down with the English"'.

Underpinning this Protestant Irish patriotism was the apparent removal of the Catholic threat. Freedom from fear was essential to the development of Protestant patriotism in the eighteenth century. Its growth in the 1730s and 1740s drove a wedge between Protestants in Ireland and in England and thus helped bring an end to that Protestant consensus, on an Anglo-Irish basis, which had earlier been a mainstay of the Protestant position in Ireland. English politicians during the 1740s and 1750s were perennially suspicious of Irish Protestants. Their patriotic rhetoric aroused misgivings in the minds of successive English governments concerning their reliability and loyalty. Not surprisingly, by the late 1750s the English government had begun to reappraise its relationship with and attitude towards Irish Catholics; some British ministers may even have seen merit in cultivating a good understanding with Irish Catholics, or with Irish Presbyterians, if only to bring home to Irish Protestants the vulnerability of their position in Ireland. Central to this reappraisal was the perception that Ireland was becoming more and more difficult to govern by the usual means, a perception confirmed by the stormy course of Irish politics in the 1740s and especially in the 1750s.

Political conflict

An early indication that the serene political world of the 1720s and 1730s was drawing to a close was provided by the so-called 'Lucas affair', the unfolding of which throughout the 1740s revealed the existence of a political nation out of doors (if mostly in the Dublin area).[4] Charles Lucas, a Dublin apothecary, had cast himself in the role of champion of the Common Council, the lower house of Dublin Corporation, and had demanded that the power of the sheriff and aldermen be curbed and that municipal reform be carried out. Predictably, Lucas's demands, and those of his colleague, James Digges LaTouche, were given short shrift by the vested interests on the corporation and he and LaTouche were forced off the Common Council in 1744. Within a few years, however, they had set their sights on higher game and stood for Parliament for the Dublin City constituency on a programme of municipal reform. A flood of electoral addresses poured from Lucas's pen during and after the campaign and, in a remarkably robust style, he found space to denounce not only the corporation but also the whole nature of Ireland's constitutional subordination to England. In unrestrained prose, Lucas claimed that Ireland had never been conquered, that the restrictions on the Irish legislature were a usurpation by the British Parliament and that all rebellions in Ireland had, in one way or another, been the result of 'English treachery, oppression and tyranny'. Again, although Lucas himself was the descendant of a Cromwellian settler (and vigorously anti-Catholic), he saw nothing incongruous in appealing to precedents from the reign of Henry II. Molyneux too was pressed into service, as was Swift.

Lucas's tireless (and frequently tiresome) patriot polemics caused such grave concern in Dublin Castle that Harrington, the lord lieutenant, declared that it was 'absolutely necessary to put a stop to his proceedings'. The Irish political establishment was only too happy to oblige, for his description of the 'undertakers' as 'those worst of land pirates' and, equally, his denunciation of their followers as 'corrupt slaves or senseless dolts', had aroused the ire of both Boyle and Stone. In October 1749 the Irish House of Commons condemned Lucas's election addresses, declared him to be an enemy of the country and ordered his imprisonment. Lucas promptly fled into exile, thereby bringing the first phase of the 'affair' to an end. However, the reverberations of the episode rumbled on for some years.

Lucas's polemics had found an audience outside the walls of the Irish Parliament, and his denunciation of English 'tyranny', and his depiction of Irish 'slavery', had evoked a popular response that, in the eyes of British ministers, was little short of alarming. Lucas had begun a process of politicisation that would ultimately prove deeply corrosive of the existing political structure. He had shown that 'patriotism' could be popular; that there existed outside Parliament a constituency that was critical of Ireland's subordination; and that highly coloured rhetoric about English oppression, and Irish liberty, evoked a response. This last lesson was not lost on at least one of the undertakers.

Even though they had cooperated in the attempt to ruin Lucas, relations between the three leading undertakers had become fraught. Stone had been very confidential with two recent lords lieutenant, Chesterfield (1745–6) and Harrington (1747–50), and this had aroused Boyle's suspicions. Stone clearly saw himself as taking a part not unlike that of an earlier archbishop of Armagh, Hugh Boulter, in acting as spokesman for the resident 'English interest' in Ireland. Stone relished such a role and since after the Lucas affair it was not difficult to represent the 'English interest' as a beleaguered one, he began to covet a much more powerful position for himself at Dublin Castle. Moreover, he had started to cultivate a good understanding with the Ponsonby connection, for while he had a contempt for John Ponsonby's abilities, his support would be vital. 'English principles' he wrote, 'must be imported in Irish bottoms' into the Irish House of Commons.

The reappointment in 1751 of the duke of Dorset, Stone's former patron, as lord lieutenant of Ireland offered Stone his opportunity. Dorset brought his son, Lord George Sackville, as his chief secretary with him to Dublin and, despite later protestations to the contrary, Sackville ('hot, hauty [sic], ambitious and obstinate', as a contemporary described him) was determined from an early date on a showdown with Boyle. In association with Stone and Ponsonby he set about undermining Boyle's position. Boyle, for his part, determined to resist, and he set out to demonstrate in the most unequivocal way that without his support government in Ireland simply could not be carried on.

Following some preliminary skirmishing in the parliamentary session of 1751–2, matters came to a head in the session of 1753 over the important constitutional issue of a Money bill which had been altered in England. The Money bill which became the focus for parliamentary attention throughout 1753 was not, in fact, the customary grant by the Irish Parliament to the crown for the necessary expenses of government; rather, it referred to a proposed bill to deal with an extraordinary state of affairs at the Irish Treasury.

In brief, in the years 1749, 1751 and 1753, after all expenses had been paid, there still remained in the Treasury a substantial – and unprecedented – surplus. To whom did the this surplus belong? Who was to decide on its disposal? The Irish House of Commons, or at least those members who followed Boyle, claimed that the money belonged to the Commons to be disposed of as it saw fit. On the other hand, while Dublin Castle had little quarrel with the ultimate destination of the surplus, it considered it of vital constitutional significance that the king's 'previous consent' be obtained to any proposed appropriation of the sum involved. This was the sticking point and it was on this specific issue that the Castle and Boyle divided. When the vote was taken the result was a victory for Boyle and his allies; the altered Money bill was rejected. A shaken Stone called for immediate and widespread dismissals of those in receipt of government pay who had supported Boyle. The duke of Newcastle, however, despite his avowed determination to secure, support and maintain, 'the king's interest and authority . . . and the constitution of Ireland as connected with and dependent upon this kingdom', was, in fact, much more cautious about his strategy. Only a few dismissals were made, and Newcastle quickly decided that conciliation would be the best policy to follow, especially in view of an approaching war with France. Accordingly, in April 1755, Dorset was replaced by Lord Hartington who set about patching up the quarrel between the Castle and the 'patriots'. He was successful in his efforts to smooth things over, but the price paid was a high one. Boyle agreed to make room for Ponsonby as parliamentary manager, and he resigned from the speakership in return for an earldom and a pension of £2,000 a year for twenty-one years. Ponsonby became speaker in his stead and those who had been dismissed were suitably recompensed. Only Stone lost out, but his fall from grace proved to be temporary. By the time of the duke of Bedford's viceroyalty (1757–60) all three men were acting together as lords justices to govern Ireland in the absence of the lord lieutenant.

The grounds on which Boyle chose to fight, the conduct and tone of his campaign, its final outcome and its overall impact on Irish political life, and on English perceptions of Ireland, were of the utmost significance for the future. By taking his stand on both constitutional and national grounds and by appealing to public opinion in the country, Boyle and his allies had moved the issue at stake far beyond the merely personal. At the opening of the critical session of 1753 Sackville was outraged to find that 'the Speaker's friends had set him up as the protector of the liberties of Ireland', while Ponsonby was attacked for his connections to the Devonshire family in England. Such attacks set the tone for what was increasingly portrayed as an Irish national struggle against an overbearing English government.

So far as the altered Money bill was concerned, Boyle had claimed that there was no need for the king's consent to dispose of what was 'in reality the money of the nation' and he had sought the approval of the 'Protestants of Ireland' who were the 'voice of the nation' for his actions. Dire warnings were broadcast as to the likely repercussions if the altered Money bill were accepted in Ireland. 'It is publicly given out,' protested Sackville, 'that if the Commons submit in this particular, there is an end to all liberty in this country', while Stone reported the opposition as declaring that 'they and their children are to be slaves, if that Bill . . . should be suffered to pass here'. The conflict was depicted as 'the last struggle of Ireland'. Those Members of Parliament who were suspected of being favourably disposed towards the Castle were bombarded with instructions couched 'in the most indecent terms' from their constituencies and as a result it was, wrote Dorset, 'no easy task' to keep them steady. Throughout the country numerous 'patriot' clubs were formed at which debates were held, resolutions passed, and addresses drawn up. Dozens of pamphlets were produced ('each press groaned under the heavy weight of the strange productions of the day'), mostly with the express purpose of identifying the fate of the Money bill with the fate of Boyle, and the fate of both with the fate of the Protestant nation.

The outcome of the dispute turned popular enthusiasm against Boyle; once idolised he was now execrated in the popular prints. None the less 'patriot' sentiment remained a powerful force in Irish political life and the conviction remained strong that Ireland's grievances ought to be redressed, that the constitutional relationship between England and Ireland ought to be adjusted in Ireland's favour, that vigilance was required to ensure that it was not altered in the opposite direction and that, perhaps, some reform of the Irish parliamentary structure itself was needed. As Lord Charlemont put it some years later, the dispute had taught Irishmen that 'Ireland had or ought to have a constitution'. It also taught Irish politicians that opposition was not just popular but profitable; and it provided them with a model and a precedent for a successful opposition. One writer commented prophetically: 'We have been taught to play a game that many will be too apt to practice and possibly find a way to play back on those who taught it to us.'

The heightened political consciousness that resulted from Boyle's campaign could not be wished away: in this respect Boyle's betrayal of the popular cause was as educative as was his opposition. The serious riots in Dublin in 1759 – the occasion was the rumour of a union between the British and Irish Parliaments – were attributed to the greater political awareness produced by the Money bill dispute. What Boyle and his allies had done was to introduce the Protestants of Ireland to the delights of popular politics: they had bypassed the Irish Parliament and sought to pressurise the British government by appealing to Protestant opinion in the country – an opinion hitherto ignored by all, save the likes of Lucas. Indeed, it was even rumoured that Boyle had gone one better than Lucas in that, through the agency of Anthony Malone, a Member of Parliament who had strong Catholic connections, he had sought to woo Catholics and Dissenters to support his campaign.

Such tactics altered profoundly the conditions of political life and, indeed, the very content of politics in Ireland. English suspicions that Irish politicians had aimed at independence had been aroused by the reception accorded Lucas and were now strengthened by the response to the rhetoric of the Boyle camp in the course of the Money bill dispute. Not surprisingly, English politicians began to take a closer interest in what was going on in Ireland. Boyle had appealed to Protestant opinion outside Parliament and, in doing so, he had consciously extended the boundaries of the Irish political nation. But this strategy was a double-edged one: if Boyle sought to appeal to a Protestant nation out of doors, then the British government could always counteract this tactic by making overtures to the Irish Presbyterians, or to the Irish Catholics, or to both. Moreover, Catholics and Presbyterians who sought to advance their position in Ireland could take advantage of the strained relations between the British government and the Irish Parliament. In 1756 it was reported that Irish Catholics were pleased that a war with France was likely but also that they were delighted 'at the unhappy divisions among our Protestant gentlemen'. It was no coincidence that at a time of strain between English and Irish politicians, and of divisions among Irish Protestants themselves, the hitherto largely silent Catholic community should have set up a committee to lobby on its behalf for various concessions. Admittedly, this committee for most of its first ten years did little save exist; but

its very existence was further proof that the contours of the political map of
Ireland were changing. The emergence on to the political stage of what was soon
known as 'the Catholic question' was yet more evidence that the old, limited and
narrowly defined, sphere of Irish politics was being enlarged.

The Catholic question

The gradual re-emergence of the Catholic question in the early decades of the
eighteenth century was not only an unwelcome development for Irish Protestants,
but also quite an unexpected one.[5] As a result of the Jacobite war (1688–91),
and the ensuing 'shipwreck' of the Irish Catholics, Protestant Ireland had been
confident that its long trial had finally come to an end. The crushing military
defeat of the Catholics in 1691, the further confiscations of Catholic land in the
1690s, the subsequent departure abroad of thousands of Irish recruits for service
overseas and the rapid implementation of a series of anti-Catholic Penal Laws, all
appeared to have resolved once and for all the struggle for power within Ireland,
the main theme of seventeenth-century Irish history. It was further evident that
the Irish Parliament would be a Protestant Parliament for a Protestant people,
and that this would be a further safeguard for the Protestants' position. There
was also an expectation that English goodwill would continue, and that Irish and
English Protestants would remain equal partners in the 'Glorious Revolution'.
All of these considerations must surely have enabled Irish Protestants to face
the future confident that they had finally become, as Jonathan Swift would
style them, 'the whole people of Ireland'. The reality, however, would be rather
different, and in the decades after 1690 the various props of Protestant confidence
would prove to be either brittle or illusory. The result was that by 1760 something
called the Catholic question – i.e. the matter of the re-admission to full civil,
religious and political equality of Irish Catholics – had arrived on the agenda of
both Irish and Anglo-Irish politics; and from then on there was to be nothing
but the Catholic question.

One Protestant safeguard that soon proved hollow was that offered by the
passing of a series of Penal Laws aimed at copperfastening Protestant hegemony,
and at further diminishing whatever social and political authority Catholics
retained after the Jacobite wars. There had been earlier anti-Catholic laws, but
the new ones (some of them in flat contravention of the terms agreed by the
articles of Limerick), especially the 1697 Act banishing Catholic bishops from
Ireland and the 1704 Act to prevent the further growth of popery, which concerned such matters as the ownership and bequeathing of land, were much more
far-reaching. If these laws had been fully implemented, they would have resulted

in the near elimination of Catholicism in Ireland within a generation. As is well known, these laws were not generally enforced. Certainly, those directed at the practice of the Catholic religion, and at the presence of Catholic priests in Ireland, were almost entirely a dead letter. This is not to say that there was no risk attached to practising the Catholic religion. Some priests were imprisoned and deported, while the need for Catholics to worship well away from the public gaze could have tragic consequences. In 1746 a mass house concealed in Pill Lane, Dublin, collapsed causing the death of nine worshippers and a priest. And yet, the evidence is clear that it was during the so-called penal era that the Catholic church, in numbers, priests, churches and organisation underwent a large expansion.

So far as the Penal Laws against the Catholic laity were concerned, the situation was more complex. The laws that denied Catholics an education at home or abroad, that precluded their admission to the more lucrative professions or subjected them to various indignities at odds with their status – they had no right to bear arms and their horses were liable to seizure for a pittance – were widely ignored, or could be circumvented by those with wealth, local influence or foreign connections. Such restrictions were in reality more irksome than oppressive, although individual Catholics from time to time did undoubtedly feel the full force of the law; it would be wrong, centuries later, to dismiss these penalties as immaterial. On the other hand, where Catholic landowning was concerned, the impact of penal legislation was much more serious. Catholics were forbidden to purchase land or to inherit it, and they were not allowed in their wills to assign their land as they saw fit. Notoriously, if any son converted to Protestantism, then he inherited the whole estate; otherwise, on the death of the father, the estate had to be broken up among all the male children. Catholics were also restricted to shorter leases than Protestants. In general, these laws against the Catholic interest in land were enforced; indeed, they enforced themselves since transactions had to be registered. Transgressions were always likely to be exposed by a 'discoverer' – a sort of freelance bounty-hunter – and this opened up a vista of time-consuming and financially draining litigation. Not surprisingly, such laws led to a large number of conversions among Catholic landowners (over seven hundred by the 1730s) and a concurrent further diminution in the amount of land owned by Catholics.

Was conversion to Protestantism the ultimate purpose of the Penal Laws? The fact that no significant missionary endeavour was undertaken strongly suggests that there was little interest, at least at a high level, in evangelising the Catholic masses. Preaching the word to the people inevitably meant mastering the vernacular language, in this case Gaelic; but such an undertaking cut directly across the centuries-old policy of anglicisation, and apart from a brief flirtation with preaching in Gaelic in the 1720s, nothing came of it. Some Protestant clergy purported to be scandalised at the lack of effort put into protestantising the Catholic masses and they put the blame squarely on Protestant laymen, claiming that they enjoyed being an elite, viewed anxiously any influx of convert gentlemen into their ranks and feared an expansion in the authority of Protestant clergy if they were entrusted with a conversion mission. And as ever, cost factors were an added deterrent to any programme of proselytism. Against all that, there were always some, both lay and clerical, who called for a strong missionary endeavour, pointing out – rightly – that so long as Protestants remained a minority in Ireland, then permanent security would prove elusive. It seems likely that, in the first flush of a providential victory, a conversion impulse lay behind some of the earlier penal legislation; but equally, it is clear that, by the 1730s, Irish Protestants had resigned themselves to, or had seen the advantages of, constituting a minority, an elite, in Ireland. True, the Penal Laws would be kept on the statute book, but more as an earnest of good intentions than as a blueprint or strategy for transforming the religious geography of Ireland. And therein lay the dangers for the future: penal legislation, without any systematic or concerted missionary activity and, hence, a willing – or a weary – acceptance of minority status, meant inevitably that the laws would be seen as little more than an intolerable, and by the 1740s, indefensible, system of petty oppression. Worse, these laws would ultimately have to go: but when would they be repealed? And who would have the credit with Irish Catholics for their removal? In truth, when it embraced the Penal Laws, Protestant Ireland had donned a straitjacket.

Penal legislation, then, on the face of it, offered little protection against a Catholic resurgence; in fact, it may even have promoted it, for the laws erected a screen behind which Catholic power could grow surreptitiously. Whatever their original intention, the Penal Laws would not help make Ireland British, or Catholics Protestant, and nor would they keep Irish Catholics either poor or powerless. Paradoxically, yet accurately, Catholic revival, as much, if not more, than Catholic oppression, is a central theme of the eighteenth century. By 1760, when a suitable opportunity beckoned, Catholics would be able to take advantage of it, and with authority, press their claims not just for redress of grievances but for admission to the body politic.

It was the late Maureen Wall, a historian at University College Dublin, who first drew attention to the phenomenon of substantial Catholic wealth in the period of the Penal Laws. In a famous article published in 1958 she pulled together the scattered pieces of evidence relating to Catholic wealth and she argued that, taken together, these provided clear proof of 'the rise of a Catholic middle class in eighteenth-century Ireland'. Subsequent research by others has done much to amplify and refine her argument, and it is now clear that the period 1690 to 1760, so far from being a penal era in which Catholics were uniformly downtrodden and oppressed, in fact witnessed a considerable Catholic resurgence.

Central to this Catholic revival was the development of elaborate networks of Catholic gentry families, sometimes based on a single county (Galway or perhaps Wexford) but more often based on a cluster of counties (for example, the Tipperary–Kilkenny–Cork–Waterford connection). These Catholic families of gentry, near-gentry, or strong farmer stock had managed to survive the shipwreck of the Jacobite war and, in what was clearly a successful survival strategy, married into one another's families, found jobs for one another's younger sons and entered into mutual trade. Moreover, involvement in trade and commerce was almost entirely unaffected by the Penal Laws, and Irish Catholics (like other outcasts such as French Protestants and Jews everywhere) were free to enter into what aristocratic society everywhere regarded as a base profession. As a result of Catholics trading with Spain, France and the West Indies, came the construction of an intricate trade and kinship network that reached from county to county, from rural to urban Ireland, and beyond, to the major ports of continental Europe and British north America. The extent of Catholic commercial wealth should not be exaggerated: Catholics remained proportionately underrepresented compared to Protestants in the mercantile sector. None the less much Catholic wealth derived from trade, and the argument that this money was bottled up by the Penal Laws and thus prevented from benefiting the Irish economy was on occasion adduced as a reason for relaxing some of those laws from the 1740s on.

In addition, and notwithstanding the Penal Laws directed against what remained of the Catholic landed interest, the eighteenth century witnessed a rising Catholic interest in land. This requires explanation. If one takes the narrow view and equates 'interest' in land with ownership of land, then undoubtedly the amount of land owned by Catholics fell during the first decades of the century (from 14 per cent in 1702 to single digits within fifty years). But there was more to landed interest than title conveying the fee simple or outright ownership. Much land was held by Catholics on advantageous leases, and this should be taken into account in any assessment. Admittedly, Catholics were restricted to a maximum lease of thirty-one years' duration and while such a lease was later represented as a heavy grievance, it was in fact a favourable one, much more so than the shorter leases currently on offer in England and Scotland. It is clear, for example, that the generous number of years granted allowed some Catholic families such as the O'Connells of Derrynane, county Kerry, the family of Daniel O'Connell, the Liberator, to take part in lease speculation. Such speculation was perfectly legal under the Penal Laws. Less legal, but still relatively common, was possession by Catholic gentry families of a thirty-one year lease renewable for ever which in effect gave the leaseholder what amounted to a permanent interest in the land in question.

Again, land transactions by Catholics were, as we have seen, liable to 'discovery'. To head off this threat it was relatively common for vulnerable or anxious Catholics to arrange to have their land dealings 'discovered' by friendly agents and thus legalised. Thus while there were some two thousand 'discoveries' made of illegal land transactions in Ireland between 1708 and 1778 at least 90 per cent of them were collusive or friendly actions designed to benefit the current possessor. Finally, if the estates owned by 'converts' are placed in the scale of the landed interest on the Catholic side (and this is where contemporaries were inclined to put them), and the whole is added to land held by Catholics on favourable leases, or on 'protection' or owned outright, then it is clear that there was a considerable and growing Catholic interest in land, just as there was a substantial Catholic involvement in trade.

Catholic expansion in trade and the growth of Catholic interest in land were mirrored by a comparable development of the Catholic church structure. Despite cash inducements to conform, there were to be remarkably few defections from the Catholic priesthood and equally there were very few prosecutions of Catholic clergy under penal legislation. Provided they were registered according to the 1704 Act, Catholic clergy were free to conduct their affairs without interference and from an early date in the eighteenth century a Catholic hierarchy had been installed. The problems which this hierarchy faced – clerical indiscipline, widespread poverty and the occasional scandal – were not all that different from those of the rival and established Church of Ireland.

Until 1766, when the papacy ceased to recognise the heirs of James II as the lawful kings of England, appointments to and promotions within the Irish Catholic hierarchy were more or less in the gift of the exiled Stuart, or Jacobite, court at St Germain-en-Laye, just outside Paris. However, while the bishops may have owed their appointments to the Stuarts, few saw any need to advocate resistance to the Hanoverian usurpers, and the Catholic hierarchy throughout the eighteenth century consistently preferred the quiet paths of diplomacy to open confrontation with the state. In the absence of any credible lay alternative it was not surprising that the clergy and the bishops should have taken on a leadership role for the Catholics of Ireland; nor is it surprising that when a lay leadership did emerge, the bishops were loath to abandon their position. When, for example, a largely lay 'Catholic Committee' began to meet regularly in the late 1750s and sought to draw public attention to Catholic grievances, its activities received less than whole-hearted support from the bishops. The hierarchy was suspicious of lay Catholics daring to draw up a list of Catholic doctrines in order to assuage Protestant anxieties, and nor was it persuaded that Catholics ought in fact to draw attention to themselves by issuing public addresses. It was to be of crucial importance for the future development of the Irish state and society that when the Irish Catholic church lost its links to the Stuarts in the 1760s it found itself enjoying a freedom from both lay and state control that was unparalleled in Europe, a freedom that it fiercely guarded thereafter. In short, it was during the penal era that the Catholic church was able to constitute itself as that quasi-autonomous state-within-a-state that was to be its dominant characteristic in the nineteenth century.

The Catholic Committee that emerged in the 1750s, and which the hierarchy in general viewed with a jaundiced eye, was the brainchild of Charles O'Conor and John Curry. Curry's family had lost its estate as a result of the Jacobite wars, and his father had gone into trade. However, he had succeeded in sending his son to Paris and Rheims where he had studied medicine before returning to practise in Dublin. Like the Curry family the O'Conors had lost much of their estate in the seventeenth century. However, they had managed to hang on to around 800 acres of poor land in county Roscommon and with this property, and an advantageous marriage, Charles O'Conor's family had staged a modest recovery. Both Curry and O'Conor were persuaded that a proper understanding of Irish history – particularly early Irish history and the events of the seventeenth century – was crucial to advancing the cause of Irish Catholics. O'Conor was concerned to refute the aspersions of English historians that before the arrival of the English Ireland had languished in barbarism and savagery, while Curry was adamant that the 1641 rebellion should not be viewed simply as a Catholic attempt at the extirpation of Irish Protestants. Needless to say, Curry's and O'Conor's criticism of the two foundation myths of the English in Ireland drew fire from Protestant writers (and from some Catholics, fearful at raising such questions), but their efforts signalled the end of Catholic quiescence and the beginnings of a Catholic challenge to the intellectual props of the Penal Laws.

The existence of a Catholic hierarchy, the emergence by the 1750s of a 'Catholic middle class' and the setting up of a Catholic Committee proved vital in enabling Irish Catholics to take advantage of the changed political climate, and to press for progress on 'the Catholic question'. The Money bill dispute of the 1750s, as we have seen, had not only revealed deep divisions within the Irish Protestant political world but had also had a marked impact on English perceptions of the loyalty and political reliability of Irish Protestants. The chemistry of the Anglo-Irish political relationship was changing – and Catholics were poised to take advantage of this. From 1760, if not before, it made sense for British ministers to keep on good terms with Irish Catholics, if only to remind Irish Protestants that though they might regard themselves as 'the whole people of

Ireland', there was another people on the island who could equally lay claim to the title.

The perceived international weakness of the papacy, the consequent disappearance of the Catholic threat on a European basis and the final collapse of the Stuart cause were additional boosts to this more flexible and, from an Irish Catholic point of view, favourable attitude. For nearly two hundred years, a shared anti-Catholicism had been a vital bond between English and Irish Protestants. The end of any credible international Catholic conspiracy and the consequent decline of anti-Catholicism in England, at least at elite level, meant that Irish Protestants found themselves speaking a language of fear, alarm and terror that few English Protestants now understood. To their astonishment Irish Protestants would increasingly have to explain their fears, and justify their exclusionist Penal Laws, in terms that British ministers no longer found acceptable, indeed sometimes found risible or positively dangerous to British interests.

The ending of papal recognition of the Stuart line in 1766 finally brought closure to what had long been an anachronistic attachment for Irish Catholics. For decades before then the political and dynastic reality had been that the Stuart cause was finished. Twenty years earlier, Catholic Ireland had not stirred when the Stuart cause had secured military victories in Scotland, only to collapse at Culloden (1746). True, Irish poets writing in Gaelic might continue to ignore the Stuart failure: their *aislingí* or vision poems predicting the return of the gallant Stuart heroes and anticipating the downfall of the Hanoverian Georges continued to be written, and sung; but such sentiments were more rooted in sentimentality rather than reality.

Lastly, the emergence of the Catholic question in the 1760s was intimately linked to the founding of the first British empire. With the successful conclusion of the Seven Years' War (1756–63), Britain found itself in possession of a great empire on which famously 'the sun never set' – in India, Canada and north America. Henceforth, the concerns, anxieties and fears of Irish Protestants would be pushed into a distant second place by the pressing manpower needs of the armed forces of the crown. If a single overarching explanation for the emergence of the Catholic question, and for the timing of the repeal of the Penal Laws in the late eighteenth century, is to be sought, it is to be found in the expansion of empire, and especially in the scale and extent of warfare from the 1760s on.

There is of course a huge irony in this: the Catholic question in the early eighteenth century had also been linked to war, for Irish Catholics then were rightly viewed as loyal to the ousted James II, and later to his son, Charles. Nor was this just a paper loyalty, for in addition to the 15,000 or so Catholic soldiers who entered the Irish regiments in French service after the defeat at Aughrim, until the 1740s when numbers dwindled there was an annual recruitment of around a thousand Catholic Irish, officers and men, into France's Irish Brigade, a group of regiments which professed loyalty to the Stuarts, and which constituted in theory an Irish standing army abroad (see figure 4.1). As a result of this Irish military establishment overseas, wars and rumours of war had ever been occasions of danger for Irish Catholics at home. For example in 1715 and in 1745, when forces loyal to the Stuarts staged insurrections in Scotland, and in 1743, at the outbreak of the War of Austrian Succession, Irish Catholics, because of their suspect loyalties, had found themselves the object of additional security measures.

But from mid-century on all this changed: war would henceforth mean opportunity rather than danger for Irish Catholics; it would mean opportunity to parade their loyalty, to draw up addresses of support and, especially, to barter recruits for concessions. Military necessity, essentially the manpower requirements of the British army, tasked with providing garrisons for the greatest empire the world had seen since Roman times, provides the key for the emergence of the Catholic question in the 1760s, and for its persistence thereafter. For the remainder of the century, British generals and politicians turned their attention to Ireland, where it was pointed out that 'there was a weapon of war yet untried by Britain' – the wholesale enlistment of Irish Catholics into the armed forces of the crown.

Ireland had not been a recruiting ground for the British army in the early eighteenth century – at least not officially. After the experience of James II's 'Catholicke designe', a major part of which had involved 'catholicising' the army in Ireland, there was agreement that it would have been foolhardy to permit the enlistment of Irish Catholics, as it were, 'to guard us from themselves'. Nor were recruiting parties authorised to enlist Irish Protestants for the lower ranks; any depletion of Protestant strength in Ireland would, it was felt, damage the Protestant interest there and, in any case, if Irish Protestants were permitted to serve the king, there was always the danger that wily papists might pretend to be Protestants, and thus gain access to the army and to arms training. It was deemed safest, therefore, to bar all Irish from the lower ranks of the armed forces (although Irish Protestants could serve as officers); and in general this rule seems to have been enforced.

The outbreak of war in 1756, however, led to an urgent reconsideration of these exclusionist policies. Already in 1745 the ban on Irish Protestant recruits to the lower ranks had been lifted; and those Catholic Highlanders who had fought for Charles Stuart a few years earlier in Scotland were permitted to enlist in the king's army in 1756. By 1760 there is compelling evidence that a blind eye was being turned to the recruitment of Irish Catholics into the ranks, particularly

4.1 Remember Fontenoy: a largely fictional representation of the battle of Fontenoy, 1745, in which the Irish regiments in French service distinguished themselves. The battle was 'rediscovered' by Irish nationalists in the nineteenth century. National Library of Ireland.

where the regiments concerned were destined for foreign parts. In that year the lord lieutenant, the duke of Bedford, was authorised to enlist Irish Catholics into the marines and into the specialist Irish artillery. More open recruiting procedures were not yet possible, but clearly the pressures of war were transforming principle into pragmatism where Irish Catholic recruitment were concerned.

This transformation was clearly revealed in 1762, when the Catholic Lord Trimleston, probably at the instigation of the British government, 'offered' to help recruit six regiments of Irish Catholics to serve either the elector of Hanover (that is, George III under his German title), or the king of Portugal, a British ally. These proposals were given serious consideration by the British government and were laid before the Irish Parliament – which promptly rejected them. The approaching end of the war, and with it the end of large-scale recruiting, caused Trimleston's proposal to lose urgency; but though his scheme came to nothing considerable significance attaches to it. Trimleston's assertion of Catholic loyalty was welcomed; his claim that Catholics wished to help militarily in defending the empire was tacitly accepted; and the stratagem adopted by the British government, in having Trimleston sponsor the offer, was one that would be tried again. In a future war the British government would be intent on gaining Catholic recruits for the army, and it would not be averse to sponsoring Catholic relief in return. By 1760 the British government had begun to court the Irish Catholics, and the Irish Catholics, despite the penal code, were able make a positive response; how would Protestant Ireland react to this new and potentially destabilising development?

The Townshend viceroyalty, 1767–72

The ten years after the settlement of the dispute between Stone and Boyle (now earl of Shannon) witnessed ever stronger confirmation of British suspicions that the current manner of governing Ireland was profoundly unsatisfactory.[6] These years also witnessed the growth of a conviction that something ought to be done about it. During the Seven Years' War (1756–63) the Irish Parliament, despite its professed pleasure at the success of British arms, proved to be less than generous where funding those arms was concerned. Irish (Protestant) recruitment into the armed forces of the crown also proved to be remarkably sluggish. During the Bedford viceroyalty there were frequent Irish protests at the foreign-born beneficiaries of the Irish pension list, and at the large number of Irish absentee landlords who clearly did not deem Ireland worthy of their residence and whose absence was – apparently – deeply resented. These were precisely the sort of contentious issues which the undertakers were supposed to stifle; and their failure to do so was usually attributed to their courting popularity or to their incompetence.

However, if the undertakers' management of the Irish Parliament in the early 1760s was clearly slipping, their appetite for government patronage showed no sign of diminishing – if anything the reverse. The new king, George III, in his youthful idealism – he was just twenty-two years old on his accession in 1760 – was especially critical of his supposed Irish servants' alleged rapacity in this regard. In fairness, the increase in the undertakers' demands was a reflection of the new difficulties which they had to deal with. The Irish House of Commons in the early 1760s was much more difficult to control than it had been previously; yet to British ministers, the undertakers' requests, and perceived incompetence, were further evidence of the deplorable state of English government in Ireland.

In early 1765, following the deaths in rapid succession of both Boyle and Stone, the Cabinet of George Grenville, the British prime minister, resolved to seize the opportunity that was now offered and decided that for the future lords lieutenant should reside constantly in Ireland. For many decades, the undertakers had deputised for lords lieutenant during their customary lengthy absences from Ireland, and this had added to their influence. Requiring constant residence as a condition of appointment for future lords lieutenant was seen as a key measure to curb the power of the undertakers. However, this policy of requiring constant residence of future chief governors appears to have been laid aside almost as soon as it was agreed. The next two appointees to Dublin made no such commitment: one, indeed, so far from being a constant resident in Ireland was, in fact, a constant absentee, for he never set foot in the country. Nor did the appointment of Lord Townshend as lord lieutenant in August 1767 mark any significant change in policy. There is no foundation for the belief that Townshend came to Ireland with a predetermined plan to 'bring administration back to the Castle'. And yet Townshend did reside constantly in Ireland during the five years of his viceroyalty; under his aegis a new system of governing Ireland was introduced; and his viceroyalty did mark the end of the 'age of the undertakers'. How can this be explained?

Townshend was sent to Ireland with one clear instruction: to obtain the consent of the Irish Parliament to an increase or augmentation in the number of soldiers from 12,000 to 15,325 paid for by Ireland. George III was a firm supporter of the scheme and he and his ministers were most anxious that the Irish Parliament agree to it. It was as a result of the difficulties encountered in winning Irish parliamentary approval for this scheme that Townshend decided that the system of government in Ireland needed to be radically reformed. The rejection by the Irish House of Commons of the augmentation scheme, followed a year later by its refusal to accept a Money bill because it had not originated in the

Commons, persuaded Townshend himself that major changes were needed in Ireland. Nothing less than a new system in which the lord lieutenant and his chief secretary would occupy central positions was required. Instead of relying on undertakers for parliamentary support for the king's measures, Townshend determined that a party of lord lieutenant's 'friends' or 'Castle party', should be formed and rewarded by government patronage.

For nearly five years Townshend struggled to implement his new system and by the time he left Ireland, in late 1772, he could justly claim to have brought power back to the Castle. The great undertakers were no longer able to dictate terms to, or negotiate as equals with, the lord lieutenant. The oligarchy had been broken. From 1772 on the lord lieutenant headed and his chief secretary directed in Parliament a 'Castle party' which would undertake the king's business. From 1772 forward the lord lieutenant was in effect the leading undertaker in Ireland. He would also be the chief dispenser of patronage. Townshend had wrested control over the Irish Revenue Board and its patronage from John Ponsonby and that constituted his abiding achievement. Ponsonby had made full use of Revenue Board patronage to consolidate his power, and his hold over it had given him immense influence throughout the country. Townshend brought the Revenue Board back to the Castle and thus acquired for himself and for future lords lieutenant control over its patronage. Without this patronage, the task of maintaining a 'Castle party' would have been much more difficult. As it was, the 'Castle party' set up by Townshend survived until the Union in 1801: but the 'age of the undertakers' was over by 1772.

Ireland and the American Revolution

On the surface, the Harcourt viceroyalty (1772–6) appeared to put the seal on the achievements of Townshend.[7] Lord Shannon, one of those undertakers dethroned by Townshend, became a supporter of the Castle; and sensationally, Henry Flood, a leading patriot politician who had been a thorn in Townshend's side, seemingly recognised the futility of continuing in opposition and accepted Harcourt's offer of the lucrative office of Irish vice-treasurer. In general, compared to the stormy parliamentary sessions of the Townshend viceroyalty, Irish political life appeared moribund in the years after 1772. At this point, however, the developing crisis among the British colonies in north America began to intrude into Irish affairs; not for the last time, Irish politics would respond to external stimuli.[7]

Shortly after Flood's appointment was announced, the attention of the Irish House of Commons had been directed towards events in north America where disturbances had broken out between the British army and armed colonists. With some difficulty a majority of the Commons was persuaded to condemn the American colonists as rebels and to agree to the dispatch of four thousand Irish soldiers to 'negotiate' with them. As isolated skirmishes gave way to full-scale war in north America, Ireland became deeply involved in this crisis of the British empire. By the time the war ended in 1783 not only had the American colonies successfully seized their independence, but Irish patriot politicians had taken the opportunity afforded them by the imperial crisis to readjust the constitutional relationship between Ireland and England; some were even contemplating reconfiguring the relationship between the Irish Parliament and the Irish people.

Ireland's interest in the British colonies in north America and in their dispute with the mother country was understandable. During the seventeenth and throughout the eighteenth century, tens of thousands of Irish emigrants had made the journey to the New World and, by the 1770s, an Irish presence was well established there. A majority of the hundred thousand emigrants estimated to have sailed from Ireland for the north American colonies between1700 and 1776 were Presbyterians from Ulster, and they established and maintained vital communication links between their new home and the old one. At one time it was thought that those Presbyterians who emigrated were invariably to be found in the ranks of those in favour of American resistance to Britain; but recent research has revised this rather romantic view. It now seems clear that while a majority of Presbyterians from the north of Ireland – soon to be dubbed Scotch-Irish – undoubtedly favoured the revolutionary cause (e.g. in Pennsylvania), an indeterminate number, swayed by local factors in their particular colony, espoused the loyalist side (e.g. in North Carolina). Those who supported George Washington and the continental army attracted most attention, for almost all had relatives in Ulster. William Steele Dickson, a Presbyterian minister in county Down, and later a prominent United Irishman, was by no means a solitary voice in revealing his political sympathies by preaching vigorously against what he called 'the unnatural, impolitic and unprincipled war in America'. And the British minister Lord Shelburne reported that 'in every Protestant or Dissenter's house the established toast is success to the Americans'.

In addition to these kinship ties might be added trade links with the British colonies of north America; the result was a tightly woven network of business and family contacts stretching from Ireland to the colonies. Irish-American trade consisted mostly of provisions – butter, salted beef, salted pork, salted fish (this last was used mostly as slave food on the plantations) and linen cloth to America, for which, in return, Ireland received large amounts of flax seed, rum, staves and sometimes wheat and flour. By the terms of the Navigation Acts of the seventeenth century and later restrictive legislation, Ireland was not permitted to trade with the colonies on an equal basis with England or Scotland. It is unlikely, however, regardless of the loud resentment that these restrictions aroused in Ireland that they in fact made much difference to the overall pattern, or indeed volume, of Irish colonial trade in the eighteenth century. They did, however, have the effect of distinguishing Ireland from Britain where colonial trade was concerned and, given the stormy course of Anglo-American relations in the 1760s, when non-importation agreements were a favoured weapon on the colonial side, Irish trade undoubtedly benefited from being marked out from British commerce in this way. During the Stamp Act controversy of the mid-1760s, for example, Irish goods were specifically excluded from the colonial non-importation agreements and there was a similar exemption favouring Ireland in the colonial resistance to the Charles Townshend duties of the late 1760s.

However, as the troubles deepened between mother country and colonies, in the early 1770s, attitudes in the colonies hardened and Ireland was no longer so favoured. When a trade war broke out following the passing of the punitive Coercive Acts in 1774, Ireland found itself, despite the best efforts of Benjamin Franklin, denied the privilege of shipping its linens and provisions directly to the colonies. This development was all the more damaging because Ireland's linen industry had been in deep recession since the late 1760s, a recession which had prompted a substantial outflow of Presbyterian weavers to the colonies in north America. Irish anger at this turn of events, however, was directed more at the British, and their inept handling of the crisis, than at the colonists and their determination not to yield to Britain's threats; that anger was further fuelled in February 1776 by Dublin Castle's imposition of a total embargo on the export of Irish provisions to the colonies. This wartime embargo aroused a storm of protest because it was blamed – unfairly – for the generally depressed state of the Irish economy. But the embargo was especially denounced because it was taken as confirmation of the thoughtless way in which Irish commercial interests were handled by England. The latent Irish resentment against English restrictions on Irish trade, a factor at least since the Cattle Acts of the 1660s, was thus reawakened. Again, because these restrictions were viewed as a product of Ireland's constitutional subordination to England, a potent fusion of commercial with constitutional grievances was effected.

Constitutional issues were of course in the air, for the war between mother country and colonies had been preceded, and would be accompanied by, furious debate on the respective obligations of each to the other, on the location of sovereignty in the empire and on the rights of the imperial Parliament over the colonies. These issues were argued in a series of pamphlets, letters and printed speeches, most of which held some resonance for Ireland; not surprisingly, appropriate lessons were drawn. It was argued, for example, that if the British government succeeded in taxing the colonists without their consent, then Ireland would surely be next on the list for such oppressive treatment; America's struggle, as Benjamin Franklin and others pointed out, was ultimately that of Ireland. Again, it was evident that what the colonists were struggling to defend, essentially the right to legislate for themselves, Ireland did not even possess. Finally, the very discussion of such matters as rights, sovereignty and representation could not but have an impact on Irish politics, for the Irish political structure would not come well out of any scrutiny couched in these terms. It could hardly be ignored, for example, that while Irish Protestant, and Presbyterian, opinion clearly thought favourably of the Americans, Irish Members in the Irish Parliament had been brought, however reluctantly, to condemn them as rebels, and to authorise the dispatch of troops to suppress their 'rebellion'. The divergence between Parliament and people could hardly be more obvious. And yet the question remained: how could Irish public opinion be brought to bear on the Irish Parliament?

The general election of 1776 brought no significant influx of 'patriot' Members: Harcourt and Blaquiere distributed large amounts of government patronage, made a number of peerage promotions and the elections passed off quietly. But political difficulties for the administrations in England and Ireland were mounting. The debates in the British Parliament concerning restrictions on Irish trade did nothing to soothe Irish tempers. Again, under the pressure of war in America the British government was reappraising its traditional exclusionist policies where Catholic recruitment into the armed forces of the crown was concerned – and this too was a worrying development. A new and untested Dublin Castle team of Lord Buckinghamshire as lord lieutenant, and Sir Richard Heron as chief secretary, added to the air of uncertainty with which the new Parliament opened in October 1777. Finally, the news from America, hitherto sombre, now turned disastrous. The British defeat at Saratoga (October 1777) was followed, early in 1778, by the entry of France into the war on the side of the Americans. England's difficulty might yet prove to be Ireland's opportunity.

The first group to benefit from English setbacks in the war for America was Irish Catholics. Throughout the 1770s, as relations between Britain and the American colonies had deteriorated, more and more Catholic recruits were taken into the armed forces. Not surprisingly Irish Protestants grew apprehensive at this development: there were protests at the open recruitment of Catholics into the East India Company army, and in 1777 alarm was expressed at reports that ten thousand Catholics were to be enlisted for the defence of Ireland. Irish Protestant sympathy with the colonists was increased by the fear that the British government appeared intent on arming Irish Catholics, French Canadian Catholics and even American Catholics to coerce American Protestants; and there were suspicions that the British government in its eternal quest for men was not above offering Catholic relief in return for Catholic recruits.

Nor were these suspicions groundless. From the late 1770s there was in fact a plan to offer concessions to the Catholics of England, Scotland and, especially Ireland, in order to help recruitment and at the same time to help fix the loyalty of the various Catholic populations, and so enable North's government to present a 'united front' against the rebellious Americans. The scheme involved the Scottish 'projector', and general busybody, Sir John Dalrymple, who was authorised by the British prime minister, Lord North, to sound out various Catholic leaders in Scotland and in England on a proposal of concessions in return for recruits. The response was encouraging: but given the number of English and Scottish Catholics (about 110,000 out of a combined population of over 7 million) North cannot have expected great things from Catholic relief in Britain. It seems clear that Ireland, and Irish Catholics, were the objects aimed at all along.

The terms of the English Catholic Relief Act of 1778 were chosen with a strict eye as to what would go down well in Ireland. Introduced by Luke Gardiner, who had been on record from an early date as a supporter of Catholic recruitment into the British army, an Irish Relief bill closely modelled on the English Act was put through the Irish Parliament in June 1778. When enacted the Act removed most of the barriers which had been placed in the way of Catholics acquiring an interest in Irish land: Catholics were now permitted to take leases for up to 999 years, although the fee simple – outright ownership – still eluded them. As important, it was now legal for Catholics to bequeath land without having to gavel it (i.e. divide the land among all the sons).

Catholic gratitude for these concessions was soon forthcoming. When the government stockpurse for recruits ran out, it was the wealthy Catholic merchant, George Goold, who offered to advance the government some 6,000 guineas 'and if necessary as much more tomorrow' in order to make up the shortfall; and the Catholic hierarchy proclaimed various fasts for the success of British arms in north America. Archbishop Thomas Troy of Dublin, one of its number, looked forward unashamedly to the downfall of 'the Puritan party, calvinistical and republican' in the American colonies. The Relief Act of 1778, in short, set the seal on Catholic support for the American war, and firmly and publicly established the British government as the sponsors and protectors of the Irish Catholic.

War with the rebellious colonists in America, and soon war with France and Spain, which entered the conflict as their allies, certainly offered the chance for Irish Catholics to parade their loyalty; but the hostilities also held major strategic implications for Ireland. France had long been cast as the chief foreign ally of Irish Catholics and that country had been the refuge of Irish Catholics for decades. Moreover, as we have seen, the French army had a number of Irish regiments, though by the 1770s, it was the officers, and much less so the men, who were Irish. It was also known that an assortment of invasion plans for Ireland was readily available in Paris. During the Seven Years' War Captain François Thurot, a French privateer, had made a brief landing at Carrickfergus, county Antrim, and when war broke out again in 1778, a further French incursion was expected. It was soon claimed that Ireland's defences were ill-prepared to resist an anticipated attack and much was made of a letter from the chief secretary, Richard Heron, in which he appeared to admit that there were only a few hundred troops available for the defence of Belfast. In actual fact, while some four thousand men had indeed been dispatched to the American colonies, as many as nine thousand still remained in the country. This debate over Ireland's defence capabilities had arisen partly through misunderstanding but also because those active in promoting a new paramilitary force, variously described as the Volunteers or independent companies, had quickly seized on Dublin Castle's alleged negligence, and used it to justify their existence and their role in the defence of Ireland.

The Volunteers sprang directly from the Irish militia, a body which had been embodied by Dublin Castle at various times in the eighteenth century, but one which had latterly fallen into disuse. To this extent, the Volunteers were not entirely a new force: perhaps as many as half of the officers had previously held militia commissions; and the militia's purpose, as specified in 1715, 'of suppressing . . . all such insurrections and rebellions, and repelling of invasions' would have fitted the Volunteers' self-proclaimed aims. There was a strong tradition of self-defence among Protestants in Ireland, for Irish Protestants of all ranks had long been accustomed to forming bands or posses with which to pursue agrarian insurgents such as the Whiteboys, or to monitor the movements of suspicious Catholics in their area when danger threatened. In these respects, once again, the Volunteers of 1778 were building on existing foundations. Some thirty local armed bands have been identified in the period 1772–7, and the naming of Volunteer companies after such 'Protestant' victories as the Boyne, Aughrim, Enniskillen, even Culloden (to mention only the names chosen in the Cork area in 1778) suggests a close affinity with an earlier anti-Catholic tradition.

The early conduct of the Volunteers for the most part offered some reassurance to those who might have viewed the whole business with some alarm. Volunteer companies were quick to proffer their services for the defence of Ireland when rumours of invasion were in the air in June 1779 and again in September 1781. While regular military opinion was scornful of their value in repelling a foreign army, it was felt that they could prove a serviceable riot police. Indeed, it was as a police force that the Volunteers primarily distinguished themselves. In Waterford they did duty for regular troops when these were called away on an invasion scare. Similarly, when a bill was introduced into the Irish Parliament to outlaw textile workers' combinations, protest meetings were held by those affected in Dublin. As a precaution against possible public disorder, Volunteer companies had gathered to maintain the public peace. More spectacularly – and clearly redolent of that earlier tradition out of which the Volunteers sprang – in 1779 Protestant landlords had mobilised the Volunteers on the Kilkenny/Tipperary borders in hot pursuit of local agrarian insurgents and killed five of them.

The avowed Protestantism of the Volunteers – at least in the early days of the movement – was also a comfort to those who were worried by 'so many thousand men in arms without a commission from the Crown'. The 'Protestant' nomenclature of Volunteer companies has already been noted, but equally their composition should be stressed. In Ulster, in particular, Presbyterians formed a significant element in the rank and file of the Volunteers, and Presbyterian ministers frequently combined preaching with parading. Members of the established church were also well represented in the ranks. And yet, while all of this was reassuring, the novelty of the Volunteers of 1778 should not be underestimated, nor the threat that they posed to the established order ignored. Despite their links with an earlier tradition, their protestations of loyalty, their Protestantism, their middle-class composition (they had to pay for their own uniforms, and have plenty of free time for drilling) and their economic conservatism, there are strong grounds for concluding that the militarisation and then the destabilisation of Irish society in the later eighteenth century was accelerated by the Volunteers.

In the first instance the Volunteer companies, unlike the militia or the earlier armed bands, were independent of Dublin Castle, and would neither accept pay (arms were a different matter) from the government nor permit their officers to be so appointed. It is, perhaps, possible that if the lord lieutenant, Buckinghamshire, had shown more assertiveness in the early days of volunteering, he might have established some Castle control over the companies; but through inertia as much as incompetence the opportunity was missed, and by the spring of 1779 the independence of the Volunteer companies was an established fact. The officers of the Volunteers would henceforth be elected by the men not commissioned by the crown. Admittedly, officers tended to be elected from among the ranks of those who, in general, combined social with political authority in their area; as we have seen, many of them had a background in the militia. But not all officers were so distinguished, and there was always the chance that those elected could, if found unsatisfactory, be turned out. This military democracy espoused by the Volunteers was thoroughly corrosive of that deferential society that prevailed everywhere throughout Ireland.

From an early date there were some ominous signs that the Volunteers might prove to be a rather wayward force. Their attitude towards Catholics, for example, was by no means uniformly hostile. Nor, it may be added, did all Catholics view them as the enemy. The fact was that, by the 1770s, the Catholic threat was widely perceived to be negligible; from Derry, for example, it was claimed that the local Volunteers were 'under no apprehensions from the Papists', and it was a similar story elsewhere. The Volunteers even gave a cautious welcome to the Catholic Relief measure of 1778, and, for their part, Catholics generally (the hierarchy, however, remained resolutely suspicious) cheered on the Volunteers, tried to set up their own Catholic independent companies (in Wexford and Waterford), sought leave to join existing bodies and, as early as June 1779, did in fact gain entry to some corps. It was the absence of any discernible Catholic threat (and the remoteness of the possibility of an invasion) that enabled the Volunteers to turn their attention to parliamentary and constitutional matters. Had there been a genuine Catholic (or French) threat, it would not have been possible for the Volunteers to enter the political arena.

Lastly, the Volunteers, in contrast to earlier armed and independent bands, were not content merely with a local presence and throughout 1779 they created first a regional, and then a nationwide, structure for the numerous companies that sprang up. From having a nationwide organisation – it is only in mid-1779 that we can talk of 'the Volunteers' as opposed to individual volunteer corps – it was but a short step to seeking a national role. From the summer of 1779, the Volunteers' attention was centred on the redress of Ireland's grievances. Patriot opinion in Ireland, hitherto inchoate and unfocused, had acquired a forum and the Volunteers had quickly found a role.

'A free trade'

Initially, the Volunteers focused their attention and their resentment on the time-honoured grievance of British restrictions on Irish trade. There had been a few signs in the spring of 1778 that the British government was contemplating a change in its commercial policy where Ireland was concerned, but the abrupt extension, in May 1778, of the earlier trade embargo to cover trading with the French, as well as the Americans, seemed to rule out significant concessions. Irish trade had remained in the doldrums throughout the 1770s, sacrificed once again, so it was claimed, on the altar of English self-interest. The Volunteers could scarcely have found a more popular cause; even such stalwart supporters of the British government as John Beresford, head of the Irish Revenue Board, citing widespread distress now called for the removal of at least some trade restrictions.

As pressure for concession mounted throughout the summer and autumn of 1779, the hapless Castle duo of Buckinghamshire and Heron found themselves more and more isolated. In the House of Commons supposed government supporters were nowhere to be seen, while the growing patriot group, sensing the Castle's disarray (and sniffing victory), proposed motions claiming that only 'a free trade' (i.e. a trade free from restrictions) could save Ireland from ruin and threatened a short Money bill if concessions were not made. A near bankrupt Treasury added to the Castle's woes: to meet routine expenses, £30,000 had had to be borrowed a year earlier from the banking firm of La Touche and a further £50,000 was later advanced from the Bank of England. By April 1779 the British Treasury was forced to undertake the payment of Irish regiments serving abroad because the Irish exchequer could no longer meet this expense. In Dublin a non-importation agreement against British goods was launched by leading 'citizens' gathered at the Tholsel, and the Volunteers were eager to police this embargo. Those who refused to comply, or those who were backsliders, soon found their names published in the local press.

The Volunteers were vital to the work of maintaining the pressure on the Irish Parliament, and through it on Dublin Castle and ultimately on the British government of Lord North. On 4 November, the birthday of William III, the Volunteers paraded at the king's statue in College Green, and draped their cannons with placards demanding 'A Free Trade or —'. Buckinghamshire attempted to pass off this demonstration as a purely traditional one and he claimed that only some seven hundred Volunteers attended; but Castle supporters were profoundly alarmed at the menacing posture which the Volunteers had come to adopt. Ten days after the demonstration at King William's statue, 'a great crowd' gathered in College Green and manhandled Members of Parliament, forcing them to swear to support a short (for only six months) Money bill 'and God knows what besides', as one witness observed. Ominously, it was reported that magistrates in the city had refused to call on the military to disperse the crowd. In the Irish House of Commons there were claims that English Acts of Parliament could not bind Ireland, that the lack of an appellate jurisdiction in Ireland was a grievance and that exports of wool from Ireland should go ahead with or without legal sanction. On 26 November 1779, a short Money bill was passed by 138 votes to 100 and the Castle's humiliation was complete.

At this point, news was received that the long-awaited concessions were to be granted and that Ireland was, after all, to have 'a free trade'. Ireland was to be permitted direct access to colonial trade, 'upon equal conditions with Great Britain', and all the securities, allowances and restrictions by which Anglo-Irish trade was controlled would be henceforth regularised by the Irish Parliament. Furthermore, Irish subjects were to be admitted into the Turkey company and

Irish ports were to be opened to the trade of the Levant. In the light of these concessions, Buckinghamshire was confident that no more 'peevish questions' would be raised. His confidence in this respect might have been fuelled by the knowledge that concessions for Irish Presbyterians, similar in (symbolic) importance to those awarded recently to Irish Catholics, were also in the pipeline.

In general, Irish Presbyterians, in the face of the Penal Laws directed against them and against other Dissenters, had maintained a dignified silence. These Penal Laws against Presbyterians had always been galling, but their effects had long been mitigated by a series of Indemnity Acts. By the 1770s Presbyterian grievances over such matters as the legality of their marriages, the validity of a Dissenting minister's orders and their access to burial grounds had been largely resolved. Moreover, as Presbyterians had never been deprived of the vote, or of the right, if elected, to take their seat in the Irish House of Commons, they had always been able to voice, however inadequately, their grievances. In addition, a small sum of money, the *regium donum*, disbursed among their ministers by royal warrant further tempered their resentment at their treatment by the members of the established church. But tempered or not, there was resentment: Presbyterians did not want sops, concessions or Acts of indemnity. They wanted an end to the sacramental test, as the clause in the 1704 Act 'to prevent the further growth of popery', was known. This excluded from public office all those who refused to take communion according to the rites of the established church, and it was designedly aimed at them. Above all, Presbyterians wanted an end to the second-class status which they had been forced to endure in the Ireland of the ascendancy. Their chance had come with the outbreak of the American War of Independence and the consequent attempt to confirm Catholic loyalties through concessions.

When the Catholic Relief bill had been making its way through the Irish House of Commons in June 1778, those opposed to its progress had attempted to sabotage it by tagging on a clause repealing the sacramental test of 1704. This clause was struck out in London but that was not the end of the matter, for within a year the 'heads' of a bill designed to remove the offending test were introduced and passed through the Irish parliamentary stages with great speed. As a result, by the end of 1779, Catholic relief, Presbyterian relief and concessions on trade, had all been accepted by the British government; but any hopes on the British side that these concessions would put an end to Irish agitation, or to 'peevish questions', proved short lived.

Behind the merits, or otherwise, of Britain's restrictions on Irish trade there had always lain, as Buckinghamshire put it, 'the constitutional question of the legislative power of Great Britain to restrain the commerce of Ireland' and, indeed, the power generally of the British Parliament to pass laws to bind Ireland.

Such issues would not go away with the announcement of the trade concessions, or even with the concessions to Irish Catholics or Dissenters. By the end of February 1780 Poynings' law, *habeas corpus*, the tenure of Irish judges and the need for an Irish Mutiny Act had all been raised in the Irish House of Commons, and it was evident that there would be further discussion of these issues in the months to come.

The American crisis, economic recession, the emergence of the Volunteers and the struggle for a free trade had helped create and direct a powerful new force in Irish life: public opinion. 'I cannot make myself responsible for the conduct of a popular assembly', wailed Buckinghamshire, declaring that 'no retrospective knowledge of Ireland can enable any man to form a judgement of the present situation.' When he reminded Irish Members of Parliament that Britain was at war and that contentious matters should be kept back until peace was signed, Henry Grattan, the foremost patriot Member bluntly replied that 'when Britain was at war, advantages for Ireland were to be looked for', and it was clear that what he had in mind were constitutional points. The concessions made previously had merely whetted appetites for further changes that would go to the heart of the Anglo-Irish connection.

With the departure of the luckless Buckinghamshire and Heron for England in 1780 and their replacement by Lord Carlisle and William Eden, Irish politics at the national level entered a period of lull, for the Irish Parliament was not scheduled to meet until September 1781. Political and constitutional questions, however, would not sleep during these eighteen months, for a new political agenda had been drawn up and the Volunteers remained mobilised and ready to forward it. Already, in January 1780, the Newry Volunteers had called for the election of committees of correspondence in all the trading towns, in order to keep the pressure on Britain. In June Volunteers in Dublin passed resolutions to the effect that only the 'King, Lords and Commons of Ireland' were competent to make laws binding Ireland, and later there were calls for a dissolution of Parliament and for a new non-importation agreement to exert pressure on Britain.

On 15 September 1781 Carlisle wrote to Hillsborough, the secretary of state, outlining the problems he anticipated in the coming session and proposing his solutions. He was certain that constitutional questions would be raised but equally he was confident that he could divert them and that he would be able to parry demands for legislative independence. On other matters, he was not so sure; there would be an attempt to limit the Irish Mutiny Act and, possibly, one to give judges in Ireland a tenure the same as that of their fellow judges in England. Almost certainly, there would be a demand for an Irish Habeas Corpus Act. In addition, some Members wanted the Post Office transferred to Ireland

and there was grumbling about the disparity in the bounty payable on refined sugar imported into Ireland and England, and about British failure to intercede in a trade dispute with Portugal. Finally, he revealed that if the subject of the Volunteers came up, and it assuredly would, his plan was to flatter them and to praise their efforts in defending Ireland rather than criticise, much less denounce, them.

Hillsborough's reply underlined the British government's total hostility to any substantial constitutional change: Irish legislative independence had to be opposed *totis viribus*; no amendment to Poynings' law was to be permitted; the Post Office could not be interfered with; the tenure for Irish judges was to be unchanged; and finally, Hillsborough professed himself doubtful as to the wisdom of flattering the Volunteers, indeed he was even hostile to the term 'Volunteer corps', which Carlisle had proposed to employ.

Until December 1781 this policy of general firmness appeared to be working. Carlisle and Eden proved dextrous at managing the Irish House of Commons. A motion praising the Volunteers was allowed to pass unopposed, thus denying the opposition in the Irish House of Commons a popular point on which to unite. At the same time Eden made substantial efforts to build up the old Castle party and, as a result of his success (on one occasion he managed to meet fifty-three Members of Parliament separately between 8 am and 2 pm) government majorities became more respectable. Flood, however, remained a problem. His continued opposition now led to his dismissal. In this way, Carlisle served notice that loyalty was expected from all office-holders; and Eden emphasised this point by entering into numerous engagements to secure the support of previously hostile, or 'doubtful' Members. The results were soon apparent and a number of government victories were recorded over contentious matters in the Commons. In particular, the Castle recorded a resounding victory (135 votes to 66) in a debate on Poynings' law, in which the recently dismissed Flood had led the opposition attack. This victory, with others, was encouraging but there was still cause for concern. The American victory at Yorktown, Virginia (October 1781) had virtually signalled the end of the American war, and North's position as prime minister could hardly be sustained much longer.

Then again, Carlisle was concerned at what might be called the tone of Irish political life. Although motions calling for constitutional changes had been defeated, he well knew that it was always open to 'the popular orators' to raise such issues again, and since in his view Irish Members constantly sought popularity, anything might happen. While attacks on Poynings' law had been defeated with ease too much should not be made of this; the fact was, claimed Carlisle, 'the independence of the Irish legislature is become the creed of the Kingdom'. Then, towards the end of December 1781 there was an unexpected but significant development. Carlisle reported that 'some measures are to be proposed after the [Christmas] recess for the further relief of the Roman Catholicks of this kingdom'. In sum, notwithstanding the victories for the Castle in the last months of 1781, there were numerous indications that the crisis in the state was far from over.

The Constitution of 1782

Since the passing of the Relief Act of 1778, Catholics in Ireland had continued to look to the British government for further relaxation of the Penal Laws. At the same time they had continued to stress their loyalty by sending in numerous addresses to the king, and their leaders had encouraged recruiting for the British armed forces. Archbishop Troy had resumed discussions with Luke Gardiner and other sympathisers and he was optimistic that further boons would be forthcoming. However, while elements within the Catholic hierarchy, together with the traditionally conservative leadership of the Catholic Committee, continued to stress Catholics' attachment to government, a new, more forceful leadership, best represented by John Keogh, a wealthy Dublin merchant, was prepared to explore other ways to bring pressure on government to redress Catholic grievances.

Keogh was a member of the Catholic Committee and of the Volunteers and, despite the opposition of the older Catholic leaders, there is clear evidence that many other Catholics had by late 1779 joined Volunteer corps in such places as Dundalk, Kilkenny and Armagh. Elements within the Volunteers professed to welcome this development and indeed to encourage it: Joseph Pollock, writing in the *Belfast Newsletter*, stressed the point that 'unless we lay aside all rancor or prejudice on account of distinctions either political or religious' there would be no progress 'towards shaking off the shackles of an usurping English people'. Equally, there were 'patriots' who reprobated any attempt at Catholic assertiveness on the grounds that it sowed dissension. The earl of Charlemont, a Volunteer commander, remained resolutely opposed to further Catholic relief, fearing that it would produce divisions within the Volunteer movement; and Henry Flood revealed his attitude towards Catholics by posing the key question: if the Catholics were given more power, '[c]an a Protestant constitution survive?'

In short, the revival of the Catholic question, as Carlisle recognised, offered the possibility of splitting the patriots, and before long he was pondering 'how far it may be either eligible or necessary for government to interest themselves in it, upon one side or the other'. Carlisle's reflections on this point were given urgency by the rapid revival of patriot feeling in Parliament and in the country. Equally, they were sharpened by the approaching collapse of North's government, for in a series of parliamentary divisions over the ministry's American policy held between early February and mid-March 1782, North's parliamentary majority crumbled. The Rockingham Whigs led by Lords Rockingham and Shelburne and by Charles James Fox took power in London; all three were associated with Grattan and Flood, the leading figures in the Irish opposition.

On 22 February, claiming that the 'present embarrassed situation' of British government was the best moment to strike, Grattan moved yet another declaration of Ireland's legislative independence. Once again, however, his action proved premature and the motion was rejected by 137 votes to 68. Carlisle drew little comfort from his victory: it had been an ominous feature of the debate that no speaker on either side had accepted that British laws could bind Ireland; and it was clear that the claim to legislative independence would never be abandoned because 'it has been spread with such industry that every rank and order in the nation are possess'd of it'.

The Volunteers had contributed much to this public mood. Representatives of some 136 corps had met at Dungannon, county Tyrone, in mid-February 1782 and had issued a call for legislative independence. Moreover, in a startling reversal of traditional attitudes, the Volunteers had professed to welcome the relaxation of the Penal Laws against those whom they called 'our Roman Catholick fellow subjects'. Hitherto the derogatory 'papist' had been the preferred term for Irish Catholics, and Protestant armed bodies had assembled over the decades to keep a close eye on them. This Volunteer declaration, however, effectively extended common citizenship to Irish Catholics. At the same time it deprived Dublin Castle of a key weapon. The question of relief for Irish Catholics had always had the potential to create divisions among the patriots, but this declaration meant that Dublin Castle had to abandon at least for the time being any attempt to play the Catholic card and create dissension in patriot ranks.

The Irish Parliament reconvened following the Easter recess on 16 April, and Grattan, secure in the knowledge that it could not be resisted, moved for the third time a motion calling for Irish legislative independence. There was no opposition. Irish Members of Parliament were convinced that the new Rockingham government in London was disposed to grant major concessions for Ireland and, as a result, Grattan's speech was little more than, as J. C. Beckett, a leading historian of this episode, put it, 'a hymn of triumph over a victory already won'. The duke of Portland, the new lord lieutenant, saw, so to speak, the writing on the wall, and informed his political masters in London that he considered 'the question as carried', believing there was no point in further discussion let alone negotiation, and urged them to accept the *fait accompli*.

On 18 May 1782, Shelburne told Portland that the British government had determined 'to meet the wishes of the Irish people'. The Declaratory Act ('the

Sixth of George I') was to be repealed by the British Parliament, an Irish biennial Mutiny Act was to be allowed and major modifications to Poynings' law were to be conceded. Quickly embodied into a bill drafted by Barry Yelverton, the powers of both the Irish and English privy councils were restricted. For the first time, formally rather than, as heretofore, informally, the Irish Parliament would now have the initiative where legislation was concerned. Irish judges were to hold office with the same terms of tenure as their English fellow judges, and the appellate jurisdiction of the Irish House of Lords was restored. These various bits and pieces of legislation made up what a later generation would call 'the Constitution of 1782', or even the 'revolution of 1782'.

Surprisingly, the Catholic Relief Act of 1782 has rarely been considered among the elements which constituted that 'Constitution' (or revolution). Yet the Catholic Relief Acts – there were in fact two of them for legislative convenience – went through at the same time as the other items of legislation and can best be seen as part of the same process by which relationships within Ireland, and between Ireland and England, underwent adjustment. The Act permitted Catholics to own land (with certain exceptions) on the same terms as Irish Protestants, and it freed Catholic priests from the penalties decreed against Catholic ecclesiastics. It also permitted Catholics who had taken the oath of allegiance of 1774 to open schools under licence from the local Protestant bishop. In a sense, it was the fact of Catholic relief rather than the content that mattered in 1782.

Once the Volunteers and, perhaps reluctantly, the patriots had backed Catholic demands for further relaxation of the Penal Laws, the British government for the first time had found itself confronting 'the whole of this country' and had realised that further resistance was futile. This was that 'sacred truth' that Grattan would refer to some months later when he reflected on the key lesson of the events of the spring of 1782. 'Intestine divisions', he told the Volunteers, had hitherto weakened the national cause, but 'your policy and my decided opinion to adopt the Catholic body' changed that. He believed that 'the Irish Protestant should never be free until the Irish Catholic ceased to be a slave' and that 'by the charter of toleration those intestine divisions...ceased and with them the domination of Great Britain has departed'. Similar extravagant sentiments were voiced on the Catholic side. The Catholic activist Charles O'Conor reflected that 'lately we are become a free and independent people and that description alone comprises the happiest revolution we have had here for 700 years past ... We are united in a single creed of politics.' And yet, for more cautious observers, there was much to reflect on both in what had been gained by the 'constitution of 1782' and in the means used to secure victory.

What had been won by the constitutional victories of 1782? Certainly, the formal subordination of the Irish to the British Parliament, enshrined in the

Declaratory Act and Poynings' law, had more or less gone, but the informal subordination of the 'Irish' government to the British government remained and, with it, the attendant problems of parliamentary management and control. After 1782 the Irish executive was still a branch of the British government, with its leading members appointed by and answerable to London. This had been a fundamental flaw in the Irish legislative system before 1782 and all that the new arrangements of 1782 had done was to exacerbate it. After 1782 the popular tone of Irish politics, the presence of a dedicated opposition and the existence of an informed public opinion simply meant that the Irish House of Commons would be more resistant than before to control by the executive. Again, while the initiative in legislation had been finally gained by the Irish Parliament, the pre-1782 'heads of bills' procedure had already allowed it the major say in formulating legislation, and it is hard to claim that the end of the little-used Declaratory Act, and the curtailment of the moribund Poynings' law, marked revolutionary advances for Irish legislative freedom.

If a question mark can be placed against the Irish constitutional victories of 1782, further doubts can be raised at the manner of those alleged triumphs. The reality was that Ireland had taken advantage of England's difficulties over the war with its colonies in North America to demand trade and constitutional concessions. However, two could play at that game: just as England's difficulty in 1782 had been Ireland's opportunity, so too Ireland's difficulty could offer England an opening – a grim truth borne out by the government of William Pitt taking advantage of the terror generated by the Irish rebellion of 1798 to push through a parliamentary union in 1800. It would be an exaggeration to claim that the union was embedded in the legislative independence of 1782, but realistically, the only options available should the Irish Parliament remain unreformed were union or separation. And again, the fact that the Catholic question had emerged full-blown on to the political agenda of both countries in 1782 was a further cause for concern. Could Irish politicians deal with this contentious issue in an effective and practical way – or would they pass the buck to the British and allow them to pose as the Catholics' friends?

More than anything, however, the use of the Volunteers, a paramilitary extra-parliamentary body, to force concessions from the British government ought to have given cause for concern. An end to British legislative restrictions on Irish trade had been sought for decades. Similarly, the Declaratory Act and Poynings' law had long been criticised in newspapers, denounced in Parliament and written against in pamphlets – all to no avail. The perception went abroad that only an Irishman with a musket could command attention from the British. It would be incorrect to claim that the Volunteers had brought the gun into Irish politics – armed force had never been far from the surface in Ireland – but they appeared to have done so successfully, and had been cheered to the echo as a result. This lesson was not lost on others who duly noted that while speeches, argument and petitions undoubtedly had their place in Irish politics, the fact remained – if one really wanted things done, one got a gun. A paramilitary tradition in Irish politics was launched by the Volunteers of 1782 and that tradition, whether nationalist or Unionist, loyalist or republican, has continued to shape and delimit the contours of Irish political activity. The force of argument had been trumped by the argument of force. Constitutional politics, however defined, undoubtedly triumphed in 1782 but the perception that they had only done so through the threat of paramilitary force proved both enduring and inspiring. The triumph of 1782, in the end, was a dear-bought victory.

Parliamentary reform and the Catholic question

The celebrations over the achievement of the 'Constitution of 1782' did not last long. The first sour note was struck by Henry Flood who, in an effort to consolidate his standing as the leader of the patriots, pronounced the 'simple repeal' of the Declaratory Act, a cornerstone of the 'Constitution of 1782' to be entirely inadequate. He demanded that the British government formally renounce its declared right to legislate for Ireland. Reaction to Flood's initiative was unfavourable: Grattan swiftly declared himself satisfied with 'simple repeal'; British ministers were outraged at the overt impugning of their good faith and the Dublin wits were quick to point out that, logically, Flood's position was untenable (a renunciation could, after all, itself be renounced). Overall, Flood's campaign smacked too much of mischief-making with a view to self-promotion. None the less it attracted support from the Volunteers and as a result Flood's personal grudge became a major national issue.

The Volunteers had been without a defined mandate since the victory of April 1782 and the approaching end of the American war promised to make them entirely redundant. Flood's doubts about 'simple repeal' offered them a new role as guardians of the Constitution and they quickly put their weight behind his demand. Addresses and resolutions from Volunteer companies calling for renunciation were drawn up and, in January 1783, this further concession was granted: the British Parliament was brought to renounce its claim to legislate for Ireland. In the eyes of some the 'Constitution of 1782' was now complete. In fact, all that the struggle for 'renunciation' had achieved was to highlight the deep residual distrust with which English policy and English politicians were viewed in Ireland and to reveal the unsatisfactory nature of the 'Constitution of 1782'. 'Renunciation' did nothing to render Irish independence any more secure; it may, in fact, have weakened it, not just because it pitted Flood against Grattan but because it increased British anxiety at what had been already given away to Ireland. Having just been forced to part with the American colonies, Ireland was simply too important to be allowed to drift away on its own; and this was apparently what it was bent on doing. On the British side, therefore, the pressure grew for a treaty that would unequivocally reaffirm Ireland's position within the empire, and its connection with Britain. British capitulation over 'renunciation' fuelled patriot hopes that their next venture might meet with equal success. Having at last adjusted the constitutional connection between England and Ireland to their satisfaction, the patriots would now seek to alter the political relationship between the Irish Parliament and the Irish people.

Perhaps surprisingly, the question of parliamentary reform had hitherto attracted little attention in the Irish Parliament.[8] Admittedly, the Octennial Act of 1768, putting a limit to the duration of an Irish Parliament, had been achieved and at general elections every eight years or so since then the custom had grown up, in some of the more open constituencies, for voters to seek to extract promises, or at least statements of voting intent, from candidates. The prime focus of patriot endeavour, however, had been fixed on the Anglo-Irish nexus, rather than on the equally flawed relationship between the Irish Parliament and the Irish people. With the winning of the 'Constitution of 1782', however, the question of parliamentary reform was tentatively raised with a view to safeguarding the legislative gains and ensuring that there would be no backsliding by Irish Members of Parliament. However, once the struggle over 'renunciation' had been satisfactorily concluded, the issue of reform was brought forward in a sustained manner. Articles appeared in the *Dublin Evening Post*, the *Freeman's Journal* and the *Hibernian Journal* in January 1783 pointing out the numerous anomalies in the Irish representation and stressing how vulnerable such absurdities rendered the gains of 1778–83. The whole panoply of 'rotten boroughs', 'pocket boroughs', non-resident voters, bizarre franchises, underrepresentation of the counties as opposed to the boroughs and general resentment at aristocratic domination was paraded in the public prints. The Volunteers, as ever, eager to pick up the ball and run with it, were soon calling for a more equal representation of the people in Parliament; and a convention to draw up a plan for parliamentary reform was scheduled to meet in Dublin on 10 November 1783.

Reaction in London to the Irish demand for parliamentary reform was intensely hostile. Portland, no longer chief governor, but now a self-proclaimed Irish expert, pronounced it 'high treason' even to suggest parliamentary reform in Ireland; the former prime minister, North, more restrained, spoke of 'insurmountable difficulties', while Fox claimed excitedly that if reform were conceded

'Ireland is irretrievably lost forever' and he forecast 'either a total separation or a civil war between us'. The new lord lieutenant, Northington, was, however, reassuring: he conceded that the proposed convention was a dangerous development but he was certain that because of the political incompatibity of those involved in reform, it would be in his power to 'perplex its proceedings and create confusion in its deliberations'. He was well aware of a certain nervousness, even among reformers, at the spectacle of the Volunteers, a paramilitary body, and now, with the American war over, a redundant one, seeking to perpetuate their importance by dictating to the elected representatives of the 'Irish nation' in the matter of parliamentary reform. Moreover, he could see that there were serious divisions between Flood and Grattan, and between Charlemont and the earl bishop of Derry, another Volunteer leader, on such matters as the content of the reform proposals and the strategy to be pursued in order to achieve them. Crucially, Northington recognised that the question of political rights for Irish Catholics, on its own, had the capacity to wreck the campaign for parliamentary reform.

The National Convention opened in Dublin on 10 November with appropriate ceremony and celebration. No business was transacted that day. The next day, George Ogle, an anti-Catholic firebrand and later a leading Orangeman – scarcely a person to be considered in the confidence of the Catholic leaders – announced that he had it on good authority that Irish Catholics did not lay claim to any share in the political process, that they did not seek the vote, much less seats in Parliament. The Catholic Committee some hours later dismissed Ogle's message as 'totally unknown and unauthorised by us'; but by then the damage had been done. With unseemly alacrity, the delegates, with but a few contrary voices, had seized on Ogle's statement and, with clear signs of relief, had resolved to exclude all consideration of Catholic claims from their discussions. Later in the week, following claim and counterclaim, the earl bishop delivered to the convention some resolutions of the Catholic Committee endorsing the claims of Catholics to participate in the reform programme, but these served only to heighten alarm among moderates and the question of Catholic eligibility was not reopened. The reform convention was palpably floundering.

At this critical juncture Henry Flood took command. He was adamant that Catholics could not with safety be given any political rights and he now stepped forward to galvanise the delegates into action. Within a few days, a very moderate series of reform proposals had been adopted under Flood's guidance. Formed by him into a parliamentary bill, it sought to bring about a tiny increase in the electorate – one estimate had it that no more than five hundred Protestants could benefit. There was also provision for the enlargement of the boundaries of decayed boroughs; three-year (instead of eight-year) Parliaments were provided for; and government office-holders were to be excluded from the House of Commons. There was no reference to Catholics. Flood, tactlessly dressed in his Volunteer uniform, quickly bore the bill to the Irish House of Commons and sought leave to introduce it. A noisy debate then ensued in which passions ran high: Irish Members, having recently won legislative independence, were not about to yield it up 'at the point of a bayonet' or sacrifice it to 'an armed assembly'. Leave to introduce the bill was denied by 158 votes to 49, the majority availing themselves of the opportunity to declare their 'perfect satisfaction' with the Constitution. Thus rebuffed, the reformers and the Volunteers were at a loss to know what to do next; having been accustomed to triumph, they had never given any thought to rejection.

A further National Congress was summoned for October 1784, but this met with a poor response for, by then, enthusiasm for reform (i.e. further failure) had fallen to a low ebb. There had been a decline in the number and, it was darkly alleged, the quality of the Volunteers over the previous year: certainly there were many more Catholics among their ranks; and this change in the composition of the patriot force caused nervousness. Again, a trade recession had provoked serious disturbances in Dublin and elsewhere and these further stiffened the resolve of those hostile to reform, and might indeed have frightened off some of the more moderate reformers. Dublin Castle's determination to play the 'Catholic card' in order to remind all right-thinking Protestants of the reality of the Catholic menace had its effect. Rumours of popish plots and French intrigues were shamelessly played up and circulated. Further disarray was caused by the public quarrels between those who supported Charlemont in his determination to exclude Catholics from all part in politics and those who, like the earl bishop, took the opposite point of view. Firm action by Dublin Castle also added to the reformers' discomfiture: William Sharman, a leading reformer, was dismissed from his post as collector at Lisburn; and John Fitzgibbon, newly appointed attorney general, and later to be a mainspring of union, threatened to prosecute those sheriffs who summoned a meeting to elect delegates to a national congress.

The Congress of October 1784 broke up having accomplished little; as Thomas Orde, the chief secretary, explained, 'the reason is plainly to be found in the jarring interests of religion and property'. By the end of 1784 the only hope for parliamentary reform in Ireland lay in its success in England where William Pitt, the prime minister since late 1783, was on record as being a keen supporter. Constitutionally, Ireland may have been a sister kingdom, with, in theory, an equal legislature; but practical politics dictated that the greater country should lead and the lesser follow. When Pitt's bill went down to defeat in the British House of Commons in April 1785 it really killed any chance reform had in Ireland.

The Irish reform movement failed, first, because the vested interests in the Irish Parliament were too well entrenched. The great parliamentary families of Shannon, Ponsonby, Ely, Leinster and Devonshire (and a host of lesser fry) had backed legislative independence because it had cost nothing, would render them 'popular' and might even enhance the price of their boroughs: but parliamentary reform threatened both their political 'interests' and their pockets, and was therefore to be resisted. Self-interest joined with wider political calculation to engender caution, for the results of parliamentary reform were literally incalculable. In addition, as we have seen, the British government, and British politicians of all parties, were unalterably opposed to reform in Ireland, foreseeing enormous problems if the Irish Parliament were freed from aristocratic control and made more popular. English political control in Ireland, already diminished by the 'Constitution of 1782', would be further weakened by a widening of the boundaries of the Irish political nation. Parliamentary management, despite the adjustment of 1782, was still the prime duty of the lord lieutenant and his chief secretary and it would be rendered well-nigh impossible if parliamentary reform were conceded, as both current and previous holders of these offices constantly proclaimed. These reasons – internal opposition from powerful interests, external resistance to reform in Ireland – go some way towards explaining the failure of parliamentary reform; but the key reason may be located elsewhere.

The reform movement in Ireland did not succeed either in mobilising public opinion, or in generating anything like the pressure necessary to win concessions. It never acquired the status of a national demand and the reason for this is evident. The Catholic question, wrote George Tandy, a leading Dublin reformer, was 'the rock we have split on'; the Catholic question, echoed Dr William Drennan, a leading Belfast reformer, 'was our ruin'. Both were right. The exclusion of Catholics from the reform proposals, the unseemly haste with which Ogle's 'message' was acted upon, the resolute refusal to contemplate enlisting the Catholics' support in the campaign, all combined to render the movement for parliamentary reform a sectarian demand by a minority interest. The Catholic Relief Acts of 1779 and 1782 had brought the Catholics into the political arena, and though still voteless in elections as well as seatless in the legislature, Catholics could no longer be ignored and it was an act of folly for the reformers to attempt to do so. Shorn of Catholic support, the agitation for reform could always be dismissed as sectional, sectarian, partial, interested or the product of envy, frustration and resentment. With Catholic support, it could not have been other than national. This conclusion was the central one drawn by reformers when, some years later, and under the inspiration of the French Revolution, they set out once again to campaign for parliamentary reform. The origins of the Society of United Irishmen of 1791 are thus to be properly located in the lessons learnt from the debacle of the earlier reform movement. In 1785, however, reform was a lost cause in Ireland.

In the event, those Irish politicians who had argued that parliamentary reform was not necessary were to an extent vindicated by the stout defence which the Irish Parliament now offered in its opposition to Pitt's wide-ranging proposals for a commercial and defensive treaty in 1785. Just as the Irish Parliament had refused to be intimidated by the Volunteers, so too it refused to be browbeaten by Pitt and his agents. Perhaps the legislative independence of the Irish Parliament was going to mean something after all?

Orde's commercial propositions, 1785

At the time of the concessions that constituted the 'Constitution of 1782', there had been much discussion among British and Irish politicians about the need to conclude a precise treaty between the two countries in order to reaffirm Anglo-Irish union. On the British side few doubted that some such arrangement was necessary to preserve 'the remaining connection between [Ireland and Britain]'. The opportunity for such a 'final adjustment' came in late 1784. John Beresford and John Foster, respectively chief commissioner of the Irish Revenue Board and chancellor of the Irish exchequer, were anxious to expand Ireland's trade by winning fresh concessions from, and confirming old ones with, Britain in the area of Anglo-Irish trade. To that end, they sought permission for Ireland to re-export British colonial goods to Britain itself. Additionally, they wanted an equalisation of duties at the lowest level between Ireland and Britain, a guarantee that Irish linen would remain duty free into Britain and an agreement that while bounties on exports would be discontinued those on Irish corn (Foster's brainchild) would be retained and that Irish corn would enjoy a preference in the British market.

William Pitt, for his part, had long been impressed with the desirability of putting the Anglo-Irish relationship on a new, firmer footing. However, his plans, though never wholly formulated, were much wider in scope than those of Foster and Beresford and ranged in their concerns from the imperial to the local. There were three distinct elements to his policy: parliamentary reform in Ireland on a Protestant basis; the substitution of an Irish Protestant militia for the religiously promiscuous Volunteers; and finally, an imperial treaty which would both reaffirm Britain's sovereignity and fix (Foster preferred 'rivet') Ireland's position within the empire. What Pitt appears to have been aiming at was a junction of the Protestant interest in Ireland with that in Britain. This united Protestant front would then set its face resolutely against the demands of Irish Catholics (and possibly Irish Presbyterians) while bidding defiance to those

Catholic powers (France and Spain) which had tilted the balance against Britain in the American war.

Before any of this could be accomplished, however, Pitt accepted that a commercial arrangement with Ireland, loosely based on that proposed by Foster, should be undertaken. Pitt's scheme was wider than Foster's, embracing commerce certainly, but also bringing in both constitutional and defence points not included in the original proposal. Specifically, Pitt maintained that the constitutional connection between Ireland and England would be strengthened immeasurably by Ireland agreeing to pay a defined annual contribution towards imperial naval charges. To this end, Foster's original scheme, against his wishes, was expanded during discussions in London with Pitt and his advisers, and ten propositions were submitted to the Irish Parliament in February 1785 for its consideration. Here an opposition conducted by Grattan was mounted, the ten propositions were increased to eleven, and two important amendments were made, again contrary to Foster's wishes. These gave Ireland, first, a greater say in how its contribution towards naval charges would be spent, and second, they provided that Ireland need not make any contribution at all in time of peace unless its budget balanced.

These resolutions on their arrival in London immediately, and predictably, came under fire. Commercial interests, ably orchestrated by members of the parliamentary opposition to Pitt, protested against the generosity of the provisions and forecast ruin for themselves if they passed into law. Pitt himself was aghast at the provision that no contribution would be made unless the Irish budget balanced and he moved to have that struck out. He further insisted on widening the scope of the provisions to bring in general imperial matters. In the face of commercial clamour and ministerial misgivings the eleven propositions now expanded to twenty. What had begun life as a modest Anglo-Irish trade arrangement had now taken on the character of an elaborate imperial treaty, complete with defence and constitutional provisions. Britain's position as general superintendent of the empire was to be copperfastened in the most resounding way.

The twenty British resolutions, as Foster had warned, elicited a storm of protest on their arrival in Ireland and were denounced in a series of addresses as being destructive of the Constitution as well as the trade of Ireland. In the Irish Parliament, where the proposals had been cast in the form of a bill in August 1785, opposition soon centred on the implications for Ireland's legislative independence if the proposals passed. In particular, the fourth proposition quickly gained notoriety, for it demanded that the Irish Parliament should agree to enact in the future whatever trade laws were passed in the Parliament of Great Britain. Much of the criticism directed at the bill or indeed at the twenty resolutions on which it was loosely based was ill conceived and ill informed. Grattan in particular made a fool of himself by revealing his lack of understanding of commercial matters; and other hostile speakers were scarcely better briefed. None the less, in the debates on the commercial propositions cogent argument was swept away by lofty rhetoric, and those who spoke in favour of the measure were drowned out by patriotic oratory. The solid commercial advantages of the plan were ignored while the threat to Irish legislative independence was highlighted. In the vote, the result was so close that Dublin Castle had to consider it a defeat, and the bill was withdrawn.

The failure of the commercial propositions was significant. It was first, a humiliating rebuff for Pitt, exposing him as politically naive and as a poor judge of the mood of Irish politicians. Moreover, he felt this rejection deeply and thereafter had scant regard for Irish politicians, or their vaunted 'Constitution of 1782'. Second, Pitt was confirmed in his view that the 'mutual faith and understanding' that Foster had claimed to be the new basis of the Anglo-Irish relationship was well-nigh worthless. By 1785 Pitt was perhaps as hostile towards 'the Constitution of 1782' as the most uncompromising Irish reformer. Third, the collapse of the commercial propositions inevitably meant an end to those more grandiose schemes involving a possible parliamentary reform and the formation of a Protestant militia which he had at one time contemplated for Ireland. Parliamentary reform – on a Protestant basis only – had, perhaps, never been likely, if only because Dublin Castle had set its face against it; but the proposed Protestant militia to absorb the Volunteers had been regarded by Dublin Castle as highly desirable. In the aftermath of the 'defeat' on the commercial propositions, there would be no imperial treaty and there could be no Irish Protestant militia and no parliamentary reform. Pitt's defeat over the commercial propositions meant that the anomalous, ambiguous and dangerously vague relationship between England and Ireland would remain unreformed and that the much sought-after 'final adjustment' would continue to prove elusive.

Finally, it was noted that in the various debates on the commercial propositions the idea of 'an Union' (as contemporaries had it) was brought into the open for the first time. Lord North, for example, protested in the British House of Commons that the commercial privileges to be offered to Ireland should have accompanied a union between the two countries. Grattan, too, took up this point but, for his part, he denounced Pitt's commercial proposal as, in effect, a covert union, claiming in debate that it was nothing but 'an incipient and a creeping Union: a virtual Union', and concluding that, in opposing the bill, he considered himself to be voting against 'an Union'. It would be wrong to say that from this point on Pitt worked for a parliamentary union, but equally it is clear that union was now on the political agenda of both countries, that it had its spokesmen and that its merits were openly canvassed. In any discussion of the origins of the Act of Union, this move from private space to public forum, a shift that occurred during discussion of the commercial propositions, has to be given prominence.

The next controversy to upset Anglo-Irish relations, the so-called regency crisis of 1788, further prompted a discussion of the merits or otherwise of union. The details of this 'crisis' need not detain us. George III was pronounced deranged in October 1788 and a regent was to be appointed during what was hoped would be a short incapacity. Matters were initially complicated by the fact that the obvious candidate for regent, George's son, the prince of Wales, was a firm friend of Pitt's leading rival, Charles James Fox. Pitt therefore proposed that the prince be appointed, though with restricted powers; Fox agreed with the appointment, but understandably was opposed to the condition of restricted powers. Matters were further complicated when the Irish Parliament sought to intervene in the wrangle over the regent's powers. A new prime minister in England, a likely consequence of the prince of Wales succeeding his father with full powers, was bound to result in a new lord lieutenant in Ireland, and those Irish politicians who were close to Fox – such as Grattan and the Ponsonbys – were expected to profit from this change. In addition, George III was also king of Ireland and the appointment of a regent was held to fall within the Irish Parliament's powers; hence, intervening in this matter would assert Irish legislative independence in the most unmistakable manner. As a result, Irish politicians surged towards what they thought would be the winning side and, casting caution to the winds, passed an address calling on the prince to take up his responsibilities with unrestricted powers. A small parliamentary delegation was sent off to bring this missive to the prince in person (the lord lieutenant had refused to convey it through the normal channel), but soon after the delegates' arrival in London, George III recovered his wits and the 'crisis' was over. The whole affair, commented W. W. Grenville, an English politician, had been 'the most absurd and ridiculous farce'. Farce or not, a degree of significance attaches to the episode, for it once again demonstrated to Pitt the flawed nature of the 'Constitution of 1782' and it confirmed his worst fears about the unpredictability of the 'giddy' Irish Parliament.

John Fitzgibbon, later earl of Clare and lord chancellor of Ireland, had been one of the few to stand their ground when others – dubbed the 'Regency rats' by the lord lieutenant, Buckingham – had rushed to jump on the prince's bandwagon, and he had endorsed Pitt's reading of the situation. Fitzgibbon was convinced that the Irish Parliament's intervention into the regency debate had actually undermined the common monarchy which had provided a hitherto unchallengeable bond between the two countries. What would have happened, mused Fitzgibbon, if the Irish Parliament had chosen someone other than the candidate of the British Parliament – a member of the Stuart family, say – for the position of regent? The conclusion was clear: because of Irish assertiveness during the regency crisis, an independent Irish Parliament and the 'Constitution of 1782' could now be seen as a threat to the connection. By 1789 'the dear ties of love and mutual affection' and the security offered by a common king had been shown to be quite insufficient to keep the Anglo-Irish relationship on a secure footing. By that date, and largely as a result of the failure – in every way – to reform the 'Constitution of 1782', not only was 'an Union' on the agenda but the danger of separation had been revealed. Finally, by that date the sectarianisation of Irish society was well under way and it is to this ominous development – so much at odds with the spirit of 1782 – that we now turn.

Ascendancy defined

Serious agrarian disturbances had broken out in the province of Munster in the mid-1780s and they had proved difficult to suppress. These disturbances and the demands for tithe reform which they gave rise to sparked off a confused and acrimonious discussion on the nature of the Irish state, the role of the Church of Ireland within that state and, in effect, the composition of the Irish nation. The ensuing debate revealed clearly not only the ambiguous nature of the 'Constitution of 1782' but also the deep-seated anxieties that would do so much to undermine that arrangement.

The agrarian disturbances that occurred in the 1780s were by no means unprecedented. Indeed, at various times from the 1690s on there had been agrarian unrest (notably in Connacht during the years 1711 to 1712) but with the outbreak of the Whiteboy disturbances in 1761, agrarian unrest became endemic in Ireland, and from the 1760s through to the end of the nineteenth century and beyond the country was never to be entirely clear of the phenomenon of 'Whiteboyism', the generic (if misleading) title given to all rural disturbances.

The Whiteboys had risen first in county Tipperary towards the end of 1761 and their protests were directed primarily at the enclosure of commonage in the county and at the exactions of tithe-farmers and tithe proctors. The fencing-off of common fields for grazing purposes meant that such lands could not be used for tillage cultivation and this caused anger, particularly among the local labourers and cottiers who had relied on access to commonage in order to improve their modest lot. Inevitably, other grievances were quickly aired and wage rates, food prices and levels of tithe were denounced.

Tithe was a charge on the produce of the land levied annually and payable by all farmers to the clergy of the Church of Ireland. Perhaps tithe had been of small importance at one time: but as the Irish population increased from the mid-decades of the eighteenth century and as more and more land was brought under cultivation so more and more people found themselves paying tithe. Curiously, there seems to have been little resentment at the fact that tithe was a tax payable by a largely Catholic peasantry in support of the clergy of the established church. Instead, anger was directed at the amount of tithe and at the many anomalies in its application. Hostility was especially directed at tithe-farmers (individuals, usually laymen and often Catholics, who purchased the right to tithe from the local rector for a fixed sum of money) and tithe proctors (agents of tithe-farmers or of the clergyman who assessed the produce for tithe and collected it). A tithe-farmer, claimed Henry Grattan, was, first and foremost, 'an adventurer' or speculator, and the tithe proctor got his profit by his shilling in the pound on what he had levied; in neither case was there any visible connection between levying tithe and promoting religion.

The Whiteboy agitation rumbled on through the 1760s and into the 1770s, spreading from Tipperary into Kilkenny and beyond. There were attacks on tithe-farmers and proctors, and ditches were levelled, walls knocked down and some cattle were killed. Wage rates and food prices were posted in prominent places by the insurgents and those who refused to comply might expect a nocturnal visit. While undoubtedly serious, the Whiteboy movement was never formidable: a number of tithe proctors suffered humiliating punishments, some were whipped or mutilated, but relatively few people were killed. The movement had no ostensible political content and nor was there any attack on landlordism or even on the principle of tithe itself. Despite the efforts of some of the Protestant gentry of Munster, determined to find 'French gold' behind a new 'popish plot', Dublin Castle and the military authorities were not deceived. Judicial repression was moderate, although eight men were executed for the slaying of two soldiers during an attempted rescue of prisoners in 1765. On one occasion, however, matters got out of hand: Father Nicholas Sheehy, reputedly a Whiteboy leader and certainly 'outspoken, socially committed', as Sean Connolly has described him, suffered what amounted to 'assassination by legal process' in 1766. This case revealed the tensions seething beneath the apparently placid surface of Irish provincial life. Four years later, Sheehy's executioner was himself stoned to death by a large crowd.

Agrarian protest was not a prerogative of the Catholics. In the 1760s the Presbyterian Oak Boys of Armagh protested against the levying of county cess, or tax, for the purpose of improving internal communications: since they never went anywhere, they claimed, why should they pay for better roads and bridges? And in the early 1770s there was trouble on the Templepatrick, county Antrim, estate of the bankrupt absentee landlord, the earl of Donegall. What these disturbances revealed was that between Presbyterian tenants in Ulster and Catholic labourers and cottiers in Munster combustible material was plentiful in the Irish countryside. They also indicated that, whatever may have been the proximate cause of the initial protest, grievances over tithe quickly came to prominence. Reassuringly, the 'insurgents' appeared to have no political agenda (the Whiteboys' predilection for Jacobite tunes hardly constituted a threat to the dynasty) nor did they enjoy leadership from among the rural elite, Protestant or Catholic. By and large, the authorities viewed these disturbances simply as protests, and sometimes they voiced sympathy with the protestors, though not with their actions. In general, the low level of violence employed by the Whiteboys and others tended to be matched by a certain circumspection on the part of those charged with repressing them. That said, neither of the sister kingdoms of Scotland and England were to witness anything comparable to the agrarian insurgency in Ireland, and the endemic nature of Irish 'Whiteboyism' throughout the nineteenth century contributed mightily to the image and reputation of Ireland as a savage, lawless country.

The depredations of the Whiteboys had not prompted a debate on their activities but those of the Rightboys of the 1780s did, and a 'paper war' erupted as to the meaning and significance of Irish rural violence. During this pamphlet debate there was heard, at first uncertainly and then, perhaps, more confidently a new watchword which ever since has come to sum up the rule of the English in Ireland in the long eighteenth century. By the end of the 1780s that 'Irish nation' which had won the 'Constitution of 1782', as if startled (and perhaps threatened) by success, had begun to appreciate the merits of provincial dominance and appeared ready to retreat behind the buckler of 'Protestant ascendancy'.

At first glance, the Rightboys appeared to have been cut from the same cloth as the Whiteboys and it was, in fact, common for contemporaries to refer to the followers of 'Captain Right' as Whiteboys. This confusion is understandable. Like the Whiteboys of the 1760s and 1770s, the Rightboys stressed their adherence to a code of behaviour that had general rather than local applicability. Again, few of their grievances were new. True, they protested at the high fees demanded by their own Catholic priests for sick visits, baptisms, funerals and marriages, and such grievances were new; but their complaints about the levels of tithe, rents, wages and prices had been heard before and would come up again in the future. Moreover, they had in common with the Whiteboys a low level of violence, limited aims (a reduction was sought in tithe, though not its abolition) and a localised area of operation. And yet, despite these similarities, there were important differences between the Whiteboys and the Rightboys and it was these, and the different contexts within which each acted, that produced the crisis of 1785 to 1788.

In the first instance, the Rightboys, unlike the Whiteboys, were reasonably effective in pursuit of their aims: certainly the Catholic church heeded their protests and published lists of lower fees for administering the sacraments. Crucially, the Rightboys appear to have been broad church in their social composition. In the Whiteboy agitation, farmers and graziers had generally been cast as enemies of the insurgents, but in the Rightboy movement social divisions were to an extent bridged, and the landed, the landless and even some Protestant gentry took part. 'Estated gentlemen' or 'gentlemen Rightboys' played an important role during the Rightboy disturbances, providing leadership and direction but also, by their presence, introducing a worrying element of division into what had hitherto been a united Protestant response to rural disorder. With clear signs that the Rightboy grievances over tithe were viewed sympathetically by some Members of the Irish Parliament, senior members of the Church of Ireland, apparently friendless and seemingly beleaguered, resolved to fight back by identifying the fortunes of the established church with the future stability of the Protestant state. There were encouraging signs that such a campaign might prove effective.

The rise of the Volunteers, the winning of the 'Constitution of 1782', the passing of Catholic Relief Acts and the successful rebuff to Pitt's commercial propositions had, no doubt, been exciting developments, flattering to Protestant pride; but they had also been productive of anxiety for the future. This anxiety stemmed from a consciousness that the political structure in Ireland was shifting at about the same time that the Anglo-Irish relationship was being reconfigured. The rapid growth of the Volunteers was both a symptom of, and an agent for, further change. The Volunteers had drawn on a long tradition of Protestant self-help, but the force, as noted, was ultimately a destabilising one in Irish politics. Moreover, the Volunteers had since 1782, and even before, begun to enlist Catholics into their ranks, and with the open enlistment of members of that religion into the British army and the East India Company army Protestant anxieties about the future were further fuelled. The right to bear arms was a key attribute of full citizenship, and so too was service in the armed forces. For these reasons they were highly prized Protestant privileges. However, Catholics carrying muskets – formally or informally – challenged both of these prerogatives, and revived historically potent images. In county Armagh this issue of Catholics bearing arms was one cause of the sectarian feuding that broke out in the late 1780s, and which by 1795 saw the emergence of both the Orange Order and the Defender movement. Here, as in other areas, the old order was clearly changing.

The rapid progress of the Catholic question especially gave cause for concern if not yet for alarm. Almost all religious restrictions on Catholics or on their acquiring landed property had been removed but, while there may have been a general welcome from Protestants for these concessions, there was by no means unanimity among them about the next step. Serious divisions existed among Protestants concerning political rights for Catholics, and these disagreements had crippled the movement for parliamentary reform. There was, however, no sign that the Catholic question would go away; indeed, the opposite, for there was every indication that the issue of political rights for Catholics would never rest. Parliamentary independence was, no doubt, very welcome and snubs to the British were no doubt exhilarating; but there was every chance that Catholics would press Protestants to act on the libertarian rhetoric of 1782 and admit them to the 'Irish nation'. As well, there was every danger that the British, seemingly rejected by the Irish Protestant, might seek an ally in the Irish Catholic. Then again, rogue elements within Protestant Ireland – and the Rightboy protest had shown that these existed – might side with the Catholics (whether for electoral advantage, or in the interests of justice, it made no difference). Irish Presbyterians, too, might be persuaded to make common cause with the Catholics. In short, the unanswered questions of 1782 – In whose interest was the arrangement made? What was the Irish nation? – would continue to be posed – a most disturbing prospect.

Protestant anxieties in this respect were further heightened in the late 1780s by a number of unsettling developments. There were, for example, a number of applications from Catholics for ancestral outlawries dating back many decades to be reversed. Even more disconcerting, some Catholics, believing that the penal era was now closed, began to petition Dublin Castle for some or all of the land forfeited by their ancestors to be returned to them. There were reports in 1786 that a certain Chevalier O'Gorman, an Irish officer in the French service, was 'now in Ireland collecting accounts of Irish estates of which the Roman Catholics were dispossessed in the time of Cromwell and at the Revolution'; and Charles Vallancey, a noted, if eccentric, antiquarian professed alarm that the French had allegedly obtained copies of the records of the Irish forfeited estates for the Bibliothèque royale in Paris. On at least one occasion, there was a resort to direct action. In January 1786, Roderick O'Connor, self-styled 'king of Connaught', repossessed certain estates in county Roscommon which his ancestors had forfeited in the seventeenth century. He was quickly driven out, and while the incident had its comic side, the amount of public and private comment that it attracted suggests that it had touched a nerve. Dublin Castle, seeing advantage in heightening Protestant fears, soon uncovered French gold behind Irish disturbances, and there were stories of French officers and spies hiding out in Munster. It was into this already very fevered arena that Bishop Richard Woodward pitched his pamphlet, *The Present State of the Church of Ireland*, towards the end of 1786.

Woodward sought to arouse Protestants in Ireland to a keen sense of the danger which he was persuaded both their church and their state faced from the Whiteboys. He began by dismissing as groundless the charge that tithe oppressed the poor, he denounced the Rightboys as being in the tradition of the rebels of 1641, and he accused the Catholic authorities of conniving at the protest (conveniently ignoring the fact that some of the Rightboy protest was directed at the Catholic priests). He then proceeded to identify what he saw as the key issue: the Irish Constitution and the established church must rise and fall together. To Woodward, the matter was plain: an attack on the established church presaged an attack on the Protestant state. The Rightboys, with their anti-tithe protest, were preliminary to an attack on the link with England, the land settlement and ultimately general liberty.

Woodward's pamphlet sparked off a controversy that raged for the next twelve months and elicited some ninety publications bearing on his theme or on aspects of it. Both Catholic and Presbyterian writers made vigorous responses, for the day was long gone when Catholics would lie down and Dissenters would fall into line when the Church of Ireland cracked the whip. The Capuchin priest, Arthur O'Leary, and the Presbyterian divine, William Campbell took up their pens and, respectively, stressed Catholic loyalty and disputed the sole identification of the interests of the established church with those of the state. It was also noticeable that the term 'Protestant ascendancy' (variously capitalised and spelt) made an intermittent appearance in this debate, being mentioned some nine times by Woodward himself, and being picked up by an occasional supporter and critic.

The use of this term revealed an edgy nervousness at the way matters appeared to be moving beyond the control of the Church of Ireland and its appearance was a product of Protestant anxiety rather than of confidence, a symptom of a loss of mastery. 'Protestant ascendancy' might have sounded like a call to arms, but in fact it tolled the retreat. Since the Jacobite wars, if not before, Irish Protestants had been in the ascendancy and therefore there had been no need to devise or conceptualise the term. By the 1780s, however, in the face of the rise of the Catholic question and growing British disenchantment with Irish Protestants, the invention of the war-cry of ascendancy instead revealed a growing powerlessness – a search for the last ditch and an increasing willingness to exchange nationhood for it. The term's coinage in the mid-1780s, its circulation (however limited) later on, and then its currency in the 1790s, and beyond, marked a doubtful progress for the one-time 'whole people of Ireland'. Later, the concept would suffer further attenuation by being restricted to a social, even territorial elite. 'Drawing a line round the constitution', as John Foster described his policy of resistance to Catholic claims, proved preliminary to putting a corral around the 'Big House'. As the 1780s closed with news of stirring events in Paris, and with the term 'The

French Revolution' in the public prints, Irish Protestants could reflect on the many achievements of that decade; but there had been missed opportunities too, and many questions remained unresolved to dominate the tumultuous 1790s.

We cannot conclude from this that by 1789 the 'Constitution of 1782' was doomed to failure: hindsight can magnify its weaknesses, and while 'an Union' might have been desired by Pitt and others, it is fair to say that no one had the slightest idea that it was within the realms of practical politics. Moreover, if we move away from the major political battles of these years a case can be made for claiming that on a day-to-day, routine basis the arrangement of 1782 seemed to be functioning satisfactorily. True, Irish bills continued to be sent over to Britain for the royal assent, and these were still examined and reported on by a legal committee of the English privy council. But there were now none of those emendations, designed to proclaim British legislative superiority, which had been a feature of the pre-1782 period. Again, the number of bills respited, usually for poor draftsmanship (in practice the only option left to the privy council) was few and none was of any consequence.

Finally, a preoccupation with crisis in the Anglo-Irish parliamentary world has meant that the solid legislative achievements of the 1780s have been frequently ignored. A Corn Law was passed that proved effective in attracting corn imports into Ireland in time of scarcity; most of the trade concessions on offer in 1785 were gained piecemeal over the next ten years; and notable pieces of legislation, far in advance of anything in England, dealing with the treatment of lunacy and disease, the running of prisons and the provision of sanitation were passed by the Irish Parliament during the 1780s. Among those prominent in these 'good works' were such figures as John Foster, John Fitzgibbon, Sir John Blaquiere and John Beresford, none of whom have generally been noted for their philanthrophic endeavours. Perhaps the very complexity of political reform in an Irish context, for it could not be tackled without bringing up the Catholic question, may have encouraged such 'men of business' to shun it and instead take up social issues.

As the 1780s drew to a close with exciting news of political change in France, the verdict on the performance of the 'Constitution of 1782' thus far was a mixed one. Useful legislation had been put through, Pitt's challenge to Irish constitutional integrity (however exaggerated) had been seen off and so too had the threat posed by the Volunteers' demand for parliamentary reform. But there were also failures and these were to become crucial in the revolutionary decade. There had been no attempt to make the Irish government responsible to the Irish Parliament; nor had there been any move on parliamentary reform to make the Irish Parliament more popular and less dependent on the executive. Crucially, there had been no approach to the Catholics who continued to look firmly to the British government as their protectors. The handful of years after

1782 had offered a space within which to address these issues; but no such period of leisure was to be available in the 1790s, a decade of revolution and war abroad, and conspiracy and insurrection at home. As the Irish Parliament, under the dispensation of 1782, turned the corner into the new decade it was poorly equipped to meet the coming challenges.

II: DESCENDANCY, 1790–1830

Introduction

The 1790s were to prove the crucial decade in the making of modern Ireland.[9] During these years Irish republicanism became equated with separatism, and republican separatism, in origin the 'invention' of Irish Protestants, was to become almost wholly identified with Irish Catholics. During the 1790s armed insurrection in collaboration with a foreign power once more became established as a key weapon in the armoury of Irish revolutionaries. The decade also witnessed the beginnings of Irish and British Unionism and the emergence of a militant loyalism ably mobilised by the Orange Order. Lastly, the conclusion to that decade was profoundly and doubly ironic: first, the separatist impulse and the attempt to seize the republican moment led to Ireland being bound closer than ever to England through an Act of Union; and second, the hopes of those who at the beginning of the decade had dreamed of creating 'an Union of creeds', and substituting 'the common name of Irishman' for the then current sectarian labels of papist, Protestant and Dissenter had it seemed by 1800 perished in sectarian mayhem and bloody civil war. We may begin our examination of this tumultuous decade with the setting up of the Society of United Irishmen in Belfast in October 1791.

The United Irishmen, 1791–4

Within a matter of weeks of the opening of the States-General in Paris in May 1789 the term 'the French Revolution' had begun to make an appearance in Irish newspapers and throughout the country. Especially in Belfast and Dublin those groups who had previously been in favour of political reform drew inspiration and encouragement from the unfolding of the stirring events in France. In July 1790 the Volunteers, hitherto moribund, had marched to celebrate not the battle of the Boyne but the fall of the Bastille and in Belfast there was much talk of new clubs and new alliances. In October 1790 the lord lieutenant, Westmorland, had come into possession of a document entitled 'The Belfast Constitutional Compact', which consisted of a series of resolutions calling on Presbyterians and Catholics to make common cause against 'extorting tithe-mongers and ecclesiastical plunderers' and pledging support for the Catholics' 'just claim to the enjoyment of the rights and privileges of freeborn citizens'. This preliminary intelligence of a potential alliance between Catholics and Dissenters appeared to be confirmed during the summer of 1791, when Westmorland drew attention to a pamphlet circulating in Belfast and Dublin concerning 'the establishment of a Brotherhood'. He pronounced this to be 'a very dangerous paper'.

This discussion document was the work of Dr William Drennan, the Belfast-born but Dublin-resident Presbyterian enthusiast for reform, and it prepared the way for a club to be set up in Belfast in October 1791 (and in Dublin a month later) entitled the Society of United Irishmen. From studying the reasons for the failure of reform in the early 1780s, Drennan had reluctantly concluded that parliamentary reform in Ireland would always prove elusive until Irish Catholics were brought to lend their weight and numbers to the campaign. This marked a notable shift in his attitude. At the time of the reform agitation he had been one of those convinced that Catholics were unfit for political liberty but now in his proposal for a reform club entitled 'the Brotherhood' he had clearly had second thoughts. In his view the only conclusion to be drawn from the earlier failure was that reform without the Catholics stood no chance whatsoever of success.

At about the same time as Drennan was contemplating a new reform society, Theobald Wolfe Tone, a young Dublin barrister and a member of the Church of Ireland, was addressing himself to the question of the role of Irish Catholics in the new push for parliamentary reform. In a remarkable pamphlet, *An Argument on behalf of the Catholics of Ireland*, published in August 1791, he maintained that not only were Catholics capable of liberty but that there could be no liberty for anyone in Ireland, until 'Irishmen of all denominations' had banded together 'against the boobies and blockheads' that governed them and demanded parliamentary reform. Tone's *Argument* had a wide impact: it quickly ran through a number of editions and it was disseminated widely – even Westmorland read it and passed it on to his masters in London. More important, its publication led to Tone being invited to Belfast, the capital of Presbyterian Ulster, to attend the inaugural meeting of the new society that Drennan had called for. Once in Belfast, Tone took charge, suggesting the name of the new society – the United Irishmen – and composing its key resolutions, calling for the destruction of English influence in Irish government by means of a union of all the people, maintaining that this could only be accomplished through a thorough-going parliamentary reform and claiming that no such reform could be 'practicable, efficacious, or just', which did not include Catholics.

Tone's pamphlet made an impact because it was relentlessly realistic, both in its reasons for the failure of the previous reform movement and in its signposting the way forward. He argued that the much vaunted 'Constitution of 1782' was grossly defective and had merely resulted in increased 'corruption' in the Irish Parliament. Directly addressing the question of the Catholics' capacity for liberty, Tone concluded on the basis of events in France that Catholics could, in fact, be trusted. 'Look at France', he urged his readers, 'where is the intolerance of popish bigotry now?' Had not the pope been burned in effigy in Paris? Who would now attend to the 'rusty and extinguished thunderbolts of the Vatican?' Moreover, in pointing to the 200,000 French Catholics who had elected the Protestant, St Etienne, to the National Assembly meeting in Paris, Tone was consciously appealing to a strong prophetic or millenarian strain in Irish Presbyterianism by encouraging the belief that the extraordinary events in France – the downfall of the most Catholic monarchy of the most Catholic country in the world through the agency of Catholics themselves – heralded nothing less than the imminent downfall of the pope, and even of international Catholicism itself. The question about the Catholics' capacity for liberty had been clearly answered: if French Catholics could promote liberty then so too could Irish Catholics. Irish Presbyterians, for their part, were being invited, through their participation in an alliance with Irish Catholics, to be part of God's plan as revealed in the collapse of the Catholic monarchy of France.

However, if this was the essence of Tone's appeal for the Dissenters, for Catholics it was all rather different, and there can be no doubt that an alliance along the lines proposed by Tone could hardly be other than extremely problematic. In the first instance Presbyterians had ever been the most implacable enemies of Catholics and Catholicism, historically far more hostile than the members of the established church. Indeed, part of the scorn which Dissenters had for Churchmen stemmed from their belief that the Church of Ireland espoused a sort of low-tension Catholicism. Much history would have to be repressed before a genuine alliance could take place. More than this, however, Catholics were well aware of how shabbily they had been treated in the recent past by the Presbyterian reformers of the early 1780s. These latter, it will be recalled, had made overtures to Irish Catholics in 1782 at their Dungannon meeting of Volunteer delegates; but then at the later reform conventions they had dumped them. In short, the reformers – Presbyterians foremost among them – had let the Catholics down in the 1780s; why should Catholics trust them now? And then, of course, there was the British government which for a generation had been the object of Irish Catholics' prayers and addresses. Indeed, the credit for previous Catholic relief measures had been claimed by the British government, for it had urged a reluctant Dublin Castle to undertake them and had pushed them through a lethargic, often hostile Irish Parliament. Why should Irish Catholics run the risk of sacrificing the goodwill of the British government by entering into an alliance with those whose capacity to deliver on their promises was questionable, or with those whose very bona fides were suspect? At the same time it was obvious that certain tactical advantages could be won by the Catholics if they or their leaders could impress upon the British government that only through the granting of significant concessions could the threat posed to English government in Ireland by the proposed Catholic–Dissenter alliance be averted.

This was the argument used most forcefully and frequently by the secretary of the Catholic Committee, Richard Burke (son of the Irish-born English statesman, Edmund Burke) during the years 1791–2 and, undoubtedly, it had an effect on the British government and through the government on Dublin Castle. Time after time members of the British government sought to impress upon a sceptical Dublin Castle administration the danger posed by an alliance of Catholic and Presbyterian reformers and the necessity to head off any such junction through substantial and immediate concessions to Irish Catholics. The outbreak of war on the continent in 1792 and the near certainty that Britain would be drawn in (duly confirmed in January 1793 when France declared war on Britain and Ireland) lent an added urgency to concession. Timely relief for Irish Catholics would, it was argued, help construct a coalition of those unalterably opposed to all that the French Revolution was held to represent. Concessions to Irish Catholics would also significantly promote the war effort. From the outbreak of hostilities, Irish Catholic manpower was targeted both for recruitment to the armed forces of the crown and to defend Ireland. For these reasons in the years 1792 to 1793 British ministers displayed an impatience with the 'panics and apprehensions' of Dublin Castle and of Irish Protestant politicians with regard to concessions to Irish Catholics.

In 1792 a minor Catholic Relief Act was put through the Irish Parliament but a year later a much more substantial one was enacted. This gave Irish Catholics the vote in county elections on the same terms as Irish Protestants (and ultimately made possible Daniel O'Connell's victory in the struggle for Catholic emancipation in 1828). It was no coincidence that the 1793 Catholic Relief Act was accompanied by another piece of legislation setting up an Irish militia some twenty thousand strong of which Irish Catholics would form the overwhelming majority. Having gained the vote, Irish Catholics were now expected to defend Ireland.

Concessions to Irish Catholics were central to the British government's (less so Dublin Castle's) strategy for dealing with the threat posed by United Irishmen and their campaign for parliamentary reform. As before, any reform of Parliament was ruled out on grounds of political expediency but, additionally, the United

Irish demand was denounced as merely a ruse to disguise a much more subversive plan – the total separation of Ireland from England. A letter written by Tone had fallen into the authorities' hands and in it he had, in fact, expressed approval for separation. His remarks were much cited as an expression of the 'real' sentiments of so-called Irish reformers.

In pursuit of their stated goal of a parliamentary reform that would include Catholics, the United Irishmen determined to use those instruments that had earlier proved serviceable in the winning of the 'Constitution of 1782'. Thus they planned to mobilise the Volunteers once more and they determined to convene reform conventions on the model of the Dungannon convention of 1782. In addition, they planned to propagate their cause through the medium of print. To that end, a newspaper, the *Northern Star*, was set up in Belfast in early 1792. It presented its readership with a heady mix of 'true' and exciting news about France and it offered an incisive commentary on events in Ireland. The *Northern Star* also kept its readers informed on the debate raging on the revolution in France with, from the beginning, the trenchant opinions of Tom Paine, the English radical, on the events there filling many columns. Each issue contained a number of poetical, satirical and humorous pieces, all of which were designed to undermine deference to the existing authorities and, ultimately, to politicise the masses. The paper was published twice a week and rapidly attained a circulation of four thousand, making it for a time the most widely diffused publication in Ireland. Until its printing presses were wrecked by men of the Monaghan militia in 1797, it was the authentic voice of Irish and, especially, Presbyterian radicalism.

The United Irish strategy to achieve parliamentary reform appeared to be based on the assumption that Dublin Castle would take no action against them and that, because the abuses of the current political system – in their eyes – were so glaring, they could not be effectively defended. Neither of these assumptions turned out to be correct and Dublin Castle, from the beginning, identified the United Irishmen as secret revolutionaries whose demand for parliamentary reform was only a smokescreen for their real objective, to separate Ireland from Britain and to set up an Irish republic. Their challenge, therefore, had to be seen off. Hence the major concessions to Irish Catholics or at least to the Catholic middle classes, for it was believed that Catholic relief would detach that body from any active support for, or involvement with, the United Irishmen. Again, the outbreak of war in February 1793 gave Dublin Castle its opportunity to move decisively against any radical group that was both outspokenly pro-French and anti-war. Professed and public admiration for the French and their revolutionary activities was possibly permissible before 1793, but with the outbreak of hostilities such sentiments became akin to treason.

Measures were soon taken to harass the membership of the United Irishmen. A Convention Act was passed in 1793 which, by outlawing conventions purporting to have a representative character, closed off to the United Irishmen the established method of putting pressure on the government. Similarly, when a section of the Volunteers sought to reconstitute itself as a 'National Guard' on the French model, the opportunity was seized to order the disbandment of the entire force. This removed any danger that the United Irishmen might engage the Volunteers in the reform campaign. The potent fusion of popular, parliamentary and paramilitary forces that had – at least in rosy memory – won the 'Constitution of 1782', would not be permitted to recur. Moreover, in a further show of the Castle's determination, leading United Irishmen, notably the editors of the *Northern Star*, were arrested on charges of seditious libel for criticising government policy; a secret committee of the Irish House of Lords was set up in order to investigate (i.e. substantiate) allegations that the United Irishmen were involved in treasonable activities with the French; and in March 1793 a 'military riot' took place in Belfast, during which gangs of soldiers attempted to overawe the town's radicals by breaking their windows and sometimes their heads. Then, in May 1794, on the foot of revelations of treasonable communications between a French emissary, the Reverend William Jackson, and various members of the Society of United Irishmen (including Theobald Wolfe Tone and Archibald Hamilton Rowan), the society itself was suppressed by government decree. It did re-emerge a short time later, but now it had become a secret, oath-bound conspiracy, dedicated to seeking military support from revolutionary France in order to achieve an Irish republic. In the government's eyes, from the beginning it had never been anything else.

France and Ireland

The French military interest in Ireland after the outbreak of war in 1793 was entirely predictable. The new revolutionary government in France may have renounced what it regarded as the disgraceful secret diplomacy of the old order, and may have turned its back on the equally decadent military practices of the *ancien régime*, but it well knew that France could not ignore what had become by repetition almost an axiom of eighteenth-century French military strategy: Ireland was England's weak point. Hence, throughout the eighteenth century, French officers of the old royal army had, as an exercise at military college, frequently been set the task of planning a landing on Irish soil and they had studied the French expeditions to Bantry Bay in county Cork in 1689 and 1690. The French well knew that Ireland supplied large numbers of men and matériel to the British armed forces and they were also persuaded that Ireland had a disaffected, Catholic population. This combination of the loyal and disloyal was ripe for mischief-making. In addition, and this was new, the revolutionary government in Paris blamed the British government, and especially the prime minister, William Pitt, for the devastating civil war that raged in Brittany and then in La Vendée in the years after 1793. Because the overthrow of the old order in France was, at least in the eyes of the revolutionaries in Paris, incontestably the most brilliant event in the history of the world, only the distribution of 'Pitt's gold' by royalist agents could explain the apparent explosion of rage against it in these provinces. How better to pay Pitt back in his own coin than by making Ireland England's La Vendée? In short, after 1793, on various grounds, there could be no question of France not intervening in Ireland: the only questions were how, when and where.

On the face of it, Jackson's mission to assess the situation on the ground in Ireland had proved a failure. Constantly spied on from his landing on the south coast of England to his arrival at Dublin, his capture had always been at the authorities' discretion. And yet his arrest and the seizure of his papers had the effect of further fuelling the revolutionary movement. Tone had written a lengthy memorandum for Jackson detailing the reasons why a French invasion would be welcomed, or at least accepted, by a majority of the people of Ireland. Compromised by this document which fell into the authorities' hands, Tone had no choice but to enter into an agreement with Dublin Castle to exile himself to the United States in return for not being prosecuted at law in Ireland.

The appointment in late 1794 of a reform-minded lord lieutenant, Earl Fitzwilliam, may have raised Tone's hopes that he would be permitted to remain in Ireland. Fitzwilliam, heavily influenced by Edmund Burke, was convinced that only by bringing in full Catholic emancipation could Irish Catholics be kept apart from the republican Presbyterians. Accordingly, soon after his arrival in Ireland in January 1795, he moved speedily on the Catholic question. He also opened negotiations with the Catholic hierarchy about state aid for a new Catholic seminary at Maynooth, county Kildare, to replace the Irish colleges closed during the upheavals in France. (These discussions were to be successfully concluded under Fitzwilliam's successor, Camden, and he laid the first stone of the new St Patrick's College, Maynooth, in April 1796.) However, Fitzwilliam's reckless action, for so it appeared to London and to powerful interests within Dublin Castle, on the question of Catholics sitting in the Irish Parliament led to his sensational dismissal in February 1795, barely six weeks after his arrival in Ireland.

Having delayed his departure for nearly a year, Tone eventually sailed for America in June 1795, for Fitzwilliam's removal from office had left him no option. The disavowal of Fitzwilliam's plans to admit Catholics to the Irish Parliament effectively closed off any possibility of averting the coming confrontation between Dublin Castle and the United Irishmen. Before Tone left he had consulted with leading United Irishmen, notably Thomas Addis Emmet and Samuel Neilson, and had secured agreement that his sojourn in the United States would be a brief one and that, at the first opportunity, he would travel to France to promote the cause of a French invasion of Ireland. Jackson's mission might not have been entirely in vain.

While Tone from his exile in the United States – a country he quickly came to detest – plotted his journey to France, the newly re-formed and secret United Irish society steadily planned its revolution in Ireland (figure 4.2). First, a major effort was undertaken to create a mass movement. As before, the idea of politicising the masses remained a given. The United Irishmen had from the beginning defined themselves by print and this continued. Newspapers, pamphlets, songs, satires and prophecies (these latter were uniformly favourable to a world turned upside down) continued to fall from its presses. Quite what effect any or all of this outpouring of print had on the populace at large is anyone's guess; at worst, perhaps, the literary effusions may have modestly contributed to the revolutionary atmosphere of the 1790s; at best, they had the potential to make every man (and woman) a citizen.

'Virtual' recruitment to the United Irishmen through the diffusion of radical publications in order to promote politicisation was one way to boost numbers; but more threatening by far was the swearing-in of large numbers in order to transform the Society of United Irishmen from a socially rather restricted club that operated on a Belfast–Dublin axis to a mass-based secret organisation that was nationwide. Throughout 1796 and 1797, at the direction of Arthur O'Connor and Lord Edward FitzGerald, two well-born enthusiasts for an Irish republic and a French invasion, tens of thousands of tenants, labourers, cottiers and textile workers, on the United Irishmen's own figures, were administered the two oaths of membership: the first, to keep secret everything about the United Irishmen, and the second the oath of loyalty to the society and its aims. The huge numbers would be used as an additional reason why the French should invade Ireland. Quite what reliance could, in fact, be placed on these extraordinary figures – by 1797, several hundred thousand were reportedly sworn into the conspiracy – remained to be seen. Certainly, the authorities had no choice but to take them seriously and adopt severe counter-measures; but a huge consolation for Dublin Castle must have been the fatal flaw at the heart of the republican plan, for, while the United Irishmen might build a mass organisation or organise a secret society, they could not have a movement that was both mass based and secret.

4.2 *The Shamrock*, December 1890: imaginative representation of a meeting in 1795 on Cave Hill, Belfast, at which Theobald Wolfe Tone, Thomas Russell and Samuel Neilson, all leading United Irishmen, took an oath together to set up an Irish Republic that would be separate from and independent of Britain. That the three men were Protestant would foster the dangerous illusion that Irish Protestant resistance to Home Rule in the late nineteenth century could be ignored. National Library of Ireland.

In their quest for numbers the United Irishmen also sought to form some sort of alliance or partnership with the largely agrarian secret society, the Defenders. Originating in sectarian feuding in county Armagh in the late 1780s, by the mid-1790s the Defenders, almost entirely Catholic, were to be found in around a dozen counties in south Ulster and north Leinster. On the face of it there ought to have been no possibility of any accommodation between the United Irishmen and the Defenders, for the latter appeared to be everything that the United Irishmen were not: rabidly sectarian, hugely violent, largely rural-based, drawn from the ranks of 'poor, labouring' people, and apocalyptic rather than enlightened in their aspirations. Urged on by the French, who saw in the Defenders a body of armed men similar to those who were waging relentless insurgency against them in western France and who could therefore do the same against George III's soldiers, some northern leaders of the United Irishmen, such as Henry Joy McCracken, sought to enlist the Defenders into the ranks of the United Irishmen. By 1797 there were reports that they had been successful in this object in large areas of south Ulster, though as ever, quite how firm any such alliance could be remained to be seen.

In addition to their efforts to recruit ordinary people to their ranks, the United Irishmen, as a dedicated revolutionary body, sought to suborn – to seduce from their duty – as many of the armed forces of the crown as they could. While Irish soldiers in regular regiments, such as the artillery, were not ignored, it was the Irish militia formed in 1793 that appeared to offer the most promising recruits in this respect. This force, at its peak about twenty thousand strong, was based on the territorial division of the Irish county and consisted (mostly) of a Catholic rank and file and (mostly) Protestant officers. It was both a defence force and a nursery for the regular army. However, based on its overwhelming Catholic complexion, at least in the ranks, and the furious rioting that had left over one hundred dead at its formation, there were grave fears as to its reliability. For their part, the United Irishmen were breezily confident that they could 'turn' the Irish militia into United Irishmen in uniform. Very often members of the United Irishmen would seek to befriend Catholic militiamen in taverns, ply them with drink, turn the conversation to politics and then swear them into the United Irish organisation. Many hundreds were so sworn in and a number went on to bring their fellow militiamen into the conspiracy. Emboldened by their apparent success in this area, the United Irishmen boasted that if a French army landed in Ireland substantial numbers of the armed forces of the crown, most especially members of the Irish militia, would throw down their weapons and side with them. And Theobald Wolfe Tone, when urging the French government to mount an invasion of Ireland, argued that it was 'a moral certainty' that a majority of the Irish militia would desert to any French force that arrived in Ireland.

Outside Ireland agents of the United Irishmen were active in promoting their cause in England and Scotland. The United Irishmen certainly sought an Irish republic with French assistance; but they also envisaged republics in Scotland and in England as well. Therefore emissaries were dispatched to liaise with disaffected republican groups in these countries. United Irish agents, notably Father James Quigley (executed in 1798 at Maidstone, Kent), were active among the Irish communities which had established themselves in the textile towns of Lancashire, and Quigley played a leading role in setting up the republican society, the United Britons. Similarly, another United Irishman, Valentine Lawless, was based in London where he was in contact with pro-French, republican elements in the capital. Elsewhere in England an attempt was made to recruit United Irishmen among the sailors of the Royal Navy. A significant proportion of that navy's seamen were Irish, and several thousand had been recently rounded up as suspects in Ireland and sent to the fleet to serve. The United Irish emissary, William Duckett, sought to exploit their resentment at their fate and, additionally, to sow disaffection among those stationed on the fleets in the naval bases at the Nore and Spithead. In short, while sometimes derided for their amateurishness, the United Irishmen throughout the years 1796 and 1797 were putting together a formidable conspiracy. Only France and French military assistance remained to complete the plan.

In January 1796 Theobald Wolfe Tone left his uncongenial exile in the United States and sailed for France (figure 4.3); his mission, to forward a French invasion of Ireland. Against all the odds, Tone made an impact on French ministers and he was rewarded with a commission in the French army and an assurance that he would accompany the planned expedition to Ireland. Tone had not suggested an expedition to the French; rather his arrival in Paris had coincided with French ambitions to undertake such a project. However, he did contribute to the plan by constantly urging haste on the French, by patiently answering questions put to him by General Lazare Hoche who was to lead the expedition and by drawing up memoranda to assist the French authorities in their planning. In December 1796 a major French expedition, consisting of forty-five vessels, carrying 14,750 soldiers, sailed from Brest. The French fleet evaded the British blockade at Brest, and a large portion of it arrived in Bantry Bay, county Cork, on 21 December. There, however, atrocious weather ruled out a landing, and two weeks later, the French ships limped back to Brest having accomplished nothing. 'England has not had such an escape since the Spanish Armada', was Tone's apt comment on the whole venture.

This French expedition, though a failure, marked a turning point, both in the military history of Ireland in the 1790s and in the progress of the United Irish conspiracy. The Royal Navy had been badly caught out by the French arrival off

4.3 Theobald Wolfe Tone seeking to interest Napoleon Bonaparte in an invasion of Ireland in 1797. Tone did meet Bonaparte several times but nothing came of these meetings. National Library of Ireland.

Ireland, for it had never seriously considered that the enemy had the capability to mount such an expedition and, therefore, had ignored all intelligence to the contrary. As for Dublin Castle, from an early date it had viewed the main threat to security of Ireland as coming from internal insurgency rather than from French invasion. It had accordingly deployed its forces in small detachments on counter-insurgency duty throughout the many disturbed counties. As a result, had the French landed in the south-west of Ireland, it would have taken nine days to assemble a large force with which to oppose it, and it was entirely probable that within that time Cork would have fallen to the enemy. The failed French expedition to Bantry Bay had revealed the inadequacy of both the Castle's and the Admiralty's planning. Moreover, while 'Protestant winds' had prevented the French from disembarking their army, they could evidently not be relied upon in the future if, as seemed likely, the French returned. Again, the success of the French in reaching Bantry Bay had afforded a huge propaganda coup to the United Irishmen. For years, there had been much boasting in radical circles that the French were planning an invasion of Ireland, but such claims had been derided by the authorities. Bantry Bay was the perfect riposte to those who had doubted that the French had entered into partnership with the United Irishmen.

In early 1797 Dublin Castle, urged on by the London government, embarked on a draconian counter-insurgency policy designed to ensure that, if the French did return, there would be little or no United Irish organisation in existence to greet them. Of course, the Castle had already been pursuing a determined policy of crushing the United Irishmen and their Defender allies in the years before the French expedition to Bantry Bay. In 1796 the so-called Insurrection Act had been passed by the Irish Parliament and this had, in effect, removed all safeguards possessed by subjects at Common Law. *Habeas corpus* had been suspended and those who were deemed 'suspect' could be summarily arrested and imprisoned; as noted, many of those swept up were sent to serve in the Royal Navy. The tendering of oaths was made a capital offence, while taking an oath could lead to transportation for life. Magistrates could 'proclaim' whole counties as being 'out of the law', and impose curfews in districts that were disturbed. Nor did Dublin Castle lack either the will or the manpower to enforce such legislation.

As noted above, a militia force had been embodied in 1793, and this had been followed in September 1796 by the formation of a Yeomanry which by the end of the year numbered twenty thousand. The militia was generally to be deployed to defend Ireland, and thus spare regular soldiers from that task, for the latter's services were required in what appeared to be more important theatres of war, such as the West Indies. By contrast, the numerous Yeomanry corps would serve in the districts where they were recruited, searching for arms and combating local subversives. The formation of a Yeomanry was welcomed as offering an outlet for loyalist energies and from its formation the Yeomanry had a strong Protestant and, indeed, Orange hue.

In the aftermath of Bantry Bay, the Orange Order, formed in September 1795, came into its own as an adjunct to the Yeomanry. The Order had been set up largely on the initiative of lower-class Protestants in county Armagh, fearful of the growth of Catholic Defenderism and concerned at the apparently unchallenged rise of the United Irishmen with their non-denominational message. By the close of 1796 the Order had won the approval and patronage of well-to-do Protestant gentry leaders. Some army officers engaged on counter-insurgency duties in Ulster were likewise content to make use of Orangeism, seeing in its strongholds in mid-Ulster a potent barrier to the spread of the United message into west Ulster and north Connacht. Against that, Dublin Castle throughout 1796 had voiced its deep concern at the Orange Order's activities and its spread; but in the aftermath of the French scare at Bantry Bay the Castle was brought to pocket its misgivings about the movement and prepared to turn a blind eye to its excesses; in the end, the Orange Order was indisputably loyal and that was what counted. We may note that neither the militia nor the Yeomanry nor, be it said, the small number of regular army detachments operating in Ireland, had much respect for the niceties of the law in carrying out their duties. With the hearty support of Dublin Castle and urged on by their superior officers, the armed forces of the crown set about breaking up the United Irish organisation and terrorising United Irish and Defender suspects.

Dublin Castle also, in the months after Bantry Bay, set about purifying its forces by purging the subversive elements that had gained a hold in the Irish militia and other units. In the summer of 1797 a series of courts martial were held throughout the country at which some twenty soldiers were sentenced to be executed for having been sworn into the United Irishmen. Scores of others were sentenced to severe flogging, transportation to Botany Bay or to serve in regiments abroad for life. Notably, in a very public display of official terror that was aimed at both disaffected soldiers and at their mentors, the United Irishmen of Belfast, in May 1797 four members of the Monaghan militia, following court martial, were paraded from Belfast to the large army base at Blaris Moor, some ten miles distant, where they were there shot to death by their fellow militiamen.

In addition to these new repressive laws and to the new forces, now largely purged of disaffection, that would implement them, the Castle could add an extensive spy network that would supply it with information on the plans and personnel of the United Irishmen. From its earliest days the authorities had placed the Society of United Irishmen under close surveillance. The meetings of the Dublin branch, even though these were entirely open and above board, were reported on regularly by the informer Thomas Collins in the years 1791 to 1794; and after the Society's suppression in 1794, a stream of information from renegade United Irishmen poured into Dublin Castle. For example, in 1796, John Smith, alias William Bird, and Edward John Newell, a miniature portrait painter, passed on to the authorities copious amounts of gossip and, on occasion, hard information concerning the activities of the Belfast United Irishmen. It was a similar story in Dublin, where Francis Higgins, editor of the *Freeman's*

Journal and known colloquially as the 'Sham Squire', ran a group of agents on behalf of the Castle. He was able to keep Edward Cooke, under-secretary at Dublin Castle, and the manager of the Castle's intelligence network, in touch with developments in the capital. It was Higgins who recruited Francis Magan, a barrister and United Irishmen, to his circle and it was Magan who would reveal to Higgins the whereabouts of Lord Edward FitzGerald, whose arrest in May 1798 was to prove such a blow to the revolutionaries.

Outside Dublin and Belfast the Castle was kept well informed by the likes of Leonard MacNally (code-name 'J. W.'), a leading barrister who acted regularly for the United Irishmen, and a person whose legal duties took him all over the country. Regular briefings were also sent in by the postmasters of principal Irish towns, whose duties included intercepting, opening, copying, resealing and passing on suspicious letters. Similarly, customs officers were useful sources of information in coastal towns around Ireland and, from all parts, came letters to Dublin Castle from local busybodies eager to report on and denounce their neighbours. Beyond Ireland, from Hamburg, the United Irish envoy, Samuel Turner, sent into the British government detailed and accurate information on the plans and activities of the United Irishmen on the continent.

We should not exaggerate the extent of Dublin Castle's knowledge of the United Irish plans up to 1797: without an appropriate structure for collating, appraising and disseminating intelligence, much valuable information was simply wasted – as for example, the reports in late 1796 that a French invasion fleet was preparing at Brest with Ireland as its destination. But throughout 1797 and beyond there were signs that Dublin Castle was improving its intelligence gathering and processing capabilities and, as a result, the Castle was able to make a number of key arrests – for example, the capture of almost the entire Leinster leadership in Oliver Bond's house in March 1798.

By the spring of 1798, then, it appeared that Dublin Castle had been successful in its determination to destroy the United Irishmen's capacity for insurrection: many of its leaders were in prison or had taken flight, its organisation was in disarray and there seemed no possibility of French assistance. In this latter respect we may note that in May 1798 a major French expeditionary force had indeed left France under its charismatic commander, Napoleon Bonaparte; but its destination had been Egypt, not Ireland. And yet, on the night of the 23/4 May, as planned, the mail coaches leaving Dublin were seized as a signal to those United Irishmen outside the capital that the revolutionary moment had come. However, with the failure of Dublin to rise as planned – a failure largely attributable to the recent arrest of Lord Edward FitzGerald a few days earlier – the rebellion, when it came, was distinguished everywhere by a lack of concert and by a lack of focus. Uprisings outside the capital had been intended by the

United Irishmen as supporting acts – sideshows – to the main event in Dublin but, with the failure of Dublin to act, they now found themselves promoted to centre-stage. In the lack of coordination between the rebel theatres of insurgency lay the salvation of Dublin Castle and British rule in Ireland.

The 1798 rebellion

The initial outbreak of the rebellion was confined to a ring of counties surrounding Dublin; and it was when the fighting in counties Kildare, Carlow, Wicklow and Meath had been largely suppressed and the capital secured that news arrived of a major rebel success in county Wexford. On 29 May 1798 a terse communiqué was issued from Dublin Castle confirming the rumours that had swept the city a day earlier. For the first time in the rebellion, a detachment of soldiers – in this case over a hundred men of the North Cork militia – had been cut to pieces in an open engagement at Oulart, county Wexford.[10] The eruption of Wexford was a most unexpected (as well as most unwelcome) development for Dublin Castle, for the county had, by and large, escaped official scrutiny in the months and years before the rebellion. The Castle had had very few informants (or informers) in Wexford and, most unwisely, had clearly considered this lack of information as pointing towards a general quiescence among the people there. Accordingly, the garrison in that county numbered only a few hundred men.

Two developments pitched Wexford over the edge and into full-scale rebellion. The first of these was the campaign of terror unleashed, particularly to the north of the county, from mid-May 1798 on. Reports of half-hangings, floggings, pitch-cappings and house-burnings conducted principally by the North Cork militia, under the direction of loyalist magistrates, inflamed that part of county Wexford that bordered on Wicklow and induced panic everywhere. On 26 May came stunning news of the summary execution of some thirty-four suspected United Irishmen at Dunlavin, in south Wicklow; and there was a further report that at Carnew, across the border in Wexford, thirty-five prisoners had been shot. Fevered rumours of extirpation now appeared to have substance. In terror, the peasantry – United Irishmen or not – prepared to resist. The second precipitating factor was the very fact of a rebel triumph at Oulart. This victory in an open engagement, the first such for the rebels anywhere, electrified the county, tempting many to join in who might otherwise have hung back. Undoubtedly, it also had the effect of reigniting the rebellion in those areas near Dublin in which it had shown every sign of petering out; and in a broader context, news of the rebels' success at Oulart sparked off renewed efforts to raise the hitherto peaceful north-east of Ireland, principally counties Antrim and Down.

On 29 May, under the command of Father Murphy of Boolavogue, a priest who had been in dispute with his bishop and who had reluctantly stepped forward as leader, the Wexford insurgents, gaining strength as they advanced, stormed Enniscorthy. The defences of the town were swept aside by means of a stampede of cattle and behind the terrified animals came the rebels. The next day, the rebel army, by now possibly fifteen thousand strong, turned its attention to Wexford town. Plans to defend the county capital were given up on news of the destruction of the approaching relief column and the town was abandoned by its defenders. The fall of Wexford was the climax of the rebellion in the south-east: thereafter, it was diminuendo, for the rebels met with devastating defeats at New Ross, Arklow and Newtownbarry, and these had the effect of coralling them within the county. Demoralised, and having suffered thousands of casualties, the rebels fell back to regroup on Vinegar Hill, outside Enniscorthy.

While rebellion had been raging in the south-east, Ulster generally had been quiet. On receipt of news of the fighting in Leinster, there had been a stormy meeting of the Ulster Provincial Council of the United Irishmen on 29 May, at which there had been loud protests at the failure to rise in support. The existing leadership was accused of having 'completely betrayed the people both of Leinster and Ulster', and it was promptly deposed. New men, Henry Joy McCracken among them, were now appointed, and plans were hurriedly made for a rising. On 7 June a large number of rebels assembled in different parts of county Antrim. In Ballymena, the green flag was raised over the market house and there were attacks on Larne, Glenarm, Carrickfergus, Toomebridge and Ballymoney. The rebels, almost entirely Presbyterian, captured Antrim Town but (figure 4.4), after a few hours, were driven out 'with great slaughter' by artillery fire. An attempted mobilisation in county Derry came to nothing and by the evening of 8 June, the Antrim rebels had lost heart and had begun drifting home. Some weeks later McCracken was captured and executed.

As the rising in county Antrim, and elsewhere, was petering out, the United Irishmen in the adjacent county Down began to assemble their forces on 10 June (known, thereafter, as 'Pike Sunday') under the command of Henry Munro, a shopkeeper from Newtownards, and a direct descendant of General Robert Munro who had commanded the Scottish force in Ulster in the wars of the 1640s. At Ballynahinch, some 12 miles from Belfast, the rebels were routed on 12–13 June, suffering several hundred casualties. Military losses were three killed and some thirty wounded. 'General' Munro was captured, and, a few days later, hanged outside his front door. The rebellion in the north-east was over.

With the rebels scattered in the north, attention shifted once again to those still 'out' in Wexford, and the army laid plans to attack their camp at Vinegar Hill. On 21 June General Gerard Lake, in order to prevent a rebel break-out,

4.4 Highly imaginative centennial image of another Protestant United Irish leader, Henry Joy McCracken, leading the attack on Antrim Town during the 1798 rebellion. He was later executed. National Library of Ireland.

attempted to surround Vinegar Hill with four columns of soldiers numbering some twenty thousand men. With this manoeuvre nearly completed, battle was then joined. It lasted about two hours: the rebels were mercilessly shelled; artillery carried the day. 'The rebels made a tolerable good fight of it' wrote Lake, and he then pronounced the 'carnage . . . dreadful' among them. Hundreds may have fallen on the field of battle, though numbers did manage to escape, for Lake's attempted encirclement of Vinegar Hill was ineffective. A 'little war' continued in the Wicklow mountains for some time, but in effect, after Vinegar Hill, the rebellion in the south-east was over.

In defeat rebel discipline had collapsed in some places. After the reverse at New Ross, about one hundred Protestants had been burned to death in a barn at Scullabogue; and now, following the disaster at Vinegar Hill, about seventy Protestant prisoners were piked to death on the bridge at Wexford town. The army repaid these atrocities with interest: the mopping-up operations after Vinegar Hill resembled, to the fury of the newly appointed lord lieutenant, Marquis Cornwallis, little more than universal rape, plunder and murder. Retribution for the rebel leaders was swift and generally uncompromising. Bagenal Harvey, Cornelius Grogan, Mathew Keogh and Anthony Perry – all Wexford commanders, or reputedly so and, incidentally, all Protestants – were executed, their heads cut off and stuck on spikes outside the courthouse in Wexford town. A similar fate awaited Father John Murphy, the hero of Oulart and Enniscorthy, or a latterday mixture of Attila, Genghis Khan and Tamerlane, as loyalists viewed him.

For a brief period in late summer there appeared a prospect that the rebellion might flare up again. On 22 August a French force of some eleven hundred men under the command of General Humbert waded ashore at Kilcummin Strand, near Killala, county Mayo. Humbert scored a striking victory over government forces at Castlebar, but then his campaign ran out of steam. In the absence of reinforcements from France or large-scale insurgency elsewhere in Ireland the signal victory at Castlebar was revealed as merely an empty triumph. On 8 September at Ballinamuck, county Longford, Humbert's force, vastly outnumbered, laid down its arms. The French were treated as honoured prisoners of war, but those Irish auxiliaries who had recklessly joined them were promptly massacred. A month later Theobald Wolfe Tone was captured as he came ashore at Lough Swilly in the north-west. He was court-martialled in Dublin and sentenced to death but cheated the hangman by cutting his throat. The rebellion was finally over: around ten thousand rebels (including a high proportion of non-combatants), and about six hundred soldiers had been slain, and large areas of the country had been effectively laid waste.

The rebels had failed because they lacked coordination and because, with one or two exceptions, their leaders had had no time to instil even a modicum of military discipline and training into the numbers that flocked to them. In addition, the arrests during the 'pre-rebellion' had been very disruptive, for the rebels, thereafter, had generally lacked both a leadership structure and a coherent strategy. The result was that it was often difficult or impossible, so the youthful Wexford rebel, Miles Byrne, later claimed in his memoirs, to know who had given which order and for what reason, and this indecision caused confusion and led to a loss of morale. The rebel failure to take Dublin at the outset had been crucial, depriving the rebellion of a focus and preventing the formation of some sort of representative assembly in the capital. From that point on the staggered outbreak of rebellion played into the government's hands: 'We may be thankful', wrote one loyalist, 'that the insurgents have acted so little in unison and have presented us with the means of beating them separately.'

Again, the failure of the French to intervene decisively had contributed to the rebel defeat. A substantial French force would have offered discipline, leadership, weaponry, recognition and perhaps, an overall strategy; the absence of the French had deprived the rebels of all of these. Finally, the rebellion had failed because Catholic Ireland, by and large, had sided with the government. The Catholic hierarchy, in particular had offered strong support to the government: no word of criticism was voiced of the government policy of 'the bayonet, the gibbet and the lash'; the rebels had been immediately excommunicated; and those priests who sided with the rebels – a derisory 70 out of 1,800 in the country – were denounced as troublemakers and drunks. In the inelegant phrase of Bishop Caulfield, the Catholic bishop of Ferns, county Wexford, such rebel priests were 'the very faeces of the church'. In the end the bedrock of Catholic loyalty, or quiescence, had helped Dublin Castle ride out the storm.

From the beginning, the rebellion had taken on a sectarian cast. Such a development was always likely, and may even have been inevitable, given the balance of power within the Protestant state, given that state's interpretation of the entire United Irish project and given its determination to fly its flag above the stronghold of Protestant ascendancy. No doubt also, the 'Orange' hue of the military excesses during the 'pre-rebellion' was hugely conducive to this development. In the opening days of the rebellion, the rebels at Dunboyne, county Meath, had succumbed to their desire for revenge and had subscribed to the agenda drawn up by the confessional state: 'The rebels took seven prisoners', it was reported, 'four of them Protestant were massacred, the three Papists were let go.' At Rathangan, county Meath, some nineteen Protestants were led out and massacred; by contrast, Catholic loyalists were spared. Within days of the rebellion's outbreak, Camden, the lord lieutenant, had exclaimed that 'party and religious prejudice has literally made the Protestant part of the country mad'; and his successor, Cornwallis, glumly recorded that 'the conversation even at my table always turns on hanging, shooting, burning etc etc., and if a priest has been put to death, the greatest joy is expressed by the whole company'. The 1641 comet, it seemed, was once again visible.

And yet, for all the talk of a 'popish plot' to extirpate Protestants, informed contemporaries were wary of seeing nothing but sectarianism in the rising. For every loyalist who saw nothing but a religious 'phrensy', there was another who observed discrepancies and discordances in this picture. The Irish-born chief secretary, Lord Castlereagh, claimed that the rebellion was in fact a 'Jacobinical' or French-inspired rising, 'pursuing its object with Popish instruments'; and John Colclough of Wexford, whose uncle, like himself a Protestant, was hanged for his role in the rebellion, pointed out reasonably enough that 'one can hardly think that it was the original intention of the United men to murder all the Protestants, for many of the heads of them were of that persuasion'.

That Protestants were murdered because they were Protestants cannot be denied, nor should the many instances of naked sectarianism be brushed aside. Such actions were entirely condemned by the rebel leaders. Eighteenth-century Ireland was a profoundly sectarian state wedded to the principle of Protestant ascendancy; and developments in the 1790s had heightened sectarian consciousness everywhere. It was all too easy for evil individuals to exact a personal revenge during the communal disorder attendant on rebellion; but massacre was not rebel policy. The burnings at Scullabogue and the pikings at Wexford Bridge can be attributed to the rebels' collapse of discipline provoked by defeat rather than to any settled plan.

Ironically, the rebellion in the north bore many of the hallmarks of a religious war, for the rebels were largely Presbyterian while their opponents were adherents of the established church (or Catholic soldiers). In the aftermath of the rebellion, however, this religious division was downplayed, and every effort was made to separate the rising in Antrim and Down from the tumult in the south-east. Those Presbyterian United Irishmen who had fought at Ballynahinch and elsewhere consoled themselves in later years with the thought that they had largely battled alone. The promised contingents of Defenders had seldom materialised. In any case, prudence determined that a veil be cast over the exploits of those Presbyterians who had espoused the republican cause; and the Orange Order beckoned. It was reported that, by late 1798, large numbers of former rebels were crowding into the Order with a view of 'screening themselves'; and by the middle of 1799, observers were commenting on the 'astonishing change in the public mind' in Ulster: 'The word "Protestant" which was becoming obsolete in the north has regained its influence and all of that description seem to be drawing closer together.' This accommodation between members of the Church of Ireland and the Presbyterian church proceeded very quickly indeed. When in 1801 Sir Richard Musgrave published his violently anti-Catholic history of the rebellion, so far had public amnesia about the rebellion in Ulster taken hold that he was able to devote a mere twelve pages to events in Antrim and Down compared to over six hundred pages spent describing the sectarian mayhem in Leinster. The monochrome interpretation of the rebellion as an onslaught by

Catholics on Protestants was thus put in place, and awkward details about Presbyterian participation and Church of Ireland leaders were not to be allowed to intrude.

The 1798 rebellion and its aftermath shattered existing relationships within Ireland, awakening atavistic fears and evoking memories of 1641. The very fact that a rebellion had occurred at all also called into question the future of the Irish political structure. In a notable departure from precedent that revealed clearly the close connection between military and political affairs, Camden's successor, Cornwallis, had been appointed both commander-in-chief of the armed forces in Ireland and lord lieutenant, and he had been charged not only with crushing the rebellion, but also with seizing the opportunity the crisis offered to put through a legislative union between Ireland and England. The Irish Parliament was to be yet another casualty of the 1798 rebellion, part-victim but also part-perpetrator.

Passing the Union

When William Pitt learned of the outbreak of insurrection in Ireland, his immediate thought was that this crisis offered the perfect opportunity to move for a legislative Union between England and Ireland.[11] In this respect Pitt's reaction was no different from that of previous British ministers faced with difficulties in Ireland. There had been mention of a Union at various points in the previous thirty years: at the time of the free trade agitation in the late 1770s; when the constitutional concessions of 1782 had been demanded; during the controversy over the commercial propositions of 1785; and, especially, during the crisis provoked by the Catholic question in 1793. But always such talk had been dismissed as premature, for it was recognised that there was no possibility of the Irish Parliament voting itself out of existence. Undoubtedly, the Catholic Relief Acts of 1792 and 1793 had advanced substantially the cause of Union, for Catholics were now within the walls of the Protestant Constitution and some Protestants took fright at this. From 1793 on there was an identifiable pro-Union lobby in both countries. The primary difficulty, however, remained: the consent of the members of the Irish Parliament to a British invitation to commit political suicide would not be forthcoming. However, at a stroke, the rebellion changed the prospects for Union, and British ministers and their Irish allies hastened to seize the opportunity that opened. The Unionist moment had finally come; but it might pass, and therefore there could be no question of postponing the matter until quieter times had arrived. It is vital to act, wrote one Unionist, 'while the terror of the late rebellion is fresh', and George III signalled his agreement for 'using the present moment of terror for frightening the supporters of the Castle into a Union'. Accordingly, Cornwallis and Lord Castlereagh were entrusted with a dual mandate: first, to crush rebellion and then to put through a legislative Union.

Union would have been inconceivable without the 1798 rebellion. The violence of that year had delivered a profound shock both to the political structure and to the self-confidence of the ascendancy. True, there were those who rightly pointed to the fact that the rebellion had been largely crushed by Irish soldiers before the arrival of substantial British reinforcements, but the balance of the evidence suggests that a hard lesson had been learnt: legislative independence and military prowess were all very well, but it was glumly acknowledged that without British power 'the Protestant interest of this country could not stand on its legs for a single day'. A Union fitted in well with this new perception, seemingly offering Irish Protestants long-term security and comfort in return for ditching their Parliament, now cast as a Trojan horse within the walls of the ascendancy.

What was a Union between Ireland and England supposed to accomplish? As Pitt saw it, a Union would give the perfect riposte to those who had in the rebellion sought separation and, to that extent, Union was not just a key instrument of counter-insurgency but also a vital strategic imperative, drawing England and Ireland closer and closer into an imperial Union, so as to frustrate those Irish Jacobins and their French allies who had sought to prise them apart. Indeed, in his main speech, in January 1799, advocating the Union proposals in the British House of Commons, Pitt made much of this imperial point. However, he also made frequent reference to other concerns. On a constitutional level, Union could be seen as the final solution to those problems that had been bedevilling Anglo-Irish relations since 1782. In particular, Pitt stressed the profoundly unsatisfactory nature of the 'Constitution of 1782', the failure to reform it and the ever present danger of a clash between two 'independent' legislatures – a clash, he claimed, only narrowly averted at the time of the regency crisis. Moreover, it was only in a united Parliament, he maintained, that the Catholic question could be solved with benefit to Irish Catholics and without danger to Irish Protestants. Since 1793, Catholics by and large had had the vote in Ireland (though not in England), and it was assumed, on no very clear grounds, that the right, if elected, to sit in the Irish Parliament, must soon follow. However, given the Catholics' overwhelming preponderance in the Irish population (a ratio of 4:1), and given the assumption that Catholics would only vote for other Catholics, there would soon be a Catholic majority in the Irish Parliament, and hence an end to ascendancy, and even to the connection between Ireland and England. In Pitt's eyes, only a legislative Union could avert this catastrophe for Protestant Ireland and for the British empire.

Pitt also looked to the future, and to the benefits which he was assured would stem from Union and, after the fashion of those Tudor lords deputy with their programmes for Irish reform, he promised that after Union Ireland would gain commercial advantages, capital would flow into the country and there would be an infusion of 'English manners and English industry', so that Ireland would prosper from Union with England as much as Scotland had done since 1707. Pitt further drew a picture of the imperial Parliament sitting as an impartial legislature, removed from the clamour and prejudice of local factions, calmly and dispassionately adjudicating in the interests of all on the various knotty problems that might arise within the entire empire. It would be an assembly where contentious issues such as the tithe question, the provision of salaries for Catholic priests or even 'Catholic emancipation' could be coolly deliberated on. Pitt closed on a note that revealed fully his commitment to the task ahead, for he promised that he would never desist from seeking to accomplish a Union 'on which I am persuaded depends the internal tranquillity of Ireland, the interest of the British empire at large and, I hope I may add, the happiness of a great part of the habitable world'. Central to Pitt's understanding of Ireland was the view that the Irish Parliament had failed, that Irish politicians had failed and that there could now be no alternative to Union. (A similar verdict on Northern Ireland would be reached by British ministers in 1972.) Pitt's unflattering verdict on the Irish political structure and on Irish politicians, his firm conviction that there was no viable alternative to Union, and his resolute determination not to rest until that was accomplished, were all well calculated to ensure ultimate victory.

In Ireland a number of different, contradictory strands can be identified in the pro-Union camp. First, some took the view that since Union was the clearly preferred solution of the British government, then resistance was not just futile, but even disloyal. John Beresford, chief commissioner of the Irish Revenue Board and long-time member of the Dublin Castle Cabinet, which advised the lords lieutenant, had been a follower of Pitt for many years and he was accustomed to doing Pitt's bidding. An instinctive conservative, Beresford none the less accepted the force of Pitt's arguments: Irish Catholics were 'barbarous, ignorant and ferocious'; Irish Presbyterians were 'republicans in their hearts'; members of the Church of Ireland were politically and financially bankrupt. Reluctantly, he drew the appropriate conclusion: without a Union 'we shall be lost'.

Similarly, Lord Castlereagh followed Pitt's line of argument. In his eyes, the Irish Parliament had ever been an irrelevance, but now, with a mighty war being waged and the future of the British empire at stake, it was a positive obstacle in the way of victory. He could see no solution to the 'anomalous and unnatural government of Ireland' save a Union. Only in a united legislature could the contentious issues of contemporary Irish life be firmly and coolly dealt with, and

Irish Protestants 'feeling less exposed, would become more confident and liberal'. Edward Cooke, the Castle under-secretary, shared this view. Everywhere Cooke looked, he saw problems: the United Irishmen sought separation or else, equally objectionable, the destruction of the established church. He feared that if the Catholics gained admission to the Irish Parliament they would immediately seek parliamentary reform and, if the Catholics got this, 'what then becomes of the church establishment?' He concluded, 'difficulties appear on all sides, and the knot is then cut with an Union'.

Finally, perhaps the firmest, certainly the most long-standing public advocate of Union was John Fitzgibbon, earl of Clare, lord chancellor of Ireland. Clare had been moving towards a pro-union position during the 1780s, but the events of 1793 and, especially, the way in which the important Catholic Relief Act of that year had been pushed through the Irish Parliament, convinced him that the 'independent' Irish Parliament, so far from being an abiding achievement of the Protestant nation, was in fact a standing threat to the Protestant ascendancy, and that only in a Union with Britain could the Protestants of Ireland find security. Clare's dominance of the Irish House of Lords, his forensic brilliance in debate and his insistence that the only choice was Union or separation and that, in the latter case, England would have to reconquer Ireland by the sword, gave him a commanding influence in the Union negotiations. Moreover, his harsh articulation of the underside of the ascendancy position – that it rested on outright plunder, bad title and naked confiscation – together with his bleak diagnosis of both the Irish character, and the Irish governing elite – combined to make him a formidable Unionist, held in awe by supporters and opponents alike.

It was in the range of arguments articulated by these members of the Dublin Castle 'Junto', that the strength of the Unionist case resided. By contrast, those who opposed Union could not aspire to unanimity, and frequently contradicted one another. The leading opposition politicians, Henry Grattan and George Ponsonby, were opposed to Union on the grounds that the 1782 settlement was a 'final adjustment' and they maintained that, in any case, a decision to end the Irish Parliament was *ultra vires* for that institution to take. These arguments were easily brushed aside by the Castle speakers: the 1782 settlement was clearly not cast in bronze; and no institution relishes being told that certain measures are beyond its competence. Grattan's case was not helped by the fact that he was widely hated by the 'Protestant Ascendancy men' as (Cooke dubbed them), and he was frequently taunted with being a crypto-United Irishman. At the time of the Union debates his influence was near nil in the Irish Parliament. Similarly, Grattan's advocacy of Catholic emancipation and his claim that this was, in fact, compatible with a defence of the Protestant ascendancy merely confirmed his reputation for impracticality. As for the Ponsonby group, they were regarded as being merely the Irish wing of the British Whig party, eager to make mischief for Pitt and equally anxious to further their own interests. Fatally, neither Grattan nor Ponsonby could come up with any convincing alternative to Union, and their unwillingness or inability to recognise that the rebellion had changed everything merely confirmed them as vain visionaries or impractical politicians.

The most effective opposition to Union came from a quarter not normally associated with either Grattan or Ponsonby: John Foster, speaker of the Irish House of Commons. He swiftly announced his hostility to the measure and until it was passed he remained its most formidable opponent. It is not too much to say that, but for Foster's determined opposition, the Unionist case would have been unanswerable. Foster's influence stemmed first from his office: as speaker he held a pivotal position in the Irish Commons; then, from his reputation as a financial and economics expert; and finally from his well-attested ascendancy credentials. On all three counts, he denounced Union. The Irish Parliament could, in fact, work very well but only if ill-informed British ministers would stop interfering in its business. Again, Foster felt that the terms offered to Ireland under the proposed Union were unfavourable – a free trade area was not at all suitable for Ireland's industries, and the financial burden it was expected to bear under the proposed Union was too heavy. But especially, Foster, *pace* Clare, opposed Union on the grounds that it would ultimately mean the end of the Protestant ascendancy. Clare had concluded that only in a Union could Irish Protestants find security; Foster was equally adamant that Union constituted a real threat to the ascendancy. He anticipated a speedy concession on the Catholic question in the new united British legislature and, in this, he was at one with the Orange Order whose opposition to Union was based on the fear that it would prove to be (indeed was calculated to be) a gateway to Catholic emancipation.

Essentially, however, Foster was persuaded of the general unwisdom of Irish Protestants, in effect, placing their future in the hands of British ministers and British political parties. Those same British ministers had not, hitherto, shown much understanding of, or solicitude for, the cares and anxieties of Irish Protestants. Indeed, a case could be made for blaming the whole mess on Pitt and his fellow ministers: in 1793, they had needlessly browbeaten the Irish Parliament into permitting Catholics to vote on the same terms as Protestants; and in 1795, they had sent Fitzwilliam to Ireland where he had recklessly aroused Catholic expectations and then dashed them. Most recently, they had dispatched the soft and ineffective (so loyalists regarded him) Cornwallis to Ireland, and he had quickly signalled his contempt for people like Foster by snubbing them. And yet, it was now seriously proposed to give such people full control over

the destiny of the Protestants of Ireland? Given the fickleness of British politicians and ministers, Foster understandably feared the worst in the post-Union
world.

Individuals such as Foster and Grattan, and officials like Castlereagh and
Clare, took their positions on the Union question; and their arguments encompassed the range of opinion on both sides. Union, however, would have to be
approved by a majority in the Irish Parliament, and here the matter would be
decided, not merely by public argument, but also by private calculation. Obviously, on many occasions there could be no difference between the two spheres,
and the eighteenth century was not too concerned to keep them apart. The early
terms for Union, for example, provided for only one Member of Parliament per
county (there were then two members per county), proposed a bizarre system
of rotating borough representation and omitted all mention of compensation
for the proprietors of those constituencies destined to be axed under the new
arrangement. There was even a suspicion that a general election (i.e. immense
trouble, plus ruinous expense) would be held immediately after Union passed. No
wonder that, when these terms were laid before the Irish Parliament in January
1799, they met with a dusty response and the narrow Castle victory – 106 votes
to 105 – had to be construed as a moral defeat. Concern at the public terms
had blended with a determination to defend private interests in such a way as
to produce a shock reverse for the Castle. Castlereagh, shaken by the setback,
could only plead a lack of preparation on his part.

In order to placate the county members the Union terms were substantially
altered. There would still be 100 Members of Parliament from Irish constituencies in the united Parliament but the mix would now be rather different. The
current arrangement, whereby two members were returned, was to be continued under the Union; a rational plan, based on the hearthmoney tax returns
(a proxy for population), was eventually brought in to determine which boroughs should be scrapped; and perhaps most telling of all, a sum of £15,000
was offered in compensation to all of those who could establish ownership of
boroughs that would lose their representation. 'The plan of representation is
universally approved' noted Castlereagh at the end of 1799, 'and the £15,000,
and no dissolution [of Parliament], most popular.'

Equally 'popular' was the British government's decision, following the reverse
in January 1799, to 'buy up the fee simple of Irish corruption' through the
unprecedented disbursement of large quantities of the 'loaves and fishes' of
Irish patronage, peerages, pensions, places and promises. In addition to the
carrot, the Castle did not hesitate to employ the stick: all Members of the Irish
House of Commons or their patrons who persisted in opposition were warned
that such conduct would be considered as 'an absolute separation . . . from all

connexion with his majesty's government'. There were a number of high-profile dismissals: the prime serjeant, James FitzGerald and the chancellor of the Irish exchequer, Sir John Parnell, were both sacked for their opposition to Union; and the Castle took every opportunity to have pro-Union members returned to Parliament while denying election writs for those constituencies where an anti-Unionist was expected to win.

None of these tactics was illegal or corrupt, and the piece of doggerel that posed the question: 'How did they pass the Union?' and answered it,

> by perjury and fraud,
> by slaves who sold their land for gold
> as Judas sold his god

was wide of the mark. Admittedly, eyebrows were raised at the Castle becoming involved in moving or refusing writs for election, and in advancing money for the purchase of seats: but such actions were improper rather than illegal. There were precedents for both and the opponents of Union were not above buying seats for the likes of Grattan. In any case, it would be wholly misleading to focus unduly on the 'bargain and sale' nature of Irish politics, for the fact was a majority could not be purchased in the Irish Parliament. In 1782 there had been no prospect of buying off the advocates of constititutional change, nor in 1785 had there been any chance of paying off the opponents of the commercial propositions. Similarly, in 1799 it was recognised that a parliamentary majority could only be maintained if public opinion, the 'real sense of the country', was behind it. The Castle recognised this truth of Irish politics: Union 'must be written up, spoken up, intrigued up, drunk up, sung up, and bribed up', Cooke had noted presciently in October 1798. Almost certainly as much time and effort went into soliciting addresses, commissioning pamphlets and moulding public opinion as was devoted to the disposal of patronage. It was a measure of the Castle's success in this respect that it received some seventy-six pro-Union addresses, as opposed to fifty from anti-Unionist sources. It was claimed that these latter addresses contained more signatures than those of their opponents, but Castlereagh was able to retort that those in favour of Union represented the property of the country, and he alleged that £1,000,000 of property was in favour of Union to £350,000 against.

Again, despite Foster's dire warnings as to the effect of Union on Irish industry and trade, it was noticeable that these interests tended to be generally pro-Union. Admittedly and inevitably, Dublin saw no future for itself as a deposed capital, and those involved in the law, in property and in the luxury trades joined in opposition to the measure. Dublin's understandable anti-Unionism also infected the adjacent counties of Meath and Louth; but elsewhere it was a different story. Cloth manufacturers, graziers and provision merchants in Connacht and Munster had benefited from the war and both Galway and Cork looked forward to further gains. These areas were solidly Unionist, as were the important trading counties of Antrim and Londonderry in Ulster. Belfast was regarded as pro-Unionist: it was reported that the city 'rather favours the measure of a Union'; and an impressive civic dinner was organised for Cornwallis when he stopped there during his pro-Union campaign tour around Ireland. It proved impossible, however, to get up a pro-Unionist address from the town; and Belfast's reputation as the citadel of Unionism should be dated to a later period. Any explanation for the success of Union that fails to take into account the real support for the measure from important commercial areas must surely be incomplete. That said, for most of the nineteenth century the perception that the Union had been purchased, that it had been passed by a 'corrupt bargain' and that it therefore lacked moral legitimacy was a central part of the rhetorical armoury of those who would seek to end or mend that arrangement.

Finally, what role did the Catholics and the Catholic question play in the Union negotiations? There was no mention of Catholic relief in the Union terms; but against that, Cornwallis and Castlereagh had succeeded in preventing a clause excluding Catholics for ever from entry into Parliament being incorporated into the Union terms. Moreover, both men had sought to enlist Catholic influence, particularly that of the hierarchy, in support of Union and in this they had also been successful. Admittedly, it had not been difficult to win Catholic support: Catholics and their bishops would shed few tears over the loss of the Irish Parliament, an institution forever associated with the Penal Laws, the repression of the 1790s and an aversion to Catholic emancipation. And the fact that the hated Orange faction was hostile to Union was an added incentive to step forward in support. Contrary to what was later claimed, it had not been neccessary to promise Catholic emancipation in return for support, and no such promise had been made. On the other hand, it is probable that both Castlereagh and Cornwallis in their discussions with the Catholics had stressed how Union would open the way to emancipation; indeed Pitt had said much the same in his speeches on Union. It is likely too that Cornwallis was less than guarded in private conversation with the likes of Archbishop Troy of Dublin. In any case, it was well recognised that one of the main objectives of Union was to permit a safe solution to the Catholic question, and Catholic hopes were understandably high that emancipation would be theirs when Union was passed.

Catholic support for Union was crucial to its success. At first glance, this statement seems absurd. There were no Catholic Members of Parliament, and there was no general election for Catholic votes to play a part. Admittedly, at the Newry by-election in 1799, the Catholic voters had 'stuck together like the Macedonian phalanx' in support of the Castle's candidate, Isaac Corry; but this had hardly been essential to the passing of the Union. Nor had Catholic numbers been evident in support of Union. There had been seventy-six pro-Union addresses, of which only eleven had emanated from identifiably Catholic groups. Moreover, the Catholics had not even been united: Dublin Catholics had heard the twenty-six-year-old barrister, Daniel O'Connell, denounce the Union as a bad bargain for the Catholics of Ireland and claim that he would prefer the reimposition of the Penal Laws to Union. Again, it was self-evident that the Act of Union had been passed by the Irish House of Commons and the Irish House of Lords: how could Catholics have been influential, much less crucial?

Certainly, this theme was taken up both at the time and later by those opposed to the Catholic claims in the united Parliament. The Catholics, it was claimed, had played no part in passing the Act of Union, their support was dismissed as of no consequence and later there were those who affected to doubt that the Catholics had even been pro-Union. And yet such views were shortsighted in the extreme. The professional politicians and managers in Dublin Castle were under no illusions as to how the Union was carried. In August 1799 Castlereagh told Pitt in the clearest terms that 'circumstanced as the Parliamentary interests and the Protestant feelings then were, the measure could not be carried if the Catholics were embarked in an active opposition to it'; while Cornwallis, rarely regarded as politically astute, reportedly claimed that 'if they [Catholics] would act heartily in support [of Union], the Protestants would not resist the efforts of British government assisted by the population of the kingdom'. Cooke commented: 'I believe his position to be true'; and he confirmed that 'the question will be carried by the Catholics'. The reality was that the British government did not dare impose a legislative Union if the Catholic hierarchy – the only available leadership in Catholic Ireland – were opposed; and Catholic acquiesence in the Union measure had denied the anti-Union party that legitimation that their opposition needed in order to resist the British government effectively.

Twenty years earlier, Catholic support for, and membership of, the Volunteers had been decisive in forcing the hand of the British government over the 'Constitution of 1782'; Catholic exclusion from the parliamentary reform movement in the 1780s had been equally decisive in ensuring its failure; Catholic demands in 1792/3 could not be resisted. Even before the union had been proposed, William Wyndham, one of the more thoughtful members of Pitt's government, in surveying the Irish political scene had concluded that the Catholics 'after all, are the body of people that must decide the fate of Ireland'. The Union negotiations showed the truth of this remark; but the next hundred years were spent attempting to deny its implications.

English images of Ireland

In the autumn of 1800 Castlereagh could finally relax: the Union had passed and would come into force at midnight on the last day of the year. 'I feel very proud of myself', he wrote to a colleague, 'of being less an Irishman and more an Englishman than hitherto.'[12] This striking statement, an expression of longing as much as of expectation, is worthy of consideration on two counts. First, it encapsulated perhaps the most problematic aspects of Union – those involving questions of nation, nationality and nationalism. Second, it highlighted that measure's greatest irony: at the very moment of legislative Union, the two countries were in fact moving further and further apart – industrially, agriculturally, demographically and, not least, religiously. There was, of course, no further geographic separation, but the Irish Sea, whatever Castlereagh might hope, would prove to be more than a ha-ha between England and Ireland and, though the two countries were now united, the 'join' would be painfully evident.

In all the public argumentation and special pleading that had accompanied the Union negotiations there had been little that had touched directly on what might be called nationalist issues, principally the implications for the Protestant nation of the loss of that most potent symbol of nationhood – the Irish Parliament. The reality was that Protestant nationalism – or at least one strand in it – that had seemed so vibrant in 1782, seeking and welcoming an accommodation with the Catholics of Ireland, had barely survived the shock of the 1798 rebellion. Hence, Grattan's 'nationalist' objections to Union had not been received with any enthusiasm, a marked contrast to the near-hysteria that had drowned the commercial propositions of 1785, which Grattan had helped orchestrate. Similarly, John Foster, the main opponent of Union, had regarded an Irish Parliament as a vital bulwark of the Protestant interest in Ireland, and he had no confidence that Westminster could be relied upon to undertake that duty from afar. But his 'national' objections to rule from London failed to win over other members of the Irish Parliament.

Outside the Irish Parliament, however, the nationalist argument – that Ireland would be diminished by the loss of its Parliament – would be heard rather more clearly, possibly an indication as to how out of touch the Irish Parliament had become by 1800. Thus, the United Irishman, Dr William Drennan, protested at the fate that lay in store for Ireland – 'to be known in future only as a sound in the title of the sovereign'; and a correspondent of the lawyer and future Catholic activist, Denys Scully, expressed his sorrow at the likelihood that Union, a measure 'so contrary and opposite to the wishes of the Irish people', would become law and that Irish people would then become 'in the true and literal sense "West Britons"'.

Ireland's standing in the world mattered little to Castlereagh or to those like him who sought a second identity in Englishness: he, and they, would find, however, that the England they sought to associate with had changed and that, as 'Irishmen', they could not become Englishmen or even British. They would discover, as the English Catholic activist, Charles Butler, noted that there was 'an unaccountable something which depreciates the talents of the Irish in the estimation of the English'. It may be suggested that that 'unaccountable something' was little more than prejudice based on ignorance.

English politicians, and indeed the English public, knew little of Ireland at the time of the Union. While the Union would give a great fillip to Irish writing in that it provided a stimulus to Irish writers to explain their country to the English, that was work for the future, for the Irish novelist, i.e. the writer who chose to set his or her stories in Ireland was, at the time of Union, largely unknown. As well, while the period 1775–1850 has been labelled the 'great age of Irish travel writing', in fact up to 1800 major accounts were scarce, and the most important of those that were written at the time were published much later. Not many English visited Ireland for pleasure, few of those who did published their impressions, and fewer still had anything worthwhile to say. The casual tourist – a rare enough bird, in marked contrast to those who visited Scotland – followed carefully insulated itineraries, 'handed about from one country gentleman to another who are interested to conceal the true state of the country'. What was known about Ireland came from a number of sources.

There was what we may call the inherited English view of Ireland; a mixture of tales of the wild Irish and amusing anecdotes of Irish 'bulls', heiress-hunters and native braggadocio, all of which were revealed for inspection in the writings of such English and Irish dramatists and novelists as Farquahar, Sheridan and Fielding. In addition, a folk memory of ineradicable popish superstition and barbarism had been recently revived, and invigorated, by scarifying accounts and graphic illustrations of the cruelties and mayhem of the 1798 rebellion. From his vantage point in Dublin Castle, Edward Cooke had forecast that Catholic emancipation, so far from being granted following the passing of the Union, would in fact fall victim to 'the conduct and prejudices of 200 years . . . [and] . . . a constitution purchased by the blood of martyrs and patriots who perished at the stake in Smithfield, and fell upon the banks of the Boyne and on the plains of Aughrim'. Throughout the 1790s English newspapers and magazines had carried detailed coverage of Irish disturbances; for example, the London *Times* had regaled its readers with long accounts of Defender outrages in the early part of the decade, while its coverage of the 1798 rebellion was both extensive and frequently sensational. Such lurid reporting of sectarian insurgency in Ireland seemed calculated to reinforce the English public's view of Ireland as an 'enemy' country, rather than as a potential partner.

A further element reinforcing these negative images and perceptions was the letters sent by Irishmen and Irishwomen resident in Ireland to correspondents in England; the impact of these writings, often confirming and elaborating on stereotypes, can only be guessed at but must surely have been profound. Some Irish politicians clearly felt obliged to pander to English perceptions of Ireland by dwelling on (and warming up) the violence of Irish life, happily shocking their English colleagues with 'all the terrific tales' they could collect. In the 1790s, the correspondence carried on by the likes of John Beresford, or John Fitzgibbon, earl of Clare, with leading British politicians, notably Lord Auckland, was especially influential in this regard, providing, as it were, a quasi-official running commentary on events and personalities in Ireland during that period. Clare's letters in particular revealed his deeply pessimistic view of human nature, recorded his view of the Irish as variously unregenerate, savage, barbaric (if Catholic), naive, foolish, giddy (if Protestant) and puritan, republican and levelling (if Presbyterian) and, above all, stressed his conviction of the futility of all attempts at reform in an Irish context. These dispatches, in the guise of private letters, had an impact on English elite perceptions of Ireland and the Irish, for they were circulated within the governing circle in London (possibly including the king).

A further source of information about Ireland were the letters sent back by English politicians, or English-born bishops in Ireland. It seemed to be expected that, in addition to the normal official correspondence, a lord lieutenant or chief secretary or chief justice would compose a statement of his reflections on Ireland and the Irish. Frequently, these were of such length that they can only have been meant for circulation, and perhaps publication. Most of the leading officials in Dublin Castle in the 1780s and 1790s wrote freely to correspondents, delivering their uniformly unfavourable verdicts on Irish politicians, voicing their conviction of the dangers of Irish reform, revealing their discovery of the ignorance and superstition of the Catholic Irish and stating their suspicions of the Irish Presbyterians.

A final source of information about Ireland was the English and Scottish army officers who served there. Arriving in Ireland clutching a sword in the manner of their Tudor and Stuart predecessors, a number of them took up a pen to record their impressions of the country and its inhabitants. In general English officers found the Irish gentry contemptible, by turns cowardly and oppressive and always uncouth, while Irish officers in the Irish Yeomanry and militia were uniformly regarded as savage, sectarian and incompetent. At the highest levels, the private letters and public statements of the two most recent commanders-in-chief, Abercromby and Cornwallis, had eloquently expressed their wholly unfavourable opinion of the Irish governing elite, both political and military. The causes of the troubles in Ireland also attracted the attention of some officers and, usually in their explanations, they stressed the malign state of social relations in that country, and the oppression visited on the poor by the well-to-do. Many officers concluded that military force alone could maintain order in Ireland: 'The people of Ireland are and will long continue to be ripe for general insurrection', wrote Colonel Robert Crauford, later to win fame for his daring in the Peninsular war.

These unflattering views of Ireland, its peoples and its prospects were seriously at odds with the buoyant public message contained in Unionist speeches and declarations. The glaring discrepancy between the negative English perception of what Ireland was (one shared at both popular and elite levels) and the positive act of seeking to unite with such a regressive country (a country in every respect the perceived antithesis of England itself) was a flaw at the heart of Union. By 1800 England was becoming more Protestant, Ireland more Catholic. And, just as Englishness and Protestantism had long been synonymous, so too the Catholics of Ireland had become, as a Catholic broadsheet had it, 'the Nation of the Irish'. England and Englishness were seen as civilised, cultured and familiar; Ireland and Irishness were burlesque, barbaric and alien. England was becoming wealthier, Ireland poorer; moreover unlike Scottish poverty, Irish poverty was intensely visible, for massive population growth, concentrated at the bottom of the social scale, was flooding the Irish highways and especially the Irish landscape with a mass of destitute humanity. Scotland's natural beauties could be admired, but in Ireland the masses got in the way of similar breathtaking views; and the negative perception of Ireland was reinforced.

Again, by the end of the century, English nationalism, as a result of interminable wars with France, was in full spate. Ireland, however, was a probable ally of the hated enemy, France. Even Cornwallis had to concede that Britain should for strategic purposes consider 'the majority of the Irish people as enemies', and a few years after Union the future duke of Wellington, himself Irish-born, declared: 'I lay it down as decided, that Ireland, in a view to military operations, must be considered as an enemy's country.' With such opinions and judgements commonplace in Ireland and England at the time of the Union, it was no wonder that Cornwallis (and others) began to have their doubts. Irish politicians, mused Cornwallis, shortly before his departure from Ireland, had many merits but these were outweighed by their strong prejudices, though he conceded that English politicians had these too. He then continued:

> They assert and I speak from high authority amongst them that the Catholics of Ireland, seven tenths of the population of the country never

can be good subjects to a Protestant government. What then have we done? We have united ourselves to a people whom we ought to have destroyed.

The first thirty years would be crucial to the success of the Union; but already in 1800 the signs were clearly not propitious.

Post-Union Ireland

Little thought had been given to what the structure of government would be in post-Union Ireland. A separate executive for Ireland, complete with its own lord lieutenant, chief secretary, under-secretaries, commander-in-chief (though no separate Irish staff), and various legal and financial officers, including a lord chancellorship and a chancellor of the exchequer, appears to have been assumed, rather than decided upon and they were all continued after the Union. Revealingly, the one item of post-Union government that had received prompt attention was the question of the Irish Parliament building. The building was quickly sold to the Bank of Ireland on condition that it carry out extensive alterations expressly designed to prevent the building from ever again being used as a legislative assembly.

So far as reform legislation was concerned, post-Union Ireland proved a disappointment. This was all the more surprising in that, if there was one thing upon which all agreed, it was that Union would open the way to legislative change and improvement. In their speeches and statements on Union Pitt, Cornwallis and Castlereagh had all given their various audiences to understand that an entire legislative programme – something on tithes, perhaps provision of government pay for Catholic priests or subventions for internal improvements, even, especially, a breakthrough on the Catholic question – would swiftly follow the enactment of a Union. Indeed, some anti-Unionists had opposed Union precisely because they believed it would open the way to further unfavourable innovation. All were proved mistaken, at least in the short term. Any notion of reforming the operation of the tithe system in Ireland was speedily abandoned in the face of protests from the established (and united) churches of Great Britain and Ireland; and state pay for Catholic priests, though brought up from time to time in the years after Union had been effectively ruled out by George III at an early date. Even those English administrators anxious to introduce what Charles Abbot, the first post-Union chief secretary, called 'British standards' into Irish government found their way blocked. On his appointment, Abbot had speedily launched an investigation into the jobs, duties and fees of the Irish Revenue Board; but this inquiry was soon abandoned in the face of howls of outrage. Chief secretaries might fume privately about Ireland being 'delivered over to Irish animosities, prejudices and corruptions', and others might demand that 'the profligacy of Ireland before the Union', a result of the 'looseness of Irish morals [which] is as striking as any part of their character' should not be continued after the Union; but in the end, little was done administratively, or legislatively, to mark the new regime. There are a number of reasons which help explain this paralysis: but central to them all was the failure to act on the Catholic question.

The resolution of the Catholic question, essentially the passing of an Act enabling Catholics, if elected, to take their seats in the new united legislature, had been the anticipated coping-stone to Union. Key members of the Pitt government – Pitt himself, Grenville and Dundas – and the entire Dublin Castle team of Cornwallis, Castlereagh and Cooke were in favour of such a measure as an essential follow-up to Union. In the event, in the first of a number of upheavals involving Ireland that would disrupt the British political structure periodically throughout the nineteenth century, and beyond, Pitt was refused leave by the king to introduce a 'Catholic' bill, and he and his leading ministers had no option but to resign. Their resignations were followed shortly by those of Cornwallis, Castlereagh and Cooke.

George III's resistance to the Catholic claims won him popularity, not just amongst loyalists and Orangemen in Ireland, but in England too where a native nationalism with its xenophobic (particularly anti-French) outlook and its anti-Catholic tone was running high. In addition, the established churches were well aware of (and apprehensive at) the likely results of concessions to Irish Catholics: a strengthened demand for similar concessions to all manner of religious Dissenters (Presbyterians, Quakers, Jews, even Methodists), and the Anglican bishops in Ireland and England were therefore generally hostile to Catholic relief. Irish politicians too had their own reasons for being less than enthusiastic about Catholic emancipation. Catholics had the county franchise since 1793 but they could only vote for Protestant candidates. If Catholics were permitted to stand for Parliament, it was assumed (wrongly) that their votes would automatically go to their co-religionists; and hence Irish Members of Parliament, at least in private, were cool on the idea of full civic equality for Catholics.

Pitt's ministry was succeeded by that of Henry Addington, and it was reported that the guiding principle of his government was simply to resist Catholic emancipation. Within weeks of the passing of the Act of Union, then, that measure had begun to take on the character of a new Penal Law, at least in the eyes of Irish Catholics who a year earlier had been among its staunchest supporters. The Union now appeared to be as flawed and as incomplete as that other 'final settlement' which it had replaced, the 'Constitution of 1782'. Unlike the situation in 1782, however, there could be no agitation for parliamentary reform, for there was no Irish Parliament to reform: there could only be a campaign on behalf of Catholic emancipation or, alternatively, one to repeal the Union. Ironically, a Union which was designed to put an end to the Irish question, in fact only shifted the location of the debate without really altering its terms. Once Catholic emancipation had been ruled out by George III, and once 'anti-popery' had become the stock-in-trade, the very cement, of a succession of English governments, then it was inevitable that Irish politics would continue to be entirely dominated by the Catholic question. It may be argued that, had Catholic emancipation been conceded in 1801, it would only have brought forward by thirty years the campaign against tithe and for repeal of the Union. Equally, it could be claimed that concession had never previously brought about conciliation, but instead had always fuelled further demands. However, the failure to complete the Union in 1801 rendered certain what must have remained uncertain. In the absence of an Irish Parliament, the struggle for Catholic emancipation could not fail to become a national struggle with religion at its heart: 'the Nation of the Irish' against the English Parliament and Dublin Castle; and that contest would prove the crucible in which the Irish (Catholic) nation was forged.

In its campaign of resistance to the Catholics, Dublin Castle would need every ally it could find, and this necessarily would mean recourse to the 'Orange faction'. Once the British government cut the Catholics adrift after 1801 it had no choice but to settle for sectarian government in Ireland and this, in turn, meant reliance on the ascendancy. There were some advantages to this: the experienced and very able Foster quickly returned to the Castle fold, and despite Abbot's determination that he was not to be allowed to 'get upon the coachbox', he soon took a lead and other anti-Unionists had followed his example. Moreover, the predominantly Protestant, largely Orange, military armament, the Yeomanry, was a reassuring, though turbulent peace-keeping and policing force, one that Dublin Castle was only too glad to have at its disposal in the event of invasion or insurgency. The price of such support, however, was that 'Union principles' or 'British standards' had to be jettisoned lest they provoked unrest among the government's Irish Protestant supporters or perhaps substantiated the opposition's argument that there was something rotten in the state of Ireland. In this way, the decision to head off the Catholics in 1801 determined the entire shape of post-Union politics, at least up to the surrender of Catholic emancipation in 1829.

Union in the end, for all the rhetoric, the promises, and the cheery forecasts, merely meant the destruction of the Irish Parliament; but herein lay the difficulty. That Parliament with all its faults had screened England from Ireland.

Its removal, however, laid bare the relationship, revealed its lovelessness and rendered its long-term continuance problematic.

Law, order and the Catholic question

Two issues dominated the first twenty years of the Union: law and order, and the Catholic question. Neither was, of course, new, but Union meant that the impact of each would be rather different from before, for a united legislature offered each question a fresh context and a different setting to the old Irish Parliament. 'Irish crime', in particular, was made to bear an additional burden. Before Union its endemic nature had seemed a pressing reason to do away with the Irish Parliament widely held responsible for the law and order breakdown. After Union, however, continuing Irish disorder legitimised both the English presence in Ireland and the enactment of a draconian series of repressive laws. Indeed, because Irish crime was so useful in excusing English inaction on reform and validating emergency legislation, historians ought to be wary of accepting at face value English reports of its endemic nature and barbaric character. The unique quality of 'Irish crime', like the uniquely regressive elements within 'Irish' Catholicism, might turn out on examination to be a creation of the English official mind. There was plenty of savage violence in England, but it served no political purpose to dwell on it and hence it rarely figured in official discourse. By contrast, Irish crime carried a heavy political freight: its universalism was necessary and its savagery was vital for the validation of the English presence and mission in Ireland. Those who voiced polite scepticism on the matter of universal Irish crime were given short shrift.

The passing of the Act of Union coincided with an alarming shortage of food and agrarian disturbances in Ireland. From all over the country, but especially from Connacht and the south-west, came reports of extreme distress accompanied by outrages. In late 1799, and throughout 1800 the price of corn in Ireland rose steeply as a result of a very poor harvest. With corn prices rising, the potato crop, hit by an unseasonal drought, was unable to meet demand and by August 1800 it was claimed that seed pototoes, destined for the next year's harvest, were being consumed by the peasantry. Dublin Castle responded energetically to this developing crisis: Castlereagh defied the wrath of the British Home Office (for corn was scarce in Britain too) and issued a proclamation offering a bounty on the import of American corn and rice to Ireland. He justified this step as a necessary measure of counter-insurgency, for from many quarters came accounts of nocturnal attacks. The province of Connacht in particular was badly hit by an epidemic of cattle-houghing (animals were crippled by having their hamstrings slashed so that they could not be driven to market) and it was a similar story in counties Cork, Limerick, Tipperary and Waterford. Even the approaches to Dublin saw attacks on cattle.

There was general agreement among observers that misery and want lay behind these outrages rather than disaffection or subversion. On occasion there was a demand for appropriate reforms and even a note of sympathy from elite observers which caused the civil and military authorities some anxiety. Within a few years, however, in the face of continual agrarian crime, English patience and understanding had grown rather thin and new, more sombre explanations were proffered. In this shift from sympathy to antipathy, the abortive rebellion of Robert Emmet is of prime importance.

Essentially, Robert Emmet's *émeute* was the last gasp of the 1798 rebellion. Undismayed by the crushing of that insurrection, Emmet had planned another, in which he would put into practice the lessons learnt from the previous attempt. He resolved this time that there would be no distractions caused by expectation of French assistance, that the centre of the rising would be Dublin itself and that the whole was to be cloaked in impenetrable secrecy. In this latter resolve Emmet succeeded only too well. Michael Dwyer, the Wicklow insurgent, who had remained 'outstanding' in the mountains since the 1798 rebellion was a party to the conspiracy, and so too was Thomas Russell who had sat out the 1798 rebellion in an Irish gaol; but Emmet's detailed plans were only known fully to Emmet himself.

In July 1803 those plans went awry when his munitions store in Thomas Street, Dublin, went up in flames and alerted the authorities to the existence of the plot. There were some desultory disturbances both in the city (Lord Chief Justice Kilwarden was the most prominent casualty) and in nearby county Kildare, especially around the village of Maynooth; but Ulster remained tranquil, despite the best efforts of Russell; and the 'rising' was crushed. The leading conspirators were quickly arrested: among those subsequently executed were Emmet and Russell, while scores of their followers were transported to Botany Bay. Notwithstanding the Protestantism of both Emmet and Russell, the rising was quickly dubbed a 'popish affair' and it was seized on by loyalists as confirmation of their warnings about Catholic plots. The key role played by the largely Protestant Yeomanry in mobilising rapidly to protect vulnerable locations and to secure the streets of the capital was equally reassuring to them, for that force was by now firmly identified as the military wing of loyalism. Dublin Castle, though it attempted to deny it, was caught completely unawares and its failure to anticipate the rising was much criticised, loyalists gleefully pointing out that an Irish Parliament would not have been so remiss.

4.5 Triumph in defeat. Robert Emmet's speech from the dock following his death sentence in 1803 was to echo down through the nineteenth century. National Library of Ireland.

The embarrassment and shock caused to Dublin Castle by Emmet (figure 4.5) and his fellow-conspirators had profound repercussions. Wickham, the luckless chief secretary (like Augustine Birrell in 1916) did not survive the rebellion: an interview with Emmet and a letter to him from Emmet shortly before his execution brought about some sort of nervous collapse, and he retired to private life. More important, in the years after the Emmet conspiracy, there was a perceptible shift in the attitude of successive British governments towards Ireland. The attempt to govern Ireland on 'Union principles' was now tacitly abandoned, and loyalists, hitherto ignored or despised, found themselves courted and their views regarded. Moreover, with reform ruled out and with all pretence of making a 'nominal' Union a 'real' Union given up, at least for the time being, Irish crime was viewed in a much more sinister light. It was still a product of wretchedness; but it was now perceived to have a rooted quality about it, and it was viewed as the outward expression of an innate flaw of the Irish (Catholic) character.

Loyalists, of course, had been saying this for a long time: the writings of Edmund Spenser and Sir Arthur Chichester had been key texts with them; what was different in post-Emmet Ireland was that the same language was now heard regularly in Dublin Castle. If Irish crime was natural, then nothing could be done about it, except enforce a stern repression; if Irish bloodlust was innate, then it could not be removed by reform, only curtailed by fear. At one time disturbances in Ireland had been advanced as something that would disappear under Union; within five years of Union, however, Irish disorder had been pronounced irremediable, thus excusing the lack of ameliorative reform. The Catholicism of the Irish – unlike the Catholicism of inhabitants of continental countries – was to be reprobated as both symptom and cause of their unique degeneracy and depravity. Ireland, concluded the lord lieutenant, Lord Whitworth, in 1814, 'is not to be governed as England is: the character and the spirit of the governed are completely different', and he argued that it was only through a large military force that 'the lower orders can be kept down'. By that date, the Union aspiration had gone: Ireland would be held rather than governed. But this might not prove all that easy; years earlier Castlereagh had put his finger on the inherent difficulty in this strategy. Since there was now no Irish Parliament to approve repressive legislation, perhaps, he had written, 'if she [England] is to govern Ireland upon a garrison principle . . . she has parted as well with her most effectual means as with her most perfect justification'.

It would be tedious to examine in detail all the disturbances which occurred in various parts of Ireland in the first two decades of the nineteenth century. However, some observations may be made about their causes, the composition of the insurgent bands and the official reaction. In general, three cycles of violence can be identified in these decades: the first, from 1799 to 1803 we have already looked at; the second occurred from 1806 to 1816, when the Caravats and Shanavests were active in east Munster and further afield; and finally, there were major disturbances during the years 1819–23 when the Ribbonmen and the followers of 'Captain Rock' wreaked havoc in the south and west of Ireland. No year, however, was entirely free of disturbances; it was often impossible to separate Thresher from Caravat, Shanavest from Ribbonman, and all of these from the followers of Captain Rock; and those contemporaries who regarded all Ireland during the early nineteenth century[13] as a single, gigantic, 'theatre of disorder' might be forgiven their rash generalisation.

All of these disturbances testify to the astonishing degree of economic and social change sweeping across rural Ireland at that time. Population growth was concentrated at the bottom of the Irish demographic pyramid (i.e. among the poor), and put great pressure on the existing structure of landholding. Subdivision of tenancies into smaller and smaller holdings increased dramatically, effectively denying the landlord anything more than a tenuous hold on his estate. For example, in 1800 Maurice FitzGerald had given out leases on his estate on Valentia Island, county Kerry, to thirteen substantial tenants for a term of three lives with each getting some 400–500 acres. These middlemen had soon become absentees, and had allowed unchecked subdivision with the result that four hundred tenants in 1800 had become eight thousand thirty years later. FitzGerald's experience was replicated elsewhere, and everywhere it was the ubiquitous, nutritious and fickle potato that fed the rising population. Moreover, wartime demand for foodstuffs – cereal and beef – meant (at least up to 1815) that there was money to be made in agriculture and in stock-rearing. But such activities sharply curtailed the amount of land available for potato cultivation and led to the conflict at the heart of Irish rural disturbances in the pre-Famine period, the antipathy between on the one hand, the large farmers, middlemen and graziers and, on the other, the small farmers, labourers, cottiers and the landless.

This early struggle for the land certainly had elements of the landlord–tenant conflict of the later nineteenth century, for the small farmers and cottiers were frequently tenants or subtenants of the marginally better-off strong farmers. However, the conflict lacked the potent ingredients of nationality and religion which would be features of the later struggle, for both the large farmers and the labourers in pre-Famine Ireland were usually Irish and mostly Catholic; nor can their rivalry be seen as a contest between winners and losers, for at this time the difference between such categories was frequently notional. Central to the conflict were differing reactions to the impact of economic change, for the spread of the market economy with its cash transactions, its profits from forestalling and hoarding and from grazing was being challenged by the proponents of a 'moral' economy where cheap food and readily available land were held to be basic rights. The acrimony between these two clusters of interests may have been sharpened by food crises, land shortage, partial harvest failures, rising rents, tithes and a general immiseration; but it was fundamentally shaped by those who sought to benefit from modernisation and those who feared it – a theme that would have long legs in the history of modern Ireland.

The struggle between the Caravats and Shanavests which ebbed and flowed between 1806 and 1816 showed clearly the class divisions within rural Ireland and revealed a precocious willingness on both sides to resort to murderous violence in pursuit of class objectives. The Caravats were in general in the old Whiteboy tradition and they purported to act in defence of the rights of the poor. Hence they swore to punish anyone who took a farm from which another had been evicted, sought to curtail the level and incidence of tithe, tried to force down food prices and occasionally abducted the daughters of wealthy farmers with a view to forcing them into marriage. Time and time again, they launched attacks on 'strangers', i.e. tenants/labourers who had left their original county to live and work in another, and who therefore represented unwelcome competition.

By contrast the Shanavests were composed of those who had to some extent profited from the Napoleonic wartime boom in Ireland, and these graziers and strong farmers banded together in the face of the onslaught from those who had not so benefited. The Shanavests were vigilantes rather than social bandits; they had only a rudimentary social programme; and by intimidation and murder (and giving information to the authorities), they sought to maintain their position in rural society and see off the challenge from their labourers and the rest of the rural proletariat. Resolute military action in 1811, when the affected areas in Munster were flooded with soldiers, brought the troubles between Caravats and Shanavests to a temporary close.

The lull in hostilities at this time owed much to the ending of wartime prosperity, leading to some degree of misery for all rural classes. Certainly the serious disturbances which occurred in Munster from 1813 to 1816 appear to represent a broad social coalition of protesters and while Caravats and Shanavests were involved, the class basis of their antagonism is difficult to establish. Once again, there were attacks on those alleged to have taken lands formerly held by others, and from Borrisoleigh, county Tipperary, came reports that over thirty families were ordered to quit because they were 'strangers', though they had been settled there nearly twenty years. Ominously, the violence was not confined to the lower ranks and among the ten people murdered in the area around Clonmel in the years 1814–15 were two prominent magistrates.

Further sustained disturbances, probably owing much to the spread of 'Ribbonism' (Catholic rural insurgency) from west and south Ulster, broke out in 1819 in Connacht, and by 1821 had appeared to fuse with the Rockite agitation, so-called because the participants swore to obey the mythical 'Captain Rock'. As in earlier outbreaks, the grievances of the rural poor were at issue in all of these disturbances: rents, tithes, taxes, even priests' dues and fees were on the protesters' agenda, and, once again, the counties of Cork, Kerry, Limerick and Clare were the prime centres for the troubles. However, in addition, there was now an unmistakable sectarian note to the protests: 'The bloody Protestant time is expired, and they shall be slaughtered like dogs' was reportedly one slogan. This overtly anti-Protestant sentiment was new – though, needless to say, some Protestant commentators affected to have detected it in every disturbance since the 1760s – and, in the early 1820s, it took on a more sinister edge with the widespread propagation of the apocalyptic prophecies of Pastorini.

Pastorini was the pen-name of the English Catholic bishop, Charles Walmsley, who had written some thirty years earlier a series of prophecies based on the Book of Revelations forecasting the destruction of the Protestant church precisely fifty years after 1771. These had been published in several editions since the 1790s but from at least 1814 his prophecies had been circulated in broadsheet format suitable for pasting up in a public place; and as the favoured dates for the end of Protestantism were 1821 and, especially, 1825, the popular excitement in the early 1820s can be readily understood. Again, as in earlier disturbances, there were frequent attacks on elite figures and those representing law and order: and there was at least one sensational assassination. Late in 1821 Major Richard Going, at the time in charge of policing county Limerick, was waylaid and shot dead on his way home. His murder, it was reported, was announced by 'a joyous shout through the country, which re-echoed from place to place: lighted heaps of straw were also at night exhibited on the different hills in triumph'. Going had been a much-hated figure to the local insurgents, for he had been indefatigable in their pursuit. He was also an Orangeman, and rumour had it that he had buried a wounded prisoner in quicklime.

The Rockite movement was essentially millenarian in that it looked forward to the destruction of Protestantism by divine intervention, and its participants were convinced that the achievement of this apocalyptic vision would herald the coming of a new order in the world. Such millennial dreams were by no means unusual in Irish popular disturbances, but the formidable extent of the Rockite agitation was new and revealed clearly the combustible material in the Irish countryside. The Rockite movement only subsided when the affected areas were flooded with 'Peelers' (as Irish secretary, Sir Robert Peel's, new police were dubbed), and by large numbers of regular soldiers. The fact that the fateful year 1825 passed without cataclysm no doubt helped reduce tension. It might also be suggested that the towering influence of the Catholic leader, Daniel O'Connell, in the late 1820s – for O'Connell was truly a messianic figure – helped divert millennial energies into more constitutional, but no less millennial, paths.

Dublin Castle sought in vain to repress these disturbances in the post-Union decades. Attempts had been made in the 1780s and 1790s to set up a rural constabulary for Ireland charged with dealing with agrarian crime, but these had been swept away in the insurgency and counter-insurgency of the 1790s. Since the time of Union, Dublin Castle had little option but to rely on the military force of militia, Yeomanry and regular army, and it well recognised that there were major problems with all of these. The militia, with its largely Catholic rank and file, was suspect since the 1798 rebellion; the Yeomanry was an undisciplined, 'Orange', force, more likely to stir up trouble than restore order; and the regulars were needed abroad to fight the French. In any case, regular army officers detested acting in support of the civil authorities in Ireland. Much reliance, therefore, had to be placed on the magistracy; but its members were universally recognised to be inefficient, often corrupt and frequently reluctant to undertake any measure that might jeopardise their election prospects. One commentator even alleged that, so partisan were the magistrates in his area, that 'they secretly chuckled at the news' of an attack on a lowly tithe-farmer or process server. One or two chief secretaries did contemplate reform of the magistracy, but they backed off when they realised the opposition that they would encounter. Instead, alarmed by the rising crime figures and the poor conviction rate (less than 30 per cent compared to over 60 per cent in England), official attention focused on police reform.

In 1808 an important start was made when Sir Arthur Wellesley, then chief secretary, managed to pilot through the united Parliament an Act which set up an essentially new force with a new jurisdiction for the city of Dublin and its environs. His object was to make the capital secure in the event of troops having to be withdrawn to meet an emergency in the countryside. At a stroke Dublin became the most heavily policed city in the British empire, with its police force entirely under the control of the Castle. There remained, however, the pressing problem of creating an efficient rural police force.

On his arrival in Ireland in 1812 as chief secretary, Sir Robert Peel had protested at the current policy of relying heavily on the armed forces of the crown to preserve or restore order: but, like others before him (and after him) he had quickly realised that little could be done with the Irish magistracy. 'Half our disorders and disturbances', he declared, 'arise from the negligence of some [magistrates] and [the] corruption and party spirit of others.' Peel, therefore, determined to make the provision of an effective, centrally controlled police force a priority of his term of office. In 1814 his Peace Preservation Act was passed by which, at the request of local magistrates or on the authority of the lord lieutenant, a police force of up to fifty constables from outside the county, accompanied by a stipendiary magistrate (a salaried government lawyer), again from outside the county, would be sent into the disturbed area. His authority would be paramount over the county magistrates. Local control in matters of law and order finally came to an end: the state would police the localities. Moreover, for the first time, and in a significant breakthrough, Catholics were to be allowed to serve in the police (lower ranks only). Previous schemes for rural constabularies had foundered on the need to restrict recruitment exclusively to Protestants. However, in many of the more disturbed areas of Ireland, the Protestant population had been simply too small to maintain such a force. Finally, the expenses of these new 'flying columns' of police were to be borne by the local authorities, though later (1820) they were to be shared between central and county government. Peel's initiative was 'revolutionary', in that it set up a centrally organised and Castle-controlled force, one that could bypass local opposition, override local jealousies and, in theory, beat down local prejudices.

Progress at implementing the new force was slow; by 1819 only some thirteen counties had the 'Peelers', and most of these were in the south and west – Ulster, for example, continued to be policed almost entirely by the Yeomanry – but the force moved into more counties in the 1820s, and it laid the foundations for the Irish constabulary of the later nineteenth century. The new police proved particularly effective when they were twinned with regular troops, and the small rise in felony convictions detected in the 1820s may be attributed to their activities. By 1825, then, Dublin, and Ireland generally, were more intensively policed than London and England; the bases of their respective police forces were entirely different; and the laws under which they operated had little in common with one another. Once again, under the Union, England and Ireland were drawing apart in a vital area of public policy.

What was the significance of these agrarian disorders that were such a feature of the first two decades of the nineteenth century? Obviously, their prevalence proved conclusively – at least in English eyes – that there was something wrong with Ireland. In attempting to isolate that rotten element, however, and to apportion blame for the disturbances, disagreement began. There was, of course, some common ground. Predictably, the magistracy was a convenient scapegoat. There was general agreement too that there was much at fault in the Irish attitude towards the law. Lord Redesdale, reflecting on his experience as Irish lord chancellor declared in 1821 'that in all ranks of people, high and low, rich and poor, native Irish, pure English, mixed breeds, Catholic, Protestant, whatever were their origins, whatever their religious or political creeds, few were disposed thoroughly to obey the law'. Unlike in England, where the law was regarded as a neutral instrument, in Ireland the 'law' was perceived as a vigorously partisan weapon, to be applied or waived as the occasion demanded. A bemused Peel himself had commented, some years earlier, that most people in Ireland seemed to regard the law as offering a rough guide to action, rather than a binding mandate. 'I believe there are nine persons in ten', he continued,

> who are convinced that the government is in no way bound by an Act of the legislature, and has a general power over the lives and property and liberty of the people. Nay, I think the majority have the same idea of the government which the natives of India are said to have of the East India Company.

These weaknesses in Irish society, part structural (the absence of a vigorous governing elite or, conversely, the presence of a useless one), and part moral (a universal reluctance to obey the law or accept its impartiality) certainly exercised the minds of concerned observers; but there were always those who favoured other competing, overarching explanations. Inevitably, there were those who saw in Irish outrages irrefutable evidence of innate flaws in the character of the Irish Catholic and, indeed, further confirmation of the judgements of a string of writers from Gerald of Wales through Edmund Spenser and on to Sir John Temple and latterly, Sir Richard Musgrave. This is what George Cornwall Lewis was getting at, in his 1836 study of Irish disturbances, when he referred to those officials who were convinced 'that there is an innate and indelible tendency in the Irish to disturbance and outrage; that Ireland has been cut off by nature from the rest of the civilised world, and been foredoomed to a state of endless disorder'. Others professed to see all agrarian disturbances as yet another round in the seemingly endless struggle for sectarian mastery which seemed to have provided the central theme of Irish history since the sixteenth century.

Certainly, material for this thesis was not lacking: the Rockite movement fitted it well enough, for the apocalyptic vision of the followers of Captain Rock offered little comfort to Protestants. Moreover, the British soldiers deployed against the Rockites were generally Protestant and paraded to the local Church of Ireland each Sunday, while the police force set up by Sir Robert Peel to combat local disturbances soon had several Orange lodges within it. 'Law and order' thereby became sectarianised, and in any case, as one commentator pointed out, even where religion appeared to play no role in disturbances, none the less, 'where the actors are of one sect and the victim of another, it does not fail to sanction the crime'. The perilous situation of isolated Protestant families in the early 1820s lent further weight to this notion of a beleaguered Protestantism about to be stormed by a resurgent Catholicism. From time to time there were reports of both Protestants and Catholics in certain areas leaving their homes at night, for fear of being massacred in their beds. And in the early decades of the nineteenth century, hundreds of thousands of Irish Protestants, perhaps as many as half a million between 1815 and 1844, left an Ireland that had become increasingly uncomfortable to them.

By the 1820s this belief in a national movement against both British rule and the Church of Ireland was becoming almost an orthodoxy in government circles. In the early years of the century, some officials had professed to see endemic Irish crime as the product of nothing more sinister than universal Irish poverty and misery. But as time went on, and disturbances spread, gained in ferocity, took on an anti-Protestant colouring and – especially – seemed impervious to repression a different verdict was returned, one that stressed innate Irish savagery and anti-Protestantism; and any who questioned this bleak view found themselves denounced. For example, in 1814 a judge had claimed in an impassioned address from the bench that in all his years on circuit he had never found evidence of any conspiracy against government. On the contrary, he had frequently come across those 'deep-rooted and neglected causes', such as 'extraordinary rents for lands' and farm holdings auctioned with 'no gratitude, no preference, no predilection for the ancient tenantry'. An outraged Dublin Castle launched an inquiry into his conduct. His description of Protestant clergy in pursuit of their tithes – 'gospel crusaders, belonging to the church militant, thinking of anything but feeding the hungry and clothing the naked' was particularly resented, and his denial (based on his experience in Kilkenny and Tipperary) that there was any need for emergency legislation in Ireland provoked additional fury.

Similarly, when a few years later, Charles Grant, chief secretary in succession to Peel, attempted a cool and dispassionate assessment of agrarian crime in Ireland, he quickly ran into trouble. At an early date, the naive Grant had protested that it was 'not doing justice to the people' of Ireland to represent them as 'rebellious', and he condemned what he called the 'powerful bias in the gentry to call in military aid'. Accordingly, he advised that the number of troops in Ireland should be reduced from 25,000 to 18,000 or, preferably, 12,000. This proposal was particularly resented, for it called into question the cherished assumption that Ireland was an enemy country, with a populace ever ready for rebellion. Grant's remarks were loudly criticised, and he was darkly accused of Roman Catholic leanings. Inevitably, he was replaced in December 1821. Grant had been a coming man on his appointment to the chief secretaryship of Ireland; he spent the next fifty years in the political wilderness.

Grant's views were regarded as subversive; much more to the liking of Dublin Castle was a report on the disturbances in county Limerick in the early 1820s, penned by two of the most experienced police officers in Ireland, Richard Willcocks and George Warburton. These two men identified what they saw as the root of the problem. This was that they were confronted everywhere by 'an immense, unemployed and consequently dissatisfied population which has for a series of years indulged in lawless, idle and disorderly habits and pursuits'. This population had long been accustomed to swearing 'illegal oaths' and resisting the laws. The fatal result of all this was that there was a 'pre-existing disposition' on the part of the local inhabitants and of the Irish generally, to seize every opportunity for mayhem. Nor was this propensity for lawlessness a local problem in the Limerick area, and nor was the violence aimless. On the contrary, they wrote, there was a 'systematic proceeding in all these disturbances' which had as their ultimate object the destruction of the Protestant religion, the seizure of church land and the recovery of the confiscated estates. Their fears in these respects were, no doubt, further fuelled by the nationwide agitation of the Catholic question under the generalship of Daniel O'Connell. It is to this movement that we now turn.

Catholic emancipation (i)

So far from Catholic emancipation accompanying Union, within a short time of the passing of that measure, it was widely recognised that emancipation would be incomparably more difficult in a united legislature than in the old Irish Parliament.[14] The formation of the Addington administration, following the resignation of Pitt, on an avowedly anti-Catholic basis, the continued obduracy of George III on the matter and the nationalistic (and anti-Catholic) tone of English society all guaranteed that emancipation for Irish Catholics would be neither easy nor prompt. Moreover, it was widely recognised that concessions for Irish Catholics held serious implications for the status of other minority religions (in a United Kingdom context) such as Jews, Presbyterians and other Dissenters from the established church. Anglican bishops, already under pressure from the Methodist and evangelical advance, were determined to hold the line against the Catholics. In addition, admitting Catholics to sit in the united Parliament meant bringing up the whole question of parliamentary reform. The war against Bonaparte would require the participation of the British (and Irish) masses to bring it to a successful conclusion, but there would be strong resistance to recognising their efforts in any tangible way. There was, for example, little desire to reward military service with a measure of parliamentary reform, and there was a fear that Catholic emancipation by opening up Westminster to Irish Catholics might, in fact, open the door to wider, more unwelcome changes in Britain. Then again, the current Irish parliamentary representation would, it was claimed, be thrown into turmoil if Catholics could be elected to Westminster.

The 1793 Relief Act had awarded the franchise to Irish Catholics on the same terms as Irish Protestants, but at that date the Irish Parliament had been essentially a 'borough' Parliament, with the large majority of the members (234 out of 300) being returned for boroughs which were either tightly controlled or owned outright by political magnates. Elections, much less 'free votes', in these boroughs were almost entirely unknown: successful representatives were selected, nominated by the patron or else purchased their seats. The Catholic electorate created, at least notionally in 1793, could only operate in the county constituencies which returned roughly 20 per cent of the Members of Parliament. However, the Act of Union changed all this. Irish representation after 1801 was henceforth centred predominantly in the counties – sixty four Members out of a total of a hundred. Here Catholic votes counted, and 'political agronomy' – the deliberate increase of the number of Catholic electors – would lead in time to greater Catholic influence in the county constituencies. This influence could, however, only be exercised in the election of Protestant candidates. It would be a potent argument against giving Catholics the right to sit in Parliament that, through their voting strength in the counties, they would speedily dominate the Irish representation; they would then seek an Irish Parliament; and, ultimately, they would go on to demand Irish independence.

The first few years after the Union saw little movement on the Catholic question. Lord Hardwicke, Cornwallis's successor, saw it as his prime duty to deflect all discussion of the matter, and Pitt's continued exclusion from office helped him in this task. The Catholics saw Pitt as their patron; his message to Archbishop Troy of Dublin counselling patience in the matter of relief had been well received; and Catholic leaders were reluctant to proceed without his guidance. This is not to say that religious harmony or Christian forbearance reigned in Ireland in the aftermath of Union. On the contrary, as a Protestant evangelical mission got under way in Ireland with Protestant preachers haranguing Catholic crowds (sometimes in Irish) and distributing Bibles among them, and as proselytism among Catholic soldiers in the British armed forces or among the Catholic poor attending charity schools began to excite concern among the Catholic hierarchy, Catholic–Protestant relations deteriorated and sectarianism became rampant.

Some Catholic bishops issued strict injunctions against Catholics marrying Protestants without a binding commitment that the children of such a union would be raised as Catholics; and the Protestant Bishop of Killala protested that the local parish priest had refused permission for the bishop's (Catholic) servants to attend household prayer with him. The unseemly public quarrel in 1803 between Lord Redesdale, the new lord chancellor in succession to Clare, and the senior Irish Catholic peer, Lord Fingall, over whether or not Catholics could ever be loyal to a Protestant prince, did nothing to improve matters; and a series of sectarian brawls, the occasional chapel-burning, and the odd murder heightened sectarian tensions. The publication in 1801 of Musgrave's history of the 1798 rebellion in which he traced its origins to the Vatican angered the Catholic hierarchy, and the claim that Emmet's rebellion, despite the Protestantism of the main leaders, 'originated with the papists exclusively' and had as its object another massacre of Protestants on the model of 1641, aroused further resentment. All of these developments made it certain that when the Catholic question appeared on the political agenda once again, it would be more sectarianised than before; at issue now would be the future of Protestant ascendancy in Ireland.

Late in 1804 a meeting attended by some thirty-five Catholic merchants, doctors, lawyers and a few landowners took place at the home of the Dublin merchant, James Ryan: its object – to discuss the presentation to Westminster of a petition calling for Catholic emancipation. Following a heated discussion, it was agreed to present such a petition and Pitt was asked to take charge of it in Parliament. When he refused, his rival, Charles James Fox was approached. Fox accepted, and the petition was duly rejected by 336 to 124 in the Commons, and by 178 to 49 in the Lords. This rebuff was confirmed a year later when the so-called 'Ministry of all the Talents', led by Fox and Lord Grenville, was dismissed for daring to suggest a minor measure of concession for Irish Catholics. The cause of Catholic emancipation was seemingly going nowhere. Indeed, if anything, it seemed to be regressing, for a new issue shortly arose to distract the energies of the Catholic body, divide its supporters and delight its enemies.

'Nothing was ever so unfortunate as the Veto', the English Catholic writer, Charles Butler, remarked ruefully in 1810 and certainly that issue, coming as it did on the heels of the downfall of the 'Talents' ministry, completed the disarray into which the Catholic body had fallen. A government veto on the appointment of Catholic bishops had been mooted, on and off, since the 1770s when the lifting of the penal curtain had revealed a nationwide Catholic hierarchy totally outside government control. In 1799 Troy and most of the other Catholic bishops had reluctantly agreed that a restricted veto could be accorded the government, but George III's hostility meant that the matter was quickly dropped. Then, in the spring of 1808, Grenville mentioned in debate that he had it on the authority of John Milner, an English priest who acted for the Irish hierarchy, that the Irish bishops were prepared to allow the crown a limited veto on episcopal appointments. However, when the Irish hierarchy came together to discuss the matter in September 1808, it decided that such a concession would be inexpedient at that time. For the next twelve years or so a furious controversy ensued within the Catholic body and among its parliamentary friends.

At first glance, the whole 'veto controversy' appeared to have been an unfortunate case of much ado about nothing: trivial in its essence, yet malign in its influence. Even if a veto had been conceded, there was never any indication that this would have altered the disposition of George III or, after 1810, his son the Prince Regent or their governments towards the Catholics. Only those in favour of Catholic emancipation fought over the veto issue; those opposed to concession were either unmoved or, more commonly, were frankly delighted at the uproar and at the allegations of lying, heresy and even insanity that were soon being bandied about by the protagonists in the struggle. And yet, tiresome though the dispute was, and pointless also in that it could only hold up but not move on the Catholic cause, some significance attaches to it.

Perhaps the most striking, and surely the most revealing, feature of the veto controversy was the near hysteria that surrounded its discussion and which quickly drove out rational argument. The furore revealed clearly a degree of disaffection, and a sense of alienation among some of the bishops, most of the lower clergy, 'the great bulk of the new proprietors of the mercantile and almost the whole of the peasantry', that had hitherto been more suspected than understood. What had been possible in 1799 – for the bishops had been agreeable to it then – was unthinkable ten years later. This hostility against a government veto was traced by one observer to 'the hereditary hatred which seven centuries of oppression has inspired in the Irish mind'; but it is more likely that the experience of the previous twenty years, and especially the difficulties of the post-Union decade, were sufficient to produce the emotional outburst against a veto. The Catholic hierarchy was the only national institution available to Irish Catholics and therefore to concede a veto to the English government would be to tarnish its national dimension, to anglicise it and thus render it hateful. In the veto controversy, the clergy and the laity were drawn into a common political arena. Even the supposed conservative members of the hierarchy viewed the scheme with alarm, and bishops and parish priests pledged their assistance in the campaign for Catholic emancipation. And yet the dispute was not really about religion, much less theology; it was not even about politics; in the end, the veto controversy was a national question, and the fact that English Catholic bishops were prepared to contemplate a veto only served to highlight the national issue. In the outcry over the veto, the Irish Catholic nation found its voice for the first time, and the whole episode witnessed the first major expression of Catholic nationalism in the nineteenth century. It also marked the arrival of Daniel O'Connell as the unchallenged leader of the Irish Catholics.

Born in 1775, of strong farming stock in county Kerry, O'Connell's life until 1800 was largely uneventful. He had been in Paris at the start of the revolution but, despite speculation to the contrary, there is no evidence that the scenes he witnessed there left him with a lifelong commitment to non-violence or pacifism. He then trained as a lawyer in London but his experience there hardly filled him with affection for the English. Almost certainly he was a member of the United Irishmen in Dublin, but he took no part in the 1798 rebellion. What made an indelible impression on him was his religion, for he was an Irish Catholic and, as he never ceased to proclaim, he loved his religion because it was Irish and because it was Catholic. Irish Protestants, by contrast, are no better than 'foreigners to us because they are of a different religion'.

O'Connell bestrode in equal measure the Gaelic-speaking world of deliverance, millenarian dreams and vision poetry and the English-speaking world of the political philosophers William Godwin and Jeremy Bentham. His mastery of both spheres rendered him an altogether new and immense force in Irish and English life; equally it offered him opportunities for deceit, deception and dissembling that were denied to monocultural and monolingual individuals. No Englishman could understand him: he was clearly not a gentleman, for his 'word' seemed never to be a binding commitment; yet his command of the language of politics and of the tactics of party politics placed him recognisably within the British parliamentary tradition. Similarly, he was an enigma to his Irish subordinates (these were all he had, for he would brook no rival), displaying real warmth and generosity on many occasions, but proving merciless in debates and vindictive in his emnities. Perhaps it was the masses who understood *An Counsiléar* (=the counsellor or lawyer) best, for they could see in him the incarnation of their dreams and aspirations. All – labourer, landless, cottier or strong farmer – despite their furious rivalries that would manifest themselves in competing agrarian secret societies – could see themselves in him and they responded to his call. Not surprisingly, the Irish folklore archives are stuffed with tales and stories about O'Connell (Bonaparte comes a distant second), casting him in the role of a Gaelic Messiah or Gaelic hero, tracing his ancestry back to the earliest gods and investing him with appropriate traits – boundless sexual energy being one of the more notable, with none other than Queen Victoria reportedly succumbing to his charms. And in the anglophone world of popular music O'Connell was to figure prominently, for he was to be the most 'ballad-ised' of all the Irish national leaders. He was a man driven – possessed, some claimed – by history, by religion and by a sense of grievance, both personal and for his people. His target, for all that it might seem to shift from decade to decade, if not year to year, was ultimately the destruction of the Protestant ascendancy.

O'Connell had first come to public prominence in his well-publicised opposition to Union. As we have seen, at a meeting of Dublin Catholics in 1799 he had declared that he would prefer the re-enactment of the Penal Code to a Union, for Union meant laying 'his country at the feet of strangers', and reducing Ireland 'to the abject condition of a province'. His remarks caused some embarrassment to the Catholic hierarchy, anxious to represent Irish Catholics as being solid for Union. With the passing of Union O'Connell devoted his attention to building up his legal practice and until 1807 Denys Scully occupied the leading position in Catholic circles. However, O'Connell continued to play his part, and his forecast in 1800 that 'foreigners' could not be trusted to do justice to Irish Catholics, was triumphantly borne out by the contemptuous rejection of Catholic claims for emancipation in 1801, 1805 and 1807. O'Connell was vindicated in his opposition to Union, but his demands for a more aggressive Catholic campaign ran up against the traditional caution and pragmatism of the Catholic leaders. The 'veto controversy' gave O'Connell his opportunity to take control of the Catholic agitation, but his opposition to the concession of securities on the appointment of Catholic bishops was principled and practical rather than opportunist. The 'old' Catholic leadership, believing that an alliance with English political sympathisers was vital, and impressed with arguments in favour of a limited veto from Irish Protestant supporters, such as Henry Grattan and Lord Plunket, the Irish lord chancellor, were inclined to view the question dispassionately; but O'Connell would have none of it, and his views prevailed.

Thereafter he remained a scourge of anyone suspected by him of harbouring 'vetoist' thoughts, only relaxing his vigilance in the mid-1820s when the idea of a veto was finally abandoned by its supporters.

With O'Connell the dominant force in Catholic affairs after 1808, it was inevitable that a more aggressive policy would be pursued. He believed that the Catholic masses must bring their weight and their numbers to bear on the issue. In O'Connell's view, their energies were being wasted in bloody and futile agrarian disputes between the various social and economic classes in the Irish countryside, and he resolved to harness those energies in pursuit of emancipation. Accordingly, he determined to keep up the pressure on Westminster by transmitting what amounted to an annual petition in favour of emancipation. These petitions were organised under the supervision of a Catholic Committee which itself, by undergoing a constant metamorphosis, became an instrument of the Catholic campaign. The Committee, like some primitive amoeba, after a slow start, grew rapidly: in 1806 it numbered thirty-six members; in 1807, a twenty-one-man group managed the petition; then in 1809 a forty-two-man committee was constituted to take charge; and in 1811 there was a scheme unfolded to elect ten members from each of the Irish counties, and a Catholic Convention of some 434 members was projected. By this stage, Dublin Castle had grown alarmed, and the then lord lieutenant and chief secretary, Richmond and Wellesley-Pole, resolved to take decisive action. Both men believed that the Catholic Assembly which resembled, some said, the Jacobite Parliament of 1688, clearly breached the terms of the Convention Act of 1793, which had outlawed any gathering purporting to have a representative function. Magistrates were ordered to take action, and Catholic leaders were warned of the consequences of their participation in the proposed assembly. A series of prosecutions was launched and the threatened Catholic Convention never actually met.

The aggression of the Catholics in the years 1808–12 stemmed in the first instance from the passions stirred up by the veto controversy and from the commanding position which O'Connell had gained in Catholic circles. The Catholic hierarchy was eager to associate itself with his strategy, and many of its members played a key role in organising the signing of the petitions in the parishes. The palpable dislike – even hatred – felt for Richmond and Wellesley-Pole by the Catholic leaders also made it easier to adopt a policy at odds with the traditional one of seeking concessions by negotiations and diplomacy. In the end, however, the year 1812 ended in disappointment and frustration. It was not just that the Catholic Convention had failed to meet: more disheartening was the clear evidence that the prince of Wales was lost to the Catholic cause.

In 1810 George III had been retired due to ill health (he died in 1820), and his son had succeeded him as Prince Regent with rather limited powers. From 1812 on, however, he would in theory be his own master, and Catholic hopes were high that a quick resolution of the Catholic question would be forthcoming. Since 1801 it had been an article of faith among the Catholics that the old king was the main obstacle to their claims, and accordingly the Catholic mood was buoyant when his son succeeded him. The prince of Wales had long been on record as favourable to the Catholic claims, and his broadmindedness over the years in selecting a number of Catholic mistresses had been seen as a good omen. The Prince Regent, however, quickly revealed himself to be as bigoted an opponent of the Catholics as his father. He retained as prime minister Spencer Perceval, an evangelical Protestant strongly opposed to the Catholic claims, and when Perceval was assassinated in 1812 he made no attempt to bring in an administration friendly to the Catholics. He even endorsed the action of Dublin Castle in disrupting the proposed Catholic Convention. The conclusion was clear – the Prince Regent was lost to the Catholic cause. The year 1812 therefore closed in disappointment for the Catholics.

Admittedly, the new ministry led by Lord Liverpool professed to regard Catholic emancipation as an 'open question', for it had not proved possible to recruit an entirely anti-Catholic Cabinet; but it remained to be seen whether this 'non-policy' marked an advance on outright hostility. Another favourable sign was that there had been a majority in favour of examining the Catholic claims in the House of Commons in 1812, and another was recorded in 1813: but ominously both involved the concession of some form of government veto. A decade of struggle appeared to have produced nothing, and the second decade of the nineteenth century proved just as barren, for the resolute opposition of the chief secretary, Sir Robert Peel, along with fresh divisions amongst the Catholics, and the end of the Napoleonic wars, all combined to remove all hopes of progress on the Catholic question.

Sir Robert Peel arrived in Ireland as chief secretary in 1812 and he stayed until 1818. Probably the most politically gifted holder of that office until the late nineteenth century, he proved a formidable adversary to O'Connell during his time in Ireland. He engineered the wrecking by amendments of the Catholic bill of 1813; he instigated the prosecution of the printer and publisher of the *Dublin Evening Press* (the Catholic mouthpiece) in 1813; and in 1814, he grasped the nettle, and banned the Catholic Board on the grounds that its existence con-travened the Convention Act. In addition, on every occasion in the House of Commons his voice was raised in opposition to the Catholic claims. He had a knack of articulating the resentments, prejudices and grievances of the Tory backbenchers and backwoodsmen (much as O'Connell had with the Irish peas-antry), and this rendered him truly formidable in debate. While he held the office of chief secretary, the Catholic cause appeared lost.

Admittedly, Peel was not wholly responsible for the lack of progress during the decade 1810 to 1820 for, during this decade, the Catholic leaders were distinguished more by their quarrels among themselves than by their efforts on behalf of emancipation. Predictably, O'Connell proved an abrasive leader and a number of those hitherto prominent found his leadership a bruising experience. In rapid succession he broke with pro-Catholic stalwarts such as Edward Hay, then with Denys Scully, then with the earl of Donoughmore. Parliamentary friends of the Catholics such as Grenville and Grattan found themselves denounced as traitors. Embarrassingly, in 1816, two rival Catholic petitions were circulating. Not surprisingly, Lord Whitworth, Richmond's successor, concluded that there were positive advantages to the anti-emancipation cause in allowing a Catholic Board to exist, for he predicted that it would 'sow the seed of discord among the great Catholic body and [disgust] those whom it was most in their interests to conciliate'.

Finally, the successful conclusion of the war against Bonaparte altered the international context in which the agitation for the repeal of anti-Catholic legislation had been set for decades. Since the Seven Years' War (1756–63), concessions for Irish Catholics had ever been associated with Britain's involvement in war, in that it had been standard British policy, in effect, to barter concessions for recruits. Admittedly, there had been few concessions since 1795, and the attempt in 1807 to extend the benefits of the 1793 Act to soldiers and sailors throughout Britain had come to nothing. None the less, so long as war lasted, and so long as Catholic recruits were vital to the war effort, it could always be argued that military necessity, imperial interests, or even, common gratitude demanded that concessions should be made. Victory over France, however, removed whatever pressure there may have been to conciliate the Catholics and although the British Catholic Board and the Irish Catholic hierarchy both claimed emancipation as the reward for Catholic exertions against Bonaparte, their pleas were completely ignored.

By the early 1820s the Catholic campaign appeared to have completely run out of steam. True, in 1821, Plunket's bills, offering a partial emancipation, did get through the House of Commons but once again, because they provided for a limited government veto on episcopal appointments, O'Connell was totally opposed to them and he expressed his relief when 'the present rascally' bills were defeated in the Lords. It seemed certain that emancipation would not be achieved unless accompanied by an unacceptable 'Bill of Pains and Penalties'. The death of George III in 1820 had clearly made no difference. A disillusioned and disheartened O'Connell contemplated changing his entire political strategy by putting parliamentary reform at the top of his agenda. In Catholic eyes, twenty years, and more, of the Union had merely served to confirm that measure as in effect a Penal Law. Great Britain and Ireland may have been united, but alienation rather than integration had been the result. From the sober drawing-rooms of the Catholic middle class where O'Connell held sway, to the tumultuous landscapes of the millenarian Catholic peasants led by Captain Rock, a Catholic consciousness was being shaped and a Catholic nation was being formed. But how to harness that consciousness? And how to bring Catholic numbers into the political arena? Could Protestant Ireland yet prove vulnerable?

Catholic emancipation (ii)

In some respects the passage of Plunket's bills through the House of Commons and their subsequent failure in the Lords can be seen as a turning point in the campaign for Catholic emancipation.[15] Clearly the tide of parliamentary opinion, at least in the lower house, was running strongly in favour of the 'Catholics'. Moreover, Plunket's bills had encumbered emancipation with humiliating securities, one of which would have permitted the British government to scrutinise correspondence between Irish Catholic bishops and the Vatican. The defeat of these bills, even though they had been accompanied with such a humiliating rider, meant that, thereafter, all talk of vetoes, oaths and other securities designed to assuage Protestant fears was abandoned. With or without shameful concessions, all emancipation proposals and annual petitions (now dubbed 'annual farces' by O'Connell) apparently were doomed to failure. A new strategy was required, for it was now clear that emancipation would never be given; it could only be taken.

The formation of a Catholic Association in April 1823, the brainchild of O'Connell and his lieutenant, Richard Sheil, signalled the opening of a new, more aggressive, campaign. The Association differed from the Catholic Board that it replaced in that its aim was specifically not to organise another petition which would give rise to a parliamentary bill. Instead, its goal was much wider – no less than the politicisation of all manner of Catholic grievances, and then the mobilisation of the Catholic masses and classes. Hence, issues as varied as the burden of tithe, the provision of Catholic chaplains in Newgate prison, disputes over burial grounds, anti-Catholicism in the armed forces and bias in the judiciary were all addressed in rapid succession. The message was clear: emancipation would not merely benefit the handful of well-off Catholics who could conceivably contemplate a parliamentary career; rather its benefits would reach down to touch even the most humble. The provision of a 'Catholic rent', a subscription of one penny per month, to be levied at all levels throughout Ireland, served to bind the Catholic masses to the Catholic leadership. By Christmas 1824 some £7,500 had been collected, and more money was coming in. In addition, in what was essentially a new departure, this 'Catholic rent', was being collected at parish level largely through the agency of Catholic priests.

Hitherto, the Catholic clergy, perhaps dismayed by the furious rows that had raged over the various 'veto' questions, or perhaps restrained by older priests and bishops, who had been ordained in 'Penal' days and hence were more deferential, had been reluctant to become involved in the campaign for Catholic emancipation. By 1824, however, the veto issue was gone, and the Catholic church in Ireland now found itself under sustained attack by evangelical elements within the Church of Ireland, eager to proselytise Irish Catholics through the inauguration of what was dubbed a 'Second Reformation'. Younger priests, in particular, those educated at Maynooth, were not prepared to look the other way in the face of perceived Protestant 'aggression', and they eagerly threw themselves into the political arena as the best way of combating Protestant assertiveness. The sectarian tone of Irish public life and politics was further stoked up not only by the inflammatory statements and provocative actions of these Protestant missionaries, but also, on the other side, by the circulation among the Catholic peasantry of the prophecies of Pastorini. Not surprisingly, in this atmosphere of poisonous sectarian rancour, the Catholic Association with its Catholic rent levied under the auspices of the local Catholic clergy was quickly deemed the harbinger of nothing less than 'an Irish Revolution'.

In response to demands for action from alarmed Protestants in Ireland, Sir Robert Peel resolved to outlaw the Catholic Association by Act of Parliament. This was done in 1825. However, in a short while O'Connell riposted by setting up a New Catholic Association which, like the old, harnessed the energies of the Catholic masses and classes. In the interests of government authority and the public peace this game could not be allowed to continue. Peel reluctantly turned his mind to the question he now posed: 'how to grant emancipation in such a way as to preserve the Protestant interest in Ireland'. In a real sense, Peel was dependent on O'Connell to come up with that plausible crisis which would allow him to yield under duress, and which at the same time would enable him to bring in securities with which to safeguard Protestant Ireland.

It was the Waterford election of 1826 that set in train the campaign that would culminate in Daniel O'Connell's electoral triumph in Clare in 1828, which in turn offered Peel and Wellington the opportunity to make the concession on emancipation, and to bring in those securities for Irish Protestants that they believed necessary. In the Waterford election, local Catholic activists (be it said in the face of Daniel O'Connell's misgivings) decided to run a Protestant candidate, though one in favour of Catholic emancipation, against the seemingly impregnable Beresford interest, long and firmly identified as hostile to Catholic claims. After a campaign of heightened sectarian animosity, in which Catholic priests urged the largely Catholic 40-shilling freehold voter to vote for his religion, rather than for his (Protestant) landlord, the Beresford candidate was defeated. There were similar 'freeholder revolts' in other county constituencies, with the landlord being rejected in favour of the priest. In public Peel professed to be sanguine about these ominous developments, but in private he recognised that the time for decision was not far off. In the event, the speedy consideration of the Catholic question, which he might have anticipated, was denied him by the onset of a period of governmental instability in London. Only in January 1828, with the formation of a government headed by the duke of Wellington, and with Peel, once again, as home secretary, could he turn his attention to Ireland.

Now, however, rather sooner than he had anticipated, there arrived that crisis which made action imperative. In June 1828 O'Connell announced his candidacy in a by-election for county Clare, even though if elected he would be unable to take his seat. His opponent was Vesey FitzGerald, a Protestant Member, though one who supported Catholic emancipation, and O'Connell's plan was to demonstrate that, in the next general election, he could plunge Ireland into chaos. O'Connell's victory in Clare was never in doubt: the freeholders resolutely followed their priests and deserted their landlords. Ominously, a Protestant backlash to these developments was now revealed with anti-Catholic Brunswick clubs, determined to resist concessions to Catholics, forming in Ulster and elsewhere. Wellington and Peel knew the game was up: speedy action was imperative if a civil war was to be averted. Catholic emancipation was duly conceded in April 1829, accompanied by laws which abolished outright the 40-shilling freehold franchise (as many as 400,000 lost their votes), and banned the Catholic Association. Spitefully, O'Connell's election victory was also overturned, and he would have to run again for election in county Clare. Catholic emancipation had been passed at last, but the delay meant that it would never be regarded as a boon.

Assessment

The true significance of O'Connell's triumph in the struggle for Catholic emancipation lay more in the means employed to bring it about than in the victory gained, for the right to sit in the united Parliament could be exercised at that time only by a handful of Catholics. Under O'Connell's inspired leadership, the Catholic masses of rural Ireland were enlisted into the campaign for emancipation. This had proved no easy task, for furious tensions and raging rivalries concerning class, wealth and land had long seethed just beneath (and sometimes above) the surface of Irish life. None the less by focusing on the single goal of emancipation, by appealing to a shared Catholic consciousness and by harping on historic and current grievances and resentments O'Connell had managed to keep these divisions at bay. For the first time in Irish history, Catholic numbers – or in O'Connell's words, the 'electricity of public opinion' – had been devastatingly deployed in a political movement and, to the evident dismay of the governing class in both Ireland and England, the 'quantity' had carried the day over the 'quality'.

O'Connell's demotic leadership, coupled with his demonic energy, had been crucial in forging this powerful weapon with which to strike down Protestant privilege and blast deference to the powers-that-be. On the platform his impassioned oratory by turns flattered his people and cajoled them, and denounced their enemies. In addition, his clever and barbed asides and his instinctive gestures, phrases and throwaway remarks – sometimes in Gaelic – that were implicitly understood by them, all marked O'Connell out as the embodiment of every aspiration held by his audience. 'The finest peasantry in the world' – O'Connell's term for his followers – loved him; and in the folklore of Gaelic Ireland, it would be O'Connell who would predominate among the political subjects.

It should be noted, however, that the invention of the strategy of mass participatory democracy in peaceful pursuit of a political objective was made possible by the liberalism of the British state. Any attempt at armed force would have been ruthlessly crushed by the British authorities, but Britain was a liberal state in which the rule of law prevailed, and as such it was vulnerable to O'Connell's tactics. It was O'Connell's genius to have spotted this. We may note in passing that a peaceful campaign similar to that waged by O'Connell in, say, Catholic Poland held by the Orthodox Russians would have been given short (and bloody) shrift. Russia was not a liberal state.

The campaign for Catholic emancipation raised a huge question mark against the future of the Union, and in many ways the outcome of that struggle determined the later political history of the nineteenth century. The Act of Union had once been heralded as the gateway to emancipation: instead it had rapidly taken on the status of a grievance. Emancipation had been conceded only when civil war threatened, and this would strengthen the hand of those who argued that the Union could never offer good government to Ireland, and that only self-government would do that. In addition, just as the passing of the Act of Union had damaged the Protestant governing elite, so too the winning of Catholic emancipation marked a further grave erosion of its political power. After 1829 the ascendancy was on borrowed time. Continental sociologists, notably the Frenchmen, Alexis de Tocqueville and Gustave de Beaumont, noted this, and were so impressed with the spectacle of a democracy triumphing over an aristocracy, while avoiding – unlike France – bloody revolution, that they undertook a research trip to Ireland in 1835 to investigate the phenomenon more fully.

Lastly, it was ominous that the first peaceful mass movement in Irish, indeed in European history, had turned essentially on a religious question. True, Catholic emancipation was ostensibly about Catholic access to politics, but the campaign to achieve it had been conducted along the lines of a religious revival with Catholic priests as cheerleaders, and no one could be in any doubt that this was a religious contest between the religion of the Irish and the religion of the English. Famously, O'Connell had confessed that he loved his religion because it was Irish and because it was Catholic; infamously, he had sneeringly dismissed Irish Protestants as 'foreigners'. There was, of course, much more to O'Connell than this sectarianism, but after 1829 the Catholics were indisputably the people of Ireland, and O'Connell was their leader. Could he and they be comfortable in a Protestant British state? And what of Irish Protestants? Could they forge a role for themselves in the new Ireland of Daniel O'Connell? Or were they doomed to be trampled in the onward march of Irish Catholic nationalism?

5 FROM UNION TO DISUNION: IRELAND, 1830-1914

Introduction

In 1829 Sir Robert Peel warned that the settlement of the Catholic question would not be the settlement of Ireland. His prediction proved accurate. Daniel O'Connell swiftly turned, or returned, to his long-term goal of repealing the Act of Union, and from 1830 until the break-up of the Irish polity into two rival states in 1921 the political history of Ireland largely revolved around various movements dedicated to ending or defending the Union. The moderate nationalist demand for limited self-government within the empire and the grudging acceptance of this in some, not all, British political circles from the 1880s on quickly evoked a response in the shape of militant Unionism. Those Unionists who pledged themselves to defending the Union regarded the entire 'Home Rule' project as simply a cloak for 'Rome Rule', as a stepping-stone to separatism and as an open assault on the integrity of the British empire. Seen in these lights, the Irish nationalist demand for Home Rule was nothing other than a Catholic conspiracy that had to be defeated whatever the cost.

Ending or defending the Union, by and large, would set the limits for Irish politics at the national level during the nineteenth century; but equally, huge efforts would be devoted by successive British governments during this period to what we might call 'mending the Union', that is, to demonstrating that good government, rather than self-government, could meet Ireland's legitimate needs. Beginning in the 1830s a series of reforms were brought in that sought to address the treatment of poverty, the provision of education, the grievance of tithe, the status of the Church of Ireland, the problem of law and order, the organisation of local government, the exercise of the franchise and much else besides. The most radical of these reforms would deal with landlord–tenant relations and by the early twentieth century a revolution in landownership had been achieved in Ireland. In effect, through the agency of the British treasury, a few thousand large landowners would be bought out by hundreds of thousands of their tenants, and a peasant proprietorship, unlike anywhere else, would be created.

However, if these reforms were supposed to eliminate the desire for self-government, their authors were to be badly mistaken. The demand for Home Rule, if not for total separation, persisted regardless of all concessions (and in spite of all setbacks and rejections). In September 1914, a few weeks after the outbreak of the Great War, a measure for Irish self-government finally reached the statute books, only to be suspended for the duration of hostilities, and with a rider that the counties of Antrim, Down, Fermanagh, Tyrone, Armagh and Londonderry were to be excluded from its provisions. Ironically, the outbreak of war with Germany had the effect of ruling out, or at least postponing, a different conflict – one between nationalists and Unionists in Ireland. Had the war with Germany ended at Christmas 1914, as many had predicted, hostilities within Ireland might well have taken its place. But the war dragged on until 1918, and when it was over, Ireland had been transformed by sacrifice abroad and by insurrection at home.

I: TESTING THE UNION, 1830–70

Repeal

It was inevitable that the winning of Catholic emancipation would disappoint those who had been most enthusiastic for it. Like the union of the two kingdoms, emancipation had been held out as a panacea for all Irish ills, a cure-all for grievances at every level of Catholic society; but this was never likely to be the case. O'Connell surely sensed as much, and his swift decision to mount a further campaign, this time to repeal the Act of Union, can best be seen as his attempt to hold together the coalition of forces that had won emancipation and which threatened to fall apart in the ensuing disillusion.

Like the able politician that he was, O'Connell resolutely refused to spell out precisely what he meant by 'repeal'. On the face of it he was demanding the repeal of the Irish Act of Union, but he surely could not have desired the return of the old Irish Parliament, for that had been an entirely Protestant body. The members of the old Irish House of Commons had been elected under a variety of franchises, now no longer operative, and a majority had been returned from borough constituencies most of which had since disappeared. As a slogan, 'repeal' (or 'repale' as O'Connell's opponents mocked his accent) had the considerable merit of being both pithy and opaque, and O'Connell's adoring troops, eager for another struggle under his messianic leadership, duly fell in behind it. It is clear, however, that the goal of ending the Act of Union did not engage the enthusiasm of his followers as much as Catholic emancipation. Indeed, it is not even certain that O'Connell himself regarded it as anything other than an *in terrorem* measure, i.e. as a way of gaining leverage with the British government, for he was quite prepared to switch to conventional politics when the time seemed right. Thus, by the time the Liberator died in 1847, during a pilgrimage to Rome, the movement for repeal had run out of steam.

The insurmountable problem that O'Connell had encountered where repeal was concerned was one that lay athwart all later movements that sought to create, or re-create, a devolved legislative assembly in Ireland. No matter what protestations of loyalty to the British connection were made by those in favour of such a course, no matter how indignantly accusations of separatism were denied, the reality was that until the 1880s, and after, in Britain and among Irish Protestants generally, the objective of Irish self-government, however described or circumscribed, was held to be completely illegitimate, wholly inadmissible and utterly destructive. O'Connell, and those who came after him, might claim that repeal (or Home Rule) was both loyal and national and, on occasion, 'God save the Queen' might be played at meetings convened to demand self-government, but few Unionists were persuaded or fooled. In Britain Irish self-government was viewed as a stepping-stone to Irish separatism and had, therefore, to be resisted at all costs up to, and including, war. It was axiomatic that the Union of Great Britain and Ireland was central to Britain's imperial greatness and the very notion of 'disunion' aroused the same dread that 'secession' did in the contemporary United States of America.

Equally, for Irish Protestants, Union was perceived as vital to their identity, well-being and way of life, and hence the connection had to be maintained at all costs. Whatever ambivalence there had been among Irish Protestants concerning Union in 1801 had, in the face of the rise of Catholic Ireland, almost entirely disappeared by 1830. At the time of the Catholic emancipation crisis, and faced with a choice between widespread public disorder or Catholic emancipation, Peel had wisely opted for concession upon face-saving terms: but confronted with the options of civil war or repeal of the Act of Union, no British government between 1801 and 1886 would have hesitated to go to war to maintain the Union. And after that date Irish Protestants were quite prepared to keep their British allies up to the mark in that respect. In short, when O'Connell declared for repeal, his campaign could not but end in failure; perhaps he knew this.

Certainly, this suggestion might help explain quite why O'Connell from an early date was prepared to 'park' the repeal demand and seek an accommodation with the new Whig government in London. O'Connell dressed up this new strategy as 'testing the Union', the clear inference being that the Union would fail the test because no British government, no matter how well-intentioned towards Ireland, could possibly do for Ireland what self-government alone could achieve. But there is more than a hint that O'Connell – like Isaac Butt and John Redmond decades later – rather enjoyed the club-like atmosphere of Westminster. Certainly he fitted in well into the smoke-filled rooms where deals were done and intrigues plotted, and the suspicion remains that he came to prefer that urbane world to the tumult of a long-drawn out and ultimately futile repeal campaign in Ireland.

That said, O'Connell's determination to press the new prime minister, Lord Melbourne, and his Whig government to commit to reform in Ireland and to deliver on its promises in that regard bore fruit throughout the 1830s. It helped that the Whig government of the 1830s was a self-consciously modernising one, resolved to bring in much-needed reforms on a whole range of topics; and so O'Connell was pushing against an open door in advocating state action in Ireland. Whatever the springs of policy, by the end of the decade a transformation had taken place in the administration of Ireland, and O'Connell could point to his alliance with the Whigs as helping to influence, if not to direct, the shape of those changes.

Out of the many reforms that were brought in during the 1830s, four – those purporting to tackle the problems of tithe, municipal corporations, ignorance and poverty – might be selected as illustrating the extent, the limit and the impact of state action during this period. As we have seen, tithe, the obligation to contribute to the upkeep of the established Protestant church in Ireland, without regard for the contributor's confessional allegiance, had long been a grievance in the Irish countryside, featuring prominently since the 1760s among the targets of the Whiteboys, Rightboys and such-like agrarian secret societies. However, in 1830 tithe, from being just one of a lengthy list of grievances, moved decisively centre stage. It did so for two reasons. First, the amount of tithe to be paid had risen in line with agricultural prices and hence the grievance pinched rather more. But second, and far more important, in the aftermath of Catholic emancipation, and buoyed up by success in that struggle, the Catholic masses regarded the payment of tithe to an alien church in the same light as the denial of a seat in Parliament to O'Connell's better-off supporters – an insupportable affront. Given their mean condition O'Connell's army of peasants could have no realistic aspiration to parliamentary representation, but an end to tithe would constitute for them both a tangible reward for their role in winning emancipation and another victory over their Protestant masters.

In so far as it would combine elements of political direction, clerical spon-sorship, mass disobedience and naked violence, the 'tithe war' that began in Graiguemanagh, county Kilkenny, in 1830 and spread swiftly through southern Ireland after that can be seen as a dress rehearsal for the Land War of the 1880s.

Similarly, in the muddled response of the authorities (inept military repression mixed with erratic concession), and in the priests' and politicians' growing fear of widespread and unmanageable civil disorder, can be seen some of the elements which led to a backing-off on both sides in that later conflict. A widely enforced 'tithe strike' led to less than one-third of tithe being collected by 1835; but rival massacres of tithe protesters at Newtownbarry, county Wexford, and of police at Carrickshock, county Kilkenny, revealed the volcanic furies just at, or beneath, the surface of Irish rural life, and forced a rethink on all sides. The result was commutation, with tithe henceforth to be paid by the landlord (and recouped by him as a charge on rent), associated arrears to be paid by the government and, crucially, the poorest cultivators in the countryside – yearly tenants and tenants-at-will – to be made exempt from any payment. Tithe had not been abolished, but it was now made invisible, and another mass peasant protest had had its victory. Fifty years earlier, in the old Irish Parliament, a modest proposal to examine the tithe question had provoked a crisis in church–state relations and had been squashed. Now, under a very different dispensation, the unfairness, if not the iniquity of tithe, had been conceded. Far-sighted observers mused: if an onslaught on tithe could prove successful, could an assault on rent, that other 'Protestant tax', be far behind?

The sectarianism that accompanied much of the anti-tithe agitation was replicated in the debate over the future of Irish municipal corporations. Since Cromwellian times these had been bastions of the Protestant ascendancy, notionally tasked not with advancing urban improvement but, like the old Irish Parliament, with furthering the Protestant interest and promoting the Protestant religion. Whatever their original, theoretical remit, by the 1830s their inefficiency, corruption and utter lack of civic responsibility had become matters of public notoriety. Of course, Irish corporations were not unique in these respects, for their English counterparts were almost equally useless. However, when it came to reform there was to be a marked difference in the approach adopted in both countries.

In England the Municipal Reform Act of 1835 gave new powers to corporations, granted the franchise to all ratepayers and allowed them to elect their own sheriff and control their local police. For Ireland it was to be rather different. Five years of bitter and prolonged parliamentary debate resulted in the Municipal Corporation Act of 1840, a compromise measure which so far from rationalising and making Irish corporations more responsible, in fact abolished the vast majority of them, leaving only ten in place in the bigger urban centres. As with the future of the old Irish Parliament, the key difficulty here was that any attempt to open up municipal corporations to the breath of public opinion meant inevitably that there would be a Catholic takeover of many, perhaps most, of them. As a result, rather that permit the 'enemy' to seize these Protestant redoubts, those opposed to any change – Irish Protestants, generally, and their Tory allies in Britain – preferred, as with the old Irish Parliament, to see them destroyed. Protestant fears in this regard were not groundless. In 1841 O'Connell became the first Catholic lord mayor of Dublin since the seventeenth century, a triumph as symbolic as his earlier parliamentary one of a decade before.

Possession of the municipal franchise and the conduct of local government were, for the most part, matters of concern to a minority of Irish people; but it was different with the introduction of an Irish Poor Law. Since the late eighteenth century Ireland's population had been increasing dramatically and had risen from around 5 million at the time of the Union to some 8 million in 1841. In England a more modest rate of population growth had been accompanied by a large-scale migration into towns and cities where manufacturing work was to be had but in Ireland there was no such movement from the countryside, and nor was there any surge in factory jobs to absorb the increase. By the 1830s the Irish people were even more overwhelmingly rural dwelling than before and as heavily involved in agriculture as ever. As a result of the huge rise in population among the very poor, Irish poverty, already much commented on at the time of Union, and regularly reported on since, had by the 1830s become vastly more visible. An accompanying dependence on the fickle potato crop completed the picture of a population mired in poverty, subject to growing immiseration and increasingly exposed to calamity.

What could be done to manage this poverty? Alleviating it, or indeed, eliminating it, was not really the objective, for this would require sweeping structural changes to the Irish economy and, if only on grounds of expense, was considered to be work for another day. There was, in fact, no clear consensus on what should be done, and various solutions were canvassed, usually involving a mixture of state-assisted emigration, a programme of public works and the consolidation of landholdings. In the end the Whig government, on ideological grounds hostile to the notion of state intervention to tackle poverty, decided that a system of workhouses, similar to those recently set up in England should be established in Ireland. Arguments that the needs of the poor of Ireland were wholly different from those of England were brushed aside, a one-size-fits-all solution was adopted, and the principle was enunciated that Irish property should pay for Irish poverty. By 1842 around 120 workhouses had been built, and indoor relief was being offered to some forty thousand destitute.

Irish workhouses have had a bad press and few historians have had a good word to say about them. The poor regarded them as worse than prison, and surely the stated attempt to make life within doors 'less eligible', or less comfortable, than that outside, so as to discourage the indolent, the feckless and the workshy, must have strained the official imagination. Notoriously, the system proved inadequate when the Famine struck. None the less, the workhouses did offer some system of relief where none, save private charity, had existed before and, in fairness, they were never designed to cope with large-scale starvation. By 1849 some 900,000 Irish poor were being relieved in them, a figure not contemplated (a ceiling of 80,000 had been envisaged) when the system was first instituted. In addition, as the boards of guardians set up to run them were to be elected locally, there would be opportunities for public service, hitherto denied or otherwise rare, not just for Protestants, but for middle-class Catholics and, after 1898, for women too. As the range of duties within the remit of these boards swelled over the coming decades to include sanitation, public health, vagrancy, orphans and district dispensaries, a cadre of local government officials, a significant number of whom proved to be aspirant national politicians, was being silently created.

Mass poverty was widely regarded in British government circles as a key cause of Irish disaffection and 'agitation' and so too was mass ignorance. The Poor Law was designed to defuse the first, the creation of a national system of elementary education in 1831 was expressly focused on the second. Prior to 1831 the provision of education in Ireland at the elementary level was extremely patchy. The Kildare Place Society, founded in 1811, operated a number of schools that were intended to be non-denominational, but the Catholic church eventually denounced them as instruments of proselytisation, and hence their appeal to Catholic parents was very limited. What provision there was for Catholics consisted of a large number, perhaps nine thousand, 'hedge', or pay, schools of widely differing standards, conducted by itinerant teachers, whose qualifications varied greatly. Originating in the era of the Penal Laws, by the 1820s these hedge schools catered for between 300,000 and 400,000 pupils (not all Catholic). In addition, a small number of schools were owned and run by the newly established Irish Christian Brothers.

To bring some uniformity to this situation, and to attempt a radical piece of religious engineering, the Whig government decided that a national system of elementary education would be set up for Ireland, one in which the guiding principle was to be non-denominational. The various religious interests involved paid lipservice to this notion of all-children-together and within a short period the guiding principle had been abandoned in the face of protests by the religious denominations. The result was emphatically not what the government had intended: a national system of publicly funded elementary education that was controlled by the Catholic church where it was in the ascendancy, by the Presbyterians where they dominated and by the Church of Ireland where its members were in a local majority. What had been envisaged as a system of religiously integrated education, one that would smooth away the rough edges of confessional enmity among the young, within a short time had become almost entirely sectarianised.

This is not to say that the national school system was ineffective. On the contrary, within fifty years it had brought about a massive improvement in literacy in Ireland to the extent that two-thirds of all young people aged between six and fifteen years old were able to read and write in English. This proportion was ahead of what had been achieved in England, where a similar national system of elementary education was not created until 1878. (We might note, however, that compulsory primary education in Ireland lagged behind that for England.) These figures have impressed later historians, who have claimed that the national school system was 'the greatest single benefit of the British connection in the middle decades of the nineteenth century', and have pointed to Ireland's grim uniqueness in that, while its per capita income placed it at, or near, the bottom of the European league in the mid-nineteenth century, its literacy rates placed it near the top of the corresponding table. Moreover, this literacy was in English, for the Irish language was discouraged in the national schools, and this presumably gave intending emigrants to the United States, or Britain, an important advantage in making their way in their new countries. Importantly, literacy in English also enabled the Irish to read the literature of the nation (and of the *Nation* newspaper), to sing its songs, recite its poetry and, especially, to resent the failure to create a state for that nation.

The replacement of the Whig administration of Lord Melbourne with a Tory one led by Sir Robert Peel in 1841 brought to a shuddering halt all cooperation or compact between O'Connell and the government, for between the two men there existed a deep-seated antipathy. O'Connell promptly announced the resumption of his repeal campaign, claiming that since even a sympathetic government such as that of Lord Melbourne had proved incapable of quenching the Irish thirst for self-government, there was no possibility that a Tory government, headed by 'Orange' Peel, would be any more successful in this regard.

The resumption of hostilities, however, should not be allowed to mask the scale of the achievements of the 1830s. By the end of that decade not only had the administration of Ireland been greatly extended, but the spirit that informed it had been changed. What had been previously an instrument in the hands of the adherents of the Protestant ascendancy had by the early 1840s become more rational, centralised and even-handed. It had also become much more efficient as, under the direction of such functionaries as the under-secretary at Dublin Castle, Thomas Drummond, the chief Poor Law commissioner George Nicholls, and the head to the Ordnance Survey, Thomas Larcom, steps were taken to bring the Irish administrative infrastructure up to, and often beyond, the standard that existed in the sister kingdom. Drummond was particularly important in this area, whether signalling the end of an unthinking Castle support for Irish landowners by announcing that 'property has its duties as well as its rights', or by centralising control of police in Ireland (apparently made necessary because of local prejudices), or by spotting the potential of railways in Ireland (first line opened in 1834). Larcom, too, was an important moderniser: through his efforts, and those of his colleagues in the Ordnance Survey, Ireland was to be much more comprehensively mapped than Britain. In short, by the early 1840s, a skeletal administrative structure had been laid down for Ireland, one to which further layers could be added, and one which was to last, by and large, until the end of the twentieth century. More immediately, however, Protestant loss of hegemony at the local level in much of southern Ireland meant that Protestant hold on power at the national level was considerably weakened; conversely, where Protestants were in a majority, as they were in many areas of Ulster, these new administrative structures passed into their hands, and further empowered them.

O'Connell and Young Ireland

O'Connell's peremptory return to his campaign to repeal the Act of Union was ill advised: Peel was by no means as hostile to Ireland and the Irish as O'Connell claimed, nor was he as wedded to the Protestant ascendancy as his soubriquet 'Orange' suggested. That said, he was resolutely hostile to any weakening of Union, and he was determined to face down O'Connell over his campaign for repeal. To Peel, the whole idea of repeal was a dangerous nonsense, but he had to concede that O'Connell could conjure up much Irish support for it. How to account for that? On the one hand, Peel believed that a large amount of Irish support for repeal stemmed from abject adulation of O'Connell himself. The only answer to such mindlessness was firmness in resistance to O'Connell. Against that, Peel was convinced that more thoughtful repealers, such as the Catholic clergy and their bishops, could be detached from O'Connell's campaign if they could be brought to see the positive benefits of the Union.

Peel's policy in the early 1840s, aptly described as one of 'iron-handed rec-onciliation', was considerably successful in the short term. In the face of the government's firm resolve, O'Connell's repeal campaign quickly ran into sand, and while he was able to attract large numbers to his 'monster meetings' to demand repeal (see map 8), his bombast proved ineffective against Peel's deter-mination. A particularly galling setback for O'Connell occurred when the gov-ernment banned a planned monster meeting at Clontarf in October 1843 and, rather than risk disorder, he had to call it off. Previous meetings at Trim in March

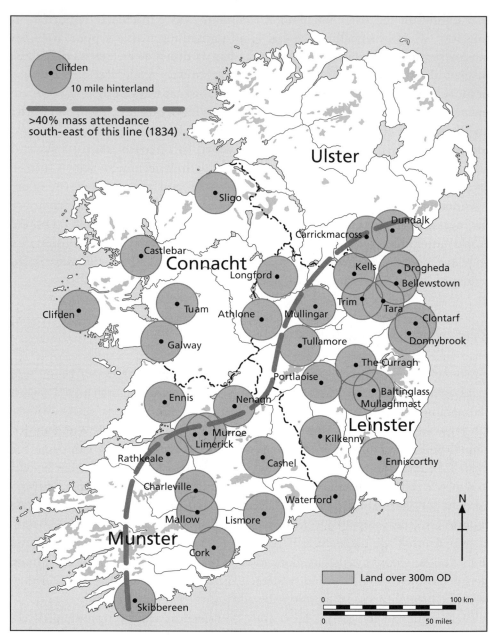

Map 8 Repeal meetings held in 1843

and at Tara Hill in August of that year had attracted hundreds of thousands but had achieved precisely nothing. In 1844, Peel moved against O'Connell himself, and he was put on trial on charges of conspiracy for which he was duly convicted and sentenced to twelve months' imprisonment. He was released after a few months, but it was evident that the repeal campaign was going nowhere.

While O'Connell was being faced down, Peel was busy cosying up to the Catholic bishops. Despite emancipation in 1829 many grievances remained and the bishops found Peel unexpectedly sympathetic to their concerns. Maynooth College, the main Catholic seminary, hitherto run on a modest budget, was awarded a capital sum of £30,000 from the government and had its annual grant trebled from £9,000 to nearly £30,000. Similarly, an Act was passed enabling the Catholic church to benefit from charitable bequests. For their part, the Catholic bishops grudgingly acknowledged some merit in Peel's proposals for university education in Ireland (though they later backtracked). Perhaps Union with the Protestant British state was not such a bad thing after all – especially as there appeared to be no alternative.

Of course, there was no possibility of entirely detaching the Catholic clergy from the Irish people, or even from the O'Connellite campaign; but Peel's strategy marked a refreshing break from the traditional one of seeing the Catholic clergy as the inveterate enemy of English government in Ireland, with Irish Protestants and their clergy cast as its natural ally. However, and herein lay the dangers, concessions to Irish Catholic bishops would win Peel few friends in his own party; they contributed massively to growing divisions within the repeal movement concerning the way forward, and especially over the ultimate purpose of winning its own Parliament for Ireland. It was this last point – the purpose of an Irish Parliament – that was to prove the proximate cause of a split within the repeal movement.

In the struggle for Catholic emancipation, O'Connell had been the undisputed leader, almost entirely above criticism from his followers; but it was all rather different when he turned his attention to repeal in the 1840s. Here his leadership came under searching scrutiny from a group of largely Protestant repealers who clustered around the Trinity-educated journalist, Thomas Davis, and who soon became known collectively as Young Ireland. For O'Connell the re-establishment of the Irish Parliament was the first step in giving good government to Ireland. He viewed with equanimity, and probably with approval, the undoubted fact that any new Parliament would be largely Catholic in membership. And he saw repeal as reversing the historic wrongs done to Catholic Ireland. For Davis and his colleagues – John Mitchel, Charles Gavan Duffy, William Smith O'Brien and John Blake Dillon were the most prominent – it was all rather different, for they saw in repeal merely the first step in the regeneration of Ireland and they were appalled at the vista of a Catholic ascendancy replacing the Protestant one. Certainly, O'Connell's clear understanding that 'Catholic' and 'Irish' were interchangeable and that Catholic numbers necessarily meant that they must rule offered them little comfort in this respect.

Davis and the others were in agreement with O'Connell that self-government was vital to a nation's well-being; but where they moved beyond him was in their mystical reverence for the very notion of the nation. To them, the nation was a product of history, language and literature, and every nation had an undeniable right to self-rule. Ireland fitted all their criteria: the Irish or 'Celts' were racially distinct from the Saxons; they had a glorious history; and they had their own Gaelic language. Young Ireland's mission was to publicise these attributes.[1] Hence a weekly newspaper, *Nation*, edited by Charles Gavan Duffy, was brought out in 1842 and soon attained a readership of ten thousand. As well as current news items, its readers were regaled with stirring poems, rousing or sentimental ballads and exciting stories, all designed to instil patriotic fervour. To that end, Irish heroism and resistance were highlighted while Saxon perfidy was denounced.

All that was missing, the Young Irelanders felt, was a genuine national literature, a literature that would serve the needs of the nation. Literary merit was, of course, desirable in this national literature but not essential. To meet this need, a Library of Ireland was instituted to bring cheap editions of inspiring works, historical, and literary, to the widest readership (and, thanks to the national school system, there was now an expanding public for such books). O'Connell had no particular problem with much of this, though the constant harping on about battles and massacres, and the note of martial pride that infused much of Young Ireland's writings, would have caused him some unease, for he was resolutely committed to staying within the law in his campaign. Essentially, where O'Connell and Young Ireland parted company, was over the role of religion. For O'Connell, with his belief that Catholic and Irish were merely two words for the one thing, it was natural that Catholics must rule, given that they were the clear majority in Ireland. Young Ireland, for its part, argued that confessional religion was a private matter and that the public religion they espoused – nationalism – was the only true faith. As one of their poems put it:

> What matter that at different shrines we pray unto our God?
> What matter that at different times our fathers won this sod?

To which of course the answer was that it mattered a lot to a Catholic middle class, convinced that its church was despised; and it also mattered a lot to Catholic tenant farmers, who believed that the land confiscations of the seventeenth century were quite simply a historic crime that demanded redress. It was all very well for Davis and his friends to claim that religion was a private affair, and to urge all Irish people to worship publicly at the altar of nationalism, eschewing all denominational advantage; but there can be little doubt that the fervour with which Young Ireland bowed down before an all-embracing, non-denominational nationalism was sharpened by a chilling recognition of the

THE KILKENNY CATS; OR, OLD AND YOUNG IRELAND "COMING TO THE SCRATCH."

"Oh, leave them alone,
They'll fight to the bone,
And leave naught but their tails behind 'em."

Punch, 8 Aug. 1846.

5.1 Kilkenny Cats. Old Ireland confronting Young Ireland. National Library of Ireland.

bleak future for the Protestants of Ireland if, and when, the Catholic 'quantity' would triumph over the Protestant 'quality'.

It was probably inevitable that O'Connell and Young Ireland would quarrel (figure 5.1): O'Connell was old and they young, by the mid-1840s he was tired, and they had grown impatient. He had never been comfortable with questioning of his leadership, much less criticism of his tactics; and Young Ireland's profound distaste for O'Connell's continual flirtation with Westminster politicians and his involvement in their intrigues, compromises and alliances swiftly led to open argument. There was also a sharp division of opinion between O'Connell and Young Ireland over the provision of university education for Ireland. Ultimately, O'Connell followed the majority of the Catholic bishops in their opposition to 'Godless colleges', while Young Ireland was in favour of the proposed institutions precisely because of their lack of religious affiliation. A breach between the two might have occurred over this matter; in the event, the proximate cause of the rupture between O'Connell and Young Ireland stemmed from a newspaper article written by John Mitchel that addressed the question of ambush tactics in a military conflict. O'Connell seized on this item as proof of Young Ireland's martial intentions and he issued the movement with an ultimatum to disavow violence under all circumstances or else. Rather than yield to such an ultimatum,

(a)

5.2 Two examples of Daniel O'Connell's colourful style of electioneering in which historic memory of persecution and religious discrimination were joined together in an appeal to the electorate.
(a) A vote for O'Connell is a vote for Catholicism.
(b) Repeal as a Catholic crusade. National Library of Ireland.

and protesting that such a demand was extraordinary, even esoteric, since they had no plans for insurrection, the Young Irelanders seceded in a body from O'Connell's movement in July 1846.

As a phenomenon, 'the split' has not been unknown in Irish history; in fact there have been so many that a well-worn jibe testifies to its prominence on the early agenda of any new movement. But rarely has the cause of the division been at once so fatuous and, in the circumstances, so obscene. For while O'Connell and Duffy and the others (but not Davis who had died aged thirty in September) bickered over theories of violence, the legitimacy of force and the possible intentions of the Young Irelanders, first reports had come in of the arrival of potato blight and by the end of 1845 it was evident that millions were facing starvation. In the face of this all-too-grim and pressing reality, the theoretical debates between O'Connell and the Young Irelanders over the justification for insurrection had more than a whiff of irrelevance (figure 5.2).

(b)

 5.2 (cont.)

Famine

In 1841 the Irish census revealed that just over 8 million lived on the island; and, by 1845, when the potato blight struck, that figure was probably closer to 8.5 million. By 1851, when the Famine had run its course, the census of that year showed that the Irish population had fallen by over 20 per cent, with one million dead from starvation and disease and another million or so having fled to Britain or north America.[2] Thereafter, very heavy outflows of people remained the order of the day. In 1861, as a result of sustained emigration, a further fall of 11.5 per cent was recorded; and in 1871, the reduction over the previous ten years was 6.7 per cent. In just thirty years the population of Ireland had fallen by approximately one-third, with nearly 3 million people missing from the record. And so it continued: by 1921 some 8 million people who had been born in Ireland were living elsewhere, mostly in the United States; and the population of Ireland was to decline further in most decades down to the late twentieth century.

The Great Famine of the 1840s marks a watershed in modern Irish history. Of course, there had been famines before in Irish history, and there had been heavy emigration before the 1840s, and changes in family structure, farm size, marriage patterns, agricultural output, religious practice, even political outlook, can be detected before the arrival of the potato blight. None the less the extraordinary intensity of the Great Famine (map 9), that is to say, the compression into a few years of changes that would ordinarily have taken decades to work through, moves it decisively beyond the role of a mere accelerator of earlier trends. Especially, the Famine set in train the unprecedented mass emigration which thoroughly reconfigured Irish life and society in the later nineteenth and twentieth centuries. From the 1850s on, with the formation of an Irish nation abroad, the history of Ireland and the history of the Irish people decisively diverge, with profound consequences for both Ireland and the Irish.

The Great Famine had a single immediate cause, the arrival from north America of potato blight, *phytophora infestans*, in September 1845. As the blight was spread largely by wind-blown spores, it was not confined to Ireland, and large areas of Europe, notably France, Germany, the Netherlands and northern Scotland, were also badly affected; but in no other country in Europe was so high a proportion of the population – at least 4 million out of 8 million – so entirely dependent on the potato; and the loss of one-third of the potatoes in the autumn of 1845 put that number at risk. Worse was to follow, for three-quarters of the potato crop failed in 1846, and since almost no seed potatoes were sown that year, the crop in 1847 was tiny. In 1848 output recovered slightly, but until 1851 potato production barely rose above a quarter of that gathered in in 1844.

The huge dependence of the mass of the Irish people on the potato stemmed from the sharp surge in population over the fifty years before the outbreak of the Great Famine. The high-yielding potato made this rise in population possible in two ways. First, because as little as one acre sufficed to produce enough food for a family, the need for a smallholding on which sufficient potatoes could be cultivated – a prime obstacle to marriage – was effectively overcome. And second, the nutritional value of the potato, when supplemented with milk, fish and cabbage, led to a healthier and taller (at least as shown in army recruitment musters) population than elsewhere in Europe. The potato is the only food which, eaten to the exclusion of all others, will not cause a serious vitamin deficiency.

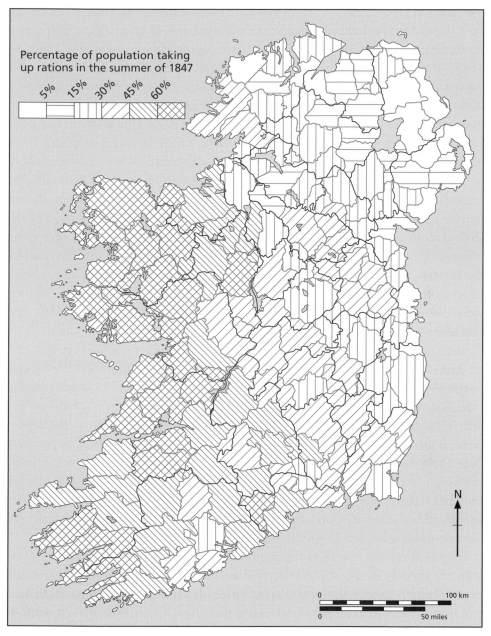

Map 9 Famine severity

This potato diet produced a fall in mortality rates, especially among nursing mothers, and with more mothers and babies surviving the rigours of childbirth and childhood, the number of young adults who would, in time, marry and become parents grew very rapidly. Contrary to what many observers claimed, the Irish did not marry younger than the people of other countries, but they did have a high rate of marriage and of marital fertility: celibacy and illegitimacy were rare in pre-Famine Ireland. Finally, the plentiful supply of a cheap, nutritious, if monotonous, food, the potato, was complemented by the general availability of turf for heating and cooking. Cheap fuel and ready food might suggest that compared to other peasant populations in Europe, especially eastern Europe, the Irish peasant may not have been so badly off. However, these advantages were more than offset by deteriorating social and economic conditions from 1815 on.

In the first place the Irish population rise which brought numbers from 2.5 million in 1750 to 5 million in 1800 and ultimately to 8.5 million in 1845 had not been accompanied as in England, or later in France and Germany, by increasing urbanisation or industrialisation. Rather the increase in population had led to growing immiseration. Especially west of a line from Derry to Cork the Irish growth in population remained not just rooted to the land but ever more mired in poverty, for the increase in numbers was disproportionately among the poorest strata of Irish society. It is a chilling thought that the millions who existed on tiny holdings were, comparatively speaking, the lucky ones, for they were out-numbered comprehensively by those who were entirely landless and thus even more at risk.

Some idea of what Irish poverty meant in the early nineteenth century can be gained from a consideration of Irish housing. This was graded for official purposes into four classes with the first class, brick-built and slated, being the best, and the fourth class, little more than sod huts, being the worst. Fully 60 per cent of the Irish population lived in fourth-class housing. By the 1840s the dependence on the potato had become overwhelming, with at least half the population dependent exclusively on potatoes and milk. As population had grown, greater pressure had been placed on existing resources of land with smaller and smaller holdings having to provide the necessary food for their owner. As a result, more prolific, if less reliable, sorts of potato such as the 'lumper' came to be preferred over the tastier, but less high-yielding, 'black', 'cup' or 'apple' varieties.

Despite these gloomy facts the outlook for the poverty-stricken Irish masses was not entirely desperate. Already by the early 1840s, emigration, primarily from eastern Ireland, was running at over a hundred thousand per annum, Britain and the United States being the favoured destinations. Undoubtedly, even without the Famine, emigration would have continued, would have grown in volume and would have relieved pressure on resources. Again, by the early 1840s there are indications that the surge in population was slowing down and further relieving pressure. Moreover, while there had been food shortages before the 1840s, they had been localised or regionalised, and had proved short-lived. Neither the Irish nor British governments had hesitated to purchase oatmeal abroad, and the crisis had passed with little excess mortality. With a population density comparable to that of Britain or Belgium, Ireland was not particularly overpopulated in 1845, and there is an argument to be made that had the Irish population remained unaffected by famine, emigration to an industrialising Britain and the United States might have resolved the Irish 'problem' without the intervention of mass death. It was not to be: as noted earlier, the potato blight of 1845 destroyed a much higher proportion of the staple food than had been ruined previously by inclement weather. Moreover, it destroyed the potato throughout Ireland, leaving very few areas untouched. And it destroyed the potato crop, by and large, for the remainder of the decade. It is scarcely an exaggeration to claim that this extraordinary, unprecedented and lethal combination burst on Ireland with all the impact of a nuclear explosion. How would the authorities react?

The view taken in the years after the Famine that successive governments and administrators failed in their duty of preventing mass famine death in Ireland has not been successfully challenged by recent research. The prime minister in 1845 was Sir Robert Peel and his immediate reaction was the time-honoured (and honourable) one of having the British government purchase food abroad, and then to set up a Special Relief Commission to oversee its distribution in Ireland. Peel also authorised the provision of some public work schemes, though the pay on these, to protect the labour market, was lower than the local rate. But Peel, as prime minister, was not to last, and his rather pragmatic view of government responsibilities in the face of famine accompanied him out of office. Those who took his place were much more doctrinaire in their approach. Some held an unshakeable faith in market forces, if left alone, to remedy all deficiencies in the economy. Others, more pious, were persuaded that the Famine was a righteous punishment from God on the Irish for their popery, and that as a nation of incorrigible workshy slackers, they had it coming. Still others, equally devout, welcomed famine as literally a heaven-sent opportunity to solve the Irish problem of gross overpopulation through a thorough-going transformation of Irish society. Most were certain that it was no function of the British state to subsidise Irish misery. Most were fearful of the costs involved in alleviating starvation in Ireland. Most were adamant that Irish property – i.e. Irish landlords – should pay for Irish poverty.

The outcome of these conflicting impulses was a relief policy that at best was inefficient and inconsistent and at worst was callous and ineffective (figure 5.3). A high point of administrative endeavour might be the feeding of some 3 million a day, and the provision of work for some three-quarters of a million, early in 1847. A low point would be the amendment to the Poor Law Act, again in 1847, which allowed outdoor relief, but refused it to any family in possession of more than one-quarter of an acre of land: a clause designed to cut the impoverished masses adrift from their tiny holdings. A further low point occurred, yet again in 1847,

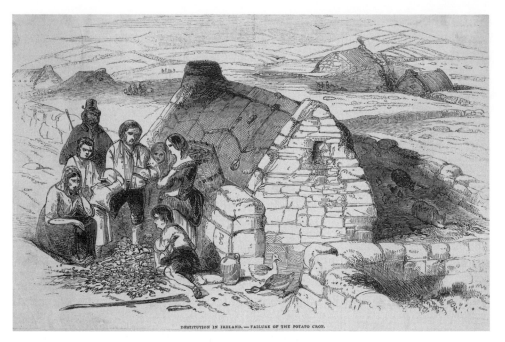

DESTITUTION IN IRELAND.—FAILURE OF THE POTATO CROP.

5.3 Illustrations of the misery of Ireland during the Great Famine left little to the imagination. National Library of Ireland.

when the Famine was, in effect, declared to be at an end. Exceptional relief measures were, therefore, unwarranted, the soup kitchens were dismantled and the burden of relief was thrown once again on to the already failing workhouse system.

So unimpressive – indeed, paltry – did these relief measures appear to some contemporaries (and to some later commentators) that they concluded that they were in fact designed to fail, and that the British government all along intended to let the Famine exact its shocking toll among the Irish. This was the view of the Presbyterian radical, and later revolutionary, John Mitchel, who claimed famously that while the potato blight might indeed have been sent by Almighty God, the actual Famine had been man-made. He and others like him laid a charge of mass murder against the British government for its refusal to ban food exports from Ireland throughout the Famine years. Mitchel claimed that had those exports been embargoed by the British government there would have been enough food for everyone. Again, he and others pointed to the mass evictions that were a feature of the Famine years and which led to several hundred thousands of cottiers and smallholders being unceremoniously turfed out on to the roadside and, in effect, forced to shift for themselves. Very many perished in this way. Others cited the £20 million sterling paid out as compensation for slave-owners in the West Indies in 1834. Later, the staggering £69 million squandered on a pointless war in the Crimea in the 1850s would be added to the accusations. These sums were contrasted with the British government's contribution for relief in Ireland, barely £7 million; and this for a country that was fiscally a part of the United Kingdom and for which the British government had entire responsibility. We may note that British tax revenues were running at around £55 million per annum, and that the sum advanced by the imperial treasury for Irish relief was easily eclipsed by the money raised from donations in Ireland.

Moreover, even those anxious to acquit the British government of genocidal intent were given cause for reflection by some of the more celebrated (or infamous) utterances of those writing about the Famine in Ireland, or charged with doing something about it. The London *Times*, for example, does not come well out of a review of its Famine reportage. It announced 'for our parts we regard the potato blight as a blessing', castigated 'the indolent Irish for their preference for relief over labour' and gleefully looked forward to the day when an Irishman in Connemara would be as scarce as a red Indian in Manhattan. Similar sentiments can be found in that other heavyweight print of the British political establishment, the *Economist*. Meanwhile at the treasury in London, Charles Trevelyan, the senior civil servant entrusted with overseeing spending on relief, welcomed the onset of the Famine, in his view brought about 'by a direct stroke of an all-wise and all-merciful providence [as] the appointed time of Ireland's regeneration'. He and others like him agonised privately that the Famine might not eliminate completely the surplus population, and thus 'this great opportunity' offered by the Great Famine might be let slip.

None of this is evidence, much less proof, of the British government's genocidal intent during the Irish Famine. There was, in fact, no such intent, and Mitchel and those who thought like him were wide of the mark in claiming that it was an artificial or contrived Famine, and that the relief measures were carefully calculated to do the most damage. There was no policy of genocide; there was instead a sincere belief that it was God who in His infinite and inscrutable wisdom had sent 'this sharp but effectual remedy', this fearful instrument, to punish the Irish for their popery, to purge them of their irredeemable idleness, but then to permit them to 'fully participate in the social health and physical prosperity of Britain' (Trevelyan). Central to this providentialism was an economic ideology that made a fetish of *laissez-faire* and market forces, and which demonised 'waste', 'dependency' and 'laziness', all key attributes of the 'nation of beggars'. (This economic ideology so maddened Mitchel that he later became an active supporter of plantation slavery, as representing, in his view, the very antithesis of heartless *laissez-faire*.) Again, so far as the export of food was concerned, much more food came into Ireland than went out during the Famine; and what did go out was mostly grain which formed a small proportion of the normal diet. Nor do comparisons between money spent on Famine relief and money spent on wars make much sense: no government in nineteenth-century Europe held it to be its prime responsibility to relieve humanitarian disasters: but all were prepared to spend whatever it took to win wars. The Dutch government of the 1840s, for example, was not particularly generous in relieving distress in its country. And of course, as we have been forcefully reminded, 'the Great Famine was no ordinary subsistence crisis', i.e. in its scale, intensity and duration it was unprecedented, and any government in the nineteenth century however well disposed would have found it difficult to meet, and overcome, the huge challenges posed by that catastrophe.

Irish poverty was not the fault of the British government, and it was poverty that made the Irish people vulnerable to Famine. None the less, when all the excuses and explanations are made, when the callous remarks and the insensitive rejoicing at misfortune are ignored and when due acknowledgement is accorded to prevailing ideology – an ideology shared by many Irish too – the stark fact remains: in the course of a few years, in a country united 'forever' to the most advanced economy in the world, at least one million died of starvation and disease. It is not too difficult to see how the words 'needlessly', 'intentionally' and 'deliberately' crept into the popular memory of those dreadful years.

The impact of the Famine was devastating for the lower strata of Irish society. The landless labourer, or landholder with a tiny parcel of land, a class that had been numbered in millions on the eve of the Famine, and that had far outnumbered their social superiors, the tenant farmers, all but disappeared from the Irish rural landscape in the sixty years after the Famine. During the Famine years they had been hard hit by food shortages which brought about excess mortality and, in the decades down to the First World War, the increasing swing to cattle production away from tillage (potato production never recovered after the Famine) meant that there was little demand for their labour. True, the numbers of Irish farmers also decreased in the later nineteenth century – they were down by a quarter between 1851 and 1914 – but the figures for farm labourers fell by two-thirds over the same period. Where once the labourers had been the largest class in the Irish countryside, by the time of the Great War they had all but disappeared and the social structure of rural Ireland was revolutionised as a result. The key unit was still the farm, but this was generally larger through consolidation after the Famine years, and the family home was often more comfortable than before the Famine. Crucially, the agricultural labourer had been washed away from the landscape, and with his virtual disappearance, and with the removal of the threat that he and his class had posed to the farmers above them, the way was cleared for the tenant farmers, now unchallenged from below, to begin their onslaught on the landlords with the ambition that they would be the proprietors in their turn.

Essentially, the Great Famine turned Ireland into an emigrant society: no European country in the nineteenth century would lose so high a percentage of its population to the emigrant ship as Ireland. It is true, of course, that since the early eighteenth century emigration had been a very important feature of Irish society, with many tens of thousands choosing to make their homes in the British colonies of north America, and elsewhere. This largely Presbyterian outflow had been superseded in the early nineteenth century by the numbers of Catholic Irish heading for the United States, and on the eve of the Famine, as noted, emigration was siphoning off an estimated hundred thousand per annum. In the circumstances, however, it is not the number who were leaving that impresses; rather it is the number of those who chose to battle it out in Ireland that is remarkable. The Famine broke the will to resist emigration, and the numbers who had gone before now constituted a resource base – in tickets, contacts and hospitality – for those who would come after. Previous outflows before the Famine had been orderly, with the winter months being avoided because of the danger from storms; but with the onset of hunger, emigration roared unchecked through all the seasons. This headlong flight continued through the early 1850s. Later, as the business of getting people out of the country as expeditiously and as painlessly as possible became the principal Irish industry, elements of judgement would enter into the timing and the destination of those leaving; but there was to be no change in the decision to go – that had been made at or before conception. It is in this latter respect that the Famine revolutionised Irish society.

Emigration in pre-Famine Ireland was an important, even striking feature of that society (figure 5.4): but post-Famine Ireland was an emigrant society, i.e. a society constructed around the necessity to remove huge numbers of its population. The best comparison here, perhaps, is with the pre-Civil War American south. At one time this had been a society in which there was slavery; by 1850, maybe earlier, it had become a slave society, to the preservation and consolidation of which, everything – ideology, politics and economics, not to mention penal code, women's dress, literature and popular religion – was directed. Similarly in Ireland, an emigrant society would emerge from the Famine years, one in which almost everything and everyone colluded to ship the surplus majority overseas, and conspired to do so in the interests of those selected to stay behind.

The virtual end to subdivision brought in its train a sharp decline in the frequency of marriage: in pre-Famine times, as elsewhere in Europe, nine out of ten Irish had married, but by 1900 Ireland was firmly at the bottom of the European marriage table, with barely six out of ten taking the plunge – though the large element of cold calculation in post-Famine matchmaking makes that

Supplement Gratis with "UNITED IRELAND." Saturday, Sept. 19th, 1885.

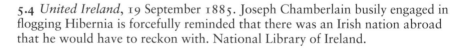

AN ERROR IN CALCULATION.

MR. CH———N.—We are thirty-four millions against your four, and by G——, if you give us any of your infernal tongue———
IRISH-AMERICAN.—Thirty-four millions against four! Hullo, stranger, draw it mild! YOU are forgetting ME! There are fifteen millions more where I came from

5.4 *United Ireland*, 19 September 1885. Joseph Chamberlain busily engaged in flogging Hibernia is forcefully reminded that there was an Irish nation abroad that he would have to reckon with. National Library of Ireland.

expression quite inappropriate. The need to defend the integrity of the family farm meant that only one son (not always the eldest) could inherit; for the other siblings, there was nothing for it but to leave, or else to stay on as a 'relative assisting', i.e. skivvying in the house or labouring about the farm for one's brother, but with no realistic possibility of a mate or a smallholding. If marriage was out of the question because of the impossibility of obtaining land or a dowry; if the possibility of inheriting was gone because another had been anointed to take over; if the only prospect was backbreaking and thankless work 'assisting' on a sibling's farm – and if everyone else was leaving – then, why resist? The chances of illicit sexual encounter were seemingly remote, for the priests, reflecting the values of their parishioners, were determined to stamp it out. Despite their best efforts, we may note that in 1870 the Royal Irish Constabulary recorded 563 brothels in Ireland. In short, the emigrant ship beckoned, and the mechanism was in place to transport the Irish masses. Those who had gone earlier encouraged those who remained to follow, and those chosen to stay cheered the emigrant on his or her way – as well they might, for the maintenance of their standard of living, let alone its improvement, was directly related to the constant outflow of potential competitors.

It is instructive that, uniquely among other emigrant groups who journeyed to north America, the Irish took the precaution of abandoning their native language and of learning English prior to embarkation for the New World. Irish society – right down to the middle of the twentieth century – required massive and sustained emigration in order to preserve its habits and values. This human haemorrhage out of Ireland in the hundred years after the Famine may not explain fully every political, economic or social, development during that period; but there is nothing that it does not help explain. This absolute requirement to preserve an emigrant society, not the struggle to end landlordism, nor the clamour for Home Rule, much less the demand for state sovereignty, or even the quest for the republic, is the key driver of modern Irish history. When emigration began to dry up from the 1960s on, that emigrant society with its ethos of the four 'Fs' – faith, farm, family and farewell – would begin to disintegrate rapidly.

A heavy outflow of people was a feature of nearly every county in Ireland in the decades after the Famine. Concealed within this statement are differences in terms of numbers and destinations. Thus, the years of the Great Famine witnessed heavy emigration from the eastern counties of Ireland, but it was in the post-Famine decades that Connacht and Munster experienced the greatest outward population movement. While all counties dispatched their surpluses to the United States, Ulster counties were highest for numbers to New Zealand, Canada and Britain, while Munster counties were to the fore in emigrants choosing Australia. For all counties, the United States of America was the main choice, with fully half of the 5 million who emigrated between 1850 and 1920 travelling there. Within that figure, however, the Connacht counties were overrepresented in their preference for that destination.

The average Irish emigrant, in so far as there was one, was young, typically aged between twenty and twenty-four years and was as likely (more likely, towards 1900) to be a female as a male. Again, the Irish emigrant was overwhelmingly single, for while family emigration before the Famine had been common, it was much less so thereafter. In so far as Irish emigration drew predominantly on young single men and women in roughly equal measure, it distinguished itself from the outflows of other European countries, where single men, and often entire family units, were the norm. Irish emigrants also marked themselves off by their reluctance to go back to Ireland: of all European emigrants to the United States, the Irish were the least likely to make the return journey. Some 58 out of 100 Italians would go back to the old country, and some 22 out of 100 Germans, but only 6 out of every 100 Irish. The presence of large numbers of suitable Irish marriage partners in the United States might partly account for the fact that, for the most part, emigration from Ireland was for keeps. However, a reluctance to return to Ireland did not mean that the emigrants ceased to think about the country. On the contrary, they took an abiding interest in Irish politics and developments. More dramatically – and probably with greater impact – Irish emigrants, especially females, revealed their attachment to those left behind by the remittance of substantial sums of money: between 1860 and 1880, some $30 million – two-fifths of which was in the form of prepaid tickets – was sent to relatives in Ireland by Irish emigrants in the United States, and as late as the 1950s emigrant remittances constituted some 2 per cent of southern Ireland's gross national product.

The nineteenth-century Irish emigrant was typically English speaking and, to an extent, literate in English (women less so than men), though both would have a knowledge of Irish. Speaking English, no matter how imperfectly, and with some reading ability in that language, the Irish were, in theory, privileged over all other continental emigrants to the United States and to other anglophone countries. However, whatever advantage accrued to the Irish emigrant from speaking English was entirely lost because of his or her attachment to Catholicism, for the favoured destination of most, the United States of America, yielded to no country in its resolute hostility to the adherents of that faith. Furthermore, while most nineteenth-century Irish emigrants, male or female, came from a rural background, and most would have had experience of farm work, this emphatically did not mean that agriculture would be the favoured occupation for those travelling to the United States. The vast majority settled in urban areas. In 1870 three-quarters of the Irish in the United States lived in cities, and in 1900 New York was second only to Dublin in the number of Irish residents. But a stubborn adherence to Catholicism, derided and feared as a foreign superstition headed by a foreign prince, and a marked preference for the urban ghetto rather than that rural idyll allegedly at the heart of the American self-image, clearly identified the Irish as quite un-American, and more than offset the advantage that they had derived from speaking English.

If a background of farm work was considered by the Irish emigrant to be of no account once he set foot in the United States, other experiences were not so easily forgotten. Those emigrants who left from the 1830s onwards were highly politicised as a result of the various agitations – Catholic emancipation, the tithe war and the campaign for repeal of the Union – which had involved the masses.

The skills acquired in these campaigns would be useful in a relatively open, democratic society. To an extent unknown among other emigrant groups, the nineteenth-century Irish emigrants arrived with an understanding of the democratic process, and how to use its instruments – voting, turn-out, registration, organisation, committees, meetings, political agendas and such like. They also, almost certainly, had experience of what we may call 'politics out of doors', i.e the agrarian insurgencies that had marked every decade since the 1760s; and the methods of 'Captain Rock' could also prove serviceable in the rough and tumble of American city politics. Above all, religion could be deployed to advantage in the political game, for despite the best efforts of Thomas Davis to educate the Irish to substitute race for religion, they had not proved adept pupils. The notion of the cheery Celt engaged in a ceaseless struggle with the surly Saxon had been ahead of its time, and race had played no part in the great agitations in Ireland during the first half of the nineteenth century. But religion had and, under the tutelage of O'Connell and later Catholic leaders, the Catholic emigrant arrived conscious of the persecuted status of his religion (for O'Connell had rarely failed to remind his audience of this), totally convinced of its oneness with Irishness and well aware of the necessity for ethnic solidarity. Few other emigrant groups could bring such potent, varied and valuable experiences to the political arena.

To all of the above, the post-Famine Irish Catholic emigrant brought a visceral hatred of England (Britain was rarely acknowledged) as the author of all his or her trials and tribulations. Mitchel's message of the Famine as attempted genocide – and he was not alone in promoting this – was accepted by and large unquestioningly by the huddled masses who found themselves decanted on to the shores of the Hudson, or sheltering in the emigrant camps at Grosse Ile in Quebec. The stock elements in Mitchel's indictment – the food ships sailing out of Irish ports as the poor starved, the 'coffin' ships foundering at sea, the mass evictions of those unable to pay their rent, the concept of humanitarian relief as a cloak for mass murder – all made sense to those who saw emigration as exile, who regarded themselves as the uprooted and who, already psychologically disoriented by the manner of their departure, found themselves despised for their religion, for their 'race' and for their poverty.

Nor were matters helped by the poor average performance of the Irish immigrant in the New World. Studies suggest a strong residential and occupational immobility among the Irish, at least until the early twentieth century. That is to say, the Irish continued for the first few generations after the Famine to occupy the worst-paid jobs while residing in the least salubrious neighbourhoods of the main east-coast cities. Yankee prejudice can account for some of this: it has been noted that those Irish who moved to Chicago or to the west coast, where there was no white, Anglo-Saxon and Protestant (WASP) establishment to oppose them, tended to climb the social and occupational ladder much more swiftly than those who remained on the east coast. It is also possible that those Irish who prospered in the west may have done so because they possessed greater ambition than those who remained in the east. In a real sense whether to move from the east coast and head elsewhere, or to remain where he or she had landed, was the first genuine migration choice that the Irish emigrant had to make. As we have seen the initial decision to leave Ireland was not really made, it was simply assumed. And yet, whether east coast or west coast, New York or San Francisco, the Irish emigrant nurtured a bitter enmity towards England. Perhaps this hatred for 'England' as the author of all their misfortunes was especially nourished among the Famine emigrants, but successive waves of emigrants equally and eagerly embraced it. A bitter crop was thereby sown and a rich harvest was to be reaped in the next century and a half, as the Irish in America went on to found, fund and support various groups and movements dedicated to achieving Irish independence: on occasion, numbers of these Irish Americans would use violence to achieve that end.

The emergence of the land question

If the agricultural labourer as a category was the most visible casualty of the Great Famine, the Irish landlord, his polar opposite in the class structure, was not far behind. Not that many landlords died during the Famine – Major Denis Mahon of Roscommon was assassinated and a few others may have died from disease – but none perished from starvation. And yet the Famine marked an irreversible point in the fortunes of Irish landlords as the central authority figures in Ireland. True, the Union of 1801 had been a blow to their political standing, for its necessity was based on the British belief that Irish landlords, the key political class, were no longer able to rule. And Catholic emancipation, provoked by freeholder revolts at elections, had shown that their power to command seats at Westminster was coming under threat. Admittedly, as late as 1852 two-thirds (68 out of 104) of Ireland's Members of Parliament came from landed stock; but this high percentage cloaked a vital truth – after the Famine there seemed to be no way back for the Irish landlord class.

During the Famine, because of the British insistence that Irish 'property' was liable for the costs of relief, Irish landlords found themselves facing ever higher bills for public works, soup kitchens, workhouses and such like. These additional sums were demanded at a time when, for obvious reasons, rental income was in sharp decline. The historic profligacy of earlier generations of landlords – whether at the racetrack or in the bedroom, it mattered not – had already led to heavy indebtedness before the Famine but the large bills for famine relief and the reduced income from rent during the Famine years brought disaster. By 1845 perhaps 10 per cent of Irish landlords had been bankrupted, and three times as many were facing that fate.

Nor was there much sympathy for their financial plight. English and Scottish economists were quick to lay most of the blame for Ireland's poor economic performance at the door of Irish landlords, while British politicians in general gazed uncomprehendingly, and with less and less sympathy, at a class that appeared to perform no function beyond that of being the prime recipient of rent. Fortunately for British policy-makers, there was a historic remedy to hand for this state of affairs. Just as the descendants of the medieval colonists, as a class, had been found wanting in the sixteenth century and were replaced by new settlers from the 1550s on, so the Great Famine had revealed the failure of the Irish landlord class, and they were now to be replaced by new, more market-oriented landlords, preferably English or Scottish.

This was the thinking that lay behind the passing of the Encumbered Estates Act of 1849 which set up a court to facilitate the sale of indebted estates to interested investors. Within a few years about a quarter of the island of Ireland had changed hands, and some five thousand new purchasers found themselves in possession of tidy estates. This was a revolution in landowning comparable to some degree with that of the seventeenth century, and like that revolution it failed to produce the desired results. Contrary to the intention of those behind the Act, the new owners turned out to be overwhelmingly Irish, with the younger sons of gentry families, shopkeepers and solicitors prominent among them. Few were progressive in their methods of farming, or were zealous for improvement. Despite later allegations that the new owners proved grasping and avaricious – in contrast, apparently, to their fondly remembered predecessors, who had been bankrupted by gambling, ruined by improvident matches or bled white through paying for poor relief – the new men were not, in fact, any better or worse than those whom they succeeded. What the Encumbered Estates Act did do was reduce by about 30 per cent the amount of rent paid to absentee landlords, for centuries the *bêtes noires* of English and Irish commentators on Irish affairs; but it achieved this end because the new landlords lived predominantly in Dublin not in London or Edinburgh. It is a moot point whether this reduction in absentee rent brought forward at all the desired improvement in Irish agriculture, or indeed whether the Encumbered Estates Act itself achieved any of the goals held out for it.

However, the Act is noteworthy in three ways, one direct and two indirect. First, there was the very fact of parliamentary intervention into the Irish land market. This was quite unprecedented: certainly, nothing like it was contemplated for either England or Scotland; and this initial Act inevitably opened the door to further parliamentary intervention. Second, the thinking behind the new Act was that a new class of landlords had to be brought in because the old one was deemed to have failed. But if landlords could simply be parachuted in without regard to ancestry, moral fibre, local connection or social authority, what was to stop tenants aspiring to be landowners in their turn? After all, they knew at least as much about agriculture as solicitors and shopkeepers, they lived on the land and, in any case, were they not continually told that they were the true heirs of those whose estates had been confiscated in the Conquest? Lastly, the Encumbered Estates Act marked an important stage in the emergence of the land question as the key issue in Irish politics, a position it would occupy for the remainder of the nineteenth century, and beyond.[3] Quite what the essence of that question was to be at any given time remains to be seen, but land, its owner-ship, and occupancy (rarely its use) was now becoming central to Irish national politics in a way that it had not been since the seventeenth century. The Famine had brought the landlord question to the fore and in attempting to deal with that issue the entire question of Irish land moved centre stage. Already in 1849, James Fintan Lalor, a Young Irelander, had claimed that 'the land question contains, and the legislative question does not contain, the material from which victory is manufactured'. At the time, little attention was paid to Lalor's prioritising the agrarian over the national question; but his voice proved prophetic. It might not be sufficient to repeal the Union; the Conquest might have to go too.

Post-Famine politics

It is not surprising that the two decades after the Famine have been categorised as constituting 'an era of fragmentation in political terms'.[4] The revolutionary, the constitutional, the agrarian and the sectarian, all competed for pre-eminence during this period. However, by the early 1870s the picture was clearer, and these strands had fused, even if no consensus had emerged on their relative rankings in the Irish political agenda.

A sign that the Famine had brought the land question to the fore was a renewed demand in 1850 from Ulster (Presbyterian) tenants headed by Sharman Crawford to have their cherished 'Ulster custom' enshrined into law. In theory and in practice this custom was a goodwill payment made by the incoming tenant to the one who was, for whatever reason, vacating the holding. It was a payment made without the landlord's permission or, very often, without his knowledge and it appears to have owed its origins to unsettled conditions during the seventeenth-century Ulster plantation. It was unknown in English land law or custom and hence there was a difficulty in grasping what it was about or accepting the tenants' argument that the lack of legal backing for it was a genuine grievance. Fortunately, the concept of the 'Ulster custom' was quickly redefined, and rapidly became associated with the notion of compensation to the outgoing tenant for any improvement he had made on his farm. This was easily understood by English law-makers. Compensation for improvement, in fact, had little to do with the Ulster custom but it accorded well with English notions of fair play and honest reward: it also fitted in well with the current stereotype of avaricious and capricious Irish landlords, heartlessly evicting model tenants without so much as a penny for their efforts in draining meadows, planting orchards and constructing outbuildings.

Ulster tenants had no success with their claim for a legal basis for the custom but they received a boost when farmers elsewhere in Ireland, agitated by a run of poor agricultural prices, took up this demand. In 1852 a tenant league headed by Charles Gavan Duffy, a former Young Irelander, and Frederick Lucas, an English Catholic journalist, was established to secure legal backing for the Ulster custom or 'free sale', and for its extension throughout Ireland. In addition, and with an eye to a catchy slogan, they sought 'a fair rent' and 'fixity of tenure': the three 'Fs' were born. In truth, they had been conceived before the Famine; but that disaster had served to bring them quickly to term. Irish tenant farmers had emerged as the undisputed winners from the Famine, and they now had their eyes on the prize.

By coincidence, and entirely separately from this agitation over land tenure, there had been an outburst of anti-Catholic rioting in England in the early 1850s, a reminder that such benightedness was not confined to Ireland. Outraged Irish Catholics demanded that their parliamentary representatives should assert the pope's claim to award titles to his bishops in England (for the pontiff's temerity in this respect lay behind the violence) and, in general, that they should protect Catholic rights. Irish Members of Parliament in the 1840s, the so-called O'Connell's 'tail', had been dutiful in this respect, and those elected under a wider franchise in the early 1850s, quickly dubbed 'the Irish Brigade' or, more dismissively, 'the Pope's Brass Band', were to prove equally zealous. However, as well as protecting Catholic interests, they also adopted the programme of the three 'Fs', and called themselves the Independent Irish Party.

For those like Charles Gavan Duffy who had long longed for the day when an all-Ireland, non-sectarian organisation would come into existence, it was understandable that enthusiasm for this campaign of Presbyterian and Catholic farmers to secure tenants' rights would cloud their judgement. Duffy was to portray this new departure grandiosely as the League of North and South, complete with Catholics and Protestants, arm in arm on the one road, whistling the one tune. Predictably, the high hopes excited by its formation fell far short of realisation. At Westminster, party discipline was non-existent, and several Members – John Sadleir and William Keogh were the best known – quickly succumbed to the lure of office and entered government employ. Improved agricultural prices saw a waning of enthusiasm for the Tenant League. Most seriously, however, the League's prominent identification with 'Catholic issues', and the influential role played by some Catholic priests in its deliberations, swiftly led to the departure of its Presbyterian tenant farmers. A shared dislike for, or hostility to, landlords, and a common desire for improved tenurial terms, could not overcome the sectarianism at the heart of Irish public life. By 1858 the Independent Irish Party had broken up, and the League of North and South was no more; Charles Gavan Duffy's pulse, it appeared, had raced in vain.

But while progress on the constitutional/agrarian front appeared to be at a standstill, important developments were taking place, for off-stage and clandestinely the Irish revolutionary movement was being reinvented (figure 5.5). Already in 1848 the popular memory of revolt had been to an extent revitalised by an attack on police at Ballingarry, County Tipperary. The insurgents, about a hundred in total, were led by William Smith O'Brien, Terence Bellew Mac-Manus and James Stephens, all formerly members of the Young Ireland group. The attack was repulsed and the rising – if it can be so described – was quickly suppressed, and swiftly derided as the 'battle of widow McCormack's cabbage-patch'. Two insurgents were killed but there were no policemen casualties and, happily, the British state saw no need for exemplary punishment. The ringleaders were, indeed, sentenced to a traitor's death, but this punishment was commuted to transportation for life to Australia. A precedent for state clemency in Irish popular insurrections was thereby set that, when departed from following Fenian attacks in 1867, was to convulse nationalist Ireland.

The Young Ireland insurrection was a confused affair. Despite later claims it owed little to resentment against England on account of the Great Famine; on the contrary, it appeared to have been staged more in emulation of republican uprisings in Paris and elsewhere in 1848, the so-called 'Year of Revolutions'. And yet, for all its farcical aspects, it was to be an important link between the United Irishmen of 1798, Robert Emmet in 1803 and the later Fenian and Easter week insurrections. No doubt if historical DNA testing had been available in 1848, it would have shown no real apostolic succession between the Young Ireland rebellion and earlier and later efforts. However, in the romantic imagination of Irish nationalists, and later in Irish popular memory, there would be a clear linkage, and this was what counted. The actual fighting on the ground would be disregarded, but much attention would be paid to the conduct of the conspirators at their trials, and much pride taken in their Emmet-like speeches from the dock. The British attitude, unsurprisingly, was entirely different. The

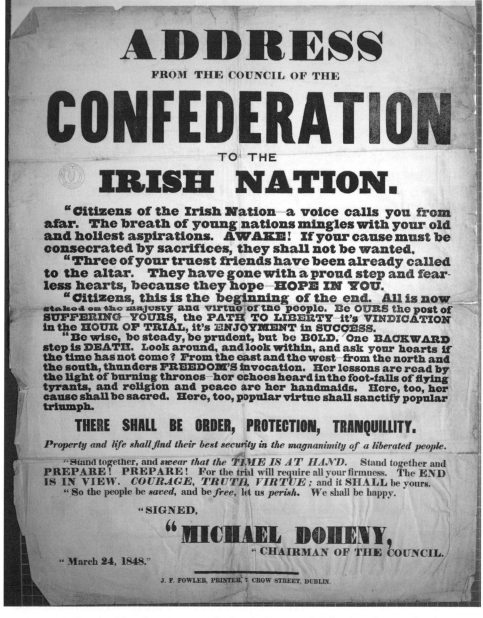

ADDRESS

FROM THE COUNCIL OF THE

CONFEDERATION

TO THE

IRISH NATION.

"Citizens of the Irish Nation—a voice calls you from afar. The breath of young nations mingles with your old and holiest aspirations. AWAKE! If your cause must be consecrated by sacrifices, they shall not be wanted.

"Three of your truest friends have been already called to the altar. They have gone with a proud step and fearless hearts, because they hope—HOPE IN YOU.

"Citizens, this is the beginning of the end. All is now staked on the majesty and virtue of the people. Be OURS the post of SUFFERING—YOURS, the PATH TO LIBERTY—it's VINDICATION in the HOUR OF TRIAL, it's ENJOYMENT in SUCCESS.

"Be wise, be steady, be prudent, but be BOLD. One BACKWARD step is DEATH. Look around, and look within, and ask your hearts if the time has not come? From the east and the west—from the north and the south, thunders FREEDOM'S invocation. Her lessons are read by the light of burning thrones—her echoes heard in the foot-falls of flying tyrants, and religion and peace are her handmaids. Here, too, her cause shall be sacred. Here, too, popular virtue shall sanctify popular triumph.

THERE SHALL BE ORDER, PROTECTION, TRANQUILLITY.

Property and life shall find their best security in the magnanimity of a liberated people.

"Stand together, and *swear that the TIME IS AT HAND.* Stand together and PREPARE! PREPARE! For the trial will require all your firmness. The END IS IN VIEW. *COURAGE, TRUTH, VIRTUE;* and it SHALL be yours. "So the people be *saved,* and be *free,* let us *perish.* We shall be happy.

"SIGNED,

"MICHAEL DOHENY,

"CHAIRMAN OF THE COUNCIL.

" March 24, 1848."

J. F. FOWLER, PRINTER, 7 CROW STREET, DUBLIN.

5.5 Inspired by the 1848 revolution in France, Michael Doheny, a leading member of Young Ireland, issued a call to arms in Ireland. National Library of Ireland.

very fact that any sort of uprising, no matter how futile, could have occurred at a time when the British state was embarked on – in its eyes – a major project of Famine relief in Ireland was deeply shocking. A further campaign of vituperation of things Irish ensued; perhaps the highpoint was reached when the eminent Victorian man of letters, Thomas Carlyle, in reaction to news of the 1848 rebellion, snarled that the Irish were 'starved rats' fit only to be squashed by 'Elephant England'.

After the Young Ireland rebellion revolutionary conspiracy was never off the Irish agenda. James Stephens, one of the leaders in 1848, had evaded arrest and fled to Paris, then the capital of revolutionary Europe. In all he spent nearly seven years there, by his own account learning the craft of the revolutionary from French and Italian theoreticians. On his return to Ireland in 1856 he set about organising a revolutionary society on the model of the Carbonari of Italy, and in Dublin on St Patrick's day 1858 he founded the secret organisation known later as the IRB (there was uncertainty as to whether these initials stood for Irish Revolutionary Brotherhood or Irish Republican Brotherhood). A year later, in April 1859, in New York, a sister organisation, the Fenian Brotherhood, was set up by John O'Mahony, another refugee from the 1848 rebellion. The aim of the Fenians, as members of the two societies came to be known, was to secure a republic for Ireland by force of arms. Other organisations – the United Irish Society, say, or even the Young Irelanders – had begun as constitutional or cultural pressure groups, and had only turned to armed insurrection when they had failed to achieve their objectives by legal means; but the Fenians from the beginning turned their back on politics, and dedicated themselves to an Irish republic to be established by war. Britain had failed to heed the force of argument; it would now be treated to the argument of force.

The Fenians recruited rapidly in Ireland, Britain, the United States and beyond: by 1864 there may have been over sixty thousand Fenians in Ireland, hundreds of Irish soldiers in the British army appear to have been sworn in and the movement was popular with those Irish serving in both the Union and Confederate armies in the American Civil War. In Ireland Fenianism appealed to those who felt uprooted by the huge changes under way after the Famine. In particular, town labourers, retail clerks, shop assistants – urban workers in general (but not farmers until later) – found in Fenianism a vehicle for their aspirations and for their energies. Conspiracy offered a release from the tedium of everyday life and the recreational attractions of Fenianism ought not to be ignored. No doubt, also, it gave men something to do while waiting to board the emigrant ship and, equally, it gave the Irish immigrant a sense of self-importance, no matter how much at odds with his (or her) despised situation in the host country. There was, however, and there remained, enough solid conviction at the heart of Fenianism to ensure that the pure separatist ideal would survive every setback. Ironically, in its emphasis on principle, sacrifice, stoicism, manliness and endurance, Fenianism was a very Victorian thing, for the Fenian cherished respectability; that was a key part of the movement's attraction.

Given that any type of self-government for Ireland, no matter how limited, was regarded by all British governments (until 1885) as a dangerous absurdity to be resisted at all costs, and given that, in the third quarter of the nineteenth century, the British empire was militarily the greatest since that of Rome, a Fenian declaration of war with the objective of setting up an independent and separate Irish republic could scarcely have been viewed in London with anything other than amused disdain. Fenian leaders, however, were confident of ultimate victory. They were certain that a major war, in which Britain would be heavily engaged, could not be long delayed and that this crisis would offer the opportunity to strike. In addition they counted on their ability to suborn a significant proportion of the Irish soldiers serving in the British army: in 1855 possibly 50 per cent of the rank and file in the army were Irish Catholic. Again, the large numbers of disaffected Irish emigrants in Britain, Australia, New Zealand and, especially, in the United States – in Stephens's words 'that second Ireland beyond the reach of British power' – could be enlisted in the cause and persuaded to supply arms, funds or leadership. Lastly, the Fenians concluded that their superior morale (as they saw it), their organisational secrecy and their ability to select the moment to strike, more than made up for all disparities between them and the might of the British empire.

In the event the performance of the Fenians during the 1860s tended to confirm the more derisory estimations of the threat they posed. Admittedly, that decade began with a major publicity coup for the new organisation. The Young Irelander, Thomas Bellew MacManus, had died in San Francisco in January 1861, and a Fenian front organisation, the National Brotherhood of St Patrick, brought his remains back to Ireland for what had many of the trappings of a state funeral. Despite the open hostility of the Catholic archbishop of Dublin and Dublin Castle to the entire venture, thousands turned out to line the route of the cortege in Dublin, and the Fenians had their public triumph. Thereafter, however, matters went downhill. Stephens proved to be both dilatory and dictatorial in his methods; he proclaimed a 'year of victory' in 1865, and then again in 1866, but both years came and went without any stir. Moreover, for one who stressed the need for the utmost secrecy, it was altogether odd that Stephens should lend his support to a newspaper, *The Irish People*, which promoted itself as the public organ of Fenianism. Organisationally too the movement left much to be desired: it was quickly riddled with informers, and swiftly split into warring factions, divided over whether an attack on Canada, or insurrection in Ireland, offered the better chance of success. Nor did fortune favour their most ambitious hope: a promising dispute between Great Britain and the United States over the former's aid to the Confederacy during the Civil War stubbornly refused to escalate into an all-out war. In addition the Irish and English authorities proved vigilant and resourceful in combating the Fenian conspiracy: disaffected regiments were quietly shipped overseas, the *Irish People* office was raided, and most of the leadership were arrested before the Fenians could act. Almost inevitably, therefore, when the Fenians, or some of them, took to the field in March 1867 around Dublin and in parts of Munster, the result was yet another fiasco. Some twelve men, Fenians and police, died in the confused exchange of shots. Scores were arrested. As with the Young Ireland insurgents in 1848, the British state saw no need for exemplary executions, and those found guilty were sentenced to terms of imprisonment, or to transportation to Western Australia.

It is possible that had matters ended with this, then Fenianism might have dwindled to a recurring footnote in the history of Irish conspiracies. What saved it from this fate was the drama of the rescue in September 1867 of Fenian prisoners from a police-van in Manchester and its fatal consequences. During the escape, Sergeant Charles Brett, on escort duty, was fatally wounded. Three Fenians, William Allen, Michael Larkin and Michael O'Brien – later dubbed the 'Manchester Martyrs' – were tried for murder. Their plausible defence, that they had not intended to injure any one but that the fatal shot had been fired merely to break the lock of the police-van, was dismissed and they were sentenced to death. The conviction of the three men and their public execution (figure 5.6) shocked a nationalist Ireland that had been largely unmoved by the absurd Fenian insurrection months earlier – or rather, had been moved to condemn it as 'wicked and mad'. It was as if a long-standing tacit understanding that Irish rebels should not pay the supreme price had been shattered, for no Irish rebel had been executed since the Emmet rebellion of 1803. The manly bearing of the three men (widely admired), their speeches from the dock (speedily circulated) and their defiant cry of 'God save Ireland' (soon incorporated into a rousing marching song) electrified nationalist Ireland, and served to ensure that their unquenchable idealism and ready sacrifice and, by extension, the entire Fenian enterprise of the 1860s, would be recalled with national pride in years to come. God might or might not save Ireland, but the 'Manchester Martyrs' had certainly saved Fenianism from ignominy and ridicule. It would be premature to say that a terrible beauty had been born; but it had certainly quickened in the womb.

One of those who pleaded with the authorities not to execute Allen, Larkin and O'Brien was Paul Cullen, Catholic archbishop of Dublin since 1852 and a cardinal since 1866 – the first Irishman to be so honoured, at least in modern times. Cullen was no friend to the Fenians or their republican project; indeed he was markedly lukewarm on the demand for Irish self-government. His long experience in Rome had instilled in him a horror of secret societies; he regarded republicans – both Italian and Irish – as the enemy of his church; and he believed that the Union could still deliver all that Catholic Ireland wanted. But while Cullen took his religion from Rome – he was the most 'Roman' Catholic prelate since Rinuccini – he took his politics from Ireland, and he feared the impact that Fenian 'martyrdom' might have on his Catholic countrymen. Fenianism, he

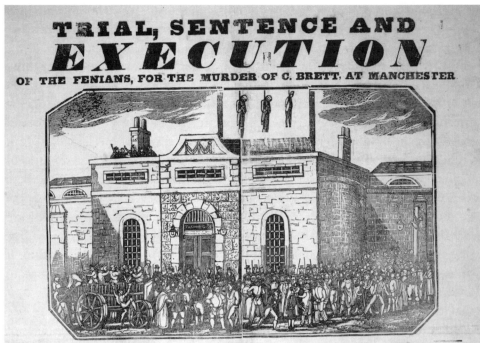

5.6 The execution of the 'Manchester Martyrs', an event which shocked nationalist Ireland. National Library of Ireland.

believed, had come about because of the lack of the Catholic church's involvement in politics; it was time for the priests to re-engage and to give a lead.

It was under the aegis of Cullen that what has become known as the 'devotional revolution', by which the Irish Catholic church became progressively more 'Romanised', was considerably accelerated. This was a process that had begun in the 1820s, when traditional, sometimes semi-pagan, religious practices – patterns, wakes and local pilgrimages, often accompanied by disorder – began gradually to be eliminated. In their place came a new emphasis on clerical control, so that the parish missions, sermons and confraternities became vital features of religious practice. With the growing clericalisation of the Catholic religion there was a very significant increase in the social and political authority of the clergy. The result was the emergence of that clericalised society in which priests were central and in which almost no activity lay outside their remit – a society that was to survive largely unchecked until final quarter of the twentieth century. It was during the long reign of Cardinal Cullen that the 'devotional revolution' finally triumphed.

Two others were caught up in the aftermath of the Fenian conspiracy: Isaac Butt (figure 5.7), a Member of Parliament and lawyer, who acted for the defence in a number of Fenian trials; and William Ewart Gladstone, leader of the Liberal Party, and prime minister from 1868 to 1874. Butt had been a founding editor of the *Dublin University Magazine*, a journal which attempted to promote a patriotism that combined loyalty to the Union with love of Gaelic culture and enthusiasm for Irish antiquity. A Protestant and a conservative, Butt had opposed O'Connell in the 1840s, but since then his political views had evolved. He had become a noted critic of the British 'misgovernment' of Ireland, and he was an unlikely admirer of those Fenians he defended as a barrister. In 1868 he began an amnesty movement to have them released from prison or exile and, in 1870, he founded the Home Government Association, whose parliamentary candidates pledged themselves to achieving limited self-government for Ireland within the empire. The Irish Home Rule party that was to last until 1918 was born.

Gladstone too was affected, even disturbed, by the Fenians, and particularly by a Fenian outrage at Clerkenwell prison, London, in December 1867. In the course of an attempted gaol-break an explosion demolished a nearby tenement, killing several of the inhabitants and causing numerous injuries. Michael Barrett, a Fenian, was executed for this crime the following May. Barrett is known to legal historians because he was to be the last man hanged in public in England; but more important, the Clerkenwell incident, for which Barrett bore some responsibility, appears to have crystallised in Gladstone's mind the conviction that something would have to be done for Ireland. He would be, so to speak, tough on Fenianism (he resisted an amnesty for them, for example), but he would

5.7 Portrait of Isaac Butt, leader of the Home Government Association and pioneer Home Ruler. National Library of Ireland.

be equally tough on the cause of Fenianism, which he identified as, basically, injustice. Gladstone was then the newly made leader of the Liberals, a party that in 1868 gained office. Necessarily, considerations of party interest entered fully into his calculations. He concluded that Ireland ought to be governed according to 'Irish ideas' of what was right and fitting. He believed that a strategy of, as he put it, 'drawing a line between the fenians and the people of Ireland', offered the best hope for the preservation of the Union and the empire. He was confident that this policy would prove popular with the (recently expanded) British and Irish electorate, and that it would dish the Tory Party led by Benjamin Disraeli, who had earlier (and memorably) dismissed the Irish question as merely 'the Pope one day, potatoes the next'.

One of Gladstone's first actions as prime minister was to proceed with the disestablishment of the Church of Ireland, whose position as the established church, he noted loftily, evoked 'painful and bitter memories of ascendancy'. This was a shrewd move on his part. Knocking the Church of Ireland off its pedestal would appeal to his nonconformist supporters in England and to his Presbyterian supporters in Scotland and Ulster. As well, quite cynically, disestablishment could plausibly be presented as righting a long-standing injustice, for it was notorious that the Church of Ireland, for all its alleged wealth and privilege, ministered to a small minority – one-eighth – of the Irish people. In a utilitarian age this was difficult to defend. Disestablishment as a policy had the added advantage of meeting one of Cardinal Cullen's short-term goals. Cullen and his fellow bishops wanted an end put to the official pre-eminence of the Church of Ireland, but they professed no desire for Catholicism to succeed it as the official state church. Then again, they had no need to do so, for they well knew that Catholic equality in the eyes of the state would, over the coming years, in practice, mean Catholic dominance. Gladstone's proposal, along with various other initiatives on the Irish tenant right and on education, recalled Peel's overtures to the Catholic church a generation earlier, and raised once again the prospect of some sort of constructive partnership between the Irish Catholic hierarchy and a great British party through which the grievances of Ireland could be redressed.

The Irish Church Act formally disestablishing the Church of Ireland was passed in July 1869 and came into force on 1 January 1871. It had an easy passage at Westminster, for the Church of Ireland had few friends there. In Ireland opposition to it was, by and large, confined to those directly affected, and the whole process had an air of inevitability about it. Whether or not a great injustice had been righted might well be debated, but what was incontestable was that an important article in the Act of Union had been removed. According to that Act, the Church of Ireland and the Church of England were to be joined 'for ever'; now one had been cast adrift. More was to follow, for having disestablished the Church of Ireland, Gladstone, perhaps unwittingly, set about the disestablishment of the Irish landlord class. With the unhorsing of the Church of Ireland, Irish landlords as a class had been left dangerously exposed as the sole obstacle to peace and harmony in Ireland. It was time to act against them.

Gladstone's Land Act of 1870 was an attempt to understand the Irish land question from an Irish perspective. For the first time 'Irish ideas', i.e. ideas in conflict with orthodox political economy, or in flat opposition to absolute property rights, were to be accorded due weight rather than dismissed out of hand. The Land Act implicitly accepted that Ireland was a different country from England, that the duties and responsibilities of Irish landlords were quite unlike those of English landlords (and were likely to remain so), and that the English record in Ireland had been one of incompetence and failure. The Act gave the force of law to the customary tenant right (the 'Ulster custom') where it existed; it made provision for compensation for those tenants evicted for reasons other than failure to pay their rent and it offered similar compensation for improvement if a tenant gave up his holding. The Act went through the Commons and Lords after a languid struggle. Only the arch-conservative Lord Salisbury made a stand in the Lords: very pertinently he asked why Irish farmers should be privileged over sacked unemployed dockers and coalminers in Britain who were left to shift for themselves, when (put) out of work; less pertinently, he groaned, where was this all going to end? His protest came to nothing, and the Act duly passed. It was to be almost entirely irrelevant to Irish needs or desires.

The Act changed very little: it did deliver a modified version of the three 'Fs' that had been sought by tenants since the 1850s; but it did so especially in Ulster, where they had been the practice anyway. Much of the rest of Ireland remained untouched in respect of free sale and fixity of tenure. Evictions were certainly harder to enforce than before, but there was no sharp drop after 1870; and since a very large proportion of evictions were for non-payment of rent, they were beyond the reach of Gladstone's Land Act. In so far as rents and other tenurial matters – including the precise definition of the 'Ulster custom' – would in future be matters for special land courts, it is likely that the main beneficiaries of the Act were country solicitors. Moreover, if Gladstone hoped that his Act would in some way create a new situation in the Irish countryside, where a benign landlord class would be warmly embraced by a tenantry abjectly grateful for a type of dual ownership – and there is some evidence that this is, in fact, what he envisaged – then he was to be badly mistaken.

The Land Act of 1870 hastened the demise of Irish landlordism. In the twenty years since the Famine, Irish tenants had done well in terms of maximising agricultural profits while keeping rent increases at bay. By 1870 they could sense that they had the landlords on the run. Why settle for fair rent when there was a good prospect of no rent to pay? Why settle for dual ownership when the prize of single ownership beckoned? The burgeoning nationalist press of the 1860s, headed by the *Irish Catholic Magazine*, had never ceased to remind the tenant farmers that the landlords were English and foreign, that they were Protestant, and that their ancestors in the seventeenth century had obtained their estates by forfeiture (i.e. theft). It mattered not that this was a gross distortion of the actual situation (in 1870, 38 per cent of landlords were Irish Catholics, albeit owning at most 15 per cent of Irish land), or indeed a misreading of the historical record (purchase, as much as confiscation, explained the pattern of Irish landlordism); what counted for the tenants was the giddy prospect of being the landowners in their turn. Already, tucked away in a corner of the 1870 Land Act, was what proved to be the signpost to the future outcome of the Irish land question. Against Gladstone's better judgement, he was forced to include a short, much circumscribed, series of clauses allowing for the purchase by tenants of their holdings from their landlords. These 'Bright' clauses, named after the politician who had prevailed on Gladstone to include them, were to be the germ of the policy adopted by Conservative governments in the late nineteenth and early twentieth centuries. The implementation of that policy would result in the transformation of Ireland into a predominantly owner-occupier society.

Assessment

How stood the Union in 1870?[5] On the face of it, despite the persistence of the Irish demand for some form of self-government, whether from the Fenians or from Butt's Home Government Association, the Union appeared to be working. Gladstone, the leader of a great British political party, was evidently seeking to conduct Irish affairs according to 'Irish ideas', and he had already delivered the important symbolic concession of disestablishment, and he had proved open to new thinking on the land question. Moreover, with the Liberals in power, there seemed every prospect of further legislative initiatives that would meet all Irish desires, short of self-government. Two vignettes seem to encapsulate the Catholic nationalist progress at this period: in 1868, Thomas O'Hagan became Irish lord chancellor: he was the first Catholic to occupy the top legal position in Ireland since the reign of James II. And in 1870 Cardinal Cullen, a 'Prince of the Church', resplendent in his robes and sporting a cardinal's red hat, dined at the side of Edward, prince of Wales, in Dublin Castle; a historic first (for both). Could the hitherto unimaginable yet become commonplace in Ireland?

On a broader front, those of an optimistic cast of mind could point to the growing closeness of the Anglo-Irish relationship throughout the nineteenth century. For example, improved transport in the shape of cross-channel steamers and internal railways was playing its part by reducing the time hitherto involved in travelling. Great Britain and Ireland had been brought closer together: the journey from Dublin to London, a three- to five-day trip in 1800, had shrunk to an overnight journey by 1870, and the fare was lower, relatively speaking. As a result, Ireland by 1870 had become rather less foreign, distinctive or exotic. Improved communications too, along with the invention of photography, had contributed mightily to the rapid development of Irish holiday resorts such as

Killarney, by 1870 much frequented by well-to-do English visitors. (The Famine clearances also played their part, by getting rid of those starving wretches who, in earlier times, had had the temerity to ruin the view.) Royal personages, rare birds for centuries before 1820, took advantage of faster communications and made frequent tours to Ireland. Queen Victoria visited in 1849, 1853 and 1861, and was always well received by cheering crowds. An unkind critic might suggest that the thousands who turned out to pay their last respects to the Young Irelander, Terence Bellew MacManus, in December 1861, might prove to be more or less similar in composition to those who had cheered Victoria to the echo a few months earlier; honouring Ireland's patriot dead, and gawping at visiting royalty, would never be incompatible.

The emergence of a common cultural zone for the arts (theatre, painting, popular fiction and music hall) appeared to close the gap still further, for Dublin and London shared similar preferences in all of these. The mid-nineteenth century has not been reckoned a golden age of Irish writing in English: at least, the poet, William Butler Yeats, modestly pronounced it to be vastly inferior to the output of his own day; and since he said it, it must be true. However, whatever later critical dismissiveness, the 'sensational' plays of Dion Boucicault, the 'rollicking' novels of Charles Lever, the comic novels of Samuel Lover and the heartwarming fiction of Mrs Anna Hall enjoyed huge popularity, not only on both sides of the Irish Sea, but in the United States as well. Conversely, the novels of English writers, such as Anthony Trollope who published *Phineas Finn* (1869), in which he wrote about an on-the-make Irish Catholic in London, and those of Charles Dickens (who visited in 1869) found a ready market in Ireland. Less visible, perhaps, though perhaps more impressive, Irish journalists were making their collective way into the top echelons of the English newpapers. It was later claimed that by 1870 a majority of the sub-editors of the anti-Home Rule *Morning Post* were, in fact, pro-Home Rule Irish journalists, and it was rumoured that Irish scribes held a near-monopoly of parliamentary reporting. Finally, by the 1870s the work of Irish artists such as Daniel Maclise or John Butler Yeats (father of Willliam and Jack) was popular in Britain, while 'Irish' subjects such as famine, emigration or evictions were very often on display. Ford Madox Brown's *The Irish Girl*, a stunning portrait of a poor Irish emigrant, was exhibited to great acclaim in London in 1861. Irish models, such as the 'slightly scandalous' Caroline Norton or Joanna Hiffernan were also in demand by both English and foreign artists. And in the new art of photography the Irishwoman Julia Margaret Cameron was a pioneer and was much admired for her portraits of her Irish servant girl, Mary Ryan. In short, by 1870, while some English Members of Parliament might have privately moaned that they were sick hearing about Ireland, neither their constituents nor the wider public appear to have shared these sentiments, at least where literature and the arts were concerned.

Moreover, by the 1870s the middle classes of England and Ireland espoused shared values on such vital matters as the position of women, the centrality of the family, the virtue of work, the importance of religion and the evils of alcohol; in a word, whether English or Irish, they both embraced respectability. Indeed, the Irish apostle of temperance, Fr Theobald Mathew, had at one time sounded quite English himself in deploring the 'depravity of the Irish peasant', and linking his fall directly to his love of the demon drink. We may note, however, that some of Mathew's followers preferred to denounce drink as an insidious English weapon deployed to keep the Irish under subjection. Such tactlessness could be left to one side, however, for a shared distaste for excessive drinking and public drunkenness was what mattered to the English and Irish respectable classes. Donnybrook Fair in Dublin, for example, for many years a byword for all sorts of excess, was brought to an end by clerical opposition in the mid-1850s.

Importantly, these common attitudes were increasingly voiced in the English language. By 1870 spoken Irish was in full retreat, and the number of monoglot Irish speakers was fast dwindling: by that date, if the census returns are to be relied upon, the monoglots, whose strength was a key determinant of the 'health' of the language, accounted for just one in every two hundred of the population. Thus an aspiration first mooted hundreds of years before, to make Ireland entirely English speaking, appeared in 1870 to be on the brink of total success. Could Ireland yet be a little England, or a New Zealand in the northern hemisphere? Surely then, with the end of a distinctive language, all talk of a republic, all demand for repeal, and all clamour for Home Rule, would fade away?

In addition, and once again no small matter, since 1800, Irish soldiers, teachers, doctors and engineers and, latterly, missionaries, had proved enthusiastic imperialists, achieving by 1870 a prominent presence at all levels, save the very highest, within the British empire. One of the promises held out for the Union of 1801 had been that Ireland and Irishmen would profit from easier access to the British empire and, mostly, this promise had been fulfilled. With the passing of Catholic emancipation in 1829, what was known as 'the colonial patronage' was deployed to open careers abroad to the emerging Irish Catholic middle classes. Again, Irish priests and nuns, who in the years after the Famine were deemed surplus to pastoral requirements in the home country, began to find outlets for their energies in the empire. And so too did bright Catholic youths, educated in the newly established second-level Catholic schools, such as those at Blackrock and Terenure (both strongly supported by the then Archbishop Cullen in 1860). The graduates of these colleges, and of those run by the Irish Christian Brothers, proved well able to compete successfully in the annual examinations held for the imperial civil service. An 'Irish empire' was being created.

And if the administration of the British empire had taken on an Irish Catholic hue by 1870, so too had its defence. True, it was Irish Protestants who dominated the Indian Army staff by 1870 (generally, they were too down-at-heel to get into 'smart' regiments at home), but it was Irish Catholics who were overrepresented in the 'thin red line' of the lesser ranks. True, the proportion of Irish in the armed forces would fall over the following decades in line with the declining Irish population (and the high level of emigration), but Irish soldiers continued to be overrepresented in the British army until the Great War. Moreover, their exploits were a source of pride to their fellow countrymen. Irish servicemen performed well in the difficult circumstances of the Indian Mutiny of 1857; this was known because the famous war correspondent W. H. Russell of *The Times* was himself Irish, and he was not slow to highlight the reckless bravery of his countrymen, notably at the storming of Delhi. In the Crimean War too, two years earlier, which Russell also reported for *The Times*, he revealed to the world the selflessness not only of Florence Nightingale and her nurses, but also of the group of Irish Sisters of Mercy, who cared for sick and wounded soldiers in that war. It was a genuine source of Irish national pride that the first two Victoria Crosses, a newly established medal for valour, went to an Irish soldier and to an Irish sailor. In all, one-third of the Victoria Crosses awarded during the Crimean War went to Irish servicemen. This bond of empire was a powerful one, tying Ireland and Britain together throughout the nineteenth century, and defying attempts to pull them apart. Some thirty years later, in 1899, Irish unease at the Boer War, the first imperial conflict since the American Revolution with 'whites' on both sides, would, perhaps, signal the beginning of Irish disenchantment with the Empire.

By 1870 the overwhelming majority of Irish Protestants, whether members of the Church of Ireland or Presbyterians, were wholly committed to retaining the Act of Union. Since 1800, there had been a growth in evangelical Christianity and this had gradually brought about a rapprochement between adherents of the Church of Ireland and of the Presbyterian church. The theological gap between members of church and kirk remained wide but, on a practical level, it had narrowed considerably. Especially from the 1830s on (Catholic emancipation was a huge spur here), significant numbers of each faith eschewed formal theology, fell into the embrace of a personal God and jointly and willingly 'came to Jesus' during a series of religious revivals, of which that of 1859 was probably the most noteworthy. Disestablishment in 1869, by removing legal distinctions between the Church of Ireland and the Irish Presbyterians, cleared the way for the formation of a pan-Protestant front in the face of the renewed Catholic threat.

As noted, Protestant opinion had not been wholly in favour of Union in 1800, and as late as the 1830s, there had been measurable anti-Unionist sentiment among Dublin Protestants; but by 1870, with a few notable exceptions, Protestants recognised the demand for self-government as one that belonged almost exclusively to Catholics. And even these Protestant exceptions might have backed some form of Irish self-government in the belief that Irish Protestants, as the natural rulers, must dominate any such arrangement. But for the large majority of Irish Protestants, whatever their condition or social class, self-government for Ireland was solely and simply about Catholic power, and on that ground had to be seen off, if only as a debt owed to history.

On another level Protestant consciousness had been sharpened and moulded by the expansion of Orangeism and by the proliferation of sectarian confrontations. Successive Party Processions Acts (1850, 1860) designed to limit Orange parades were studiously, and with impunity, either ignored or ingeniously circumvented. The Orange Order might have begun life in rural Armagh in the 1790s, but it had proved adept at migrating to the urban centres of Ulster and beyond. Orangeism especially found a home in Belfast, a town no larger than Newry or Drogheda in 1800 but a very large one by 1870 that, with its manufacturing industries, resembled the great industrial cities in Britain. However, if Belfast and the northeast industrialised in the nineteenth century, industrialisation had not brought modernisation and the sectarian rivalries of the drumlin country of south Ulster had migrated to the factories, shipyards and mills of Belfast. By 1870 Belfast was visibly a success, industrially and economically; equally, it was a religiously divided city, with sectarian rioting nearly every year, sometimes resulting in loss of life. Protestant loyalty to the Union in nineteenth-century Ireland was the elephant in the room so far as Irish nationalists were concerned; for the most part, it has remained so.

That neither common imperial nor cultural bonds much diminished the Irish Catholic desire for self-rule can be ascribed, in the first instance, to the fact that the broad mass of the Irish people (wilfully ignoring the presence of a substantial Protestant minority) saw itself as pre-eminently a Catholic nation that could never be comfortable in a Protestant state, no matter how well disposed or neutral that state might be or claim to be. Ominously, by 1870 Catholic consciousness was rising, as was Catholic assertiveness. One source of this was Cardinal Cullen's leadership of the Catholic church in Ireland, for he played a key role in the developing clericalism of Irish society. Whether in building schools, disciplining his priests, instigating parish missions, attending the Vatican Council or, apart from the occasional splendid dinner, steadfastly keeping his distance from Dublin Castle, Cullen displayed outstanding leadership qualities. While Catholic lay achievement had become visible, especially in the professions, trades, civil service and police, there was still a yawning (and a gnawing) gap between entitlement and accomplishment. By 1870 Catholics were still much underrepresented in the law and medicine – the only two professions that counted – but they had made the 'greasy till' their own, for they constituted over 80 per cent of Irish shopkeepers, fishmongers, publicans and butchers. Catholics also made up over 70 per cent of the Irish police, though not of the higher ranks. These percentages were important, for if the eighteenth century could be characterised as an age when 'quality' counted, then the following century was increasingly one when quantity mattered more. In short, by 1870 Catholic numbers formed an unanswerable argument in favour of Catholic advancement in a way that they had not fifty years earlier. But while, by that date, there had been some significant Catholic advances, the fact was that a Protestant population that constituted barely 25 per cent of the total numbers still controlled over 75 per cent of the wealth of Ireland. Not surprisingly, the middle class of Catholic Ireland was becoming impatient at its failure to secure the levers of power and increasingly frustrated, as it saw matters, at the slow pace of access.

The 'Irish nation' overseas was also frustrated at the lack of progress on the question of self-government. The presence of over a million Irish immigrants in the United States, and the continuing exodus from Ireland of thousands more on a monthly basis, was regarded as a standing indictment of the Union. The Catholic Irish in America laid the blame for all their misfortunes at England's door, and they were oblivious to any reforms, or proposed legislative changes, short of Home Rule for Ireland. So long as this was the case, the Catholic Irish at home would never be allowed to rest easy under English Protestant rule. Gladstone had to concede that emigration was 'another word for banishment' to the Irish, but he had no remedy for its persistence. Perhaps this was just as well for the standing of the Liberal Party in Ireland, because no sector of Irish society would have welcomed any legal restrictions on emigration; and most would have opposed any back-to-Ireland campaign sponsored by the British government. The rapid emergence of this Irish nation abroad is a key political fact of Irish history between the Great Famine and the Great War. No Irish politician could be unaware of its potential, no British politician could be insouciant about its influence and its existence was a standing reproach to the Union.

Consider John Devoy (1842–1928). Irish born, he enlisted in the French Foreign Legion in his youth, and thereafter became a professional revolutionary who, from his first involvement with the Fenians in 1861, lived to see the larger part of Ireland independent. He spent over sixty years in the United States and appears never to have let a day pass without plotting the downfall of English rule in Ireland. Similarly, consider Jeremiah O'Donovan Rossa, likewise an early Fenian who was born in the famine-decimated town of Skibbereen, west Cork.

He was imprisoned in an English prison in harsh conditions from 1865 to 1871. In the months before the passing of Gladstone's Land Act he was elected a Member of Parliament, though as a serving prisoner he was unable to take his seat. On his release, he went to the United States, where he organised a 'skirmishing fund' to finance attacks on mainland Britain. Then, finally, consider those who remain anonymous, those hundreds of thousands of Irish in America who, mindful of the Famine and out of self-respect and as a debt owed to posterity, would support with their money, their influence and, occasionally, their person, any attempt to do down English rule in Ireland. In truth, enough dragon's teeth had been sown by 1870 to make an observer fearful of the coming harvest.

The stark fact was that by 1870 the Union of 1801 still showed few signs of bedding down, of being seen as normal and unremarkable. From the beginning there continued to be a separate Irish administration, headed by a viceroy and chief secretary, and its existence had not been conducive to integration, let alone assimilation. From the outset, there had been an Irish question, in a way that there had never been a Scottish, much less a Welsh (or an English) question. Or rather, the English question was the question of Ireland. In a real sense, it did not matter what constituted the Irish question at any given time up to 1870. Catholic emancipation, administrative reform, famine relief, tenant right, agrarian agitation? They were all as one, for what they signalled and signified was that Ireland was different, separate and distinct; that it was a country that required new laws, demanded new thinking and posed new challenges that required new responses. But to what end? Once all or indeed any of these were conceded, once 'Irish ideas' on property, for example, however bizarre to English ears, were accepted as having the same validity as those in currency elsewhere in the United Kingdom, then what was the point of Union? Certainly, England got little, if anything, from its 'exploitation' of Ireland; and if Ireland was not very profitable, by 1870 it was apparently not strategically indispensable (or so the Royal Navy had concluded). In the end, however, the greatest danger for Union in 1870 was that it had not passed quietly into history; on the contrary, seven decades on, mending, ending or defending the Union, was still a very live issue in Irish politics.

II: ENDING AND DEFENDING THE UNION: IRELAND 1870–1914

Isaac Butt and Charles Stewart Parnell

In May 1870 Isaac Butt launched the Home Government Association with the aim of winning a large measure of self-government for Ireland.[6] On the face of it Butt's credentials for the leadership of such an organisation did not appear promising. Essentially, the demand for Home Rule had been set in an O'Connellite mould some thirty years earlier and ever since it had been represented as the manifest destiny of the Catholic people of Ireland. A Protestant Tory, with a Trinity College background and a history of opposition to O'Connell himself, surely Butt had no business putting himself at the head of an organisation whose object was the attainment of what was seen as a largely Catholic demand? However, as noted, Butt was no ordinary Tory or Protestant. He yielded to none in his admiration for the fortitude of the Fenians, many of whom he had defended in the courts in the late 1860s and, oddly, he displayed a devotion to the Virgin Mary, regularly saying the rosary. These eccentricities aside, the reality was that Butt took up the quest for Irish self-government because he had become deeply disillusioned with the British administration of Ireland and because he believed that Irish Protestants and Tories had no option but to come to terms with the new forces (Fenianism being the latest) emerging in Irish life, and to seek to manage them. Following the disestablishment of the Church of Ireland and the passing of the Land Act of 1870, Butt and others like him, were heartily sick of Gladstone and were convinced that little reliance could be placed on British expressions of support for the Protestants of Ireland. The way things were going, Irish Protestants, like Butt, might have no future in Ireland unless they selflessly and patriotically put themselves forward as leaders of the Irish people. There were, however, two problems with this strategy: the first was that Butt was not much of a leader; the second, and much more difficult one, was the question of whether or not there was a single Irish people.

Some sixty-one Irish Members of Parliament, fairly evenly divided between Liberals and Conservatives, and with a healthy religious mix, had turned up at the inaugural meeting of the Home Government Association at the Bilton Hotel, Dublin, and initially matters had appeared promising. As with O'Connell, little time was devoted to the specifics of Home Rule (Butt himself appears to have favoured home-rule-all-round for Ireland, Scotland and Wales – a federalist solution on the Canadian model) and, instead, attention focused on the creation of a Home Rule 'party' or 'grouping' at Westminster. To an extent, this tactic paid off: by 1874, following the establishment of a Home Rule League a year earlier with Butt as president, some fifty-nine alleged, though not avowed, Home Rule Members were returned to Parliament. However, this impressive total cannot be taken as the product of an enthusiastic and swift endorsement by the Irish electorate of the notion of self-rule, or Butt's idea of it. It was noticeable, for example, that Home Rule candidates for election did best when, as well as claiming to be in favour of self-government, they publicly supported 'Catholic' demands for religiously denominated education, or when they denounced the inadequacies of the 1870 Land Act. Home Rule, Catholic demands and farmers' grievances, to Butt's chagrin, appeared to be seamlessly linked and many Protestants quickly took fright at what appeared to be the Catholic tone of the Home Rule campaign.

Nor were those elected under the banner of Home Rule any more committed to it on its own than the Irish electorate. An alarming number of so-called Home Rule Members of Parliament soon began to treat Home Rule as a mere flag of convenience, while a few even ventured to jump ship and oppose the demand in the House of Commons. Butt, for all his courtroom skills, was poorly equipped with the man-management techniques required to deal with this indiscipline. For long periods he appeared at a loss to know what to do in order to make a splash at Westminster, possibly because he may not have viewed this failure as in fact a shortcoming. He was too much of a gentleman to relish the hurly-burly of politics, and rather too polite to press his point. Butt raised the question of Home Rule only twice between 1874 and 1876 in Parliament, and quietly accepted the resounding rebuff (458 votes to 61 in June 1874, 291 to 61 in July 1876) which he received. He saw the House of Commons as a sort of gentleman's club whose traditions were to be respected; and he was outraged when a few of his 'followers', notably J. G. Biggar, a Belfast provisions merchant, and Charles Stewart Parnell, a young Wicklow landlord, thought and began to behave otherwise. In any case, Butt's personal life and his finances were quite chaotic and, on their own, might have made his leadership untenable. He was sometimes accosted at public meetings by the mothers of children he had fathered, and who now sought money from him. He was frequently in hiding from creditors; and even a 'dig-out' by wealthy well-wishers failed to remove his financial worries.

Perhaps surprisingly, given its professed abhorrence of 'politics', the Fenian leadership, notably John Devoy in America, had offered support to Butt's organisation. It had done so largely out of gratitude for his efforts on their behalf, for he had not only defended them ably in the courts but had set up an Amnesty Association pledged to achieve the early release of those incarcerated (thirty-three Fenians were in fact freed in 1871). Perhaps also the Fenians had no other option, for it was clear that no matter what the leadership commanded, individual Fenians in the constituencies were determined to be politically active. However, the Fenians grew disillusioned with Butt's less than masterful leadership (John Mitchel, the former Young Irelander, revolutionary and pro-slavery activist, damningly dubbed him 'Anything Butt'), and their attention shifted to another Protestant Home Ruler, Charles Stewart Parnell.

Parnell had caught the eye of advanced nationalists by his laconic defence of those Fenians convicted of murder in 1868 – to loud dissent in the House of Commons, he had flatly denied that they were, in fact, guilty of murder. His imperviousness to further howls of outrage from fellow Members, when he and a few like-minded Members (Biggar and F. H. O'Donnell were the most prominent) embarked on a policy of 'obstruction' in the House of Commons, marked him out as someone to watch. By their single-minded and ruthless exploitation of the lax rules of procedure at Westminster, the 'obstructionists' set out to ensure that if Irish affairs were not attended to in Parliament, then precious little business of any sort would be dealt with. Such tactics, as well as being noticed favourably by the Fenians, also commanded much admiration among Irish nationalists in Britain, who promptly showed their displeasure with Butt by electing Parnell, in August 1877, to the presidency of the Home Rule Confederation of Great Britain in August 1877. Butt's ideal of having a safe Protestant pair of hands steering the Home Rule movement, in order to maintain control and secure a soft landing, was coming closer to fulfilment; ironically, only Butt himself stood in the way. When Parnell's presidency was confirmed at a Home Rule convention in Dublin the following year, Butt was effectively displaced. However, if he had been an unlikely leader of a an Irish nationalist movement, so too was Parnell. Like Butt he was a Protestant and a conservative on social issues, but he was also a landlord and, additionally, he had an English accent and he disliked funerals; the last two at least, then and now, major barriers to political success in Ireland. But Parnell hated the English because (he believed) they despised him and the Irish, and he resolved to stand up to them and this was enough to make up for other deficiencies. An enviable ability to deploy silence as an offensive weapon no doubt helped. Perhaps Michael Davitt, a guarded admirer in the 1880s, put it best: Parnell was 'an Englishman of the strongest type, moulded for an Irish purpose'.

It is likely that the Butt–Parnell rivalry for control of the Home Rule movement would have remained confined to the halls of the Palace of Westminster or to the convention rooms of Irish and British provincial cities but for the eruption of the Irish rural masses on to the political stage – not as extras, but as players. This extraordinary and unprecedented development can be traced immediately to a run of poor harvests in Ireland from 1877 on and, then, to a widespread fear among the farming classes that a famine on the scale of that of the 1840s loomed. Irish farmers in general had improved their lot, relatively speaking, since the Famine decade (better houses, higher income and a more varied diet were all noted by observers); but most tenants had little security for any of these improvements in their conditions. In the late 1870s Ireland found itself engulfed in a general agricultural depression that would be characterised by low prices throughout the Atlantic world for thirty years. With this general downturn in rural fortunes everywhere, the threat of famine loomed, especially in the west of

Ireland where the potato crop had failed in 1877 and 1878. The coincidence of general depression and harvest failure threatened to set at nought all the gains that had been achieved by the farmers since the 1850s. Faced with ruin – as they saw it – the farmers prepared to resist; and that meant a refusal to pay rent until times improved.

Three further ingredients need to be added to the pot in order to explain (however inadequately) the explosion of rhetoric, rage and resistance that characterised the activities of the Land League, set up in 1879, and the ensuing Land War of 1879 to 1882. First, there can be no doubt that since the 1850s a process of politicisation had taken place among the farming classes which ensured that future rural crises would not, as heretofore, be accepted with resignation as the will of God. The extension of the franchise, and the introduction of a secret ballot at elections (1872), had given the masses some political clout. Moreover, the growth of literacy, the spread of a 'nationalist' provincial press, and the dissemination of historicist propaganda, portraying the tenant farmer as the only 'true Irishman', with the landlord as an alien oppressor, had had a huge impact. Previously, when there had been a rural crisis, the farmers had turned to the landlords for relief; but when the harvest failed in 1877 (and in 1878 and 1879), they turned on them as the architects of their misfortune. Second, and allied closely to the first point, since the 1850s there had been a growing confidence among the farming classes that they were the rightful owners of the land, and that the landlords, whether Irish born, long-time resident or just unfortunate enough to be either English or Scottish purchasers were all in fact mere intruders who served no useful economic purpose and, worse, prevented the tenant farmer from coming into his own. Lastly, and equally important, was the presence in Mayo, the birth-place of the Land League, of a dedicated group of agitators who were determined to make an end of landlordism. James Daly, editor of the *Connaught Telegraph*, a Fenian and a large farmer in his own right, was by far the most significant of their number. He played a pivotal role by supplying through his newspaper the inflammatory rhetoric of landlord injustice, historic dispossession and moral justification without which a 'land' war could scarcely have been contemplated. Equally, his extensive grazing interests, and his standing as a prominent Fenian, gave him the authority to take on an early and crucial leadership role in the struggle to awaken the west.

Neither Parnell, nor for that matter, Butt, had any role in the agrarian agitation that led to the setting up of the Land League in October 1879; but Parnell, ever with an eye to the main chance, saw in that organisation a way to mobilise the tenant farmers behind the demand for Home Rule. And so too did Michael Davitt, though his ultimate ambitions certainly went far beyond Parnell's. Davitt's family had suffered eviction from their holding in Mayo in 1850 and, after settling in Haslingden, near Manchester, he had worked in the cotton mills, where he had suffered a serious accident, losing his right arm. He had then joined the Fenians and took part in gun-running for which he served seven years' imprisonment in Dartmoor. His release in December 1877 came precisely at a time when the potato crop had failed in the west of Ireland, and when tenant-right agitation was beginning in Mayo, in Connacht and elsewhere. Davitt had meetings with Parnell in London and in Dublin – each emerged with a respect for the other's qualities of leadership – and, in January 1878, he travelled to the west of Ireland to see the situation for himself. In Mayo Davitt was the guest of James Daly and everywhere he went, he was, as he described it, 'received like a prince'. More important, he came away a convinced agrarian radical, more than ever persuaded that the land question held the key to the national question.

In July 1878 Davitt went to New York for discussions with John Devoy on the possible shape of a 'new departure' in Irish politics. This encapsulated nothing less than the bringing together of the constitutional, insurrectionary and agrarian strands of the national movement under the acknowledged leadership of Parnell in order to resolve the land question on the basis of tenant ownership. And to solve it, moreover, not by violence, but by the moral force of overwhelming numbers. The landlords were, in this view, an alien garrison that kept Ireland in subjection on behalf of the British; their passing, therefore, would clear the way for self-government. Parnell, a landlord himself, agreed with this analysis, but with the important proviso that he saw the land question as preventing Irish landlords from taking up that leadership role for which he believed they were naturally fitted. Resolving or removing the land question, in Parnell's mind, would enable landlord energies to flow into the national movement. Thirty years earlier, Fintan Lalor had predicted that the land question would be the engine that would draw the Home Rule train to its destination. Could it be that his prediction was finally going to come to pass?

Devoy was genuine in his approval for the proposed new departure. Not all Fenians were as well disposed, a significant number of them remaining wedded, among other things, to the idea of an invasion of Canada, or bombing attacks on London, or even selective assassination. However, the Irish American press, notably Patrick Ford's *Irish World*, was noticeably enthusiastic and that in effect decided the matter. Devoy set out for Europe for further discussions and he, Davitt and Parnell met in Dublin in April 1879. All three agreed to prioritise the land question on the basis of a national campaign. Devoy received assurances that the Catholic church would be kept at arm's length and that all federal schemes involving devolution in Wales and Scotland would be abandoned. Moreover, it was agreed that when the number of Home Rule Members of Parliament had reached a majority they were to withdraw from Westminster and set up an assembly in Dublin. On 20 April, two weeks after the meeting between Davitt, Parnell and Devoy, and following a campaign by Daly's *Connaught Telegraph*, the land agitation was 'officially' launched at a mass meeting in Irishtown, county Mayo. A handbill advertising the gathering made no attempt to play down its potential significance:

> From the china towers of Pekin to the round towers of Ireland, from the cabins of Connemara to the kraals of Kaffirland, from the wattled homes of the isles of Polynesia to the wigwams of North America, the cry is: 'Down with invaders! Down with tyrants!'

Landlords (good or bad, it made no difference) would have to go, and so too would the Conquest. Nor would the onslaught stop there: unbelievably, in a village in the west of Ireland, the dismantling of the United Kingdom, and then of the British empire, was being contemplated, and may even have been begun.

Land War and Land Acts

In October 1879 the Irish National Land League was founded in Dublin with Parnell as president and with Davitt as one of its secretaries; the fusion of the political and the agrarian and the insurrectionary (for the Fenians were in support) was now complete.[7] The League's aims were nothing less than the end of landlordism and the creation of an owner-occupying farming class; or, in numerical terms, to replace around three thousand large proprietors with several hundred thousand small proprietors; or, as its slogan had it, to take back 'The Land for the People'. The League called for the payment of rent only as a last resort ('at the point of a bayonet', in Parnell's words); it offered financial and legal support for tenants who were victimised (American dollars were vital here); and it urged that those landlords or their agents as well as farmers or labourers who proved recalcitrant should be sent into a 'moral Coventry', i.e. boycotted, after the name of its first victim on the estate of Lord Erne at Lough Mask, county Mayo, in September 1880 (figure 5.8). (Fortunately for Captain Charles Boycott, a volunteer group of northern Orangemen came to his rescue and saved his harvest.) The League's message was conveyed to its supporters by a series of mass meetings at which impassioned rhetoric competed with martial music played by marching bands to keep up the spirits of the 'risen people'. Such activities were, more or less, legal, though the element of intimidation and victimisation inherent in 'boycotting' ought not to be ignored (figures 5.9, 5.10).

5.8 Captain Boycott out walking under the watchful eye of soldiers. National Library of Ireland.

(a)

5.9 The Land War was a subject of international interest. (a) A French journal depicts the difficult position of Captain Boycott and his family. (b) A highly fanciful depiction of an engagement between Land League activists and soldiers.

(b)

5.9 (*cont.*)

5.10 Boycotting: picture from the *Illustrated London News*, 1 January 1881. National Library of Ireland.

But what we might call 'moral action' was accompanied by the full panoply of agrarian 'outrages' perpetrated by the mythical 'Captain Moonlight' and his fellow insurgents. By the end of 1880 such crimes were running at twenty-five times the level of 1878 and included shootings, beatings, maiming (of animals), murders (Viscount Mountmorres in county Galway was a notable high-profile casualty), the disruption of fox-hunting (*not* from concern for animal welfare) and the dispatch of threatening letters (once again, literacy had proved its usefulness). None of these was approved of by the League – they were certainly not its policy – but they added immeasurably to the picture of a countryside, and a country, in revolt. So too did the reaction of the authorities: Parnell, Davitt and other activists were arrested and eventually imprisoned in the winter of 1881–2, a severe 'coercion' act was put through by the chief secretary, W. E. Forster, who also authorised a bulk order for the Irish police of buckshot cartridges (the rubber bullets of the 1880s), thus earning for himself a memorable soubriquet. Inevitably, in October 1881, the Land League itself was suppressed by 'Buckshot' Forster 'as an unlawful and criminal association'.

However, the British government's policy was not wholly one of fighting fire with fire, for Gladstone, once again prime minister, had turned his attention – or had been forced to attend – to the problems of Irish land. A new, far-reaching Land Bill was prepared through the autumn and winter of 1880–1, almost entirely by Gladstone acting on his own, taking his own counsel, without any consultation with Irish Members of Parliament and without taking any soundings in Ireland. True, he did turn for inspiration to various reports of various committees of inquiry into Irish agrarian conditions. More worryingly, he had even immersed himself in Irish history: from his researches in that field, he had concluded that the Act of Union of 1800 had been passed on a fraudulent basis, and this discovery strengthened his resolve to act boldly. This combination of the parliamentary, the political and the academic probably guaranteed that he would get things wrong. So it proved. Gladstone's 1881 Land Act had some merits: it conceded fixity of tenure, free sale (of a tenant's interest in the holding) and a fair rent; but it was fatally flawed, for its author held that the concession of these three 'Fs' would solve the land question. The reality was that the ambitions of Irish tenants had moved far beyond these demands, and the three 'Fs' had always been more important as a political slogan than as a reality. To reiterate, Irish tenants wanted to become landowners, and since the 1881 Act did not advance that prospect by much (the land purchase clauses were inadequate), it constituted in their eyes little more than a piece of legislation on behalf of Irish landlords (figure 5.11). Certainly, those Irish Members who supported Parnell saw no need to extol its merits.

5.11 Hibernia bound to the stake by Gladstone is assaulted by the Orange and Royal factions. *Weekly Freeman*, 24 December 1881. National Library of Ireland.

Having been comprehensively ignored in its drafting, Parnell's party fought its passage line by line through the House of Commons, while Parnell himself responded to it by demanding that the terms of the Act be put to the test. In point of fact Parnell was worried lest the perceived benefits of the Act might beguile his followers into abandoning their campaign for an end to landlordism.

Paradoxically, as a conservative property owner, he was also concerned lest matters get out of hand in Ireland, a worry shared by the Catholic bishops. Hence the suppression of the Land League by Forster was not entirely unwelcome, while Parnell's own incarceration in Kilmainham gaol for sedition was also not without its advantages. It gave him the opportunity to put his signature to a call for 'no rent' to be paid, which endeared him to his more advanced followers; it allowed him to join the pantheon of imprisoned Irish patriots, and thus strengthen his 'national' credentials; and it gave him time to improve his aim through target practice (he was allowed an air-gun in his cell). The major drawback for Parnell was that he was now available to his parliamentary colleagues who knew where they could reach him. He may never have forgiven Gladstone for that.

A way out of this impasse was swiftly found. By the terms of the so-called Kilmainham treaty, an informal agreement concluded with Gladstone, Parnell was released from prison on promising to withdraw the 'no rent' manifesto and on offering to use his best influence to stop agrarian 'outrages'. In return Gladstone would revisit his Land Act with a view to improving its deficient features, notably its land purchase provisions and those sections dealing with tenants who owed arrears of rent (and who were therefore excluded from the Act's benefits). The resignation of the tough-minded Forster on 2 May 1882, in disgust at Gladstone's surrender to – as he saw it – the forces of disorder, was an added bonus for Parnell. However, the murder a few days later by members of the Invincibles, a Fenian splinter group, of Forster's successor as chief secretary, Lord Frederick Cavendish, and of T. H. Burke, the under-secretary, while walking in Phoenix Park, rather spoilt Parnell's triumph.

For Parnell the murder of the Dublin Castle officials (figure 5.12) was further proof that the land agitation needed to be stopped. The Land League had outlived its usefulness; it had successfully harnessed the agrarian to the political, but it was past time for the politicians to reassert themselves. A new body, the Irish National League, was set up ostensibly to replace the Land League but it was in fact little more than an electoral organisation for the parliamentary party, which by now was firmly under Parnell's sole control. A possible rival, Michael Davitt, who had begun to call for land nationalisation, in his view the only real meaning of 'The Land for the People', was in effect excluded; and another perceived threat, the Ladies' Land League, which had done important work in monitoring the progress of the Land War and in assisting evicted tenants, and which was headed by the remarkable Anna Parnell, Charles's sister, was also wound up; Anna appears never to have spoken to her brother again.

So far as Parnell was concerned, the Land War (figure 5.13) was over by May 1882 and, in general, historians have been prepared to follow his view on this matter, for the struggle for Home Rule quickly moved to the centre of the political

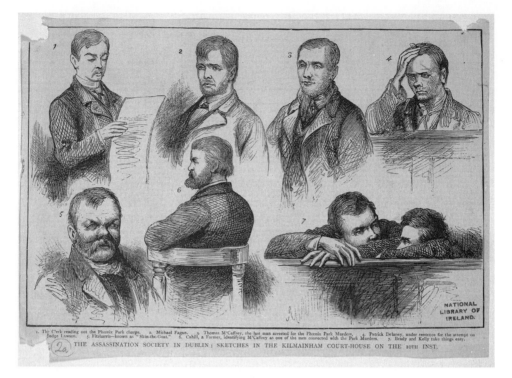

5.12 Sketches of the Invincibles during their trial for the assassination of Cavendish and Burke. National Library of Ireland.

stage, while the land question rather faded into the background. However, on any reading of the matter, a series of struggles for the land continued unabated for the next twenty years, during which time a series of Acts – Ashbourne's in 1885, Balfour's in 1891 and, crucially, that of Wyndham in 1903 – had progressively committed the resources of the British treasury to buying out Irish landlords, and enabling their agricultural tenants to become owner-occupiers. Nor had these Acts been passed in an unbidden, or disinterested, manner: on the contrary, separate agricultural crises had accompanied them, and energetic campaigns of the kind made famous (or infamous) by the Land League had preceded them. Thus Ashbourne's Act of 1885 was to an extent a response to continuing protest at the inadequacies of Gladstone's Land Act of 1881, while Wyndham's Act of 1903 was triggered by the United Irish League's demands for tenant ownership of holdings.

And yet, for all that, there is a sense in which Parnell's decision to call a halt to the Land War in 1882 was well founded, for by the time he had in effect pronounced that struggle to be at an end, the landlords had been outmanoeuvred, and all that remained was to determine the conditions of their surrender.

5.13 Land War poster. The central message is all too clear. National Library of Ireland.

(a)

BATTERING RAM "BACK WITH THEM, AWAY WITH THEM. 1771. W.L.

5.14 Evictions. (a) Deployment of a battering ram to bring down the walls and the roof of a cottage. (b) Aftermath of an eviction at Kilrush, county Clare. The thatched cottage was destroyed to prevent any possibility of the tenant re-entering it. Irish Photographic Archive.

Admittedly this process was to take more than twenty years and, arguably, even continued into the 1920s in the Irish Free State when the Land Commission took over the collection of rents and the redistribution of the remaining landlord land: but the Land League had the landlords on the run in 1882, for the moral case against landlordism had been made by then. With the 'Fall of Feudalism', as Davitt entitled his stirring account of the Land War, the democratisation of Irish society could proceed apace; but so too would the construction of something that looked like an alternative government, for the agrarian radicals had their own structures, courts and sanctions. In addition, passive resistance, the central feature of the campaigns in the 1880s as well as in the early 1900s, proved vital in consolidating Catholic rural community identity and ultimately in forging an Irish national consciousness. In an important sense, 'the west', where the Land War began, proved to be the cradle of the modern Irish nation; it has not failed to remind the rest of the country of this ever since.

There was, inevitably, a downside to all this (figure 5.14). As a result of the Land War, the entire Irish population appeared to be divided (or reduced) into

(b)

5.14 (*cont.*)

landlord or tenant, with no room for the town dweller, the emigrant or the labourer, and nor for the northern loyalist, torn between competing objectives, anxious to get rid of landlords, but also wishing to come to the rescue of fellow Protestants. In the end, whatever Davitt had contemplated, 'The Land for the People' had proved an empty slogan, and had come to mean simply the land for the occupying tenant. The agricultural labourer along the western seaboard, the slum-dwellers of Dublin or Cork or Belfast, and the Irish denizens, male and female, of Manhattan, Manchester or Melbourne were strictly excluded from all consideration, much less participation, in the various Land Acts. Only the occupier, not the farm labourer, not the emigrant or the exile, whether internal or external, was eligible to share in the buy-out of the landlords and the bounty of the British treasury.

The creation of an owner-occupying landed class within the space of some thirty years can rightly be regarded as a revolution, but it had the effect of copperfastening the pre-existing social conservatism of Irish rural life. Did successive Conservative leaders and chief secretaries recognise that this would be the case? After all, it was they who, by and large, put through the revolution in landowning in Ireland in the late nineteenth and early twentieth centuries. Did Lord Salisbury, the Conservative Party leader for much of this period, correctly intuit that property-owners, even Irish ones intellectually on a par with the Hottentots (his comparison), would prove, if not natural conservatives, then very reluctant Home Rulers or wholly improbable revolutionaries? Certainly, the consequent conservatism, not to say reactionary nature of Irish society, north and south, especially in its social structure, religious fervour and sexual mores must have proved gratifying to him (had he deigned to notice). Whatever Salisbury's personal feelings, the impact of the Land War and the later Land Acts was immense, and would continue to shape Irish society well into the twentieth century.

Most profoundly, perhaps, the revolution effected by land purchase could not but ordain that the emigrant exodus would continue to flow on, largely unchecked. Ireland by 1920 had become a society of owner-occupiers, a large majority of whom owned farms that were barely viable in an economic sense. More than ever, such a society would need a continual haemorrhage, even an annual blood sacrifice, of its surplus citizens in order validate its social structure and to offer (barren) consolation to those held unworthy to wed and thus deemed surplus. Because unlicensed, unbridled or casual procreation threatened the interests of a peasant proprietorship, celibacy and chastity (and emigration) had to be urged on the many in order that the few could maintain some modest comfort at home. The sleight of hand by which the outcome of the Land War was represented as a victory for all the people, except the landlords, no doubt also helped. In point of fact, as some contemporaries observed, Irish landlords did rather well out of land purchase. Given that they were offered government money for their uneconomic estates, along with generous bonuses as inducements to sell (and given that they would be spared the burden of rent-collecting with its attendant drawbacks of legal challenge, passive resistance and, on occasion, attempted assassination), it was no wonder that by the early twentieth century the pressure for land purchase was coming from the landlords.

There is, however, a further objection that may be raised to the notion of the resolution of the land question as an unalloyed triumph for the people against an oppressive landlord class. Over a period of fifty years, discussion of this question had centred almost entirely on issues of ownership, morality, (dis)possession and tenure. But it had rarely, if ever, focused on the use to which the land would be put once the tenants came into possession. When that vital question came to be raised in the 1890s, and in the early twentieth century, by that enthusiast for agricultural efficiency, Horace Plunkett, it was given short shrift. The land question had never been about maximising yields, nor had it been about the aggressive marketing of produce. For good or ill, it had been a morality play; but in the end, possession not performance, and tenure rather than technique had been what counted. That legacy was to dog the Irish economy until the end of the twentieth century.

Home Rule

In 1882, as noted above, the Land War was largely abandoned by Parnell: he declared that it was over, that it was won and that that was that. It had served its purpose in unleashing energies that could now be harnessed to the national cause. He turned his attention to creating a parliamentary party that would be firmly under his control. A degree of discipline, unthinkable under Butt, was rapidly imposed on Irish Members of Parliament who sought election on the Home Rule ticket. In essence, a new type of political party was being created. In 1884 a rule was introduced that a parliamentary candidate, in order to secure endorsement by the party, had to take a pledge to 'sit, act and vote' with the party at Westminster and, in addition, to step down, if called upon to do so by a majority of his colleagues. Moreover, in a radical departure from contemporary practice, the Irish Parliamentary Party began to pay its Members with monies remitted through the American counterpart to the Irish Land League. Such payments for salaries and, significantly, for election expenses not only helped reinforce discipline, but they rendered Irish Members largely immune to the attractions of office. In addition, the Catholic church in Ireland, after some heart-searching, chose to ignore a papal condemnation of Parnell and his party (obtained at the behest of the British government) and, in effect, anointed him as the patron saint of the national cause. True, Parnell was a Protestant and a (perceived) Fenian fellow-traveller, and neither of these appealed to the Catholic hierarchy. But Parnell was a 'bad' Protestant, i.e. not a practising one; he kept the Fenians at arm's length; and he had welcomed the Catholic clergy into his constituency organisations. Crucially, he deferred to the bishops on all educational matters. In the end, this was what mattered most to them. Lastly, electoral reform in 1884 boosted the number of voters in Ireland from 250,000 to over 750,000 and this, too, helped reinforce party discipline as well as making the party ever more national. Parnell could now take his place as the 'uncrowned king of Ireland', secure in the knowledge that his 'subjects' had just increased threefold.

What was the Irish Parliamentary Party for? Ostensibly and avowedly it sought Home Rule for Ireland: but since the two major British parties had ruled that out, its options appeared very limited. Would it align itself automatically with the Liberal Party led by W. E. Gladstone – who had, after all, delivered the 1881 Land Act – or would it seek to be truly independent and tack hither and thither between the Liberal and Conservative Parties, as advantage beckoned? Certainly, Parnell tended towards the latter course. He had little time for the pompous and moralising Gladstone whom he blamed for his incarceration in Kilmainham gaol. Much more to Parnell's liking was the up-and-coming Conservative radical (and maverick), Lord Randolph Churchill, who had taken a very public 'patriot' stance during the time when his father, the duke of Marlborough, had been lord lieutenant in Ireland. Might it be the Conservatives who, with their new blood and their fresh thinking, would take a cold, hard look at the Anglo-Irish relationship and decide that the only way to protect the Union was to concede a limited form of Home Rule? After all, by the mid-1880s, it was clear that they were not at all sentimental about their supposed natural allies, the Irish landlords; and the next twenty years were to bear that out. Was it possible that the Conservative Party might, in fact, bring forward some form of self-government to Ireland? And of course, if they chose that option, they could conceivably deliver the House of Lords with its large, in-built Conservative majority in favour of this policy shift.

There were a few indications that the Conservatives were contemplating a policy change. The Conservative lord lieutenant, Lord Carnarvon, made noises in favour of some form of Home Rule, and held secret discussions with Parnell. Lord Randolph Churchill publicly disassociated the Conservatives from reliance on coercion where Ireland was concerned, and he seemed to be moving towards some new departure in Irish policy. In addition, the Conservative minister, Lord Ashbourne, had brought in a further measure of land purchase for Ireland in the late summer of 1885. Even Salisbury, the Conservative Party leader, and one not generally regarded as sympathetic to Irish concerns, was enough of a politician to realise that Liberal and Conservative strength was quite evenly balanced in mainland Britain and that, therefore, the 'Irish vote' in Manchester, Liverpool, Newcastle and elsewhere could make a significant difference on election day, possibly determining the outcome in as many as thirty seats. The beneficiary of this Celtic surge at the ballot box would have a very good chance of taking power. Perhaps the time had come for the Conservative Party to change its stance on Irish self-government?

Parnell was sufficiently impressed by what appeared to be these positive signs from the Conservatives (and equally struck by the total lack of anything remotely comparable coming from Gladstone and the Liberals) to urge Irish voters in Britain to support Conservative candidates in the general election of November 1885. The result of the general election was a Liberal majority of eighty-five seats over the Conservatives within Britain, a figure which, by a delicious irony, was exactly the size of Parnell's Irish nationalist party. However, when Irish Conservative seats were added to Salisbury's tally and when the solitary Irish nationalist seat in Britain (for the Scotland division in Liverpool) was added to Parnell's, it became clear that the Conservatives would take power almost entirely reliant on the votes of Parnell's party. It was at this moment – to be precise, on 17 December 1885 – that Gladstone's son, Herbert, disclosed to the press that his father had become a convert to Home Rule for Ireland. This sensational news changed everything: for the first time since the Act of Union a major British political party, or at least its leader, had declared in favour of Home Rule. An idea that had hitherto been regarded by British politicians of all stripes as inadmissible, at a stroke had had legitimacy conferred on it. In response to Gladstone's 'outing' as a closet Home Ruler, the Conservatives promptly ceased whatever flirtation they had been conducting with the notion of Irish self-government. Salisbury angrily rejected outright Gladstone's plan for an Irish legislature as calculated to destroy both the United Kingdom and the British empire; and Lord Randolph Churchill began to threaten to use the 'Orange card' to defeat Home Rule. For his part, Parnell wasted no time in ousting the Salisbury government, and in February 1886, Gladstone duly became prime minister, pledged to bring in Home Rule for Ireland.

Gladstone's 'conversion' to Home Rule puzzled contemporaries and it has intrigued historians ever since. On one level, his adoption of Home Rule did seem to mark the logical terminus for his long-stated aim of offering justice to Ireland. First, the Church of Ireland was disestablished, second, the landlords were felled and, then, the Irish were offered a limited form of self-government or Home Rule. Certainly the strong moral arguments with which Gladstone defended his new policy could give grounds for believing that his entire programme for Ireland should be viewed as a seamless garment, designed to seek atonement for past wrongs and to bring closure to an age-old problem. However, this conclusion should be resisted. Gladstone was a consummate party politician and each of his policy decisions (or departures) on Ireland have to be viewed in this context. His Liberal Party was an unwieldy coalition of disparate interests that had hitherto been held together through a series of moral crusades. Another campaign, in his judgement, was required to keep it together and to keep it focused. Gladstone had sensed that the political world in which the Liberal Party had formerly thrived was changing rapidly. He believed that the Conservative Party was benefiting disproportionately from the recent enlargement of the electorate. This had facilitated the emergence of a Tory democracy, comprising the urban working-class or lower-middle-class voter, both of whom were shamelessly wedded to empire and increasingly dazzled by the monarchy. By contrast, the 'Celtic fringe' constituency of the rural, the religious and the far-flung, sober, serious and high-minded, all of which had been the mainstay of the Liberals, was palpably shrinking. In addition, there was always the possibility that the Conservatives might beat the Liberals to it and declare in favour of Home Rule for Ireland. Viewed in these lights, Gladstone's conversion to Home Rule can be understood, first, as a pre-emptive ploy to force the Conservatives to come clean on their Irish policy and, second, and more important, as an attempt to reinvigorate his party with moral purpose and thus stave off the evil day of Tory electoral triumph. Naked political advantage lay behind Gladstone's adoption of Home Rule; but God had whispered in his ear that it was the right thing to do.

Unfortunately for Gladstone, God had neglected to divulge this message to some of the more prominent politicians in the Liberal Party and, before long, the GOM (Grand Old Man) had a fight on his hands. Long-time allies such as Joseph Chamberlain threatened to desert the party, and it was quickly revealed that Gladstone's decision to go for Home Rule would bring about a split in the Liberals. Undeterred by threats of resignation from some close colleagues – or perhaps invigorated by them – Gladstone pressed on, resolutely resisting all advice, ignoring all warnings and dismissing all criticism. His Home Rule bill was presented to the House of Commons and awarded its first reading on 14 April 1886.

In the light of the howls of outrage with which Gladstone's conversion to Home Rule had been greeted and given the dire predictions of disintegration, destruction and collapse that allegedly lay in store for the United Kingdom and the British empire should his bill pass, the actual amount of self-government that he proposed for Ireland was modest. The loaded word 'Parliament' was completely avoided; instead, there was to be an assembly of two orders, one representing Irish wealth and the Irish nobility, the other representing the rest. The range of responsibilities which would pass to this new legislature was very limited, with matters affecting taxation, tariffs, foreign policy, policing or religion being all expressly excluded from its concerns. Its sole remit seemed to be to collect the monies owed by the growing number of owner-occupiers; scarcely a task that set the flags waving, the trumpets blowing or the pulse racing. Moreover, Irish Members of Parliament would no longer attend at Westminster. This may have been the bill's major attraction for British Liberals. To get rid of Parnell and his ruffianly crew of parliamentarians (by 1885, the majority were both Catholic and unlanded, a sea-change since 1868) was an aspiration shared by many Liberals and Conservatives. However, and notwithstanding the absence of Irish Members, Westminster would still retain sovereignty over the Dublin assembly and the lord lieutenancy would remain in place as a symbol of that authority. Gladstone had steeped himself in Irish history while preparing this bill and he had come away from his studies much impressed with the so-called 'Grattan's Parliament' of 1782 to 1800, but also distressed at the corruption which he thought had accompanied the passing of the Irish Act of Union, and which – in his eyes – made the case for Home Rule morally unanswerable.

On any reading Gladstone's plan for Home Rule for Ireland was so deeply flawed that it would almost certainly have proved unworkable. For one thing, excluding Irish Members of Parliament from Westminster, while stating that that legislature would remain responsible for Irish revenue, would inevitably have raised the protest cry of 'no taxation without representation'. Again, Gladstone's prescription of two 'orders' sitting in the new assembly was clearly a recipe for confrontation and/or stalemate, since the first order – comprising those 'marked out by leisure, wealth and station' (in Gladstone's unhappy formulation) – were to have a veto over the second order, who, presumably, would possess none of these attributes. Needless to say, given that Gladstone had impatiently waved away any suggestion that the Protestant majority in the north-east of Ireland might require certain safeguards, their very vocal concerns for their future attracted no special provision. Perhaps the most startling reaction to Gladstone's Home Rule initiative was that of Parnell, who quickly declared the measure to be 'a final settlement'. Given the major discrepancies between Parnell's ideas on Home Rule and those enshrined in Gladstone's plan, notably on tariffs and revenue-raising, such an endorsement had to be viewed with extreme scepticism. Not surprisingly, when confronted with such an ill-conceived and, indeed, barely intelligible scheme some Members of Parliament argued that complete independence for Ireland made more sense than what was now proposed by Gladstone.

There were other weighty objections to Gladstone's course of action. His historical case for Irish Home Rule was based on a very imperfect reading of late eighteenth-century Irish history, as the historian and Irish Unionist W. E. H. Lecky, was quick to point out. (Gladstone had quoted Lecky's work in support of his case.) More important, it was incontestable that the issue of Home Rule for Ireland had figured nowhere in the election literature or speeches of the main British parties in the previous general election in Britain, and thus Gladstone had no mandate to introduce such an important measure. (As noted, he had also kept his party colleagues completely in the dark regarding his intentions.) In addition, the financial terms rightly gave rise to much criticism from Conservatives and caused misgivings even among Home Rulers. Finally, in his haste to get in first and to trump the Conservatives with his Home Rule card, Gladstone had miscalculated badly. His declaration in favour of Home Rule had had the unforeseen effect of transforming the Conservative Party into the party of the Union, and had thus resolved whatever identity crisis that party had been undergoing since the days of Disraeli. Gladstone's adoption of Home Rule had invigorated, not the Liberal Party, but its Conservative rival. He had torn apart his own party and, in effect, guaranteed a lengthy period of Tory governments (1886–92, 1896–1906).

Gladstone's Home Rule bill was rejected by 341 votes to 311, with over 90 Liberals, led by Chamberlain, voting with the Conservatives, and the government fell. A subsequent general election produced a Conservative majority, and Lord

Salisbury entered office as prime minister in July 1886. While these political developments had been taking place at Westminster rioting had broken out on the streets of Belfast early in June and had continued throughout the summer. These violent protests highlighted what was to become the crucial objection to Home Rule for Ireland: it would be resisted by force. This prospect or threat was pithily summed up by Lord Randolph Churchill in a speech to opponents of Home Rule (soon to be dubbed Unionists) in Belfast in February 1886: 'Ulster will fight, and Ulster will be right.'

Ulster will fight

The opposition of the Protestants of Ulster to Home Rule could have been predicted. Ulster had been perhaps the province most opposed to Union in 1800, but O'Connell's campaign for Catholic emancipation had brought about a swift change of attitude. An apparently resurgent Catholicism had rekindled historic fears of massacre and domination. In addition, and to an extent in reaction to this threat, there had been a coming together of members of the Presbyterian and Church of Ireland churches in a pan-Protestant evangelicalism. Equally important, perhaps, were the visible signs that so far as Ulster was concerned, the Union had delivered on the economic promises held out for it. In the decades after 1800 there had been a rapid expansion of a commercial and manufacturing economy centred on a fast-growing Belfast (population of 20,000 in 1800 but over 200,000 by 1886) so that by the 1880s the region, with its textile, engineering and ship-building industries, bore more resemblance to Glasgow and its hinterland than to anywhere else in Ireland. Harland and Wolff, the Belfast ship-building firm, had launched 1000 tonnes of shipping in 1850, but that had risen to nearly 14,000 tonnes in 1880, or approaching 20 per cent of the output for the whole United Kingdom. 'Look at Belfast and be a Repealer if you can', so Henry Cooke, the Presbyterian leader, had mocked O'Connell in the 1840s; but by 1886 that taunt had become a threat.

It was Belfast that was to be the core of resistance to Home Rule; it was Belfast that made determined opposition to Home Rule possible; and, ultimately, it was Belfast that made partition feasible. These are sweeping statements, but together they recognise a central truth about the anti-Home Rule or Unionist struggle in the years up to the outbreak of the Great War: that it was Belfast's commercial wealth and Belfast's muscle that saw off the threat of the imposition of Home Rule for all Ireland. True, Irish Unionism from its beginnings in 1886 had been a broad church, an unlikely alliance in which southern landlords rubbed shoulders with northern captains of industry, where shipyard workers saw eye to eye with Protestant tenant farmers, and where patrician scholars, like Lecky, made common cause with Portadown Orangemen; but the various elements had not been equal in the struggle.

Southern Irish Unionists could drape resistance with that social authority that came from landed wealth and they might offer the leadership skills of those accustomed to command. They would also offer valuable contacts with, and support from, the highest reaches of British society (and the British army). All of these were important. Rural Ulster, too – or at any rate that part of it that was Protestant – would take a lead in opposing Home Rule, not least in persuading British (and to an extent, world) opinion that the population of 'Ulster' consisted entirely of Protestants, all of whom were utterly opposed to Home Rule. At one time, Presbyterian tenant farmers, because of their embrace of the United Irish message in the 1790s and their turn-out in 1798, had been regarded as possible recruits to the cause of Home Rule. However, the boons of the 1881 Land Act and, even more, the land purchase clauses in Ashbourne's Act of 1885, had killed completely whatever conceivable interest they might have had in self-government. When put to the trial, they would prove resolute opponents of the Catholic conspiracy that was Home Rule, as they saw it. Yet in the end, for all that the southern opponents of Home Rule offered by way of leadership and entrées to high political circles in Britain and, for all that the tenant farmers of Protestant Ulster would prove staunch, it would be Belfast with its commercial wealth, its industrial clout, its local government structure and its Protestant majority and ethos that would determine the outcome of the struggle. It was, in the end, Belfast that was the key argument against Home Rule.

In 1886, however, that argument did not need to be deployed. The Home Rule bill, offering a very modest amount of self-government, went down to speedy defeat; had it made it to the House of Lords, it would have suffered rejection there; and, in quick order, a Conservative government led by Salisbury and firmly opposed to Home Rule, succeeded that of Gladstone and his now-split Liberals. In these circumstances, what was there for Ulster opponents of Irish Home Rule to be worried about? The riots in Belfast which accompanied the bill's progress, and then became bloodier when it had failed, appeared to have had their own internal dynamic, divorced from parliamentary proceedings. In 1886 Ulster would not need to fight.

Ulster was, however, right to be concerned. Gladstone's emergence as a Home Ruler had been a huge shock. His land legislation had been popular in Ulster but with his declaration in favour of Home Rule, he was instantly cast as the great apostate, or the arch-betrayer, a character well known in Ulster folk history. In Protestant memory, sedulously cultivated since the 1600s, the only way that the plantation could be undone, and 'Fortress Ulster' taken, was through betrayal. In this view Gladstone's conversion to Home Rule, i.e. Rome Rule, was treachery, not so pure and not so simple. Given the very limited measure of self-government that his bill offered, the howls of outrage that greeted it, must have seemed extravagant, if not hysterical, to Gladstone. From his historical studies, he was wedded to the notion of the Presbyterian tenant as a gallant United Irishman, bravely marching on Antrim, Saintfield and Ballynahinch in the 1798 rebellion. He believed that the Orange Order was responsible for much of the trouble in 1798 and that it had stirred up all the current protests. And he remained confident that the figurative descendants of the United Irish leaders, Henry Joy McCracken and 'General' Henry Munro, would soon come to their senses.

In other words, Gladstone's capacity for self-delusion (though he was not alone in this) was boundless. What he failed to realise was that Home Rule was not really about Home Rule at all; nor, in fairness, were those opposed to it merely concerned about maintaining the Union. Therefore, arguments about whether or not a prospective Home Rule government would pursue a 'free trade', or a rabidly protectionist policy, or whether its education policy would slavishly follow the dictates of the Catholic church or the values of the Liberal Party, or even whether there would be a parliament or an assembly in Dublin were all irrelevant. Equally, Conservative and Liberal Unionist claims that Home Rule posed a deadly threat to the integrity of the British empire were just as wide of the mark. Home Rule, like the Land War, was about undoing the Conquest and, so far as Ulster Unionists were concerned, it was about undoing the plantation. In short, what fuelled the demand for Home Rule was partly the intoxication of grievance, but ultimately it was hatred of England, pure and simple. Nowhere was this better understood than in Ulster, and especially in Belfast. Those opposed to Home Rule – Unionists as they came to be known – cared little about the Union as such, for English betrayal ran through it like the letters in a stick of rock; but as a settler people they did care a lot about the plantation, and they well remembered the Irish rising of 1641, the siege of Derry between 1689 and 1690, and the battle of the Boyne, and they were to be further reminded of them all during the Home Rule crisis, for all were prominent features in the public prints of 1886, and later. Ulster Unionism was about maintaining the seventeenth-century plantation, and Unionists believed that Home Rule was about undoing it; that is why Home Rule had to be resisted whatever the cost.

But while determined to defeat what they saw as a nefarious conspiracy, Ulster Unionists were well aware of their vulnerability. Although they might speak and act as if the population of the nine-county province of Ulster was entirely Protestant, the fact was that, while Protestants did indeed hold a majority, it was a narrow one. That slim confessional majority had proved quite brittle in electoral terms, for Parnell's party had won sixteen seats to fifteen Unionist in Ulster in the

1886 general election. From the beginning, however, Ulster Unionists warned that the Home Rule issue would not be decided by parliamentary majorities. Just as worrying as the delicate constituency and demographic balance, were the deep social and class divisions within Ulster Unionism, for the shipyard worker had little in common with the captain of industry, and landlord–tenant rivalries could be as sharp in Ulster as elsewhere. T. W. Russell was to exploit them. Much effort, and no little ingenuity, would have to be deployed by Unionists to maintain the myth of a monolithic 'Ulster', and to paper over fissiparous tendencies within their ranks. Again, Unionists were conscious of the impact on public opinion of the phenomenon of rogue Protestants who threw in their lot with the Home Rule party. Parnell, of course, was the most prominent Protestant Home Ruler, but he was joined by no fewer than twelve co-religionists in the nationalist party. In response, Unionists dismissed such disgraceful backsliding as the customary betrayal, which had ever stained the history of Protestants in Ireland, and which had hitherto been overcome. Be that as it may, socially divided, outgunned in the electoral shoot-out of 1886, mindful of the existence of Protestant recidivists and aware of a slim demographic majority in the nine counties, Ulster Unionists had much to ponder on when they resolved to see off the threat of Home Rule.

The true strength of Ulster Unionism lay in Belfast and its environs. In Belfast Protestants were in an overwhelming majority and while, in 1861, the proportion of Catholics had reached 34 per cent of the city's population, by the 1880s that percentage was in decline. In 1881 Catholics numbered 60,000 out of a population of over 200,000 (about 29 per cent); but by 1911, though the city had grown to nearly 400,000, the Catholic proportion had slumped to under a quarter. Fewer Catholics were coming to the city – its reputation for persistent sectarian rioting was probably the main factor here – and more Catholics were leaving in search of better opportunities, for job discrimination against Catholics was endemic. In addition, intense residential segregation, similar to that found in racially divided cities in the American south, had the effect of corralling Catholics together and screening them from view. Those Catholics to be found in Belfast were hugely overrepresented in the ranks of the unskilled or semi-skilled workers, and servants. In stark contrast, middle-class Belfast, professional Belfast, and commercial Belfast, were essentially Catholic-free zones. For example, in 1900 Catholics constituted less than 3 per cent of the membership of the Belfast Chamber of Commerce. These religious, class, employment and residential fissures that distinguished Belfast in the late nineteenth century were crucial in determining that there would be all-out resistance to Home Rule in Ulster. To Ulster Unionists, Irish Home Rule, however circumscribed, meant nothing less than a social revolution on an awesome scale, one that would place the Catholic underclass over them, and one that would succeed, where previous attempts in 1641 and 1688 had failed, in destroying them as a people apart, and in wrecking the Ulster that they had built. Belfast would provide the core of Ulster's resistance, and Ulster would put the steel in the Irish Unionist argument against Home Rule.

As noted, Ulster was not required to fight in 1886, for the emergence of a hundred or so Liberal Unionists within Gladstone's Liberal Party brought about the defeat of Home Rule. But Ulster did need to stay vigilant, for the Liberals remained committed, at least ostensibly, to some form of self-government for Ireland. Moreover the Conservative Party under Salisbury might not always prove resolute in its opposition, though that said, given the electoral credit, not to mention their new identity, to be gained as *the* party of the Union and of the empire, the risk of its embracing Parnell and his party was remote. It was the weakness of Unionism that made watchfulness essential. The fissiparous tendencies already noted within the Unionist family, north and south, meant that there was a constant danger of fragmentation along class or geographical lines. The interests of northern Unionists did not always coincide with the needs of the southern Unionists; the requirements for the expansion of commercial wealth might just as easily collide with those needed for the protection of rental income. Again, the shipyardman – to take just one type of industrial worker – surely could not be forever expected to accept – grimly, glumly or gladly – the leadership of those captains of industry responsible for his low wages and poor living conditions. In order for Unionism to remain intact as a cross-class, inter-Protestant and islandwide movement it had to remain focused on the catastrophic nature of the threat posed by the smallest piece of Irish Home Rule. Even when that threat seemed in abeyance, as it was for most of the period 1886 to 1906, constant vigilance and absolute readiness to resist were required.

The Orange Order was vital to this process. For most of the nineteenth century it had been rather looked down upon by the respectable Protestant middle classes because of its association with rowdyism and rioting. But that sniffy disapproval was sapped by the Order's resolute resistance to the attempted 'invasion' of Ulster by the Land League in the early 1880s, and it wholly disappeared under the shock of Gladstone's conversion to Home Rule in 1886. From that date on the Order expanded greatly, especially in urban areas, where it provided a network of fraternal clubs, within which Conservatives and Liberal Unionists of all classes, and of all Protestant denominations, could meet, plan resistance and, not least, reinforce each other's horror at the thought of what Home Rule might bring.

There was a brief flurry of excitement when Gladstone became prime minister for the fourth time in August 1892. The following February he introduced another Home Rule bill, which passed the House of Commons, only to go down to a crushing defeat (419 votes to 41) in the House of Lords in September 1893. This crisis, if it can be called that, was marked by further evidence of the determination of Unionists in Ulster to resist. In June 1892, an 'Ulster Convention' was held in the Botanic Gardens in Belfast, at which some 12,000 Conservative and Liberal Unionist delegates had declared that they would have nothing to do with Home Rule. And this was followed up by a more menacing meeting of Orangemen in the Ulster Hall a month after Gladstone had introduced his Home Rule bill. At this gathering, the redoubtable William Johnston of Bally-kilbeg, who had defied the British government over a ban on provocative Orange processions as long ago as 1867, carried a resolution in favour of meeting Home Rule with passive resistance. Once again, however, this crisis swiftly passed, and Orangemen were not required to back up their words with swords. Following the defeat of his Home Rule bill, Gladstone retired from politics and he was replaced as prime minister by the earl of Rosebery, a Liberal who regarded Irish Home Rule as a millstone around his party's neck, and who placed it far down its agenda. Rosebery himself was succeeded as prime minister by Salisbury in June 1895, and for the next ten years a Conservative and Liberal Unionist alliance formed the government. Home Rule, in this circumstance, seemed forlorn.

And yet Ulster's vigilance remained undimmed during these ten years. If anything, Ulster's position as a place apart, with its people as a race apart, Protestant and British, was cemented during these years. The writing of Ulster history as an epic, even biblical, narrative, with set-pieces clustered around the plantation, the 1641 rebellion and the siege of Derry in 1689 continued apace. Culturally too, there was a renewed emphasis on the Ulster dialect and on stories, folk tales, even topography special to Ulster, all of which was designed to underpin its declared and imagined political distance and difference from the other peoples on the island.

Moreover, during these ten years, Ulster was moving decisively to the front and centre in the opposition to Home Rule. When the Conservative chief secretary, George Wyndham, abetted by the leading southern Irish Unionist, Lord Dun-raven, suggested in 1904 that some form of 'devolution' might be introduced, there was fury in Ulster Unionist circles. It was now abundantly clear that the Conservative and Unionist Party was not immune to the virus of Home Rule (for 'devolution' was another word for it). It was further evident that even southern Unionists could not be counted on to remain stalwart. In short order, Wyndham's resignation was demanded and obtained and, significantly, an Ulster Unionist Council was set up to safeguard and promote the interests of Ulster Unionists as opposed to Irish Unionists. In 1905 there was as yet no hint of partition: Ulster Unionists would continue to look to their allies in the Conservative Party to defeat Home Rule for all Ireland; and they would maintain cooperation with the southern Unionists – indeed, they would even be led by one. But after 1905, there could be no mistaking that the Protestant working classes and commercial middle classes of Ulster would constitute the core of the resistance, and that, by 1905, the nature of that resistance had changed: the Ulsterisation of Unionism had taken place. True, patrician denunciation of Home Rule would continue to be heard, and impassioned constitutional and legal arguments would continue to be made. But it would now be Belfast steel that would decide the issue; perhaps this had always been the case.

The fall of Parnell

Unionist opposition to Home Rule had not much engaged the attention of the Irish Parliamentary Party in 1886, and nor did it do so thereafter. In fairness Gladstone himself was not all that concerned at protests against his bills of 1886 and 1893, and he made no attempt, in either of them, to introduce specific safeguards that would reduce anti-Home Rule clamour in Ulster, or anywhere else. Gladstone viewed such opposition as a mixture of bluster and bullying that would quickly die down, and was best ignored. Irish nationalist Members of Parliament, by and large, agreed with this analysis. In any case, to concede that the Unionists had genuine concerns that had to be addressed would in fact force the admission that the 'Irish people' were not as one on the question of Home Rule. Ulster Unionists might put about the myth that Ulster was entirely Protestant; but Irish nationalists would hold to their own myth of an undivided nation on the island of Ireland.

The defeat of Home Rule in 1886 had been a setback, but Parnell and his party could look forward with some confidence to its reintroduction when their new best friends, the Liberals under Gladstone, would return to power. Parnell's ascendancy over his party and the country was then unchallenged: he was, wrote the *Freeman's Journal* 'the personal embodiment of the Irish nation', and there were even grounds for believing that 'Parnellism' was replacing Irish nationalism in the affections of his adoring public. Parnell appeared to grow in stature in consequence of the outcome of a judicial inquiry into his record on violence and disorder. In a series of articles published by the London *Times* in 1888 that newspaper had purported to show that not only was Parnell soft on Irish crime, but that his denunciation of the 1882 Phoenix Park murders had been bogus. He appeared to be fully vindicated when one of his chief accusers was unmasked as a forger (and subsequently committed suicide). Parnell's reputation soared. An invitation to visit Gladstone's house at Hawarden to discuss Home Rule with the GOM in December 1889 amply confirmed his status as the leader of the Irish people and as a prime-minister-in-waiting himself.

Ten days after Parnell's stay at Hawarden, the news broke in the *Freeman's Journal* that he was to be named in divorce proceedings brought by Captain William O'Shea (later revealed as prompted and paid by *The Times* newspaper) against his wife and Parnell's long-time lover, Mrs Katherine O'Shea. Initially it appeared that Parnell would weather the crisis but, when eventually the unseemly revelations of his fugitive visits to the Eltham home of Mrs O'Shea emerged from the court in November 1890, his future seemed less secure. Certainly, the Irish Parliamentary Party expressed the utmost confidence in his continued leadership, but Gladstone was ominously silent. Already, the keepers of the nonconformist conscience in the Liberal Party had privately intimated to senior party figures that because of the divorce they would not have Parnell as a partner under any circumstances. After the Irish Parliamentary Party voted unanimously to support Parnell, Gladstone broke cover and declared publicly that Parnell's continued position at the head of the Irish Parliamentary Party would render his own leadership of the Liberal Party 'almost a nullity'. In effect, he was saying that the Irish party had to choose between the Liberal alliance with a real prospect of Home Rule or Parnell himself.

From this point on, matters unravelled with terrifying swiftness. Parnell bluntly told Gladstone to mind his own business; but then the Irish party rowed back on its assurances of support for Parnell, with a majority walking out of Committee Room Fifteen in the House of Commons. Then, the Catholic bishops in Ireland, at first reluctantly, and then with gusto, waded into the controversy, voicing their firm opinion that Parnell should withdraw from public life. Crucially, Irish opinion in the United States was almost entirely hostile to Parnell's continued leadership with only three out of sixty-three Irish American newspapers reportedly backing him. Between 1890 and 1891 a string of by-election results in Ireland showed that anti-Parnellite feeling was in the ascendant. Parnell, however, refused to bow before the storm of abuse and he became more and more extreme in his speeches, renouncing the Liberal alliance, attacking Gladstone and, apparently, even making an appeal to militant Fenians. For their part, former colleagues, now enemies, within the party – most prominently Timothy Healy, John Dillon and William O'Brien – were well able to match, and even exceed him, in the abuse that they heaped on Parnell (and on Mrs Katherine Parnell, for he had married her in June 1891). Indeed so violent, not to say outrageous, were the attacks, particularly those by Healy, on both Parnell and his wife that an observer might well conclude that the divorce was merely a proxy issue for a long-standing and deep-rooted hatred of Parnell that was now out in the open. Worn out by campaigning in a hostile environment, Parnell died in

October 1891, aged forty-five. Too much should not be read into the circumstances of his death: Parnell had been in poor health for some time, his father and grandfather had both died young, and he was a heavy smoker. Even so the word 'tragic' is not misplaced.

Parnell's final year, and the manner of his passing, seemed to be a tragedy on the Greek model, and it is tempting to attribute cosmic significance to his rapid rise and even swifter destruction. Certainly, contemporary writers, earnestly and anxiously debating the notion of an Irish literature, and seeking Irish themes for their work, could not but be struck by the spectacle of the aristocratic hero seemingly brought down by the craw-thumping middle classes. The youthful William Butler Yeats and James Joyce each in their own way saw the fall as crystallising all that was deplorable and rotten in the state of Ireland. Others ransacked history – or the Bible – for the meaning of the Parnell saga. To the advanced nationalist Constance Markievicz (née Gore-Booth), Parnell had been a Moses, prevented by cowards from leading his people to the chosen land. For his part, Gladstone, unfortunately still engrossed in his studies of Irish history, preferred to see Parnell as another sixteenth-century earl of Kildare who had tried to take on Henry VIII (i.e. Gladstone himself) and had failed. Other contemporaries claimed that he had never, in fact, died or gone away, and there were a number of sightings of him (or his ghost) in later years. All of which testified to the huge effect he had on people around him and to the palpable sense of loss or of emptiness that seemed to pervade the 1890s. However, while in no way seeking to diminish the impact of his death, a sense of proportion is needed.

Gladstone brought the Liberal Party to accept, however reluctantly, that Home Rule was to be the party's Irish policy. In so far as Parnell was instrumental in this process, it was to be his crowning achievement. Unfortunately for Parnell, however, once an alliance with the Liberals was gained, he and his party were its prisoner, for there was no room now for parliamentary independence. After Parnell's death, both Parnellite and anti-Parnellite Members accepted as much and professed loyalty to the Liberals, and they did so because the Liberals offered the only realistic prospect of delivering Home Rule. For Parnell to turn his back on Gladstone, or the Liberal Party, made no sense whatsoever. His rejection of Gladstone appeared to be sparked as much by petulance at the Liberal leader's perceived moralising as by rational political calculation.

Can Parnell's death be seen as a watershed in the political history of Ireland? After 1886 Home Rule depended entirely on the Liberals, but that might be no bad thing: Gladstone would demonstrate his bona fides in this respect by bringing in a second Home Rule bill in 1893, and in 1905 his successor, Henry Campbell-Bannerman, would promise to bring in another. In short, after 1886

Parnell was not at all central to Home Rule: had he lived he could hardly have altered, or speeded up, its progress. It is even difficult to maintain that Parnell's refusal to accept that his leadership had lost all moral authority split his party in 1890–1. Parnell's party was essentially a coalition held together by the force of his personality and the mystique of his leadership. However, the venom that was spewed out during those last few months of Parnell's life, when some of his party lieutenants turned on him, was clear evidence that some sort of explosion could not be long delayed. The uproar over the divorce proceedings merely brought to a head pre-existing tensions within the party. The continued war between Parnellites and anti-Parnellites in the 1890s is easily explained but the explanation for the much more deadly strife within the ranks of the anti-Parnellites – between those who looked to John Dillon's leadership and those who followed T. M. Healy – is complex. This division, which remained central to Irish politics for over a decade and more, might be seen as the outcome of a debate that had been going on in cultural circles in Ireland since the early 1880s, perhaps even from the time of the Young Ireland group, and which had loosely revolved around a single question: what was the point of Home Rule?

Culture wars

One answer to this question had been that self-government or Home Rule (though this term was only coined in 1873) would mean better, more efficient, more responsive government for Ireland. Certainly O'Connell had ostensibly viewed his campaign for the repeal of the Act of Union in this light. That the realities of Irish confessional demography would inevitably put Catholics into the driving seat was another undoubted advantage in his eyes. By contrast, Isaac Butt viewed 'Home Government' – his formulation – as a way of keeping wrong-headed English initiatives for Ireland at bay and also as offering an opportunity for Irish Protestants to reassert their natural capacity for leadership. Parnell seems, likewise, to have believed that, when Home Rule was implemented, Protestant landlords like himself would somehow reclaim their role as the Irish governing class. What was missing in any of this was an indication that self-government might, or indeed, ought, to have a cultural dimension, that the whole object was pointless if it did not lead to the regeneration of Ireland.[8]

But while Irish political leaders had, for the most part, studiously avoided all questions of identity and cultural purpose, there had been those, throughout the century, who had persisted in raising these issues. Admittedly, they had not spoken with the one voice. The Young Irelanders, for example, had been exasperated and dismayed at O'Connell's seeming indifference to the cultural potential of his repeal campaign, while Sir Samuel Ferguson, a Protestant, a Unionist and a prominent Gaelic scholar, had argued in the 1860s that cultural nationalism could prove to be an alternative to self-government or political nationalism. Little was heard of these debates outside the narrow circles of the *Dublin University Magazine*, the Royal Irish Academy and Trinity College Dublin, and it was not until after Parnell's death that the issues they raised received both a wider airing and a more earnest interrogation.

In November 1892 Douglas Hyde delivered a presidential address to the National Literary Society in which he called for the 'de-anglicising of the Irish people' through the revival of Irish as a spoken language (map 10). This clarion call led to the setting up a year later of the Gaelic League with Hyde as its president. Hyde was a Protestant, indeed he was a clergyman's son, and he was increasingly concerned at the apparently bleak future in store for his people – the Protestants of Ireland. Hyde can be seen as part of an apostolic succession that included Davis and Ferguson. His remedy was not all that different from theirs, in that he sought by reviving the Irish language to create a vital cultural space that Protestants and Catholics could occupy jointly. The Irish language was, he argued, denominationally blind, and it was therefore a positive unifying force, unlike religion, class or indeed politics. As Hyde surveyed the threatening spectacle of the English-speaking, Catholic middle classes 'crawling' (his word) into positions once monopolised by Irish Protestants, he would probably have found it difficult to say whether it was the religious, class or political aspects of this social climbing that most disgusted him.

Hyde intended the Gaelic League to be resolutely apolitical, even anti-political, and he was equally determined to keep the language issue non-sectarian. He was to be unsuccessful in both these endeavours. Whether Hyde liked it or not, the Irish language was soon seen as a 'Catholic' possession, and it became more so by the early years of the new century. There may have been a few Protestant ministers in the League's ranks, but it was the large number of Catholic priests who caught the eye. Their ultimately successful efforts to have the language made a compulsory subject for matriculation in the National University of Ireland, set up in 1908, created further resentment among Protestants. Similarly, it was unrealistic to portray Irish as a non-political issue: in the Ireland of the 1890s, and later, every public question had its political dimension, and Irish was no exception. From an early date, the language revival movement was a home for advanced nationalists, usually from the predominantly anglophone east of Ireland, and a knowledge of Irish had become a touchstone for those who yearned to fashion a new Gaelic identity for themselves. Hyde's vision – and it was not his alone – was not to be realised.

While Hyde's aim had been to revive Irish as a spoken language, he was also concerned to reveal or recover its literary jewels, hitherto obscured, through

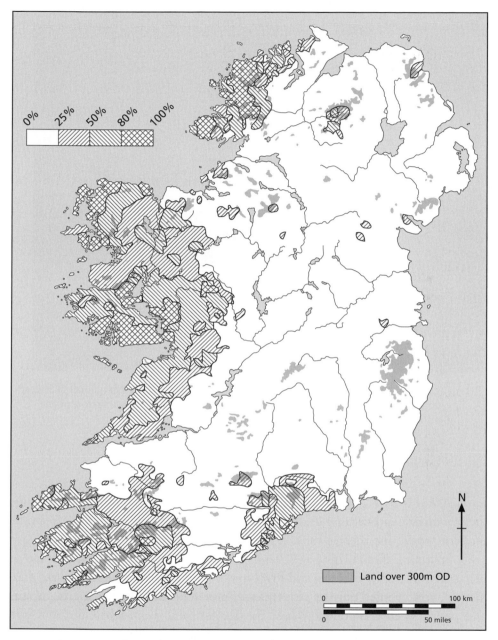

0% 25% 50% 80% 100%

N

Land over 300m OD

0   100 km

0   50 miles

Map 10 Irish speakers as percentage of population in 1911

prejudice against the peasant patois. His efforts in this respect coincided with those of William Butler Yeats, Lady Gregory, John Millington Synge and others who, in revolt at the talentless buffoonery and shameless shamrockery that, in their view, had hitherto characterised much of Irish writing, self-consciously sought to realise a new national literature in English, one that would be

(a)

5.15 Another Ireland: scenes such as these from the Aran Islands off the west coast of Ireland, *c.* 1900 had a powerful impact on the imagination of the cultural revivalists. Irish Photographic Archive.
(a) Women washing clothes.
(b) Young boy watching a girl carrying seaweed.
(c) Women carrying turf.

'unmistakably Irish', yet cosmopolitan rather than insular, and possess genuine literary merit. And because Yeats and his circle were in headlong flight from the modern world, the themes for this new literature were to be found, largely, in pre-Christian Ireland. This pagan land possessed the inestimable advantage of being free of both Catholics and Protestants (and grubby middle classes) and, instead, was peopled only by peasants and aristocrats and by heroes, magicians and poets. In contemporary Ireland the closest to this pre-lapsarian idyll was apparently the province of Connacht, and it was along the western seaboard, and on the Aran Islands (figure 5.15), that Lady Gregory and J. M. Synge found inspiration.

Some fifty years earlier, Thomas Davis, like Yeats, had called for a national literature for Ireland, but there was a crucial difference between their respective visions. So far as Davis was concerned, his national literature would promote the idea of the nation, but he had held that, while literary merit was desirable

(b)

(c)

5.15 (cont.)

for this enterprise, it was not essential. Yeats disagreed profoundly: literary excellence, in his view, was fundamental, and so too was artistic freedom. For much of the time, these distinctions made no difference, at least in terms of audience, for the plays put on at the Irish Literary Theatre set up by Yeats, Lady Gregory and Edward Martyn in 1899 won both plaudits and brickbats. Yeats's play *The Countess Cathleen* (1899) aroused much protest for its less than favourable view of the Irish peasant, but *Cathleen Ni Houlihan* (1902), which he devised with Lady Gregory, won nationalist approval for its stirring, rousing qualities. However, there would come a point when those who espoused what we might call the superlative image of the Irish peasant would be moved to protest violently at any perceived slight on him (or her). Those who held that the Irish were the most pious, most noble and bravest race on earth were not about to allow their heroes to be portrayed in a mocking or disparaging way. The first performances of Synge's *The Playboy of the Western World* (1907) provoked rioting in the Abbey Theatre; the moment had arrived when the artist's need for creative freedom had run up against the nationalist's demand for an uncritical literature that promoted the national ideal.

The literary revival spearheaded by Yeats and his circle has sometimes been seen as a reaction to the fall of Parnell, as an attempt by culture to fill the void left by politics. Yeats himself favoured this interpretation, and while there is something in it, it should not be pushed too far. The origins of the revival can be traced generally to the growing fear of Protestant Ireland since the time of the Land War, if not O'Connell, that it would be swamped by the apparently inexorable rise of the Catholic masses, ill educated and philistine; hence the retreat to the more congenial world of pagan Ireland where aristocrats, or poets, were always in charge, and where magic and mystery were the order of the day. More precisely, the first stirrings of revival can be sourced to the period before the Chief's fall. In a real sense, it was Parnell's ascendancy, and Parnell's success, that generated the energy to address the questions of national identity and national purpose that underlay the literary movement. Equally, it was the explosion of bitterness, attendant on his fall, that poisoned the atmosphere within which the debate on the role of a national literature would be conducted.

Already, even before Parnell's death, there were indications that defining the national ideal or purpose would be far from easy. In November 1884 the Gaelic Athletic Association (GAA) had been formed with a mission to wean Irish people away from what were known as 'garrison games' (such as cricket, rugby and lawn tennis), and to bring them to enjoy instead Gaelic football and hurling. Of course, the GAA can be seen simply as an Irish expression of the growth of spectator sports everywhere in Britain and north America in the late nineteenth century; but the Association had an avowedly nationalist character – it was never just a sporting body – and from the beginning it was more or less under Fenian control. It was also a focus for anti-British and anti-army sentiment that was clearly growing in Ireland from the 1880s on. The official visit of Edward, prince of Wales in 1885, for example, provoked numerous protests both before and during his stay. His mother, Victoria, was pilloried as the 'Famine Queen', Disraeli's alleged glee at the Famine was once again brought up, a miniature coffin was thrown at the royal party in Cork and, rather tactlessly, there was public rejoicing at the Mahdi's defeat of 'Gordon of Khartoum' in the Sudan. The GAA added its mite to this mood by banning members of the British army from playing its games or joining its organisation. The exclusion was undoubtedly prompted by hostility to the army but there is also some suggestion that dislike of the stern competition offered by teams of footballing – and very fit – soldiers was a subsidiary cause.

The level of recruitment to the British army, once very high in Ireland, also began to level out in the 1890s. From being an honourable situation in the 1850s, by the turn of the century 'going for a sojer' was seen as something shameful and off-duty soldiers were liable to be heckled in public. *Inghinidhe na hÉireann* (Daughters of Ireland), an advanced nationalist women's pressure group, set up under Maud Gonne's leadership in 1900 to protest the visit of Queen Victoria in that year, also took as one of its objectives to discourage Irish recruitment to the British army. Imperial woes in South Africa added to the mood of disenchantment with the British Empire and with its army. Irish nationalist opinion was firmly on the side of the Boers in their struggle against an oppressive imperial state. The Boer War (1899–1902), with its widely perceived aggression against 'white' subjects, turned many Irish nationalists against the Empire. By way of contrast, we may note that just as the prince of Wales was hissed in Cork, he was hurrahed in loyalist Ulster; and while nationalist Ireland was in general opposed to the Boer War, Ulster Protestants had no qualms about enforcing imperial rule in South Africa. Indeed, service in the British army during the Boer War was to be a common bond among a number of later leaders of Ulster Unionism. Even in matters apparently far removed from the Irish question, 'Ulster' and 'Ireland' were drawing decisively apart.

For D. P. Moran the separation could not come quickly enough. Moran was the editor of a weekly periodical, *The Leader*, set up by him in 1900 and destined to last for forty years under his stewardship. Talented rather than brilliant, and irascible, indefatigable and insulting – though hugely influential – he brought the cultural debate centred on the ultimate purpose of Home Rule to new heights (or depths) of vituperation. Almost from its first issue, *The Leader* had the Ulster Unionists in its sights, and his message was clear: they should shut up and accept that the future was to be Green and Catholic. If they did not relish that prospect then they could have partition and good riddance. Yeats and his circle also came under hostile fire: their declared ambition to construct a shared cultural space was denounced as a dangerous nonsense, and their attempt to create an Irish literature in English was rubbished as impossible of realisation. It is relatively easy to jot down a number of the targets of Moran – a shortlist might include Theobald Wolfe Tone, Daniel O'Connell, Thomas Davis, the Irish Parliamentary Party, 'Grattan's Parliament' ('a fraud'), the 1798 centenary celebrations ('a sham'), Irish literature in English ('a mongrel thing'), Protestants generally ('sourfaces'), socially aspirant Catholics ('Shoneens'), Irish nationalists ('Sulky West Britons') and, unforgivably, the Irish liquor interest ('Mr Bung') – but it is rather more difficult to itemise those of which he approved. Self-confessedly, he stood for 'Irish Ireland', by which he seems to have meant an Ireland that was genuinely separate and independent. Typically, he was entirely dismissive of the bogus Home Rule that the Irish Parliamentary Party championed, for it could not lead to national regeneration. His ideal was an Ireland in which the Irish language and Irish culture were dominant, and in which Catholicism was, in effect, the state religion. But he despised the contemporary idealisation of Irish peasant life and especially of pre-Christian Ireland, and he was an earnest advocate of Irish industrial development and cultural self-sufficiency, all of which set him apart from Yeats, Synge and Lady Gregory.

In the general welter of assertion, argument and accusation, punctuated by the occasional fistfight, that characterised public debate in Ireland in the 1890s and 1900s, yet another dissident voice could be heard taking issue with both Moran and Yeats. In March 1899, Arthur Griffith, a Dublin printer and journalist who had spent a short time in South Africa, began publishing a newspaper, *United Irishman*, whose concerns were similar to those of Moran's *Leader*. Unlike Moran, however, Griffith took a more favourable view of the late eighteenth-century Irish Parliament and of the legacy and achievements of the Protestant patriots, T. W. Tone and Thomas Davis. On the other hand, he yielded to no one in his denunciation of Yeats and Synge for what he saw as the immorality and degeneracy in their poems and plays. He was a separatist and he revered the rebels of the past – '98, '48 and '67 were his lucky numbers – but he recognised that another armed rebellion was out of the question, and he accepted that not all nationalists would go as far as separation. His solution was a dual monarchy – to keep Irish royalists happy – on the Austro-Hungarian model and, just as Hungarian deputies had withdrawn from the imperial parliament in Vienna, so he urged Irish Members to abstain from Westminster, a course of action that had in fact been first mooted as long ago as O'Connell's time. Especially, Griffith was an economic nationalist, whose advocacy of protectionism for nascent Irish industries, while sincere, was based on a misreading of Friedrich List's *National*

System of Political Economy (London, 1885). Similarly, it is only fair to point out that his understanding of recent Hungarian history was rather tenuous.

However, what he might have lacked in his understanding of the constitutional and financial intricacies of *Mitteleuropa* he more than made up for by his indefatigable work on behalf of his vision of what Ireland could be. He was an accomplished organiser, a talented journalist and a prolific pamphleteer. In 1900 he formed Cumann na nGaedheal as a sort of umbrella organisation for like-minded nationalist groups; and in 1903 he formed the National Council in order to mount protests against the visit to Ireland of the newly crowned Edward VII. Following the National Council's success in elections for Dublin corporation in 1905, it adopted the policy of *Sinn Féin* (= Ourselves), in essence, the espousal of a programme of economic and cultural self-sufficiency. Griffith's Sinn Féin – for the policy became the name of the party – was not a republican party, though it had many republicans in its ranks, and it did succeed in harnessing the energies of young Irish nationalists, in revolt, and perhaps revulsion, at that centre of paralysis that was the Irish Parliamentary Party after Parnell. Officially, the 'Green Hungarian Band', as Moran gleefully dubbed Sinn Féin, remained wedded to a dual monarchy, but very many of its supporters almost certainly favoured a more drastic solution to Anglo-Irish relations.

Two further voices can be added to the Babel that characterised the fifteen years or so after Parnell's death: the voice of women, and the voice of labour. Neither was particularly concerned with issues of Irish identity, Irish culture or even Irish self-government, yet both in their own ways had a contribution to make on all of these questions. Moreover, while both had previously been active, they had not been well attended to. If they chose to speak out and act at this moment, it may have been because Parnell's death appeared to open a space for dissenting groups to act, and especially for dissenting voices to be heard.

There had never been any sort of golden age for Irish women, but there are good grounds for claiming that the sixty years after the Famine saw a deterioration in their situation. In the first instance, female employment fell markedly, while that of men remained steady: the census for 1881 recorded 815,000 women in paid work, that for 1911 returned a figure of around 430,000. In 1861, 56 per cent of houseworkers were female, but that figure had risen to 85 per cent fifty years later. By 1911 a third of all occupations had no female employed in them; the figure had been a fifth twenty years earlier. During the same period women were more likely to end up in workhouses, or other charitable institutions, than men. There were far more girls than boys in orphanages, and female beggars out-numbered males by three to one. In addition, beginning in 1864, a moral panic over the health of recruits to the armed forces led to the passing of various 'contagious diseases' Acts. These Acts specifically targeted women in named garrisons, principally the military camp at the Curragh, county Kildare, and provided for their compulsory examination on suspicion of being infected with venereal disease. It is eloquent testimony to the high regard in which Victorian women were held (no men were to be subject to these tests), that the term 'contagious diseases' had hitherto only been used in connection with cattle ailments. It is scarcely surprising that faced with decreasing chances of obtaining paid work, confronted with the bleak prospect of 'assisting' on the family farm with all the humiliation (and sexual risk) which that entailed, and with little hope of contracting a marriage unless in possession of a dowry, some 1,700,000 Irish women (a higher figure than for men) chose to emigrate from Ireland during the half century following the Famine.

And yet, perhaps this is too dismal a picture of the condition of Irish women? The collapse of paid employment for women might well be overstated as a result of errors in recording female workers. It has also been suggested that the flight of women from the workplace may in fact have been a conscious choice. Late nineteenth-century Ireland witnessed an increase in household consumption, and 'new' areas of expertise in childcare, cooking, sewing and knitting had opened up within the home. Compared to the toil of agricultural work, to the tedium of such factory work as there was, and to the near-slavery of domestic service, housework, with its real possibility for budgetary control over the home, the management of their own time, even the prospect of earning a few shillings from the hens, might have appeared to many women a sensible option to take.

Even emigration can be seen as offering Irish women, if not liberation, then the potential for it. The New World opened opportunities for advancement to Irish women that were simply not available at home. Admittedly the statistics on Irish women emigrants to the United States in the decades after 1850 make for depressing reading: Irish women topped the lists for drunkenness, prostitution, arrests and imprisonment in all the large east-coast cities. By the 1880s, however, new careers for them were becoming available as schoolteachers, clerks and nurses, and Irish women were crowding into them. It was noticeable that, from the 1880s on, Irish women began to seek marriage partners outside the Irish community. Marrying 'out', or exogamy, appears to have frequently led to an improvement in condition.

Such, in brief, were the experiences of poor, or working-class, women in the fifty years after the Famine, but for middle-class or well-born women it was all rather different. It had ever been so. In the eighteenth century, society hostesses and the wives of prominent politicians had played some role in political affairs. And on the other side, so to speak, the female relations of leading revolutionaries had carved out a role for themselves. Matilda Tone, the widow of Theobald

Wolfe Tone, lived until 1848, the epitome of republican widowhood, zealously guarding the flame of Tone's memory. Equally, Mary-Ann McCracken, the sister of Henry Joy who was executed in 1798, selflessly took care of her brother's illegitimate offspring, and fearlessly involved herself in any number of philanthrophic causes over the first five decades of the nineteenth century. It was, in fact, philanthrophy, a desire to help those less fortunate, rather than politics, that led middle-class women into the national arena. That said, philanthrophic campaigns almost always had political effects, so that, in reality, little distinction can be made between the two. The Belfast Presbyterian, Isabella Tod, for example, was an activist in the temperance movement, an advocate of educational opportunity for women and a tireless worker for the welfare of female ex-prisoners. She also conducted a spirited campaign against the Contagious Diseases Acts (repealed 1885). Almost inevitably, she then directed her attention to securing parliamentary votes for women. She was also a Liberal Unionist who campaigned energetically in Britain and Ireland against Gladstone's Home Rule bills.

On the nationalist side, some women came to political action after having received their education from Irish nuns. The number of female religious in Ireland had risen dramatically from around 120 in 1800 to over 8,000 in 1900 and, by this latter date, they constituted almost a quarter of professional adult women workers. Most of these religious were involved in charitable work with the poor, the sick and other unfortunates, but some were members of teaching orders working in national schools and in the (few) intermediate schools. It was a sign of the advance of the Catholic bourgeoisie that, in 1883, the Dominican convent school, and, a few years later, the Loreto convent school (both in Dublin), were opened to prepare the daughters of the Catholic middle classes for a university education. (By 1900, there were some three thousand male students attending university in Ireland, but just ninety-one women, out of a total population of 4.5 million.) It was also a sign of something that the annual results for competitive examinations provided the occasion for much sectarian muscle-flexing and point-scoring between Catholic convents and Protestant colleges, such as Alexandra College (established in 1866).

Can it be doubted that nuns generally, and teaching nuns in particular, provided positive role models for their youthful charges? Here were women in charge, managing institutions, controlling finances and acting independently of men. It is not surprising that more than a few of the middle-class products of these Catholic schools were unwilling to accept exclusion from the public sphere from the 1880s on, and began to assert themselves. The experience of Hannah Sheehy might be taken as a case in point. The daughter of an Irish nationalist Member of Parliament, she was educated by the Dominican nuns in Eccles

Street, Dublin. She then attended university and was affronted in 1902 with the realisation that in the eyes of the law her 'status as a woman was worse than [that accorded to criminals, infants and lunatics]'. She went on to be a lifelong feminist.

By the time of Hannah Sheehy's realisation of her low status, a women's suffrage society dedicated to winning the vote for women in parliamentary elections had been formed with branches in Belfast, Dublin and elsewhere. Already in 1896 some hundred thousand Irish women had been enfranchised and made eligible to stand for election as Poor Law guardians. In 1898 the Local Government (Ireland) Act established the same franchise as the earlier Poor Law legislation. Irish women were still excluded (until 1911) from membership of county and county borough councils, and the vote in parliamentary elections was still some way off; but there could be no denying that, at the turn of the new century, Irish women were undergoing a powerful consciousness-raising experience and that they were entering the public arena to an unprecedented extent.

The voice of labour, too, was making itself heard in late nineteenth-century Ireland. Given the marked absence of industrialisation (outside the north-east of Ireland), it is not perhaps surprising that trades unionism was rarely heard in nineteenth-century Ireland. What passed for industry, once again outside the north-east of the island, was in fact largely pre-industrial in structure, involving, as it did, little more than the processing and transport of agricultural produce. Even Guinness's brewery in Dublin, by 1900 the largest in the world with over three thousand employees, does little to qualify that statement. The reality was that outside east Ulster, Dublin, and to some extent Cork, there was next to no manufacturing or, indeed, any export-oriented activity (except emigration). In any case, the achievement of the Land War, and subsequent agitations, had been in effect to reduce the bulk of the population of Ireland to simple categories of landlord and tenant. As a result, while the interests of the craft worker (they numbered about sixty thousand, with well over half in Belfast alone) could be represented by the Irish Trades Union Congress, set up in 1894, those of the factory operative, the docker or the 'general' or casual labourer – and of this latter category there was a large pool – were largely ignored.

Three factors lay behind the emerging labour unrest of the 1890s and early twentieth century. The first was the example of English 'new unionism', in which the so-called unskilled in London, beginning with the dockers in 1889, had demonstrated that they had, in fact, a valuable skill, and that they could win better conditions from the employers. Could the unskilled or semi-skilled in Dublin or Belfast follow suit? The second was the arrival in Ireland at different dates of two charismatic labour organisers, both of Irish emigrant parentage: James Larkin, who arrived in Belfast in 1907 to organise the dockers there, and

James Connolly who, after a period as a labour organiser in the United States, arrived in Dublin in 1910.

By far the most important factor, however, was the spectacle and scandal of the most appalling poverty in Dublin. The Irish capital's housing might not have been the worst in the world, but it was certainly among the most notorious. In 1900 some 37 per cent of families lived in one-room accommodation – the comparable percentage figure for London was 15 per cent, for Cork 11 per cent and, strikingly, for Belfast 1 per cent. And inevitably, along with wretched housing went poor diet, irregular and badly paid employment and very high rates of typhoid and tuberculosis. Though conditions in rural Ireland had improved after the Famine, with measurable growth in, say, disposable income, post office savings, diet, housing and longevity, these had not been matched in Dublin. The Connachtman (or woman) with a life expectancy of 62.3 (or 62.6) years in the early 1900s could consider himself/herself fortunate compared to his/her Dublin counterpart who could reckon on living no longer than 51.5 years for a man, and 55.8 years for a woman. The disparity in infant mortality was even more startling: in 1914, the figure was 87 per 1000 for Ireland overall (better than both England and Scotland), but 196 per 1000 for Dublin. As we shall see, not everything was rosy in rural Ireland – the so-called congested districts along the west coast from Donegal to Kerry, could exhibit comparable deprivation to Dublin; but the misery of the capital's slums really was shocking. Equally appalling, perhaps, was the fact that the city fathers on Dublin Corporation, in general cheerleaders for the Irish Parliamentary Party, and eager, eloquent exponents of the iniquity of British rule, saw no need to undertake any sort of drastic remedy, possibly because they felt nothing could be done until Home Rule was achieved, or perhaps because a number were themselves the beneficial owners of tenement slums.

For a labour organiser like Larkin, Belfast offered special challenges. Its skilled workers in ship-building and engineering – a labour aristocracy if ever there was one – looked down on the wretchedly paid, unskilled workers. To some extent, this division, here and elsewhere, almost directly mirrored the segregation of the city into Protestant and Catholic; but there was a snag, for Protestants were also well represented among the ranks of the unskilled in Belfast; caution and some guile were called for by the employers. As for Larkin, he would have difficulty in mobilising the workers and, at the same time, meeting the sectarian counter-challenge that would inevitably come.

Even before Larkin's arrival, maverick elements within the predominantly Protestant workforce had emerged to challenge the easy equation of Protestant worker, Unionist supporter and quiescent employee. William Walker, a ship-yard worker and member of the Belfast Independent Labour Party, had caused

Protestant employers a few headaches at the turn of the century, and so too had Thomas H. Sloan, with his recall of the supposed radical philosophy of the early Orange Order; but both had been reeled in, though not without difficulty. As if in atonement and in order to seek redemption, both thereafter espoused a particularly virulent species of anti-Catholicism.

For a short time, it looked as if the efforts of Larkin would succeed in bringing together the divided workers of Belfast. In May 1907 he organised the Belfast dockers in a strike that for a time united Protestant and Catholic workers. Other workers came out in sympathy, notably Protestant and Catholic policemen (they were replaced by troops) but in the end the iron grip of sectarianism reasserted itself, and the experiment fizzled out in communal rioting in August. Discouraged, Larkin moved on to Dublin, where he was joined by Connolly in 1910, and the pair set about organising the ubiquitous 'general labourer' of that city. The authorities in Belfast, however, could rest easy.

That the voices of Yeats, Moran, Griffith, Larkin and Sheehy (or Isabella Tod) – it is hard to say which of these would be most affronted by their inclusion on such a list – came to be heard in the fifteen years after Parnell's death did not mean that the customary clamour of conventional politics was drowned out. Far from it: the rhetorical combat of Unionist and nationalist continued unabated, though with less intensity, during these years. The conflict betweeen Unionism and nationalism was seen as normal, their rivalry was accepted and their partisans were returned in election after election. All other voices could be classed as 'noises off', sometimes irritating, often provoking – even occasionally stimulating – but rarely threatening to disrupt the central political drama on the Irish public stage. And yet, it might not always prove so. There was a certain impatience, a real urgency and a definite menace to some of these seemingly peripheral discourses which, if fused, harnessed and directed, might yet spell serious trouble for the dominant Unionist and nationalist interests. At the very least, they ought to have been aware that complacency was not an option.

Killing Home Rule

The Conservative Party was in power for most of the period, 1886 to 1906, after 1895 with its Liberal Unionist allies. For Ireland this meant a period of 'constructive Unionism', principally associated with the Balfour brothers, Arthur and Gerald, and with George Wyndham, chief secretaries 1887–91, 1895–1900 and 1900–5 respectively. It would be easy (and perhaps tempting!) to dismiss the notion of 'constructive Unionism' as something of an oxymoron, for the Conservative or Unionist Party had long been cast as the 'stupid' party in British politics. And yet, beginning with Catholic emancipation, some of the more far-reaching changes in Irish society had been implemented by that party. As we have seen, it was the Conservatives who accelerated the process by which some three hundred thousand Irish tenants became owner-occupiers over the period 1880–1910 and, in the period after 1886, they appear to have set out to show that there was an alternative to self-government, viz. good government. Contrary to what has sometimes been claimed, not least by Gerald Balfour himself, this most certainly did not amount to any idea of 'killing Home Rule by kindness'. The Conservatives saw Home Rule as a millstone around the Liberals' neck, had no wish to see it 'killed off' and were only too delighted to bring it up on every occasion that offered. By adopting Home Rule the Liberals had offered their opponents not so much an own goal as an open net, and the Conservative-Unionist Party was determined to score at will.

That said, the Balfour brothers, in their different ways, were keen to govern efficiently, but they were also pragmatists. The dictum of Arthur that he would be 'as relentless as Cromwell ... [but] ... as radical as any reformer' where Ireland was concerned, was essentially meaningless: he was neither. Indeed he could be neither, for these options were not available. He was, of course, soon nicknamed 'Bloody Balfour' on account of the 'massacre' at Mitchelstown, county Cork, in September 1887 (three fatalities), though the tempting alliteration might have proved irresistible in any case. In essence Arthur Balfour believed Irish nationalism was another word for socialism, and had therefore to be defeated. His brother Gerald agreed. He was an academic philosopher and therefore accustomed to stealing other people's ideas, and he was utterly unencumbered with blueprints or scruples where Ireland was concerned. The mission of the Balfour brothers – in so far as there was one – was to keep Ireland out of the news, to keep Conservative voters in England contented (not easy where Ireland was concerned), to remain on good terms with Irish Conservatives (again, not easy) and finally, to keep on board those Liberal Unionists (especially Chamberlain) who had broken with Gladstone over Home Rule (hence, no matter how tempting or desirable, Cromwellian-style rule was not on). In all of these areas, the Brothers Balfour managed quite well.

By the time he left Ireland in 1891 'Bloody' Balfour, his soubriquet notwithstanding, could look back on a record of some achievement. True, he had brought in another Crimes Act – an English audience would expect nothing less – but he had also seen off the anti-rent movement known as the Plan of Campaign, and he had brought in important Acts relating to light railways, technical instruction (both in 1889) and in 1891, land purchase (£33 million was earmarked for this). This latter Act also set up the Congested Districts Board (CDB) with a brief to rejuvenate the economy of the western seaboard of Ireland, an area initially stretching from Donegal to Kerry but eventually covering a third of the entire island. Within this zone acute poverty was held to hamper business initiative, and to remedy this, *inter alia*, local industries were to be promoted, migration assisted, uneconomic holdings combined, cottage industries fostered, harbours and piers built and light railroads constructed. Few of these initiatives were in fact successful, and there are some grounds for arguing that a Congested *Dublin* Board might have better served the needs of Ireland, including the 'agricultural slums' (Wyndham's term) of the west. The congested districts remained stubbornly untransformed. Still, the CDB proved popular, perhaps because it distributed substantial funds (by 1910, it had a budget of £250,000 per annum) without inquiring too closely into how effectively the money would be managed or spent. A tradition of government largesse was thereby established that has since proved enduring.

Similarly, when his brother Gerald left Ireland in 1900, he too was not without his accomplishments. A new Land Act (1896) had removed some of the barriers to tenant purchase – though there was still no inducement for, let alone compulsion on, landlords to sell. By another Act the way was cleared for the Irish to take to the roads in automobiles. The enormity of this mistake would only become apparent a century later, but as early as 1911, the Irish census would have a new entry for 'chauffeur', of which there were 1,349; and by 1914, there were some 4,500 cars in Ireland.

Gerald Balfour's most notable achievement was the passing of the Local Government (Ireland) Act of 1898. To a large extent this was aimed at bringing local government in Ireland into line with the position that had pertained in Britain since 1888, and all talk that it was a cunning Balfourian plan to offer local government to the Irish as a substitute for self-government can be ignored. None the less in Ireland its effects were altogether more dramatic than in Britain; they were certainly more long-lasting; they may even have been revolutionary. At a stroke, the last bastion of the ascendancy, the non-elected, gentry-dominated grand juries that had governed Ireland at local level were swept away, to be replaced by elected county and district councils. The democratisation of local government in 1898 caused more damage to Irish, particularly southern Irish, landlords than the Land War, and it fatally undermined southern Unionism. Already their estates were being broken up, and progressively bought out from under them. Already, their social role in the Irish countryside was swiftly sliding away from them, and now their political authority had been terminated. Small wonder that in the delirium induced by decline, decay and defeat, southern landlords might begin to harbour hitherto forbidden ideas on devolution, or entertain previously unthinkable thoughts on accommodation with the new forces that were in the ascendant in Ireland in the new century.

Sadly, they could not expect any sympathy for their plight in London, while tough-minded Ulster Conservatives and Liberal Unionists – no shrinking violets in their ranks – would give a robust answer to such heretical stirrings.

Balfour's term as chief secretary was also noteworthy for his establishment of the Department of Agriculture and Technical Instruction (DATI) in 1899. He did so at the urging of that Protestant do-gooder, busybody and all-round meddler, Sir Horace Plunkett, who had been instrumental in setting up cooperative creameries in order to promote quality, enhance marketing and produce efficiencies. DATI, however, proved unwieldy, having under its charge such disparate areas of Irish life as fisheries, statistics, agricultural education, the geological survey, plant diseases and the National Museum and the National Library (both opened officially in 1890). Disputes over jurisdiction arose between the new department and the CDB, there were personality clashes, and Plunkett, who was vice-president of DATI, was soon sidelined. At bottom, the problem was that the entire thrust of a generation of land legislation for Ireland had been to establish the small family farm as the 'normal' unit in the Irish countryside; but the typical small farmer now, or soon, to be basking in a proprietorial glow, had one eye fixed on his heir and the other focused on the emigration of his surplus children. He had little time at all for Plunkett's vision of agricultural efficiency to be achieved through cooperation. Given that Plunkett had a regrettable tendency to categorise his political opponents as either 'priests' or 'hags', surely his admonitions and strivings could be dismissed as just another Protestant ploy?

To say as much is not to underestimate Plunkett's achievement in promoting the cooperative movement as the remedy for 'agricultural backwardness' (his term) among Irish farmers. Beginning in 1891 at Doneraile, county Cork, cooperatives spread across southern Ireland, and by the early twentieth century, there were more than 876 of them. Whether they made much difference to the quality or quantity of Irish produce is debatable – there is no clear break in the figures for Irish agricultural productivity between 1870 and 1920. And certainly, Irish economic historians tend to see Plunkett as rather a marginal figure. In any case, he received scant reward for his pains: his creameries proved a tempting target for crown forces during the Irish War of Independence; and Plunkett's own house was burned down by anti-treaty republicans in January 1923. He left Ireland shortly afterwards.

George Wyndham became chief secretary in 1900 and, to continue the Cromwellian note sounded by Arthur Balfour, he passed 'like a lightning' through Dublin Castle. Unlike the Balfours Wyndham had an agenda, or rather he had several. He was depressed at the evidence of military failings revealed in the Boer War and attributed these to the lack of able-bodied Irishmen coming into the British army. He saw the Irish, for all their faults, as members of the

'Aryan race' and therefore regarded the undernourished condition of the poor of Ireland – the usual body of recruits – as actually a threat to the defence of the Empire. Of Irish background himself – he was distantly related to the United Irishman and revolutionary, Lord Edward FitzGerald – he saw Ireland as 'a land of sorcery' and particularly admired the 'Celtic twilight' motif in some of the work of Yeats and Lady Gregory. In addition he had a special sympathy for Catholicism and was keen on promoting a Catholic university on the grounds that it might help civilise Ireland and thus strengthen the Empire. He was, of course, a conservative on social matters – for him the natural order of things was Eton, the Guards and Westminster – but he could be radical in other areas. Perhaps inevitably, his success was spectacular, and so too was his failure.

In Irish history Wyndham is forever associated with land purchase, and the Act that colloquially bears his name is generally regarded as the final piece of the legislation that comprehensively revolutionised the landowning structure of Ireland. With some qualifications, this popular verdict can stand. True, the genesis of Wyndham's Land Act of 1903 lay, not with him, but with a group of southern Irish landlords who, in fact, urged it upon him. But it was he who fought to make available 'unlimited' British credit in order not only to enable the landlords to be bought out, but also to offer them significant inducements to sell up. Again, although there were many difficulties with the 1903 Act, and later legislation was required to facilitate tenants wishing to purchase and to put pressure on landlords to sell, the key commitment had been the one enshrined in Wyndham's Act: the resources of the British treasury would be used to reverse, once and for all, a system of landholding instituted at the point of a sword in the seventeenth century.

Wyndham's triumph was to be short lived. He had enticed to Dublin as his under-secretary, an Irish-born (and Catholic) forty-year veteran of the Indian administration, Sir Antony MacDonnell: and it was MacDonnell who had in fact drafted the Land Act of 1903. Emboldened by his success, and impressed by the consensual way in which the Land Act had been received, MacDonnell now turned his fertile mind to further strengthening the Union through a measure of administrative devolution. This was not at all a new idea. The Irish Local Government Act of 1898, and the setting up of the DATI a year later, had involved a certain amount of devolution and decentralisation, and a further instalment could be represented as simply good governance rather than innovation. In 1871 there had been a mere 5,800 civil servants but, by 1911, there were over 27,000 working in some thirty-nine departments. Surely some representative council overseeing their work could not be objected to? However, as we have seen, the proposals brought forward by the southern Unionist landlord, Lord Dunraven (with MacDonnell's encouragement) did in fact meet with a storm of criticism, especially from Ulster Unionists. They swiftly attacked the plan as, in effect, 'Home Rule by stealth'. The unfortunate MacDonnell and his boss, Wyndham, stood condemned for heresy. Dunraven, for his part, was denounced as the dupe of a Dublin Castle conspiracy. In the marked absence of support from London Wyndham was forced to resign in March 1905.

MacDonnell's ideas, and those of Wyndham (though there is some dispute about how much he knew about them), represented both the logical conclusion of 'constructive Unionism' and its innate limitations. Some species of devolved government had been inherent in the Balfour brothers' policies from the beginning: 'constructive Unionism' was always going to be about 'home rule' rather than 'Home Rule'; and thus MacDonnell and Wyndham were treading well-trodden ground. What had changed was that, first, the Conservative-Unionist Party by 1905 was facing electoral defeat in the next general election and was not, therefore, amenable to embracing electorally unpopular Irish initiatives. To an English electorate all Irish initiatives were unpopular.

But, second, and more important, Ulster Unionists had come under sustained pressure from a variety of 'fringe' loyalist movements, and their apparent monolith had begun to fragment. 'Not responsive enough to the needs of Presbyterian tenant farmers' was one accusation (voiced by T. W. Russell, and his associates), 'hostile to the interests of the Protestant workingman' was another (by William Walker, and his allies) and overall Ulster Unionists stood charged with neglecting Protestant interests and being 'soft' on the Catholic menace (the Orange Order). In the face of these serious challenges, Ulster Unionists, consciously or not, magnified a modest devolution proposal, emanating, after all, from their Conservative and southern Unionist friends into a full-scale Home Rule project. They did so in order to re-establish party unity and to encourage vigilance in the face of the eternal Catholic threat (notoriously, MacDonnell was a Catholic, and even Wyndham was suspect on that score). A 'Home Rule' crisis, indeed any crisis, was, and remained, essential to Ulster Unionism (figure 5.16): the absence of crisis encouraged party mavericks to break ranks, caused party discipline to fray and opened party fissures best concealed. The formation of an Ulster Unionist Council in March 1905 in the aftermath of the devolution crisis sent a signal that the interests of defenders of the Union, north and south, might not always be in harmony.

The Home Rule crisis

For most of the decade following Parnell's death, Irish Members of Parliament at Westminster had offered the Irish Home-Rulers in Ireland a pitiful spectacle

5.16 No Home Rule: humorous propaganda against the Home Rule plot. National Museum of Ireland.

of ineptitude and mutual recrimination. Of course, given the vituperation that had accompanied the 'split' – allegations of theft, even murder were routine – the continued division between pro- and anti-Parnell Members could have been expected. What was scarcely believable – and what constituted the real scandal – was that the anti-Parnellite Members were themselves bitterly divided into two camps, those who looked to T. M. Healy's leadership and those who followed John Dillon. As a result Irish nationalists made little impact at Westminster during the 1890s. When a royal commission revealed that Ireland had indeed been overtaxed (a common nationalist complaint) for most of the nineteenth century, Irish Members, because of their suspicions of each other, were unable to make political capital out of this revelation. Nor were they able to forget their differences at the time of Gladstone's second Home Rule bill in 1893.

Eventually, however, even Irish Members seem to have realised the danger in pursuing their own vendettas to the near-exclusion of Irish matters. In 1898, William O'Brien, a long-standing anti-Parnellite, who had quitted national politics in disgust and moved to Mayo, was sufficiently disturbed by the plight of smallholders along the west coast of Ireland to set up a new organisation to do something about it. He also sought to reawaken a popular grassroots nationalism and to make irrelevant the main Irish issue of the time, the various post-Parnell rivalries. His United Irish League (its name was a homage to the rebels of 1798, whose centenary was about to be celebrated) had some success in assisting smaller tenants in their disputes with the large graziers or 'ranchers'. Embarrassingly, these latter very often turned out to be supporters of the Irish Parliamentary Party. In political terms, however, the United Irish League's significance lies in the fact that the spread of its branches brought Irish Members of Parliament to their senses and more or less forced them to come together under a single leader. In what looked like a replay of the 1882 junction between the Land League and Parnell's party, a suitably anaemic (or 'vampirised') United Irish League now became a sort of constituency organisation for the reunited party under the leadership of John Redmond. A furious and disillusioned O'Brien was forced out of the United Irish League in 1903.

The lacklustre performance and self-indulgent antics of Irish Members at Westminster following Parnell's death has frequently been adduced to explain an apparent disillusionment with politics during the same period. Certainly, Irish Members had made little, or no, intervention into the culture wars of the 1890s, nor had they much to say about the Ulster question, nor about labour unrest (only two Irish Members out of eighty-plus could plausibly be described as of working-class stock) nor, indeed, about the growing movement in favour of votes for women (apparently most Irish Members were opposed, but their silence makes it difficult to be certain). Again, their sheer ineffectiveness in the House of Commons, their unashamed embeddedness in the metro-clubland of London and their grubby pursuit of partisan advantage, lent weight to Arthur Griffith's denunciation of what he saw as the scourge of 'parliamentarianism'. By 1906 Irish Members at Westminster had acquired an 'image problem'. It was still dogging them in 1918.

And yet, despite all the odds, the Irish parliamentary party had survived – older, shabbier and grubbier, but recognisably similar to what it had been in its Parnellite heyday. And when in January 1906 the Liberals were returned to power with a huge majority, this represented good news. Surely the moment for Home Rule had finally arrived. Perhaps now the wilderness years would be forgotten and quietly forgiven by the Irish nationalist electorate? Admittedly, the Liberals had not highlighted their commitment to Home Rule in their general election manifesto, but it had remained one of their foundation policies. It was, according to Sir Henry Campbell-Bannerman, their new leader, nothing less than a 'sacred trust' owed to Gladstone. In short, notwithstanding all the trials since the fall, the Irish parliamentary party was in 1906 still unchallenged for the votes of nationalist Ireland and, by and large, the party would remain unchallengeable until 1914.

'Sacred trust' or not, the new Liberal government was in no hurry to bring in a Home Rule bill for Ireland. Instead, it appeared content to pursue a policy of what might be called 'constructive Liberalism' that could perhaps dent the Irish Parliamentary Party's own rather nervous enthusiasm for self-government. Accordingly, another attempt was made to introduce administrative devolution for Ireland: this time the proposal was that eight Irish departments would be controlled by a partly elected Irish council. This scheme was brought in by Augustine Birrell, the new chief secretary and, like the previous one introduced by Wyndham, it too failed, and for much the same reasons. Predictably, Unionists dismissed it as 'creeping Home Rule', while Irish nationalist Members rejected it on the grounds that it was intended as a substitute for Home Rule, rather than a step towards that goal.

Undaunted, Birrell pressed on with further concessions to Irish nationalist opinion. The British Old Age Pensions Act of 1908 applied to Ireland: a pension of five shillings a week was made available to those aged seventy or over. Proof that one had attained that venerable age could be provided by claiming to recall the 'Night of the Big Wind' of 1839, when something approaching a hurricane had swept Ireland. Remarkably, no fewer than 128 per cent of the anticipated age cohort claimed to have full memory of this event, a take-up rate for the pension which excited both indignation and amusement at Westminster. Also in 1908 two new universities were set up in Ireland: one in Belfast (Queen's University), and the other, the National University of Ireland, with constituent colleges in Dublin, Galway and Cork. At a stroke, the 'university question', the solution to which had defied some of the best brains in church and state in the nineteenth century, was resolved and removed from politics. No one appears to have noticed that setting up two universities, each organised on a different basis, directed at different religious communities, and located in different parts of the country, might presage some form of partition. A year later, Birrell put through an important Land Act which allowed landlords to be compulsorily bought out by the CDB. Such reforms as these were all well and good, but Irish opinion was becoming impatient: where was the Home Rule bill that the Liberals were pledged to introduce?

It is likely that such a measure would have been further postponed but for a major political upheaval in England. In 1909 David Lloyd George, the Liberal chancellor of the exchequer, had brought in the so-called 'People's Budget', which, while it did propose a tax on land, also raised taxes on both tobacco and liquor. In a fit of petulance – though madness might be more apt – the Conservative-dominated House of Lords, unprecedentedly, rejected this budget and Britain was plunged into a constitutional crisis. A general election was held on the issue in January 1910, the result of which was that the Liberals were returned with a much reduced majority over the Conservatives, and with a dependence on Irish nationalists for an overall majority. In the face of continuing constitutional impasse, a second general election was held in December 1910, and this duly confirmed the earlier result. The Liberals were once again returned to power, reliant on the votes of the Irish Parliamentary Party.

In August 1911 the Liberals succeeded in passing the Parliament Act which did away with the House of Lords' veto over Money bills and which limited its veto powers over other bills to two years only. In April 1912 as the reward for his Irish allies' support – or as the price demanded for it – Henry (his wife hated his given name, Herbert, and he stopped using it) Asquith, the prime minister, introduced a Home Rule bill for Ireland. Assuming that the House of Lords would throw out that measure in successive parliamentary sessions, under the terms of the Parliament Act, John Redmond and his parliamentary colleagues could look forward confidently to seeing Home Rule pass into law some time in 1914. Was the long gestation for Irish nationalism about to end in issue?

The first thing to note about the crisis provoked by the third Home Rule bill is that in almost every way it was radically different to the previous two. That of 1886 had been essentially confined to Westminster and its fall-out had been mostly limited to the political parties there: that of 1893 had been swiftly snuffed out by the House of Lords. But the Home Rule bill of 1912, in contrast to the earlier ones, had every prospect of passing into law. Of course, once Gladstone, the leader of a great political party, had pledged that party in 1886 to implement Home Rule for Ireland, it was probably inevitable that some such measure at some future time would be passed. One of the lessons of Irish history had been that British governments had generally got what they wanted, from Catholic Relief Acts in the 1790s, to the Union itself and to near-compulsory land purchase in Ireland. What was new in 1912 was the manner in which Home Rule would pass into law. The Parliament Act had been devised as a way of exacting revenge on the Lords for its action in blocking the 'People's Budget', but to use it to steamroller Irish Home Rule on to the statute book appeared improper or, in the eyes of some, even illegal. From the outset, therefore, opponents of the measure could defend their threats with reference to the allegedly unconstitutional way by which Home Rule was being driven into law.

From an early date Ulster Unionists had been alive to the threat posed by the Parliament Act. Even before Asquith had introduced a Home Rule bill, some

50,000 Orangemen and Unionists had warned in September 1911 against using the Parliament Act to force Home Rule through the House of Lords. Ominously, in January 1912 Orange Order leaders had sought licences from magistrates to conduct armed drilling in defence of the Constitution. Thus, when the Home Rule bill was introduced in April, resistance to its passing had already begun to mobilise, and given that its opponents had nearly a further three years to prepare against 'doomsday' – its coming into law – it was evident that the crisis provoked by the third Home Rule bill would be no ordinary one.

The leadership of the contending parties in 1912 was radically different from what it had been at the earlier crises. In 1886 Lord Randolph Churchill had cut an unlikely figure as a leader of Irish Conservative resistance to Home Rule: but Unionism in 1912 was led by the charismatic Edward Carson, a southern Unionist, admittedly, but one who was determined to use the opposition to Home Rule of 'the Protestant province of Ulster' to scupper the whole project. In this endeavour, he was supported by James Craig, a Boer War veteran and Ulster businessman who would work assiduously to ensure that the threat posed by Ulster's opposition to Home Rule was entirely genuine. He would also prepare the ground to convene a provisional government in Ulster, should that be necessary. Lastly, these men enjoyed – at least outwardly – the full confidence of the new Conservative leader, Andrew Bonar Law, Canadian-born of Ulster Presbyterian stock.

At a demonstration at Balmoral, on the outskirts of Belfast, two days before Asquith introduced his Home Rule bill, Bonar Law had announced that he could conceive of no lengths to which the Unionists might go in their opposition to that measure in which he and his party would not support them. Altogether less militant statements from O'Connell, Parnell and Dillon in previous years had led to their swift incarceration: but Bonar Law would face no such penalty, for restraint was no longer valued, at least on the Unionist side. Those in favour of Home Rule, however, still clung to moderation. In opposition to the formidable team of Carson, Craig and Bonar Law, the nationalist camp could only field H. H. Asquith and John Redmond. The first was the deeply unimpressive and indecisive prime minister, and the second had emerged as leader of the Irish Parliamentary Party in 1900 solely because he was the least unacceptable candidate for the position. He was also someone whose thirty-two years' membership at the Westminister 'club', to put it mildly, had ill prepared him for handling the crisis that now unfolded. The result was that as one set of leaders made ready for armed resistance, the other prepared for a debate: it was a one-sided contest.

Finally, the crisis precipitated by the introduction of the third Home Rule bill was different from earlier ones because Ireland had changed markedly in the intervening twenty or so years. Fresh voices – strident, assertive, dogmatic and impatient – were being heard with greater frequency and increasing volume. A new militancy, for example, was entering the women's campaign for the vote. The Irish Women's Suffrage Federation was set up in August 1911 and brought together into a national body a number of regional 'votes-for-women' organisations. Their protests and demonstrations sometimes turned violent: the luckless Asquith was ambushed by suffragettes (to distinguish them from their more moderate suffragist sisters) when he visited Dublin in July 1912. (A hatchet, or axe, was thrown at him and narrowly missed his head, but grazed Redmond; some suffragettes defended the action by claiming that it had been a small axe and not very sharp.) Opponents of women's suffrage also abandoned moderation: meetings held to protest at the continued denial of the vote were frequently broken up by thugs. In April 1914, Cumann na mBan, a women's counterpart to the Irish Volunteers, was formed. It was not, of course, a feminist movement, indeed it was avowedly quite the opposite, but its formation harked back to the Ladies Land League and rekindled militancy among women.

Elsewhere trade union activists found themselves in violent confrontation with employers. In August 1911 foundrymen in Wexford had been subjected to a lock-out when they sought to join Larkin's Irish Transport and General Workers' Union (ITGU). In July 1912 the by-now traditional expulsion of Catholics from the shipyard in Belfast (they tended to creep back outside the marching season) also witnessed a purge from the workforce of Protestant trade unionists, socialists and other undesirables. And in August 1913 some four hundred Dublin employers headed by the redoubtable William Martin Murphy, former nationalist Member of Parliament and owner of the *Irish Catholic* and *Irish Independent* newspapers, embarked on a full-scale lock-out in Dublin in order to crush the ITGU. The lock-out was marked by attacks carried out on the workers by the police and by members of the Ancient Order of Hibernians, a Catholic fraternal organisation modelled on the Orange Order, and enlisted on the side of the bosses. Employer-sponsored violence elicited a response from the workers in November 1913, when Connolly set up a Citizen Army, about two hundred strong, which had as its objective the protection of those denied work. This initiative came too late to affect the result of the lock-out. Had the workers been tenant farmers, the outcome might have been rather different: but in January 1914, after enduring sixteen months without pay, the starving strikers had little option but to accept the harsh conditions laid down by their employers for a return to work. The Citizen Army, however, was not stood down (figure 5.17).

Lastly, by 1912, a new generation of Irish nationalists was emerging that regarded the Irish Parliamentary Party with ill-disguised contempt. Some of its members were not so new. In 1907 the fifty-year old Thomas Clarke, a lifelong republican, had returned to Ireland after spending many years in prison for his

5.17 Incident during the Dublin lock-out of 1913. National Museum of Ireland.

role in bomb attacks in London. He was determined to revitalise or, if need be, reignite the Fenian flame which seemed all but extinguished. Clarke would be joined by others, more youthful than he, though no less committed to republican separatism; among their ranks, Bulmer Hobson, founder with Constance Markievicz of a Fenian youth movement, Patrick Pearse, poet and educationalist, and Sean MacDermott, journalist. What these doctrinaire republicans had in common was a profound suspicion of 'parliamentarianism', their term for futile and disgraceful toadying at Westminster. They also shared a corresponding yearning for war as an instrument of both personal liberation and national regeneration. In this bloody aspiration they had much in common with similarly alienated groups across Europe. What they were certain of was that the Irish Parliamentary Party had been given its last chance to deliver Home Rule, though whether even that achievement would have dented their admiration and enthusiasm for armed force must remain an open question.

The clamour, indeed the rage, of these various dissident groups, the menacing tone of their respective newspapers and the chilling adulation of bloodshed that infused some of their prayers, prose-writings and songs formed an essential backdrop to the fast-developing crisis over Ulster's opposition to Home Rule. By

1912, when the Home Rule crisis broke, political moderation, reasoned debate and polite disagreement were being denounced on all sides as shameful, spineless and worthless; public space in Ireland was being rapidly militarised. Nowhere was this bellicose note more stridently struck than in Ulster.

Militarisation

In September 1912 over 250,000 Unionists publicly signed a Solemn League and Covenant by which they pledged themselves before God never to accept Home Rule. Signing the Covenant was, however, merely a gesture, albeit an impressive one. Altogether more substantial was the formation of the Ulster Volunteer Force (UVF) in early 1913. This body soon numbered upwards of ninety thousand and represented a hugely visible military mobilisation of Protestant opinion. One precedent for such a formation might be found in the Volunteers of 1778 who had come together to defend Ireland against the French during the American War of Independence, and had then moved on swiftly to play a political role in the 1780s. Then again, a forerunner might be located in the Laggan army of the 1640s which had ably and bloodily defended the Protestants of Ulster during that time of crisis. In either case, the UVF was rooted in pre-Union Ulster history and in a settler folk memory of self-reliance and self-defence.

At a stroke the formation of the UVF altered decisively the current rules of political debate in Ireland: Unionists had adopted the Fenian dictum – if the force of argument did not work, then the argument of force must take its place. The UVF was initially poorly equipped (steps were soon afoot to remedy this) but it enjoyed the training skills of former British army officers, and with its dispatch riders, mobile field hospitals and women's auxiliaries it was in its organisation someways in advance of regular army units in Britain. Without guns the UVF could be blithely dismissed as a comic-opera army; but such a view was no longer tenable after the spectacular gun-running exploits of 24–5 April 1914. In a matter of hours some 25,000 rifles and 5 million rounds of ammunition, purchased in Germany, were successfully landed at Larne, Bangor and Donaghadee; overnight, the UVF became perhaps the best equipped force, apart from the British army, in the United Kingdom. True, not every UVF member could be issued with a rifle and a pouch of bullets, and there would always be problems with matching ammunition to weapons, and artillery was non-existent; but these deficiencies were more than compensated for by the force's motivation and its size. Not perhaps since the 1640s, when Oliver Cromwell's New Model Army had successfully blended religion and politics in principled aggression, had such a force emerged in Britain or Ireland. The UVF, in short, was absolutely formidable. It was also illegal, or at least its importation of arms was. Neither Craig nor Carson, nor indeed senior members of the Conservative Party, were unduly troubled by this. Far from it: not only did they condone gun-running, they positively celebrated it, for now the key weapon – the UVF – to scotch Home Rule for all of Ireland was in place. In the process, paramilitarism was given a boost, and parliamentarianism – however defined – was put to the test.

It could have been predicted that Redmond's and Asquith's reaction to the arming of Ulster Unionists would be hesitant and indecisive. By temperament and experience neither was cut out for crisis management. They seemed power-less to act effectively as Unionists relentlessly ratcheted up the tension. Even when British officers at the military camp at the Curragh, in what was an unprecedented intervention into politics, declared that they would rather resign their commis-sions than act against the UVF, Asquith dithered and no one was disciplined. If the British army was, in effect, saying that it would not be used to coerce Ulster into a Home Rule arrangement, then perhaps the rival Irish Volunteers (IV) might be used for this purpose?

This force had been set up in nationalist Ireland in November 1913 in response to the founding of the UVF. Within a short period of time it numbered 160,000. Its governing council was dominated by members of the Irish Parliamentary Party (though the party had initially opposed the force), and by members of the Irish Republican Brotherhood (IRB), now enjoying a resurgence and long skilled at inserting its men into nationalist organisations. From its inception, the IV lacked firearms but, again in emulation of the UVF, steps were soon afoot to import weapons. At this point the comparison with their northern counterparts ceased. The UVF had imported a very large cargo of modern weapons and ammunition under conditions of strict secrecy: the IV attempted a publicity stunt at Howth, a seaport north of Dublin, where they brought ashore a yachtful of out-of-date weapons in broad daylight. On their way back to Dublin, laden with their prizes, the Volunteers were intercepted at Batchelor's Walk, along the River Liffey in central Dublin, by a detachment of the King's Own Scottish Borderers, a regiment not then or subsequently renowned for its sympathy for Irish nationalists. In the confusion that ensued four people were shot dead (including a woman whose son was in the British army), and a number wounded. Not surprisingly, though somewhat unfairly, nationalist opinion drew the lesson that, while Unionists bent on defying the will of Parliament could import arms with impunity, those who acted in support of lawful government ran the risk of being shot. By July 1914, then, two rival military formations, the UVF and the IV, each with a radically different understanding of what was at stake, confronted each other in Ireland.

At this point, it might be apposite to inquire whether the third Home Rule bill, that had conjured up these rival military formations and brought Ireland to the brink of civil war was, in fact, that 'threatening and fearful spectacle' that presaged catastrophe for the Protestants of Ireland and especially those of Ulster. On the face of it, the answer must be no. Unlike the 1886 bill, that of 1912 contained a provision for the comforting and reassuring presence of forty-two Irish Members at Westminster. On the other hand, as in the 1893 Home Rule bill, the lord lieutenant was to head the new Irish executive, whose powers along with those of the assembly and senate were to be very limited. On one reading, then, the Home Rule Bill appeared to be the reverse of separatism in so far as it sought to strengthen the Union; on another, it might be argued that Home Rule, as envisaged in 1912, was little more than an attempt by the British government to create an agency that would see to the collection of land purchase payments. What was so terrible about either of these interpretations that necessitated the creation of an army to resist them? Once again the answer was that the very term 'Home Rule', irrespective of what it, in fact, offered in the matter of self-government, was deemed by the vast majority of Ulster Protestants to be quite simply an engine for their destruction that must be resisted at any price.

Further 'proof' of the malignity and magnitude of the threat had recently appeared in the successful campaign for compulsory Irish in schools, and especially in the promulgation in 1907 of the *Ne Temere* papal decree. This had directed that the children in a 'mixed marriage', i.e. a union between a Catholic and a Protestant, must be brought up as Catholics. Given that the number of such unions (in Ulster at any rate) was in fact very small, the reaction of Ulster Protestants was entirely disproportionate and may even have bordered on the deranged. None the less their outrage at this contentious decree elicited that rarity from Asquith – a concession. The Home Rule bill duly contained a clause addressing the issue of mixed marriages; predictably Unionist opposition to the bill was not assuaged by this figleaf of protection from a perceived universal Catholic conspiracy. In short, Ulster Protestants' fear of an apocalypse on a biblical scale should Home Rule be implemented explains the ferocity of their opposition to that measure.

And yet it had been evident since 1886 that Ireland would surely in time have some form of Home Rule. How could the historical inevitability – so to speak – of the onward march of the Irish nation be squared with the equally historical and irresistible determination of Unionists that Home Rule should not pass? From the 1880s on one answer that was suggested was that of partition. No one was enthusiastic about this solution. Southern Unionists' perennial fears that they would be abandoned by their northern colleagues and left to shift for themselves would be realised. The Conservatives under Bonar Law who had wanted to use Ulster to wreck the entire Home Rule project would have to admit defeat, and so too would Carson, for this had been his plan all along.

Irish nationalists naturally would be hostile to the idea of a divided Ireland and for Redmond and the Irish Parliamentary Party, given the volatile public mood outside Ulster, such a concession might prove their undoing in electoral terms. Even Ulster Unionists were cool on the idea, for it brought into the light their guilty secret: there was no such thing as the 'Protestant province of Ulster'. Their dilemma was an acute one. If nine-county Ulster were excluded from Home Rule, the arrangement might be short lived, for the province was evenly balanced between Protestant and Catholic. Against that, if only the six north-east counties where Protestants overall had a large majority were proposed for exclusion, then that meant abandoning their fellow Protestants (and Ulster Covenant signers) in counties Monaghan, Donegal and Cavan (where presumably they would be swiftly overwhelmed by Gaelic speakers brandishing *Ne Temere* decrees).

By 1913, however, it seems clear that some idea of exclusion for parts of Ulster had been accepted reluctantly by both Carson and Redmond, and only the details (essentially, perpetual or temporary division, and involving four, six or nine counties) remained to be addressed. In 1914 there really was no alternative: the British army was not about to coerce the Protestants of Ulster; the IV were incapable of doing so; and, crucially, the UVF was not bluffing. The gun-running on the part of the UVF in April 1914 had effectively decided the matter. Partition would not last a few years or, as Carson put it, there could be no 'stay of execution' followed by unification. Instead, partition would be permanent, and the area hived off would encompass the six counties of Antrim, Down, Armagh, Fermanagh, Tyrone and Londonderry where Protestants were in a majority of three to two over Catholics. As a result, southern Unionists and Ulster outliers would have to fend for themselves. Pragmatism, realism and ruthlessness had triumphed: 'Ulster' Unionists would defend what they could and, if that meant defying Parliament, tearing up the Covenant, abandoning their brethren in Donegal, Cavan and Monaghan, and betraying their southern Unionist leader, Sir Edward Carson, and his people then so be it. This is not to downplay the anxiety these issues caused after 1916.

While the map of a soon-to-be-partitioned Ireland was taking mental shape in the early months of 1914, events elsewhere in continental Europe were conspiring to drive both Ulster and the Irish question off the front page of the newspapers. In June 1914 Archduke Franz Ferdinand, heir to the Habsburg throne, was assassinated in Sarajevo by a Slav nationalist, and this set in train a series of French, German, Russian and British military mobilisations that, in August, saw Britain and France at war with Germany. In the meantime, the Irish Home Rule bill had been proceeding bumpily on its way to the statute books. It duly passed into law in September 1914, but with an amending Act suspending its operation until 'not later than' the end of the continental war, and with a separate commitment that 'Ulster', not yet defined, would not be encompassed within its

5.18 John Redmond addressing a pro-war rally in Dublin, *c.* 1914. Irish Photographic Archive.

reach. For Redmond and the Irish Parliamentary Party, the passing of the Home Rule Act was undoubtedly a victory and they sought to capitalise on it. Redmond initially offered the IV and, bizarrely, the UVF as defenders of Ireland during the war; but then on 20 September at Woodenbridge, county Wicklow, in a fateful speech that parroted the offer of Carson in respect of the UVF, he further pledged the IV to serve 'wherever the firing line extended'.

Redmond, like most obervers, was convinced that the war between Britain and Germany would be a short, sharp affair on the model of the Franco-Prussian war of 1870. He was determined that in the ensuing and, as he saw it, inevitable victory parade along Sackville Street, probably around Christmas 1914, the Irish Army (formerly the IV) would be appropriately honoured for its part in the defeat of Germany. Home Rule would then be conceded and Ireland, or twenty-six (hopefully, twenty-eight) counties of it, would take its place along with Canada, Australia and South Africa, as a (lesser) self-governing white entity within the Empire. England's difficulty, in Redmond's eyes, was Ireland's opportunity to demonstrate its loyalty to king and Empire (figure 5.18).

Redmond's offer of the IV was in essence a gamble. Where the British army was concerned, there had been unmistakable signs over the previous twenty years that public opinion in Ireland was, at best, lukewarm about Irish enlistment into its ranks, at worst, verging on the downright hostile. Equally, admiration for the British Empire had been fading quickly over the same period. Redmond's strategy was particularly risky, for one of the few lessons to be learned from Irish history was that the outcome of Irish wars, i.e. wars involving Ireland, was quite unpredictable. Still, there was a chance that Redmond might pluck triumph out of the nettled danger that opened before him in September 1914. Everything would depend on a short war and a victorious conclusion. Already, however, two weeks before he had spoken at Woodenbridge, pledging the lives of the IV as a token of his commitment to the British war effort, a small group of equally committed republicans and socialists had met in Dublin, and had determined that the war must not pass without an Irish insurrection. 'England's difficulty is Ireland's opportunity' was a lesson that they, too, had learned from Irish history, though not in the same sense as Redmond.

6 THE MAKING OF THE TWO IRELANDS, 1914–45

Introduction

War in its various guises shaped and defined the Irish experience during this period. Most obviously, the world wars book-ending these years had a major impact on the two Irelands. During the First World War what would emerge in the early 1920s as the separate entities of Northern Ireland and the Irish Free State (though the outline of some such arrangement could be discerned in 1914) would make similar contributions to the British war effort and would endure similar losses. However, the memory of sacrifice would be wholly different in the two states. Again, the Second World War affected both parts of the island. Because of its constitutional connection with Britain, Northern Ireland was committed on the Allied side and thus was to be directly affected in terms of air-raids, wartime industrial expansion and the presence of hundreds of thousands of Allied troops. Sharing wartime adversity – though not conscription – and enjoying the thrill of eventual triumph, brought a growing solidarity with 'mainland' Britain that did much to strengthen the Union and copperfasten partition. With regard to Ireland (or Éire in the Irish language) – as the Irish Free State was described after the new Constitution of 1937 – it might be claimed that because it remained resolutely neutral in the Second World War it must therefore have largely escaped the effects of that conflict. But this is true only if the direct effects of war – massive air-raids, strict rationing, heavy casualties or actual invasion – are taken into account. In fact Ireland was greatly influenced by the war but in ways that were subtle and opaque, although no less profound for that.

There were other 'wars' too. The Easter Rising of 1916, a planned national uprising that in the event was confined largely to the centre of Dublin, pitted Irish insurgents against British soldiers, many of whom were themselves Irish. Over four hundred rebels, soldiers and bystanders died during a week's fighting. The Rising's immediate impact was twofold: it struck down Home Rule, for the rebels had proclaimed a republic and – an unintended consequence – it confirmed the partition of Ireland, with only the details remaining to be ironed out. It may also have made a further passage of arms inevitable, for the newly stated objective of a republic, and thus the separation of Ireland or the larger part thereof from British sovereignty, remained quite unthinkable to any British government of the time. Ostensibly, the Irish War of Independence – or 'Tan war', so described after the Irish Republican Army's most noted opponents – fought between 1919 and 1921, was an early Irish example of what was to become commonplace in the twentieth century – a war of national liberation. But there was more than a whiff of sectarian civil war about it: southern Irish Protestants found themselves disproportionately represented among the casualties, and so too did the socially marginalised, for there was more than a hint of class war about it as well. In Northern Ireland – the new six-county state finally hived off from the remainder of the island in 1921 as part of a solution to the Irish question – the armed conflict that accompanied its birth was much more openly sectarian, with the hundreds killed being routinely classified by their confessional allegiance. The murderous disturbances in Northern Ireland in the early 1920s left a legacy of bitterness and set a tone in public life that was to persist for many decades.

And so, too, did the outbreak of hostilities in June 1922 between those who accepted the terms of the recently concluded Anglo-Irish Treaty, which offered those in arms more than Home Rule, and those who flatly rejected the Treaty on the grounds that its terms fell far short of a republic. The Irish civil war between pro- and anti-Treaty forces was not at all as destructive as the near-contemporary Finnish civil war, or the later Spanish Civil War, and its scale is perhaps better captured by its Irish name, *Cogadh na gCarad*, or the war of the comrades. Still, it was vicious enough, and before it was over in April 1923, perhaps a thousand had been killed on both sides (compare this figure with about thirty thousand dead in Finland with a similar population) and there had been numerous atrocities, official reprisals and much destruction of public buildings and private property. Stances and positions taken up in the Irish civil war were to shape politics in the south of Ireland over subsequent decades, and waving the 'bloody shirt' would be for long a key electoral tactic.

Two world wars, at least one civil war and a war for independence, along with low-intensity confessional conflict, attempted ethnic and social cleansing, and post-conflict score-settling indelibly marked the Irish experience: the shadow of the gunman was never far from the two Irelands during the years 1914 to 1945. But surprisingly, military rule, north or south, though threatened at certain times, was not to be Ireland's fate, and in the end it was the politicians who triumphed over the soldiers. The reasons for this unlikely and, in the context of other states set up in Europe at the end of the First World War, exceptional, outcome may be debated – embedded, even genetic Irish acceptance of English democratic norms has been often cited as a cause – but another explanation might focus on the absence from the Irish stage of two types of conflict that might easily have led to martial law, military government and the rule of the generals. First, Ireland was not subjected to an invasion during these years, and while Britain and Germany might have contemplated such a course of action in 1940–1, in the event both drew back, with benign consequences for the survival of democratic government in both the fledgeling Irish states. Second, the full-scale Irish war that threatened, and had even seemed inevitable in the autumn of 1914, and that might have been touched off again in 1922 – the war between loyalist and Protestant Ulster and nationalist and Catholic Ireland – failed to materialise, minor engagements apart, and this was crucial to the grudging acceptance, north and south, of the primacy of civilian rule. Few other small countries in Europe were to be spared invasion in the first fifty years of the twentieth century, and some were to endure catastrophic civil war as well.

That said, neither northern or southern Ireland could lay claim to being an unalloyed success story in the first fifty years of the twentieth century. In the latter case, a bloodless 'economic war' with Britain in the 1930s probably caused disruption to the southern Irish economy, and also damaged that of Northern Ireland. Indeed, it might well be argued that less fortunate countries that had endured invasion, experienced civil war and suffered enemy occupation appear to have performed rather better in terms of economic growth and social welfare than either of the two Irelands.

The Easter Rising

The Great War is the essential context within which to assess the Easter Rising of 1916 and the confused public response both to the Rising and its suppression (mingled pride, outrage and sorrow)[1]. The outbreak of war in August 1914 was greeted by many in Britain as an intoxicating release from the pressures of everyday life, a welcome opportunity to test one's manhood in the fire of war and as a most timely distraction from the seemingly permanent crisis engendered by the Irish question. War fever was widespread in Britain and so too was hatred of the 'Hun'. By contrast, in Ireland reaction to news of hostilities was rather more muted, and there was little jingoism. Notwithstanding, the war was and remained generally popular (figure 6.1) and 'pro-German' sentiment was almost non-existent, a contrast to the 'pro-Boer' views trenchantly voiced in 1899. Tellingly, tens of thousands of Irishmen, north and south, swiftly answered the calls of Carson and Redmond and marched off to war. Of the 50,000 Irish who

6.1 Recruitment posters to encourage Irish enlistment, 1914–15. National Library of Ireland.

enlisted in the first six months, some 30,000 were members of the UVF who entered *en bloc* to form the 36th (Ulster) Division. They were permitted, indeed encouraged, to preserve their pre-war identity and were allowed to retain their own officers and colours. The remainder of the first wave of recruits were mostly Irish National Volunteers, so called to distinguish them from the 12,000 or so

6.1 (*cont.*)

IVs who rejected Redmond's plea. There was, however, to be no such 'national' gesture extended to them as had been allowed to the UVF, for Lord Kitchener, the recently appointed recruitment supremo, would have none of it. Kitchener, like the duke of Wellington, may have been Irish born, but neither liked to be reminded of it and neither had time for Irish nationalism. The last thing Kitchener wanted to see was anything that looked like an Irish army; Wellington would have concurred.

6.2 Irish soldiers at the front during the Great War. National Museum of Ireland.

The apparent contrast in treatment between the UVF men and those of the Irish National Volunteers was much commented on at the time and Redmond and his lieutenant, John Dillon, were scathing in their criticism. However, Kitchener's churlishness, in the event, made little difference to Irish recruitment which, after the initial surge, fell off in mid-1915, in this mirroring the response in England and Scotland. In all around 200,000 men from Ireland would see service in the British armed forces from 1914 to 1918 (about 30,000 died) and while this figure certainly did not satisfy the War Office, which regarded the Irish as incorrigible slackers and persisted throughout the war in drawing up plans for Irish conscription, it was in fact quite a respectable one. Indeed, given that the age structure of the Irish male population was somewhat distorted through decades of emigration, and given that the rural basis of much of Irish society outside the east coast meant that enlistment would always be sluggish – for it was the towns and cities rather than the countryside that were the prime recruiting areas everywhere in Britain and Ireland – the final figure might be judged a very respectable one indeed.

The war was, initially, a popular cause in Ireland (figure 6.2) and while a certain cooling in enthusiasm can be detected from 1915 on, by and large it remained so to the end. After all, the war boosted the Irish economy, and Irish farmers and their sons saw agricultural prices rise sharply due to wartime demand. Similarly, there was a fall in unemployment, though wages remained low. And for those who took the king's shilling, there was – no small consideration – the 'separation money' paid to their next of kin, usually wives or mothers. However, it would be wrong to labour the point of 'economic conscription' or to view military service, in the absence of emigration (paused for the duration of the war), merely as a kind of assisted passage abroad. Many enlisted for reasons of patriotism, duty and obligation, having concluded that German aggression was a threat to free societies and that, therefore, an Allied victory was in Ireland's interest. What is striking is not the large numbers who joined up in the early days, but the, admittedly rather smaller, numbers who continued to volunteer for military service long after the lengthy casualty lists and the ghastly realities of trench warfare had revealed that such an undertaking was exceptionally hazardous.

But while the need to prosecute the war itself may have been accepted in Ireland, and the enlistment figures certainly suggest this, any thought of replacing voluntary service with forced conscription was completely ruled out. When, in April 1918, such a plan was announced, it convulsed Ireland and had the war not soon ended its implementation might have sparked another insurrection. Even so, despite the conscription crisis, nearly ten thousand Irishmen enlisted voluntarily in the last three months of the war.

For members of the IRB, such as Patrick Pearse, Tom Clarke, Joseph Plunkett and Thomas MacDonagh, all of whom occupied key positions in the IV, the outbreak of war offered a perfect – indeed probably the only – opportunity in their lifetime for an insurrection. They excoriated the previous hundred years of – more or less – international peace as a period of frustration, shame and disgrace, as a time during which, in Pearse's view, 'Ireland has not known the exhilaration of war'. By contrast, the first year of hostilities had been 'the most glorious in the history of Europe'. Fortunately for these IRB conspirators, the conflict had defied the predictions of a large majority of military or civilian commentators by failing to be over in a short time. Had the war ended at Christmas 1914, or even in 1915, as many had forecast, there would probably have been no rising, for while Pearse and his colleagues would display a gift for conspiracy, they would show little talent for military planning. And yet the fact that the planned rising would take place during a war, one in which things were generally going badly for Britain and its allies, and one in which horrendous casualties were commonplace on the Western Front and elsewhere, could only mean that stern military repression had to be expected. Were the conspirators aware of any or all of this?

Such a crushing response was made all the more certain when, following the outbreak of war in August 1914, there had begun what had amounted to a speedy militarisation of Asquith's government – the appointment of Field Marshal Lord

Kitchener was an early sign of this process. In May 1915 a coalition Cabinet that included selected Conservatives and Unionists, was formed, and Sir Edward Carson was made attorney general. By 1916 the generals and their Conservative allies were firmly in the driving seat, and Asquith, though still prime minister, was little more than a figurehead; nationalist disturbances in Ireland, should they occur would not be viewed indulgently.

Was serious trouble in Ireland likely? From an early date Dublin Castle and British naval intelligence were aware of a plot, largely orchestrated by Roger Casement, a former British Foreign Office consul, but now an ardent pro-German Irish nationalist, and by John Devoy, the American-based 'Fenian Chief', to seek German military assistance. Casement's efforts in this quest came to nothing and, in the absence of a significant German threat, it was easy for the Castle to dismiss the rumour of a rising as either exaggerated and/or unfounded. Augustine Birrell, the chief secretary, in retrospect looking and sounding more and more like William Wickham, his counterpart at the time of Emmet's rising in 1803, believed that any move against the advanced nationalist IV, now being dubbed the Sinn Féin Volunteers, might, in fact, spark off the very disturbances that the government was keen to avoid. And of course, the tens of thousands of Irish serving at the front, the clear evidence of the popularity of the war among farmers and 'separation' women, and the warm support given to recruitment by Redmond and his colleagues in the Irish Parliamentary Party – even the moderate enlistment figures – surely meant that it would be madness to stage a rebellion that must mean flying in the face of Irish public opinion by attacking the British army, an army that had very many Irishmen in it.

None of these apparently unfavourable circumstances unduly troubled any of the conspirators self-tasked with organising an insurrection in wartime Ireland. Such inconvenient facts counted for nothing when set alongside the divine mandate for armed action entrusted to the current generation of would-be revolutionaries by their deceased predecessors. The only anxious thought that might have crossed their minds was that they might be too late, and that Ireland might have been irretrievably denationalised. The 'frozen' Home Rule Act, with its paltry measure of self-government, along with Irish participation in a war fought on behalf of the 'Robber Empire' (Connolly) and, especially, Redmond's continued leadership of nationalist Ireland and his cheer-leadership of the recruitment drive, were all seen as shocking evidence of a craven loss of nationality and viewed as standing affronts to separatists. Along with the English connection, these disgraceful stains on Irish national honour could only be washed away by bloodshed.

The IRB was a secret organisation, which, after the Volunteer split in the autumn of 1914, had retained almost entire control of the break-away IV, who had repudiated the leadership of Redmond. Eoin MacNeill, a professor of early Irish history at University College Dublin, was the ostensible commander of this small force, but he was not a member of the IRB and he was strong-minded enough not to be its stooge. His view was that the Volunteers could only be called into action in a crisis – say, an attempt at mass arrests, or a move to disarm them, or even the introduction of conscription – but this was not the view of Pearse, Tom Clarke and their fellow plotters. In December 1915 a military council within the IRB was set up, and this secret group within a secret organisation decided on a rising at Easter 1916. Along with military planning, there went a massive effort at deception. James Connolly, the leader of the socialist Citizen Army, was brought into the secret in January 1916 for fear that he might unilaterally and prematurely strike for a workers' republic, but all others were kept in the dark. In a sense the Easter Rising would see the first staging of a 'Guns 'n Roses' concert.

Few members of the IRB supreme council were in on the planned rising, MacNeill was repeatedly lied to as Pearse regularly pooh-poohed the idea of a rising, and ordinary Volunteers themselves had little idea of what was going on. In any case Volunteers were frequently out drilling at weekends and on holy days so that the authorities would see nothing amiss when the real turn-out was authorised for Easter Sunday, 23 April 1916. One particularly impressive exercise had been held on St Patrick's day 1916 and saw the successful deployment of 1,400 Volunteers in Dublin, and some 4,500 elsewhere. In effect, the Volunteers had seized and, for a time, had held control of key points in the country; had this been a dry run for the real thing at Easter?

The Rising was planned to coincide with, and was contingent upon, the arrival of a cargo of German rifles and ammunition but when the ship carrying these had to be scuttled near Cork on 20 April to avoid capture, it looked as if the game was up. The capture of Casement, fresh from a German submarine, on Banna Strand, county Kerry, near where the guns were to have been landed, was a further setback. At the St Patrick's day mobilisation earlier that year the authorities had complacently noted that fewer than half of the Volunteers had been armed and now, with no expectation of German military assistance, the would-be insurgents would lack all kinds of modern weaponry and munitions. Not surprisingly, British naval intelligence, having broken the German codes (though it would never dream of informing Dublin Castle that it had done so, or of passing on the intelligence gained) concluded that the danger had passed. And as if to confirm this conclusion, MacNeill, learning that he had been duped all along as to the intentions of Pearse and his associates, issued an order countermanding a nationwide mobilisation of the Volunteers to be held on Easter Sunday, 23 April. The 'Guns 'n Roses' concert planned for Sackville Street, it seemed, was off.

In the event, undaunted by this series of setbacks or by the confusion engendered by conflicting commands, the leaders of the conspiracy assembled at Liberty Hall, the Transport Union headquarters in Dublin city centre, and unanimously resolved to press ahead with their plans. They would lead their men (and some women) on Easter Monday to seize and hold a number of public buildings in Dublin, and elsewhere, and they would proclaim an Irish republic. But now they could have no hope of success. What was going on?

The rebel leaders – a mixture of poets, playwrights, socialists, educationalists, mystics and professional revolutionaries (with some a blend of all of these) – were clear on only one thing: come what may, they had to have a rising before the war ended. To have failed to do so would have been the ultimate disgrace, a grotesque and unforgivable betrayal of preceding generations, who had not enjoyed so favourable a moment since the French revolutionary wars. However, that did not mean that their entire project was little more than self-indulgent heroics, conducted at the expense of the ordinary people of Dublin who would inevitably have to bear the cost of their actions. Their plan to acquire German arms and, in the manner of Humbert in 1798, even foreign military assistance, was not entirely far-fetched, and the possibility that their protest in arms in Dublin might be accompanied by a German breakthrough on the Western Front should not be entirely ruled out. Had the *Aud* got through with its cargo of German arms, had MacNeill not countermanded the mobilisation scheduled for Sunday 23 April, had the Rising gone off as planned and had 'our gallant allies', as the Easter Proclamation described the Germans, done their bit in France, then perhaps all might have been changed utterly.

It was not to be; and by midday on Easter Sunday, it was clear that it was not going to be; so why proceed on Easter Monday with what could only be a fragmented rising? Why embark on a course of action that must result in a serious loss of life, and certainly in failure? It was not as if Ireland at Easter 1916 was groaning under an intolerable tyranny. In fact, as noted, the war had brought measurable benefits to the Irish economy, there was as yet no conscription and wartime restrictions on free speech were irksome rather than oppressive. Even the Volunteers had been allowed to parade, drill and conduct their manoeuvres during the preceding years, and surely this was proof that a liberal (and probably unwise) indulgence had been extended to them. Why then stage a rising that within a twenty-four hour period, 23–4 April 1916, had moved from being a just-about-possible enterprise to being an entirely forlorn hope?

Pride cannot be ruled out: to have spent well over a year – even, in one or two cases, a lifetime – in planning and preparation, and dreaming – and then to have meekly folded tents, and stolen away at the first major setback, would have confirmed all the worst English stereotypes of Irish rebels – 1803 and 1867 *redivivus*. Hence, there could be no turning back: even after the news of the failure of German weapons to arrive was received, there was a determination to make a protest in arms, to mount an insurrection that would redeem past failure, atone for present complicity in an imperial war and summon future generations to the cause. Even so, it is improbable that what became known as a blood sacrifice lay behind the rising. If that had been the object why wait for arms from Germany? And why surrender after six days rather than, like the Jews at Masada, fight to the last man?

Perhaps some of Pearse's more blood-curdling utterances, along with his fusion of pagan belief and Christian doctrine about dying in order to redeem the world, or at least Ireland, could lend themselves to that interpretation? And, of course, the choice of Easter, with its central Christian message of death and resurrection, adds to this theory. However, Pearse's views were not those of the entire leadership and others – such as Connolly and probably MacDermott – may have expected the rising to ignite a nationwide insurrection. And Easter seems to have been chosen in order to coincide with an anticipated German offensive on the Western Front rather than for its religious significance.

And yet doubts linger. Despite a planning process that had gone on for nearly a year, the Volunteers who turned out on Easter Monday were poorly equipped with food and water, no supply system seems to have been set up and the places selected for seizure had more visual or dramatic importance than military value. A number of them were actually overlooked by taller buildings: for example, St Stephen's Green was occupied and trenches dug, but then was quickly and prudently abandoned for this very reason. For a rising that sought to emulate that of Robert Emmet, it is surprising that Dublin Castle was not made the focus of attention. Almost certainly the rebels could have taken it, but poor intelligence about the numbers defending this powerful symbol of British rule appears to have led the attackers – men from the Citizen Army – to back off. It seems that few, if any, of the buildings to be seized had been properly reconnoitred by the Volunteers beforehand. Among the entire rebel military command, only the comparatively junior Eamon de Valera appreciated the importance of reconnaissance.

Again, it was all very well to capture Boland's mill, Jacob's biscuit factory (where the Volunteers quickly tired of rations of chocolate cake), the South Dublin Union and, famously, the General Post Office, outside which Pearse read the Proclamation of the Irish Republic to a bemused audience of passersby; but little thought seems to have been given to lines of communication between these sites. And of course, the confusion sparked by MacNeill's order countermanding the nationwide Volunteer mobilisation for Easter Sunday meant inevitably that any turn-out on Easter Monday would be almost entirely confined to Dublin itself, and to those places within range of the ubiquitous Lucania bicycle, the essential transport of the revolutionaries. In short, months of planning appear to have produced possibly the most chaotic insurrection in Irish history. Even the printing of the Proclamation of the Irish Republic – the key document of the Rising – had not gone to plan. Production had begun around noon on Easter Sunday, but because there was not enough type available the top and bottom had to be set separately, and the work was not completed until early on Easter Monday morning. Astonishingly, had the rising gone ahead as planned on Easter Sunday, there would have been no proclamation to accompany it and to explain the rebels' purpose.

The wording of the Proclamation (figure 6.3) is usually attributed to Pearse, with some assistance from Connolly, and it firmly situated the rebels of 1916 within an alleged three-hundred-year-old tradition of asserting national sovereignty. It acknowledged that the IRB was behind the Rising, and it made explicit reference to support from a key element of the Irish diaspora – Ireland's 'exiled children in America' – and a more guarded one to the Germans. The Irish Republic 'as a Sovereign Independent State' was duly proclaimed, and a provisional government was declared. Perhaps surprisingly, there was no overt mention in the Proclamation of Ulster Unionists, whose mobilisation in arms had brought Ireland to the brink of civil war two years earlier. However, a reference to ignoring differences 'carefully fostered by an alien government', while 'cherishing all the children of the nation equally', the latter phrase usually taken as a socialist commitment inserted by Connolly, was probably a reference to Irish Unionists, whose resistance to any form of Irish self-government tended in advanced nationalist circles to be dismissed as a ploy devised by a 'foreign government' (i.e. Britain) to prevent Ireland's march to freedom.

In all, around 1,500 Volunteers, along with a few hundred members of the Irish Citizen Army, took part in the Rising. About one hundred women, mostly members of Cumann na mBan, also served in a support role – as doctors, as nurses (on Pearse's orders Nurse Elizabeth O'Farrell would later begin the process of surrender at the General Post Office), as messengers (Mollie Adrian was particularly resourceful in delivering Pearse's orders) and as secretaries. Connolly, famously, was accompanied everywhere by his secretary, Winifred Carney, armed with her typewriter, and when he was unable to carry on because of the severity of his wounds Dr Kathleen Lynn took command of his men. Constance Markievicz of the Citizen Army was also prominent, being second-in-command to Michael Mallin at Stephen's Green, though often acting as if she were the leader. In general, women were kept out of combat; alone of all the military commanders of the Easter Rising, only Eamon de Valera, in charge at Boland's mill, refused to have any about the place in any role whatsoever. (Possibly a pointer to his views about the proper place of women, later enshrined in the 1937 Constitution.)

POBLACHT NA H EIREANN.

THE PROVISIONAL GOVERNMENT OF THE IRISH REPUBLIC TO THE PEOPLE OF IRELAND.

IRISHMEN AND IRISHWOMEN: In the name of God and of the dead generations from which she receives her old tradition of nationhood, Ireland, through us, summons her children to her flag and strikes for her freedom.

Having organised and trained her manhood through her secret revolutionary organisation, the Irish Republican Brotherhood, and through her open military organisations, the Irish Volunteers and the Irish Citizen Army, having patiently perfected her discipline, having resolutely waited for the right moment to reveal itself, she now seizes that moment, and, supported by her exiled children in America and by gallant allies in Europe, but relying in the first on her own strength, she strikes in full confidence of victory.

We declare the right of the people of Ireland to the ownership of Ireland, and to the unfettered control of Irish destinies, to be sovereign and indefeasible. The long usurpation of that right by a foreign people and government has not extinguished the right, nor can it ever be extinguished except by the destruction of the Irish people. In every generation the Irish people have asserted their right to national freedom and sovereignty; six times during the past three hundred years they have asserted it in arms. Standing on that fundamental right and again asserting it in arms in the face of the world, we hereby proclaim the Irish Republic as a Sovereign Independent State, and we pledge our lives and the lives of our comrades-in-arms to the cause of its freedom, of its welfare, and of its exaltation among the nations.

The Irish Republic is entitled to, and hereby claims, the allegiance of every Irishman and Irishwoman. The Republic guarantees religious and civil liberty, equal rights and equal opportunities to all its citizens, and declares its resolve to pursue the happiness and prosperity of the whole nation and of all its parts, cherishing all the children of the nation equally, and oblivious of the differences carefully fostered by an alien government, which have divided a minority from the majority in the past.

Until our arms have brought the opportune moment for the establishment of a permanent National Government, representative of the whole people of Ireland and elected by the suffrages of all her men and women, the Provisional Government, hereby constituted, will administer the civil and military affairs of the Republic in trust for the people.

We place the cause of the Irish Republic under the protection of the Most High God, Whose blessing we invoke upon our arms, and we pray that no one who serves that cause will dishonour it by cowardice, inhumanity, or rapine. In this supreme hour the Irish nation must, by its valour and discipline and by the readiness of its children to sacrifice themselves for the common good, prove itself worthy of the august destiny to which it is called.

Signed on Behalf of the Provisional Government,

THOMAS J. CLARKE,

SEAN Mac DIARMADA. THOMAS MacDONAGH,

P. H. PEARSE. EAMONN CEANNT,

JAMES CONNOLLY. JOSEPH PLUNKETT.

6.3 Easter Proclamation, 1916. National Museum of Ireland.

6.4 Eamon de Valera under arrest, 1916. National Museum of Ireland.

The military response to the takeover of large areas of central Dublin was sluggish but by Tuesday morning reinforcements had been rushed to the city and martial law had been declared (figure 6.4). The failure of the Rising to take on a national dimension was reassuring for army commanders. Admittedly, one of the deadlier encounters that week had taken place at Ashbourne, county Meath, some miles from Dublin, in which the local Volunteers, under the command of Thomas Ashe, had successfully ambushed a contingent of Royal Irish Constabulary, and inflicted serious casualties. But attempts to mobilise Volunteers in Galway, Tipperary and Cork had little success. Given that there was only a small garrison in the Dublin area, for there was no official perception of a real threat, the actual repression of the Rising was greatly assisted by the presence in Dublin of Irish soldiers on leave from the Flanders killing-fields or on recruiting duty. These were quickly drafted into the battle for Dublin, and vicious street-fighting ensued for the next three to four days. When Pearse surrendered on 29 April around 450 had been killed, of whom 64 were rebels, 132 were soldiers, and the remainder were civilians; some three thousand were injured, mostly civilians. Artillery had been deployed to murderous effect; and contrary to Connolly's alleged claim that the army of the capitalists would never be ordered to destroy the capitalists' property, O'Connell Street and other areas were mercilessly shelled and reduced to ruins (figure 6.5). Over three hundred buildings were damaged, Liberty Hall was completely destroyed and the insurance bill for the week's destruction would run to over £3 million.

Inevitably, there were military excesses, most of which involved non-combatants. At Portobello barracks, J. C. Bowen Colthurst, an apparently deranged officer in the Royal Irish Rifles, summarily executed two journalists, along with Francis Sheehy-Skeffington, husband of Hannah, and like his wife a prominent supporter of women's rights, and also a vegetarian, pacifist, non-smoker, non-drinker and well-known Dublin 'character' who had been out and about trying to prevent looting. (It is not known which, if any, of these attributes or activities had ignited Bowen Colthurst's ire.) Elsewhere in Dublin soldiers of the South Staffordshire regiment appear to have shot out of hand thirteen prisoners in North King Street. In circumstances of close quarter combat amid a civilian population (and it is salient that neither rebels nor soldiers had any prior experience of this type of war), it is perhaps surprising that there were so few 'regrettable incidents', as the new commander-in-chief, General Sir John Maxwell, awkwardly styled these shootings. By way of grisly comparison we might note that the rebels' 'gallant allies in Europe' had shot hundreds of innocent civilians in their capture of Louvain and other towns in Belgium in 1914. They had also deliberately dynamited the world-famous university library of Louvain.[2] This latter act of vandalism attracted some notice in the public prints, and might be seen as a possible precedent for the destruction of the Public Record Office of Ireland in 1922 by anti-Treaty forces.

Initial reactions to the Rising were mixed, appear to have been rather class-specific and changed markedly over the week. They ran the gamut from bafflement, to indifference, to outrage at the destruction, to admiration of the rebels' heroism and then on to further outrage at the manner of its suppression. Redmond and his colleagues in the Irish Parliamentary Party were angry at the damage done to the Home Rule cause and, more self-interestedly, concerned at the damage done to them. Generally, the Dublin propertied classes were outraged at what appeared to be the wanton destruction of much of central Dublin. Anger at the damage to property – and specifically to his own Imperial Hotel on O'Connell Street, occupied by men from the Citizen Army – may have led William Martin Murphy to call for the head of James Connolly. Murphy clearly saw the Rising as a re-run of the Dublin lock-out of 1913 (and possibly

6.5 Aftermath: the area around the General Post Office after the Easter Rising. Royal Irish Academy.

6.5 (cont.)

Connolly did too). Less elevated witnesses also made their displeasure clear. The 'separation women', furious at the betrayal of their menfolk serving in France and elsewhere, were prominent among those who barracked and levelled abuse at the rebels. However, as the fighting continued initial outrage was succeeded by a kind of grudging respect for the courage of the rebels. Their 'superb bravery and skill' was noted by, among others, John Dillon, in Dublin on leave from Westminster, and thus well placed to sense a change of mood among the popu- lace. And, in its turn, this qualified admiration was replaced by further outrage, but this time at the British military authorities for their cover-up of the killing of Sheehy-Skeffington and the others and for their execution of the rebel leaders.

Scores of rebels were tried by court-martial and sentenced to death. In all fifteen were shot over a period of two weeks, including all the signatories to the Proclamation; only de Valera among the senior military commanders had his sentence commuted, not because of his American birth, as sometimes claimed, but because by the time he was tried the politicians had finally managed to wrest the initiative back from a military command bent on swift retribution. But the damage had been done: the firing squads at dawn, the secretive nature of the trials that preceded them and the affecting circumstances that surrounded some of the executions caused a revulsion of feeling, and ensured that the lasting response to the Rising, at least in nationalist Ireland, would be one of pride.

Those executed were all Catholics – Connolly, the Marxist socialist, prudently had the last rites before his execution, and so too did the atheist Tom Clarke. Even Roger Casement, a Protestant, and the last of the leaders of Easter 1916 to be sentenced (though he had been arrested before the fighting began), was received into the Catholic church shortly before his lonely death by hanging in Pentonville prison in August 1916. The Catholicity of the Rising was important and, coupled with the undoubted piety of some of the rebels, quickly led to a cult growing up around their memory, complete with ribbons, lapel badges and *in memoriam* cards. By July the *Catholic Bulletin* had begun publishing what was, in effect, a martyrology of the leaders. Just as the execution of the Manchester Martyrs nearly fifty years before had excited the sympathy of many who had had little time for the Fenians, so too the episodic executions – three shot on 3 May, four on 4 May, one on 5 May and so on – after trials of dubious legality, had the effect of making the Rising genuinely popular. Lastly, and crucially, these executions were accompanied by a round-up of thousands of suspects, and this swoop completed the sea-change in Irish public opinion regarding the Rising.

Almost from the beginning, the authorities had claimed that 'Sinn Féiners' had been behind the Rising, and the whole affair was quickly described as the 'Sinn Féin' rebellion. In fact, these assumptions were wholly unwarranted and merely showed how defective was Dublin Castle's intelligence. The military operation to arrest those supposedly implicated was based on information that was at least ten years old and the swoops on suspects were heavy-handed, fiercely resented and ultimately counter-productive. Some 3,340 men and 79 women, allegedly all rebel sympathisers (i.e. mostly prominent nationalists or 'Sinn Féiners'), were arrested within a week, half of whom were promptly released; but the remainder, including five women, were deported along with the surrendered rebels to prisons in England and Scotland. The large majority of rebels was sent on to Frongoch internment camp in Wales. There, in the incessant rain, they would have ample time on their hands to mull over the events of Easter week 1916 and to plan for the future.

The Rising was over: what now? Asquith called for a 'new departure', and hurried over to Ireland on 12 May 1916. He was able to put a stop to the executions and he secured better rations for the rebel prisoners; but he also recognised that the black arts of his colleague, the 'Welsh Wizard', David Lloyd George, were required for any wider settlement. In the aftermath of the Rising the policy options available were very limited. Home Rule, the attainment of which had absorbed the energies of generations of constitutional nationalists, had been buried in the rubble of the General Post Office. It was unlikely that it could be exhumed, and new life breathed into it: if anything, there was every danger that Redmond and his Irish Party might join it in the grave. He and they had denounced both the Rising *and* the manner of its suppression; but such even-handedness pleased no one.

In fairness, Redmond was in an unenviable position. He was not a member of the coalition government (he had turned down a Cabinet position in May 1915), but his whole-hearted support for Irish recruitment meant that he looked and acted as if he were. It was this perception that led to him bearing the blame for military actions beyond his control. In a sense, the Rising had been as much directed against him and his party as against the English connection, and there was nothing that Lloyd George could do to alter this. Nor was there much that Redmond could do to regain the commanding position that he had held in 1914. Those Irish National Volunteers who had answered his call to arms had disappeared into the mud of Flanders. A new national narrative, forged in the fires of Easter week, was being fashioned around the heroics of the rival IV and there was no room for Redmond's men in it.

From a Unionist perspective, the Easter Rising had borne out all their dire warnings about inherent nationalist disloyalty and genetic separatist tendencies. Carson, thankfully, had the decency to refrain from baying for rebel blood, for he well knew that, had things gone differently, he might have been reading out a proclamation similar to that of Pearse on the steps of Belfast City Hall. The Easter Rising had finally made partition inevitable, and Carson recognised that what for him had always been a tactic had finally become the goal of his followers. As early as June 1916 Lloyd George had come up with the outlines of the future settlement: Home Rule for Ireland would be implemented immediately, and the six north-eastern counties would be excluded from the scheme, at least until the end of the war. There was, as yet, no word of a separate Parliament for the six counties, nor was it determined how long their exclusion would last; it was not even clear whether the Home Rule on offer was the same as that which had been 'frozen' in August 1914; but, in the aftermath of the Rising, the future shape of the two Irelands was plain to see. The Ulster Unionist Council accepted this plan, and so too did a convention of nationalists from the six counties meeting in Belfast on 23 June 1916. Redmond and his party refused to go along with it, but their rejection of partition carried little conviction. In any case, in a time of war, bullets rather than ballots, and blood rather than argument, would settle it: on 1 July, the 36th (Ulster) Division – i.e. mostly the pre-war UVF – took part in the Somme offensive and sustained shattering casualties. By nightfall some 5,500 of them had been killed, wounded or listed as missing; just as the republic had been sealed with blood in the Rising, so too had partition by the sacrifice at the Somme.

Aftermath

The Rising had been dubbed the Sinn Féin rebellion, and undoubtedly the party of Arthur Griffith was its principal beneficiary. British military repression had made the Rising popular, while the Irish Parliamentary Party's attempt to have it both ways – appalled at the Rising, appalled at the manner of its suppression – was to cost them electorally. Moreover, in so far as virulent anti-British feeling had been aroused by the execution of Pearse and his comrades, by the shooting of Sheehy-Skeffington and others and by the mass arrest of 'sympathisers', then Redmond and his party, as the perceived partners of the British, were bound to suffer at the polls. Redmond was further hurt by doubts over his attitude towards partition, and he was jeered for his failure to prevent the execution of Casement. His candid admission that he had been deceived by the British further damaged his reputation and his party's morale. Probably only a spell in prison for Redmond and Dillon could have slowed the electoral slide of the Irish Party, but even this boost was denied them.

Meanwhile, Sinn Féin, 'the party of the Rising', was expanding its organisation and actively recruiting new members. A key constituent of this fresh intake was the rebel internees, all of whom were freed by Christmas 1916, with those convicted before the courts being released in June 1917. These men (and one woman, Countess Markievicz (figure 6.6) were mostly young, fit and confident. They had used their sojourn in prison to become acquainted with each other, form networks, identify rivals and plan future strategy. They emerged from gaol with a clear idea of the Ireland they wanted and, thus empowered, they had chosen Sinn Féin as the vehicle to overtake the Irish Party and realise that vision. In April 1917 Sinn Féin could muster only 166 clubs and around 11,000 members but by October this number had risen to 1,200 clubs with over 150,000 members. They had also notched up four by-election successes over the Irish party.

Perhaps the most notable – certainly the most symbolic – of these victories was de Valera's victory in East Clare in July, where he took the seat left vacant as a result of the death in Flanders of Willie Redmond, John Redmond's brother. In October de Valera followed up this triumph by being elected president of Sinn Féin, Arthur Griffith gracefully stepping aside. Within twenty-four hours de Valera had also been made president of the IV – a fusion of the political and the not-at-all-political in the hands of one person that had not been achieved since Parnell had brought the Land League and the Irish Parliamentary Party

6.6 Militarisation was gender blind. Constance Markievicz in military uniform, 1915. National Library of Ireland.

under his control a generation earlier. The awkward fact that Sinn Féin was still technically a monarchical party was artfully side-stepped by de Valera's formulation (Parnell would have been proud of it) that, once a republic had been achieved the Irish people could chose whatever form of government they wanted, presumably including a monarchy. In September 1917 the death on hunger strike of Thomas Ashe, the victor of the Ashbourne ambush in April

1916, further convulsed nationalist Ireland and strengthened Sinn Féin. Ashe's ghastly death – he expired while being forcibly fed in Mountjoy gaol – could only reaffirm the core principle of Easter week, self-sacrifice in a noble cause and, inevitably, made Redmond's party look, once again, ignoble, cheap and tawdry. By the end of 1917 Sinn Féin seemed unstoppable.

Moreover, the Irish Parliamentary Party's engagement with the Irish Convention brought it no advantage and may even have damaged it further. The Convention was a Lloyd George initiative aimed at promoting Redmond's men at the expense of Sinn Féin, and to that end a major constitutional conference of interested parties was to be held in Dublin to discuss further settlement proposals. The Convention duly met in July 1917 and it continued to sit until April 1918. But its work was crippled from the start, for Sinn Féin ignored it and the Ulster Unionist leadership refused to take part. Only the southern Unionists, the Irish Parliamentary Party and some independents were represented and, while the debates make for interesting reading – they were probably the last frank discussion of Unionist–nationalist fears and anxieties until the 1990s – there was an unavoidable air of irrelevance about the entire proceedings.

Any hope that Redmond's party might recover ground lost, or even hold their existing ground, faded in 1918. The threatened German breakthrough in Flanders in the spring of 1918 brought the hugely contentious issue of conscription for Ireland (it had been in force in Britain since 1916) once again to the fore. The arguments heard then were once again deployed in favour of and against such a drastic course of action; but this time what had changed was that the imminent threat of German victory outweighed all other worries about widespread resistance in Ireland, and the British government was duly authorised to extend conscription to this country.

For the Irish Parliamentary Party, this was the last straw and, led by John Dillon, replacing Redmond who had died on 6 March, its members withdrew in protest from Westminster and reconvened in Dublin. In April, at a conference in the Mansion House in the centre of the city, members of the Irish Parliamentary Party joined with representatives of Sinn Féin and the Labour Party to concert their undying opposition to conscription. Irish Catholic bishops offered them their support and encouragement, and a one-day strike was called. The British government reacted by uncovering a 'German plot' and organising a round-up of over seventy agitators, almost all of them Sinn Féiners. Fortunately, the German offensive faltered then failed in France, the pressing necessity for conscription in Ireland faded overnight and the alleged plotters were freed some months later. But the damage had been done. The Irish Parliamentary Party had once again been shown as, at best, irresolute and ineffective – why had they not withdrawn from Westminster in the aftermath of the Rising? – while Sinn Féin had clearly emerged as the new voice of a resurgent nationalist Ireland. The Catholic bishops, recognising the way the wind was blowing, scrambled to reposition themselves. They professed to be impressed by de Valera's anxiety to defer to them, especially on educational matters; equally, they were reassured by his insistence that one Easter Rising was quite enough and that there were no plans for a reprise.

The end for the Irish Parliamentary Party came suddenly and decisively in the general election of December 1918. Electoral reform had just given the vote to all men over twenty-one and to most women over thirty, with the result that the Irish electorate had trebled to over two million. When the final votes were counted the Irish Parliamentary Party had just about disappeared from the scene. It entered the general election with sixty-eight seats, and it came out with just six, five of which were in Ulster (where a church-brokered pact had stopped Irish Parliamentary Party and Sinn Féin candidates from squaring up to one another). By contrast, Sinn Féin had gone into the election with just seven seats and emerged with the grand total of seventy-three. Unionists advanced from eighteen to twenty-six seats. This was an electoral rout possibly unprecedented in modern European history: a political party that had articulated in Westminster the aspirations of moderate Irish nationalists for nearly fifty years, a party that, as late as 1917, seemed reasonably secure electorally and a party that had gone on (and on and on and on – as the wags had it) to win some form of Home Rule, had seemingly vanished overnight.

The Irish Parliamentary Party was essentially a casualty of the Great War. As the militarisation of Irish society in the pre-war decades had proceeded, the party had looked increasingly uncertain and ill at ease, lacking a vocabulary with which to speak to the new nationalism and, like the Liberals, totally out of its depth where militant Unionism was concerned. Its crass attempt to position itself at the head of the IV in June 1914, as if the Volunteers were just another potential political rival to be seamlessly absorbed, was misconceived and was strongly resented by advanced nationalists. Redmond's role as a recruiting sergeant for the British army backfired on the party still more. Not only were his efforts unacknowledged by the War Office but, by sending tens of thousands of Volunteers to their death and many more to disillusionment, he effectively undermined the party's support base in Ireland. His refusal to take office under Asquith was probably the correct decision, and bought a little time; but his handling of the Easter week crisis was inept. Had the war ended quickly, perhaps the party might have struggled on, but by Christmas 1914 it was clear that there was no early end in sight and yet Redmond had persevered with a policy that only made sense if peace was around the corner.

Admittedly, the Irish Parliamentary Party still appeared vibrant in 1914 and it had continued to win by-elections until the end of 1916. However, appearances

6.7 Large crowd in College Green, Dublin, celebrating the return of the 16th Irish Division from the war, 1919. Irish Photographic Archive.

were deceptive. A post-mortem might conclude that, while the Irish Parliamentary Party had been badly mauled by the Ulster uprising of 1912–14, and that Easter 1916 had inflicted further wounds, in the end it had been the interminable war, with its martial rhetoric and its mass slaughter, both of which privileged confrontation and disparaged compromise, that had brought about the party's demise. The Irish Party, like the Liberal Party, had been conceived in gentler times: neither could function, let alone flourish, in an era of total war; and both were ultimately to be consigned to the dustbin of history (figure 6.7).

Those elected for Sinn Féin were pledged not to take their seats at Westminster and instead to assemble in Dublin where they would constitute a Dáil, or Parliament. They would then proceed immediately to set up a parallel administration to the current British one. The Sinn Féin Members of Parliament – or those of them not in prison – duly gathered in the Mansion House, Dublin, on 21 January 1919, declared independence, ratified the republic proclaimed on Easter Monday and issued the 'democratic programme', a document setting out the economic and social goals of the new government. On the same day, at

Soloheadbeg, county Tipperary, two members of the Royal Irish Constabulary guarding gelignite were shot dead by a group of IV, soon to be known as the Irish Republican Army (IRA). These killings sent a clear message that there existed on the ground in the localities a steely resolve to implement by violence the lofty sentiments of the various Dáil declarations of that day. The ambush was not in any sense authorised by the Dáil in Dublin: indeed, nearly two years were to elapse before the new government formally accepted responsibility for IRA operations; but, for all that, Soloheadbeg was the Irish Lexington.

The Irish wars, 1919–23

The Irish War of Independence, 'Anglo-Irish war' or 'Tan war' – it would be tedious to elucidate the conflicting claims embedded in the varied nomenclature – lasted until a truce was concluded in July 1921.[3] By comparison with other twentieth-century wars of national liberation, it was a small-scale affair, rather resembling those native uprisings that had broken out in areas of Mesopotamia following the collapse of the Turkish empire in 1918,[4] or perhaps one of those 'little wars' waged in remote areas of the Empire during Queen Victoria's reign. Despite claims to the contrary, it was not a titanic struggle for national liberation on the scale of later struggles witnessed in Vietnam and Algeria. Leinster (especially Dublin City, figure 6.8) and Munster (especially Cork and Tipperary) witnessed most of the action, with Connacht largely untouched and Ulster (notably Belfast and Derry) so consumed with confessional struggles that it had little time for the wider picture. Throughout the war large areas of Ireland remained relatively untroubled. That said, hundreds died and thousands were injured during the period of hostilities.

Members of the Royal Irish Constabulary, in the front line from the beginning, were quickly judged to be unsuited to a guerrilla struggle, and they were soon supplemented in January 1920 with several thousand British recruits, instantly dubbed, because of their motley uniform, the 'Black and Tans' (figure 6.9). These, in turn, were reinforced by a paramilitary force of ex-army officers, who were attached as auxiliaries to the Royal Irish Constabulary. These 'Auxies' (figure 6.10) had been blooded in the Great War, had no desire to settle back into humdrum civilian life thereafter and relished the opportunity offered by conflict in Ireland to sustain a comradeship forged in action on the Western Front and elsewhere. In modern parlance, they were undoubtedly dysfunctional and their excesses, particularly against civilians, were a dismal proof of this. But they were probably the finest armament to be deployed in Ireland by an English government since the 1650s, and their hard-living (and drinking) ways,

6.8 British soldiers searching a car in Dublin, 1921. National Museum of Ireland.

their derring-do and devil-may-care attitude won even the grudging admiration of their IRA opponents. Civilians, having borne the brunt of their attention, might beg to differ. In addition, some forty thousand regular army soldiers were deployed throughout Ireland, especially in the most troubled areas.

The 'Anglo-Irish war' went through a number of phases: from the murder of individual Royal Irish Constabulary members (1919), through to a concerted attack on various Royal Irish Constabulary barracks (1920) and then on to large-scale engagements against British troops (1921). A short list of major incidents in the war might include the assassinations of Lt Col. G. B. F. Smyth, shot in Cork but a native of Banbridge, county Down (July 1920) and, a month later, of District Inspector Swanzy in Lisburn, county Down – both of whose deaths sparked murderous rioting in Lisburn and environs; Kevin Barry's execution in November 1920, the first since the Easter rebellion, and particularly poignant given Barry's youth and student status; the sack – the word is not too strong – of Balbriggan, county Dublin, and of Mallow and Cork City in 1920 by elements of crown forces; the shooting dead of fourteen alleged British intelligence agents on 'Bloody Sunday' (21 November 1920), followed, later that day, by a devastating

6.9 'Black and Tans' check out premises in Dublin. National Museum of Ireland.

reprisal attack by 'Black and Tans' on spectators at a Gaelic football match in Croke Park, and finally, a week later, by the annihilation of an eighteen-man patrol of 'Auxies' at Kilmichael, county Cork. Perhaps inevitably, such incidents as these have tended to colour the popular memory.

The 'Tan war', to give it its most nationalist title, was later remembered as one of gallant flying columns, lonely patrols, hair-breadth escapes, deadly ambushes and poignant death-cell scenes. In fact the war was, in very large measure, a grim, dour and unglamorous struggle that fell heaviest on those who were only slightly, if at all, involved. Civilian casualties from 1919 to 1921 formed at least half of those killed and, in the months before the truce, they may have risen to 80 per cent. Favourite targets of the IRA, apart from soldiers and policemen, were informers or 'touts', a catch-all category that appears to have included the likes of tinkers, tramps, ex-servicemen and Protestants, none of whom fitted the dominant republican stereotype. For their part, the 'Auxies' and 'Black and Tans' made little effort to distinguish between rebels and non-combatants in disturbed areas and, believing that all Catholics (or even, all Irish) were inherently disloyal,

6.10 Auxiliaries on patrol, 1921. National Library of Ireland.

were happy to blaze away promiscuously. In all, some 400 police, 150 military and an estimated 750 IRA and civilians died before the truce came into effect on 9 July 1921 (figure 6.11).

Even while hostilities had been at their bloodiest, efforts had been made to secure some form of settlement and, by the time of the truce, more than the outlines were visible. Ireland was to be partitioned between Northern Ireland and Southern Ireland. The former was to remain part of the United Kingdom and was to consist of six counties of the province of Ulster. Craig and Carson had rejected any suggestion that Northern Ireland might include all of the province, on the pragmatic grounds that Unionist control, given the sectarian arithmetic, could only be guaranteed in the smaller area. Moreover, partition was to be permanent: all suggestion of a six-year trial period for the new arrangement had been given up in 1916. Most dramatically, the area was to have its own Parliament and government, though both were limited in their powers, and sovereignty was to reside at Westminster.

Given Northern Ireland's explosive sectarian history since 1886 (at least), and its current murderous furies (eighteen killed in Derry, in June 1920, and every indication of more to come), it might have been assumed that some provision for

6.11 Members of Cumann na mBan recite the rosary outside Mountjoy prison as Thomas Traynor is being executed, 25 April 1921. Irish Photographic Archive.

the protection of the rights of the Catholic minority would have been included in the Government of Ireland Act (1920) that established partition between north and south. But this was not done: British ministers and politicians were anxious to be rid of the Ulster question once and for all, and they had no desire to be seen directly governing Irish nationalists. The logic of this stance was that contentious matters such as policing, education, and law and order would become, in the first instance, the responsibility of the new Northern Ireland government. There should, therefore, be little or no running off to Westminster with complaints or demands for intervention. What all this meant was that the Ulster Unionists who had led the opposition to Home Rule to the brink of civil war, and who had sworn a covenant with God never to accept it, had now, with some heart-searching, abandoned their co-religionists in Cavan, Monaghan and Donegal and had embraced Home Rule – for themselves alone.

The Government of Ireland Act passed in the dying days of 1920 also provided for a government and Parliament for Southern Ireland, as the twenty-six-county remnant was to be known. But because this offered nothing like the republic that had been proclaimed, and that was then being fought for, it was almost entirely ignored. Admittedly, in 'Southern Ireland' all candidates in the general election provided for by the Act were returned unopposed: and the 124 Sinn Féin Members of Parliament (out of 128) thus elected proceeded to set up a second

Dáil, once again in the Mansion House, from which to govern the country. Since the inauguration in January 1919 of the first Dáil, much progress had, in fact, been made in setting up a parallel, *de facto*, government in those areas where republicans held sway. At the national level, Michael Collins, a veteran of Easter week, and a graduate of Frongoch, acted as minister of finance. He was conspicuously successful in raising loans for the new regime; he was equally impressive as IRA director of intelligence in which role he ordered the assassination of any detective who got close to him or his activities, and he masterminded the elimination of the 'Cairo gang' of British agents on 'Bloody Sunday'. The president of Sinn Féin, Eamon de Valera, had escaped from Lincoln gaol in February 1919, and, a few months later, had gone to the United States (returning in December 1920) where he lobbied on behalf of the Irish cause. Whatever his lobbying skills he proved to be a natural fund raiser, collecting some $5 million which proved vital in ensuring that the 'war' could continue.

Another 1916 veteran, W. T. Cosgrave, had been appointed minister for local government and, with some help from local Sinn Féin 'muscle', he too had been effective in persuading district and county councils throughout the country to accept the Dáil's authority. Sinn Féin courts, designed to supplant the official courts, were also a notable success: barristers (though few solicitors) were prepared to appear in them, and there were many indications that the quality of justice dispensed was acceptable, even preferred by the public. Given that much of this activity had to be conducted in secret, and often by ministers on the run, the achievement of the first and second Dáil in constructing a parallel administration, in fund-raising and in propagating where possible the Sinn Féin cause to an international audience, should not be underestimated. The violence of the IRA during the War of Independence, 1919 to 1921, might have stolen the headlines, and the reprisals of their military opponents might have evoked outrage (or elicited applause), but the behind-the-scenes work of the provisional Sinn Féin government was of genuine revolutionary potential. Ireland, or at least twenty-six counties of it, was quietly slipping away from mother England.

The truce came into effect on 11 July 1921 and, in October, a five-man Sinn Féin delegation headed by Michael Collins and Arthur Griffith – but not including de Valera, for reasons that are still obscure – went to London to negotiate agreement with the British authorities on the future constitutional shape of Ireland. On 6 December, following two months of intensive talks, the Anglo-Irish Treaty was signed in London. This document was the subject of impassioned and frequently embittered debate in the Dáil, and was finally approved by the narrow margin of sixty-four votes to fifty-seven on 7 January 1922. During the sessions given over to the Treaty some speakers swore that they would not be bound by any majority vote, and that they would remain faithful to the oath they had sworn to the Irish Republic. When the final vote was taken Sinn Féin's unity had shattered, and the threat of civil war loomed. The Treaty was broadly approved by the electorate of the Irish Free State – as the new entity was styled – in a general election held in June 1922. By that date, however, matters had taken a grave turn, for those opposed to the Treaty had occupied and fortified certain buildings in central Dublin, notably the Four Courts complex. In addition, they had taken over military barracks elsewhere in the country, and disarmed any pro-Treaty IRA members they found in them. They were, in effect, bidding defiance to the newly created provisional government, and to its chairman, Michael Collins. On 28 June, under pressure from the British (and some Irish pro-Treatyites) to take action (especially following the assassination, erroneously blamed on an anti-Treaty IRA unit, of Field Marshal Sir Henry Wilson on the steps of his London home) forces under the command of the provisional government commenced shelling the Four Courts – the Irish Fort Sumter – and the civil war had begun.

It was by no means inevitable that the twelve-month period from the truce to the opening bombardment on anti-Treaty positions in Dublin would end in civil war, but it is not difficult to see how it might appear so. The privileging of the martial over the mundane, begun with the formation of the UVF and IV, and sustained by the mass deaths of the Great War, had been mightily reinforced in Ireland by the sacrifices and heroics of Easter week and the Anglo-Irish war. Too many people in Ireland were not only prepared to die for what they believed but ready to kill as well. Ireland was little different in this respect from Finland, Germany and parts of the now fragmented Habsburg and Turkish empires. The restraint traditionally afforded in crisis situations by a powerful state apparatus was absent from Ireland (and other war zones in central and eastern Europe) at this time, and in its place there was a power vacuum, a situation that would always make any peaceful settlement elusive.

Moreover, from Easter Monday 1916 to the truce of 1921, the primary goal sought had been a sovereign all-Ireland republic; but this had never been a realistic ambition. Indeed by the time of the truce, partition was an established fact; in a real sense, the truce itself had only been possible because Northern Ireland was up and running, and thus off the agenda. And the status of a republic, sovereign and separate, for the remainder of Ireland was inadmissible. Democratic states – as opposed to ramshackle empires – simply do not permit the secession of portions of 'their' territory. As the assassinated Sir Henry Wilson, the Irish-born former Chief of the Imperial General Staff, and sometime adviser to the Northern Ireland government, had repeatedly pointed out, Ireland was 'vital' to Britain's strategic interests, and he placed its retention within the empire well ahead of that of India, Egypt or Mesopotamia. Nor was it helpful to insist, as some IRA commanders did, that Britain had been brought to its knees by the IRA's onslaught during the Anglo-Irish war and that, therefore, it would have little option but to accept a republic. Britain was a warfare state and, as such, was infinitely prepared to sustain casualties in defence of perceived national interests. Equally, the British state was well organised to wage war in pursuit of those objectives. In any case, having just emerged victorious in the Great War, Britain was not about to accept humiliation in Ireland. When the chief British negotiator, Lloyd George, promised 'terrible war' if his terms were not agreed, it would have been most unwise to have dismissed his threat as a bluff.

Essentially, the Treaty offered twenty-six-county Ireland a 'dominion status' within the British commonwealth, comparable to that enjoyed by Canada and Australia, with sovereignty still residing in London, and with key monarchical symbols retained, such as the governor-generalship, the crown on official seals, an oath of fidelity to the monarch and of allegiance to the new Free State. Also retained by Britain were a number of Irish ports judged necessary for its continued defence. All of this was far from a republic; but it was also very far from the Home Rule arrangement that had been on offer in 1914. Full fiscal autonomy, no interference from Westminster on Irish internal affairs, the evacuation of the British army – and the establishment of an Irish one – and a role on the international stage were just a few of the main gains. As Collins put it, while the Treaty did not offer full freedom, it did offer the freedom to gain that freedom. We may note that in the opinion of some later commentators the Constitution of 1922, which enshrined the Treaty's major provisions, meant that the Irish Free State was a republic in all but name.

The thorny issue of partition might have proved a deal-breaker, but it had been cleverly brushed aside by Lloyd George's offer of a Boundary Commission (but not a plebiscite – they were for defeated nations, like Germany) which would pronounce on Northern Ireland's borders. The southern delegates were apparently assured that Northern Ireland would be rendered unviable by the Commission's cuts and population transfers; Ulster Unionists for their part were reassured that any changes would be minimal. The 'rabbit' of a Boundary Commission produced by Lloyd George out of his top hat was such a transparent ruse that only those willing or eager to be tricked could have fallen for it. Just as the Parliamentary Reform Convention in Dublin in 1783 had concluded, on the basis of implausible hearsay evidence, that Catholics did not want the vote and had quickly moved on, so too the Sinn Féin delegates in London (and their colleagues in Dublin), with unseemly haste, abandoned northern Catholics, and settled for a Boundary Commission whose remit was deliberately left vague. The fact that in all the charge and counter-charge of the Treaty debates hardly any mention was made of partition seems to point to the conclusion that, irrespective

6.12 Anti-Treaty rally in Dublin. Irish Photographic Archive.

of whether one approved of the Treaty or not, privately there was an acceptance (and perhaps a sense of relief?) that partition was here to stay. The British promise of a Boundary Commission was seized upon by both sides because it offered a way of seeming to do something about partition without actually having to do anything.

De Valera had dismissed the Treaty out of hand (figure 6.12), but his opposition to it was compromised by his refusal to join the delegation to London. It was all too easy, therefore, to chide him for opposing it because it was not his Treaty. However, unlike the other opponents of the Treaty he did bring forward his own proposal, labelled 'document no. 2', and providing for 'external association'. That this was not a casual solution opportunistically tossed out (or plucked from *his* top hat) is shown by the fact that, when in power after 1932, he immediately returned to it in his negotiations with British ministers, much to their bemusement. (De Valera's formula was quite visionary and was to form the basis of the future relationship between the Republic of India and the British crown in 1950.) In 1922, however, those who opposed the Treaty were equally unmoved by both 'external association' espoused by de Valera, or the 'dominion status' brought back by Collins. Neither set the pulse racing – who would die (or kill) for 'external association'? – and a ballad in favour of either option was surely impossible. For many IRA veterans who had been in combat and who had lost comrades, there could be no compromise with the holy grail of the republic. It was notable, too, that all six female *Teachtaí Dála* (TDs) or deputies, almost all of whom were mothers, widows or sisters of dead heroes, came out against the Treaty; they made it abundantly clear that, in their opposition to it, they were prepared to fight to the last man, so to speak. Most of the IRA commanders in the localities also declared against the Treaty, but headquarters staff in Dublin in general supported and stayed loyal to Collins. This was to be crucial to the success of the pro-Treaty side in the coming struggle.

That said, it would be wrong to see the line-up of pro- and anti-Treaty forces purely in terms of democrats against diehards, or even republicans versus anti-republicans. The victors in the civil war were certainly successful in portraying their opponents as 'irregulars', wedded to the gun and resolutely opposed to all politics and majority decisions. And some anti-Treatyites undoubtedly did despise civilian authority and the compromises necessary in a democracy. But not all; and the majority of those who opposed the Treaty were to settle down very comfortably into political life after the formation of their party, Fianna Fáil, in 1926. For their part, the anti-Treatyites branded their opponents as traitors to, and betrayers of, the republican ideal. But the reality was that, in 1922, neither side had a monopoly on republicanism or democracy.

Valiant efforts have been made by historians to categorise those in favour, or opposed to, the Treaty in socio-economic terms, and it does appear that the less well-off, residing in counties furthest from Dublin and, curiously, those in areas less involved in the earlier hostilities, were to be found in the anti-Treaty camp. There were, of course, major exceptions – writers such as Ernie O'Malley, Frank O'Connor and Sean O'Faolain – were to be found in the anti-Treaty ranks, and none of these could be classed among the socially marginal. By contrast, those in favour of the Treaty, by and large, encompassed the great and the good: the Catholic hierarchy came down decisively in favour of the Treaty and so too did the war-weary Catholic propertied classes and large farmers, fearful of expropriation and dispossession. Against that, for many IRA men, loyalty to the charismatic Collins was paramount: 'his' men were to be found everywhere, on every rung of the social ladder, taking their stand on the principle that what was good enough for 'Mick' Collins was good enough for them. Ideology and class struggle have their limits in explaining the line-up in the Irish civil war (see figures 6.13–6.25).

The war began with an act worthy of the Jacobins of the Year II, or of the Taleban of the year 2001 or, more pertinently, of the German demolition of the Louvain university library in 1914: the destruction of the Public Record Office, within the Four Courts buildings, along with its archive of historical

6.13 Group of newly enlisted members of the National Army during the Irish civil war, 1922. Irish Photographic Archive.

6.14 Michael Collins addressing a pro-Treaty rally in Cork (*c.* 1921). Irish Photographic Archive.

6.15 Attack on the anti-Treaty forces occupying the Four Courts: the opening shots in the Irish civil war. Irish Photographic Archive.

6.16 The Four Courts blazing. Irish Photographic Archive.

6.17 Mixed group of National Army soldiers (*c.* 1922–3) along with civilians and dog peer confidently into the camera. Irish Photographic Archive.

6.18 National Army soldiers receive a blessing from a Catholic priest. Irish Photographic Archive.

6.19 National Army soldiers, fresh from their triumph at the Four Courts, on board ship bound for county Kerry. Irish Photographic Archive.

6.20 National Army soldiers in action at O'Connell Street, Dublin during the civil war. Irish Photographic Archive.

6.21 Another shot of the same incident. Irish Photographic Archive.

6.22 Shattered dream. General Michael Collins at Portobello Barracks, Dublin, *c.* 1922. Irish Photographic Archive.

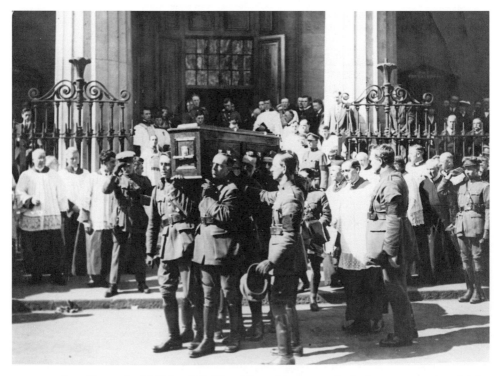

6.23 Funeral of Michael Collins. Note the strong clerical representation. Irish Photographic Archive.

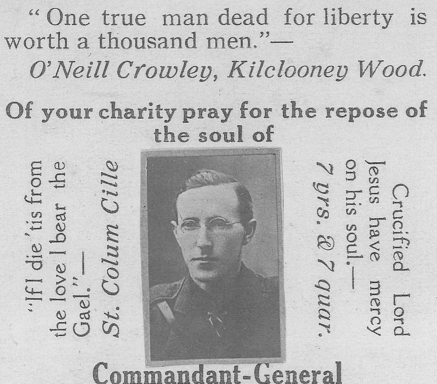

"One true man dead for liberty is worth a thousand men."—
O'Neill Crowley, Kilclooney Wood.

Of your charity pray for the repose of the soul of

"If I die 'tis from the love I bear the Gael."—St. Colum Cille

7 yrs. & 7 quar.

Crucified Lord Jesus have mercy on his soul.—

Commandant-General
LIAM LYNCH (White Chief)

Leader of the Irish Republican Army of Counties Cork, Kerry and Waterford during the Black and Tan Terror, and later Chief of Staff of Irish Republican Army, who died fighting for Ireland on the Knockmealdown Mountains, Tuesday, April 10th, 1923. Age 29 Years. R.I.P.

Beannact De le na Anam.

6.24 Memorial card for Liam Lynch, military leader of the anti-Treaty forces. The reference to 'White Chief' suggests comparison with the defeat of the 'Whites' in the Russian Civil War. Desmond Fitzgerald Papers, University College Dublin Archives.

6.25 Cartoon by Constance Markievicz attacking the activities of the Free State government during the Irish civil war. Irish Photographic Archive.

manuscripts relating to the history of Ireland from medieval to modern times. This could hardly be described as an accidental explosion: the stockpiling of petrol, paraffin and munitions in the building by anti-Treaty forces was a clear statement of an intent to obliterate Irish official memory, and thus permit the creation of a new history beginning at year zero.

Those opposed to the Treaty, however, had repeated the error made by the Easter Monday rebels by barricading themselves in buildings in Dublin city centre that were barely defensible, at least not in the long term. With the aid of artillery borrowed from the British, the anti-Treaty occupiers were driven from their strongholds; for the second time in six years, O'Connell Street lay in ruins. The war continued in the countryside and, from an early date, Free State forces under the command of Michael Collins and Richard Mulcahy showed a determination and vigour in its prosecution. A large army of some 40,000 men was mobilised and equipped from British arsenals, and slowly the areas of the country held by anti-Treaty forces were squeezed. Cork and Kerry, Limerick and Clare were all occupied by December 1922. Collins himself had been shot dead in an ambush on 22 August in his native Cork, and his death further envenomed an already embittered atmosphere. Reprisal executions began to be carried out by Free State authorities three months after Collins's death (seventy-seven in all, between November 1922 and May 1923), unofficial vengeance was also exacted on 'irregulars' by members of Collins's 'squad', and there were any number of grisly atrocities on both sides, particularly in Kerry. A feature of the later stages of the conflict was the widespread burning of the country residences of Protestant gentry; the blackened skeletons of the 'Big Houses' were to stand for decades as silent witnesses to the excesses of the Irish civil war. In April 1923 the death of Liam Lynch, chief of staff of the anti-Treaty forces, hastened the end of hostilities. His successor, Frank Aiken, ordered the IRA still fighting to dump arms and to await another day.

By the spring of 1923, then, the gunsmoke had begun to clear, and the shape of the two Irelands was coming into the light. In the Irish Free State pro-Treaty forces had carried the day against those who had rejected the Treaty and the way was open for a government led by W. T. Cosgrave to implement its vision of the Ireland, or at least twenty-six counties of it, that it had fought for. In Northern Ireland, the threat posed by the IRA to the new state – perhaps as grave as that offered by anti-Treaty forces south of the border – had been seen off through the combined efforts of the paramilitary Special Constabulary and the British army. The intense sectarian rioting of 1922, which had left hundreds dead and injured (disproportionately Catholics), had ceased, at least for the time being. Sir James Craig, the prime minister, and his Unionist colleagues could now focus their efforts on consolidating their state. That both Northern Ireland and the Irish Free State had been born in bloodshed was ominous for the future. In 1914, although partition in some form had been conceded, the precise geographical or constitutional contours of neither state had been foreseen or planned. And this was a danger: what could be done so quickly could just as easily be undone, while the cult of the gunman in or out of uniform, north and south, scarcely offered any reassurance for a peaceful political future.

State-building, north and south

In 1923 A. J. Balfour, Irish chief secretary in the late 1880s, and forever associated with firm government, contemplated contemporary Ireland and was moved to ask defiantly: 'What was the Ireland which the Free State took over?' He then answered his own question, '[it was] the Ireland that we made'. There was much in what he said. There was almost no area of government, law, education or social policy that did not bear the stamp of the former rulers.[5] The government of the Irish Free State was not essentially dissimilar to that in London, with ministers being responsible for their departments and with an executive council or cabinet being set up, chaired by a president (W. T. Cosgrave was the first). One crucial difference was that elections, north and south, were to be by proportional representation rather than the British 'first-past-the-post-system', and this offered an advantage for smaller parties. As important as the structure was the ethos: and here there was no discernible difference between the outlook of Cosgrave and his ministerial colleagues, and their counterparts in Britain and the Commonwealth. The Irish Free State may or may not have come about as a result of a revolution, but this was a revolution on the eighteenth-century American model, i.e. one singularly lacking in revolutionaries (figure 6.26). As Kevin O'Higgins, one of Cosgrave's more dynamic ministers, was to put it, those in power in the South 'were the most conservative revolutionaries that ever put through a successful revolution'. Except in respect of the Irish language – and this was an important exception – there was absolutely no plan to transform Ireland socially or economically; if anything, the reverse. Financial rigour of the most stringent kind, a firm adherence the rule of law, glacial tolerance of minorities and a desire to consolidate the 'revolution' (however defined), were the objectives.

There was above all a determination to make the transition from what was essentially a British crown colony to a self-governing Free State as painless, as seamless and as reassuring as possible. This process was aided enormously by the retention of much of the pre-existing civil service. Out of some 28,000 civil servants around 21,000 elected to stay on in the Irish Free State (population *c.* 3 million) with the remainder going to Northern Ireland (population *c.* 1,300,000), to Britain or out on pension. The proportion of civil servants to population was impressive and, undoubtedly, would have been the envy of any state escaping from British rule over the next fifty years. Social insurance schemes for health and unemployment were in place, and so too was the old age pension at 10 shillings per week for the over-seventies.

The Irish Free State had also inherited a well-developed, if sprawling, administrative apparatus in which these civil servants could function. The existing

6.26 The revolutionaries: members of the Cosgrave government at a function, early 1920s. Irish Photographic Archive.

forty-seven boards or offices of the old days were speedily consolidated into eleven departments, with two entirely new ones – finance and external affairs – being set up. A further guarantee, more or less, of financial stability and rectitude was that the Irish pound was to trade at parity with sterling (this remained the case until 1979). Had there been any desire to shake off British fiscal shackles – and there is no sign that there was – on its own this key currency connection between the Irish Free State and Britain would have made financial adventures highly unlikely.

The Irish Free State even inherited the Royal Irish Constabulary; and though it was rapidly replaced by an unarmed body, *An Garda Siochána*, the latter kept on a large proportion of the previous force. Every effort was made to roll back earlier innovation. Irish law (and lawyers), for example, had had a brief, though rather successful, flirtation with the radical 'Dáil courts', which had practised mediation and arbitration; but these courts were quickly discontinued, and the barristers were brought back to the straight and narrow of English jurisprudence, complete with antiquated legal dress and very unrepublican modes of address. Elsewhere, to audible sighs of relief, the bailiff, the taxman and the rent collector

6.27 The revolutionary: Sir James Craig, third from right, at the opening of the Northern Ireland Parliament in Belfast City Hall, June 1921. Irish Photographic Archive.

came in from the cold; the propertied classes could relax – 'revolution' would not now take place.

The situation in Northern Ireland, as might be expected, was rather similar to that in the Free State. A bicameral legislature was set up with the lower house, as in the Free State, to be elected by a system of proportional representation, and the upper house, or Senate, being mostly elected by the lower house. Craig, like his counterpart in the Free State, W. T. Cosgrave, was, to put it mildly, no radical in social or economic matters; and even if he were, his hands were tied by a British treasury which was, at least initially, anxious about the potential costs of regional devolution, and determined not to let them get out of hand. Some 90 per cent of Northern Ireland tax revenues went straight to the British exchequer, and the imperial contribution (mostly for defence) was always a first call on the Northern Ireland budget. The Northern Ireland Parliament had little or no control over income tax levels, or the rates for customs and excise.

For Craig (figure 6.27) and his colleagues, however, the main threat to the existence of Northern Ireland was neither fiscal nor financial; it was the IRA which was determined to destroy the state. In response to this threat, measures similar to, though perhaps not as harsh as, those deployed in the Irish Free State during the civil war were brought in. The UVF had been reconstituted in 1920 and, having shown its capacity for sectarian murder in Belfast and elsewhere, was absorbed into the newly created paramilitary Special Constabulary, a type of Yeomanry in the spirit, if not on the model, of their predecessors of 1798. The Specials ('A' were full-time, 'B' were part-time, 'C' were reserve and the whole numbered around 20,000) were deployed against the IRA. In this role, the various 'Specials' did achieve some successes, but these tended to be accompanied by excesses against northern Catholics in general. It may be noted that while control over finances was denied the Unionist government, at an early date it was allowed to assume full responsibility for law and order in Northern Ireland. The militarisation of the police in Northern Ireland would continue for the next fifty years, and this, along with the role of the police as a Unionist Party militia, was to play a key role in confirming Catholic alienation from the state. So too was the severely partial deployment of that force: draconian legislation aimed at squashing the republican menace, such as internment and flogging – though not summary execution of prisoners, as in the Free State – were all introduced; but these measures were rarely if ever employed against freelance loyalist gunmen, who seemed to be able to expel Catholics from their homes and work, and frequently to murder them, with impunity. The figures for Belfast are quite stark: in 1922, although Catholics made up between 25 and 30 per cent of the population they accounted for over 60 per cent of the casualties, and represented the vast majority of those driven out. 'Emergency' legislation in Northern Ireland was designed for use against 'Sinn Féiners' only.

The IRA had been temporarily beaten back by the summer of 1922 and, in this respect, so far as the Unionist government was concerned, the Irish civil war could not have been more timely. It had split the IRA and Sinn Féin, and had diverted the attention of the Free State government, and especially Collins, away from Northern Ireland and on to more pressing concerns such as the survival of their own state. Collins's untimely end, too, had been a boost. Admittedly, in early 1922, he and Craig had developed a glimmer of a working relationship that might have come to something; but against this, among all the members of the Free State government, only Collins seems to have been a hawk on Northern Ireland. His death removed a potentially formidable foe and there was no one else to take his place.

Another threat to Unionist control of Northern Ireland was that posed by dissident or maverick Unionists and, in 1922, Craig resolved to take action against them by abolishing proportional representation in local elections. (In 1929 single-member constituences became the norm for all elections in

Northern Ireland.) Craig's reasoning was that proportional representation blurred the issues and advantaged small parties, such as Labour or dissident Unionists. He much preferred that every election, at local or national level, should in essence be a referendum on the existence of the state. As late as 1938 he could declare that 'one question and one question only' (the Constitution), would be put before the northern electorate. In 1922 the British government had strongly resisted the abolition of proportional representation but then, in the face of the Unionist government's threat to resign, it had reluctantly acquiesced. It was not until 1940 that any British government was moved to intervene again in Northern Ireland's internal affairs.

The Irish Free State and Northern Ireland, then, were both born in bloodshed, were to share a similar governmental structure and their politicians were basically of the same outlook – agreed on the need for financial soundness in the conduct of affairs and on the necessity for a large role for the state (a legacy of British rule). Indeed, politicians, north and south, actually seemed to be cut from the same cloth as their counterparts in Westminster: Cosgrave, for example, so far from looking like a crazed gunman, it was reported, 'looks rather like the general manager of a railway company'.

The two states also shared common economic problems. In 1914 the north-east of Ireland, soon to become Northern Ireland, was much more economically advanced – measured by manufacturing industry, high-value exports and falling dependence on agriculture – than the rest of the island. The north's industrial base had long been a prime Unionist argument against Home Rule. But by 1922 this 'fact' had a huge question mark against it. A postwar recession had hit key industries such as ship-building, linen manufacture (female workers were the majority here) and engineering in Northern Ireland, and the 'gap' between the two economies was closing. Northern Ireland, like the Irish Free State, fell back on its agricultural sector. By the mid-1920s neither economy was looking particularly modern or advanced, for unemployment was high and rising: 25 per cent in Northern Ireland, and only emigration was keeping the number of jobless in the Irish Free State from soaring even higher.

Throughout the period up to 1939 it would be hard to say which of the 'statelets' was pulling ahead. In fairness, none of the ministers, north or south, charged with the conduct of economic affairs during these years felt that it was his responsibility to alter this state of affairs. Wedded to a policy of low taxation, few if any deemed it necessary or, indeed, desirable, to involve themselves in what were seen as suspect socialist job-creation measures. Frugal, efficient management, not innovation or 'economic growth', was their watchword, and given that there were major global problems undermining 'the market' throughout the inter-war period, their hesitation in this regard may have been well founded.

Economic affairs up to 1932 were not, then, a major preoccupation of Cosgrave's government. There had been a sort of assumption that now that the English yoke, so to speak, had been more or less cast off, then Ireland's woes, particularly emigration (long held to be an English ploy to ruin Ireland), would wind down rapidly, without anyone actually having to do anything about them. There was also a lazy expectation that, with independence, would inevitably come an improvement in living standards: again, no one need do anything. Partition, too, would prove temporary; the Boundary Commission would see to that. But solutions to all of these problems would prove elusive, perhaps because solutions were never really sought. Actively not having an economic policy seemed central to the mindset of Irish Cabinet ministers in the 1920s. True, the Shannon hydroelectric project was begun (in 1924) and completed (in 1929): but rather than trumpeting this achievement as a major triumph, the Cosgrave government appeared to view the whole enterprise rather shamefacedly, and made little political capital out of it. After the excitement of the Anglo-Irish war, and the shattering experience of the civil war, there was a rush for stability.

Emigration, checked during the Great War, resumed in the 1920s and, as before, proved central to Irish immobilism. For all the hand-wringing evoked by the spectacle of Irish citizens leaving the state in droves, self-interest continued to demand, and the structure of landholding in Irish society required, that a very large out-migration must continue in order for that society to maintain itself. Throughout the 1920s an official disregard for manufacturing industry and, as was the situation under British rule, a privileging of the agricultural sector, meant inevitably that the surplus population on the land would have to travel.

Similarly, there was little or no movement, only talk and songs, on partition. Its manifest private advantages (as opposed to the wretched, and wholly hypocritical, public laments for the 'lost province') had quickly become evident. The ghastly tribe of recalcitrant and benighted Unionists had been, thankfully, corralled behind the border and as a result Dublin could pursue its own agendas where language revival, economic matters and moral issues were concerned, without having to face northern clamour.

Any attempt to do anything that might conceivably undermine partition was silently ruled out. For a short time northern Catholic teachers who boycotted the state system in Northern Ireland had their salaries paid by the Free State authorities, but this was discontinued within a year. More substantially, there was to be no seat in the Dáil for elected representatives of northern nationalists, who for a time pursued – in the best Sinn Féin tradition – an abstentionist policy from the Northern Ireland Parliament. Nor did either of the main parties in the Free State, Fianna Fáil or Cumann na nGaedheal (after 1934, Fine Gael), see fit to organise in the 'fourth green field'. Even when in 1925 the Boundary

Commission, the promise of whose redrawings had apparently been sufficient to move forward the Treaty negotiations, failed to deliver on the high hopes held out for it, the official reaction was very muted. Publicly, southern ministers might fume and protest: but yet Cosgrave would go to London and enter into, in his words, 'a damned good bargain', with the British and Northern Ireland governments to shelve the Commission's report and recognise the border as a fixed international boundary. Partition, along with emigration, were the twin pillars on which southern Irish society would be constructed in the period post-1922. Both of the main parties would continue to denounce them as evil legacies of British rule; but both also guiltily recognised that the first allowed democratic rule to bed itself down, while the second permitted the creation of a society that was both manageable and malleable.

And yet the picture for the 1920s was not entirely one of immobilism. In two areas some progress may be noted. First, Ireland's position 'among the nations of the world' was enhanced by joining the newly formed League of Nations in September 1923. Apart from the glow of pride, this step brought the added satisfaction of irritating British ministers, who had believed that 'their' dominions were ineligible for membership. De Valera too was to criticise this move, though on different grounds, but when in office in the 1930s he took an active part in the League, denouncing Great Power aggression (along with the evils of partition). The Cosgrave government also established full diplomatic relations with the United States, and it set up legations elsewhere. Such forwardness in diplomatic matters caused much consternation in the British Foreign Office. Cosgrave's actions also caught the attention of other dominions in the Commonwealth – as the British Empire was gradually being renamed – who were quite as anxious as the Irish Free State to enhance their independence. Joint pressure from the Irish Free State, South Africa and Canada was to lead in 1931 to the Statute of Westminster in which was enshrined a much wider definition of dominion status. Perhaps Collins's conviction that the Treaty would be a stepping-stone to freedom might yet be vindicated.

Second, by 1932, when Cosgrave handed over power to Eamon de Valera and his Fianna Fáil party, some progress had been made towards the construction of a truly Gaelic and Catholic society (figure 6.28). It is important to realise that the dream of a genuinely Gaelic Ireland had been cherished on all sides of Irish nationalism since at least the 1890s, and that its realisation in the 1920s was regarded, not so much as the coping-stone of the Irish revolution but as fundamental to the whole revolutionary project itself. Given a choice between ending partition, stemming emigration or reviving the Irish language, few of the revolutionaries would have hesitated. Hence, the Irish language, or Gaelic, was accorded major status in the Free State Constitution (1922), and the Cosgrave

6.28 Mass being celebrated on O'Connell Bridge during the Eucharistic Congress, 1932. Irish Photographic Archive.

government moved swiftly to establish an Irish language test as a condition of entry into, and promotion within, the civil service. More than this, of course, was needed to reverse a decline in Irish-speakers that had been in train since the Famine, and for far longer than that where monoglot Irish speakers were concerned. In 1919 a minister for Irish had been appointed, whose brief also included education, and this had signalled that the task of reviving the language was to be entrusted to the teachers (and children) within the national school system.

Under the Cosgrave government Irish was to be made compulsory in the primary schools, and subjects such as drawing and nature studies were to be elbowed off the curriculum in order to make way for it. The task of language revival, or substitution, was entrusted to the primary schools because it was believed that the 'English only' national schools in the nineteenth century had effectively destroyed Irish and that, therefore, these same schools should now be the prime agency in undoing the damage. The first part of this claim was highly suspect, ignoring as it did, for example, the long history of language decline, the key importance of Irish emigration to anglophone countries and other socio-economic factors to do with language shift. The second part was equally questionable. Reviving a language solely through teaching it throughout the primary school system, regardless of its currency in the home or in the local area, had never been attempted anywhere else in the world. A few voices were raised in protest at children bearing the main burden of restoring Irish, but such criticism was brushed aside, and the experiment was proceeded with. The results were profoundly disappointing: the English language maintained its relentless advance, colonising more and more Gaeltacht (= Irish-speaking) areas.

Before berating the teachers or their pupils for their failure to achieve the sacred national goal entrusted to them, we might consider the efforts of their political masters in this respect. True, many of the founding fathers had been involved in the Gaelic League; but very few Dáil debates were conducted through Irish, and Cabinet meetings were always held in English. In later years few politicians would make speeches in Irish, few wrote letters in Irish and fewer still made any attempt to conduct government business through the medium of the Irish language. (It is instructive in this respect that a knowledge of Irish, while desirable, is not a requirement for a historian who wishes to study the archives of the main actors in the Irish Free State in the decades after 1922.) Given the lack of official recognition of Irish in the business of the state throughout the first decades of independence – and given the persistence of a cluster of adverse economic factors that undermined the language – it is scarcely surprising that the revival project was a resounding failure. What is astonishing, however, is that this clear lack of success was never seen as a reason to redirect energies, or to refocus on the problem of replacing English with Irish. Instead, ever stricter regulations were prescribed for the primary schools, and the nation's teachers were subjected to ever shriller exhortation in this area. Significantly, when Cosgrave's government was succeeded by de Valera's, there was to be no let up in this regard, rather a greater authoritarianism. But a Gaelic Ireland, like an end to partition or to emigration, remained resolutely unachievable.

By contrast a Catholic Ireland, i.e. one in which a Catholic moral code was enshrined in law, might not prove so elusive (figure 6.29). Since the emergence of a Catholic nation in the nineteenth century, there had always been an aspiration for an appropriate state that would reflect that nation's values. The removal of Northern Ireland meant that this task would be all the easier. In 1925 divorce was banned in the Irish Free State, artificial contraception was outlawed – there was never any question of permitting abortion – and throughout the 1920s there was an unrelenting onslaught on 'evil literature', culminating in the Censorship of Publications Act of 1929, which set up a board with powers to censor or ban publications for obscenity or indecency. Earlier, the Censorship of Films Act of 1923 had sought to protect the Irish citizen from 'the menace of Hollywood'.

6.29 Attempted revolution in Dublin. Cartoon from *Dublin Opinion* satirising the obsession with matters of private morality in the new Irish Free State. The perceived weight of clerical influence is very evident. Irish Photographic Archive.

It is easy to scoff at the *mentalité* that lay behind these laws, but we must remember that similar legislation was not unusual in either Europe or the United States at the time. There was a widespread feeling that the Great War had broken down barriers where sexual relations were concerned and throughout the Western world there was alarm at the apparent unchecked spread of sexually transmitted diseases, especially syphilis, which was held to primarily affect men. As a result in almost every country in Europe censorship laws were strengthened and sexual freedoms were reined in. The League of Nations, for example, was particularly exercised about the availability of 'evil literature', and appeared to approve of such legislation. In this near-universal atmosphere of moral panic, it is therefore scarcely surprising that freelance volunteer rescue squads made ready in Ireland to rid the country of 'filth'. English newspapers such as the *News of the World* were a prime object of opprobrium, being sometimes seized and burned; and there were strident demands for the taxing or banning of certain English magazines on the grounds that they might carry information, or even hints, on contraception – a practice indelibly linked with prostitution in the minds of clergy and others. That these papers were English was an added reason for prohibiting their importation, for 'England' was regularly denounced as the *fons et origo* of depravity and sexual licence, and it was claimed that its army had introduced syphilis into Ireland. (It was, admittedly, perplexing that syphilis rates had continued to rise long after the British soldiers had gone, but this puzzle could be explained by Irish women having consorted in their thousands with the departed enemy, thus remaining infected.)

Women generally were objects of suspicion, and there was much alarming comment on them as temptresses, lurking in the popular dance halls or as all-too-willing companions, keen to go for jaunts in the motor cars that were now becoming common. Single mothers, in particular, found the Irish Free State a cold place, and their children too faced a bleak future educated or, all too often, incarcerated in a number of religious, though scarcely Christian, institutions. Many of them would emerge from this experience as damaged adults, given to drink and depression and fit only to shuffle on to the ferry to England. It goes without saying that there was no country in Europe, or in the English-speaking world, where the single mother was viewed indulgently or where her child was cherished. At the same time it seems that both were treated particularly harshly in the Irish Free State, because both threatened those pillars of Irish society, the family unit, property and its safe transmission, and a (largely fictional) self-image of chastity.

Above all, it was axiomatic that the literature of the English contained within it the bacillus that might destroy Catholic Ireland, that it was 'unhealthy' – a word that now took on the meaning that 'degenerate' had in the sixteenth century – and that therefore extraordinary vigilance was required to prevent it entering into the Irish bloodstream. The Censorship Board set to work and, urged on by vigilance groups like the Catholic Truth Society (founded in 1911) or the Legion of Mary (founded in 1925) the bin of banned books filled appreciably: within a short time, 120 books a year were tumbling into it. Some of the works brought to the board's attention were undoubtedly devoid of literary merit; but many, possibly most, were not. It has been calculated that some 70 per cent of the books reviewed in the *Times Literary Supplement* were banned in Ireland, and a list of those authors so stigmatised would form a 'who's who' of modern literature. By contrast, we may note that nothing published in the Irish language – however risqué – was ever censored, nor were books banned whose subject matter was explicitly anti-Protestant, pro-fascist or anti-Semitic.

That said, censorship was routine throughout the Western world: the only difference was in its degree, and at least Ireland never came close to the book-burning orgy of the early years of Hitler's regime in Germany. Again, while many Irish writers were no doubt distraught at the non-availability of the works of modernist authors, most Irish readers were, perhaps, just as pleased to reach for a Zane Grey western or a Georgette Heyer romance. So long as books such as *West of the Pecos* or *Regency Buck* were readily available, few Irish readers appear to have missed the works of Aldous Huxley, Radclyffe Hall or Bertrand Russell. Escapism, whether in print or celluloid, commanded the Irish public's loyalty: Dan Breen's *My Fight for Irish Freedom* (a sort of Irish western) was published in 1931 and achieved a popular success, and two of the biggest sellers in Ireland in 1937 were the programme for the coronation of George VI, and a handbook on emigration to England put out by the *Irish Independent*.

There was also the cinema, for the Irish, more so than the Scots or the English, proved to be inveterate and determined attenders at 'the pictures'. In 1935 there were some 165 cinemas in the Irish Free State, selling around 20 million tickets a year, and despite constant – and clearly futile – fulminations from the pulpits about the 'Los Angelisation' of Ireland, and the 'aphrodisiac influence of the cinema' (Michael Browne, later bishop of Galway), attendance at picture-houses continued to soar. In short, while high culture, or at least its manifestation as modernist literature, was in effect barred from Ireland as 'unhealthy', unsuitable, evil or dangerous, popular culture – the world of the Hollywood gangster movies and westerns, and of trashy romances and crime thrillers, ran on regardless.

The efforts of the Cosgrave government to turn back 'the filthy modern tide' (as Yeats called it, in a different context) and to revive the Irish language did attract some criticism at the time. Those Protestants who were not afraid to put their heads above the parapet, such as W. B. Yeats or Sean O'Casey, railed at the prohibition on divorce, opposed the banning of books and were hugely critical of the elevation of Catholic moral teaching as a sort of supreme law in Ireland. But against such voices there was criticism that the government was not, in fact, doing enough to incorporate Catholic moral teaching into the law of the land, or to promote the Irish language. De Valera, and the Fianna Fáil Party, were particularly scathing of Cosgrave and his ministers for their alleged shortcomings in these areas, and they looked forward to taking office in order to dismantle the Treaty and even replace the 1922 Constitution that had been drawn up on foot of it. By 1930 there was every sign that that day might not be far off.

Cumann na nGaedheal in power

The ending of the civil war in May 1923 had left the Sinn Féin anti-Treatyites, nominally under de Valera's leadership, in considerable disarray but with an unswerving opposition to any political course that might involve recognition of the Irish Free State. De Valera eventually signalled his unwillingness to accept this negative strategy and, in March 1926, he resigned as president of Sinn

Féin. Two months later, he launched the Fianna Fáil party which immediately attracted support from twenty-one of the forty-four abstentionist deputies, and in the general election of June 1927, Fianna Fáil came a close second to the ruling Cumann na nGaedheal Party. An impassioned debate ensued within the new party over whether or not to take the hated 'oath of allegiance' in order to gain entry to the Dáil. Already in Northern Ireland, a total of five nationalist Members of Parliament had renounced abstention and entered Parliament, and this may have had some bearing on the eventual decision. However, in July 1927 the assassination of Kevin O'Higgins, minister for justice and a hate-figure to the IRA, by a gang of freelance republican gunmen brought matters to a head. Emergency legislation was brought in to deal with the crisis provoked by O'Higgins's murder, and one element of it was that those running for election in the Irish Free State had to give a prior commitment to take the oath if elected. A month later, pocketing their principles, their pride and, possibly, a pistol or two, de Valera and his followers duly trooped into the Dáil, and signed the parliamentary oath, dismissing it as 'merely an empty formula'. It must have been difficult, to put it mildly, for those who had suffered during the civil war, on both sides, to hear the alleged *casus belli* so casually dismissed.

Bringing Fianna Fáil in from the wilderness of diehard abstentionism was a signal success for the Cosgrave government, and it built on other measures which bedded down democracy in Ireland. Though the Treatyites had been the military victors in the civil war, there was to be no 'special position' for the National Army, their creation, in the new state. The force was speedily wound down (from 48,000 in 1923 to just 5,800 in 1932) and when some officers expressed their dissatisfaction at this, and at the recruitment of ex-British army officers, the government's response was dramatic. In marked contrast to Asquith's shilly-shallying when faced with the shenanigans at the Curragh in 1914, Cosgrave's government swiftly demanded, and obtained, the resignations of the army's top brass. The minister of defence, and former commander of the army, Richard Mulcahy, quit in protest. The quashing of the 'army mutiny' of March 1924 underlined the civilian credentials of the new government. Pushed out of politics, and starved of arms and equipment, the army had henceforth little option but to devote itself to show-jumping, amateur boxing and military music, at which pursuits it was to gain a great reputation during the interwar years.

Fianna Fáil's progress as a political party was astonishing. Founded in 1926, by 1932 it could contemplate removing Cosgrave and taking power itself. The party's electoral success resulted, first, from the organisational skills of its dedicated party workers – party organisation was a necessary activity that Cumann na nGaedheal had wholly neglected and, second, from the attractiveness of its (fairly radical) social policies, for example, on housing, and from its commitment to implement protection if elected. There was also a progressive disillusionment on the part of a growing proportion of the electorate with the Cosgrave government's measures. Its reduction of the old age pension, from 10 shillings to 9 shillings in 1924, had neither been forgiven nor forgotten, and its apparent inability to do anything about partition, emigration or even the revival of Irish aroused discontent and produced disillusion. A perception of conservatism and pro-British outlook, quite unjustified, allied to its heavy-handed tactics on the eve of the election in prosecuting the *Irish Press* for seditious libel, added to the government's growing unpopularity. The *Irish Press* had been set up in 1931 as the 'national organ' of the Fianna Fáil Party, and it quickly achieved a high circulation. It was an effective propagandist for the cause of an 'Irish Ireland', and it missed no opportunity to attack the *Irish Independent* or the *Irish Times*, respectively the newspapers of the Cumann na nGaedheal Party and of the now-faded ascendancy. In short, Fianna Fáil appealed to those who had not done well out of the new state – the small farmer, the town labourer, women and the poor – to all those who looked for more radical social and economic policies that might realise some of the hopes held out for Irish independence. And if such policies trod on the toes of the former British masters then so much the better.

In February 1932 Fianna Fáil easily outscored Cumann na nGaedheal in the general election, seventy-two seats to fifty-seven seats and, with the support of the handful of Labour deputies, took office. By any standards, this was a remarkable turnaround. De Valera and his colleagues had been defeated in the civil war less than a decade earlier, but now, constitutionally, were poised to supplant those who had vanquished them in that conflict. This was an outcome that many in Ireland and Britain viewed with profound unease. Cosgrave came under pressure to disregard the election result: in Belfast, there were fears of an invasion led by de Valera; and in London ministers waited nervously for news from Dublin. In the event, in a vital service to Irish democracy, Cumann na nGaedheal bowed out gracefully, and took on the uncongenial and unaccustomed role of opposition to a Fianna Fáil government.

It is all too easy to be critical of Cumann na nGaedheal's record in office. Arch-conservatism, married to a stern authoritarianism, made for an uncongenial atmosphere in which those who might be classified as a minority, or labelled marginal, deviant or artistic received short shrift. Protestants usually fell into one or more of these categories and a sizeable proportion took the ferry to England, or the train to Belfast. When Yeats was given the Nobel Prize, he commented, 'now perhaps they will listen to me'. Instead, the award was dismissed, as merely 'a substantial sum provided by a deceased anti-Christian manufacturer of dynamite'. The Protestant population in the twenty-six counties fell from 10 per cent to 7 per cent during the years 1911–26 and, contrary to popular myth, little of this decline was caused by hunting accidents or run-ins with the Hun. Artists of all religions or, more often, none, also made for the boat, fleeing the nets that restricted and threatened to suffocate them. Many of the less fortunate were not able to get out: for the Dublin slum-dweller, independence did indeed make a difference – but only for the worse. Overcrowding, already horrendous in 1911, had increased by 16 per cent by 1926, infant mortality was running at over 9 per cent, and there were nearly eight thousand deaths annually from tuberculosis. In truth the Irish Free State was no land for heroes.

And yet, if the survival of the state is taken as a litmus test, then Cosgrave and his colleagues did do some service. Against all the odds (a bloody civil war is rarely a guarantee of future stability), and in defiance of contemporary precedents (few of the postwar crop of new states made it to maturity), and despite temptations to resort to extra-legal measures (for example, after the murder of O'Higgins), there was to be no significant departure from civilian and constitutional rule. And when the electorate turned against Cumann na nGaedheal, Cosgrave stoically accepted the verdict and prepared to vacate his office. Just as Cosgrave had taken over the Ireland that the British made, so de Valera would inherit the state that Cosgrave had built. What would he do with it?

Northern Ireland in the interwar period

The dramatic change of government in the Irish Free State in 1932 was not replicated in Northern Ireland. A *bouleversement* of that magnitude could not be allowed, for it would inevitably presage the immediate destruction of the state. The maintenance of partition, rather than the defence of the Union, had become the *raison d'être* of Unionism and this required a one-party government and the practical exclusion of Catholics – disloyalists all – from power. As a result, a profound paralysis gripped political life north of the border. A very large number of seats in general elections went uncontested (two-thirds of Unionist Members were returned unopposed in 1932), while those that were contested rarely resulted in an upset to the sitting candidate. Cabinet ministers were seemingly appointed for life, and there were many lesser offices available to buy off the discontented or restless within Unionist ranks. At any one time, around 50 per cent of Unionist Members were government office-holders. Nationalist Members, when they did attend Parliament, were ignored or treated with contempt. By contrast, close attention was paid to fringe Orange and other extreme Protestant organisations, and to labour or temperance or tenant groups, and these could usually, not always, be guaranteed a hearing, and a hand-out, from Craig (after 1927 Lord Craigavon) and his ministers.

The Ulster Protestant League, for example, threatened to run candidates against official Unionist Members of Parliament in the early 1930s on the grounds that they were 'soft' on the Catholic menace. But this threat receded when the League was allowed to meet at Unionist headquarters in Glengall Street, Belfast, and was more or less incorporated into mainstream Unionism. Again, there could be no question of scrapping the 'B' Special paramilitary force: it would have been political suicide for any Unionist minister to seek to remove them from permanent duty, i.e. permanent pay. Stormont, the grandiose Parliament building completed in November 1932, symbolised Unionists' determination to maintain 'their' state against any perceived threats. In addition, the pageantry that surrounded the formal opening, and the unveiling of a splendid statue of Sir Edward Carson by the prince of Wales, drew Unionists of all hues together (while offering a delicious counter-blast to the celebrations surrounding the Eucharistic Congress in the Free State a few months earlier).

In so far as normal political life existed in Northern Ireland, then it did so within the Protestant and Catholic communities, but not between them, and revolved around, on the one hand, matters of security, the defence of Protestantism and the maintenance of the border, and on the other, the question of abstentionism or attendance at Stormont. Educational issues, always potentially disruptive, were not neglected but the sting was taken out of them by the ready concession of, in effect, parallel but almost equal Protestant and Catholic systems of education. Catholic schools were less well-funded than state, i.e. Protestant, schools, though all schools in Northern Ireland were better funded than their equivalents in the Free State. (By 1950, Northern Ireland, with half the population of the Irish Republic, was spending twice as much on education.) However, the Catholic bishops regarded less generous funding for their schools in Northern Ireland as a small price to pay for retaining full control over the education of Catholic youth there. Segregated education had been a much-deplored feature of Irish life since the mid-nineteenth century and it was now set to continue indefinitely into the future. Separate or denominational education mirrored pre-existing divisions between the Catholic and Protestant communities in Northern Ireland, but over the next decades it would prove to be a powerful agent for reinforcing Catholic alienation from, and Protestant loyalty to, the northern state.

Arguably, the threat to the economy was the most serious one that the Northern Ireland government faced in the interwar years, but that is a claim made from the vantage point of hindsight. As noted above, no government, north or south, saw it as its primary responsibility to 'drive economic growth' and, in any case, in a pre-Keynesian era of strict monetary control and protectionism, the economic options open to governments were severely limited. And, as we have seen, full control of finances (unlike responsibility for security) had been denied Northern Ireland by the terms of the Government of Ireland Act. In addition, and it is an important point, although some form of partition had been on the cards since 1916 and probably since 1914, no separate or 'Home Rule' government for Northern Ireland had been envisaged as late as 1919. Craig and his colleagues, unlike Cosgrave and Collins, had hurriedly to accustom themselves, first mentally, then practically, to the business of (restricted) self-government.

And yet, even with these caveats in mind the Unionist governments of Northern Ireland proved to be remarkably complacent in the 1920s and 1930s. By just about every measurement available – unemployment, wages, gross domestic product, outdoor relief, infant mortality, life expectancy, house-building, tuberculosis rates, numbers in second level or higher education, scholarships available – Northern Ireland, of all the regions in the United Kingdom, regularly and depressingly topped the list or came out bottom in the years up to the outbreak of the Second World War. (In fairness, during the interwar years, the murder rate in Northern Ireland was significantly lower than elsewhere in the United Kingdom, two to three per year, as compared to 150 in the UK generally, with a population thirty times greater. Consolingly, perhaps, a very large percentage of those murdered were not personally known to the attacker, but were done to death during civil disturbances.)

It mattered little that the Irish Free State performed marginally worse during these decades and endured a steady emigration of its citizens – something Northern Ireland was largely spared, though Catholics made up a disproportionate percentage of those who did leave; what was scandalous was the insouciance with which the Unionist government viewed these gloomy reports. As the average age of Cabinet ministers crept up from the mid-fifties in the early 1920s to the mid-sixties in the late 1930s, the frustration of top civil servants, such as Sir Wilfrid Spender, at the slow pace of change and the lack of response to pressing problems was palpable. Sir James Craig, once a formidable leader of Unionist resistance to Irish Home Rule, by the mid-1920s had run out of energy and ideas. He had seemingly settled for populist profligacy, endlessly gladhanding disaffected Unionists and Protestant splinter groups rather than confronting them, and he was increasingly erratic in his decision-making, a development possibly linked to his fondness for ever longer holidays. A visiting English civil servant put his finger on the problem: he wrote that while de Valera had decisively cut himself off from the IRA in the Free State, Craigavon had refused to sever his links with the paramilitary sectarian force, the Ulster Special Constabulary or 'B' Specials. For Craigavon the maintenance of a state of siege, the inculcation of a siege mentality and the quest for a permanent crisis that would unite Ulster Protestants and keep them in line took precedence over any long-term strategy aimed at making partition normal and the Union with Great Britain a given.

Above all, there seemed to be no recognition on the part of Unionist ministers that, so long as Catholics *as Catholics* were constantly reminded that they were a category of disloyalists rather than a constituency of citizens – and as such could expect to be subject to discrimination – then there was no prospect of partition bedding down. Equally, so long as Unionist employers were exhorted never to employ a Catholic, so long as Unionist politicians boasted that they had never done so, and so long as the Orange Order claimed in effect the primary allegiance of over 90 per cent of Unionist Members of Parliament (the remainder were either women, or mavericks) then, with 35 per cent of the population firmly excluded and left to contemplate their grievances, the permanence of the Union had to remain problematic.

On one occasion a crack appeared in the Unionist edifice. The worldwide slump, triggered by the Wall Street crash of 1929, had hit Northern Ireland hard, for its workforce in the traditional heavy industries was especially vulnerable to global depression. Unemployment soared and, by 1932, there were nearly eighty thousand out of work in Belfast alone. A substantial proportion of these men, mostly Catholic but including Protestants too, having exhausted their claim to state benefit, were dependent on outdoor relief. This was a small payment fixed upon and administered by a board of guardians, and it was really aimed at relieving those who were incapable of working rather than attending to the needs of the able-bodied workless. Perhaps predictably, Belfast's outdoor relief was much less than that of any other large city in the United Kingdom. What was less predictable was that Protestant and Catholic workers, whose mutual hostility had been the foundation of the Unionist front, would come together in opposition to the paltry sum offered and to the indignities attendant on receiving it.

In October 1932 a protest march of some sixty thousand unemployed culminated in a mass rally in the centre of Belfast. A further rally led to unprecedented non-sectarian rioting during which two men were shot dead and dozens injured. For a brief period, it appeared that a labour or even socialist front, embracing Protestant and Catholic workers, might emerge; but the moment passed. Richard Dawson Bates, the hard-line minister for home affairs, swiftly defused the crisis by timely concession – the police were declared exempt from pay cuts (unlike elsewhere in the United Kingdom), the 'B' Specials were mobilised, an IRA plot was uncovered (a 'Moscow' plot too for good measure), the draconian Special Powers Act was made permanent and the unemployed had their relief upped. Such populist policies worked: by the end of the year, the customary internecine feuding had been resumed, and the Unionist hierarchy could rest easy.

Serious sectarian rioting flared up in Belfast in the spring and summer of 1935 and left eleven dead (mostly Protestant), hundreds injured and hundreds more (mostly Catholic) expelled from their homes. The riots showed that the united working-class protest of 1932 had not been a proletarian breakthrough but merely a temporary aberration. The disturbances had broken out while Craigavon was on a three-month holiday touring South America. But he saw no need to return home, and happily left it to his eighty-three-year-old deputy, Hugh Pollock, to deal with the matter. In marked contrast to previous outbreaks of communal disorder – and surely an indication of how reassuring, if regrettable, such sectarian commotions were to those in the Unionist establishment – there was to be no independent examination into the causes or handling of the riots. Cogent Catholic allegations of inflammatory speeches directed against them, massively one-sided police operations, and judicial bias against those sent for trial, were simply swept aside. Stanley Baldwin, the then British prime minister, flatly refused a request by a hundred British Members of Parliament for an inquiry to be held, on the grounds that 'law and order' in the province were matters for the Northern Ireland government.

The first twenty years of Home Rule for Northern Ireland, then, saw little change in the sectarian structure and nature of its society and politics; if anything there was a consolidation of the forces keeping Catholic and Protestant apart. Divisions were reinforced by the construction of parallel societies, and shored up by conflicting memories of deaths, expulsions and destruction. It was entirely possible, at least in Belfast and probably Derry, less so in the countryside, to live one's entire life without becoming acquainted with, interacting in business with, or socialising with, anyone who was not 'one of us'. Whole networks of Catholic streets, schools, social clubs, religious sodalities, fraternal organisations, shops, pubs, sports, hospitals, newspapers, doctors, lawyers, employers and undertakers catered for almost all of the needs of that community. It was a similar story with the Protestant community, but with several important additions. First, Protestants had their hands on the levers of political power (for example, fifty out of sixty councillors on Belfast city council were Unionists, and through manipulation of ward boundaries they could constitute a political majority even where they were a numerical minority – as in Derry). Second, they controlled and massively dominated the police forces (less than 18 per cent – and falling – of the Royal Ulster Constabulary was Catholic in the mid-1930s, and there were no Catholics in the 'Specials'). Third, Protestants disproportionately held the highly prized jobs in the public service. In 1934 Catholics constituted just 10 per cent of the lower ranks of the Northern Ireland civil service, a lower percentage than nine years earlier. The trend continued: by 1943, they made up only 5.8 per cent of the bottom grades and there were none (out of fifty-five) at the permanent and assistant secretary level. In 1933 the minister of labour (and future prime minister), J. M. Andrews, angrily refuted the malicious allegation that of the thirty-one porters at Stormont, twenty-eight were Catholics: after a full investigation, he could state unequivocally that there were in fact thirty Protestant porters and one Catholic – and he was there only 'temporarily'.

It is true that by 1939, the Unionist governments of the interwar years could point to some significant economic and social achievements. It had been evident from an early date that Northern Ireland, with its small population base and its tiny area of economic activity, on its own could never afford to pay for the various improvements in social welfare, health insurance and old age pensions that were gradually being introduced into Britain in the 1930s. In passing, it might be noted that Unionists stoutly resisted the categorisation of Northern Ireland as a 'Special Area' within the United Kingdom, entitled to claim extra funding from London: such a designation was held to be an admission of failure and thus had to be resisted. At the same time, it was vital to overcome treasury resistance in London and win the important concession of 'step by step' social welfare advances, which would mean that those resident in Northern Ireland would suffer no loss in their entitlements from living there. By and large this point had been conceded by the late 1920s; and the British treasury, too, had been forced to turn a blind eye to Craigavon's favourite populist ploy of never allowing any aggrieved Protestant deputation or delegation to leave his presence without the promise of a cheque to assuage their wounded feelings.

However, politics mattered more than economics. In terms of social welfare entitlements, Catholics were undoubtedly better off in Northern Ireland than in the Free State, and the Catholic population of the state grew by over 10 per cent in the interwar years (the Catholic population of the Free State fell by around 3 per cent, through emigration, in the same period), but they did not have a sense of belonging there, and this was the important point. Catholics endured chronic joblessness during these years, for while they made up 35 per cent of the population, they always represented over 50 per cent of the unemployed. Again, Catholics suffered from systemic discrimination, and they were never made to feel valued and, in the end, this was what counted. The dismissal of a Catholic gardener from Stormont said it all: he had served in the forces in the Great War and possessed a 'character' from none other than the prince of Wales, but neither of these distinctions could outweigh his 'disloyalist' credentials and he had to go.

Catholic alienation would remain the Achilles' heel of the Unionist state. In order to secure the future of the Union with Great Britain, and to maintain partition, what was required was imaginative, courageous and tough-minded political leadership on the part of Unionist politicians; but this never emerged. And while Sir Wilfrid Spender might see the need to pursue inclusionist policies, in the end, the short-term goal of maintaining Protestant unity was pursued by Craigavon at the expense of a long-term strategy of accommodating parts of the Catholic community. The suffocating requirement to maintain Unionist solidarity at all costs took precedence over any more creative, generous or inclusive policy. Long after the siege was lifted the political benefits of a state of siege continued to be cherished, and the insouciant nostrum of Sir Jonah Barrington, an eighteenth-century gadfly, was embraced: why worry about posterity – what has posterity ever done for us?

Fianna Fáil in power

In the Irish Free State the dire predictions that the victory of de Valera and his Fianna Fáil Party in the 1932 election would lead to economic chaos, political instability and bloody revenge soon proved unwarranted.[6] True, in an early gesture towards his former revolutionary base, de Valera did order the immediate release of all IRA prisoners, the closure of the military tribunal that had sentenced them and the suspension (but not repeal) of the draconian Public Security Act. However, to the disappointment of some of his supporters, there was to be no declaration of a republic, or a witch-hunt over actions carried out during the civil war. The civil service, which had feared the worst, was left untroubled and so too was the National Army which had defeated the anti-Treaty forces, though the appointment of Frank Aiken, a former chief of staff of the IRA, as minister of defence, would test its loyalty. (Its patience would be tried by de Valera's instruction to halt the weekly issue of condoms to soldiers.) Again, to some surprise, Eoin O'Duffy, the Garda Commissioner, and a hate-figure with republicans, was allowed to remain in office – though within six months he had goaded de Valera into dismissing him.

There was change, of course, but it was change within continuity, for while de Valera moved to effect a number of symbolic alterations in the Anglo-Irish relationship, these would be accomplished within the framework created by the earlier patient work of the Cumann na nGaedheal government. The existing governor-general was snubbed, then replaced with a nonentity who was ordered to take no action unless instructed to, and then finally the office – 'a badge of our slavery' claimed de Valera – was abolished altogether in 1936. Judicial appeals to the English privy council were outlawed, the 'oath of allegiance' was dropped (the Senate, which had sought to delay this, now found itself in the firing line, and destined for destruction), and all reference to the crown was removed from state documents. These changes were scarcely earth-shaking, but they had the desired effects of demonstrating to the Fianna Fáil faithful – the term is not premature – that de Valera was as determined as ever to renegotiate the 1922 Treaty. They also had the huge advantage of arousing British ministers to fury. Further provocation was offered by de Valera's refusal to hand over to the British exchequer the annuities payable by Irish farmers as the price for gaining a legal title to their land under the earlier Land Acts.

The notion of refusing to pay the land annuities was one that had been circulating among left-wing republicans during the 1920s. De Valera now took it up, but with an important, though often overlooked, twist: contrary to what the likes of the socialist, Peadar O'Donnell, had called for, the annuities were still to be collected but, henceforth, were to be retained by Dublin, rather than transferred to London. De Valera's action was ostensibly aimed at rewarding and placating his supporters among the small-farming classes and, further to these ends, he soon halved the amount of annuities to be paid. However, stopping the annuities also had the effect of reopening the more contentious clauses of the 1922 Treaty. Perhaps this was the objective that de Valera aimed at all along?

British retaliation was swift: denied the Irish annuities by de Valera, the money would instead be raised by a heavy tariff imposed on a variety of Irish exports to Britain. Against the advice of his officials in the Department of Finance, de Valera ordered similar impositions on British imports into Ireland. The ensuing 'economic war' was a most unequal contest, and Irish farming interests, especially those involved in cattle-rearing suffered grievously; the quest for sovereignty would carry a high price. De Valera was adamant that at issue was Ireland's control over its own finances: but he also claimed that the farm annuities were of a piece with continued British possession of naval bases in Cork and Donegal which also infringed Irish sovereignty.

The 'economic war' ended as another war loomed. In 1938, following negotiations in London between British prime minister, Neville Chamberlain, and de Valera, the land annuities were written off in return for a one-off payment of £10 million (in place of £5 million per annum to the British exchequer) and the 'Treaty' ports were returned to Ireland. By any standards, this was an astonishing deal: the final payment to Britain for the annuities was a truly remarkable bargain, while the return of the naval bases gave 'Ireland' (as the twenty-six counties were to be called since the ratification of the new Constitution in 1937), for the first time, full sovereignty over its national territory.

The concessions by Chamberlain aroused much opposition in Britain, but they have to be seen as part of his wider, and later much criticised, policy of appeasement. In the case of de Valera's Ireland, appeasement meant little more than the redress of Ireland's financial and constitutional grievances – as identified by de Valera. Significantly, while de Valera did raise partition in his negotiations with the British he did not press it, and he may have done so purely with an eye to the optics. He did not bring up the issue of the treatment of Catholics in Northern Ireland at all. With the outbreak of war in September 1939 Ireland's refusal to allow the Royal Navy – or anyone else – the use of the recently returned ports, was roundly condemned by British politicians, particularly Winston Churchill, soon to be Chamberlain's successor as prime minister. De Valera was unperturbed: Ireland's declaration of neutrality in the ensuing world conflict was made possible by the return to Irish control of the Treaty ports, and Ireland's firm exclusion of all belligerent forces from its sovereign territory would make credible its continued neutral stance.

The economic policy that Fianna Fáil pursued on taking power in 1932 was also largely bound up with the pursuit of sovereignty. Just as an 'Irish Ireland' was the goal in cultural matters and in Anglo-Irish relations, so too an Ireland that was self-sufficient was the goal aimed at in economics. The desired outcome was an Ireland that was dependent on no one, and an Ireland whose new industries (established behind high tariff walls) would be controlled by Irish industrialists, not foreigners (including, curiously, those born in Northern Ireland). To implement this strategy, control of manufactures legislation was passed in 1932 and 1934 to ensure that foreign capital and foreign capitalists were kept at arm's length, and imported goods were burdened with heavy tariffs.

It is difficult to assess the overall result of this policy during the 1930s. The Great Depression was a huge complicating factor, for it triggered a flight from free trade throughout the developed world, and Ireland's high tariff barriers were replicated throughout Europe (those of France, for example, were much higher and more numerous). With a much smaller industrial base Ireland, though not Northern Ireland, would escape the worst effects of the depression. True, emigration to the United States practically ground to a halt because of the dire unemployment situation there, but this was compensated for by movement to Britain which now became the destination of choice for those leaving. Moreover, the Fianna Fáil government instituted an extensive state programme of house-building with some 65,000 dwellings being constructed between 1932 and 1939, and this was a major boost to the economy. Lastly, few of the regulations were strictly enforced: had they been, the Ford Motor Company could not have lasted in Cork, nor could the plants of the Lever Brothers (soap), Crosse and Blackwell (food) and Rowntree and Mackintosh (sweets) have survived elsewhere in Ireland.

In short, the picture is mixed: what can be said with confidence is, first, that the 'economic war' hit the large farmers, especially graziers, very hard, for the cross-channel cattle trade was nearly wiped out; second, government action may have raised the number of those at work by nearly 50,000 (probably the first increase since the Famine), and more generous welfare allowances and pensions helped those who were out of work; third, less-than-strict protectionism, on balance, probably benefited Irish industry and helped boost output by some 40 per cent; and, finally, that while economic conditions in Ireland were certainly not prosperous in the 1930s, they did compare favourably with Depression-hit more 'modern' economies in continental Europe. Fianna Fáil's mistake in government, and it was to be a costly one, was not that it pursued economic policies based on self-sufficiency through protection in the 1930s, but rather that it adhered to that strategy down to the 1960s, by which time it had long passed its sell-by date.

Culturally, de Valera's Ireland continued in the footsteps of the Cosgrave government – though, unlike Cosgrave, de Valera did not need phonetic flashcards when saying a few words in Irish in public. As before, the revival of the language was declared to be a national priority and Tomás Derrig, minister of education, i.e. minister for the revival of Irish, and a great language enthusiast, was tireless, and very likely tiresome, in his exhortations to teachers to fulfil the nation's destiny. He was certainly as lacking in success, and as unreflective, as earlier ideologues: Gaeltacht areas continued to shrink and the number of native speakers fell, but no one appears to have asked why, or shouted stop. In other battles along the cultural front, 'dirty' or 'unsuitable' books continued to be pulped: between 1932 and 1939 some 1,200 books and 140 magazines fell foul of the censorship board. On the other hand, theatrical productions were rarely censored, but then, they did not need to be: the Abbey played it entirely safe, while in the 1930s the Gate Theatre under the direction of Micheál MacLiammóir was slightly more adventurous; but neither really rattled the theatrical dovecots. In any case, professional theatre was for the middle-class elite; they did not want to be challenged at the theatre, and theatre managers had no intention of allowing them to be upset.

In more recondite areas of intellectual inquiry the 1930s saw some significant developments. Building on the establishment of the Irish Manuscripts Commission in 1928 – set up to locate, calendar, and publish Irish historical documents – *Irish Historical Studies* was begun in 1938 as a 'north–south' journal, dedicated to a dispassionate search for value-free (i.e. emotionally sterile, morally dubious and utterly boring) history; inevitably, its inquiries were confined to the period before 1900. In a parallel attempt at capturing, or creating an authentic history, the Irish Folklore Commission was founded in 1935 and charged with gathering the tales, customs and beliefs of the plain people of Ireland. There was a great urgency to this work, for the rural communities that were the custodians of these stories were fast disappearing. On a different level, at de Valera's prompting, the Dublin Institute for Advanced Studies was set up in June 1940, just after Mussolini declared in favour of Hitler, but before the surrender of France. Its small band of specialist areas ranged from the analysis of Early Irish texts to the study of cosmic physics; early research findings, as reported by the acerbic humorist Flann O'Brien, suggested the existence of two St Patricks, and put a question mark against the existence of God. With the fate of Western civilisation itself hanging in the balance at that time, such investigations were welcome diversions, and reassuringly confirmed that Ireland's priorities continued to lie with the spiritual, or other-worldly, rather than with the material, even in a time of war.

The Fianna Fáil government of the 1930s faced threats from both the left and the right, but it successfully faced both down. IRA enthusiasm for de Valera, never very high, quickly cooled when it became clear that he would make no precipitate move on declaring a republic, or take action on partition. Following a number of attacks on Gardaí, and the callous murder of two members of the public, the IRA and a number of other republican splinter groups were banned in 1936. By this date, the IRA may have numbered as many as four thousand members but, torn apart by ideological splits and distracted by divisions over strategy, it was never able to deploy its strength to any effect. A futile, quixotic, though deadly campaign in Britain, on the eve of the war, achieved precisely nothing in the political sense. But seven civilians were killed by explosions, and two IRA volunteers were executed. When war was declared, de Valera did not hesitate to intern IRA activists for its duration. De Valera's break with his erstwhile supporters, the 'Legion of the Rearguard', could scarcely have been more decisive.

The threat from the right was also comparatively easily seen off. Disgruntled ex-servicemen from the National Army, fearful at the prospect of de Valera taking power, mindful of the civil war, and furious at what they saw as IRA bullyboy tactics against Cumann na nGaedheal activists, formed an Army Comrades Association in February 1932.[7] Members of Cumann na nGaedheal also joined later, especially in areas of Munster badly hit by de Valera's 'economic war'. The movement was headed for a time by the dismissed Garda Commissioner, 'General' Eoin O'Duffy. Its members wore a blue shirt – hence their popular name – and sported black berets. They also adopted straight-arm salutes like those of Italian or German fascists, as well as some of their rituals. In so far as they had a coherent ideology, it was derived from Catholic social thought, as expressed in various papal encyclicals, and they also preached anti-bolshevism and anti-Semitism. Notwithstanding, their primary motivations clearly lay in civil war hatreds, and in detestation of de Valera (a 'foreign mongrel of unknown origin') for the damage wrought to the large farming interests by his 'economic war'. At their peak, they may have numbered fifty thousand, a very impressive figure on paper, but, like the IRA, they were never able to deploy their full strength, and in any case, O'Duffy was a poor leader, much given to drink, and he proved erratic, unstable, paranoid and conspiratorial. Enthusiastic backing from W. B. Yeats made little difference. Duffy eventually led a contingent of his men to Spain in November 1936 to fight for Franco and the nationalists. To the glee of his many enemies the expedition was swiftly terminated in black farce: the Dublin IRA member, and future playwright, Brendan Behan, chortled that O'Duffy's peninsular campaign had been truly remarkable in that he had returned to Ireland with more men than he had set out with. (Those volunteers who fought for the republican side in Spain were not to be so fortunate.)

The Blueshirts merged with Cumann na nGaedheal in 1933 to form the Fine Gael party (though subsequently that party has been afflicted with severe memory loss over acknowledging that O'Duffy was its first leader). In the end, for all the alarm generated by their parades, their uniform and their social theories, the Blueshirts resembled O'Connell's repeal movement of the 1840s more closely than their Nazi contemporaries, and they were put down just as easily. Emergency laws, suspended when de Valera came into power, were revived and directed against individual Blueshirts (and members of the IRA) and when a provocative march by O'Duffy and his men was banned by de Valera's government in August 1933, they meekly accepted it; a humiliating climbdown, from which the movement never really recovered. The suppression of the Blueshirt threat had the effect of establishing Fianna Fáil's democratic and non-revolutionary credentials. The party was now much more than 'slightly constitutional'; indeed it was now claiming to be the party of law and order – perhaps the importance of the Blueshirts lies here?

The reality was that the social conditions for a genuine fascist movement did not exist in Ireland in the 1930s. Economic melt-down had not occurred, and though the agricultural slump was potentially threatening, the middle and professional classes continued to do nicely, and Fianna Fáil's welfarist policies eased matters somewhat for those at the bottom of the economic ladder. To the relief of some government ministers and civil servants, emigration continued to siphon off potential troublemakers among the lower classes, and thus reduced considerably the combustible elements in Irish society. Again, the so-called 'communist menace' was a joke, for the number of communists was derisory. Meanwhile, the governing elites, whether Fianna Fáil or Fine Gael in orientation, remained wedded to the British model of democracy and wanted no reprise of the civil war. And the Catholic church offered a broad welcome to both Treatyites and their opponents; there was equality at the altar rails and, perhaps, in the confessional. True, there was plenty of fear and loathing, and there was no shortage of anxieties and resentments – the Blueshirts were one expression of these and the IRA was another – but the stifling consensus at the heart of Irish life was simply too great to be broken. Nor was that consensus fractured when de Valera took on the hugely contentious task of replacing the hated 'Free State' Constitution of 1922 with his own conception of what Ireland's basic law ought to be.

The 1937 Constitution

It is tempting to suggest that de Valera turned to framing a new constitution[8] in order to distract attention from some of the less successful outcomes of his first few years in power, notably the failure to stem the outflow of emigrants and the onset of the disastrous 'economic war' with Britain; but this is a temptation that should be resisted. De Valera had never concealed his distaste, even detestation, for what many republicans saw as a 'pagan' Constitution, in effect, imposed on the Irish people in 1922 by 'a foreign non-Catholic power', i.e. the British state. It was, therefore, probably inevitable that, with his consolidation of power following his success in the 1933 general election, his thoughts would turn to framing a new constitution. Some recasting of the 1922 document was in fact needed, for the Cumann na nGaedheal government had been steadily chipping away at it since its inception, and de Valera's early actions to remove the oath and shut off appeals to the English privy council had further undermined it.

In April 1935 de Valera instructed the legal adviser to the Department of External Affairs to begin drafting the heads of a new constitution. It is probable that de Valera, even then, had a very clear idea of what he wanted – and what he did not want – to see in the new arrangement; and he had the draftsmen at hand who could turn his vision into a reality. This was to be a constitution that reflected, and addressed, the needs and aspirations of a Catholic nation; but it was not to be a Catholic document, for de Valera entertained genuine, if wholly unrealistic, hopes that it would form a basis for the future unification of the island. It was to be a constitution that enshrined a vision of what Ireland might become, but it was not to be a visionary document that ignored Irish realities, for it was notorious that the Irish state was not coterminous with the Irish nation. It was to be a republican document and there would be no mention of the British crown: but there was to be no declaration of a republic, and even the very word, republic, would be avoided, perhaps again, in deference to northern Unionist opinion. Especially, it was to be a constitution that the Irish people – though not those cut off in Northern Ireland – would ratify, rather than the one that was forever flawed by the very fact of its imposition without a referendum in 1922. Not that the Free State Constitution of 1922 was completely binned. As the drafting process got under way, large chunks of it, primarily dealing with the courts and the Parliament or *Oireachtas*, were lifted seamlessly into the new arrangement. Some constitutional experts have, therefore, considered the 1937 Constitution as much more a continuation of the 1922 Constitution rather than a definitive or decisive break with it. (Some seventy years later, a similar argument broke out over the relationship of the Good Friday Agreement of 1998 to the St Andrews Agreement of 2006.)

It is in the nature of constitution-making – and the unfolding saga of the interpretation of the clauses of the United States Constitution, from its ratification in 1787 down to the present, is a case in point – that what exercised contemporaries about the merits, or otherwise, of various articles, would not at all be those that would draw trenchant criticism or warm praise from later generations. Thus the claim (articles 2 and 3) that the national territory was the whole island but that for practical reasons legislation passed by the Dáil would run only in the twenty-six counties was much less contentious in 1937 than it would be in later decades. Protestant and Unionist criticism, in the main, focused on the absence of any mention of the crown; 'lofty indifference', might just about sum up the attitude of Craigavon's government to the whole exercise. For their part, northern nationalists were pleased that they had not been completely airbrushed out of 'the nation'. Again, the recognition afforded 'the special position' of the Catholic church (article 44), drew little hostile comment at the time. Admittedly, republican doctrinaires complained that it marked – as did the entire document – a repudiation of the Easter week proclamation. And orthodox Catholic opinion, as voiced by John Charles McQuaid, then headmaster of Blackrock College and later archbishop of Dublin, and Edward Cahill, a Jesuit social theorist, may also have been a little disappointed by some of the formulations in the document. They might well have wanted something more unequivocal in the Constitution (the Catholic church as the 'one true church', for example) and they were not best pleased – to put it mildly – with the state's formal recognition of other Christian denominations. They particularly disliked the acceptance of the main Irish Protestant church's claim to be the 'Church of Ireland'.

Curiously, however, in the light of later condemnation of this article, there was little Protestant criticism at the time of the 'special position' of the Catholic church. Presumably this was because the population of twenty-six-county Ireland was 95 per cent Catholic and that, therefore, article 44 could be seen as simple recognition of, as the *Irish News* of Belfast put it, 'a plain fact'. Nor did northern Protestants make much fuss over this article. Indeed, the outgoing moderator of the Presbyterian Assembly, a certain Dr O'Neill, went so far as to voice his approval of the 1937 Constitution as a 'Christian' document, and expressed his gratitude for the article recognising the various religious denominations. (Inevitably, a storm of criticism burst over the unfortunate man, who had clearly forgotten his script, his position and his audience: praise for de Valera and the

new Irish Constitution from a northern Protestant cleric was simply not on.)
(The sections of article 44 addressing the position of the Catholic church were
removed by referendum in 1972.) In passing, we might note that article 44 also
afforded recognition to the 'Jewish congregations'. At a time when one of the
most cultured nations in Europe was embarking on the destruction of European
Jewry, this was a declaration that was not without risk or a certain nobility. In
the event, however, this article was to offer the Jews no protection or shelter
when the Holocaust was unleashed – possibly the grand total of sixty obtained
refuge in Ireland.

Three aspects of the proposed new Constitution elicited much adverse comment at the time. The first concerned the establishment of the new office of
president of Ireland who would be elected by a direct vote of the people. This
was perhaps the most contentious of all the articles. In the first instance there
was concern that the president might upstage the Taoiseach (prime minister),
but there was also a real fear that de Valera was preparing the ground for a
dictatorship. (For the Blueshirts of Fine Gael, fear of a dictatorship at this time
might be an example of what psychologists call projection.) In point of fact the
position of president turned out to be almost entirely a ceremonial one, though
he (a 'she' was not envisaged in the wording of the document) would be commander of the army and he would have some important functions at moments of
constitutional crisis, for example in dissolving the Dáil. He would also have the
power to refer legislation to the newly created Supreme Court. However, at a
time when dictatorships were increasingly the norm in Europe, the opposition's
alarm was quite understandable; and indeed de Valera probably did aspire to
the presidency, but he saw the office as a comfortable berth for the time when
he retired as Taoiseach, not as a stepping-stone to totalitarianism.

A second aspect that aroused much criticism, was the accusation that, despite
its ringing declaration of religious liberty and its guarantee against religious discrimination, the Constitution, in effect, enshrined the Catholic moral code as the
fundamental law of the land. Not just legislatively but constitutionally divorce
was outlawed, contraception was prohibited, even 'blasphemy' was banned – and
the latter was, presumably, to be defined by reference to Catholic doctrine. In this
regard, we may note again that some Catholic intellectuals were a little hurt at, in
their view, how little of Catholic teaching was in the Constitution; for example,
that no constitutional ban on Freemasonry (a bugbear of Fr Cahill, and others) had been introduced into it. And by comparison with other constitutions –
such as those of Great Britain or Norway – the religious aspect was rather
low key; unlike in these countries where the highest office-holders had to be a
Protestant or, in Norway's case, an Evangelical Lutheran, there was nothing in
de Valera's Constitution that positively required a president or a Taoiseach, or

6.30 Mother and widow: Mrs Pearse, mother of Patrick and William, along with Mrs Hannah Sheehy-Skeffington, at Earlsfort Terrace, Dublin, 1920s. Irish Photographic Archive.

indeed any office-holder, to be a Catholic. Also, the prohibition on divorce was hardly new; and the fact was, it was acceptable to many Protestants as well. As before, opposition to such articles, mostly, was restricted to those – writers, artists, left-wingers and the other usual suspects – who had been in the van against earlier legislation on contraception and divorce. At the time, their complaints were easily ignored, but in the 1970s and later, criticism of the 'Catholic articles' would not be so easily brushed aside.

Lastly, the Constitution attracted adverse comment at the time because of the clearly subordinate and unequal role that it envisaged for women (figure 6.30) in the new Ireland, though, once again, opposition in 1937 paled into insignificance when compared to the torrent of abuse that descended in later years on these articles in de Valera's Constitution, the basic document of 'de Valera's Ireland'. Essentially, de Valera's Constitution saw the family as the natural unit of society, regarded a woman's place (her 'life') as being 'within the home', and endeavoured to make a commitment that no 'mother' should have to work outside the home because of 'economic necessity'. Once again, it is easy to see how these articles (40.1 and 42.2 respectively), rightly, would arouse indignation because of their paternalist assumptions and because they were, even as they were being drafted, anachronistic and largely ideal.

Feminists such as Louie Bennett and Hannah Sheehy-Skeffington led the protests and they were supported by Mrs Tom Clarke, widow of the 1916 martyr, by Professor Mary Hayden of University College, Dublin, and by the Womens' Graduate Association. From Britain, the Six Point Group, an organisation that lobbied on behalf of womens' rights, claimed that the offending articles embodied 'a fascist and slave conception of women'. The protesters had some success in causing the removal of some of the more objectionable wording, particularly about the respective bodily strengths of men and women, and the latter's fitness, or otherwise, for certain tasks, but, in the crucial areas of paternalist control they failed to make any impression. It is clear that many women and mothers agreed with de Valera's construction of their role: the Constitution would not have passed – by 685,000 votes to 520,000 – if this were not the case. It is instructive, also, that a feminist attempt to keep up the fight in subsequent general elections in 1938 and 1943 proved fruitless.

The key criticisms of the offending articles, as valid in 1937 as in later decades, were these. First, even as they were being drafted, Irish women were fleeing Ireland (and the home) in their tens of thousands, and the proportion of 'mothers' to women in the country remained the lowest in Europe, largely because the proportion of unmarried women was the highest in Europe. The reality of motherhood in Ireland in the 1930s was that because of the social and economic collapse of rural Ireland, fewer Irishwomen than ever could realistically aspire to that status. Second, and damningly, de Valera made little attempt to make his vision a reality, or to transform his pious rhetoric into something practical. It stood to reason that if Irishmen were paid more then perhaps more Irishwomen could stay at home, but this did not happen, and 'economic necessity' made a mockery of de Valera's aspiration that women would not have to labour outside the house. Irish women would find employment – but in a restricted range of jobs, with inferior conditions and for lower wages than their male counterparts. Third, if an Irish mother's place was in the home, then why not reward her financially for staying there? Fianna Fáil did have some radical policies in the 1930s, at least in comparison to Cumann na nGaedheal: they upped unemployment benefit and old age pensions, and they invested in an extensive house-building programme, but on the issue of mothers, they fell short. True, it was a Fianna Fáil government that brought in children's allowances in 1944, before they were introduced in Britain, but they made them payable not to the mother but to the father (which, in too many cases, meant the local publican); seemingly, the ex-revolutionaries took fright at this attack on patriarchy. Fourth, there was a further telling contemporary argument that might be made: the proposed constitution stated that all citizens would be 'equal before the law'. It was, therefore, arguable that the offending woman/mother articles were, in effect, unconstitutional at the very moment they were being ratified. Certainly, decades later, this equality article was used to strike down, among other discriminations, the barring of women from jury service (an exclusion imposed ten years before de Valera's Constitution), the ban on married female teachers and the posting of unequal pay rates in the civil service. In other words, in assessing the various articles of the Constitution, it is important to debate the case in terms that made sense in the 1930s.

Perhaps too much emphasis has been placed on what were later denounced as the shortcomings of the 1937 Constitution? Perhaps its strengths ought to be acknowledged? It is noteworthy that the Constitution of 1937, unlike that of 1922, was submitted to the people for ratification. Popular endorsement gave the new one a legitimacy that the earlier one could never possess. Moreover, a provision for popular referendums to be held on controversial legislation was brought in to replace the article which had made provision for such, but which the Cosgrave government had jettisoned in 1928. Again, and unusually, the electoral system to be used, proportional representation through the single transferable vote system, was enshrined in the Constitution, and was not left to simple legislation. (Fianna Fáil may well have rued this article in later years, as they struggled to win an overall majority.) And to the surprise of many, the new Constitution restored the Senate, abolished a year previously. This was de Valera's nod towards vocationalism, a sop to the Catholic corporatists, intrigued by the prospect of a *via media* between capitalism and communism/fascism, as enunciated in various papal encyclicals. As a gesture, it was largely meaningless, for de Valera had no intention of allowing the second chamber to have any real power; and neither he nor his ministers had any interest in either decentralisation or in limiting the state's reach. In reality, the new Senate, for all the windy rhetoric surrounding it, and the hopes entertained for it, largely functioned as a delivery room for political wannabees, a convalescent ward for the electorally wounded, an asylum for exotics (ex-Unionists and the like) and a hospice for those near the end of their political life. It was still useful for all that.

Again, possibly borrowing from the Bill of Rights, attached to the United States Constitution as its first amendments, the 1937 Constitution reconfirmed a whole series of rights, among them a right to private property, to a good name, to protection of life, to free speech and to assembly. At a time when 'rights' of all sorts were being systematically slapped down throughout Europe, and not just in Italy, Spain, and Germany, this was a major reaffirmation of liberal democratic values. The proposed new Constitution also made provision for a powerful Supreme Court – more or less on the American model – to which appeals could be made concerning the constitutionality, or otherwise, of all laws passed by the *Oireachtas*. Little was heard of this court for the next twenty years: Irish lawyers were wedded to the British tradition of the primacy of Parliament; and a Supreme Court was seen as a foreign accretion. However, from the 1960s on, the contested cases and constitutional challenges have markedly increased, so much so that by the early 2000s, the Supreme Court, by its interpretation of the Constitution had, in effect, far outstripped the Senate as the second house; and in terms of making new law by its judgments, it may actually be usurping both houses of the *Oireachtas*. Lastly, for all its faults, *Bunreacht na hÉireann* (= the Constitution of Ireland) has endured, has performed creditably in the vastly different circumstances of Ireland in the decades after the 1930s, and has shown itself capable of renewal, essentially through referendums where constitutional change is required and through judicial scrutiny of later legislation. Once again, the favourable comparison with the basic laws of other European states since the 1930s is valid.

The Constitution set up a republic in all but name: it went some way towards establishing Irish ownership over the twenty-six counties, now renamed Ireland; and the return of the Treaty ports a year later confirmed that Ireland was now fully sovereign. All of these achievements were to be challenged with the outbreak of war in September 1939.

The Emergency and the Second World War

Even before Britain and France declared war on Germany, de Valera had announced that Ireland would remain neutral in the coming struggle.[9] Irish neutrality was widely recognised and accepted; even the London *Times* in an editorial conceded that de Valera had no real choice in the matter. There was very little dissent within Ireland at this course of action; those sentimentally and emotionally attached to Britain, some indeed prepared to fight for it, saw no option other than neutrality for an Irish government. For de Valera, neutrality during the 'Emergency' – as the Second World War was described in Ireland – was not only the supreme assertion of Irish sovereignty, it was also the only feasible policy to adopt. Any move towards participation on Britain's side would have caused convulsions in an Ireland still recovering from the civil war and still fuming (at least publicly) over partition. In any case throughout the 1930s de Valera had grown disillusioned at the failure of the League of Nations to deal with Germany or Italy. Nor was Poland's grubby collusion in the destruction of Czechoslovakia, the prelude to its own invasion by both German and Russian forces, calculated to make him believe anything other than that neutrality was the only correct and principled course to follow. In September 1939, of course, such a stance was by no means uniquely Irish, much less remarkable; apart from the principal belligerents, nearly every country in Europe declared itself neutral, and so too did the United States. However, declaring neutrality was one thing, maintaining it would prove to be quite another.

Most of those European countries that had sought to rule themselves out of the conflict soon learned quickly that declarations of neutrality offered no protection in the face of Hitler's panzer divisions. By the summer of 1940 Belgium and Holland had been invaded and by June, with the fall of France, the German juggernaut seemed unstoppable: Britain, many observers believed, would surely be the next to go under. It was during the twelve-month period between the British army's retreat from Dunkirk and Hitler's invasion of Russia, roughly June 1940 to June 1941, that Ireland's neutrality became dangerously controversial. De Valera came under huge pressure to declare for Britain and firm promises were made to him to reopen the question of partition. But de Valera refused all blandishments and remained firm to his conviction that neutrality was Ireland's best and only policy. He was not persuaded of the sincerity of the proposal on partition and nor did he believe that the British would face down Unionist resistance to unification. He also well understood the furies that bubbled away beneath the surface of Irish public life, and that would have burst into the open in the event of a pro-British declaration. As a student of Irish history, de Valera may also have been aware of the extravagant terms offered by King Charles I three hundred years earlier to Irish Catholic leaders in order to acquire an Irish army to aid him in his war with Parliament; he would also have been mindful that Charles's generosity was directly linked to his incipient defeat in England. He may also have remembered that, in 1789, Theobald Wolfe Tone, a founding father of Irish republicanism, had advised against Irish participation in England's wars.

In any case, during the dark days following the defeat of France, and throughout the battle of the Atlantic, de Valera may well have believed that Britain would lose the war, though unlike some of his colleagues he would not have welcomed a British defeat at the hands of the Third Reich. Then again, what would an Irish declaration of war have meant? The Irish army was in a lamentable position where numbers and equipment were concerned. And its situation worsened in the first few months of the war as, under pressure from the minister of finance, Sean MacEntee, the number of soldiers was actually reduced. Had Ireland entered the war the reality was that Britain would have had to defend it against German attack. But the Royal Navy and the Royal Air Force would do that anyway because, apart from Ireland's strategic position, it was a key source of food for Britain – and would become an important source of labour. By declaring for neutrality de Valera prevented a renewal of the Irish civil war which would not have been to Britain's advantage. Again, perhaps contemplating John Redmond's hasty pro-British pledge at Woodenbridge in 1914, which split the Volunteers, he was determined to preserve the unity of the Fianna Fáil party, which assuredly could not have survived any such declaration. And by keeping Ireland at peace he turned Ireland into what it had always been when Britain was at war – a prime source of recruits, workers and food.

British half-promises on partition have to be seen in this light. Such offers had to be rejected because, whatever he may have said in public, ending partition had never been a priority for de Valera – not in 1921 or in 1940: the self-determination of Ireland – by which was meant the twenty-six counties – along with the revival of Irish had always been his key objectives. Indeed, de Valera may privately have regarded Chamberlain's tentative proposals on unification in 1940 (as well as Churchill's more excited rhetoric on this matter when the United States entered the war in December 1941: 'now or never; a nation once again') as threats, not dissimilar to those uttered by Hitler. De Valera's sovereign Ireland could not have survived the ending of partition, and de Valera knew it; he also knew, by looking into his heart (a favourite ploy), that the Irish electorate would never accept a declaration of war on behalf of Britain as the price for unification. Prudence, therefore, allied to principle in his mind, and he made it clear that under no circumstances would Ireland side militarily with Britain, that the Treaty ports, recently returned to Irish control (figure 6.31), would not be made available to the Royal Navy (or to the German navy) and that Ireland would not be used as a base for the IRA to strike at Britain. He pledged that he would not waver from this position and he never did.

Admittedly the pressure on de Valera and his government to throw in Ireland's lot with Britain diminished as the tide turned firmly against Germany in 1942, largely as a result of the American entry into the war the previous year. But American direct involvement brought fresh challenges. British patience and, to an extent, sympathy with and understanding of Ireland's neutral stance – though not without the occasional waspish aside – was not matched by the more muscular diplomatic style of the Americans. The American envoy to Ireland, David Gray, had arrived in Dublin as an enthusiast for things Irish, but had soon turned into a harsh critic of de Valera's conduct of Irish neutrality, which he believed was characterised by 'specious openness' and by deception. De Valera, notwithstanding his American birth, was not prepared to bow before American pressure, and he lodged a protest at the presence of tens of thousands of American soldiers in Northern Ireland, claiming that they were propping up a 'Quisling government' at Stormont. For his part Gray constantly complained about what he regarded as the large 'enemy' presence in Dublin, and, in the anxious months before D-Day in June 1944, he demanded (to no avail) the closure of the German, Italian and Japanese legations, in the interests of security. Relations between the

6.31 Eamon de Valera with Frank Aiken on their way to inspect Spike Island, one of a number of installations and ports returned to Ireland in 1938. De Valera papers, University College Dublin Archives.

Irish government and the United States remained frosty long after the war was over.

Despite the complaint about American soldiers on Irish soil, the arrival of large numbers of GIs in Dublin, regularly decanted from the Belfast–Dublin train, and in search of general rest and recreation, was ignored by the Irish government. This was, in effect, the private face of public neutrality, and no attention could be drawn to it. It is now clear that Ireland's neutrality disproportionately benefited the Allies. In a postwar report the British secret service listed more than a dozen ways in which Irish neutrality was firmly tilted towards the Allies – among them, permission for overflights in Irish airspace, repatriation of downed British airmen (Germans were interned for the duration, possibly a more fortunate fate), sharing of weather information, monitoring shipping movements off the Irish coasts and, crucially, cooperation on intelligence matters. And of course, the huge number of Irish civilians who went to Britain on warwork, and the large number of Irish who enlisted in the British armed forces, appeared to redefine the definition of neutrality.

Perhaps fifty thousand Irish men and women would serve in the British armed forces by 1945; an impressive number given that there was no conscription. Equally striking was the large number of decorations won by these volunteers, over seven hundred in total, including seven Victoria Crosses. Historians have been reluctant to draw conclusions from these figures concerning Irish enthusiasm for the Allied cause, or indeed for Irish neutrality in the war. Instead they have stressed as motivations the desperate shortage of work in Ireland, the lust for adventure and the lure of 'real' soldiering. (As many as five thousand members of the Irish army, bored with garrison duty, wooden rifles and turf-cutting deserted and joined the British army.) However, a belief that Irish neutrality was the best policy could easily coexist with a conviction that Hitler was a menace to world civilisation who had to be brought down; an apparent contradiction aptly summed up by a cartoon in *Dublin Opinion*, in which two Irish airmen, high over a German city, endure a relentless barrage of anti-aircraft fire, only to congratulate each other: 'Thank God for de Valera, he kept us out of this war'.

Irish civilian workers also made a major contribution to the British war economy. Early on in the conflict terms were negotiated between Dublin and London which determined that Irish civilians journeying to Britain during wartime would be exempt from conscription. There was never any question of an Irish government prohibition on emigrating to Britain, even for the purpose of enlisting. Once again, it is difficult to see how unrestricted movement either to work or to enlist was compatible with any current definition of neutrality. Especially, it is hard to understand how Ireland's ostensibly neutral stance squared with the presence of a United Kingdom Permit Office in Dublin, staffed with British civil servants, issuing passes to those leaving for war work. In addition, and reminiscent of agents for the Irish regiments in French service in the eighteenth century, no fewer than thirteen recruiters – 'not all of them very reputable characters', as one report had it – acting on behalf of British munitions factories, traversed Ireland signing on potential workers. The Irish labour exchanges were furnished with lists of industrial vacancies in Britain so that the unemployed could be pointed in the right direction. Astonishingly, the Irish Department of Agriculture, at the request of the Scottish Department of Agriculture, undertook to interview Irish girls in Dublin in order to ascertain their suitability for agricultural work in Scotland. Meanwhile, the Gardaí were expected to vouch for the bona fides of those travelling. At times the figure for those travelling to Britain for war work would reach more than eight thousand per month.

The Irish government's main anxieties about this exodus were threefold. First, although some ministers and civil servants were pleased at the removal of potentially disruptive people who, in their eyes, had no stake in the country, the government itself was sensitive to the charge that it was encouraging, if not actively sponsoring, emigration. There was, therefore, a real worry that the true extent of this transfer of workers would come into the public domain. Hence, everything to do with it had to be kept confidential so far as possible, and the British government was only too pleased to accede to this. Second, there was concern at British complaints at the low standard of personal hygiene of those travelling. Following the turning back of a number of infectious or verminous workers at Holyhead, Wales, de-lousing stations for men and women were speedily set up in Dublin to address this problem. Third, there were worries expressed, privately, about what would happen when the war was over. The fear was that those workers who went to England would return to Ireland at the war's end, perhaps filled with 'leftist', welfarist ideas and would move straight into the ranks of the unemployed. Such concerns proved groundless: the wartime emigrants, by and large, did not return and remained in Britain. Nowhere in the paperwork generated by this mass transfer of Irish workers can be found any realisation, or understanding, of the shame and shock of those shunted on to the ferries, their collars turned up against the wind, clutching their cardboard suitcases, smarting from their hosing down in the Iveagh baths, and sporting around their necks an address label on which was scribbled 'British factories'. Ireland's part in the downfall of Hitler had to be kept secret: in public, Ireland's neutral stance between the belligerents had to be impeccable.

Another public–private contradiction emerges when the two Irelands' respective roles in the Second World War are considered. Ireland's stance was often criticised in public by British and American politicians, but in private its 'contribution' was tacitly, though rarely warmly, acknowledged. By contrast, Northern Ireland's war effort was publicly praised on all sides, and its important contribution was singled out by Churchill at the war's end as almost a rebuke to Ireland; yet in private, in report after report, there was much criticism of Northern Ireland's lacklustre response to the needs of the British war economy.

On the outbreak of war, Northern Ireland's unemployment figure was hovering around 20 per cent of the insured labour force, the highest figure since the state was set up in 1921. In Britain war with Germany would lead to a swift fall in unemployment, but in Northern Ireland there was actually a rise in the jobless figure. This increase was almost entirely a direct result of Northern Ireland's dependency on linen manufacture: Hitler's triumph in Norway and Denmark had caused a loss of flax supplies from the Baltic, brought about a sharp fall in output and created a figure of nearly 37 per cent unemployed in the linen industry. The rise in the jobless was also partly due to Northern Ireland's unusual constitutional position: because it was, in effect, self-governing it found itself, at least initially, with no representatives on the national wartime boards that were set up to direct the war economy and, for reasons of security and distance, munitions factories were never established there. However – and this is the salient point – those out of work in Northern Ireland did not flock to join the British armed forces. There was to be no conscription in the north, though Unionist ministers did urge its implementation. However, the feeling in London – as at the time of the Great War – was that it would be more trouble than it was worth to bring it in. In public Unionist ministers continued to call for conscription, but Sir Basil Brooke, one of the few energetic members of the Cabinet, and eventually prime minister in 1943, confided to his diary that it was 'probably a wise decision' not to introduce it, partly because of likely unrest orchestrated by the IRA and the Catholic church, but also because 'Free Staters' might cross the border and take the jobs of those away fighting for king and country.

The absence of conscription undoubtedly contributed to a mood of 'detached engagement' in Northern Ireland during the early months of the war. Enlistment in the British armed forces declined from around 2,500 per month in September 1939, to a paltry 600 per month in December 1940. In other areas, too, there was a marked lack of enthusiasm for sacrifices in the pursuit of victory. Northern Ireland firms were slow to bid for wartime contracts; there was a reluctance on their part to switch production from secure and profitable commercial business to munitions work; and even Harland and Wolff, the jewel in the crown of northern heavy industry, for a time, was denied warship orders because its prices were far above those of other shipyards. (When Harland and Wolff did eventually move to a wartime footing, there were constant complaints from the Admiralty about the quality of its work and its inability to meet targets; unions criticised its lack of canteen and welfare facilities, and highlighted its outmoded adherence to a rule whereby workers who were a few minutes late in arriving for work were shut out for the entire day.)

In December 1940 a young economist, Harold Wilson, compiled a report for the war Cabinet on Northern Ireland's contribution to the war effort. He concluded that, to date, its role had been negligible and all the more inexcusable because Northern Ireland had suffered less from enemy action than any other area of the United Kingdom. Since September 1939, he noted, 'the siren [warning of an air-raid] has sounded only five times' in Belfast, and each time it was a false alarm, in marked and deadly contrast to other British cities. (Thirty-four years later, and now prime minister, Harold Wilson most unwisely denounced those involved in the Ulster workers' strike of May 1974 as 'spongers' – an outburst possibly traceable to his wartime investigations in Northern Ireland.)

Ulster's complacency was, to an extent, shattered by the massive German air-raids on Belfast on the nights of 15–16 April and 4–5 May 1941. Perhaps a thousand died in the first raid, and nearly sixty thousand houses were damaged overall; the figure for the dead bestowed on Belfast the unenviable distinction of being the city – apart from London – that had incurred the highest casualties in a single night. The Unionist government had regarded 'this little corner of the British Empire' – as a Stormont civil servant had it – as remote from the war and had failed to take seriously the likelihood of an air-raid; hence the lack of civil defence planning and the utterly inadequate anti-aircraft weaponry. Surprisingly, however, even after the dreadful wake-up call of the Blitz, entrenched positions remained just that – entrenched. Thus there was continued opposition to northern workers moving a few miles from their home, or relocating to munitions factories in Britain. (The sectarian arithmetic in tight constituencies might be upset – Stalingrad might fall but not the Shankill.) There was also a flat refusal to adopt night-shift working in the factories, and there was stout resistance in heavy engineering firms to any dilution of 'male' jobs through the recruitment of females. In British shipyards, 9 per cent of the workers were women, in Northern Ireland, it was a derisory 2 per cent. In fairness to the unions, they could legitimately point to the absence of a trade unionist at the Cabinet table at Stormont, unlike in London where Ernest Bevin had been brought in because of his trade union credentials.

Matters scarcely improved in Northern Ireland throughout the war. In February 1943 absenteeism in the Belfast shipyards was twice to three times as bad as in Britain, resistance to 'dilution' remained undiminished, and in the aircraft manufacturers, Short and Harland, there was still no agreement on night-time shift work. The very poor take-up of female labour was especially galling to government because women had proved far more productive than men in engineering factories; the 'limited extent' (as Churchill put it in uncharacteristically delicate terms in May 1941) of Northern Ireland's contribution to the war effort was so blatant that British newspapers began to play up the theme of the 'unequal sacrifices' between the province and Britain. Particularly newsworthy, from 1942 on, was increased strike activity in engineering and ship-building; in 1944 there were even fears of an all-out general strike in these industries. Not surprisingly, in surveying Northern Ireland's wartime industrial relations' history, the *Sunday Pictorial* trumpeted that its record was 'a disgrace to both Britain and the Empire'. The figures were, admittedly, stark: Northern Ireland had 2 per cent of the insured workforce, but still accounted for 10 per cent of the working days lost during the war.

And yet despite all this, Northern Ireland had a 'good war', with Ulster-born generals, among them Sir Alan Brooke, Sir Bernard Montgomery and Sir Claude Auchinleck all achieving a high profile in the struggle against Hitler. British and American politicians remained grateful in the difficult years after the war's end. By and large, this gratitude to Northern Ireland was not based on the quality of its generals, or its people's commitment, mobilisation and energy, and nor was it a tribute to its industrial relations: rather it was an acknowledgement of its strategic location. With the loss of the Treaty ports in the south, Derry had proved vital in the battle of the Atlantic, and Lough Erne became important as a base for Sunderland flying boats over the western approaches. In deadly contrast it was claimed that denial of the southern Treaty ports had cost the lives of five thousand Allied servicemen and women ('the mackerel are fat – on the flesh of your kin' snarled the northern Irish poet Louis MacNeice). Moreover, with the formal entry of the United States into the war, Northern Ireland became a gigantic training camp for American soldiers. As many as three hundred thousand stayed there for a time, training for the invasion of Hitler's Europe. It was the contributions in these areas that Churchill saluted in his victory speech in May 1945; and it was the contrast between Northern Ireland's commitment to victory and the southern state's alleged 'frolic' with the Axis powers of Germany and Italy that he chose to highlight.

There is some evidence that under the stresses and strains of wartime adversity community relations in Northern Ireland appear to have improved somewhat. German bombs had not discriminated between Catholic and Protestant houses, and shared suffering may well have produced an encouraging thaw in what had been in the 1930s a frozen hostility. With good wages being paid in the wartime industries and with the virtual ending of unemployment by 1944, there was an improvement in living standards all round which may also have helped defuse tensions. In addition, the very experience of being in a 'world' war, of taking part in what for many was a great adventure, challenged engrained attitudes and habits in what had been both a very conservative and a divided society. The arrival of hundreds of thousands of strange and exotic Americans could not but shake conventional ideas. Again, communist Russia, once excoriated as the great Satan (and worse, IRA sponsor) was, after June 1941, rebranded as a brave ally in the fight against Nazism. As a result left-wing ideas became quite fashionable, there were demands for a more just postwar society, and the Labour vote in Northern Ireland rose substantially – to the alarm of the Unionist government.

In 1942 the publication and acceptance of the Beveridge report outlining the establishment of a welfare state in Britain when the war ended caused concerns among some Unionist ministers. There was a fear that people from the south would flood into Northern Ireland in order to avail themselves of welfare payments and would thus undermine slender Unionist majorities in certain areas. Mindful, however, of the surge in Labour support, these misgivings were put to one side and, instead, urgent assurances were sought from the treasury that when the reforms were implemented in the rest of the United Kingdom, Northern Ireland would not be left out. In short, directly as a result of the experience of the war and especially the common fears, thrills and expectations that had accompanied it, by 1945 there seemed to be a prospect of the emergence of a class-based politics, a left–right divide, rather than the simple continuation of the deadening (and all-too-recently deadly) loyalist–disloyalist division that had marked the state from its first beginnings.

The period of the 'Emergency' was equally a watershed in the history of Ireland. On one level, it marked a personal triumph for de Valera, for he was both Taoiseach and minister for external affairs throughout. He vigorously defended neutrality, maintained his party's unity, and helped heal civil war wounds by bringing pro- and anti-Treaty elements into the Irish defence forces to protect the state set up by that treaty. In addition, a large number of what might be described as ex-Unionists, Protestants and Anglo-Irish offered their services to defend Ireland during the 'Emergency', and their contribution in this regard facilitated their absorption into the new Irish state. Others, such as the IRA, who were believed to be a danger to that state and a threat to its policy of neutrality were ruthlessly dealt with. During the 'Emergency', around eight hundred members of the IRA were interned without trial or imprisoned after being convicted, six were executed and a handful died on hunger strike. These were brave men, but they understood nothing but the gun; and by their actions they might have provoked British intervention in Irish affairs or even encouraged a German invasion. De Valera's tough policy towards the IRA, formerly regarded as 'his people', would assist in the creation of a new, though no less genuine, Irish patriotism, albeit one confined to the twenty-six counties. Shared shortages – of tea, petrol, flour, fuel – and the spread of rationing also assisted in the creation of a common citizenship. (It has to be admitted that Irish shortages were nothing like those experienced in the United Kingdom, much less German-occupied Europe: visitors from Britain to Ireland during the war, after the unrelieved grimness of wartime London and the tedium of the blacked-out train journey to Holyhead, not surprisingly saw Dublin, and Ireland generally, as places of plenty and of light.)

Neutrality was policed and maintained by a draconian censorship which sought more or less successfully to prevent any news of the war getting through to the Irish population. Films were severely cut, often to the bewilderment of the audience, or banned altogether, to avoid offending the belligerent powers. Irish audiences, for example, had to wait until 1946 to see Charlie Chaplin in *The Great Dictator*: if shown during the war, explained the film censor, Richard Hayes, 'it would have meant riots and bloodshed'. (Not, perhaps, an altogether exaggerated claim, for with large crowds attending the many cinemas in Ireland, it might only take one person to start booing and jeering for a disturbance to break out.) Newsreels were a particular cause for concern. These were unashamedly propagandist ('Well done the RAF!') and had, therefore, to be shorn of any mention of the war: eventually they ceased to be shown at all.

For its part, Irish radio's output was largely confined to anodyne music pro-grammes and plays, though it did broadcast live commentary on Gaelic games and rugby (from 1944). But its propensity to broadcast government messages and ministers' speeches as 'news' quickly earned it the title Radio Fianna Fáil. To compensate for these deficiencies, the determined could always tune into the BBC for 'war news', or to German radio to hear the English-language broadcasts of celebrity fascist exiles, Francis Stuart and William Joyce (Lord Haw-Haw) and no doubt many did, at least in the early years of the war. But a shortage of radios and of batteries, and a lack of spare parts from 1943 on, sharply curtailed this eavesdropping far more effectively than censorship.

Inevitably, Irish newspapers were particular targets of the authorities. The *Irish Times* (suspect because of its largely Protestant readership), after a number of run-ins with the censor, was ordered to submit for detailed scrutiny a mock-up of the next day's paper before going to press. All newspapers and magazines – even Catholic ones – were ruthlessly purged of any potentially offending material, such as the plight of Irish missionaries captured by the Japanese. Thus weather forecasts were dropped because of their possible use to an enemy, and Irish casualties 'abroad' (i.e. in the war) could be published in the death columns, but no mention of the war, let alone the battles where the soldiers or sailors fell, was permitted in the notices. Foreign news was confined largely to Portugal (where, apparently, exciting social reforms were afoot), to Spain (ditto), to the United States (until December 1941) and to the pope's activities (*passim*). Almost no criticism of the Irish government was permitted, and thus its handling of the transfer of workers to Britain went uncontested, as did its control and rationing of supplies on the home front; nor was there any highlighting of rural decline. Frank Aiken, the Cabinet minister charged with implementing censorship, proved unrelenting in his efforts to suppress all war news, and he strove to stifle all dissent and debate. As a result of this all-pervasive media control, an Irish citizen living in Ireland might have gone through the 'Emergency' largely unaware of the ebb and flow of the war in the Pacific or with only a dim understanding of the invasion of Belgium and Holland or of the invasion of Russia or, later, of the Allied advance on Germany after the Normandy landings. Atrocity stories were routinely spiked or gutted: Russian massacres at Katyn, Japanese frightfulness in the Far East and German treatment of civilians in occupied Europe were all toned down or omitted.

Such stringent controls made sense in the early years of the war, when the outcome was unclear, Ireland lay open to invasion, and the issues at stake were far from clear-cut. Was this a war to defeat the evil of Nazism or one merely to defend the British Empire? However, from 1942 on, certainly from 1943, Allied victory seemed certain, and any direct threat to Ireland was now remote. Severe restrictions on reporting the war, at that juncture, began to appear increasingly wrong-headed and pointless, and to be directed less at maintaining neutrality than at keeping the rest of the world at bay. Crucially, by 1943 the morality of the war, unclear in 1939, had been firmly resolved in the Allies' favour: as the horrors of the Final Solution unfolded, there could be no doubt that they were fighting the good fight. It was then that a question mark was placed against Irish neutrality, and it was to remain there until the end of the war and after.

Neutrality, most were agreed, was the only realistic policy for Ireland in 1939. But did that remain the case throughout the war? The trouble was that the rationale for neutrality could scarcely be the same at the end of the war as at the beginning. Initially, it was declared in order to defend the Irish state and to preserve it from likely predators. However, with the threat to the Irish state removed by 1942, increasingly, neutrality seemed to mean little more than indifference to the outcome of the war, a position that by that date had become more and more morally indefensible. And yet de Valera rigidly continued to adhere to his policy of even-handedness between the Allies and the Axis in the face of mounting and irrefutable evidence of the true nature of Nazi rule. It was not that de Valera knew little of the reality of life in occupied Europe: on the contrary, he was particularly well informed, for he had access to a range of diplomatic reports; and Isaac Herzog, a former Rabbi of Dublin, and a personal friend, had written to him from Palestine describing the nightmare of European Jewry. Yet he chose to ignore this moral dimension to the war and he continued to do so even as the first footage of Buchenwald and Belsen concentration camps was being shown in cinemas everywhere in Europe (though not in Ireland).

De Valera's visit to the German legation in May 1945 to express his condolences on the death of Adolf Hitler was simply the final expression of this wilful blindness, but it was by far the most disastrous. There was no need for any such gesture: the leaders of other neutral countries such as Switzerland and Sweden did not follow his example, and even the German envoy, Eduard Hempel, was taken aback by it. A warm letter of congratulations to de Valera from the British Union of Fascists (along with a note boasting that Hitler had in fact escaped to Argentina) showed how the visit would be interpreted outside Ireland. And in justifying his action by pointing out that he had expressed similar condolences on the death of US president, Franklin D. Roosevelt, de Valera simply compounded his error of judgement. The clear implication here was that there was an equivalence between Hitler and Roosevelt and that, in effect, Ireland was neutral between the two. It was as if the skipper of a small craft, having successfully and against heavy odds steered his ship through dangerous seas into safer waters – and having made his point that it could be done by small ships everywhere – had then deliberately turned back and run it aground.

The explanation for de Valera's action may lie in his vision of the kind of Ireland that he dreamed of. Famously, in a radio broadcast on St Patrick's day 1943, de Valera had described his Ireland in lyrical terms as a rural idyll of 'cosy homesteads', replete with 'sturdy children', 'athletic youths' and 'comely maidens', all living in 'frugal comfort'. This Ireland had never existed and would never exist: indeed, at the time he spoke, rural Ireland itself showed every sign of being on the point of collapse. As before, de Valera had next to nothing to say about urban Ireland, though he, like other Fianna Fáil grandees, saw no incongruity in lauding the countryside and the positive virtues of a modest standard of life while, at the same time, living in a rather grand mansion in the leafy suburbs of Dublin. Ireland's neutrality nourished this vision, for behind the high fence that shut out the mad, modern, materialist world, with its excesses, its cruelties and its paganism, the notion of Ireland as a repository of all that was spiritual, not material, could be nurtured. In addition, behind the 'Green Curtain' that was neutrality, the idea of a self-sufficient Irish Ireland, independent of all, and standing as a beacon of light in a continent consumed by savagery and barbarism could be developed. Feeding this fantasy necessarily involved the development of a sense of moral superiority to the crass concerns of the wicked world beyond Ireland's shores; it also meant turning a blind eye to its inherent contradictions, not to mention its blatant absurdities. All of this came together to produce the calamitous visit by Eamon de Valera to a startled Herr Hempel to offer the sympathy of the Irish people on the death of Herr Hitler.

It may be that de Valera's action on receiving news of Hitler's death provoked Churchill into taking a sideswipe at Ireland's neutrality in a broadcast he made marking the end of hostilities and celebrating the Allies' triumph. It is more likely, however, that the onset of peace permitted emotions, diplomatically suppressed over the years, a freer rein. In his speech, Churchill saluted Northern Ireland's contribution to victory, and then contrasted its loyalty with Ireland's denial of the Treaty ports, and with its 'frolic' with the Axis powers. He also commended Britain's self-restraint in not invading Ireland. Churchill's remarks were crass. They were also entirely counter-productive in that they offered de Valera a way out of the difficulties caused by his visit to the German legation. De Valera's reply, when it came, was measured, and all the more effective for that. As was his custom, he began with an Irish history lesson, rehearsing the standard hundreds-of-years-of-oppression argument, a period far longer, he noted, than the few years when Britain had stood alone. He then expressed his sadness that Churchill could not 'find it in his heart', a deft formulation, to acknowledge this. He also flatly refused to thank Britain for not invading Ireland, and in a pointed snub to Churchill, he praised his now much maligned predecessor,

Neville Chamberlain. His reply was generally judged a triumph, a masterful assertion of Ireland's right to sovereignty, independence and its own foreign policy. It may have been de Valera's finest moment.

Assessment

The Second World War had a profound effect on the two Irelands. In Northern Ireland, as a result of the war, a real prospect had emerged of what might be called a regional identity, one that might defuse or overcome deep-seated confessional rivalries. The economic stimulus given by wartime expansion had reduced unemployment and boosted the standard of living of both Catholics and Protestants. Unemployment and poverty were by no means the whole explanation for sectarian conflict, but they had played a part. The immediate future held the promise of far-reaching welfare legislation in Northern Ireland – nothing less than the creation of a 'welfare' state – and seemed to offer some chance of reconfiguring politics there. The Northern Ireland Labour Party's wartime gains might be sustained into peace time, especially now that its sister party had been swept to power in Britain. Partition was no longer in danger – that was plain to see – not least because of the divergent paths taken by the two Irelands during the world war/Emergency. In contrast to the Great War, there had been few shared experiences between north and south, and there could be no common memory of the events of the years 1939–45. And just as partition had been copperfastened by the war, so too the other strand of Unionism – the link with Britain – had never seemed more secure than in 1945. Northern Ireland's loyalty had been praised by Churchill, and Unionist ministers were not going to let London forget the debt owed to it nor how strategically vital its naval bases had been – and might be again, as 'cold' war succeeded 'hot' war.

For Ireland the 'Emergency' had been at times an exhilarating, sobering and bewildering experience. The promise held out by the new Constitution of 1937 and the diplomatic triumph of the return of the Treaty ports had underpinned the declaration of neutrality in 1939, and made possible its successful defence. Throughout the war years, De Valera had resisted all pressures – from Allied or Axis sources – that were brought to bear on him, and he had skilfully charted a course designed to secure Ireland during the conflict. There was, of course, a price to be paid for all this, and not just in terms of wartime scarcities. By the end of the war, Ireland was diplomatically isolated. De Valera's refusal of an American demand to hand over 'war criminals' should any flee to Ireland and his condolences on Hitler's death had outraged American opinion, while his resolute neutrality had not endeared him or Ireland to the Soviet Union. The

Irish Free State may have supported Russia's entry into the League of Nations, but the Soviet Union would keep Ireland out of the United Nations for ten years after the end of the war. (For the future, we may note that when the Troubles in Northern Ireland broke out after 1969, most of the British ministers charged with dealing with the crisis had served their political apprenticeship during the war years, and their attitude towards the Irish Republic thereafter had been coloured by its declaration of neutrality during the Second World War.)

So far as the Irish economy was concerned, the 'Emergency' appeared to have shown the value of the policies aimed at securing self-sufficiency, or autarky, and pursued under Fianna Fáil during the 1930s. Ireland had not starved during the war and, while there was rationing of tea and petrol and much else, it was the Irish surpluses in foodstuffs that most struck observers, accustomed to the not-so-'frugal comfort' of life in wartime Britain. In Ireland, there seemed always to be food for sale, for export to Britain and for smuggling across the border. Crucially, and unlike the rest of Europe, Ireland did not lack fuel, for an abundance of turf made up for a lack of coal: in 1941 alone, some sixteen thousand men had been deployed on county council turf-cutting schemes.

There was, however, a great danger here: Northern Ireland may have had a 'good' war, but 'that neutral island', as Louis MacNeice labelled southern Ireland, had had a 'good' neutrality. However, surviving the war through the policies of the 1930s, could easily lead to the complacent conclusion that such might serve into the postwar world. Almost alone in Europe – Spain and Portugal were the only possible exceptions – Ireland entered the post-'Emergency' world wedded to the economic strategy of the 1930s. And not only in economics, but culturally and mentally, Ireland entered the postwar world rooted in the mindset of the 1930s. Ireland's very success in weathering the war had had the effect of validating policies pursued in the 1930s, and earlier. A strict censorship, a resolute hostility to modernism in all its forms and a key national objective centred on the revival of Irish, all surfaced intact when the flood waters of the world war had subsided. There continued, in addition, at official level a sort of shoulder-shrugging attitude to the monthly haemorrhage of Irish people to the cities of Britain. The official attitude was not so much a good riddance (though that was heard), but rather, better work in Britain than idleness in Ireland. And at least the middle classes were not leaving in droves, and therefore the social order was not threatened. This complacency in the face of an Irish exodus survived the 'Emergency' and continued untroubled into the 1950s.

Irish isolationism, already evident in the 1930s, also survived the Emergency not only unchallenged but strengthened. In about equal measure, it combined elements of moral superiority and smugness. In other words, while many, probably most, countries in Europe had known defeat, endured occupation and suffered famine, they had at least emerged from these shattering experiences declaring 'never again'. Ireland had not been a belligerent and the physical destruction it sustained during the conflict was minor; but it entered the postwar world possibly more psychologically damaged than other countries, for in Ireland the policies of the 1930s had, apparently, been a success, and hence the watchword for the future was 'same again'.

7 HUBRIS AND NEMESIS: THE TWO IRELANDS, 1945–2010

Introduction

On 8 May 2007 a power-sharing executive came into being in Northern Ireland. At its head, as first minister, was the Reverend Ian Paisley, the leader of the Democratic Unionist Party (DUP), a strongly Protestant evangelical party pledged to maintaining the Union with Great Britain. The deputy first minister, so styled, but equal in status in this new arrangement, was Mr Martin McGuinness, reputedly a member of the Army Council of the IRA and a leading member of Sinn Féin, an almost entirely Catholic party dedicated to the establishment of an all-Ireland republic. This outcome – a government drawn from the two extremes of the hitherto warring religious communities in Northern Ireland – could never have been predicted in 1945, nor indeed could it have been envisaged for much of the next sixty years. Even after its formation, observers (and some participants) continued to rub their eyes in amazement at the spectacle of what were – and remained – polar opposites sitting down together in government. And yet, this was only one of the many *bouleversements* – political, social, cultural above all economic – that utterly transformed the Irish landscape, north and south between 1945 and 2010 and that have reconfigured relations between the two Irelands and the wider world.

A short list of the most striking transformations might include the ending of large-scale emigration which, like the dreary steeples of Fermanagh and Tyrone, had constituted an apparently irreducible feature of Irish society since the 1840s. True, the annual exodus rose to new peaks in the 1950s, but from those highs it had dwindled rapidly into relative insignificance by the turn of the new century. Given that Irish society for the previous hundred and fifty years had in effect required a continuous outflow of surplus population in order to function, such a reversal had consequences that could legitimately be labelled revolutionary. Indeed, in the first decade of the third millennium the unthinkable happened as the Irish Republic witnessed an unprecedented volume of immigration and struggled to meet the numerous challenges attendant on being for the first time a host country to a multi-ethnic inflow.

In turn, the displacement of out-migration by in-migration as a key feature of contemporary Irish society was sparked by an extraordinary development in the Irish Republic – the spectacular boom in the Irish economy that began in the early 1990s and continued until 2007. By the end of the millennium, Irish growth rates were among the highest anywhere and Irish gross domestic product revealed that Ireland should be counted among the wealthiest two or three countries in the world. For over a decade Ireland's new-found prosperity, largely export driven, constituted an astonishing (and in some quarters, a galling) reversal of what had long been tacitly accepted as immutable truths about the country's irredeemable backwardness and chronic under-performance.

By way of contrast, while the 'Celtic Tiger' economy roared away in the Irish Republic from 1996 to 2007, no such animal was seen or heard in Northern Ireland. There economic growth was much less impressive, and public sector employment was hugely dominant. The reasons for Northern Ireland's under-performance between 1970 and 2000 have been much debated, but a major factor was surely the devastating impact on the economy and on business confidence of the 'Troubles', the rather anodyne term commonly applied to the murderous ethno-religious conflict that was seemingly intractable in the north from the late 1960s, and which it was hoped the formation of a power-sharing administration in 2007 would conclusively bring to an end.

At least part of the reason for the 'Troubles' was the failure of Unionist politicians in Northern Ireland to prioritise politics over economics. Northern Ireland certainly embarked on the path of economic modernisation in the 1950s and 1960s, but it did so without making any fundamental changes to its sectarian ethos or to its outmoded political architecture (or to its malign associate – the systematic discrimination against Catholics in northern Irish society). The consequences of this self-interested shortsightedness – economic progress but not political advance – led inexorably to civil strife and a wrecked economy in the decades after 1968. By contrast, it was precisely because the Irish Republic had undergone political modernisation – at least as measured by the smooth and peaceful transference of power consequent on election results – that it was able eventually to embrace economic modernisation with its stated goals of achieving high growth rates, expanding gross domestic (and national) product and attracting direct foreign investment. Economic self-sufficiency as a national goal was finally abandoned by policy-makers in the Republic in the 1960s.

A huge impetus to modernisation was given by the entry in 1972 of the Republic of Ireland into the European Economic Community, later the European Union.

(Northern Ireland – as part of the United Kingdom – joined at the same time.) In numerous ways 'Europe's' influence was profound: it was a case brought to the European Court that led to the legalisation of homosexuality in the Republic; and in many other areas and at every level – work practices, family law, fishing quotas, interest rates and a single currency – European influence permeated into Irish society. In economic affairs, the transfer of substantial development or structural funds and subsidies (notably to the agricultural sector) from Brussels to Dublin for decades after the Republic's accession caught the attention of many observers and fuelled claims that Ireland was the 'beggar of Europe', wedded to hand-outs as an alternative to generating wealth at home. Such views were misplaced and should be ignored: Ireland's 'entry into Europe' was about more than the wretched coin. For the first time since the early medieval period, Ireland – north and south – was in a position to contemplate continental Europe without having its view occluded by the island of Britain. Mentally, even psychologically, this was a huge shift, the implications of which would be teased out over many decades. And if Ireland could 'see' Europe, then Europe could now see Ireland, for despite periodic invasions, actual and threatened, the island of Ireland had been largely invisible to the continent since the end of the first millennium; this was a change of potentially great significance.

Boom conditions continued on into the first decade of the new century, but from 2001 on they were almost entirely driven by construction mania at home and by speculative property developments at home and abroad; and both in their turn were underwritten by reckless bank-lending practices. The downturn when it came at the end of 2007 had been forecast by economists. However, their warnings were dismissed by politicians on all sides and of all parties: some could see no further than bulging exchequer returns; some showed every sign of being in thrall to the property developers; still others felt that they could spend the bounty more productively than their rivals. But while a recession had been predicted, its severity had not. A 'soft landing' – comforting term – had been anticipated; instead there was a train wreck. House prices plummeted, thousands found out that their properties were worth considerably less than they had agreed to pay for them and hundreds of thousands found themselves out of work. Irish banks that were once household names for probity and prudence were revealed to be little more than poorly run casinos whose directors and executives had blithely gambled away their depositors' money in unbridled speculation, at the same time rewarding themselves with huge salaries and bonuses.

Admittedly, a global recession – the 'credit crunch' – greatly exacerbated Irish problems and transformed them into a deep crisis that threatened the very viability of the state; but the scale and the depth of the Irish depression owed their origins to domestic practices and decisions. As the number of jobless rose inexorably to 15 per cent (roughly half a million claiming the dole) and as the main banks teetered on the verge of bankruptcy national confidence hit an all-time low. In 2010 the economic and social outlook was grim. More and more, the sickening realisation dawned that the gains of the boom years of the Celtic Tiger had been squandered in the pursuit of excess. More and more, it became clear that it would be future generations that would have to live with the mess. A question first posed in the 1950s, once again returned: did Ireland have a future?

Even in the heyday, there had always been a dark side to the boom years and to the huge wealth that they generated. At its peak, prosperity emphatically had not penetrated all levels of Irish society; contrary to assumptions and assertions, not all boats rose with the rising tide; some were too firmly anchored to the sea bottom and gross inequality persisted. In the Republic the scandalous spectacle of grinding poverty and corrosive deprivation in the midst of apparent plenty, excess and greed for the chosen few led to confusion, frustration and sometimes violent resentment. Drug abuse, and the criminality associated with it, became rampant, in and of themselves a reflection of the modernisation of Irish society. So-called 'gangland killings' – largely unknown in the postwar era (outside the paramilitary sector) – were routine in all urban centres in the Republic and seemingly acceptable because of their 'in-house' character. There were seventeen 'gangland' murders in the first six months of 2009. Rarely were the killers brought to book, except by their rivals who met lethal force with lethal force.

In the Republic the health service throughout the period of the Celtic Tiger had remained very much a two-tiered one in which money continued to command speedy access to treatment while poverty, or even modest circumstances, condemned the sick to lengthy waiting lists. Even for those who apparently 'did well', debt accumulation through mortgages, exhausting commutes to work and expensive and inadequate child-care provision cut into their 'quality of life' and led to desperation, depression and a diminished sense of well-being. These negative aspects were made far worse by the economic recession that began in 2007. Greatly increased taxation and various levies of one sort or another, designed to plug enormous deficits in public finances, had the effect of plunging many thousands into straitened circumstances if not into outright poverty. Those in employment considered themselves fortunate, but there were few, faced with greater financial and job insecurity, who were not fearful of the future. Disgracefully, the billions deployed to bail out the delinquent banks in the first decade of the twenty-first century would be a charge on future, unborn generations: the Republic had eaten its children.

As noted, the Republic and Northern Ireland diverged economically over the period 1995–2007. There was, however, a convergence after that as the global economic downturn hit both with exceptional severity. Massive job losses and zero economic growth rapidly became features of both the northern and southern economies, and remained so for many years. Moreover, economic convergence during this period was mirrored by a striking coming together in social and demographic matters. Large families of ten, eleven or more children, for example, had become very rare in Ireland by the 1990s. Such feckless fecundity had usually been put forward as a historic feature of Catholic Ireland, frequently invoked as an inevitable product of an adherence to Catholic doctrine on contraception and, as often, cast up as a key reason why poor Ireland had stayed poor for so long. The new reality was that marital and extra-marital fertility levels, north and south, and between Protestants and Catholics everywhere, whatever they might have been in the past, were much the same in the twenty-first century.

In the half century after 1945 women in the Republic emerged out of the shadows to which de Valera's Constitution sought to confine them. By the first decade of the new century, they constituted a growing proportion of members of the medical and legal professions, and were increasingly prominent in politics, business and education. Female Cabinet ministers, unheard of until the 1970s, became commonplace at least in the Republic, and between 1990 and 2010 the office of president of the Republic of Ireland – an office that had been conceived entirely as a male preserve in the 1937 Constitution – was occupied by Mrs Mary Robinson, who was succeeded by Mrs Mary McAleese.

Feminist matters were less advanced in Northern Ireland, where the demands of a combat zone ensured the persistence of a sort of frontier misogyny that baulked at women having any role except that of home-maker and carer. Notoriously, Margaret 'Mo' Mowlam, Secretary of State for Northern Ireland in the 1990s, endured a torrid time there from male politicians hostile to females in charge. And so too did the Women's Coalition, a tiny group of feminist politicians whose pursuit of what was essentially a family-oriented political agenda elicited disproportionate and disgraceful abuse, once again from northern male politicians.

In matters of private morality the Ireland of the 1940s had long passed into history by the twenty-first century. In the new century at least one-third of all children, north and south, were born out of wedlock, perhaps one-third of all marriages, north and south, ended in divorce, church-celebrated marriages were on the wane everywhere and the number of cohabiting couples rose dramatically. Marriage and childbirth were conclusively divorced from one another, and divorce itself was legalised. Equally notably, gays and lesbians conducted their lives largely unmolested (though some politicians in the two Irelands might have wished otherwise). Their legal rights were protected in both parts of Ireland, and they could celebrate their sexuality, or not, as they saw fit. There were plans to offer legal status to same-sex unions. None of this could have been foreseen, even imagined, in the 1940s.

Strikingly, within a brief period, the seemingly impregnable moral monopoly wielded by the Catholic church, north and south, was shattered, and the standing enjoyed by its priesthood crumbled. This loss of authority can be traced partly to clerical sex abuse scandals and to even more damaging cover-ups by church authorities. As a result society in the Republic in the new century was markedly less clericalised and much more secularised than it had been. The days when no public event or activity could proceed without a priest or a bishop throwing in the first ball, turning the first sod or blessing the entire company, crew or audience were over. The number of vocations, male and female, to a religious life plummeted; clerical control of Catholic education ebbed rapidly; and attendance at mass was at record low levels (though attendance at clerically conducted funerals kept up mightily). At the same time, and directly related to the advance of secularisation, the number of Irish people in third-level education in the new century was a large multiple of those who attended university in 1950; and the figures were equally impressive for those completing their secondary schooling – again in marked contrast to the situation a generation earlier.

The sheer rapidity of the changes that transformed Irish society created further problems. In the Republic the retreat of the Catholic church and its clergy from the public sphere, for example, could not but raise vital questions of authority and leadership which could not easily be resolved. Mired in scandal, the bishops no longer cared or dared speak out on behalf of the Irish people. Politicians, bankers, developers and financiers were similarly reticent, for their stewardship of the economy during the boom years had bordered on the criminal. Equally, medical consultants, law officers and business tycoons kept their heads down following the revelations of rascality that had emanated from over twenty tribunals starting in the early 1990s. Who would step into the vacuum thus created? Who could command authority in Ireland in 2010? The widespread celebrations surrounding Seamus Heaney's seventieth birthday in 2009 suggested that such a person might be found among the ranks of Irish poets, novelists or playwrights rather than among the traditional professions.

In short, Ireland, at one time portrayed and, according to one's prejudices, admired or denounced as a 'place apart', a holy island or an 'anomalous state' like no other on the planet, by 2010 appeared to have become much like elsewhere, anywhere or indeed everywhere. The 'bee-loud glades' beloved of W. B. Yeats had given way to the 'bee-stung lips' of celebrities worshipped by the tabloid press, while greed, excess and profligacy were all home-grown rather than filthy foreign imports. By 2010 Irish distinctiveness had apparently vanished, and so too had Irish exceptionalism. Where once just about everything on the island was unfathomable, mysterious or exotic to the outsider, by 2010 all that remained to puzzle the traveller was the undimmed urge of the Irish to attend the funerals of distant acquaintances, the undiminished support for the field sports organised by the GAA, the unquenchable determination to drink to excess and the near total refusal to speak Irish in everyday conversation. To these we might add, perhaps, that the Irish still retained a way with words and music and dance. Were these enough for a distinctive identity?

Lastly, the setting-up of a power-sharing government in Northern Ireland was heralded as ending a 'centuries-old quarrel'; but it did so by institutionalising a sectarianism that many found repulsive and that others regarded as a deeply flawed basis for sustainable devolved government. Large numbers of alienated loyalists and disaffected republicans remained in sink estates largely beyond civil society. Power-sharing – or mandatory coalition as the DUP call it – offered them little, and was unlikely to do so in the future. Such groups were quite capable of causing mayhem and massacre, and their numbers were likely to be boosted as the recession bit deeper. Low intensity sectarian disturbances continued, with numerous assaults and the occasional murder. Immigrants to Northern Ireland came under attack, with numbers driven from their homes. By 2010 the 'Troubles' had ended, but no one could pretend that normality had returned.

Postwar Ireland

In the aftermath of the Second World War, politicians in the Irish Free State were secure, complacent and even arrogant in their vision of what they wanted Ireland to be and confident that with perseverance a Gaelic-speaking, self-sufficient, agriculturally based, Catholic moral community could finally be realised. The 'Emergency' had seemingly vindicated the policies pursued by Fianna Fáil in the 1930s towards achieving those goals; surely the electorate would be duly grateful?

Storm clouds, however, were not slow to gather on the horizon. Admittedly, one immediate anxiety concerning the plans of those who had gone to Britain during the war years turned out to be unfounded. As noted earlier, ministers and civil servants had agonised that Irish workers in Britain might be so unsporting as to return to Ireland seeking (non-existent) jobs, thereby adding to the number of unemployed. Worse, such return migrants might well harbour leftist ideas about state welfarism, and might even be infected with unmentionable contagious diseases picked up in pagan, promiscuous Britain. Happily, the Irish in Britain overwhelmingly did the right thing and stayed there to help man (and woman) that country's postwar boom. They were soon to be joined by tens of thousands of new emigrants.

Other clouds, however, did not blow over quite so easily. A wet summer in 1946 and a freezing winter in 1947 led to fuel shortages and food rationing (including bread, which had not been rationed during the 'Emergency'). A rash of strikes, too, proved troublesome; teachers, for example, embarked on a lengthy and bitter work stoppage in 1946, but they were faced down by de Valera's government which had detected the influence of the IRA behind the labour unrest. Following robust work by *An Garda Siochána*, who appeared to be unfamiliar with the concept of peaceful protest, the teachers were beaten back to work empty handed (and with more than a few sore-headed as well). Bus workers and bank officials fared little better in their disputes with their employers.

More serious than any of these was the political challenge mounted against Fianna Fáil, not from Fine Gael – for that could have been easily shrugged off – but from its own republican constituency. Some intellectual republicans came to believe that the party was flagging in its efforts to attain the sacred goals of language-change, self-sufficiency, an end to partition and even a stop to large-scale emigration. For Sean MacBride, son of an Easter week martyr and of Yeats's muse, Maud Gonne, the death on hunger strike of Sean McCaughey, an IRA *enragé* who had spent over four years naked in an underground cell in Portlaoise prison, crystallised his misgivings at the direction Fianna Fáil was taking. In July 1946, he set up Clann na Poblachta as an avowedly republican party with left-wing policies (though since these were mostly derived from papal encyclicals, fears that a red revolution was in the offing were surely exaggerated). A number of quick by-election victories for the new party revealed growing dissatisfaction with the government, and allegations – unproven – of corruption against some ministers added to voter disenchantment. In the general election held in January 1948 (figure 7.1), de Valera and the Fianna Fáil failed to secure a majority. As Winston Churchill had ruefully discovered in 1945, so de Valera was to learn to his cost in 1948 – the Irish electorate, like the British, were strangers to gratitude.

By later standards, the years 1948 to 1959 exhibited much electoral volatility and government instability. The Fianna Fáil government was replaced by a coalition headed by Fine Gael's John A. Costello, a barrister, with support from Clann na Talmhain, a largely western smallholders' party, the two Labour Parties, some independents, and Clann na Poblachta itself. This first interparty government barely lasted three years before collapsing (May 1951), and being succeeded by a Fianna Fáil government which in its turn was followed in May 1954 by a further coalition government once again led by Costello. This government survived until March 1957 when de Valera's party regained power. De Valera himself was to bow out from active politics in 1959 and he was succeeded as Taoiseach by another, though much younger 'man of 1916', Sean Lemass. With his taking office there began a long period of Fianna Fáil dominance which was to continue, with a few interruptions, for the next fifty years.

7.1 Election poster from 1948 urging the Irish electorate to return de Valera to power because of his successes since the early 1930s. Fianna Fáil papers, University College Dublin Archives.

The 1950s, with their short-lived, ineffective governments, apparently highly resistant to new thinking and each clinging to the detritus of the failed policies of economic self-suffiency, language revival and rural development, have attracted a uniformly hostile press and been depicted as the 'critical period' for Irish independence. On closer examination, however, this decade may yet prove to have been a seedbed for future recovery and growth. At first glance, any such relatively benign assessment must appear misguided, for the facts and figures are stark. Irrespective of which government was in power annual outflows of emigrants remained punishingly high (perhaps sixty thousand in 1958 alone, with around a total of four hundred thousand exiting between 1951 and 1961; and overall during the 1950s the twenty-something age cohort fell by 25 per cent). So constant was the outflow that the notion of the 'vanishing Irish' became a subject of public debate, with the *Irish Times* editorialising that it was entirely possible that if such levels of out-migration did not abate the Irish might die out 'not in the remote, unpredictable future but quite soon'.

Unemployment remained at unacceptable levels (peaking at nearly a hundred thousand in 1957), rural Ireland continued to decay (120,000 jobs in agriculture went in these years), and despite protection and import substitution there was only a very small increase in manufacturing industry. A weak domestic market and a continuing crisis over Ireland's balance of payments (a £5.5 million deficit in 1954 had soared to £35.6 million two years later) kept economic growth throughout the decade at or under 1 per cent per annum, while Irish incomes hovered at around 55 per cent of the UK level. This crisis for Irish independence was made all the more painful because it was occurring at a time when the rest of Europe, including Northern Ireland and those countries defeated in the war, was enjoying sustained economic growth, and when as the British prime minister, Harold Macmillan put it, most people had 'never had it so good'.

Even the *Belfast Newsletter*, the organ of Ulster Unionism, was moved to make sympathetic noises. As it contemplated 'Eire's' thirty-four years of independence it could not but feel 'sad and disillusioned' at the plight of the 'twenty-six counties'. There was, however, a limit to Unionist sympathy with the south's difficulties, for in April 1949 the interparty government had taken Ireland out of the Commonwealth and had declared a republic. It had also sponsored what was evidently a ludicrous campaign aimed at exposing the wrongs of partition. The British government had responded to the severance of the last constitutional links between (twenty-six-county) Ireland and Britain by passing the Ireland Act which enacted that Northern Ireland would not cease to be part of the British dominions without the consent of the Northern Ireland Parliament. Reassuringly for the newly declared Republic, the Act had also declared that Ireland was not to be regarded as a foreign country and nor were its citizens to be considered aliens: the vital safety valve of emigration to Britain would therefore remain open.

Ireland's extremely poor economic performance during the 1950s was not compensated for by advances in social matters. The decade began with a first-class, even epoch-defining, dispute between on the one hand, Dr Noel Browne, minister for health in the first Costello government and, on the other, the Catholic archbishop of Dublin, the redoubtable John Charles McQuaid, aided by the Irish Medical Association (IMA). At issue was the question of the provision of a free health scheme for pregnant mothers and for postnatal care for them and their children. Browne had already scored a major success in his efforts to bring under control, if not eradicate, the scourge of tuberculosis (TB) which was at that time rampant in Ireland and which had carried off his parents and two of his sisters. TB rates had fallen sharply and were soon in line with those in Northern Ireland and Britain.

Browne's new scheme seemed a logical step forward towards his goal of improving the health of the nation – or at least some of the most vulnerable sections of it. However, Archbishop McQuaid, and other members of the Catholic hierarchy, had multiple objections to the scheme. The principal ones were founded in Catholic social teaching. From this perspective, Browne's plan looked dangerously socialist, even totalitarian, in that it would have permitted the state to intervene in matters that were properly the preserve of parents, while the absence of a means test for treatment appeared to reward the feckless at the expense of the prudent. But behind the allegations of 'communist' medicine, there surely lurked the fear that the doctors who would work this scheme, and who would be treating and advising pregnant women and young mothers, might not be entirely sound on the question of contraception. The fact that Browne was a medical graduate of Trinity College Dublin (a bugbear of McQuaid's in particular) could offer no reassurance on this crucial matter of faith and morals. For its part, the IMA was wholly opposed to anything that smacked of socialised medicine or that threatened to turn its members into civil servants; and in McQuaid, they had a powerful ally and advocate. Faced with this formidable array of opponents, Browne discovered that his party leader, MacBride, and some of his ministerial colleagues were not prepared to back him – indeed a few viewed his discomfiture with glee – and his scheme had to be abandoned. Browne resigned in April 1951 and the interparty government was defeated at the polls a month later.

To the *Irish Times* the whole affair revealed that 'the Roman Catholic church would seem to be the effective government of this country'. In addition, not only did the controversy over the 'mother-and-child' scheme overlap with the exuberantly public Catholic celebrations of 'Holy Year' (1950) but it had also coincided with the anti-partition campaign sponsored by the same interparty government that had abjectly buckled when threatened with the crozier (or the scalpel). Ulster Unionists were quick to take advantage. Speeches and correspondence by the various parties to the dispute were republished in a pamphlet and this was duly distributed to British Members of Parliament and to prime ministers throughout the Commonwealth. Unionists had always forecast that 'Home Rule' would become 'Rome Rule': the outcome of the mother-and-child scheme had apparently proved them right (figures 7.2, 7.3).

7.2 A shop in Dublin in the 1950s. Irish Photographic Archive.

And yet it would be too simplistic to dismiss the whole affair as proof that Ireland had become a theocracy. There is evidence that Browne was abandoned not because of episcopal denunciation but because he was a threat to an already fragile coalition. Browne himself seems to have grudgingly recognised something of this: in later years he maintained that he was ousted on foot of a plot orchestrated by jealous Cabinet colleagues. Again, the incoming Fianna Fáil government brought forward substantially the same scheme a little over a year later (though free medicine was abandoned) and managed to have it enacted without opposition from the bishops. Browne was impetuous, stubborn and naive, and to an extent the author of his own downfall. He did not seek to challenge the existing profound consensus on social and religious values, but that was how it appeared. In so far as he had a target in view, it was probably the IMA, but the hierarchy obligingly had acted as a proxy for it. In Ireland, appearances are always more important than reality; it seemed that a dedicated pioneer in the area of state provision of healthcare for mothers and children had been brought

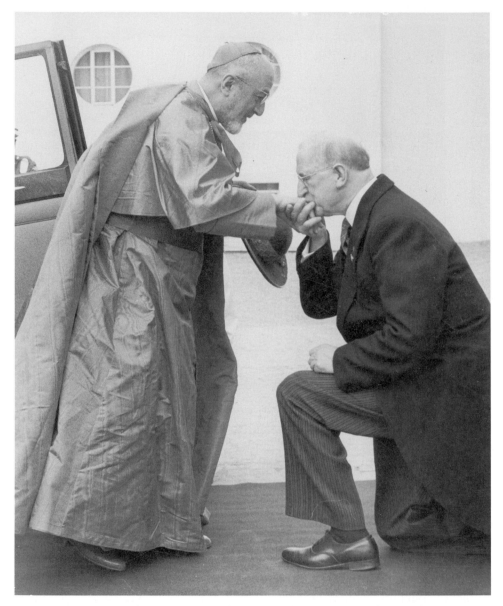

7.3 Rome Rule? Eamon de Valera paying his respects to the Papal Legate to the Patrician Congress in Dublin in 1951. De Valera papers, University College Dublin Archives.

down by an obscurantist and elitist hierarchy and that was what counted. The IMA walked away blame free.

Attachment to outdated modes of thought and action was also exhibited by the IRA during the 1950s, for despite ruinous splits, ideological confusion, long terms of imprisonment for activists (including playwright Brendan Behan) and infiltration by informers, it had resolutely refused to go away. As before, the ending of partition by violence was its goal. In the early 1950s, various raids with varying success took place on British army bases and other places where guns and ammunition were stored. In 1954, for example, a raid on Gough Barracks, county Armagh, had netted 400 weapons. Emboldened by such triumphs, the IRA embarked on 'Operation Harvest', a series of hit-and-run attacks on military barracks and government installations, notably customs posts, in Northern Ireland. The campaign began in 1956 and lasted until 1962. Some eighteen people died on both sides. It was noticeable that the Catholic minority remained almost wholly indifferent, if not hostile, to the IRA's activities. Put bluntly, so far as northern Catholics were concerned, an end to partition would mean an end to the benefits of the British welfare state along with incorporation into a country in which unemployment threatened to top a hundred thousand per annum and from which as many as seventy thousand were fleeing annually. These cold facts could scarcely be classed as inducements.

In marked contrast to a worsening economic environment and to what seemed to be a political landscape mired in the past, complete with republican irredentists, the Irish cultural scene in the 1950s exhibited a vitality that was on some levels exciting and refreshing. The works of James Joyce had all been published before the Second World War but his influence was profound in the 1950s and later. He was a hero to the writers of the 1950s and his onslaught on the self-deluding romanticism of the literary revival seemed tailor-made for an Ireland in which all aspirations seemed to be consigned to the dustbin or the passenger ferry. Similarly with Samuel Beckett. He had published *Murphy* in 1938 and had chosen to remain in France during the war during which he had served with distinction in the Resistance. In later works such as *En Attendant Godot* (1953), his 'incurable pessimism', like that of Joyce, seemed to catch the pointlessness of Ireland in the 1950s.

Waiting for Godot was given its Irish premiere in 1955 in the Pike Theatre Club run by Alan Simpson and Carolyn Swift, one of a number of major theatrical occasions seemingly at odds with the apparent general torpor of the period in matters political or economic. In 1954, again in the Pike Theatre Club, Brendan Behan's *The Quare Fellow* was premiered. This was a play about an IRA prisoner condemned to death, who like Godot never appears on stage. In 1955 in the Gaiety Theatre the actor Cyril Cusack braved the wrath of the hierarchy by staging Sean O'Casey's rather poor anti-clerical play *The Bishop's Bonfire*.

Exciting experimentation and bold innovation in the Irish theatrical world did not meet with whole-hearted approval. Far from it: in 1958 the newly inaugurated Dublin Theatre Festival had to be cancelled in the face of episcopal objections to some of its more risqué intended productions. Touchingly, if naively,

Dr McQuaid had been invited to celebrate a mass at the opening of the festival. A year earlier, and much more serious, a production at the Pike Theatre Club of Tennessee Williams's *Rose Tattoo* was shut down by the Gardaí, and Alan Simpson was arrested. He was eventually found not guilty of 'presenting for gain an indecent and profane performance', but in the interval before his acquittal his marriage had collapsed under the strain and the Pike never recovered.

And yet, for all the very public and shaming reverses, Irish theatre thrived in the 1950s: Behan and Beckett were genuinely innovative talents and, at the other end of the scale, amateur dramatic societies throughout the island brought thousands into the world of playwrights and performance – there were over three hundred societies in 1959. The literary world was equally lively: poets such as Austin Clarke and Patrick Kavanagh, and novelists such as James Plunkett, Benedict Kiely, Brian O'Nolan and Patrick Galvin sought, like Joyce, to move beyond the suffocating provincialism of nationalist Ireland and to address the world. Their task was not an easy one. Public indifference to the writer was widespread; but as menacing was a pervasive drink culture that elevated conviviality over achievement. The pub would prove as threatening to the writer as the emigrant ship to the Fenian or as the informer to the IRA. State censorship continued to bite: some six hundred books a year were banned in the 1950s (among those proscribed were the usual suspects – Sartre, Steinbeck, Hemingway, O'Connor, O'Faolain *et al.*). This figure was well up on the hundred or so per annum put on the list in the 1930s. Yet even here there were signs of a thaw, for successful protests were made at the composition of the censorship board. In the end, the apparent rage for banning may in retrospect be regarded as much as an indication of ebbing power and loss of control as of a demonstration of unchallenged and unchallengeable authority.

In short, despite outward appearances, there were more than a few signs that official Ireland – the Ireland of civil war party politics, pre-Keynesian economics, abject sycophancy towards the hierarchy and blind determination on language revival – was, under the shattering experience of the 1950s, undergoing a fundamental change in outlook. The sheer scale of the crisis was such that new ways of thinking were urgently required. In addition, the embarrassing spectacle of the 'Six Counties' – the usual designation for Northern Ireland – outperforming the Republic in just about every area was a further spur to a root and branch reappraisal of some time-honoured but now discredited policies.

Perhaps the first sign that such a rethink might be emerging can be seen in the setting up in 1948 of a Commission on Emigration. Over the next six years it went about its work, gathering evidence from the great and the good – churchmen, economists and playwrights among them; few actual emigrants were invited to participate. The Commission's eventual findings – it reported in 1954 – were hardly startling. In general, it noted gravely, men left Ireland to find work, women to find a husband. It suggested that it was not really the business of government to discover why people were leaving in droves, and certainly in the view of some commissioners the state bore little responsibility towards the emigrants. That was the church's job – and one that Archbishop McQuaid was keen to take on. So far so complacent; however, the very fact that emigration was finally seen as a fit subject for investigation was truly ground-breaking, and the recommendation that proper statistics be collected was encouraging. Emigration might have been a 'fact' about which nothing could be done, and the Irish might indeed be a 'migratory people', as some argued on the Commission, but emigration as a problem was now in the public domain in a way that it had not been previously. And it was destined to stay there, for the publication of the Commission's report could hardly have come at a worse time. The alarming *The Vanishing Irish* by John O'Brien had preceded it by a few months in 1954 and made the Commission's anodyne recommendations and suggestions seem altogether lacking in urgency, even defeatist. From now on, no Irish government could afford to ignore emigration or fail to seek ways to reduce it.

Similarly, in matters of economic policy there were some signs that the 1930s' goal of a self-sufficient Ireland was coming to an end. In 1948 the interparty government set up the Industrial Development Authority. Its remit was quite narrow, but economic planning, however limited, was about to come in from the cold. Typically, Lemass in opposition denounced it, but in office he could see its value and was content to keep it on. Direct foreign investment was the next item to be tackled. For many Republicans – de Valera and Lemass among them – this was code for British recolonisation of Ireland, and had to be resisted at all costs. And yet under the pressure of soaring unemployment, balance of payments deficits and constant budgetary crises, Lemass had something of a Damascene conversion. 'We welcome foreign investment', he announced in 1953. His 'welcome' was, however, a carefully guarded one: but even so, another cherished 'core value' was being reassessed, and this was what mattered.

In other words, when Lemass finally took over from de Valera in 1959 he was not starting with a blank sheet of paper. Economic planning, direct foreign investment and a rejection of the nostrums of the 1930s had been fashionable for some time. And in T. K. Whitaker, a young northerner just promoted to be secretary in the Department of Finance, Lemass was to find an able ally. Their relationship was not to be entirely harmonious, but it was effective. It was Whitaker who had already written the breakthrough document, 'Economic Development', in December 1958, and the Fianna Fáil government itself had produced a 'Programme for Economic Expansion'. Taken together these documents in effect announced an end to protectionism and the embrace of something

7.4 Changing Dublin: a bus bound for Dublin airport overtakes a jaunting cart, probably in the 1950s. Irish Photographic Archive.

like free trade; Ireland was to be transformed (figures 7.4–7.6 illustrate change in Ireland.) There was still much to do: both reports were scandalously light on the necessity to expand the second- and third-level educational sectors; but as Ireland turned the corner into the 1960s there was a palpable sense of movement rather than stagnation. Perhaps the chief importance of the two documents lay in the psychological boost they gave to a population apparently beaten down by repeated failure and growing apathy.

Postwar Northern Ireland

In the popular memory of northern Unionists, the two decades after the Second World War were in just about every respect the best decades of the twentieth century. This was the period when Northern Ireland was in their eyes 'a great wee place'. Popular memory can often be flawed, but in this instance there is a lot of evidence to sustain it. Curiously, for northern nationalists these decades too have acquired a certain rosy hue in the mind of those who lived through them. Admittedly, as we shall see, the Northern Ireland economy ran into difficulties once the war was over, unemployment quickly rose and remained stubbornly high by British standards (though not by those of the neighbouring state). None

7.5 Changing Dublin: children playing in the flats complexes built in the 1960s. Irish Photographic Archive.

the less the implementation on a 'step-by-step' basis of the key educational, social security and health provisions of the British welfare state undoubtedly took the sting out of economic downturn. The benefits of the welfare state, it should be stated, were not confined to 'loyalists' – though some might have wished that this were so. 'Disloyalists' took advantage (disproportionate advantage, grumbled some) of their new entitlements in terms of social welfare payments, childrens' allowances, free healthcare and educational opportunities.

Southern neutrality had been a godsend for Ulster Unionists, for it appeared to mark out clearly for British opinion that the 'Paddies' were not all alike and, as noted, Unionist ministers were not about to let Westminster forget their debt of gratitude to Northern Ireland. Admittedly, in the early postwar months the arrival of a Labour government in London did arouse anxieties, for Unionists on historic grounds had always associated themselves with the Conservative Party in Britain, and there was a small group of Labour Members who were vocal in their criticism of Unionists. In the event Labour ministers by and large viewed

7.6 Changing Dublin: nuns escort a group of young girls preparing for their first Holy Communion, under the eyes of mini-skirted girls. Mid-1960s. Irish Photographic Archive.

Northern Ireland through the benign lens of its 'contribution' during the Second World War, in contrast to the south's so-called 'neutrality' (i.e. spineless slacking). Most Labourites took a very dim view of Ireland's priest-ridden society, as soon confirmed by the debacle over the mother-and-child-scheme (a propaganda gift for Unionists). A strong current of pro-Ulster sentiment was seen when Costello's government unilaterally declared a republic and withdrew from the Commonwealth. The Labour government's response was to pass the Ireland Act (1949) which copperfastened partition, and completely wrong-footed Costello, who apparently had had no inkling of any such reaction.

Unease in Unionist government circles at the advent of a Labour government in Westminster had increased when the scale of the changes in welfare legislation was revealed. Northern Irish politicians – on both sides of the sectarian divide – were quite hostile to the proposed expansion of state control. Nationalist figures took their cue from the fulminations of northern Catholic bishops against, for example, 'socialist' medicine, while some Unionists worried about how to prevent 'Free Staters' tunnelling under the border, emerging in, say, Portadown, to claim the 'dole', and even to vote. (The Safeguarding of Employment Act of 1947 saw off this potential threat.) More controversially, Unionists sought to limit the number of children in any family eligible for child benefit, for everyone knew what Catholics were like regarding large families; but the Labour ministers were having none of it, and parity of provision between the United Kingdom and Northern Ireland was secured. For some years into the 1950s there were some desultory protests at 'socialist' legislation, and a few (some senior) Unionist romantics continued to toy with the idea of Ulster going it alone, as a dominion along the lines of Canada or Australia; but that notion could not endure a swift dose of economic realism. Like it or not Northern Ireland could not exist without Britain, and all talk to the contrary was just wishful thinking.

Within a handful of years the entire social landscape of Northern Ireland was transformed as British welfare legislation was enacted there. A cornerstone of the new structure was comprehensive social insurance. Accordingly, a National Insurance Act was passed in 1946, to be complemented by the Industrial Injuries Act which in its turn was followed in 1948 by the National Assistance Act. The workhouse had finally closed. Alongside these, a series of laws effectively boosted healthcare provision throughout Northern Ireland and began to make amends for decades of neglect. Again, the housing record of Northern Ireland had been lamentable between the wars and to remedy this the Northern Ireland Housing Trust was set up in 1945, with a target of 25,000 houses in ten years (local authorities were to be responsible for building the remaining 75,000 dwellings required). Finally, the Education Act of 1947 revolutionised access to second-level and further education in Northern Ireland. The school leaving age was to be raised to fifteen (finally achieved in 1957), and there was (a means-tested) provision of scholarships for all those eligible to enter university – a momentous change.

The construction of a welfare state in Northern Ireland could not be matched by the Republic, which continued to fall behind on just about every index of welfare, education and health provision. (In 1950, unemployment benefit was 24 shillings in the north, 15 shillings in the south; children's allowance was 5 shillings for each child after the first in the north, 2 shillings and 6 pence for each child after the second in the south.) And yet it was not all unalloyed progress in the north, for some of the many welfare boons were themselves soon to prove religiously contentious. The refusal of the Mater Hospital in Belfast, owned by a Catholic religious order, to enter fully into the National Health Service because of a principled objection to the possibility of non-Catholic control led to a row which rumbled on until a resolution was found in 1967. Similarly, while Catholic schools had the full costs of their staff met under the Education Act of 1947, they were eligible for only 65 per cent of their capital expenditure because they refused to accept some members of the local authority on to the individual secondary school's committee. This led to a stand-off until a solution emerged in 1972. Ironically, while there had been criticism from Catholics at the Unionist government's failure to pick up the entire educational bill without any conditions, the whole scheme had been denounced by red-hot Protestants as an over-generous sell-out to Catholics and they succeeded in forcing the resignation of Major Hall-Thompson, the minister of education. Lastly, the idea of building tens of thousands of houses might have seemed an attractive one. Who could possibly object? However, in certain areas of Northern Ireland, religious majorities were paper-thin, and the disposal of new houses was certain to have major implications for sectarian control. So long as few houses were being built by district councils, there was little to fight over; but a housing target of a hundred thousand within ten years – if met – could not but prove disruptive of old ways of local political management.

In short, while Northern Ireland was modernising in terms of the creation of a welfare state, little if any consideration was given to the deeply segregated and sectarian nature of its society. Throughout the 1950s the state's official discourse – as revealed by the language of various economic reports – may have stressed growth, development, foreign investment, modernisation and, above all, planning; but its public discourse – as measured by party manifestos and platform speeches – tended to reinforce the age-old watchwords of vigilance, unity, 'no surrender' and the menace of Rome. Thus at one level, Industrial Development Acts could be passed between 1945 and 1953 which offered generous incentives to foreign companies to set up in Northern Ireland, and which could genuinely be regarded as progressive and modernising. But on another level, public debate during 1953 was dominated by the question of where and when to fly the Union flag, considered by around 35 per cent of the population to be an alien symbol and a sectarian badge. In 1954 the issue was resolved by passing an Act which made it illegal to try to prevent the flying of the flag anywhere in Northern Ireland.

This attempt at modernising economically without reforming politically was a deliberate one, not a strategy that was arrived at by accident. In its favour were numerous historical precedents. John Foster, the last pre-Union speaker of the Irish Parliament, had always believed that Catholic discontent was at bottom economic and that if the lot of the peasant could be improved, then silence would descend over the question of equal political rights with Protestants. So too, one hundred years later, the whole notion of 'killing Home Rule by kindness' was based on the belief that Irish nationalism was essentially the coded expression of bread and butter grievances of Irish farmers. The fact that neither of these strategies had proved at all successful mattered little; it was the precedent that counted and conferred validation.

Sir Basil Brooke, prime minister since 1943, created Viscount Brookeborough in 1952, and probably the most gifted Unionist politician of his (or the next) generation, espoused this way forward for Northern Ireland, and this was crucial. Brookeborough had fought in the Great War, and he had been 'out' in the 'border war' of 1920–1 in Fermanagh. His Unionist credentials were thoroughly impeccable. And he could see the way the wind was blowing: in 1951 he had the unpleasant task of informing his ministers of the existence of something – um – called the – ah – United Nations Convention on Human Rights which apparently meant that religious discrimination against Catholics was unacceptable and ought no longer to be trumpeted as proof of loyalist credentials, much less as an achievement. However, instead of indicating to his bemused ministerial colleagues that the world was changing, Brookeborough instead chose to reassure them that, notwithstanding this edict, all could be well. In later years he gamely sought to cut off family allowance for the fourth or subsequent children – an obvious anti-Catholic ploy that embarrassed his friends at Westminster (but did him no harm in Ulster); and he sided with those who asserted that a Catholic could never be a member of the Unionist Party, let alone a candidate for a Unionist seat (even though he stated otherwise in private).

Brookeborough, following Brooke's elevation to the peerage, had the charisma and the credibility to have carried off a major policy shift, and to have brought within the embrace of Unionism those who hitherto had been regarded as the constant enemy. He chose not to go down that route, for his greatest fear was that while overtures to the 'disloyalists' might pay off in the future, they would certainly split the party in the present; and the here and now was the arena in which he operated. Already in the early 1950s a fiery evangelical preacher, the Reverend Ian Paisley, had appeared on the scene to denounce any signs of ecumenism, Romeward trends or overtures towards Catholics; and Unionist leaders had to take note. That said, Brookeborough's failure to educate his followers to the approaching new reality has to be seen as a missed opportunity.

By the early 1960s the figures suggest that well over 20 per cent of university students were Catholics (much higher in arts and law). It was evident that a growing Catholic middle class had lost patience with IRA irredentism, and that many had begun to vote for another type of Unionist party – the Northern Ireland Labour Party. Young Catholics were turning their backs on the suffocatingly dated Nationalist Party, and within Belfast there was little support for Sinn Féin's abstentionism. On the international scene, a charismatic pope, John XXIII, was making overtures to different faiths, while in Washingdon DC an equally charismatic president of the United States, John F. Kennedy, had already broken the mould by becoming the first Catholic to be elected leader of the 'Free World'. In short, on a number of fronts, the way was open for Brookeborough to bring in some Catholics into the party, into the system, into the state and the consequences of such a new departure would surely have been profound – not least in deploying them to defend certain 'peculiarities' (i.e. anti-democratic elements) of the electoral system. Only Brookeborough could have delivered this level of change; only he had the pedigree to refute accusations of selling out and backsliding; and only he could have seen off extremist Protestant protests. It was not to be.

In 1963 Brookeborough was succeeded as leader of Ulster Unionism and prime minister by Captain Terence O'Neill. O'Neill had emerged as leader largely because he had seemed the most likely candidate to turn back the rise of the Northern Ireland Labour Party which was threatening the Unionist grip on Belfast, but also because he spoke the language of economic modernisation – though his aristocratic drawl made his admonitions grating on the ear. It should be stressed that O'Neill did not become prime minister because he would extend the hand of friendship to Catholics. His 'contrary' credentials seemed quite sound on that score. He was of course a member of the Orange Order; in 1959 he had advertised for 'a Protestant girl for housework' in his home. (He had had trouble with Catholic servants, he explained. Quite so.) And he was quickly on record as stating that if Catholics were treated fairly, they would become like Protestants and stop having eighteen children. His double whammy here was quite extraordinary, for the crass condescension in his remark outraged Catholics, while the prospect of fair treatment for 'disloyalists' rang alarm bells for Unionists.

O'Neill was an unanchored individual, uneasy on the hustings, detached at the dispatch box and with a languid demeanour on television; he was never really at his ease anywhere except perhaps in London society. His father had been the first Westminster Member of Parliament to die in the Great War, and the orphaned O'Neill had been helped thereafter by various well-heeled and well-connected aunts, uncles and cousins. He had basically drifted during the 1930s, with a spell as *aide de camp* to the governor of South Australia, and then a period in the London Stock Exchange. As with so many others of his class, the outbreak of war came to the rescue, and a commission in the Irish Guards was quickly secured. But O'Neill did not have a particularly 'good war'; he served in intelligence (by no means an indicator of intellectual attainment – often the reverse); he won no medals for gallantry (unlike Brookeborough in the Great War) and he ended up as a lowly captain. After the war, his extended family again came to the rescue and a seat was found for him in the Bannside constituency of county Antrim.

Once elected to Stormont, his lack of adminstrative experience proved to be no handicap, while the dearth of competitive talent on Unionist backbenches ensured for him a swift progress up the greasy pole. He became a junior minister in 1948, and minister of finance in 1956. Notably, he brought proposals to the Cabinet for solving Northern Ireland's unemployment problem by draining Lough Neagh and designating the resultant landfill as county Neagh. His plan, more Don Quixote than J. M. Keynes, got nowhere.

The goal of O'Neill's premiership was economic modernisation through dedicated and detailed planning. Brookeborough had dabbled a little in this, though his heart was more into shooting and fishing; but with O'Neill the need for economic planning became all consuming. He loved the expert and, assisted and advised by the very young, and very able, Kenneth Bloomfield, deputy secretary to the Stormont Cabinet, he moved swiftly to employ them. Numerous reports were commissioned – on the economy itself, into the future of the railways, concerning the extension of the road network, the possibility of a new university and even the feasibility of a new town. Not since the early days of the Ulster plantation had so many plans been drawn up by so many experts – Cuthbert, Isles, Mathew, Lockwood, Wilson – all with the overall aim of transforming the face of Northern Ireland. Two new ministries of development, and health and social services were set up, and great efforts were expended in attracting new industries to the province to replace the older heavy industries which had been on the slide since the early 1950s. There were undoubted successes – major firms such as Michelin, Goodyear, Du Pont and British Enkalon all established large plants in Ulster. After the somnambulism of the later Brookeborough era, there appeared to be at last energy and action.

But it was economic rather than political modernisation that O'Neill aimed at. Admittedly, he did set out somewhat hesitantly to improve community relations. He had a very difficult path to tread here, but he undoubtedly made things worse by not thinking the matter through, and he certainly did not seek his Cabinet colleagues' approval for what we might call his policy of guarded *détente*. Socially gauche, angular in manner and highly secretive, he was hardly tailor-made for the grand gesture, let alone the imaginative *démarche*. Nor did he seem to realise that actions might be preferred to symbols, and in the end the latter were about all that he had to offer. A visit to a Catholic convent school and an expression of sympathy on the death of the pope apparently marked the limit of his gestures towards Catholics. And against these had to be set a flat refusal to contemplate the appointment of Catholics to public boards. Even the normally reliable *Belfast Telegraph* was moved to protest that the excuse offered – that suitable Catholic candidates were not available – simply would not wash. Further needless trampling on Catholic sensitivities occurred in other areas. The proposed new town was to be named Craigavon, hardly a designation to attract 'cross-community' support, and the new university was – following Unionist lobbying – not to go to 'Catholic' Derry lest it imperil religious balances, but was instead to be located in the sleepy 'Protestant' market town of Coleraine. The divergence between economic modernisation and political reform was plain to see. At bottom O'Neill had not the slightest understanding of northern Catholic discontent: if he thought about it at all, he seems to have regarded it as a type of behavioural disorder that would be remedied by economic progress. He was to be badly mistaken.

And yet it is important when reviewing the early years of O'Neill's premiership not to be too conscious of the coming storm. O'Neill's gestures towards Catholics, in retrospect, seemingly trivial, were quite unprecedented from Unionist leaders and attracted some favourable notices from Catholic leaders. His meeting with the southern Taoiseach, Sean Lemass, in January 1965 at Stormont was also well received in Catholic circles (less so by his Cabinet colleagues whom, typically, he had kept entirely in the dark regarding it). Following this historic meeting – the first such in forty years – the leader of the Nationalist Party, Eddie McAteer, declared that his party would take on the role of official opposition at Stormont. The fact that Paisley had condemned the visit as a sell-out to the republican enemies of Ulster probably gained some back-handed sympathy for O'Neill also.

There were other signs that the 'times they are a-changin', or at least appeared to be. This was the era of the 'swinging sixties' and young people in Belfast, Derry, Enniskillen and most areas in between, appeared to have other things on their minds than the shibboleths, slogans and dogmas of their parents' generation. Throughout Northern Ireland the music scene was dominated by showbands which played cover versions of popular hits to enthusiastic dance-goers in numerous ballrooms. By 1965 there may even have been the beginnings of an authentic Belfast sound, with the group Them, fronted by Van Morrison, to the fore. In soccer, George Best of Manchester United and Northern Ireland was reinventing the dribble and the body swerve, and in snooker a very young Alex Higgins had begun to attract attention in Belfast's clubs with his devastating potting and revolutionary use of screwback. Television was increasingly bringing the world, and world news, along with political argument and debate, into the living-room, and this too proved liberating (or disturbing). BBC Northern Ireland had begun regular television broadcasts in 1955 and by the early 1960s coverage was near universal throughout Northern Ireland, with an overspill into the Republic as far south as Dublin. A mile up the road from the BBC studios, a small group of young poets clustered around Philip Hobsbawm, a lecturer in English at Queen's University Belfast. One of this group, Seamus Heaney, went on to publish his first collection, *Death of a Naturalist*, in May 1966. With poets like Heaney, musicians like Morrison, and sportsmen like Best and Higgins, the unthinkable looked like happening: in both high and popular culture, Belfast and Northern Ireland might yet take the lead in these islands.

The Republic of Ireland in the 1960s

The 1960s were also a period of rapid change in the Republic. For the first time, the goals of national independence were identified as economic growth and wealth creation, though redistribution of resources lagged far behind as a state objective. What was certain was that language revival and ending partition would have to wait. Lemass's visit to O'Neill in January 1965 was clear proof that he had a radically different agenda from his predecessors. He had never had much time for the Irish language, and he had certainly never mastered it, but he had even less time for the vulgar anti-partitionism that pervaded official discourse in the Republic and that passed for a northern policy. Lemass bluntly pointed out that the best argument for ending partition would be the prosperity of the southern state – and that this was an argument that had not hitherto been tried. In practical terms, he also suggested that Aer Lingus, the national carrier, might consider ordering aircraft from Shorts Brothers in Belfast, and in a similar spirit of good neighbourliness, he attempted to outlaw the term, 'the Six Counties', as the customary designation of Northern Ireland in southern radio broadcasts. He had little success in this latter endeavour.

Economically, Lemass's policies have to be judged a success. Between 1959 and 1970 manufacturing jobs increased from some 160,000 to over 200,000, and most of this growth was attained by an influx of foreign capital, attracted to the Republic by a favourable tax regime and low wages. Some 350 foreign firms came to the Republic in the 1960s; and economic growth ran at around 4 per cent throughout the 1960s whereas it had been barely measurable in the 1950s. Emigration fell to under 15,000 per annum – still high, but a fraction of the exodus that had taken place on an annual basis during the bad old days in the 1950s. Perhaps the most striking sign that Lemass was prepared to discard policies that had not worked was his readiness to have Ireland join the European Economic Community, still in its infancy in the early 1960s, but clearly representing the future. The central problem here was that the Irish economy was so closely aligned to the British (75 per cent of all Irish exports went there) that the Irish entry would largely depend on the outcome of the British application. When the British request for entry was duly refused (by the French, largely on chauvinist grounds), Ireland's parallel application fell with it. None the less, the Republic had attempted to join 'Europe', and assuredly there would be another pass. (An Anglo-Irish free trade agreement concluded in December 1965 was something of a consolation prize.) Almost overnight, it appeared that autarky, self-sufficiency, irredentism, isolationism and revivalism, i.e. all the economic and cultural baggage borne resolutely forward since the 1920s, had been unceremoniously dumped.

Not everyone was happy with the abandonment of the social and cultural ideals of the 1930s or with the embrace of economic growth. A series of strikes among what had traditionally been regarded as worker-aristocrats – electricity workers, maintenance craftsmen, printers and bank officials – revealed great unease at the proposed winding down of monopolies, job protection and wage differentials. The rather warmer relations between the Irish Republic and Northern Ireland also invited some robust criticism. In the wake of its disastrous border campaign, the IRA had been rethinking its entire strategy, and it had begun to develop socialist policies designed to win working-class support north and south. It was active in the Dublin Housing Action Committee and was well represented at various 'fish-ins' designed to expose continued foreign ownership of Irish natural resources. However, it also retained its destructive capacity, and on the night of 8 March 1966 a number of volunteers blew up Nelson's pillar (figure 7.7), a well-known landmark in Dublin's O'Connell Street. A further boost for the IRA came in April 1966 with the start of the official commemoration of the fiftieth anniversary of the 1916 Rising. It is likely that IRA membership grew as ceremonies, pageants and parades were held throughout the Republic. There were also a number of commemorative ceremonies and demonstrations organised in Northern Ireland, and these were to have a further negative impact on Protestant and loyalist sensitivities, already inflamed by what was seen as Terence O'Neill's policy of 'selling-out to Republicans'.

So far as the Catholic church was concerned the 1960s were a period of change, and while ostensibly this was welcomed – the change came after all from Rome, the pope and the cardinals – there was no little trepidation, and some heartburn, at its implications. The Vatican Council had met from 1962 to 1965 and its deliberations into the organisation of the Catholic church, its dogma, its liturgy and, most unsettling, the role of the laity, had proved painful for those Irish prelates accustomed to fulsome deference, abject obedience and unquestioned authority. The whole experience was in some respects a preview for clerics of what tribunals would be like for Irish politicians a generation later.

Archbishop McQuaid had attended the Vatican Council, and on his return from Rome he had reassured the faithful that nothing had changed. But in his heart he must have known that there had in fact been what amounted to a seismic shift, though it was to be some years before its full extent would become apparent.

7.7 1966: aftermath of the blowing up of Nelson's Pillar in Dublin. Irish Photographic Archive.

In public Dr McQuaid carried on regardless: his agents attended and reported on every significant public meeting in the greater Dublin area; he ran checks on all academic appointments to University College Dublin; he succeeded in driving John Whyte, a politics lecturer who had published on church–state relations in independent Ireland, out of the same university; and he reaffirmed his 1944 ban on Catholics attending Trinity College Dublin (it was lifted in 1970). Lay zealots remained active throughout Irish society, married women were by and large absent from the workforce, and the Irish Censorship Board doggedly continued its work of keeping the nation's reading matter pure. However, keeping the nation's morals above reproach was not quite as straightforward as heretofore: in 1965, 450 ballrooms, manned by four thousand musicians and filled with 'heavin 'n' sweatin'" dancers, were difficult, if not impossible, to police adequately. Books could now be 'unbanned' after twelve years (1967) and this led to an instant flood of 'new' books emerging into the light. As well, a new – more liberal – film classification scheme was brought in. True, it was all a little late for *Country Girls* (1960) by Edna O'Brien which was proscribed, and even for *The Dark*, by John McGahern (1965), who also lost his job as a national school teacher. (His dismissal might also have come about because he had had the temerity to marry not just a foreigner but a divorcée to boot.) And yet, notwithstanding, the times were definitely 'a-changin' in the south as in the north.

BBC television had been available in the border areas since the 1950s, and from the early 1960s Téilifís Éireann had begun to broadcast. By 1970 there were well over four hundred thousand TV licences in the Republic (over four times the number taken out in 1960) and programmes such as the *Late Late Show*, hosted by Gay Byrne, were commanding large audiences for discussions on previously taboo questions of sex, religion, alcohol, contraception, family relations and women's rights. Airing an item that became known as 'the bishop and the nightie' affair would have been unthinkable even a few years earlier. Deference had not disappeared but it was receding, and into the vacuum came questioning, probing and criticism, all marking the early beginnings of secularisation. Archbishop McQuaid could not have been more wrong when he had claimed that nothing had changed after the Vatican Council.

In retrospect, perhaps the greatest change in that decade came in 1966 with the decision by the minister of education, Donogh O'Malley, to introduce free secondary education from the following year. A year earlier, the report *Investment in Education*, commissioned by the then minister of education, Patrick Hillery, and largely written by the economist Patrick Lynch, had disclosed that well over half of all children emerged from the national (primary) schools having left no trace of their existence nor indeed any record of educational attainment. This damning report repeatedly stressed that education had a vital role to play in wealth creation and that the wholly inadequate educational provision was imperilling the nation's future. These conclusions were accepted. Hitherto, education had been almost entirely viewed as the handmaiden of the language revival, and post-primary schooling had been seen as suitable only for those destined for the professions or for those contemplating a religious life; now it was to be the right of every citizen. In 1960 just 20 per cent had proceeded to secondary education; but by 1970 that figure had risen to 50 per cent, and was to grow further. Education was to remain scandalously underfunded – in 1967, Northern Ireland with half the population spent £38 per head on education, the Republic spent £17 per head – and it was not until the 1970s that the expansion of third-level and further education finally got under way. But the crucial breakthrough in this hitherto neglected sector came with the report into education and with the subsequent O'Malley initiative. It seems clear that the origins of the Celtic Tiger economy of the 1990s can be located in the decision to extend secondary education to all. In terms of the educational and social benefits, the results were incalculable.

The beginnings of the 'Troubles'

If the year 1966 has strong claims to be regarded as the key year in the crucial decade in the making of the Irish Republic, its claims are no less pressing north of the border, for this was the year when the wheels began to come off the O'Neill experiment in economic modernisation without political reform. Admittedly, there had been early signs that O'Neill's awkward initiatives towards Catholics would cause trouble among the more traditional Unionist supporters. His expression of condolences on the death of Pope John XXIII in June 1963 had aroused the ire of the Reverend Ian Paisley, founder and leader of the Free Presbyterian Church. From then on, it is fair to say that Paisley and his supporters had O'Neill in their sights as one who would betray Ulster, Protestantism and the Union. Paisley again came to the fore in 1964 when he forced the Royal Ulster Constabulary (RUC) to intervene to remove an Irish tricolour from a window in the Catholic Divis Street area of Belfast. Four nights of rioting ensued. (These disturbances have a rather deeper significance in that they drew a very young Gerry Adams into the republican movement in Belfast.) A few months later came the O'Neill/Lemass meetings which Paisley denounced as yet another sell-out of Unionism; and in February 1966 he led protests at the Belfast city council's decision to name the new bridge across the Lagan after Queen Elizabeth rather than Lord Carson. (The irony of this protest by loyalists *against* naming the bridge after the sovereign did not go unremarked.)

Paisley might have seemed like an anachronistic throwback to an earlier more anarchic period of Northern Ireland's history, but in fact he represented the future as much as the past. His support came in part from evangelical Protestants, bewildered and angry at, as they saw it, the all-too-evident Romeward slide of the mainstream Protestant churches. It was revealing that one of the most violent of Paisley's early demonstrations had been that directed against the Belfast meeting of the General Assembly of the Presbyterian Church ('soft on Rome') in June 1966, and for which he received a prison sentence. But Paisley also drew support from members of the Protestant working classes. They were not particularly evangelical or even all that religious, but they could sense that their world was changing rapidly, and in ways deeply inimical to their interests. The heavy industries, a major source of Protestant pride and identity, had all but gone and those industries that sought to replace them were proving to be anything but Protestant preserves. Working-class Protestant feelings of frustration, confusion and resentment were further fuelled by the obvious distaste with which the Unionist establishment – the lords and the squires, the captains and the majors – regarded their earthy sectarian slogans and songs. Paisley constantly proclaimed that a massive betrayal of Protestant Ulster was underway at the hands of Unionist leaders – especially Captain Terence O'Neill – and he filled his speeches with the apocalyptic rhetoric of the Old Testament. When laced with a virulent and homespun anti-Catholic sectarianism, his message as preached from his pulpits (his church had twelve congregations by 1965) and as printed in the pages of his *Protestant Telegraph* (founded 1966) exerted a powerful appeal on those fearful of all change, and anxious at what appeared to be a Catholic surge.

The phenomenon of 'Paisleyism' was much wider than Paisley's church and went far beyond the man himself: it spoke to those who were persuaded that O'Neill's policies would inevitably lead to an erosion of their Protestant identity, and it spoke on behalf of those who sensed that the outcome of O'Neill's so-called reforms would be nothing less than the cultural dispossession of their community. The plantation would be undone. Already by the mid-1960s a number of fringe Protestant organisations had sprung up – the Ulster Constitution Defence Committee, the Protestant Volunteer Corps and the re-formed UVF – and these bore witness to a profound unease on the part of loyalists at the speed and direction of change. By the mid-1960s opinion polls revealed that some 30 per cent of Protestants agreed with Paisley.

Paisley's fiery speeches and dire warnings might have had less impact had there not been ample evidence of a new assertiveness on the part of northern Catholics. By the early 1960s the Education Act of 1947 had begun to boost the hitherto small Catholic middle class in Northern Ireland with the addition of an annual cohort of university-educated and articulate young men and women. Many went into teaching, law and medicine (relatively few entered the civil service, a Protestant preserve) and they were also, it seemed to Protestants, disproportionately represented in the new broadcast media. Ostensibly, they had little time for anti-partitionism or indeed republicanism; instead they focused on discrimination in housing allocation and in the gerrymandering of electoral constituencies. For example, Dungannon council had not allocated a council house to a Catholic in over twenty years, and in Unionist-controlled councils (90 per cent of the total) there was almost an entire lack of Catholic employees at any level above manual labourer. Again, it was particularly notorious that the city of Derry, with a large Catholic majority, had had a Unionist-controlled council for the previous thirty years. Disastrously for the image of the Unionist government outside Northern Ireland, 'one man, one vote' did not apply in local government elections. Brookeborough's administration had not seen fit to follow Britain in the introduction of universal suffrage at all levels after the war and instead had continued to reward with extra votes those with a 'stake in the country', and who were overwhelmingly Protestant. Almost as embarrassing was the admission that Catholics were not allowed to join the Unionist Party, the sole party of government over the previous fifty years.

The new Catholic intelligentsia was vocal in airing these grievances in the vocabulary of civil rights derived from the United States, and they would soon adopt its anthem – 'We shall overcome' – as theirs. But they also appealed to British notions of fair play and their allegations of unequal treatment were to find a sympathetic ear among Labour Members of Parliament, some of whom – notably those of Irish background and with Irish constituents – had on their own account set up a pressure group, the Campaign for Democracy in Ulster, with a view to overturning the long-standing convention that Northern Ireland's affairs could not be raised at Westminster. Predictably, Unionists, for the most part, were enraged that Catholic accusations of widespread, systemic discrimination were not seen for what they so obviously were – bogus, fraudulent and a cover for the promotion of republican conspiracy. To Unionists of all classes it was axiomatic that because anti-partitionism, republicanism and even nationalism had so patently failed to destroy Northern Ireland over the previous fifty years, the current demands for civil rights and for an end to discrimination were simply another 'disloyalist' strategy to attain that end. From an early date a dialogue of the deaf had commenced and a dangerous impasse was swiftly reached.

A Campaign for Social Justice had been set up in 1964 by middle-class Catholics, and it sought to highlight the enormity of religious discrimination in Northern Ireland. The fact that it was set up in Dungannon, county Tyrone, a town with a Catholic majority but with a Protestant-controlled council, meant that it had a plentiful supply of damaging facts and figures to hand. In 1965 it affiliated itself to the (British) National Council of Civil Liberties and worked closely with the Campaign for Democracy in Ulster. In March 1966 consternation had been caused in Unionism by the victory of Gerry Fitt in West Belfast, a constituency which included both the nationalist Falls Road and the loyalist Shankill. Fitt was a member of the tiny Republican Labour Party and, irritatingly, a veteran of the wartime Murmansk convoys – no chance therefore of a charge of 'disloyalism' having credibility.

Elsewhere in Northern Ireland, just as loyalist fringe groups were springing up to defend their interests, so too nationalist and republican clubs were emerging, though pledged to an entirely different agenda. The bicentenary of the birth of Theobald Wolfe Tone in 1963 had seen the founding of Wolfe Tone societies 'to foster republicanism by educating the masses in their cultural and political heritage' and, as noted above, the celebration of the jubilee of the 1916 Easter Rising had given an added boost to republicanism. On Easter Sunday 1966 ten thousand marched in a republican commemoration parade on the Falls Road, Belfast – a huge provocation to those who were remembering the sacrifice of the 36th Ulster Division at the Somme fifty years earlier.

Loyalists viewed all of these bewildering but, in their eyes, clearly linked developments with mounting alarm. In 1966 stories circulated of an IRA plot to take over Belfast City Hall. O'Neill's leadership looked less and less resolute, and his perceived policy of reconciliation seemed more and more a sell-out of all that Ulster stood for. There were even rumours of a loyalist plot to assassinate him. Meanwhile, Paisley's rhetoric grew ever more envenomed, and his predictions ever more apocalyptic. Not surprisingly, in this atmosphere of loathing, fear and paranoia, elements of the newly re-formed UVF determined on action. In the early hours of 26 June 1966, a young Catholic barman, Peter Ward, was shot to death in Malvern Street in the Shankill area of Belfast. His killers were quickly apprehended and in October were sentenced to life imprisonment. The 'new' UVF was banned; but the deed was done.

Peter Ward's murder revealed that O'Neill's grand strategy of modernisation would meet with violent resistance from traditional loyalism. Paisleyite denunciation was one thing – O'Neill just possibly could have coped with that – but UVF bullets were quite another. O'Neill's policies had always been poorly conceived, and he had never seen fit to explain his ideas to his colleagues, much less master the black arts of media presentation. Certainly, his views were never really grasped or accepted by the party faithful. Whatever he may have thought (or not, for a disdainful insouciance was a trademark), it was evident that after Malvern Street he could expect murderous opposition to his declared policy of delivering – in his view – progressive change in Northern Ireland. That his grasp on both his own Cabinet (for there was a nest of opponents there) and on the historically decentralised Unionist Party was weak, multiplied his difficulties.

In early 1967, a number of socialists, left-wing republicans, trade unionists, professional people and some from an IRA background, came together to form the Northern Ireland Civil Rights Association (NICRA). Its stated aims were carefully devoid of nationalist rhetoric and instead asserted that British subjects in Northern Ireland must have the same rights as British subjects in the United Kingdom. These were eventually listed as 'one man one vote' in council elections, an end to gerrymandering, fair and transparent allocation of public housing, discrimination to be made illegal, the repeal of the Special Powers Act and the standing down of the 'B' Specials. Given the source from which they emanated – and Unionists from the outset were adamant that NICRA was nothing more than a republican front organisation – the demand for such 'rights' in their eyes was tantamount to a call for unconditional surrender.

NICRA involved itself in little more than discussion, debate and propaganda throughout 1967 and into 1968, but in August of that year it was persuaded to sponsor a civil rights march from Coalisland to Dungannon, county Tyrone, to protest at the grotesquely unfair housing allocation in the area. Austin Currie, nationalist Member of Parliament for Tyrone since 1964 and a prime example of the new Catholic – young, articulate, educated, energetic and unafraid – was behind this demonstration. Since his election he had been tireless in publicising discrimination in Tyrone, and he hoped to gain further publicity by emulating the marching strategy of the American civil rights movement. This was undoubtedly a high risk venture. In Northern Ireland, no more than in the southern United States, the protest march was not regarded as an innocent pursuit: on the contrary, those against whom it was directed saw it as an invasion of their territory, a violation of their space, and an attempt to 're-take' their stronghold. Given these perspectives, it was fortunate that the march passed off peacefully enough. Admittedly, the RUC, charged with policing it, had shown themselves to be woefully inexperienced, and their decision to re-route the march caused anger, but they did at least succeed in keeping rival protesters apart. Before peacefully dispersing, the marchers had celebrated by singing 'We shall overcome'. They were led in this song by Betty Sinclair, a (Protestant) communist and a prominent member of NICRA. The organisers might have assumed that such an action reinforced their non-sectarian credentials but those opposed to the march were not deceived, for they noted the presence of long-standing republicans among its stewards.

Impressed by the way that the Dungannon marchers had made their point, housing activists in Derry sought NICRA sponsorship for a similar protest march in October. However, Dungannon was one thing, Derry was quite another, for historically hallowed ground was at stake here. William Craig, the feisty minister for home affairs, faced with the likelihood of public disorder – Paisley and his followers were pledged to a counter-march – banned all demonstrations within the city walls. The organisers refused to accept this decision and the march went ahead on 5 October 1968. On that day, the RUC deployed water-cannon to break up the march and then quickly lost all discipline. They attacked the marchers, who included Gerry Fitt and some Westminster Members of Parliament, in Derry as observers. The ensuing police riot was memorably captured by the RTÉ cameraman Gay O'Brien, and broadcast to a stunned and then outraged audience in Ireland and then much further afield. The genie was out of the bottle.

Unfortunately for the Unionist government, the police attack on the Derry march more or less coincided with the return of students to Queen's University, Belfast at the end of the long vacation. Hitherto regarded as a prime candidate for the accolade of the most somnolent third-level institution in western Europe, under the impact of events in Derry, the university underwent a swift transformation into a hotbed of student radicalism. A loosely structured group, People's Democracy (PD), Marxist in orientation but, notwithstanding, with huge support from the large Catholic contingent within the student body, was quickly set up. It had no 'leaders' (denounced as a bourgeois affectation), nor any recorded membership and decisions taken at one meeting could be overturned at another, or indeed, later in the same meeting, when most of the audience had gone home on the last bus. It was loosely affiliated to NICRA, but it went its own way when it chose. In the recently opened and rather splendid students' union building, PD conducted interminable debates on the merits of civil disobedience, the limitations of non-violence and the theory of Marxist revolution. The *événements* in Paris in May 1968, which almost toppled General de Gaulle, were analysed and comparisons were drawn with the burgeoning student protest movement in the United States (numbers of Northern Irish students had worked there during the summer). More importantly, PD embarked on a series of protest marches and sit-ins which had the effect of keeping the thorny issues raised by the Derry march to the forefront of public attention. In late December it took a fateful decision – typically at a very poorly attended meeting, for most of the students had gone home for Christmas – to organise a 'long march' between Belfast and Derry to highlight and expose the inequities of Unionist rule and the shallowness of O'Neill's so-called reforms.

When the marchers set out 1 January 1969 they were fewer than a hundred – too insignificant seemingly to be banned by Craig – but on their journey they were subjected to continual harassment by loyalists and re-routing by the RUC, and as the march continued more students and local republicans joined it. By the time the marchers reached the outskirts of Derry they numbered several hundred. There, at Burntollet, in a well-planned ambush they were set upon and severely beaten, though luckily there were no fatalities. Their attackers were Protestant vigilantes organised by Ronald Bunting, an associate of Ian Paisley, and included a number of 'B' Specials. The RUC made little attempt to intervene. Rioting flared in Derry as the bedraggled and badly mauled students made their way into the city.

In the interval between the police riot in Derry in October 1968 and the PD march in January 1969, Terence O'Neill had struggled to regain control over events. His position was doubtless an unenviable one. Under orders from Harold Wilson to make appropriate and timely concessions, he was equally under pressure from his minister for home affairs, William Craig, to do nothing of the sort. To Craig, demands for civil rights were merely a cloak for republican subversion; equally, clamour for reform from London should be resisted. At the same time, Brian Faulkner, O'Neill's minister for commerce, and his defeated rival for the premiership, waited in the wings, ready to seize his opportunity to replace him.

For a time it had seemed that O'Neill and moderate reform might survive. In November 1968 he had announced a five-point reform plan which proposed a fair allocation of local authority housing, a review of the Special Powers Act, a reform of the whole system of local government within three years, the appointment of an ombudsman and the replacement of Derry city council by a development commission. (But not 'one man one vote' – a fatal error.) The proposals were generally well received by Catholics, less so by Protestants, but they had at least the effect of rebutting allegations of inaction from London. A dramatic broadcast to the people of Northern Ireland on 9 December – in retrospect, something of an Emmet-like speech from the dock – in which O'Neill declared that Ulster was at a crossroads and that it was time to choose which direction to take, gained him further Catholic approval – and some sceptics were won over when he sacked the truculent Craig two days later. The year ended with O'Neill – ominously looking like the manager of a struggling football team – winning an insincere vote of confidence from his parliamentary party.

The PD march from Belfast to Derry in the early days of 1969, with its exposure of the ugly sectarianism at the heart of Ulster society, and its revelation of RUC and loyalist collusion, instantly destroyed whatever credibility O'Neill might have had among the Catholic community. Further street protests ensued, and on 24 January, the slippery Faulkner resigned over O'Neill's decision to appoint a commission of inquiry into recent disturbances. His departure highlighted the deep divisions within Unionism (and made public his own vaulting ambition). O'Neill's response to this challenge was to call a snap general election. He was confident that he could see off his opponents within the Unionist Party, and that he could rally large elements of the country, including Catholics, behind him; but the results were inconclusive, few Catholics were tempted to vote for O'Neill Unionists and, ominously, O'Neill himself was only narrowly returned for his Bannside constituency, just ahead of his arch-critic, Paisley.

Captain Terence O'Neill – he clung doggedly to his absurd military title, presumably believing that it conveyed authority – resigned on 28 April 1969. He later claimed that a series of mysterious explosions, for a time attributed to republicans, and then conclusively shown to be the work of the UVF, had 'quite literally' blown him out of office: but in fact it had been the fall-out from the PD march to Derry, the loyalist ambush at Burntollet and the ensuing riot in Derry, that had undermined his position and ruined whatever chance he had of weathering the storm. Ten days before his resignation, Bernadette Devlin, prominent in PD and a fiery orator in 'La Passionaria' mould, had been elected

7.8 Civil Rights or armed insurrection? This illustration encapsulates Unionist fears that the disturbances in Northern Ireland were nothing more than a re-run of the 1916 Rebellion. National Library of Ireland.

as a Unity, i.e. pan-Catholic, candidate for the Westminster constituency of Mid-Ulster. Two days after her victory, elements of the RUC had gone on the rampage in a Catholic street in Derry and had assaulted a man who later died from his injuries. Captain O'Neill was the past; the future lay with the street-fighters, in and out of uniform.

O'Neill was succeeded as prime minister by a distant cousin, Major James Chichester-Clark, an amiable old duffer, whose main (sole?) qualification for the post was that he was not Brian Faulkner. Throughout the summer of 1969, civil disturbances continued on a regular basis and with increasing intensity (figure 7.8). In July there had been rioting between Catholics and Protestants in Derry and Dungiven during which one man was killed, and on 2–5 August Belfast also witnessed serious disturbances. A UVF bomb attack on RTÉ's headquarters at Donnybrook on 5 August was another sinister development, being the first, though by no means the last, such explosion in the Republic. However, all of these paled into relative insignificance with the outpouring of rage, violence and hatred that characterised what was to become known as the 'battle of the Bogside' over the period 12–14 August in Derry.

Entirely predictable disturbances had broken out at the annual Protestant Apprentice Boys' march on 12 August, but they had intensified as the RUC, by now utterly discredited in Catholic eyes, sought to enter the Catholic Bogside district. Graphic film of the ensuing struggle to repel them was broadcast world-wide and conveyed the impression of incipient or even actual civil war. The 'battle' was brought to an end on 14 August when the British army was called in to restore order, and the exhausted RUC retired. On 15 August serious rioting in Belfast's nationalist areas led to a number of deaths at the hands of the RUC, who had turned to the machine-gun as a weapon of choice for crowd control. In the ensuing disturbances, Bombay Street, a Catholic street on the Falls Road, was almost totally razed by loyalist mobs, and scores of Catholic houses were torched elsewhere in the city. As in Derry, so in Belfast, trouble only abated when the British army was deployed on to the streets. (It is worth noting that the British army was called in because the British 'mainland' police forces had made known their refusal to come to the aid of their over-stretched, exhausted RUC colleagues.)

It had been just under a year since the first NICRA march at Dungannon to demand civil rights and fair treatment. Yet in that short time, the Unionist regime at Stormont, in power for nearly fifty years and apparently impregnable, had been shown up as unable to maintain law and order and exposed as brittle. At the same time, the British government had been forced, much against its wishes, to move from quiet encouragement of reform to military intervention in the province's affairs. With the general officer commanding in Northern Ireland being given overall responsibility for policing, something dangerously close to direct rule from London had in effect been installed. Who could tell when or where British intervention (or meddling) would end? How had relatively straight-forward demands for civil rights, political reform and fair treatment produced such a convulsion?

The various government reports commissioned into the origins of what became known as the 'Troubles' were quite clear as to where responsiblity lay. The report of Lord Cameron (September 1969) into the Derry march of October 1968, and related matters, identified exceptionally poor leadership on all sides as being responsible for the ensuing chaos. The Hunt report (October 1969) into policing in Northern Ireland had criticised the RUC and the 'B' Specials, recommending that the RUC be disarmed and that the 'B' Specials be disbanded. And Justice Scarman, tasked with investigating the ghastly events of August 1969 in Belfast, in his report published in April 1972, had not hesitated to point the finger at the sectarian rhetoric of the Reverend Ian Paisley.

All of these reports managed to avoid the key question: why did a call for what were, after all, modest reforms – 'one man one vote' was scarcely revolutionary, or even radical, in the third quarter of the twentieth century – produce such a violently disproportionate response? Could it be that a state founded on notions of Protestant separatism, Protestant superiority and Protestant preference, simply could not entertain, let alone embrace, ideas of change, reform and inclusion? It appeared so. Northern Ireland had been set up to protect and promote the interests of northern Protestants. The persistence of the notion – not entirely far-fetched – that the new state was under permanent siege had meant that no overtures to the minority community could be contemplated or countenanced without risk to its *raison d'être*. And yet it was evident that the postwar advance of a new Catholic middle class, educated, impatient and increasingly weary of the old Nationalist Party and its rhetoric, meant that the Unionist Party simply had to cease being just a Protestant organisation and attempt to become a genuine party of the Union, seeking and drawing support from all sections. This it signally failed to do. The party's loose federal structure, which in effect strongly prioritised the local boss over the national leader, along with its high degree of penetration by the strongly anti-Catholic Orange Order, meant that it was almost incapable of delivering change even if it had wanted to. As a result, when a political party that was so identified with the state as to be almost synonymous with it, began to fragment, it could not but imperil the state. Poor and unimaginative leadership was certainly an added difficulty, but the fundamental causes of the collapse were structural and ideological.

The Republic of Ireland in the 1970s

The tumultuous events in Northern Ireland caught southern politicians, like their northern counterparts, completely by surprise. The relaxed and genial Jack Lynch had taken over as Taoiseach when Lemass had stepped down in November 1966, and he had continued the latter's policy of bilateral meetings with Terence O'Neill in December 1967 and January 1968. But as violence erupted in the north, Lynch was pressed to take a firmer stand. In August 1968, in response to the 'battle of the Bogside', he had declared – most unhelpfully, for he managed to arouse loyalist fears and nationalist hopes both of which were equally groundless – that the Irish government could 'no longer stand by' and see innocent people injured 'and perhaps worse'. Following the August pogrom in Belfast, Lynch had ordered the setting up of a number of field hospitals just south of the border for those fleeing the turmoil. However, a few of Lynch's Cabinet colleagues, notably Charles J. Haughey, minister for finance, and Neil Blaney, minister for agriculture, both of whom despised Lynch in any case, were by no means satisfied with these actions. In their view, a much more robust response to the mayhem in the north was required. Accordingly, they enlisted the assistance of James Kelly, an Irish army officer (later, and disgracefully, made a scapegoat for the whole business), and they set out to import five hundred pistols for use in the north. They also sought to hand over some Irish army weapons to the recently established Catholic defence committees in Belfast and Derry. In addition, arms training was to be offered to suitable northern defenders, and money was made available too.

When Lynch learned of this plot, which was directed more against himself than in favour of northern nationalists, he proved anything but relaxed or genial, and moved decisively. On 6 May 1970 Haughey and Blaney were sacked from the Cabinet, and were later arrested on charges of conspiring to import arms and ammunition. Blaney was quickly discharged. None of those accused, who, in addition to Haughey, included a Belgian arms dealer, a Belfast republican and an Irish army officer, was ever convicted, but the Irish public – and not for the last time – was treated to the unedifying spectacle of at least one former Cabinet minister perjuring himself under oath. Unionists, for their part, were convinced that Haughey had undertaken the funding and arming of the emerging Catholic defenders in the north, the Provisional IRA.

The 'whiff of gunsmoke' that thereafter hovered around Haughey did him no harm at all with the electorate (his first preferences soared in 1973) or indeed with Fianna Fáil stalwarts. Haughey had been first elected in 1957 and within ten years, had managed to accumulate property, racehorses, an island and an appropriate princely lifestyle, all ostensibly paid for out of a TD's modest salary. Eyebrows might have been raised at this transformation but few questions were asked. Haughey remained in the political wilderness for seven years after his dismissal, but in 1977, Lynch, following his (by Irish standards) landslide victory in the general election, most unwisely brought him back into the Cabinet as minister for health. Haughey, however, was neither chastened nor forgiving, and like Brian Faulkner he waited his chance.

The 1970s generally had not been good years for the Fianna Fáil party. A resurgent Fine Gael under the direction of the youthful Garret FitzGerald and Declan Costello had moved the party into the modern age, got rid of part-time leaders and brought forward a series of left-of-centre policies. The image of Fine Gael as the party of the big farmer and of everything that was conservative (and amateurish) in Irish society was to an extent pushed aside. In addition, the Labour Party, long the Cinderella of Irish politics and burdened with guilt about socialism, communism (and indeed any other -ism, except baptism) was being revived and reoriented by the acquisition of some celebrity candidates, notably Dr Conor Cruise O'Brien. In the early 1950s as a lowly third secretary in the Department of External Affairs he had been active in promoting anti-partitionist propaganda, and had frequently been obliged to break bread with repulsive northern nationalists in order to earn his crust. He had since seen the error of his ways and had become a trenchant critic of nationalism and anything to do with physical-force republicanism. He had also emerged as an avowed partitionist.

In March 1973, Fine Gael and Labour, having achieved agreement on a fourteen-point plan for economic and social regeneration, came together to form a coalition government. In and of itself such an agreed policy for economic growth and social reform was a breakthrough. There was a clear need for such forward thinking: the census of 1971 had recorded the first increase in the southern Irish population since the state's formation; the unravelling of Unionist power in the north held lessons for the Republic concerning the need for timely reform; and the arrival of a 'contraceptive train' at Dublin's Connolly Station in May 1971 marked the opening salvo in what ultimately became a protracted struggle for women's rights.

Organised by the Irish Women's Liberation Movement, about twenty women had travelled to Belfast, purchased contraceptives – still banned in the Republic – and on returning to Dublin, with the press duly forewarned, had flaunted their purchases in the faces of embarrassed customs officials. The excursion was an unqualified publicity triumph, but solid achievements would prove more difficult. Catholic Ireland – i.e. an Ireland where the Catholic moral code was enshrined in the law and Constitution of the land – was not about to pass quietly into history. Admittedly, the ban on Catholics attending Trinity College had been dropped in 1970 while the 'special position' of the Catholic church in the 1937 Constitution was removed by referendum in December 1972, but the hierarchy had long been indifferent to these. More significant, in the same year as the 'contraceptive train', attendance at mass regularly touched over 90 per cent, while 1971 as a whole also saw something of a surge in vocations for the religious life. In the light of this, it could hardly have come as a surprise when Senator Mary Robinson's bill legalising contraception was peremptorily denied a first reading in the Irish Senate in July 1971.

The Fine Gael–Labour coalition took office at an unfortunate period. In a referendum in May 1972 over 80 per cent of the Irish people (in a 71 per cent turn-out) had voted in favour of joining the European Economic Community and on 1 January 1973 Ireland was formally admitted as a member (along with the United Kingdom). By itself this offered reassuring evidence that the outbreak of the northern conflict had not diverted attention from economic growth as a national objective. A diminution of Ireland's sovereignty seemed a relatively small price to pay for the EEC subsidies. Nor did the EEC disappoint: between 1973 and 1991 some £13 billion in grants, subsidies and other funds were transferred to Ireland, mostly to the agricultural sector. Irish farmers had never had it so good. However, such grants were for the future: whatever high hopes were held out for membership in 1973, they were rapidly overtaken by a fivefold increase in oil prices which largely rendered redundant almost all economic planning. Consumer prices doubled within a few years, by 1974 inflation was running at 20 per cent, by 1975 the budget deficit was running at £259 million, and by January 1976 the number of unemployed had risen from around 70,000 to near 120,000, the highest since 1940. Faced with a severe hike in costs, many firms went to the wall.

Fine Gael's proposal for a wealth tax on the super-rich (many of whom were its supporters), along with Labour's urging of pay restraint on the lower paid (many of whom were its supporters), was scarcely calculated to endear the new coalition to its separate and formerly rival constituencies. In addition, Cruise O'Brien's imposition of draconian censorship over RTÉ's coverage of IRA or republican activities, which bore more than a passing resemblance to Frank Aiken's efforts during the 'Emergency', rather took the gloss off the coalition's soft left-of-centre image. Buffeted on all sides and rapidly running out of ideas, the coalition broke apart over its modest attempt to legalise contraception. Legislation was needed in this area because the Supreme Court, in a case brought by Mrs Mary McGee, had determined in December 1973 that the Act banning the import of contraceptives was unconstitutional. In the event, the proposed bill was defeated in the Dáil; onlookers watched with bemusement as the Taoiseach, Liam Cosgrave, voted against his own government's legislative proposal.

In the ensuing general election in June 1977, Jack Lynch shamelessly courted the lower-paid workers and the middle classes with promises of tax breaks, pay boosts and an end to road tax and rates. The result was a decisive victory for Fianna Fáil. Initially, Lynch, as befitting a 'bastard Keynesian', for the great economist would surely never have acknowledged his alleged follower as legitimate, attempted through a confused strategy of increased public spending and borrowing to buy his way out of the economic difficulties bequeathed by the Fine Gael–Labour coalition. However, as unemployment soared, this solution was quickly seen to be fuelling budget deficits. Lynch came under criticism from some members of his Cabinet for his financial profligacy, and from other members (Haughey tellingly stayed behind the scenes) for apparently caving in to British security demands over Northern Ireland. Lynch duly departed in December 1979: Haughey's day had finally come, and a thirty-year period of thuggery, skullduggery and sleaze was begun in Irish political life.

Whatever Haughey's plans might have been, and it is by no means certain that he had any, for winning power and enjoying it rather than using it to make a difference was his whole object, they were rapidly derailed by yet another world economic crisis in 1979 brought on once again by a steep rise in the price of oil. As had happened earlier in the 1970s the fragility of the Irish economy was once again mercilessly exposed. The decade closed with lengthy lists of jobless (now nearing two hundred thousand), a rise in emigration, soaring public debt, enormous balance of payment deficits, protest marches by disgruntled trade unionists and in January 1980 a hugely condescending (and wholly hypocritical – he was living like a prince at the time) broadcast by Haughey to the nation in which he patiently explained to the Irish people the dire state of the Irish economy and sternly enjoined on all the absolute need for belt-tightening and stringent retrenchment. His hand-made Parisian shirts, fine wines and silk socks were, of course, exempt from any and all cut-backs.

The 'Troubles', 1970–3

Economic matters, while never neglected, were perhaps the least of Northern Ireland's problems during the 1970s. During that decade, and for several decades after, a bitter war was waged between on the one hand, a Provisional IRA that had emerged in late 1969, and on the other, the British army, the RUC, the Ulster Defence Regiment (successor to the disbanded 'B' Specials), aided and sometimes hindered by loyalist paramilitaries such as the UVF and the Ulster Defence Association. Hundreds died and thousands were injured as bombings, shootings and murders were, especially in the years 1971–4, near daily and at times much more frequent occurrences.

Just as society in Northern Ireland was exploding into violence, so too the political structure of the previous fifty years was imploding. The hitherto impressive Unionist monolith had fractured between the Official Unionist Party and the Paisley-led DUP (set up in October 1971), with a number of fringe loyalist parties in the wings. On the nationalist side, a new formation, the Social and Democratic Labour Party (SDLP), led by Gerry Fitt, was founded in August 1970: it brought together remnants of the old nationalist, republican socialist parties, and individuals like John Hume of Derry who had emerged out of the struggle for civil rights. Its rival for what amounted to the Catholic vote was Sinn Féin. Admittedly, during most of the 1970s this party functioned as little more than a sort of social club for republicans not active in the armed struggle. The 'Provos', as members of the Provisional IRA were soon dubbed, like the Fenians a century earlier, disdained politics; but as the decade wore on, Sinn Féin became in fact the political wing of the Provisional IRA.

'Out of the ashes of Bombay Street arose the Provisional IRA': this well-known origin legend of the Provos does in fact go some way towards explaining their emergence. The old IRA had been barely active in Belfast in 1969, numbering only a few dozen members. Its Dublin-based leadership was strongly Marxist in outlook and following the fiasco of its border campaign had sought to move away from a discredited military strategy. It may even have sold some of its weaponry to the shadowy Free Wales Army. As a result, when in August 1969 elements of the RUC, supported by loyalist gangs, became convinced that they faced a full-scale nationalist insurrection and launched attacks on Catholic areas in Belfast and elsewhere, there was almost no response from the IRA. Humiliated by their failure to defend their areas, and stung by criticism that the initials IRA stood for 'I ran away', Belfast republicans, supported by some southern IRA members who had never approved of Marxism, and encouraged – to put it no more strongly – by some Dublin politicians, set up a clandestine Provisional Army Council in December 1969. In January 1970 there was an open and acrimonious split at the Sinn Féin annual congress. Those who sat tight became the so-called 'Official' IRA, and retained a Marxist outlook (and a military capacity); those who walked out became the Provisional IRA, self-appointed defenders of the Catholics of Northern Ireland.

It would, however, be a mistake to see the Provisional IRA as simply a product of the August 'pogrom' of 1969. Very many of those involved in the new military structure had significant 'previous' as IRA veterans, having been involved, like Joe Cahill, in the organisation since before the Second World War, or like Seán MacStiofáin and Daithí Ó Conaill, having taken part in arms raids in England or in attacks along the border with Northern Ireland in the 1950s. Others, like Gerry Adams, came from a strongly republican family, with a tradition of IRA activism on both his father's and mother's side going back at least to the War of Independence. Such men constituted a sort of officer class among the first Provos: for their part, the earliest foot-soldiers recruited to their ranks had been almost entirely radicalised by the events of August 1969 and had little prior history of republican activism.

Initially, relations between the British army and local defence committees, usually Provisional IRA dominated, were quite good, with many examples of cooperation. Undoubtedly, old-time republicans resented the British army presence on 'their' streets, but they well knew that, given the state of their training and weaponry, they could do very little about it; and in any case, ordinary Catholics in the affected areas genuinely regarded the army as their protectors. The cups of tea and ham sandwiches offered to soldiers by Catholic housewives provided excellent photo opportunities and bore testimony to Catholic gratitude. Such apparent harmony, however, was not to last, and over the next two to three years there was a total breakdown of relations between the British army and the Catholic population of working-class districts of Derry and Belfast. The reasons for this collapse have been much canvassed. Some have argued that as the Provos grew stronger they embarked on a deliberate strategy of tension and actively sought to engineer confrontations with the army, confident that massive over-reaction and further alienation would result. Others have detected the malign hand of Unionist politicians behind the escalating violence. Brian Faulkner, a man whose reputation as a hard-liner dated from the 1950s, and was based largely on his hearty support for Orange marches in Catholic areas, eventually achieved his ambition in March 1971 by succeeding Chichester-Clark as prime minister. He was sympathetic to demands for an end to 'no-go' areas where the RUC were not permitted to set foot. Yet again, others have pointed to a noticeably tougher military policy on the ground with the coming of the Tories into office in Britain, and with the appointment of Edward Heath as prime minister in June 1970.

Whatever the reasons, the stages by which the breakdown occurred can be quickly listed. The first of these was undoubtedly the Falls Road curfew of 3–5 July 1970. This was imposed by General Sir Ian Freeland in response to several nights of serious rioting and had as its objective the seizure of IRA arms which were allegedly concealed in some fifty streets in the lower Falls. The area was sealed off, residents were ordered not to leave their homes, resistance was met with CS gas, and in all around five thousand houses were searched, very many suffering extensive damage as doors were kicked in, floors ripped up and fireplaces pulled out: religious images and figurines, especially, seem to have drawn the soldiers' wrath. Under heavy army protection, two Stormont ministers toured the area, further incensing the choking and battered residents. Six civilians were killed during the operation, many more injured and a tiny number of weapons were recovered. There would be no more cups of tea for the 'squaddies'.

During 1971 the Provisional IRA began to move on to the offensive. In February 1971 the first soldier to die was shot dead under cover of a riot. (The previous August the first members of the RUC had been killed when two were blown up in an explosion near Crossmaglen, county Armagh.) Then in March three Scottish soldiers were lured from a pub and shot dead, a frightening escalation in violence that prompted a demonstration in Belfast to demand the internment of IRA leaders. Faulkner, from previous experience of the border campaign of the 1950s, was convinced that internment was the only solution to Northern Ireland's growing violence. The British army was sceptical, while Heath warned Faulkner of the likely consequences of failure. Internment, in fact, was the Stormont government's last throw of the dice.

In the small hours of 9 August, 'Operation Demetrius' was rolled out, and within twenty-four hours over 342 suspects (all republican) had been arrested. Widespread violence followed leading to seventeen deaths within forty-eight hours, the burning of more than 150 houses, and the displacement of over 7,000 people, almost entirely Catholic. Police intelligence had been very poor and out of date, resulting in the apprehension of very few of the new players in the Provisional movement. Gallingly, Joe Cahill, an IRA commander, was able to hold a press conference later that day to deny that his organisation had been damaged by internment. Deaths and injuries among soldiers and civilians soared in the weeks following internment (4 dead in the four months before internment, 114 dead in the four months after) and these figures offer striking evidence of IRA strength, ruthlessness and resilience. Disturbingly, on 17 October, the *Sunday Times* published reports of in-depth interrogation techniques being used on selected internees. Beyond question, it was evident that internment was proving an unmitigated disaster, handing a propaganda gift to the Provos, and fit to be ranked alongside the execution of the Easter week leaders as an action that served to boost the ranks of Irish rebels rather than deter and dishearten them. Faulkner's gambler's throw having failed, his (and Stormont's) days were probably numbered.

What finally destroyed all trust between Catholics and the British (and brought down the curtain on Northern Ireland's devolved government) was 'Bloody Sunday', the killing by British paratroopers of thirteen unarmed civilians in Derry on 30 January 1972. For many weeks previously the army in Derry had been dealing with an almost daily round of recreational rioting by the so-called 'young hooligans' of that city. Its patience was wearing thin at these frequent attacks, and there were well-justified fears that the IRA, as it had done many times before in Belfast and Derry, would use stone-throwing crowds as a cover for sniper fire. Tensions were therefore running high when a civil rights march was organised for the last Sunday in January 1972. The march was banned, but the NICRA organisers decided to go ahead with it anyway. When a relatively small-scale riot broke out, fully armed units of the Parachute Regiment were sent in to quell it, and immediately opened fire, killing thirteen unarmed civilians within minutes. The 'Paras' had a formidable, not to say ferocious, reputation: in republican west Belfast over a three-day period the previous August they had bagged eleven civilians, among them some IRA gunmen certainly, but also including a priest and a mother of eight. Significantly, local British army commanders were on record as complaining at their naked aggression, and they did not want them deployed to their areas. In short, the Paras were as suitable for crowd control as the RUC's Browning machine-guns of August 1969.

The carnage in Derry was therefore predictable and it drew widespread national and international condemnation: protest marches were held in many capital cities around the world; Bernadette Devlin physically attacked a complacent Reginald Maudling, the British home secretary, in the House of Commons; Jack Lynch declared a national day of mourning for those killed; and the British embassy in Dublin was burned down by an angry mob. Inevitably, violence across Northern Ireland reached new heights of intensity as recruits flocked to the Provisional IRA. In March 1972 the Abercorn restaurant was blown up by an IRA bomb which killed two and caused injuries to over one hundred, many quite horrific. In July the IRA exploded twenty-two bombs in Belfast with the loss of eleven lives and scores injured. Even the Official IRA, smaller in number and generally much less aggressive than the Provisionals, was moved to action. In February 1972 some of its members planted a bomb that killed seven civilians at the headquarters of the Parachute Regiment in Aldershot. Catholic alienation was completed when the inquiry conducted by Lord Widgery into the events in Derry on 30 January 1972 reported in April, and was broadly favourable to the army, placing the blame for the deaths squarely on NICRA for organising the march and defying the ban.

By that date Stormont had been suspended – it was abolished a year later – and direct rule from London had been implemented. The Kingship Act of 1541 had been the outcome of the Kildare rebellion of the 1530s, the old Irish Parliament had been abolished in 1800 on foot of the 1798 rebellion, and partition had been implemented in 1920 because of separate nationalist and Unionist rebellions. (Such 'adjustments' did not only apply to Ireland: the East India Company had been stripped of power in India because it was held culpable for the Great Rebellion of 1857.) Given precedents like these, there had to be a question about whether Stormont, faced with mounting violence and the withdrawal of minority consent, could survive the crisis that had unfolded with terrifying swiftness in 1969. Heavy-handed military action as seen in the Falls curfew, the imposition of internment and, fatally, 'Bloody Sunday' with its damning show of force, had all led to Catholic alienation. Together, they had made certain that the devolved administration in Northern Ireland could not go on. But what to put in its place? The quest for an answer to that question was to take up the next thirty years, and more.

Sunningdale and the power-sharing executive

An early solution to the problem of replacing the old Stormont regime was the Sunningdale Agreement of December 1973. No sooner had the British government reluctantly taken over formal, direct responsibility for Northern Ireland, than it began to cast around for ways of exiting from, as James Callaghan, the Labour home secretary, later put it, the 'Irish bog'. Several obvious ways suggested themselves: one was to devise some form of power-sharing between the main constitutional parties, viz. the Official Unionists, the SDLP and the

7.9 Members of the short-lived power-sharing executive that was brought down by the Ulster workers' strike in 1974. Brian Faulkner is third from the right, front row; Gerry Fitt is second from left, second row; John Hume is to the right in the second row from the rear. Irish Photographic Archive.

middle-class and respectable Alliance Party which had come together in April 1970 as a sort of fan club for Terence O'Neill. As a corollary to this, the so-called extremists, viz. the DUP and Sinn Féin, were to be rigorously excluded and thereby, it was hoped, marginalised. Equally, it would be necessary to bring the Irish Republic into any new arrangement so as to reassure northern nationalists. (The Irish government welcomed this. It cared little about northern nationalists, but it did suspect the perfidious 'Brits' of wanting to withdraw from the north: Irish involvement enabled it to monitor British moves and head off any such calamity.) Such a publicly defined role for the Republic meant, of course, that further strict guarantees about the constitutional position of Northern Ireland had to be given to Unionists in order to placate them and assuage their fears. Finally, in order to encourage the emergence of a wider, and more liberal body of opinion, presumed on no very clear evidence to exist in Northern Ireland, a key feature of any new dispensation had to be proportional representation rather than the divisive first-past-the-post electoral system.

Elections for an assembly were held in June 1973 and resulted in a narrow victory for those on all sides in favour of power-sharing (figure 7.9). Ominously, however, pro-Faulkner Unionists were out-numbered by those unionists opposed to power-sharing. Negotiations on the creation of a power-sharing executive and on a Council of Ireland then took place during the autumn and were concluded at an 'away-day', or days, at a civil service training centre in Sunningdale, Berkshire, over 6–9 December 1973. Surprisingly perhaps, Brian Faulkner, long-regarded as a loyalist hard-liner, had been prepared to make significant compromises. He was resolved to restore devolved government to Northern Ireland, and he maintained that since the Irish Republic had finally accepted partition and had made major concessions on security at Sunningdale, the Union with Great Britain was thereby substantially strengthened. He proclaimed a Unionist triumph. On the other hand, the nationalist side was equally victorious. Austin Currie claimed that the dream of none other than Theobald Wolfe Tone had been realised (though even the most hostile Unionist critics of Sunningdale had to concede that an Irish Republic allied to France was some way off).

There was, in fact, some anxiety that the nationalist side had won more concessions than was wise – Garret FitzGerald, perhaps gifted with the insight of his northern Presbyterian mother, had voiced concern that 'more' might in the end mean 'less' for northern nationalists. There was general recognition that the negotiating skills of the officials of the Irish Department of External Affairs had proved superior to those of their opposite numbers. (This was no aberration: the Republic of Ireland, thanks to an immensely talented group of diplomats would, for years after, continue to box far above its weight in the EEC and at the United Nations: for a number of these officials, the Sunningdale discussions would be merely a dry-run for future lengthy sessions in Brussels, and elsewhere.) The Sunningdale power-sharing executive, complete with provision for a Council of (all) Ireland, promises of security cooperation, constitutional guarantees and proportional representation came into existence on New Year's Day, 1974. It lasted barely five months. Why was this?

The arrangement was wholly premature. Unionists had not at all recovered from the shock of losing their government, Parliament and fifty-year hegemony. Faulkner's volte-face, as it seemed, on the merits of sharing power with Fitt, Currie and Hume seemed like a poisonous additional pill to swallow. Worse, if possible, the proposed Council of Ireland struck even the least paranoid (or pre-scient) Unionist as the highroad to ultimate Irish unity. What the Unionist community wanted was not power-sharing, but military victory over the IRA: then, and only then, could reconstruction, and perhaps reconciliation, begin. Significantly, the high command of the British army also looked to the outright defeat of 'republican terrorists' and would not settle for less. As for the Provisional IRA, it quickly dismissed Sunningdale as inadequate: it had sought a British commitment to withdraw from Northern Ireland, and since the new arrangement had not offered this, the Provos would continue the armed struggle. In short, it could be claimed that Sunningdale lasted such a short time because crucial elements within Northern Ireland were convinced that a military victory was not only possible but lay within their grasp. Until war-weariness replaced war-readiness, there would be little progress towards a peaceful settlement. The chilling fact was that when Sunningdale was implemented there had not yet been enough killing.

From the beginning, it was hard to see how the projected Council of Ireland and the power-sharing agreement hammered out at Sunningdale could ever meet with general Unionist acceptance. As early as 4 January 1974, the Ulster Unionist council, by a clear majority, had rejected any notion of a Council of Ireland, and in effect had repudiated Brian Faulkner as leader. He was left with no option but to resign, though he continued as chief executive in the power-sharing government. Possibly, if there had been a clear security dividend from Sunningdale, some Unionist criticism might have been stilled, and some critics won over. But there was to be no comfort in that area: a bus carrying British army personnel was blown up in Yorkshire in February with eleven deaths, and in March Billy Fox, a Protestant member of the Irish Senate, was shot dead by the IRA in county Monaghan, and shootings and explosions continued unabated in Belfast and Derry. Again, despite expectations held out at Sunningdale, extradition of terrorist suspects from the Irish Republic to Northern Ireland remained a forlorn hope.

Together with opposition from within the Ulster Unionist Party, the power-sharing executive faced relentless hostility from other influential players in Northern Ireland such as Paisley's Democratic Unionists, the Vanguard Unionist Party (Bill Craig's claque), Sinn Féin, the Provos and loyalist paramilitaries, for they had all been ignored during the negotiations and had therefore no sense of ownership of the outcome. In their separate endeavours to destroy the executive, they were unwittingly aided by the decision of Edward Heath, faced with trade union unrest in Britain, to call a snap general election for the Westminster Parliament. The election in February 1974 brought defeat for Heath and the Conservative Party, and the return of Harold Wilson as prime minister in a Labour government for a second time. However, much more dramatic were the results in Northern Ireland where those Unionists firmly opposed to Sunningdale won no fewer than eleven out of the twelve Westminster seats, with only Gerry Fitt's success in West Belfast preventing a clean sweep. No more than the Sinn Féin landslide of 1918, these results revealed a decided majority opposed to the whole Sunningdale Agreement, and gave a much-needed democratic boost to those who were prepared to take direct action against its most detested aspect: the proposed Council of Ireland.

Loyalist paramilitaries had reacted to the setting up of the executive by establishing an Ulster Army Council to oversee their activities and they had offered 'assistance' to any Unionist politicians opposed to the Council of Ireland. Separately, an Ulster Workers' Council (UWC), a loyalist grouping consisting of shop stewards and senior employees from the Harland and Wolff shipyard, the power stations and other key industries, was established in March 1974. It advocated civil disobedience if its demands for new assembly elections were not met. On 14 May a motion in the Assembly condemning power-sharing and the Council of Ireland was rejected by forty-four votes to twenty-eight – a clear repudiation of the Westminster election results – and, as threatened, the UWC called a general strike in protest.

The strike began sluggishly, and it was evident that whole-hearted support was lacking within the Protestant community, but massive intimidation by loyalist paramilitaries (now represented on the UWC), and the reluctance (or refusal) of the RUC or the British army to do anything about loyalist roadblocks, soon allowed the strike to build up a head of steam. Anti-Sunningdale Unionists such as Ian Paisley, who had typically hung back in the early days, now came on board as the strike gathered momentum. The new Secretary of State, Merlyn Rees, had no personal political capital invested in the Sunningdale Agreement, and hence had no political will to crush the strike, and certainly the British army was unenthusiastic about opening a second front in Northern Ireland. Any attempt at intervention from the Republic was seen off by massive car-bombs in Dublin and Monaghan on 17 May 1974. Scores were injured and thirty-three died. (Twenty years later, these bombs were revealed to be the work of the UVF, but because of their relative 'sophistication', there were suspicions that rogue elements within British security might have colluded in the attacks.) Loyalist workers in the power stations proved to be the trump cards: as the supply of electricity faltered, and as petrol and food ran short throughout Northern Ireland, apocalyptic predictions were made of the total collapse of civil society. Tactless remarks in a television broadcast by Harold Wilson, in which he denounced the strikers as 'sponging on Westminster and British democracy', merely had the effect of further strengthening their determination. On 28 May 1974, Faulkner and five of his Unionist colleagues on the executive resigned, the next day the Assembly was prorogued and direct rule from Westminster reinstated. Amid exuberant loyalist celebrations embracing all classes, the strike was called off, and 'normal' conditions were quickly restored. The search for a solution resumed.

The fall of 'Sunningdale' was hailed as a Unionist triumph in the same way that the fall of Stormont had been claimed as one for the nationalists. There was, however, at least one significant difference between the two. Stormont fell and with it went its exclusivist ideology. On the other hand, while the executive and the Assembly, and even the Council of Ireland, were in ruins after the Ulster workers' strike, the principles that had underpinned the whole

Sunningdale arrangement – the absolute necessity for power-sharing and for an all-Ireland dimension – had survived relatively unscathed. Apart from a brief flirtation with an internal settlement in Northern Ireland in the early 1980s, by and large British policy remained wedded to these for the next thirty years. There could be no going back to simple majority rule on the Stormont model; nor indeed would there be any British acceptance of or enthusiasm for indefinite direct rule.

In the aftermath of their victory, Unionists of all persuasions in Northern Ireland outdid one another in vowing to shun any plan that contained power-sharing and an Irish dimension. Such a double rejection was understandable – but only in the short term. By spurning both power-sharing and an Irish dimension for the next decade and more, Unionists left themselves open to an imposed settlement, even to the threat of a unilateral British withdrawal. Brian Faulkner's fate at the hands of the strikers haunted Unionist leaders and negotiators for years to come; his downfall was seen as a conclusive warning against compromise. As a result, long after the fall of Sunningdale, Unionists generally remained in flat denial of the existence of well-flagged talks continuing between London and Dublin, and they refused to recognise that the British were never going to accept direct rule as a long-term answer. In short, the destruction of the Sunningdale power-sharing executive, for all the euphoria that greeted it and for all the rapture that quickly enveloped it in Unionist mythology, turned out to be rather a Pyrrhic victory for Unionism.

The 'Troubles', 1973–80

While the search continued for a constitutional settlement which would meet the aspirations of Unionists and nationalists, the gunmen returned to centre stage. Not that they had ever gone away of course: over a thousand deaths were recorded between internment and the fall of the power-sharing executive, with the IRA being responsible for 55 per cent, loyalists for 33 per cent and the security forces for 12 per cent. Throughout 1972 and 1973 the IRA had inflicted heavy casualties on the British army and, armed with its newly invented weapon, the car-bomb, its members had set about the near systematic reconfiguration of the centres of most northern Irish towns, very often causing civilian casualties in the process. Within a few years all but 20 out of Derry's 150 shops had been blown up, and it was little better in Belfast city centre. In retaliation, loyalist death squads bent on the torture/murder of Catholics – any Catholic would do – roamed the streets of North Belfast and the byways of mid-Ulster with apparent impunity and with deadly effect. Particularly grisly were the murders in the early 1970s of some nineteen Catholics in Belfast by a gang known as the Shankill

Butchers: its leader apparently had a complex about about being named Murphy, and had sought to expunge that stain on his loyalism by slaying Catholics. He was later shot to death by the IRA.

It was particularly galling to Catholics that while membership of the IRA and associated bodies was illegal and drew stiff prison sentences, the main loyalist paramilitary organisation, the Ulster Defence Association, remained perfectly lawful until as late as 1992, even though its members were notoriously responsible for the large majority of sectarian murders of Catholic civilians. There were also credible allegations of security force collusion in some of the murders of Catholics. Suspicion fell particularly on members of the newly formed Ulster Defence Regiment (UDR), a successor to the disbanded 'B' Specials. The UDR was intended to be a non-sectarian force but since few Catholics joined it was inevitable that it would acquire some of the characteristics of the Specials: by 1989, sixteen members of the UDR were serving sentences for murder, and well over a hundred had been gaoled for terrorist offences. (Nearly two hundred members of the UDR and its successor, the Royal Irish Rifles, were to die at the hands of republican paramilitaries by the turn of the century.) Nor was the British army above suspicion of having had a hand in certain targeted assassinations of republicans. Shadowy units, such as the Military Reconnaissance Force (1972) operated outside the usual army structure and would soon have a number of 'kills' to their credit. The introduction of the elite undercover unit, the Special Air Service (SAS), in January 1976 into the conflict, following ghastly tit-for-tat sectarian murders in Armagh (fifteen Catholics and Protestants shot dead in a 48-hour period), quickly led to a number of controversial shootings.

Contemporaries found the military conflict in the 1970s so chaotic and shapeless (though deadly enough) that they preferred to use the nebulous, neutral term the 'Troubles' as a catch-all one for the violence. In retrospect, however, certain patterns can be detected in the conflict. For example, loyalist murders of Catholic civilians tended to rise sharply when suspicions were aroused that the British government was leaning towards cutting some sort of deal with nationalists or when there were reports that the British government was engaged in talks with republicans. During the so-called IRA ceasefire of February to September 1975, and on into 1976 when there was constant contact between the British authorities and the IRA, there was a marked upsurge in loyalist attacks on Catholics, probably because loyalists feared a sell-out of their interests, and because they wished to issue a warning to Catholics and to the British government. However, with the introduction of the SAS regiment, a pause in constitutional experiment and the drying-up of contacts with the IRA, loyalist murders dwindled considerably from 110 in 1976, to 19 in 1977, to 6 in 1978 and 12 in 1979. There was to be a corresponding rise in murderous attacks on Catholics by loyalist paramilitaries in the early 1990s amid renewed fears of a British betrayal.

A pattern, too, can be seen in IRA tactics. Up until the time of the Sunningdale Agreement, vicious firefights in built-up areas between the British army and IRA volunteers had been fairly common, with numerous 'bystander' casualties. However, the superior fieldcraft, equipment and numbers of the British army by and large won the day in these encounters, and large-scale shoot-outs fell off sharply after 1974. Snipings and car-bomb explosions in the cities, and roadside and culvert landmines in the countryside, however, took their place and exacted a deadly toll. Then, from 1974, as it became clear that British public opinion was comparatively unmoved by the casualty figures among its soldiers, a bombing and assassination campaign was unleashed in Britain and elsewhere. In June 1974 there was an explosion at the Houses of Parliament in London causing injuries; in October five died in explosions at pubs that were frequented by British soldiers in Guildford, Surrey, and in November, bombs in a pub in Birmingham killed twenty-one civilians and injured scores. (In a further dreadful twist, over seventeen individuals found guilty of these outrages were, it later transpired, entirely innocent and were eventually exonerated, but only after having served lengthy prison sentences.)

There were also targeted assassinations: Queen Elizabeth had a lucky escape in August 1977 when a bomb exploded just after she had left the University of Ulster at Coleraine, and so too did Prince Charles, but others were not so fortunate. The British ambassador to the Hague, Richard Sykes, was shot and killed in March 1979 and in the same month, and even more shocking, Airey Neave, the Conservative Party spokesman on Northern Ireland, was blown up in his car within the palace of Westminster by a bomb planted by the Irish National Liberation Army, a republican splinter group linked to the IRA. The aim of these IRA bombings and shootings appeared to be to sicken and terrorise the British public and the British establishment so that together they would seek a unilateral British withdrawal from Ulster. Such an objective was perhaps not entirely unrealistic: IRA contacts with the British government and the Secret Intelligence Service, MI6, since 1972 had led it to believe that a declaration to that effect was on the cards.

By the beginning of 1976, however, the IRA campaign had begun to run into sand and the 'war' had entered something of a stalemate. The British army and the RUC had taken advantage of the ceasefire of the previous year, and had recruited 'moles' among the Provos. These informers were to prove valuable but even so, overall intelligence-gathering by the authorities (by communication-interception as opposed to agents on the ground) had improved enormously since the early days of internment. The number of British soldiers in Northern Ireland had climbed steadily and together with the RUC, RUC reserve and the UDR were more than capable of keeping the IRA locked down. The IRA would still retain an infinite and indefinite capacity to sustain the 'armed struggle' and there would be dreadful 'spectaculars' from time to time, such as the assassination of the British ambassador to Ireland, Sir Christopher Ewart-Biggs, in July 1976, the blowing up of eighteen British soldiers at Warrenpoint, county Down on 27 August 1979 and the killing of Earl Mountbatten on the same day. Incidents such as these were, however, very much the exception and the annual death toll in the 'Troubles' never again reached the sickening heights of 1972–6. (At no time, for example, after 1976 did casualties from the 'Troubles' exceed road-traffic deaths in Northern Ireland.) For the remainder of the 1970s, and on through the 1980s and 1990s, the death toll hovered well under the hundred mark: such inexcusable carnage was deemed, as the Conservative home secretary, Reginald Maudling, put it in a hideous phrase, 'an acceptable level of violence'.

The IRA had responded to British army successes in terms of the arrests and deaths of key operatives by attempting, under the direction of Gerry Adams, to restructure its organisation away from the conventional brigades and companies model and towards a cellular structure that would render penetration by the British much more difficult. It also expanded its foreign support networks, achieving particular success in the United States where organisations such as the Northern Irish Aid Committee proved adept at fund-raising for the IRA and where modern weapons could be readily sourced. This reorganisation by the IRA signalled a realisation on its part that the security forces were gaining the upper hand and also, more important, that Britain had no immediate intention of quitting Northern Ireland. In the early 1970s the IRA had been wont to proclaim each year as 'the year of victory', but all this had ceased by mid-decade and they had settled down for a 'Long War' in which victory, they believed, would go to the side whose morale, endurance, patience (and ruthlessness) would prove superior.

Like the IRA, the British government also sought to adjust its policies to what it saw as the new improved security situation that had arisen by 1976. With the IRA seemingly contained, it determined to bring in a new policy of 'Ulsterisation' in which insurgency would be dealt with primarily as a law-and-order issue and in which the insurgents would be seen as criminals, not freedom fighters, guerrillas or rebels. Thus the RUC would be given primacy in the conflict with subversives, and the British army would step back. Internment without trial would be brought to an end. It had proved ineffective in curbing the IRA, it had damaged Britain's reputation abroad and it had handed the IRA a valuable propaganda weapon. Henceforth, members of the IRA and other paramilitary suspects would be put on trial in open court and, if convicted, treated as criminals, rather than as political prisoners allowed to wear their own clothes in prison, to maintain their own command structure there, to associate freely and to exercise complete control over their time. To make the conviction of terrorists/criminals easier, and to counter the threat posed by paramilitary intimidation of witnesses, jury trials were abandoned and the rules of evidence much diluted. (A reading of the 1979 Bennett report into the alleged transgressions of the security forces might prompt the thought that while the RUC made a significant contribution to 'Ulsterisation' by beating a large number of 'verbal' confessions out of IRA suspects, its actions also helped bring about its own demise twenty years later.)

The IRA naturally determined to resist the scrapping of 'special category status' for its prisoners, and on 16 September 1976, Ciaran Nugent, the first IRA man convicted under the new rules, refused the prison uniform that he was offered and, naked, elected to wrap himself in a blanket. By Christmas of that year nearly 340 IRA prisoners were 'on the blanket': a second front in the 'Long War' had opened up.

The hunger strikes

Matters quickly deteriorated in the prisons as IRA insistence on 'special status' was met with a steely rejection by the authorities. Refusal to wear prison garb resulted in a removal of privileges such as access to reading matter, television or radio. It also meant that prisoners were confined to their cells twenty-four hours a day. As the authorities tightened the screw and allegedly indulged in routine roughing-up of the prisoners (many warders were flown in from Britain on temporary contract) the IRA prisoners responded by refusing to wash or shower. The 'no-wash protest' escalated into the 'dirty protest' in which IRA prisoners refused to slop out their cells, instead turning them into *cloacae*. By 1980 there were over eight hundred republican prisoners in the Maze (a.k.a. Long Kesh) prison of whom some three hundred were on the 'dirty protest'. As the tension mounted and the stakes rose there were threats by inmates to go on hunger strike in order to achieve their demands. The initial concession of special category status had been forced from the British authorities by a hunger strike in 1972: perhaps another one would regain it?

The first hunger strike by IRA prisoners began on 27 October and was led by Brendan Hughes, a senior Belfast Provisional; it lasted fifty-three days and was called off on 18 December 1980. Three female republican prisoners also on hunger strike since 1 December (among them Mairead Farrell, later shot to death in controversial circumstances in Gibraltar in 1988) called off their protest a day later. The initial exhilaration surrounding the end of the hunger strike was quickly replaced by anger as the realisation set in that there was a fundamental disagreement between the authorities and the prisoners over what exactly had been conceded. For example, the prisoners demanded to wear their own clothes but the prison authorities insisted that they wear 'civilian-type' clothing, which was not at all the same thing: those who had been 'on the blanket' for years never did receive their own clothes. With an air of grim inevitability, a second hunger strike began on 1 March 1981 headed by Bobby Sands, a Belfast republican who was serving fourteen years for possession of a gun. This time, the prisoners agreed there was to be no fudging or premature capitulation; but the British government led by Margaret Thatcher was to prove equally intransigent, and matters moved inexorably to a tragic *dénouement*. Bobby Sands died after sixty-six days refusing food and nine other strikers were to follow him to the grave before the strike ended on 3 October 1981. A few days later, the Secretary of State for Northern Ireland, James Prior, ordered the progressive concession of the hunger-strikers' demands: before long prisoner-of-war status was in effect restored.

Bobby Sands was barely into his hunger strike when the independent (i.e. old-style nationalist) Member for Fermanagh–South Tyrone, Frank Maguire, himself a former internee, unexpectedly died and a by-election was called for 9 April. The Provisional leadership decided that Sands from his prison cell should contest the seat. This was a high risk move, rather similar to the one made by Daniel O'Connell in the Clare by-election of 1828 in pursuit of Catholic emancipation and, just as in that contest, there were weighty arguments for and against the decision to run a candidate. For example, the SDLP might not stand aside and thus Sands could lose on a split vote; and even if the SDLP were to bow out (as it did eventually) there was still a chance that the IRA candidate might lose, for the religious composition of the constituency was finely balanced. Against that, electoral success, as had weighed with O'Connell, might bring enormous rewards in terms of moral persuasion. A common criminal, as Bobby Sands was routinely depicted (or denounced) in the British press and in parliamentary statements, did not in the normal order of things get elected to Westminster. The British government's insistence on the criminalisation of the IRA would thus be exposed to ridicule. Again, if the Thatcher government stood by and allowed a duly elected Westminster Member to die on hunger strike then it might be accused of being itself criminal. In the event, Bobby Sands won the election by 30,492 votes to 29,046 for the Unionist candidate, Harry West. However, Thatcher proved to be utterly inflexible and Bobby Sands Member of Parliament went to his maker without winning the concessions that he had sought. None the less, a vital point had been made: to the thirty thousand or so who had voted for Sands, could be added the hundred thousand who followed his coffin up the

Falls Road to Milltown cemetery in Belfast. Criminals generally did not attract that sort of send-off.

So, who won the 'prison war'? On the face of it, the Thatcher government had emerged from the battle of wills triumphant. She had not conceded anything and had proved unflinching in her dismissal of the hunger-strikers' deaths. She had loftily remarked that they had chosen to end their lives, and she had grimly added that this was not an indulgence the IRA had extended to its victims. Her firmness probably helped prevent an upsurge in loyalist murders; but against that, dozens died in the riots and shootings that accompanied the deaths of the hunger-strikers.

Undoubtedly, the IRA had won a major propaganda victory: 'thugs', 'hoodlums' and 'criminals' – the normal nomenclature for the Provos – did not usually starve themselves to death in order to secure the right to wear their own clothes. At the very least, the hunger-strikers had emphatically proved that they were no ordinary convicts. They had elicited massive sympathy throughout Ireland: numerous protest marches were held, black flags were everywhere, and a major riot took place at the British embassy in Dublin. Outside Ireland, British embassies and consulates in Europe and the United States were picketed, and at least one street, in Tehran, was later named after Bobby Sands. And of course, ten men had died slow and ghastly deaths and this could not but strengthen the will of the IRA to continue the armed struggle, if only to honour the memory of those who had died and to exact retribution on those in authority held responsible. The deaths of the hunger-strikers had bestowed a certain moral legitimacy on the IRA, much more important than the oxygen of publicity that so concerned Margaret Thatcher. Just as Bombay Street, internment and 'Bloody Sunday' had created the Provisional IRA, so her unyielding stance on the hunger strikes had given a huge boost to that organisation. Lastly, Bobby Sands had won a Westminster by-election, with the seat being retained by Sinn Féin after his death, and a further two seats were won in the Dáil by hunger-strikers. Henceforward, Sinn Féin, as the unarmed wing of the IRA and as the public voice of a substantial body of nationalists might claim a say in any future settlement – a prospect equally unwelcome in Dublin and in London. The striking electoral successes of Sinn Féin had opened up the prospect of yet another front in the 'Long War', one based on political activism.

The IRA had long dismissed any idea of seeking a democratic endorsement from the Irish electorate: in its eyes, it had received full validation by the results of the 1918 general election and by the subsequent setting up of the first Dáil, and nothing further was required. After all, retorted IRA leaders, since when did the British army ever seek an electoral mandate? Moreover, the IRA recognised that continuous involvement in politics, north and south, would inevitably imply some degree of recognition for partitionist structures and this was anathema to it. In any case, many Provos shared the old Fenian disdain for political agitation, considering such a pursuit as a distraction from the armed struggle. More pragmatically, IRA leaders realised that there was always a chance of failure in the political arena and that this would invite scorn and derision and undermine the 'army's' morale. None the less, Sands's stunning victory in Fermanagh–South Tyrone was an eye-opener and further electoral successes in the south held out the promise of gaining additional ground there.

In a radical departure, Sinn Féin determined to keep the political momentum going. At its *Ard Fhéis* (annual conference) in October 1981, its new policy was unveiled by Danny Morrison, a leading Sinn Féin strategist. He ridiculed any notion that politics alone could defeat 'the Brits' and 'win the war' – this rhetoric was meant to reassure the gunmen – but he then added that surely no one would object 'if, with a ballot paper in one hand and an armalite [rifle] in the other, we take power in Ireland'. As yet, Sinn Féin remained wedded to an abstentionist policy where Stormont, the Dáil and Westminster were concerned; but they would take their seats on local bodies. (And from1986, they would enter the Dáil and whatever Stormont assemblies (but not Westminster) were on offer.) The reponse to this new departure was impressive: in elections held in Northern Ireland in October 1982 Sinn Féin polled 10 per cent of the votes to the SDLP's 18 per cent, and in the general election of June 1983, the figure rose to 13 per cent against the SDLP's 17 per cent. In a notable coup, Gerry Adams defeated the SDLP member for West Belfast.

As Morrison had forecast, the IRA's war of attrition would continue despite Sinn Féin's move into the political arena. A short list of headline-grabbing incidents might include the assassination of the Reverend Robert Bradford, Member of Parliament for South Belfast in November 1981, the attack on the Household Cavalry in London in July 1982 in which eight died, the Irish Nationalist Liberation Army bombing of a pub frequented by service personnel in Ballykelly, county Londonderry, which killed seventeen, including twelve soldiers in December 1982, the IRA bomb at the Grand Hotel in Brighton which nearly wiped out Margaret Thatcher and her Cabinet in October 1984 and the IRA mortar attack on Newry RUC station, county Down, that killed nine police in February 1985. The security forces also would chalk up their 'successes': six unarmed IRA suspects were shot dead by the RUC in Armagh in 1982, a further ten IRA members were ambushed by SAS undercover squads between December 1983 and December 1985, and by the end of 1983 a series of so-called 'supergrass' trials had seen the conviction of scores of IRA suspects, almost all of them on the uncorroborated word of a single informer.

Sinn Féin's journey along the political path, in short, appeared to have changed little, for the IRA and the security forces remained locked into a bitter, bleak, seemingly endless and pointless war; and loyalist paramilitaries would continue to take their prey where they could. And yet such a view would be quite superficial. With hindsight it is clear that Sinn Féin's electoral advance had a deep impact on the Dublin government, first, because it threatened the moderate SDLP – in its eyes, the only acceptable face of northern nationalism – and, second, because Sinn Féin, unlike the SDLP, was determined to organise in the south and win seats there, thus upsetting a political structure that had taken two generations to construct. Fresh from its moral victory in the hunger strikes, Sinn Féin might prove very attractive to idealistic but alienated and unemployed young people in the Irish Republic, gloomily facing up to the prospect of emigration or joblessness. Similarly, Sinn Féin's 'ballot paper and armalite' strategy had a galvanising effect on the British government, for the dangers of doing nothing had been revealed. Unmoved by the deaths of hunger-strikers, Margaret Thatcher's government, faced with what it saw as The Rise of Sinn Féin, quickly began to turn its mind to constitutional initiatives designed to draw the republican movement ever deeper into politics. By the grimmest of ironies, Bobby Sands, not by his death, but by his electoral victory in Fermanagh–South Tyrone, was to be the distant father of the political process that culminated in the Good Friday/Belfast Agreement of April 1998.

Politics, divorce, abortion: the Irish Republic in the 1980s

Politics in the Republic of Ireland during the 1980s largely revolved around the persistent crisis in the public finances rather than the equally persistent crisis in Northern Ireland. The dreadful state of the economy, partly home-produced and partly the product of external forces, went a long way towards forcing the emergence of coalition governments, headed either by Fine Gael or, from 1989, by Fianna Fáil as the norm in Irish politics. Most of the governments during these years were short-lived. Charles Haughey was Taoiseach from December 1979 to June 1981, and he was succeeded by a coalition government headed by Garret FitzGerald which barely lasted into the new year. Haughey and Fianna Fáil then regained power in February 1982 but this government was replaced in November by another coalition government again led by FitzGerald. This government lasted until February 1987 when, following a general election, Haughey returned to power. However, he failed to win an overall majority in June 1989 and had no choice but to endure the humiliation of entering into a coalition government with the Progressive Democrats, a political grouping formed by disgruntled Fianna Fáil members who had deserted the party in 1985, and set up for themselves. By offering some members of the Progressive Democrats important Cabinet posts, the Fianna Fáil Party was forced to abandon two of its core principles: first, that it must govern alone, untrammelled and unfettered by partners, and second, that there must be neither forgiveness nor reward for renegades. Haughey, never having been much worried by principles of any sort, would have found this sacrifice more irritating than conscience-troubling.

This rather chaotic pattern of government, so different from that of the previous thirty years and more, can to a large extent be explained by the adverse economic circumstances of the 1980s. (The exception is the Haughey government of 1982 which collapsed for reasons which had little or nothing to do with economics. It ultimately imploded in the face of a welter of accusations of sleaze, illegal phone-taps on journalists and the exertion of improper pressure on the Gardaí. There was also the small matter of the discovery of a double-murder suspect in the attorney general's apartment.) Years of profligate borrowing and spending in the 1970s, along with another oil crisis, had produced an economy in the early 1980s in which unemployment was running at 17 per cent (over 200,000 people), interest rates were well into double figures, the top rate of tax rose to 65 per cent and sparked protest marches, and the national debt stood at over 120 per cent of gross domestic product. The servicing of that debt alone meant that there was next to nothing left in the government coffers, and further borrowing was required to keep the ship of state afloat and on course.

By the end of the decade, emigration approached 70,000 per annum. This was an exodus superficially like that of the 1950s in that the emigrants were overwhelmingly young. But the difference now was that those leaving were much better educated than their predecessors, with many having third-level qualifications. In other words, apart from the human cost of this exodus, there was a huge economic one, for while Ireland was picking up the bill for the education of those who left, it was to be denied any benefit, and other countries' economies were to enjoy the use of their skills and training. There was also a palpable sense of national shame, much more developed than in the 1950s, at the spectacle of the youth of the country fleeing: television brought poignant scenes of young men and women being seen off by their parents and friends at the airports after Christmas; it was impossible to miss the near-permanent queue for visas outside the American embassy in Ballsbridge, Dublin, and there was a plethora of newspaper features concerning the inability of certain rural parishes to sustain team sports because so many of the local young people had moved abroad.

All parties agreed that drastic remedial measures were needed, but none was wholly prepared to embark on the necessary deflationary policies because they were fearful of the electoral consequences. A salutary example might be the Fine Gael–Labour coalition of the early 1980s: not only did it collapse because it could not get its stringent budget through the Dáil, it was also punished at the polls by an electorate that was unimpressed with, among other money-raising ventures, its attempt to collect a tax on children's clothes and shoes. And in 1986 the Fine Gael-led administration speedily unravelled over proposed public spending cuts. Undoubtedly Fianna Fáil came out best in this struggle between the necessity for fiscal rectitude and reform, and the need to keep the voters on side. Even it, however, had to swallow its pride in 1989 and, as noted, for the first time in its history enter into coalition. It was immeasurably helped in tackling the formidable problems that faced the country, by the decision of Alan Dukes, FitzGerald's successor as leader of Fine Gael, to 'park' opposition to the government for a time, and to support the Fianna Fáil government in implementing the required painful measures: a 2 per cent national wage agreement (a fraction of current inflation) was secured, 20,000 public servant redundancies were effected, and over £900 million was duly cut from public expenditure between 1987 and 1989. Dukes's reward for the so-called 'Tallaght strategy' was to be dumped from the leadership by his party in 1990. By contrast, Fianna Fáil unblushingly claimed the sole credit for the very fast rates of growth in the Irish economy which began to be registered from the late 1980s, and the party was to be the dominant partner in a series of coalition governments – the 'rainbow' coalition between December 1994 and June 1997 was the only one without Fianna Fáil members – that have governed the Republic of Ireland until 2010.

Apart from the last year or so, the 1980s were economically depressed, though as we shall see, there were some significant innovations which were to have a huge impact in the 1990s as the 'Celtic Tiger' (first use, 1994) began to roar; none the less the dominant images of the decade were of anti-tax protest marches, crippling strikes, a wages free-for-all, soaring inflation and especially, a return to the high rates of emigration prevalent in the 1950s. Socially, too, the decade appeared to have more than a few echoes of the 1950s about it, for the Irish obsession with abortion, divorce and contraception once again came to the fore. Their re-emergence took many people by surprise.

So far as artificial contraception – condoms and the like – was concerned, these had been available in pharmacies since 1978 but only to married couples furnished with a doctor's prescription. (Charles Haughey, the health minister who had introduced this measure, pronounced it to be an 'Irish solution to an Irish problem'.) Single people had always been able to go across the border and purchase condoms in Northern Ireland, though this was probably not a feasible option for those living in Munster or the south-east of Ireland. In 1985, however, following acrimonious debates, and despite the firm opposition of the Catholic church, the sale of condoms was made available to anyone over eighteen years of age in the Republic. (In 1992, under the pressure of the AIDS crisis, condoms were quietly made available for purchase in most public places.) As for the contraceptive pill, this had long been legally prescribed by Irish doctors for women with irregular periods, but not (at least not officially) as a contraceptive. Given the large number of prescriptions for the 'pill' that were written, Irish women appeared to have had the most irregular periods in the developed world. However, if the Catholic church experienced defeat in its efforts to prohibit artificial contraception, it was to enjoy a very qualified 'success' on the questions of abortion and divorce.

Abortion was illegal in Ireland, north and south, under the 1861 Offences against the Person Act, but it had not been specifically outlawed in the 1937 Constitution. Concerns raised about the efficacy of the current legislative prohibition on abortion can be directly traced to the papal visit by John Paul II in September 1979. Audiences of up to a million in number had turned out to see and hear His Holiness deliver several homilies in which he had denounced the IRA, calling on it to cease its campaign, and he had urged vigilance in the defence of traditional religious values. Probably with the Italian example in his mind, for a referendum had recently legalised divorce there (1974), and there was a concerted campaign in that country to legalise abortion (ultimately successful in 1981), the pope had warned against complacency on the matter of 'the dignity and sacredness of all human life, from conception to death'. His admonitions were duly noted, and in 1981 a Pro-Life Amendment Campaign, a largely lay group, was set up with the object of introducing an amendment into the 1937 Constitution to prohibit abortion. Astonishingly – for this was after all a tiny group – pledges were quickly secured from the major party leaders, Haughey and FitzGerald, to introduce appropriate amendments if and when either was in power. Haughey's government duly drew up the wording for the proposed amendment which even to a layman looked flawed, for it seemed riddled with loopholes. FitzGerald reluctantly rowed in behind his opponent's wording and the anti-abortion amendment campaign got underway in 1983. The result was the most divisive and bad-tempered debate in Irish public life since the campaign over acceptance of the Treaty in 1922.

The referendum was held on 7 September 1983 and the result was a vote in favour: but the turn-out was rather disappointing – only 54.6 per cent of those eligible voted (as opposed 71 per cent on EEC entry in 1972) – and 66.5 per cent of these supported the amendment. Ominously for the Catholic church the majority in favour of the amendment in Dublin was unimpressive. Given the moral intensity of the debate, the viciousness of the personal attacks and the general all-round consciousness-raising attendant on incessant media discussion of the rights of the unborn and of the mother, the result might be accounted something of a Pyrrhic victory for the Irish religious right. Moreover, while the anti-abortion amendment to the Constitution was certainly carried, it did not at all prove fit for purpose. In 1986 pro-life groups went to the courts to force the closure of women's clinics that were allegedly counselling women and offering them referrals to abortion clinics in England.

Then in 1992, the High Court sought to prevent a fourteen-year old rape victim – the so-called 'X' case – from travelling to the United Kingdom for an abortion. The ban on her leaving the state was appealed to the Supreme Court which overturned the decision, and unambiguously declared that abortion was permissible where the woman's life was in danger. This led to a further constitutional amendment later that year which recognised the right of the citizen to travel and to information. However, an attempt to eliminate a loophole in the prohibition on abortion by yet another constitutional amendment failed narrowly in 2002. As a result, the unintended and profoundly unsatisfactory result of twenty years of heated argument, graphic propaganda and pro-life campaigns to protect 'the unborn' has been to make abortion legal under certain conditions in Ireland, but not to make it currently available. That promises to be the unsatisfactory situation for the foreseeable future, for there is no political appetite to return to the matter, and the prospect of legislation is remote. Some five thousand Irish women per annum will presumably continue to make the journey to the abortion clinics of the United Kingdom – yet another 'Irish solution to an Irish problem'.

From the Catholic church's point of view the situation with regard to divorce proved little better. In 1986, the coalition government headed by Garret FitzGerald had sought to remove the constitutional ban on divorce. This was part of its 'constitutional crusade' which had already seen the relaxation of the sale of condoms and, absurdly, was designed to make the Republic of Ireland more attractive to Unionists. (There had earlier been abortive proposals to delete from the constitution articles 2 and 3 claiming jurisdiction over Northern Ireland.) However, following a highly alarmist campaign (one episcopal opponent claimed that the effects of the removal of the ban on divorce would be similar to the fall-out from the Chernobyl nuclear accident, and there was much irresponsible scare-mongering on the material implications of divorce), the divorce amendment was heavily defeated. Almost certainly, however, this result had less to do with adherence to the church's teachings than with fear of the possible financial consequences of a yes vote. In the event, the question of divorce in Ireland could not rest there, for something would have to be done for the estimated seventy thousand persons caught up in marriage breakdowns, and in 1995 the Irish electorate by a wafer-thin majority voted to change the Constitution so as to permit divorce under certain conditions.

In important respects, therefore, the Irish Catholic church in the 1980s, buoyed up by the facile success of the papal visit, had managed to reassert traditional religious values, as the pope had recommended. Admittedly, the ban on artificial contraception could not be maintained, but a prohibition on abortion, however imperfectly drafted, had been added by popular vote to the Constitution, and an attempt to permit divorce had been seen off, apparently for good. In addition, the courts had not been afraid to stress the religious basis to the Irish Constitution. In 1983 the Supreme Court had rejected a claim that pre-1920 British Acts that outlawed homosexual acts were repugnant to the Irish Constitution by arguing that that document had been framed in accordance with Christian doctrine that 'for hundreds of years' had regarded homosexual conduct as 'unnatural... and gravely sinful'. (In 1993, following a successful appeal to the European Court of Human Rights, homosexual conduct between consenting adults over seventeen years of age was legalised in the Republic.)

And yet, for all the ostensible 'success' that attended the assertion of traditional Catholic religious values, closer observers were not convinced. The comparatively low turn-out in the abortion referendum, surely an indication of lack of interest among the general population, along with the very narrow victory in Dublin, were both causes for concern. The adulation witnessed during the pope's visit had proven deceptive; secularisation was making much progress in Irish society. The continued decline in religious observance, though still high by continental standards, among the young, the urbanised and the skilled or semi-skilled, was evidence of this and offered further grounds for worry. There was, also, the growing realisation that for large numbers of the Republic's population 'indifference' was the dominant attitude towards the commands of the Catholic church, especially in matters of private morality. Religious vocations continued to fall steeply, from 1,400 per annum in the mid-1960s to a paltry 100 or so in the late 1990s. (In 2007 just 9 priests were ordained, while 160 died; similarly, just 2 nuns took their final vows, while 228 died. By 2009, there were roughly ten times more priests aged seventy or above as there were under forty years.)

To some extent, behind these dramatic transformations lay the growing numbers in second- and third-level education; those in the 1950s who had forecast that increased access to further education would promote secularisation had been proved correct. The Catholic church and its priests still commanded respect among all sections of the Republic's population; and the conduct of Irish missionaries in south America, their apparent embrace of 'liberation' theology, and their opposition, at considerable personal risk, to American-funded right-wing governments in the region, elicited admiration especially from the youth of Ireland. Bishop Eamonn Casey of Galway, in particular, had been prominent in criticising American policy in south America, and in June 1984 he had pointedly refused to attend a ceremony at University College, Galway, honouring the US president, Ronald Reagan, on his visit to that city. It was just possible that an Irish Catholic church that directed its attention more to social justice at home and abroad, rather than to what went on in the bedroom, might have retained the allegiance of the 'young people of Ireland', as the pope had addressed them. But it was not to be, and the 1990s were to witness a seemingly unending series of clerical sex abuse scandals that were to destroy the institutional influence of the Catholic church.

The fall of the Catholic church in Ireland

The 1990s were a nightmare for the Catholic church in Ireland. As noted, the abortion and divorce questions returned, the first in an especially virulent form in February 1992, and the Catholic church was widely blamed for the legal mess that unfolded concerning the fourteen year-old rape victim. There was a further sensation in May 1992 when news broke that Bishop Casey had, years earlier, fathered a child by Annie Murphy, an American divorcée, and had subsequently used diocesan funds to maintain the child. The country, both the pious and the snide, was agog at this revelation and Casey promptly fled. Curiously, he had been one of the two 'warm-up' acts on the pope's visit to Ireland in September 1979: the other one, Fr Michael Cleary, a deeply traditionalist priest, and like Casey, a long-time media celebrity, was revealed after his death to have fathered a child by his housekeeper and common law wife, Phyllis Hamilton. It quickly became apparent, however, that Casey and Cleary were in the halfpenny place where sexual transgressions were concerned, for worse, much worse, was to follow, as cases of clerical sex abuse of children and the vulnerable continued to fill the newspapers and airwaves with numbing regularity.

Particularly notorious was the case of Fr Brendan Smyth (figure 7.10), who had had a string of allegations concerning the abuse of minors, including orphans, lodged against him in various countries since the 1960s but who was only brought to book in 1994. He had jumped bail in 1991 when charged in Northern Ireland, and had taken refuge in his order's house south of the border. Only in January 1994 did he voluntarily return to Northern Ireland where he pleaded guilty to seventeen charges and was imprisoned. In a documentary about the case screened on Ulster Television in October 1994, two particularly disturbing revelations emerged. First, that the church authorities had known about Smyth's predatory conduct with minors for a long time, but instead of alerting the police to what were extremely serious crimes had sought to shield him by assigning him to a different parish. Damningly, they had continued to do this for nearly thirty years.

Second, and just as troubling, there was widespread outrage when it was revealed in the programme that an RUC warrant for Smyth's extradition from the Republic in 1993 had been ignored for months in the Irish attorney general's

7.10 The fall of the Catholic church in Ireland. Fr Brendan Smyth, convicted child abuser, glowers at the camera. Irish Photographic Archive.

office. The warrant was never in fact executed because Smyth returned to Belfast of his own volition. There was a further twist. The Irish attorney general at the time of the television broadcast was Harry Whelehan, and he found himself facing a barrage of ill-directed criticism and much unfounded innuendo concerning secretive Catholic circles in high places. However, when in November 1994, the then Taoiseach, Albert Reynolds, in the face of warnings from his coalition partners, stubbornly persisted in his attempt to promote Whelehan to the presidency of the High Court, his Labour coalition partners walked out and the government fell.

As further clerical sex abuse cases unfolded throughout the 1990s there was a depressing uniformity to the details: complaints about individuals had been at first ignored and when this was no longer possible those concerned were transferred to another diocese, even to another country, where typically the assaults would continue afresh. On occasion abuse victims were offered 'loans' or compensation on condition of silence. An example of the 'paedophile priest' was Fr Ivan Payne of the Dublin diocese who was finally suspended in 1995. In January 1998 he was convicted on eleven counts of sexually abusing boys over the period 1968 to 1987. Another was Fr Sean Fortune of Ferns diocese in the south-east of Ireland who had allegations laid against him as a seminarian but had discovered that such accusations in no way inhibited his progress to the priesthood. Fortune was a deeply dysfunctional sexual predator who was to commit suicide in 1999 while awaiting trial on sixty-six charges of sexual abuse against twenty-nine boys. A damning inquiry into the handling of abuse allegations in the diocese of Ferns was published in 2005; and following a thorough investigation into clerical sexual abuse in the Dublin diocese between 1975 and 2004 an even more devastating report was completed in 2009.

Was there something peculiar to Irish society that led a small minority (2–4 per cent) of Irish priests to become sexual predators and abusers? Was clerical sexual abuse a recent phenomenon or a crime that had existed for centuries? Was it a problem especially for Ireland, and for the Irish overseas? Was the brutalisation of children, in short, the Irish disease? One result of increasing secularisation in the last decades of the twentieth century was that people were no longer in awe of the clergy and were prepared to step forward and lodge complaints; and one consequence of the rapid empowerment of women in the same period was that they were not prepared to keep silent for ever in the face of abuse. Undoubtedly, outrages were no longer concealed or covered up on the same scale as previously. Can we say therefore that in the 1990s Ireland we witnessed an explosion in the reporting of the sexual abuse of children? After all, 37 cases of child sexual abuse were recorded in 1983, but 2,500 in 1995. None of these questions has been as yet satisfactorily resolved, but certain points might be made.

The sexual and physical abuse of children in Ireland was by no means confined to clerics or religious brothers: lay teachers in Ireland had their share of offenders, and so too had almost any organisation – such as those tasked with promoting competitive swimming or boy scouting – in which adults had unsupervised control over children or adolescents. And of course, the Irish family was frequently the setting for the abuse of children by their father or other relatives. Nor was child sexual abuse confined to Irish Catholics: the Kincora boys' home in east Belfast was run by born-again Christians and in the 1970s systematic sexual abuse took place there, probably with the connivance of British intelligence (MI5). Again, for historical reasons, the Catholic church had manned most organisations dealing with the vulnerable – orphans, single mothers and so on – and it is not at all surprising that its members should have featured prominently among the lists of abusers. It is altogether possible that throughout the 1960s and later, sexual predators deliberately chose to become priests in order to obtain unrestricted access to children, and it constituted a glaring failure on the part of the Catholic church that these miscreants were not quickly identified and the civil authorities alerted. In some instances, and the Ferns report identified a number of such cases, serious warning signals were ignored in the seminary, and the ordained priests went on to be abusers. In turn, these failures must raise questions about the management of the seminaries and about the spiritual formation of the would-be priests. Few if any of the sexual depredations of the clergy where children were concerned can be traced to the rule of celibacy, or indeed to homosexuality. These were in reality crimes of power, sex and class perpetrated by disturbed, sexually immature individuals wholly unsuited to priestly office who did what they did because they could, because they knew that they could get away with it and because they knew their crimes would be covered up by a church more concerned with the 'good name' of its organisation than with the punishment of priests or the protection of children.

Altogether more shattering and disturbing than the sexual abuse of children in parishes, and the persistent cover-ups, were the revelations of systemic violence – sexual, mental and physical – that had been visited on those children entrusted to the Catholic church's care in its residential gulag. Large numbers of those who had done time – the term is not too strong – in a host of church-run institutions, ranging from the state-funded and supposedly state-supervised Dickensian industrial schools, to the 'mother and baby homes', to the 'Magdalene asylums' began to come forward with their chilling stories of vicious beatings, sexual abuse, humiliation, starvation and virtual slavery. These horror stories broke piecemeal throughout the 1990s, with some becoming the subject of television programmes and even films, such as Peter Mullan's acclaimed *Magdalene Sisters* (2002). Similar stories of wickedness had been uncovered in Catholic residential institutions further afield, in Canada, Australia and the United States, often in those with an Irish Catholic flavour, ethos or connection.

Despite these earlier revelations, the publication in 2009 of the Ryan Commission report into the abuse of children in state-owned but church-run institutions from the 1930s to the 1970s came as a profound shock to Irish public opinion and caused much heart-searching, shame and anger. This massive report laid out in horrific detail a dreadful saga of systemic and systematic terrorisation of those children entrusted to the care of various religious orders over many decades. It uncovered a closed institutional world in which rape, flogging, beatings, torture and starvation were routine, one in which allegations of abuse were ignored or the accusers intimidated, one in which the perpetrators were protected and one in which those who might have done something chose to look the other way. The Irish public's sense of outrage at these findings was heightened by the apparent attempt by the religious orders concerned to wriggle out of their financial responsibilities with regard to compensation for the victims. Nearly a hundred years after Yeats had consigned 'romantic Ireland' to the grave, 'Catholic Ireland' tumbled in after it, and the *Soggarth Aroon* (=darling priest) of folk memory passed into history.

The fall from grace of the Irish Catholic church was a shock of seismic proportions, for Catholicism, along with language and nationalism, had formed the bedrock of Irish identity since at least the mid-nineteenth century. The speed of the church's collapse made it all the more shocking, for while sociologists have understandably detected fissures and tremors in the fusion between church and people dating back to the 'mother and child' crisis in 1950, and certainly to the 1960s, to most observers the crucial decade was the 1990s. By the turn of the millennium religious observance, especially in urban areas was in freefall and vocations had slumped. Especially, the church's moral authority was in tatters. Was it entirely coincidental that as the influence of the Catholic church withered and as the adjective 'priest-ridden' disappeared, the Irish Republic experienced the most striking economic advance – the so-called Celtic Tiger – in its history? And is it entirely fanciful to suggest that as the Republic's economy forged ahead and as the priest fell from the high moral ground the Republic became an altogether less threatening place for northern Unionists and that this development helped move along the peace process which had been in a long gestation since the hunger strikes of 1981?

The Celtic Tiger

The economic phenomenon known as the Celtic Tiger has been much studied and the central elements are well known. In essence, between 1987 and 2000 the southern Irish economy shed its traditional features of high unemployment, low productivity, heavy emigration and chronic wage inflation allied to a strike culture, and became the fastest growing economy in the world, according to the Organisation for Economic Cooperation and Development (OECD). Unemployment, which was running at 18 per cent in 1987, fell to 4 per cent in 2000, and between 1994 and 2000 over a thousand jobs a week were coming on stream. For many of these years Ireland was posting growth rates of between 8 and 10 per cent, similar to and often exceeding those recorded in the 'Tiger' economies in the Far East from the 1960s on. Between 1913 and the mid-1980s, Irish income had hovered at around two-thirds of the United Kingdom level, often much lower; but by the year 2000, Irish income levels had stormed into a commanding lead. In 2004 Ireland's 'quality of life', according to the *Economist*, was the best in the world: the United Kingdom's was placed twenty-ninth; and as measured by income per head, the Irish were possibly the richest people on the planet. Perhaps most strikingly, almost overnight, Ireland went from being a donor country out of which its citizens had for generations emigrated in search of work, to being a host country for tens of thousands of foreign workers mostly from the countries of eastern Europe but also from south America, who would come to Ireland seeking employment. By 2006 some four hundred thousand out of a population of around four million had been born outside Ireland. In addition, a large number of asylum seekers arrived in Ireland during the years of the Celtic Tiger – in 1990 there were 50 applications for asylum whereas in 2000 there were 11,000. What explanations can be offered for these dramatic transformations that were such features of the Celtic Tiger?

Before addressing this question, it should be immediately pointed out that these impressive statistics and Ireland's high position on various league tables did not mean that poverty had been eliminated from the Republic of Ireland, or that everyone benefited proportionately, or that generations of neglect and underfunding on social welfare, educational infrastructure or the provision of healthcare was put right within a handful of years. On the contrary, despite the economic boom, the proportion of those deemed to be living in poverty remained at over 15 per cent of the population, and Ireland was reckoned to have the second highest level of poverty in the developed world. (The United States had the highest.) The provision of healthcare remained profoundly unsatisfactory and, despite the billions that were pumped into the system in the 1990s, it continued to be so. Again, over 20 per cent of the adult population was believed to be functionally illiterate, and that percentage proved resistant to improvement.

Sadly, there was very little serious debate on what to do with the revenues that poured into the Irish exchequer during the 1990s and the years up to 2007. In the event, very large sums went to fund tax cuts for the well-to-do and the not-so-well-off, and there was a massive programme of road-building. The commuter-belt zones around Greater Dublin, such as Kildare, Meath and Wicklow certainly grew in wealth; and so too did the suburbs of Cork, Galway and Limerick. By contrast, while rural areas of Mayo, Donegal, Leitrim and Kerry made progress they showed few signs of catching up with the more urbanised sectors. Shamefully, in parts of Dublin, Cork and Limerick there remained large areas of acute social deprivation which the Celtic Tiger had entirely passed by.

Had the boom continued then matters might have been rectified. It was not to be: the 'original' Celtic Tiger faltered briefly in the early years of the new millennium, but continued economic growth was sustained by a construction-led speculative surge from 2001 to 2007. In its turn, the building industry ran into sand. Economic activity everywhere slowed right down, unemployment soared, the banking system faced collapse, government revenue shrank and the forecast for economic growth was at its lowest percentage for very many years. By 2009 there was a painful acceptance that the best use had not been made of the swollen revenues generated in the heyday of the Celtic Tiger economy. There was also a resentful realisation that those entrusted with the management of the country's finances, chiefly bankers and successive Fianna Fáil governments, had behaved recklessly or negligently during the first decade of the new century.

The reasons for the explosive growth of the Irish economy in the 1990s are well known. Economic theory had it that poorer countries could grow faster than rich ones, and much was made of the historically underdeveloped state of the Irish economy, with claims that this enabled Ireland, unencumbered by decayed industrial infrastructure, to move rapidly from being a Third World to a First World country and, so to speak, leapfrog directly into the information age. There was something in this, but it was by no means the whole story. The explanation for Ireland's unprecedented economic growth in the 1990s and early years of the new millennium must be sought in the confluence of a large number of other factors.

As noted, Ireland's postwar economic performance fell some ways short of impressive, with growth of around 2 per cent (as opposed to 6 per cent elsewhere in Europe in the 1950s and 1960s), high jobless rates and emigration at a level that raised the spectre of the 'vanishing Irish'. This picture had not changed substantially by the 1980s. Admittedly, growth rates had improved in the 1960s and 1970s but the impact of two major oil shocks in 1973–4 and 1979–81 was sufficient to derail the economic locomotive, with unemployment remaining high, and emigration too, especially in the 1980s. What had changed in these years, and would ultimately prove crucial, was a massive raising of the level of educational attainment.

In the early 1960s, Irish children held the unhappy distinction of possessing the poorest completion rates for primary and secondary cycles of education anywhere in western Europe; however, by the 1990s, Ireland was at or near the top of the OECD league table of educational achievement. In 1965 roughly 20 per cent – we think, for accurate statistics were not a priority – completed the second-level cycle, but by 1995 that had risen to 80 per cent. Dr Patrick Hillery and Donogh O'Malley were two Fianna Fáil ministers who in the 1960s cleared the way for free secondary education in the Republic. The number attending third-level colleges rose by sixfold during the same period. Fortunately, not all of this expansion was centred on the traditional universities. The regional technical colleges set up in the 1960s offered a broad vocational and technological training and attracted some 40 per cent of those who stayed on after second level. By 1990, Ireland was second (out of sixty countries) in the OECD league table for those attending third-level colleges; the United Kingdom was thirty-sixth. Moreover, these regional technical colleges – later institutes of technology – proved very responsive to government policy objectives with the result that between 1978 and 1983 engineering graduates went up 40 per cent, and the number of computer scientists rose tenfold.

There can be no doubt that the existence of this well-educated, 'high-tech', labour force was an extremely powerful inducement to choose Ireland for those multinational companies seeking access to the European single market that was set up in 1987. It was also very important that Ireland was an English-speaking country, one that had a democratic government, a well-regarded judiciary, a tolerably efficient bureaucracy, a good education system and a reasonable transport infrastructure. Ireland was also a country that was for the most part corruption free. (Admittedly, some politicians were later revealed to have been on the take but the sums involved were – apart from those garnered by Charles Haughey – rather modest. Significantly, rogue politicians at a local or national level made few attempts to put the squeeze on multinationals.)

In addition, by the late 1980s, public finances were largely under control, and a series of national wage agreements between unions and employers brokered by the government had begun to deliver moderate wage increases and curb strikes. To these features must be added the attractions of low corporation tax (12.5 per cent as against the European norm of over 30 per cent), high profit repatriation and relatively low wage levels, at least compared to other continental countries. Ireland was, moreover, a country that enjoyed an Atlantic location, and possessed valuable cultural and historical contacts with the United States. The complete package, as unveiled time and time again by Michael Killeen, the dynamic managing director of the Industrial Development Authority, proved very compelling. Presciently, pharmaceutical companies, food-processing conglomerates and information-technology firms were particularly targeted, and lured to Ireland. Foreign direct investment fuelled the rise of the Celtic Tiger: by the year 2000 Ireland had become the economy with by far the most foreign direct investment in Europe, with six times the amount of its nearest rival. Valued at some €60 billion, and yielding well over €2 billion per annum in corporate tax, this investment came overwhelmingly from the United States: by 2005 some six hundred US firms in Ireland employed 100,000 people directly, with a further 250,000 jobs supported indirectly through purchases of goods and services.

Three further economic factors may be identified. First, order was restored to Irish public finances by 1990, and maintained throughout that decade. Second, the United States was undergoing throughout the twenty years after 1980 perhaps the greatest growth period in its history: and given Ireland's dependence on the US market and on Foreign Direct Investment the significance of this extraneous factor is very clear. Lastly, under European Union structural and cohesion strategies, there was a very large transfer of funds, worth well over £20 billion to Ireland over the period 1985 to 2000. These transfers have been particularly identified as responsible for the economic boom by those who were basically incredulous that the Irish, long a byword for poverty and inefficiency, could do anything for themselves. Unionists, in particular, gloomily contemplating the complete lack of dynamism in their own economy, with its bloated public sector and relative absence of manufacturing, were quick to place great weight on handouts from Brussels to Ireland. As a region of the prosperous United Kingdom,

EU structural funds were not available on anything like the same scale to Northern Ireland. However, structural funds, while hugely welcome, were not on their own a primary, much less a sole, cause of the Celtic Tiger's advance. Other 'cohesion' (EU-speak for 'poor') countries, such as Spain, Portugal and Greece, were also in receipt of such funds, but none of them experienced an economic advance like that of Ireland. The most that economists assigned to the value of EU transfers is a very modest 0.5 per cent in an Irish growth rate that at times touched and on occasion even exceeded 10 per cent.

So far, with the exception of the educational revolution that began in the 1960s, emphasis has been laid on the specific economic factors that helped fuel and sustain the Celtic Tiger economy through the late 1980s, on through the 1990s and into the early years of the new millennium. And this is entirely appropriate; but it would be wrong-headed to ignore the essential contribution of what we might call intellectual or cultural factors. Put simply, the key question about the Celtic Tiger economy is not what caused it but why it took so long to happen. The combination of economic factors identified as fuelling Ireland's boom years would have meant little without a positive desire on the part of the Irish political classes to create wealth, raise employment levels and stem emigration; in short, to embrace modernisation.

Until the 1960s a certain mindset prevailed on all sides in Irish public life. A short list of common, widely shared attitudes might include the following: that Irish poverty was England's fault, or a result of partition; that only in the north-east of Ireland could manufacturing flourish; that the purpose of education was to revive the Irish language; that education beyond a minimal level was point-less, even unsettling, in that it might excite discontent; that foreign investment was a form of colonialism; that emigration was an unalterable and permanent feature of Irish society; that state regulation on what to read, see, and hear was beneficial; that the authority of the Catholic church was superior to that of the civil power; that intellectual isolationism and economic protectionism were to be cherished; that the study of science was best left to Protestants and that Catholics should stick to the humanities; that the proper place for women was in the home; that discussion of any of the above should be firmly discouraged; and in short, that modernisation was undesirable and was to be strongly resisted. Until such attitudes altered, softened or were replaced, no amount of transfers from Brussels, low corporation taxes or foreign direct investment could have transformed the Irish economy in the last decade of the twentieth century. Irish people had to want change and to prefer it to stasis before there could be movement.

In helping to bring about just such a changed mindset the experience of the 1950s was crucial. In that desolate decade not only did it look as if the Republic was an economic failure but, nearly as galling, Northern Ireland appeared to be a success. As a result of the near collapse of the 1950s it no longer became acceptable to treat near economic ruin, continued emigration and other material matters with a lofty disdain. A process was begun – through the establishment of commissions of inquiry, through the collection of statistics, through revolution-ising the provision and quality of education at all levels, through the establishing of government agencies designed to encourage foreign investment, through the relaxation of censorship, and through chipping away at authoritarianism in church and state – that was to transform official attitudes to wealth creation and economic growth. It was the experience of the 1950s that caused the ideologies of protectionism and isolationism of previous decades to be abandoned, and over the next thirty years the Republic of Ireland set out to modernise. As a result, when a number of favourable economic circumstances converged in the late 1980s, Ireland was ready to seize the opportunities that opened up. It was the 1990s when the Celtic Tiger began to roar; but the animal had had a long gestation.

One early indication of a radical transformation in Irish public attitudes was given in 1990 by the election of the Labour Party's Mary Robinson (figure 7.11) as president of Ireland. Her victory was something of a sensation, for not only did she thereby break a Fianna Fáil stranglehold on what was largely a ceremo-nial office (though one that was symbolically important) but she also signalled unmistakably the arrival of women into Irish public life. That Robinson's pres-idential victory was no flash in the pan was revealed by the election in 1997 of her successor, Mary McAleese who went on to serve two terms as president. The feminisation of Irish public space had been progressing piecemeal since the 1960s but the pace had accelerated in the 1980s. Few had been more active than Mary Robinson herself in leading the feminist challenge to deep-seated Irish male attitudes of exclusion and superiority. And female journalists such as Nuala O'Faolain, Nell McCafferty, Mary Holland and Geraldine Kennedy were also prominent in the 1980s in challenging male prejudices and stereotypes – simply by being brilliant at their jobs. As well, by the early 1990s there was a clear process of feminisation underway in the teaching, legal and medical pro-fessions: by the end of the decade women would dominate the ranks of those training to be teachers, doctors and lawyers. In the workforce, too, there was a huge increase in the percentage of married women – up from 5 per cent in 1966 to 40 per cent in 2000 to over 50 per cent in 2006. De Valera's homely vision of the role of Irish women as revealed in his 1937 Constitution by the early 1990s was fast fading and by the turn of the century it had gone.

It was no coincidence that the overturning of entrenched attitudes was accom-panied by a cultural revival on many fronts. From the 1960s on there was a near constant flowering in prose-writing (including works in Gaelic), poetry, Irish

7.11 Mary Robinson of the Labour Party celebrating her victory in the presidential election of 1990. Behind her is the defeated Fianna Fáil candidate, Brian Lenihan, with, to the right, Charles Haughey. Irish Photographic Archive.

music, theatre and film. Dramatists of the quality of Brian Friel, Tom Murphy and Frank McGuinness interrogated aspects of the Irish experience in stunning plays such as *Dancing at Lughnasa* (1990), *Whistle in the Dark* (1960) and *Observe the Sons of Ulster Marching towards the Somme* (1985), and their works drew huge acclaim not just in Ireland (on occasion, not even in Ireland – Murphy's

7.12 Seamus Heaney, Nobel Laureate in literature. Irish Photographic Archive.

play was rejected by the Abbey as 'rubbish') but much further afield. Irish theatre directors, too, would be feted worldwide, among them Garry Hynes of the Galway-based Druid Theatre Company, who would go on to win awards in Dublin, London and New York for *inter alia* her reimagining of J. M. Synge's, *The Playboy of the Western World*, and for her staging of Martin McDonagh's *Leenane Trilogy* (1996–7), a sort of 'Psychopath of the Western World' to be set alongside Synge's classic. And Irish actors such as Siobhán McKenna, Donal McCann, Mick Lally, Marie Mullan, Niall Tóibín and Sean McGinley were central to this endeavour. In film, too, Irish directors such as Neil Jordan had major successes with *The Long Good Friday* (1986), *The Butcher Boy* (1990) and *The Crying Game* (1992), very often casting the Irish actor Stephen Rea in a leading role.

It was a similar story with Irish novelists such as John Banville, Colm Tóibín, Patrick McCabe, John McGahern and Edna O'Brien who again have interrogated the myths that shaped Irish people's self-images and held together their lives, and in doing so have been prominent in the ranks of those who were shortlisted for or awarded such literary prizes as the Man–Booker. Irish poets such as Seamus Heaney, Medbh McGuckian, Ciarán Carson, Nuala Ní Dhomhnaill, Derek Mahon, Paul Muldoon and John Montague have emerged from under the towering presence of W. B. Yeats to create new and distinctive 'voices' – and to win numerous awards. Heaney emulated Yeats by winning the Nobel prize for literature in 1995 (figure 7.12). No doubt, many (including most of those cited above) would reject the notion of international recognition, accolades or prizewinning as a true indication of literary or indeed any other kind of merit, but that

7.13 Happy Days! The Republic of Ireland soccer team celebrating its advance to the quarter-finals of the World Cup in 1990. Irish Photographic Archive.

is not the point: by winning awards, gaining recognition, being invited to lecture in prestige universities they made the news headlines, and they undoubtedly contributed to the emergence of an Irish 'feel-good factor' in the late twentieth-century that helped prepare the ground for the Celtic Tiger.

In this latter respect, the impact on Irish consciousness made by the Irish international soccer team in qualifying for the European Championship in 1988 and for the World Cup in 1990 (figure 7.13) ought not to be ignored. Dennis Taylor's success in the 1987 World Snooker Championship was another cause for celebration; two years earlier it had been the Irish rock-star Bob Geldof who had organised the first Live Aid concert to tackle poverty in the Third World. Nor should the stunning achievements of the rock band U2 (with millions of albums sold worldwide) and the global phenomenon of the Irish dance spectaculars, *Riverdance* and *Lord of the Dance*, be underestimated in terms of boosting Irish self-esteem. Again, the triumphs of Irish racehorses, such as the triple Gold Cup winner, Arkle, and the 1981 Derby winner, Shergar (sadly, later shot by the IRA in a bungled kidnap attempt) should be noted. Irish trainers such as Tom Dreaper, Vincent O'Brien and Dermot Weld, and Irish jockeys, both on the flat, such as Kieren Fallon (many times a champion jockey) and over jumps, A. P. McCoy (ditto) made their contribution to a national mood of confidence. In short, in the last decades of the twentieth century, Ireland enjoyed success on various international stages and had, it appeared, become assured, modern and 'cool'. The Celtic Tiger would find a natural home there.

Politics and society in the Irish Republic, 1998–2010

The years 1998 to 2007 were marked by further sustained economic growth and by enormous social change in the Republic. During these years, the transformation of Irish society begun in the 1990s through in-migration proceeded dramatically. Foreign-born residents registered a 58 per cent increase to bring them to at least 14 per cent of a total Irish population of just over four million in 2006. By far the largest group of foreign nationals was Poles (150,000), followed by Chinese (60,000), then by Lithuanians and Latvians (45,000 and 30,000 respectively). In 2006, census data revealed that nearly three hundred thousand workers had entered the workforce since the early years of the new century, and of these workers almost half were foreign born. A substantial percentage were Irish emigrants returning from abroad and, as noted earlier, the proportion of married women in the workplace continued to rise. These new workers fuelled the Celtic Tiger economy during the 1990s and sustained growth until 2007, when the onset of a global economic recession, triggered by the collapse of the home loan market in the United States and spiralling fuel costs, had a huge impact on the Irish economy, notably in the financial and construction sectors. Ironically, these, together with pharmaceuticals and technology, had been to the forefront of Irish economic growth during the entire period of the Celtic Tiger.

The social impact of these foreign-born workers, and their families, was enormous. They were not spread evenly throughout the Republic, but rather clustered in certain towns and certain areas of the cities. Thus Gort, south Galway, attracted a large proportion of Brazilian meat workers because of the meat-packing plants nearby, Millstreet, county Cork, had the highest ratio of Polish residents to native-born in the state, while in Dublin the area south of Parnell Street in the city centre had over 44 per cent of its residents born outside Ireland. While the economic recession beginning in 2007 led to the return of some of these workers to their native lands, large numbers, especially those with families, remained in Ireland as the 'new Irish', and the proportion of foreign born in Ireland remained constant or continued to rise.

The implications of this massive and, it seemed, largely permanent immigration in terms of Irish social, educational and welfare policies were scarcely realised. As a country that had (falsely) prided itself on its racial distinctiveness, crudely along the lines of the superiority of the Celt over the Saxon (and anyone else), and as a people that for the most part had only ever experienced ethnic diversity in the United States or Britain, Ireland and the Irish were initially not well equipped mentally, legislatively or educationally to meet the challenges posed by scores of thousands of immigrants who had different skin colours, different religions, different languages and different *mores*. A blatant racism which formerly targeted travellers was swiftly expanded to include the new immigrants. For a time, strict enforcement of laws outlawing racial discrimination proved largely successful in driving out overt racism. However, as the Irish economy headed into recession and as immigrants continued to be disproportionately represented on the lists of the unemployed, anti-foreigner sentiment was never far from the surface of Irish public life.

From 2006 on, debate and argument centred on relatively trivial issues such as whether Islamic schoolgirls should be allowed to wear a headscarf to school, or whether Garda officers from the Sikh community be permitted to wear turbans rather that the uniform cap. The amount of heat generated by such minor matters showed clearly that knottier problems might well be potentially explosive. How was Irish citizenship to be defined? Who was or ought to be eligible? How should asylum seekers be treated and who qualified for that status? And, above all, was a policy of multiculturalism, where parity of esteem was extended to all newcomers and their culture, the desired objective, or was the full integration of the immigrant into the host society sought? At times, successive coalition governments over the period 1995 to 2005 appeared hesitant and unclear on such matters, and this led to some confusion. This lack of focus led to further problems and triggered renewed resentments against the newcomers 'taking Irish jobs', and enjoying advantages in social welfare benefits.

A further consequence of the Republic's new-found affluence between 1995 and 2007 was the rise of a rampant consumerism that swiftly elbowed an earlier generation's goal of 'frugal comfort' out of the way. Shopping was the new religion with the malls, its cathedrals: *Tesco, ergo sum* was the new mantra, *introibo ad altare Dei* was no longer heard. A large majority of homes in Dublin by 2010 had acquired a washing-machine, microwave oven, hifi apparatus and two televisions, complete with satellite or cable channels. Nearly half had a dishwasher. All of this was radically different to the position in the mid-1980s, and possession of such consumer goods put the Republic broadly in line with other western European countries. The number of private cars rose from 750,000 in 1986 to over a million in 1996 and further doubled by 2007. By 2003, car ownership in both rural and urban parts of Ireland was among the highest in the developed world. Again, during the housing boom of the 1995–2005 period, many house-owners used the combination of surplus equity on their homes along with low interest rates to travel frequently and to invest in property abroad, mostly

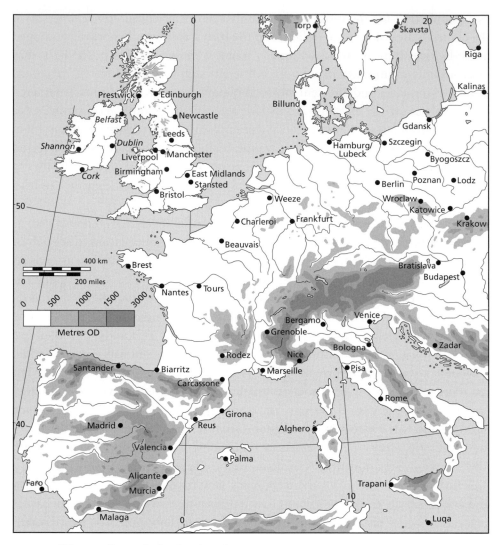

Map 11 Ryanair destinations in 2007

in Spain, but also in France, the United States, the Czech Republic, Hungary and Bulgaria. (Holidaying abroad and visiting one's property abroad were both facilitated by low-fare flights on budget airlines, a development pioneered in Europe by Ryanair (map 11), an Irish company) Internet access – a badge of modernity – became generally available: around 21 per cent of the population had it in 2001; but by 2006 nearly 50 per cent were 'on the net'.

One less desirable sign of modernity was the unbridled consumption of alcohol per capita. This rose dramatically by over 40 per cent during the decade of the 1990s, and there was a further rise in the new century. In 2009 hospital consultants reported a sharp rise in alcohol-related health problems, particularly among the young. Earlier generations of Irish people drank heavily because they were poor and needed the comfort of alcohol, but the cubs of the Celtic Tiger drank to excess because they were rich and could afford to do so. Another undesirable sign of progress was the increase in drug abuse. The supply of illegal drugs, almost unknown in the 1960s, became a multi-million euro industry: by 2006 there were well over fifteen thousand heroin users in the Republic, and cocaine and ecstasy in industrial quantities were being seized by the Gardaí. (There was a 700 per cent increase in cocaine abusers seeking treatment – 43 to 342 – between the years 2001 and 2006.) With the growth in drug use came an associated rise in the number of criminal gangs eager to import drugs and to supply users. There was also a comparable increase in the level of violence that gang members were prepared to perpetrate against rivals, the police or even investigative journalists – Veronica Guerin, shot in 1996, was a high-profile victim in this latter category. By 2010 Dublin was on course to be the gangland murder capital of western Europe. In the same year, official figures for Irish drug use tended to place Ireland at about midway in the European league table.

If the Republic's economy was the success story for the 1990s and on through to 2007, then, at least in terms of drama, it was run a close second by the revelations that emerged from a slew of tribunals set up *seriatim* in the 1990s to investigate everything from the Irish beef industry, to planning matters in the greater Dublin areas, to 'payments to politicians' and to haemophiliacs infected with contaminated blood. What these tribunals had in common was that they all proved extremely expensive, with costs running at hundreds of millions of euros. They were also on the whole slow moving, with some still investigating more than ten years after they were set up. However, they were extremely revealing about the political culture of *fin de siècle* Ireland.

There had been some allegations of corruption and wrong-doing in Irish public life in earlier decades, though in comparison with other newly arrived states, these had been few and far between. The finances of the *Irish Press*, for example, from the outset had always been something of a puzzle: so too had been those of the multi-million pound Irish Hospitals' Sweepstakes from the 1930s on; and in the 1980s, planning and rezoning decisions by various Irish county councils appeared to show that public welfare was very often cast aside in the rush for private profit and personal remuneration. By and large, however the Republic had prided itself on its reputation for probity in its public officials, a reputation that would barely survive the revelations of the tribunals of inquiry set up during the 1990s.

The first of the modern tribunals was set up in 1991 on foot of serious allegations made in a television programme of irregularities amounting to corruption in the valuable Irish beef export industry. Justice Liam Hamilton, who conducted the inquiry, duly issued a report in July 1994 which revealed that tax evasion, bogus labelling of beef and other fiddles were widespread. Curiously, his report was received with relative indifference by the Irish public, perhaps because the complexities of the beef industry were baffling, or perhaps because the findings were scarcely surprising. In any case, the major fall-out from the report was a souring of relations between the then Taoiseach, Albert Reynolds, and his coalition partners from the Labour Party. Reynolds had outraged his Labour partners by rushing out a statement claiming that the report was a total vindication of his conduct. In retrospect, it was the beginning of the end for that government.

While the Beef Tribunal was sitting, the Irish public was greatly diverted by reports of an incident in a Florida hotel on the night of 19 February 1992 involving Ben Dunne, Irish supermarket heir and one-time IRA kidnap victim, and escort girls, cocaine and the local police. The Dunne family was outraged at the negative publicity that ensued and set on foot legal moves to detach Ben Dunne from the family's multi-million pound business. Investigations into Dunne's spending quickly revealed that he had, over the years, donated £1.3 million to Charles J. Haughey for his personal use. The scandal of payments to politicians began to unfold, with many revelations of corrupt practices and sheer dishonesty emerging over the next ten years.

The McCracken Tribunal was set up in 1997 to examine matters relating to Haughey's finances and discovered that the very wealthy elite of Ireland – not just Haughey – had long enjoyed a privileged banking regime, complete with tax evasion, if required, and friendly offshore accounts in the Ansbacher (Cayman) Bank. These accounts were actually 'on-shore', and available for the use of their holders in Ireland. The McCracken report was published within seven months and was quietly devastating: Haughey was shown to have lied to the tribunal about payments to him by Dunne, and the report severely criticised him for allowing himself to be put in a position of dependency on a private citizen. As with clerical scandals, more were swift to follow. A second tribunal tasked with investigating other payments to Haughey, and to Michael Lowry, a Fine Gael politician, concluded that during his career between 1979 and 1996, Haughey had been the recipient of nearly £12 million in gifts. It was therefore no wonder that on a TD's modest salary of around £10,000 a year, he had been able to consistently spend above £300,000 a year on his property, servants, hospitality, fine wines, restaurants and bespoke shirts. Nor was it a surprise that over the same period, he had been able to amass a large estate in north Dublin, an island off Kerry, thoroughbred racehorses and a yacht.

Haughey was not the only high-profile politician to find his reputation in tatters after probing by a tribunal into their affairs. Other casualties included the minister for foreign affairs, Raphael Burke, jailed for corruption, and Liam Lawlor, TD, imprisoned on a number of occasions for refusing to cooperate with the Flood (later Mahon) Tribunal that had been set up to investigate planning irregularities in north Dublin. A host of county councillors and even the long-time assistant city and county manager for Dublin, George Redmond, found themselves under investigation and asked to explain large payments to their accounts. Similarly, Bertie Ahern, Taoiseach from 1997 to 2008, had great difficulty in explaining large sterling sums paid to him in the early 1990s, and he left office rather sooner than he had intended. Lesser individuals also found themselves in the spotlight when, often on a bank's advice, they had lodged money into an account which they duly registered as non-resident by adding a bogus foreign address. As a result of the revelations from the various tribunals, it was clear that a culture of evasion and secrecy where tax was concerned and of payments, backhanders and bribes at the highest levels had become engrained in Irish public culture. Finally, the Lindsay Tribunal into the supply of contaminated blood products to a large number of women and haemophiliacs revealed staggering levels of complacency and incompetence in a vital state agency, the Blood Transfusion Service Board.

The net result of these disquieting revelations was to increase public cynicism where politicians were concerned, and to promote disillusion with the performance of office-holders. Neither bank officials nor revenue officials came out well from most of these investigations. Strangely, however, no protest marches were held and no cars were overturned in the streets, possibly because the economy was doing well and low interest rates, pay increases, and tax cuts probably helped assuage public anger. Certainly, the party to which most of the prominent malefactors belonged – Fianna Fáil – suffered little damage at the polls and continued undisturbed as the lead partner in an unbroken series of coalition governments headed by Bertie Ahern and then Brian Cowen.

Perhaps public anger was registered in the votes on two referendums to do with the European Union, the first, or Nice, referendum held in 2001 and the second, or Lisbon, referendum held in 2008. In both cases there was a decisive vote against the proposed amendments, though in the case of Nice, this result was reversed a year later when put once again before the Irish electorate. Similarly Lisbon was resubmitted to the Irish electorate in October 2009 and this time passed. Neither of the primary rejections could be attributed to anti-European feeling, for the Irish public was, and continued to be, enthusiastically pro-European Union. Certainly, there was unease at enlarging the EU through the admission of eastern European countries (Nice), and there was also concern at what some felt were the implications for Irish neutrality of a stronger European defence force (Lisbon). Grotesque fears were voiced at the possible conscription of Irish youths into a European army and at the threat of an EU directive authorising abortion in Ireland. Overall, however, the Irish remained very much in favour of the EU from which the country had greatly benefited. The votes on Nice and especially Lisbon were essentially protest votes against a political establishment that in many ways had taken the Irish electorate for granted and against a political class which, through the revelations of the tribunals, had been to an extent exposed as corrupt and dishonest. At the same time, the many visible benefits of the Celtic Tiger helped maintain voting in regular elections along traditional lines, irrespective of what emerged from the tribunals.

By 2008 the benefits of the boom years had faded completely from view and the Republic of Ireland had moved into the greatest recession that the country had faced since the Great Famine. In the United States plummeting financial stocks and the collapse of several high-profile banks – such as Lehman Brothers – triggered a global recession which swiftly engulfed Ireland. In short order, the fragile foundations of Irish financial institutions were ruthlessly exposed, the insane lending practices of Irish banks during the years of the construction-led boom were revealed and so too was the recklessness with which the economy had been managed by politicians and public servants since the mid-1990s. In September 2008 the six principal banks in the Republic nearly capsized as waves of 'toxic' debt washed over them. This immediate danger was headed off when the government headed by Brian Cowen pledged a blanket guarantee of both all deposits and, remarkably, all existing bonds issued by the banks to other financial institutions. This action brought a welcome respite and bought some time; but it quickly became clear that nothing could save Anglo-Irish Bank, primarily a specialist commercial bank that had loaned billions of euros secured on property to developers. As property prices went into free fall in the spring and summer of 2008, this bank was left dangerously exposed. The government believed that the collapse of 'Anglo' would endanger the entire banking system and, rather than allow this to happen, the bank was therefore taken into state ownership. The deposits of all banks operating in the Republic were once again guaranteed; and billions of euros were advanced to them in order to recapitalise them.

This was by no means the end of the crisis. As the banking system teetered on the edge of collapse, business confidence in 'Ireland Inc.' ebbed rapidly. Ireland, once bracketed with Taiwan and South Korea in terms of the strength of its economy, now found itself compared to the sick men of Europe – Portugal, Italy and Greece. Irish stocks fell sharply, with the shares of the once-mighty Bank of Ireland and Allied Irish Bank that had traded at over 13 euros barely a year previously falling to under 20 cents. Construction ground to a halt, and builders' suppliers notched up large losses. To stabilise the banking system and get credit moving again the government set up the National Assets Management Agency

(NAMA) with a brief to buy up the bad debts of the banks. Since these bad debts were primarily property based, by the end of 2009 the Irish taxpayer, through NAMA, found itself the owner of, as one academic critic had it, 'ghost estates, empty office-blocks, guestless hotels and weed-choked fields'. The prospects of selling these at a profit appeared remote and the billions paid for them were a heavy charge on public finances.

To narrow the growing gap between the government's proposed expenditure and anticipated income, increasingly desperate measures were resorted to. Large sums were borrowed abroad, but with Ireland's credit rating slipping, such loans were increasingly expensive to procure. Two new advisory groups – one on taxation and the other on public spending – were set up to advise the Cowen government on ways to increase taxation and to come up with cuts in expenditure. While it waited for these to report, two emergency mini-budgets imposed various pay, health and pension levies on workers in the public sector (whose members were regularly denounced for being overpaid, underworked and enjoying job security). Despite such revenue-raising measures, the gap between income and expenditure stubbornly refused to close and further taxes were imposed towards the end of 2009. However, given that the jobless total by the end of 2009 was running at half a million (200,000 higher than the previous year), the scope for increased revenue from rises in income tax was very limited. Meanwhile the bill for social welfare payments soared.

It would be surprising if, in the face of such a savage economic meltdown, urgent voices were not raised questioning the governance of the Irish Republic. A disturbing feature of the Irish recession was the revelation of a complete failure on the part of those charged with regulating the financial sector or supervising the banks to take action against these financial institutions, and to curb their enthusiasm for reckless lending, especially to developers. There was also disquieting evidence of an unhealthy, close, even overlapping, relationship between bankers, developers and politicians which, in practical terms, appeared to rule out the possibility that any one of them could have shouted 'stop' during the construction boom years. Equally unsettling was the realisation that in the end no one would be held responsible for the near-collapse of the Irish banking system, or for the billions that had disappeared into thin air (and for which the Irish taxpayer would be liable). In some other jurisdictions, those found guilty of financial wrong-doing were led away to serve prison sentences; but not in Ireland. And yet, while some questioned whether the public institutions of the state, the electoral system or even the Constitution of 1937 were in the new millennium 'fit for purpose', such voices were surprisingly few, given the gravity of the recession. As we have seen, the sole merit of the near-collapse of the 1950s was that it had impressed upon policy-makers and politicians the necessity for a radical appraisal of existing policies; but in 2010, there was little sign of any need for an urgent rethink about Irish governance. In the end, for all the new taxes, levies, charges and cut-backs, the government's chief plan for recovery was to sit tight until the United States and the United Kingdom led the way out of recession.

From Anglo-Irish Agreement to IRA ceasefire

For Unionists in Northern Ireland, the massive economic advances in the Republic in the 1990s, the resulting immigration transforming the make-up of the Irish population and the equally decisive shifts in social attitudes, particularly where the position of the Catholic church was concerned, were all most perplexing. Abject poverty and priestly domination, in Unionist eyes, were the twin defining and inescapable features of Irish nationalism. However, as the Catholic church fell into disgrace and the southern economy roared ahead in the 1990s, these historically validated traits no longer applied. Confusingly, it now appeared as if Northern Ireland were the state lacking in modernity, mired in sectarian hatred, faced with an interminable low-intensity insurgency and, humiliatingly, governed like some colonial outpost of empire through a string of increasingly ineffective and sometimes absurd British Secretaries of State. Under the impact of dramatic economic change in the Republic, northern Unionists would be led to re-evaluate certain of their own cherished attitudes. Such rethinking, however, was for the future: as the prison protests ended in apparent defeat for republicans in October 1981, Unionists were upbeat that they would continue to hold the trump cards. They had flexed their muscles and seen off the Sunningdale power-sharing government, and the 'Iron Lady', Margaret Thatcher, had faced down the hunger-strikers' challenge to her definition of the IRA's 'armed struggle' as nothing more than 'crime, crime, crime'.

In the aftermath of the hunger strikes, Unionists were in no mood to enter into serious negotiations with northern nationalist parties. Unionism itself was divided on the question of whether to seek full integration or devolution, with the leader of the Ulster Unionists, James Molyneaux, favouring the former. However, having Northern Ireland as an undifferentiated region of the United Kingdom was not an option that the SDLP, much less Sinn Féin, would accept; and devolution, for all the safeguards offered, appeared to be simply a return to the old Stormont. Northern nationalists, having briefly enjoyed power-sharing and an Irish dimension in the Sunningdale Agreement, were not prepared to accept much less. The impasse that soon developed on constitutional matters was not all that unwelcome to Unionists.

In the early 1980s life was returning to something approaching (a very flawed) normality. The economy might have been in the doldrums, but for the professional middle classes residing in the leafy suburbs of Belfast and in the coastal towns life was good, with high incomes normal, plentiful state employment and low house prices. Top of the range motor cars such as BMWs and Mercedes for a time sold proportionately more per head of population in Northern Ireland than elsewhere in Europe. Northern Ireland's many fine grammar schools consistently out-performed all other regions in the United Kingdom, as measured by the proportion of pupils attaining the highest grades at 'A' level. (Less trumpeted was the fact that Northern Ireland had the highest percentage in the United Kingdom of young people leaving school with minimal qualifications.) On the security front, the threat from the IRA was apparently contained; many areas were quite free from trouble, and the SAS were taking the fight to the 'terrorists'. In these circumstances, loyalist paramilitary violence diminished to a handful of murders each year. In London, Margaret Thatcher looked and sounded rock solid on the Union and uncompromising where the IRA were concerned. For Unionists of all persuasions negotiations were a high-risk venture that conceivably could lead to power-sharing and all-Ireland bodies. Moreover, even if the Ulster Unionist Party of James Molyneaux was tempted to make compromises on these matters, it was evident that it would lose ground to the DUP of Ian Paisley. Why not settle for the status quo? Considerations such as these help explain the Unionist preference for stasis in the years 1981–5.

There were, however, certain dangers to this sleepwalking strategy. No British government had any enthusiasm for full integration or for open-ended direct rule or, indeed, for the long-term military engagement that both options appeared to involve. Devolution with some form of power-sharing and with an Irish dimension was the preferred cross-party solution, one to which the electoral rise of Sinn Féin had brought an added urgency. For the British, doing nothing was simply not an option. Moreover, if Unionists refused to engage in meaningful negotiations with the objective of bringing about an acceptable devolved administration in Belfast, there would always be a temptation to go over their heads and come to some arrangement with the Dublin government.

As we have seen, Dublin too had been alarmed by Sinn Féin's electoral surge and this had injected a new momentum into its search for a solution. As yet, there was no interest in talking to that party, for the SDLP remained in its eyes the voice of northern nationalism (and it also had the decency – unlike Sinn Féin – not to organise politically in the Republic). Thus, while the SDLP was invited to take part in the multi-party 'New Ireland Forum' set up by Garret FitzGerald in May 1983 to discuss the way forward, Sinn Féin was firmly excluded. The Forum duly presented its report in May 1984 and, under pressure from Charles

Haughey, expressed a preference for a united Ireland but, failing that, then a federal Ireland of north and south or joint authority between the UK and the Republic might be acceptable. Quite how Unionist consent might be gained for any these options was not addressed. Nationalists were shocked and dismayed when Margaret Thatcher summarily ticked off each of these options with 'out, out, out', and Unionists were gleeful that the 'Iron Lady' had not let them down. Their pleasure was not to last.

For reasons that are not yet wholly clear – Unionists might have suspected post-traumatic stress disorder, for she had narrowly escaped an assassination attempt a few months earlier in Brighton – in May 1985 Margaret Thatcher agreed with Garret FitzGerald that something had to be done on Northern Ireland, and that Unionists should be put under pressure to enter into meaningful negotiations. She was, in addition, persuaded that a bilateral treaty between the UK and the Republic offered every chance of a major security dividend in terms of southern cooperation in the pursuit of the IRA. Irish diplomats who had 'dined for Ireland' for a considerable length of time (and who had put their livers at risk in wooing influential players in the British media and establishment) had every reason to feel pleased with themselves. The result was the Anglo-Irish Agreement, signed at Hillsborough Castle, county Down, in November 1985. This international treaty embodied three key points. First, the Irish government was given a consultative role in various elements of the government of Northern Ireland, and was to have a permanent presence there. Second, there was a clear recognition that no change could take place in the status of Northern Ireland without the consent of the majority of its people. And lastly, Britain declared that it would not impede a united Ireland if a majority in Northern Ireland wanted it.

By any standards, this was a significant advance for the Irish Republic and for northern nationalists, for the Agreement was a clear and definitive confirmation of the need for an Irish dimension in any future constitutional settlement. A team of Irish diplomats and civil servants was to be based at Maryfield, near Belfast – because of the tight security around the complex, it was quickly dubbed 'the Bunker' by those working in it – where they would consider and review progress on various cross-border issues, including security, human rights and matters to do with rival British and Irish identities. For Unionists, this was by far the most hated feature of the Agreement and they regarded an Irish government presence in Belfast as a huge step on the road to a united Ireland. Again, Britain's blunt declaration of neutrality on, or indifference to, the future unification of Ireland was a major blow to Unionist *amour-propre*; the lovelessness of the current Union could not be made clearer. Finally, the assertion that there could be no change in the status quo without the consent of the majority was little more than a restatement of the current agreed position, and was not at all an adequate compensation.

Apart from gaining closer security cooperation from the Republic, a point which weighed heavily with Thatcher, British officials appeared to have seen the Agreement as a way to encourage Unionists to begin serious negotiations leading to the setting up of an agreed executive. If this was the case, they were to be sorely disappointed, for Unionist reaction to the Agreement was one of unbridled fury at what they regarded as a gross betrayal. There was further outrage that the negotiations leading up to the Agreement had been kept entirely secret from them, while the SDLP had been well briefed by Dublin. Nothing had prepared Unionism for this disaster: and all energies would henceforth be directed towards making it clear that 'Ulster says NO' to the Anglo-Irish Agreement (figure 7.14).

A few days after the signing, up to two hundred thousand angry Unionists demonstrated at the City Hall in Belfast. All fifteen Unionist Members at Westminster promptly resigned their seats with a view to turning the ensuing by-elections into a referendum on the Agreement. (Over 400,000 votes were duly garnered in the ensuing by-elections by anti-Agreement parties.) In March 1986, a 'day of action' was held which saw a more or less complete shutdown of industry and business life in Northern Ireland. Serious rioting directed at the RUC followed these protests, and scores of police families were forced to move home because of intimidation. Loyalist paramilitaries became far more active and, as usual when the constitutional position seemed in danger, there was an increase in the number of Catholics killed by them: by the early 1990s loyalist paramilitaries were out-murdering the IRA. Some Unionist politicians even began to flirt with paramilitarism: Paisley and his deputy, Peter Robinson, formed 'Ulster Resistance', the members of which wore rather fetching red berets and, at their parades, sported gun licences as a sign of their capacity and resolve. In August 1986 Robinson headed a short-lived 'invasion of Clontibret' in county Monaghan, for which he was duly punished by a court fine and ridicule.

These protests produced no concessions from the British government. Margaret Thatcher, famously, was 'not for turning' on this or, indeed, any other issue and the loathed Agreement remained in place. These were dark days for Unionism, not only because of the Agreement, but because there appeared to be a more general tide running in favour of nationalists. It was unsettling that the percentage of Catholics as a proportion of the population in Northern Ireland had risen from 35 per cent to 40 per cent by the later 1980s, and that Belfast was on its way to becoming a Catholic city: it acquired its first nationalist lord mayor in June 1997. Again, new anti-discrimination measures were in place, and there was a firm emphasis on fair employment practices: both of these were widely perceived by Unionists as disproportionately benefiting nationalists. It was also widely believed by Protestants that Catholic areas were attracting far greater government funding than Protestant ones for social regeneration and material

7.14 Not for turning? Democratic Unionist Peter Robinson, in 2008 first minister in a power-sharing executive with Sinn Féin, protests at the Anglo-Irish Agreement of 1985. Irish Photographic Archive.

improvement. Moreover, the banning of a controversial Orange parade in Portadown in March 1986, and the firmness with which the RUC dealt with the resulting protests, were also rather disorienting. With the Agreement still in place after years of protest, and the introduction of unwelcome employment guidelines and other changes to the political landscape, there was a palpable sense among Unionists that nationalists were 'winning'.

Unionist jitters further increased in the early months of 1988 when news broke that a series of secret talks had been held between John Hume and Gerry Adams, the respective leaders of the SDLP and Sinn Féin. The purpose of these talks was to ascertain Sinn Féin's thinking on the national question in the wake of the Anglo-Irish Agreement. Hume was to dominate the nationalist agenda for the next twenty years. Though very repetitious, he had the vision to see that without Sinn Féin no agreement could last. Sinn Féin had rejected the Agreement outright: it never did have much time for what it saw as an artificial majority on the island of Ireland having a veto over unification. None the less, Gerry Adams, with Martin McGuinness, recognised that it might be worth exploring the possibility of making advances in a peaceful (and piecemeal) way. Adams especially was keen to interrogate the British government's declaration that it would not stand in the way of a united Ireland. Could the British government be brought to promote this outcome, to persuade Unionists that Irish unification was the way forward, and to issue a declaration to that effect? Already in 1986 Sinn Féin had reversed its policy on Dáil membership and had decided that its elected members would take their seats rather than abstain. (This decision prompted a walk-out of those opposed to it who then set up Republican Sinn Féin.) The Hume–Adams talks dragged on over the early months of 1988 and while they appeared to be unproductive, they did mark a further advance for Sinn Féin along the constitutional path.

By 1990, then, Unionist protests against the Anglo-Irish Agreement had achieved little, the Hume–Adams talks had apparently led to nothing, and 'talks about talks', sponsored by the British government, between the main constitutional parties in Northern Ireland seemed to have failed. Before she was replaced by John Major in November 1990, even Margaret Thatcher had complained that the Agreement had not delivered the anticipated security dividend. If anything, matters were worse than in 1985, for a bloody stalemate had resumed in the 'Troubles', and what were euphemistically known as 'community relations' were probably at an all-time low. Loyalist murder gangs had upped their kills from around eight per annum in the years preceding the Anglo-Irish Agreement, to eighteen in the period 1986–90, and the IRA remained formidable despite reverses. In May 1987 eight members of the East Tyrone brigade of the IRA were shot by the SAS in Loughgall, county Armagh; but in November of that year, eleven Protestants were blown up by an IRA bomb at a Remembrance Day commemoration in Enniskillen, county Fermanagh. In March 1988, three members of the IRA were shot by an SAS unit in Gibraltar, but in August of that year, eight soldiers were blown up at Ballygawley, county Tyrone, and in September 1989, a further ten were killed at a Marines' barracks in Deal, Kent. In July 1990, Ian Gow, a prominent Conservative-Unionist Member of Parliament and an outspoken opponent of the Agreement, was assassinated by the IRA. All in all, the IRA, boosted by the arrival of large weapon consignments from its gallant ally, Libya, and much more tightly organised in small cells, looked as if it could maintain its 'armed struggle' indefinitely. British army intelligence tended to agree, and the Secretary of State for Northern Ireland, Peter Brooke, to the dismay of Unionists, admitted in 1990 that it was difficult to 'envisage the defeat of the IRA'.

Further talks between the constitutional parties resumed in 1991–2 and focused on three areas or 'strands': the first was relationships within Northern Ireland, the second was relationships on the island of Ireland, and the third was the relationships between the United Kingdom and the Republic of Ireland. This time, however, there was a new context to these discussions in that the collapse of communism in eastern Europe and the bringing down of the Berlin Wall had changed the international scene out of all recognition. In the first instance, the ending of the Cold War confirmed the British government's insistence that it had no long-term strategic interest in Ireland and that, in effect, it could not care less if that country became another Cuba, for there was now no USSR to station nuclear missiles there.

And second, the fall of the communist empire raised the possibility of the United States becoming more involved, even seeking a role, in settling the Irish question. Successive American governments had previously refused to intervene in what was officially regarded as an internal British matter. (A possible exception to this was Ronald Reagan's encouragement to Thatcher to proceed with what later became the Anglo-Irish Agreement in 1985. He did so, allegedly, in return for senior Democrats in the Senate going easy on his administration's conduct over Nicaragua.) Given Britain's importance as a vital diplomatic and military ally in the Cold War, no US government could seriously risk damaging its 'special relationship' with that country by meddling in Irish affairs. In general, the British view of the conflict was accepted by Washington, and US law-enforcement agencies had frequently sought to intercept arms shipments destined for Ireland and to curtail fund-raising for the IRA, deemed a terrorist organisation by the State Department. Again, since 1974 no visas had been issued to members of Sinn Féin or the IRA. From 1990 on, however, the United States was the only superpower on the planet, and the British alliance and British goodwill were no longer quite so essential. In addition, there was pressure from a powerful group of Democratic senators, headed by Edward Kennedy, who urged the United States government to help move matters along in Ireland. The 1992 election of President Bill Clinton, a Democrat with Irish roots, and keen to capture the Irish American vote, gave them a chance to exert leverage to bring about a peace settlement.

It was a daunting prospect, for the IRA and loyalist paramilitaries enjoyed – if that is the word – a killing spree in the years 1990 to 1994 that recalled the worst days of the 1970s. In February 1991, there was an IRA mortar attack on Downing Street, and a year later, eight Protestant workmen were killed at Teebane in county Tyrone. In revenge, a gun attack on a bookmaker's premises in Belfast left five Catholics dead. In April 1992 the heart was torn out of London's financial district when the Baltic Exchange was targeted in a massive blast. According to one estimate, the cost of the damage caused in this one bomb attack – in excess of £800 million – might have equalled or exceeded all the insurance paid out in 'Troubles'-related bombings in Northern Ireland since 1970. Further bombings causing destruction and casualties in Britain took place at Warrington and in London – at the NatWest Tower – in the spring of 1993. The nadir was reached in the bombing of Frizzell's fish shop on the Shankill Road, Belfast, in October 1993: nine Protestant customers died and scores of passersby were injured. Retaliatory attacks on Catholics left eleven dead, and the chilling statistic emerged that deaths from paramilitary violence in October 1993 (twenty-seven people murdered) had not been matched in a single month since the bad days of 1976. The only consolation – and it was a slim one – was the realisation on all sides that such pointless, retaliatory violence had to be brought to an end. War-weariness had finally begun to set in; but how to bring the war to a close?

This question was to dominate the period between 1992 and 1998. Further talks were held between Hume and Adams in the spring of 1993 and continued despite IRA killings. In August 1993 the two leaders released a statement in which they reaffirmed that any solution must be on an all-Ireland basis, that an internal arrangement for Northern Ireland on its own was not acceptable, and that 'all the people of Ireland' must have a say in the final outcome. This ambiguous formula might just offer the IRA the opportunity to come in from the cold. There was further pressure from Albert Reynolds of Fianna Fáil who had become Taoiseach in a Fianna Fáil–Labour Party coalition in January 1993. Largely unencumbered by republican ideology, he approached the northern 'Troubles' with a business-like briskness that was refreshing, and he had placed the quest for a settlement in Northern Ireland high on his agenda. Discussions with John Major, Thatcher's successor, culminated in the Downing Street Declaration of 15 December 1993 in which Britain reaffirmed that it had no 'selfish strategic or economic interest in Northern Ireland', stated that all it wanted was peace and reconciliation there, and declared its role to be essentially that of a facilitator in that process. For his part, Reynolds ruled out any attempt to impose a united Ireland against the wishes of the majority of Northern Ireland. In addition, and very significantly, in the event of an overall settlement, he made a commitment to hold a referendum on scrapping articles 2 and 3 of the Irish Constitution. These articles claiming ownership and jurisdiction over Northern Ireland by the Republic were particularly offensive to Unionists and were regarded by some of them as a foundation charter for the Provisional IRA.

Reaction to the Declaration was mixed. Unionists were predictably uneasy at Dublin–London talks, and suspected that there was a hidden agenda to the whole document. Moreover, since it did not appear to mark a step back from the hated Anglo-Irish Agreement, they were not at all in favour. Nor were the IRA much impressed with this Declaration: Britain had still not agreed to be a 'persuader' for unity, nor had it rejected any political interest (as opposed to economic or strategic) in Northern Ireland. Still, there was enough in it for Gerry Adams to continue the process of dialogue in order to ascertain whether strategic gains could be made if republicans replaced armed struggle with unarmed struggle.

To help matters along, the republican movement was offered some significant sweeteners. Already, an internment commemoration rally had been held at Belfast City Hall in August 1993 (possibly the first-ever republican demonstration on what had always been hallowed ground for Unionists), and in January of the following year, the ban on Sinn Féin spokesmen appearing or speaking on RTÉ radio and television was lifted. Much more sensationally, however, in the teeth of British protests and on President Clinton's direct order, a US visitor's visa was issued to Gerry Adams. (Clinton was later to claim that this visa was crucial in prompting the IRA declaration of a ceasefire in August that year.) His action in defying the British (and his own State Department) signalled very clearly that he would be his own man where 'Britain's Irish problem' was concerned, and that the 'Troubles' had just been internationalised. The IRA was impressed: a new player and a real 'persuader' had appeared on the scene. On 31 August 1994, it issued a statement declaring its commitment to 'the democratic peace process', and announcing that from midnight that day there would be 'a complete cessation of military operations'. The 'Long War' was over, and the 'Long Negotiation' had now begun.

Endgame

David Trimble, soon to be leader of the Ulster Unionists, later described the IRA ceasefire as 'the event which has caused the greatest problem to Unionists in recent years', and it was easy to see why. The near-euphoria in republican strongholds and the triumphant motorcades that followed on the announcement of a ceasefire, instantly raised Unionist fears that some dangerous, secret deal had been done between the British government and the IRA. More particularly, there was a real vagueness about the IRA declaration that brought forward Unionist protests and prompted calls for urgent clarification. The IRA's ceasefire statement had not mentioned the word 'permanent', nor was there any indication as to what would become of its arsenal of weapons and explosives, nor of what would become of the IRA itself. If its ceasefire was in fact permanent, then why would the IRA continue to hold on to its weapons? Why would it continue to exist? Predictably, neither the IRA nor Sinn Féin was about to help out Major, Paisley or Trimble on this one; the republican movement had spoken and that must be sufficient. The response of the Unionists and the government of John Major was that until the ceasefire was guaranteed 'permanent' – that word was fetishised – and until weapons were verifiably decommissioned, then Sinn Féin could not be admitted to any talks process. A loyalist paramilitary ceasefire, declared six weeks after the IRA's cessation, did little to calm nerves. Stalemate had set in.

The dangers in permitting drift were demonstrated in July 1995 when very serious disturbances took place following the refusal of permission for an Orange procession to march along a nationalist area at Drumcree, near Portadown, county Armagh. The Orangemen were eventually allowed to parade along their 'traditional' route, but only after Northern Ireland had been brought to a near-standstill through violence, riots and blocked roads. David Trimble and Ian Paisley shared the laurels of this Orange victory, filmed arm-in-arm dancing down the Garvaghy Road, the contested route. Trimble's reward was to replace the ineffective James Molyneaux as leader of the Ulster Unionist Party in September 1995.

The terminally uncharismatic Molyneaux had been much influenced by Enoch Powell, an antique Conservative who had, it seemed, never quite forgiven himself for missing the Home Rule crisis of 1886. He had relocated from his Wolverhampton constituency to South Down in 1974 in order to fight the Unionist cause. Both men had been convinced integrationists, and Molyneaux (like Redmond) had naively believed that he had a certain 'understanding' with senior Conservatives, one that was uniquely advantageous to Unionism. The hollowness of this vaunted 'special relationship' had been exposed at various times by the Anglo-Irish Agreement, the Downing Street Declaration, the British commitment to devolution and, equally, by Britain's continuing recognition of a role for Dublin in any future structures. Molyneaux, the integrationist, had to go.

His surprise successor was Trimble, the hero of Garvaghy Road. He was an altogether different proposition from Molyneaux, for he had never deviated from his conviction that devolution was the only way to preserve the Union with Britain and save Northern Ireland from the sweaty embrace of the Irish Republic. Ulster Unionists chose him as leader because he appeared to be the sort of intelligent, politically savvy, tough-minded, blunt-speaking operator required to take on Sinn Féin and the SDLP. Perhaps as important, as a result of his conduct on the Garvaghy Road, he now had credibility with hard-line Unionist voters who, fearful of the turn of events, had been deserting the party and turning to the militant Ian Paisley and his DUP. Trimble was therefore well equipped to take the fight to the enemy, without or within the Unionist community, but whether he would prove to be a leader or a tribune remained to be seen.

Trimble's chances of making an impact were aided by the very uncertain political situation in London. Major's Conservative government was beginning to disintegrate as scandal followed scandal, and as his parliamentary majority ebbed away increasingly he had to rely on the backing of Ulster Unionist Members to remain in power. Their support came with a price, one which Major was quite prepared to pay. Accordingly, he swiftly vetoed the SDLP's proposal of joint authority between London and Dublin, and he appeared firm on the need for decommissioning of weapons and explosives before Sinn Féin could be admitted to any talks. He was also adamant that no solution could be imposed and that any final agreement had to be subject to a referendum in Northern Ireland. To the IRA, this all sounded as if the Unionist veto over constitutional change was still very much in place and its impatience grew. The publication of two British and Irish government 'framework' documents in February 1995, one of which sketched in future north–south bodies while the other stressed the need for recognition of an 'Irish' identity in Northern Ireland, did little to assuage growing republican anger and frustration.

From the time of the ceasefire, the IRA's strategy had been to raise national consciousness in the Republic, to do the same among northern nationalists and to internationalise the struggle – in particular to enlist Irish American support. Little of this appeared to be happening. Admittedly, John Major had appointed a three-man international body, headed by George Mitchell, a former United States senator, to advise on decommissioning. The Mitchell report duly maintained that there could be no giving up of weapons before talks. Instead, any such decommissioning would accompany talks. Only Sinn Féin and the SDLP were pleased at this solution, Trimble and Paisley with varying degrees of intensity were opposed, while John Major very reluctantly accepted it. A visit by Bill Clinton to Ireland, north and south, was scheduled for November 1995 in order for the president to lend his weight to the peace process. However, little of this appears to have had much impression on the IRA who now regarded Major as either a puppet or a prisoner of the Unionists. As a result, sometime in December 1995, perhaps earlier, IRA leaders had taken a fateful decision to end the ceasefire. On 9 February 1996, a massive bomb exploded at Canary Wharf in London killing two people and causing damage estimated at £85 million.

It was a reflection of the gravity of the issues at stake and of the determination of the people involved that this explosion did not derail the search for a settlement. Every effort was made to maintain the momentum. Even the IRA did not follow up the Canary Wharf bomb with a sustained campaign as if indicating that, despite the ending of its ceasefire, it had not fully abandoned faith in the 'peace process'. Still, there were further explosions, notably in the centre of Manchester, which caused huge damage in June 1996, and an IRA sniper gang operating in south Armagh throughout 1996–7 notched up a number of security force 'kills', including Private Stephen Restorick, shot in February 1997, and the last British soldier to die in the 'Troubles'. (A further two British soldiers and a policeman were killed by republican dissidents on 9 March 2009.) On the other hand, when serious rioting broke out at the annual Orange parade at Drumcree in July 1996 and the British army and RUC acted heavy-handedly and disproportionately against Catholic rioters, the IRA hung back from armed retaliation. In the event the RUC once again decided to force the Orange parade along the Garvaghy Road and this led to angry protests by the SDLP and their swift withdrawal from all-party talks. These talks had been scheduled in February 1996 to take place in June, and had gone ahead as planned. The constitutional parties had roundly condemned the ending of the IRA ceasefire but had agreed that, notwithstanding, they would enter into negotiations without waiting for Sinn Féin. However, with the SDLP walk-out in the aftermath of the Drumcree riots, these talks were effectively stalled, and as Major's government lurched from crisis to crisis, the impetus behind the peace process slackened appreciably.

Fresh pressure came from London, Dublin and Washington in the new year. The general election in Britain in May 1997 resulted in a Labour landslide, and Tony Blair became prime minister. He had identified a peace settlement in Northern Ireland as a key objective and he was keen to involve President Clinton in that goal. In June 1997 a Fianna Fáil–Progressive Democrat coalition led by Bertie Ahern came to power in the Republic. Ahern possessed infinite patience and was an expert fixer and negotiator. Like his predecessor, Reynolds, he had few, if any, hang-ups about republicanism or Irish unification. He, too, put Northern Ireland and the peace process at the top of his list of priorities and, like Blair, he was anxious to involve Clinton. These three – Blair, Ahern, Clinton – together determined to press ahead with new talks and to that end certain reassurances were apparently given to Gerry Adams and Martin McGuinness, the leaders of the Sinn Féin negotiating team, for them to pass on to the IRA. At any rate, despite the by-now 'traditional' rioting at Drumcree, and the usual RUC capitulation to the Orangemen demanding to parade along their 'traditional' route, the IRA on 19 July 1997 announced the resumption of its ceasefire. Sinn Féin was brought into preliminary talks after six weeks 'quarantine', with the understanding that they would be involved in more substantive talks in September. The DUP promptly walked out, loudly protesting that neither a bullet nor an ounce of explosive had been put beyond use by republican paramilitaries, that the IRA had not been stood down and that Sinn Féin had been 'decontaminated' with indecent haste. However, Trimble and his team remained, perhaps calculating that if they left, a settlement that was not at all to their liking might be imposed on them by London and Dublin acting in concert and supported by Washington. They may also have realised that the tide of history – loosely stated, Catholic demographic growth, Protestant flight from Ulster and a changing international context – was creating an unfavourable conjuncture for Unionism. In Trimble's view, talks leading to an agreed settlement offered Unionism its best chance to influence decisively the final outcome.

The discussions that ensued were dominated by John Hume of the SDLP and David Trimble of the Ulster Unionist Party. Sinn Féin, to its chagrin, and the other tiny parties – the Women's Coalition, the Alliance Party and various loyalist fringe groups – had little input into the substantive talks. From time to time, Blair and Ahern intervened to move matters along and so too did Clinton, but police reform, decommissioning of IRA weapons, the early release of 'political' prisoners and parity of esteem for Irish and British identities remained huge sticking points. Eventually, some seventeen hours beyond the deadline fixed for the talks, the drawn out negotiations came to an end and agreement was reached at 5 pm on Good Friday, 10 April 1998.

Essentially, what had been agreed was a power-sharing arrangement that gave the representatives of each community a veto over the other. The whole structure would be overseen by a newly styled first minister and deputy first minister, one drawn from each community according to voting strength in a new devolved Assembly in which all legislation would require a 60 per cent approval. There would be no Cabinet as such, but the actions and performance of individual ministers – to be appointed according to their party strength in the Assembly – would be scrutinised by cross-party subcommittees. A British secretary of state would remain, and significantly Britain would retain responsibility for law and order. It had not proved possible to reach agreement on policing during the marathon negotiations, but the British hope was that eventually responsibility for this could be devolved to the Assembly. Various north–south bodies were to be set up with power to address cross-border matters, including tourism, transport, education, health and the environment, and these were to be subject to the Assembly and to the Dáil.

Additional aspects included the release of all paramilitary prisoners within two years if their organisations remained on ceasefire, though they stayed subject to recall to serve their sentences if they reoffended. A commitment to further strengthen fair employment and anti-discrimination legislation was given. There was also an important cultural dimension to the Good Friday Agreement. The position of the Irish language in Northern Ireland was to be enhanced, and so too was that of Ulster Scots, a dialect now elevated to the status of a language in order to balance any gains for Irish. 'Parity of esteem' was the stated goal for all symbols, identifiers and cultural markers. Lastly, the Republic agreed to submit the offending articles 2 and 3 of its Constitution to a referendum, and Britain agreed that the Anglo-Irish Agreement – still detested by Unionists – would be jettisoned and replaced by a British-Irish Agreement, which would underpin a British-Irish Council involving representatives from all the assemblies in the British Isles. Such a body was much favoured by Unionists as a counterweight to Irish nationalism. And, as before, it was reiterated that there could be no change in the constitutional position of Northern Ireland without the consent of the majority.

So, who won? Seamas Mallon of the SDLP, soon to be deputy first minister (John Hume preferred to devote his energies to international affairs), famously remarked that the Good Friday Agreement was 'Sunningdale for slow learners'. By this he meant that the central ingredients of the 1998 Agreement had been in place in 1974, and that the Unionist community in rejecting Sunningdale had, in effect, condemned Northern Ireland to nearly twenty-five years of turmoil. There was something in this verdict: certainly, the key elements in the Good Friday Agreement – power-sharing and a north–south dimension – had been present in Sunningdale; but Mallon's *bon mot* was not the whole of the matter. The IRA, after all, had flatly rejected Sunningdale. At best, it had regarded it as a first instalment, and it was determined to continue its war to win further concessions until its ultimate goal was achieved. It is highly unlikely that Sunningdale could have delivered peace, for war-readiness and war-willingness were too dominant in 1974. By contrast, the Good Friday Agreement was signed when the IRA and loyalist paramilitaries were on ceasefire, and war-weariness was near universal among all sections of the population, except for a handful of diehards on both sides. Again, the north–south bodies in the Good Friday Agreement were subject to an Assembly veto, and were firmly counterbalanced by the east–west British-Irish council. For Unionists, the Good Friday Agreement was a significant advance on Sunningdale, though as many as half did not see it that way. Particularly galling for Unionists was the early release of 'terrorists' (republican or loyalist, it was all the one to them), and loose talk about restructuring and rebranding the RUC was deeply unsettling. Nationalist jubilation was also disturbing: if 'they' were so pleased, then 'we' must have lost.

The Ulster Unionist Party, with some heart-searching, voted to support the Agreement and endorsed the leadership of David Trimble. Sinn Féin at a special

Ard Fhéis (=plenary conference) voted in favour, and so too did the SDLP. Predictably, Paisley rejected the Agreement outright, though he announced that DUP assemblymen would take their places on any executive set up under it. Paisley went on to berate Trimble as a sell-out traitor to Unionism; but he was on firmer ground in pointing out that the IRA had not given up any weapons or explosives, and that it remained in existence as the avowed military wing of Sinn Féin. Just as de Valera had rejected the Treaty of 1921, so too Paisley rejected the Good Friday Agreement because it was not *his* agreement, for he had played no part in negotiating it. Some eight years later, however, he was to settle for something – the St Andrews Agreement – that was not significantly different.

Popular endorsement was secured on 22 May 1998 when referendums on the Agreement were held simultaneously in Northern Ireland and in the Republic. The result was a massive vote in favour, with 71 per cent of the northern electorate and a North Korean-style 94 per cent of southern voters giving their approval. The northern 'yes' vote was heavily boosted by nationalists, for Unionists approved by 'only' 55 per cent. Southern voters had also agreed to remove articles 2 and 3 from the Irish Constitution and so to embrace twenty-six-county nationalism; the historic goal of uniting Ireland was finally interred. In October 1998 Trimble and Hume were jointly awarded the Nobel Peace Prize. A few months earlier, they had appeared on the stage at a U2 concert in Belfast. Could things get any better? Was the war finally over? Had Irish history come to an end?

The failure of the Good Friday Agreement

The short answer is that it had not, and those who expected that the Good Friday Agreement would mark the end of the conflict were proved wrong. Agreement might have been achieved but implementing that agreement would prove a daunting, frustrating and, above all, time-consuming task. Certainly, armed hostilities did not resume and the body count would stay low, but twelve years on, few could be confident that the Good Friday Agreement, as amended by the St Andrews Agreement of October 2006, had finally bedded down.

There are a number of reasons why the implementation of the Good Friday Agreement proved so elusive, and why it was to take eight years of further negotiation to bring about a devolved power-sharing executive that might just have a chance of surviving beyond a few months. In the first instance, the Agreement had been deliberately vague on a number of key issues, notably the decommissioning of IRA weapons, but also the early release of 'political' prisoners and the whole question of policing. What Jonathan Powell, the British government's chief negotiator, described as 'constructive ambiguity' enshrouded these matters.

Such opacity was probably necessary to secure a deal but when it came to implementation, the resolution of issues such as these would pose huge challenges. Above all, the key issue in Unionist eyes – the absolute necessity for the decommissioning of IRA weapons before a power-sharing executive could be set up – had been skirted during the negotiations leading to the Good Friday Agreement. Resolving that momentous issue would prove very difficult not only because of the sensitivity of the matter, but because Trimble up to the time of the Agreement had never sat down face to face with Gerry Adams or Martin McGuinness. He had never even spoken to either of them.

Second, Adams for Sinn Féin and Trimble for the Ulster Unionist Party, were keen students of Irish history (and, possibly, Shakespeare) and were both well aware of the toxic fall-out from previous agreements concluded with the British government. Gerry Adams was mindful that the IRA had torn itself apart over whether to accept or reject the 1921 Treaty, with Michael Collins himself falling victim in that contest. Adams was determined not to let history – as he saw it – repeat itself. More recently, David Trimble had played a major role in the overthrow of Brian Faulkner who had put his name to the Sunningdale Agreement, and he was equally anxious to avoid a similar fate. Neither leader, therefore, could, or would, move ahead of their natural supporters. This shared predicament, however, concealed some fundamental differences in the respective positions of Adams and Trimble, and these were ultimately to prove decisive for the latter's failure.

Adams was in fact immeasurably stronger than Trimble, for he was a natural politician and man-manager, who at every stage had taken great care to bring influential figures – the republican 'First Eleven' – along with him. Martin McGuinness, sometime commander of the IRA in Derry, was constantly at his side. Brian Keenan, the mastermind of the bombing campaign in Britain for which he had served many years in prison, and an iconic hard man in the Provisional IRA, was firmly in Adams's camp. And so too were Joe Cahill, an IRA activist since the 1930s and a notorious gun-runner, and Gerry Kelly, a London bomber and IRA escaper, whose support for Adams and the peace process never wavered. By keeping such men – and others like them – close to him, Adams ensured that when the inevitable split did come – in May 1998, a splinter group calling itself the Real IRA was set up – it would not be nearly as disruptive or numerically as significant as that of 1922. Also, the SDLP, although sometimes exasperated by being kept in the dark about talks between Sinn Féin and the British government, was not prepared to split the nationalist movement by moving on without Sinn Féin. Adams would face little opposition from that quarter.

By contrast, Trimble was at all times faced with a war on two fronts, and he was temperamentally ill suited to conducting either. During the negotiations leading to the Good Friday Agreement, Jeffrey Donaldson, an articulate and able member of Trimble's team, had walked out in protest and eventually defected to the DUP in 2003. In the intervening five years, however, he remained a member of the Ulster Unionist Party and from within its ranks he waged a relentless and unremitting guerrilla war against Trimble and his leadership. Trimble took no action to win him over or to silence him. Again, as was predicted, Paisley and the DUP missed no opportunity to vilify Trimble in the harshest language and accuse him of outright treachery. Beset from within the Ulster Unionist Party by hostile critics and besieged from without by those bent on destroying the party, Trimble could deploy few political skills with which to out-fox, let alone overcome his opponents. He had a volatile, even choleric, personality which was unfortunately allied to an unforgiving nature – he could probably have brought Donaldson back on board had he tried. Notoriously, he possessed a capacity for rudeness that left opponents furious and onlookers gasping in disbelief. Such traits were scarcely calculated to elicit sympathy or help move matters along.

And yet Trimble was not unintelligent and, as noted, he had closely studied Irish history, and in Sean O'Callaghan, an IRA killer-turned-police informer-turned-Trimble adviser, he had an expert to hand on IRA thinking. Could it be that when signing up to the Good Friday Agreement, Trimble had done so in the expectation that it would completely split the republican movement as the Treaty had in 1922? And that when this did not happen he was at a loss to know how to proceed? Perhaps: none the less, 'saving David Trimble' – a determination to preserve him as leader of a united party – remained central to the British government's strategy in negotiations over the implementation of the Good Friday Agreement. By the time the realisation hit home that Trimble's career could not be salvaged, and that his party was on the way out, years had been spent in futile and fruitless talks.

It would be wrong, however, to place all the blame for the eight-year stalemate that ensued once the Good Friday Agreement was signed on the rebarbative personality of Trimble, the silky evasions of Adams and on the imbalance in the opposition they faced. The IRA certainly did not help matters by stringing out its movement towards decommissioning. It pointed out that it was not a signatory to the Good Friday Agreement. It was adamant that putting its weaponry beyond use and curtailing punishment beatings and other criminal acts carried out by its members must not be construed as the actions of a defeated army or those of a surrendered foe. Equally, it was not about to be dictated to by David Trimble. Hence, the timing of decommissioning, the precise details of that exercise and the proof that it had happened were all hugely sensitive matters. Undoubtedly, the IRA could have timed its decommissioning to help Trimble politically, and it could have permitted General John de Chastelain, the Canadian expert eventually in charge of that exercise, to have been more forthcoming on what weapons and explosives he had seen destroyed, and this too might have assisted Trimble in his war with Donaldson and Paisley. A few photographs or, better, a video of IRA guns going up in smoke or being entombed in concrete might have helped steady Unionist nerves and enabled Trimble to see off his critics and remain the leader of Unionism. None of this was to happen: the IRA worked to its own schedule on decommissioning, it devised its own wording in explaining its actions and it remained steadfast in its refusal to allow any photographic record of what had happened. The last act of decommissioning took place in September 2005, by which date David Trimble and the Ulster Unionist Party had been overtaken by Ian Paisley and the DUP as the largest Unionist party.

In retrospect, it had probably been a mistake for Trimble to place such an emphasis on IRA decommissioning in advance of the establishment of a power-sharing executive. As most informed observers had noted, at the turn of the new century Europe was awash with weaponry – whether detritus from the Balkan wars, surplus from the various Middle East conflicts or as a result of the implosion of the Russian empire – and therefore, while the IRA could indeed have made a very public bonfire of its rifles, its pistols and its semtex, it could have gone on to replace them in a matter of months. Moreover, as was frequently pointed out, in other conflicts weapons decommissioning had usually proceeded alongside or even after agreement on government had been reached; it was rarely insisted on as a pre-condition. Trimble, however, dug his heels in on this issue. In fairness, even if he had wanted to step back, his critics within the Ulster Unionist Party would have been merciless in denouncing him. When in November 1999 – fully eighteen months after the Good Friday Agreement – he did enter into a short-lived power-sharing executive with Seamus Mallon of the SDLP as deputy minister, he had insisted on submitting a postdated resignation letter to be activated if the IRA failed to decommission within three months. Any such attempt by Trimble to dictate a timetable to the IRA was doomed to failure, and his resignation letter was duly delivered in February 2000. It was long evident that to secure his position Trimble needed a symbolic and public act of weapon destruction. He well knew (and so too did the IRA and Adams and everyone else, except the British government) that in Ireland the 'symbolics' were just as important as the realities. In the end, this is why the IRA denied him.

Events, too, as British premier Harold Macmillan had noted in another context, conspired against a speedy resolution of the difficult problems left unresolved by the Good Friday Agreement. From a Unionist standpoint, perhaps the most disquieting – certainly the earliest – of these was the parading of four members of the IRA cell known as the Balcombe Street gang before an adoring audience of delegates at a Sinn Féin *Ard Fhéis* in May 1998, barely a month after

the Good Friday Agreement. The four men had been imprisoned for their bombing campaign in London in the 1970s, subsequently transferred to the Republic
to serve their sentences and were now newly released. They received a ten-minute
standing ovation. Ten years on, Trimble recalled that very public adulation of
convicted terrorists as a pivotal moment after which things rapidly began to go
south – so to speak – for him.

Further shocks were to come. The annual Drumcree stand-off was approaching, but this time there was a difference. An independent Parades' Commission
had been appointed earlier in the year with a remit to approve, alter or disallow
the routes to be taken by all marchers in Northern Ireland. This was precisely
the sort of body that stoked Unionists' fears of a sell-out or betrayal of their heritage. It came as no surprise to them when the Commission refused to allow the
Orangemen's return march from Drumcree church to proceed along the nationalist Garvaghy Road. It did, however, come as a major shock to the Orange
Order when the RUC, backed up by elements of the British army, made it clear
that this time they had every intention of upholding a ban on the march along the
contested route. The ensuing mayhem in early July 1998 throughout Northern
Ireland had not been equalled in its intensity since the street protests of the early
1970s: hundreds of shootings, fire-bombings and roadblocks left the province
paralysed and the RUC reeling but, crucially, not intimidated into surrender.
The nadir was reached with the fire-bombing of a Catholic home in Ballymoney,
county Antrim, which caused the deaths of three children from the Quinn family.
An attempt by a DUP figure to claim that the fire was started by an estranged
family member was quickly squashed: and the sole sliver of silver lining from the
horror was the decision by the Orange Order, supported by Trimble, to call off
the Drumcree protest and to wind down the siege there.

The Orange Order had learned the hard way that there were unspeakable
furies at work in Northern Ireland; unfortunately, the newly formed Real IRA
had yet to take on board that lesson. On 15 August 1998, a Real IRA car-bomb
exploded in Omagh, county Tyrone, killing twenty-nine and injuring scores,
many horrifically. It was the single deadliest blast in thirty years of the 'Troubles'.
The dreadful carnage was not the objective aimed at, though it would always
remain unclear how any political goal could have been furthered by blowing
the heart out of a modest market town in central Ulster. The Real IRA quickly
announced that it was declaring a ceasefire; yet another high-priced sliver of
silver among the charred corpses and blasted lives. The Real IRA subsequently
abandoned its ceasefire, and no one was ever convicted for the Omagh bombing.

Throughout 1999 and 2000 the formation of a power-sharing executive continued to be bedevilled by the delay in decommissioning. To the Unionist slogan
of 'no guns, no government', republicans responded with 'not an ounce, not a
bullet'. Various deadlines for decommissioning – in March, May and June 1999 –

came and went, and there were periods of intensive negotiation between all sides, but progress was minimal; and 'events' continued to intrude. In late 1999 the Patten report into the future structure of the RUC was published. It was a further body-blow to Trimble's standing within Unionism and a huge boost for his critics. The proposed make-up of the new force was barely addressed by Unionist critics; instead most attention was to focus on the rebranding of the RUC as the Police Service of Northern Ireland. As always, the symbols mattered more than the details, and the loss of the 'Royal' from its title, along with a new cap badge, were seen by Unionists as a terrible betrayal of a force that had suffered grievously over the previous thirty years; others saw it as a sinister move towards the republicanisation of Northern Ireland.

Republicans, too, were scarcely making things easier for Trimble (or helping the cause of peace) by engaging in a little recreational gun-running into Ireland from Florida. Not only were the IRA not putting their weapons beyond use as promised, Unionists protested, they appeared to be actually restocking. The only consolation for Unionists of all persuasions in the summer and autumn of 1999 was that Mo Mowlam, the feisty Secretary of State for Northern Ireland, was to be replaced by Peter Mandelson. Mowlam had long been regarded by Unionists as too pro-republican in her sympathies, while her unconventional approach to the very conventional male-dominated world of Northern Ireland politics had further grated on Unionist, and some nationalist, sensitivities.

There was a brief flurry of excitement when it was announced that the IRA would embark on decommissioning in November 1999 and as a result Trimble with Seamus Mallon for the SDLP took office as first minister and deputy first minister, respectively. However, the harmony was not to last: Trimble and Mallon were not natural bedfellows and their *connubio* was troubled and strained from the beginning. Further inaction over decommissioning meant that Trimble had little to show for power-sharing, his petulance proved wearing and his standing in Unionism fell sharply. A visit to Ireland by President Clinton in November 2000 failed to speed things up. He was received with enthusiasm everywhere, but Trimble proved immune to his charms, famously leaving midway during the US president's speech for a minor engagement in Palermo, Sicily. In the elections of April/May 2001, the DUP of Paisley replaced the Ulster Unionists of Trimble as the largest party in the Assembly. Trimble's position as first minister was salvaged temporarily through a joint sleight of hand by the moderate Alliance Party and by the Women's Coalition who described themselves as Unionist and backed him. Trimble, however, had been fatally wounded and increasingly British eyes turned to Paisley as the one with whom they would have to do business.

It would be an exaggeration to claim that the Al Qaeda attacks on the World Trade Centre in New York on 11 September 2001 changed utterly the political landscape in Ireland, but there is some suggestion that in the aftermath of that devastation the IRA came to realise that its type of warfare was now wholly outmoded. Flying passenger planes into buildings crammed with office workers made IRA tactics instantly obsolete, while American opinion now turned decisively against all 'terrorists', whether Irish or Islamic. Certainly, within a few weeks the IRA announced that a quantity of its weaponry had been definitively put beyond use. The whole process had been witnessed by the Canadian observer, General John de Chastelain. But it was all a case of 'too little, too late' for David Trimble: Paisley and the DUP were in the ascendant.

A series of IRA 'own goals' completed the destruction of Trimble's position. In August 2001, even before the New York attacks, three prominent members of Sinn Féin had been arrested in Colombia, south America, charged with lending military assistance to the left-wing FARC guerrilla movement. Then in March 2002 there had been a break-in at the notorious Castlereagh police complex on the outskirts of Belfast, and a large number of police records were stolen. Many members of the force, with their families, had to move house, now that their addresses and other vital details were thought to be in the hands of the IRA. Finally, in a well coordinated operation – and one well-leaked to the media – the Sinn Féin offices at Stormont Castle were raided by police in October 2002 and evidence was seized suggesting that senior members of the RUC and British army were being actively targeted for assassination. Republicans denied all involvement in both the Castlereagh break-in and rejected allegations of spying at Stormont. Much remained curious about both these incidents. As a result of these embarrassing developments, the Good Friday Agreement and with it, David Trimble, lost further ground within the Unionist community. It was now clear to all, except perhaps Tony Blair, that Trimble had decisively cut himself off from his party and that he would never be in a position to sell any deal to the wider Unionist community.

Blair, however, remained loyal to Trimble; he refused to countenance any overtures to Paisley, reckoning that he would be even more difficult, if not impossible, to deal with; and he adhered to the policy, long after it became untenable, of supporting Trimble. Throughout these years, Blair kept in constant touch with Bertie Ahern, usually finding time at various European Community summits for a quiet word in the margins, and these brief encounters were crucial in keeping the peace process on track. Nothing, however, could be done for Trimble. In October 2003, de Chastelain gravely informed the world's media that he had witnessed a significant act of decommissioning of IRA weapons, but that he was precluded by what amounted to the seal of the confessional (or of the Provisional) from talking about it. To Unionists who had longed for some public act of repentance by the IRA, or at least some 'Kodak moment', this was wholly unacceptable. Trimble's persistence in dealing with Adams and McGuinness in order to secure decommissioning seemed foolish, naive and reckless. In the November 2003 elections the Ulster Unionist Party took a beating and Trimble's political career was over. The DUP and Sinn Féin emerged as the largest parties in Northern Ireland, and an outcome that the British and Irish governments had sought to avoid for twenty years had finally happened: undoubtedly, the extremes had triumphed, and the moderates of the Ulster Unionist Party and the SDLP had been vanquished. Where now for the Good Friday Agreement?

The St Andrews Agreement

The British and Irish governments' immediate response to the victory of the DUP was to try to cast it as the wrecking ball in Northern Ireland politics, hoping that this would bring it some bad press and publicity and that as a result, the Ulster Unionist Party and Trimble would benefit electorally. A moment's reflection ought to have revealed the bankruptcy of any such strategy. Paisley and the DUP had not climbed to the top of Unionist politics by allowing themselves to be branded by others as *enragés*. And their plan, now that they had the right-wing Unionist constituency (Trimble's one-time supporters) in their camp, was to complete their takeover of Unionism by winning over the more moderate, middle-class (or 'Flymo') vote. 'Wrecking' had served its purpose; it was now to be mothballed. Hence in February 2004, Paisley said that under certain circumstances he would be prepared to share power with republicans. If republicans gave up paramilitarism and if there was some renegotiation of strands 1 and 2 (internal relations in Northern Ireland, and north–south bodies) in the Good Friday Agreement, then a power-sharing government could be established. There was much disbelief in government circles in London and Dublin at the surprisingly moderate stance of the DUP, and large swathes of the wider public were equally incredulous. None the less, the opening had to be pursued. If a deal could be struck then there could be no doubt but that Paisley and his lieutenants, Peter Robinson and Nigel Dodds, would be able to carry their party with them, and thus deliver. For the first time in thirty years, there was no alternative Unionist Party waiting, dagger in hand, in the wings.

An 'away day' of talks was duly held at Leeds Castle in September 2004. Paisley, recently in hospital with a serious illness, took three days to arrive there by ferry and car because he had been told on medical grounds not to take a plane. He was accompanied by no fewer than six DUP negotiators. Some progress was made on decommissioning: independent observers might be accepted by the IRA for purposes of verification, though the DUP were still insisting on photographs. There was some room for manoeuvre here, and overall, though the talks went nowhere on the matter of strands 1 and 2, enough had been done and said to show that the DUP were serious about implementing (albeit with amendments) the Good Friday Agreement. In addition, the IRA appeared to accept that a unilateral destruction of its weaponry, witnessed by de Chastelain and some Northern Ireland clergymen, would be infinitely preferable to anything that looked linked to a Unionist timetable. After the inconclusive and largely futile conferences and meetings held at such stately piles as Hillsborough Castle, Weston Park, Farmleigh and Chequers (and also at more modest establishments such as Clonard monastery and various terraced houses in Derry and Belfast) all of this constituted real progress towards a settlement that could be accepted.

So far so good: but then matters went seriously down hill. First, on his return to his constituency, Paisley reverted to type and sought to reassure his followers by roaring that before they could enter government, republicans had to don 'sackcloth and ashes' to do penance for their past sins. Moreover, there was a further insistence on a photographic record of the destruction of IRA arms; none of this endeared Paisley to Adams or the IRA. Second, a few days before Christmas 2004, the IRA coolly robbed the Northern Bank in Belfast of some £30 million, at that time the largest theft of cash in British, or possibly European history. Then, third, in February 2005, members of the Provisional IRA were accused of murdering Robert McCartney following an altercation in a pub in Belfast. Dramatically, the murdered man's sisters, all members of the republican 'family', turned his death into an international incident, engaging the support of Tony Blair and President George W. Bush (2001–9) in their campaign to bring the killers to justice. Paisley's speech/sermon, the Northern Bank heist and the McCartney slaying were to set back the peace process by a year. Unionists, in particular, could not see how any confidence whatsoever could be reposed in republican bona fides following the bank robbery, which was clearly an IRA operation. That the McCartney murder was entirely unauthorised by the IRA was revealed when that organisation issued a statement suggesting that it shoot the perpetrators – an offer that was about as helpful as Paisley's 'sackcloth and ashes' oration.

The onward march of Paisley's DUP continued. In the April 2005 election Westminster campaign, the Ulster Unionist Party was totally routed and left with only one member, Sylvia Hermon, ironically a Trimble loyalist whom Trimble had treated poorly. Trimble himself lost his seat. Flushed with victory, Paisley could consider concession. Crucially, he now gave up his insistence on photographs of IRA weapon destruction, settled for independent observers to verify it and long-fingered his 'sackcloth and ashes' demand. For its part, the IRA was increasingly drawn to the idea of a unilateral decommissioning, outside any imposed timetable, so that it could never be claimed that it had acted under pressure. On 26 September 2005 de Chastelain announced that the IRA arsenal had gone and that independent witnesses had been present to view its destruction. The way was cleared for new negotiations.

These took place at St Andrews in Scotland in October 2006. Over a three-day period several amendments to the legislation enacting the Good Friday Agreement were accepted. One notable one provided for Assembly authority to be imposed over both ministers and north–south bodies: another required a ministerial 'code' to be drawn up and put on a statutory basis. Amendments such as these went a long way towards enhancing the accountability of ministers and they were inserted at the insistence of the DUP who feared that nationalist ministers might take decisions that damaged the Unionist community. These changes were undoubtedly significant, but all talk by DUP politicians that through them they had 'buried' the Good Friday Agreement was wide of the mark. A date for the setting up of a power-sharing executive in March 2007 was agreed, though it too, like most deadlines in the peace process, had to be extended. Damagingly, however, almost everything to do with policing – as had been the case with decommissioning in the Good Friday Agreement – was to be left to another day. A target date in May 2008 for the devolution of policing and criminal justice came and went with few signs of a resolution in sight. Equally, instead of detailed proposals to boost the Northern Ireland economy, there was a minor concession on domestic rates for pensioners, and a vague commitment 'to establish the most favourable financial climate' for the new executive.

None the less that any sort of agreement to share power had been reached between such sworn enemies as Sinn Féin and the DUP struck most people as nothing short of incredible (and even reprehensible, for many blamed them both for keeping the murderous hatreds going for thirty years). One factor in promoting a settlement was the eighty-year-old Paisley's keen desire to take power before he died. A serious illness in 2004 seemed to have produced some sort of change of outlook in him: and having finally seen off his lifelong enemy – the Unionist Party – he knew that there could be no real opposition to him sitting down in government with Sinn Féin. He and Robinson genuinely believed that the St Andrews Agreement copperfastened the constitutional position of Northern Ireland. As for Adams and McGuinness, they too were getting on in years and cannot have relished the spectacle of yet another generation of Catholics embarking on yet another cycle of violence. They concluded a deal with Paisley because they were persuaded that the St Andrews Agreement and the institutions to be set up under it, were, in Adams's words, 'markers on the road to achieving . . . [the reunification of Ireland]'. Quite how the aspirations of Sinn Féin and the DUP could both be accommodated remained to be seen. Finally, both sides entered into an agreement because they were aware that the Republic had embarked on a remarkable economic odyssey which had left Northern Ireland trailing in its wake. Surely, there would be a major peace

7.15 The peacemakers? Martin McGuinness, Sinn Féin, Ian Paisley, Democratic Unionist Party, Tony Blair, British prime minister and Bertie Aherne, Taoiseach, at the setting up of the power-sharing executive in Northern Ireland in 2007. Harrison photography.

dividend which would help restore the usual pecking order on the island of Ireland, i.e. Northern Ireland as the United States and the Republic as Mexico.

The power-sharing executive finally met on 8 May 2007 (figure 7.15), and Ian Paisley, as first minister, followed by Martin McGuinness, as deputy first minister, each took the oath of office in which they both swore 'to uphold the rule of law based as it is on the fundamental principles of fairness, impartiality and democratic accountability, including support for policing and the courts'. Jonathan Powell, a key player in the negotiations over nearly ten years, and a witness to this momentous event, remarked that he 'felt dizzy and slightly faint, as if I had just finished pushing a very large boulder uphill'. However, compared to the burden of those tasked with promoting peace in Northern Ireland, Sisyphus had it easy. And even though Peter Robinson trumpeted that the devolved structure 'will last', there was every chance that the boulder might roll back.

Paisley bowed out of the executive after a year and was replaced as first minister by Peter Robinson. In general, harmony characterised relations between the DUP and Sinn Féin in the executive, at least in public; but such harmony was achieved through a complete refusal or inability to take tough decisions, and paralysis rather than dynamism mostly characterised the executive. For example, a decision could not be arrived at on education where the situation remained that while the 11-plus selection method for second-level education was scrapped, nothing was done to bring in a uniform procedure to replace it. More significantly, an impasse over policing threatened ultimately to bring down the entire structure. In February 2010, following marathon negotiations that revealed all too clearly the lack of trust at the heart of the power-sharing executive, Robinson and McGuinness agreed that responsibility for law and order would be devolved to the Assembly in April of that year. Further serious difficulties remained to be resolved concerning parading, while the continued existence of the IRA army council remained contentious. Moreover, the 'peace dividend' from devolved government proved short-lived. The worldwide economic recession has affected Northern Ireland as much, if not more, than elsewhere. As economic activity slackened and unemployment rose – and the new devolved government's response to both seemed both hesitant and unsure – disillusion appeared certain to increase.

Finally, while both nationalist and Unionist communities made sacrifices in terms of their aspirations, there remained a palpable sense that Catholics had benefited disproportionately over the previous thirty years. Catholics still harboured grievances that needed to be addressed, and the McCartney murder – and later the paramilitary murder of Paul Quinn – revealed clearly the terrifying speed with which the furies could be summoned up and the capacity for extreme violence that remained in Catholic communities. In addition, the republican splinter factions, the Real IRA, and the Continuity IRA both retained a capacity for violence that nothing apparently could diminish and the shooting of two soldiers and a policeman by republican dissidents in March 2009 was evidence of this. Overall, however, Catholics as Catholics generally have vastly improved their position in the Northern Ireland state. Their identity is safeguarded, their culture promoted and strict anti-discrimination and fair employment legislation are in force.

On the other hand, there remains a very large loyalist underclass, poorly educated, mostly unskilled and socially disadvantaged who harbour a belief that their position in Northern Ireland had drastically slipped, and that their culture is no longer valued. The capacity of this section of loyalism to make mayhem through its continued tolerance for paramilitarism should not be underestimated. While such a large reservoir of hatred, rancour and resentment remains in Northern Ireland, it is hard to feel optimistic. Equally, because the devolved structures of government were expressly designed to reflect and perpetuate the sectarianism that was at the heart of the Northern Ireland state, it is only possible to feel a sort of nervous confidence where the future is concerned.

NOTES

Chapter 1

This chapter draws extensively on Dáibhí Ó Cróinín (ed.), *A New History of Ireland*. Vol. 1, *Prehistoric and Early Ireland* (Oxford, 2005); Dáibhí Ó Cróinín, *Early Medieval Ireland, 400–1200* (Harlow, 1995); T. M. Charles Edward, *Early Christian Ireland* (Cambridge, 2000). Wendy Davies (ed.), *From the Vikings to the Normans* (Oxford, 2003) is valuable for the wider context.

1 Micheline Kerney Walsh, *'Destruction by Peace': Hugh O'Neill after Kinsale* (Armagh, 1986), p. 208; Ferghal McGarry, *Eoin O'Duffy: a Self-Made Hero* (Oxford, 2005), p. 285.

2 Ó Cróinín, *Early Medieval Ireland*, pp. 14–15.

3 For these documents see Charles Doherty, 'Latin writing in Ireland c400–c1200', in Seamas Deane *et al.*, *The Field-Day Anthology of Irish Writing* (3 vols., London, 1991), 1, pp. 61–8. I have found Liam de Paor's *St Patrick's World* (Dublin, 1996) particularly illuminating.

4 Ó Cróinín, *Early Medieval Ireland*, p. 25.

5 See the informative entry under 'Tara' in S. J. Connolly (ed.), *The Oxford Companion to Irish History* (Oxford, 1998), pp. 534–5.

6 Their letter to *The Times* was published on 27 June 1902; see the letter of Vincent Salafia of TaraWatch.org to the *Irish Times*, 4 February 2002.

7 Jeanne Sheehy, *The Rediscovery of Ireland's Past: the Celtic Revival, 1830–1930* (London, 1980), pp. 103–5. For the motorway controversy see www.Irishtimes.com.

8 E. A. Thompson, *Who Was St Patrick?* (London, 1985), p. 161.

9 On St Patrick's Day see especially Mike Cronin and Darryl Adair, *The Wearing of the Green: a History of St Patrick's Day* (London, 2002) and also Bridget McCormack, *Perceptions of St Patrick in Eighteenth-century Ireland* (Dublin, 2000).

10 Discussed by Ó Cróinín, *Early Medieval Ireland*, ch. 5.

11 See F. H. A. Aalen, Kevin Whelan and Matthew Stout, *Atlas of the Irish Rural Landscape* (Cork, 1997); B. J. Graham, 'Early medieval Ireland: settlement as an indicator of economic and social transformation, c500–1100', in B. J. Graham and Lindsay Proudfoot (eds.), *An Historical Geography of Ireland* (London, 1993), pp. 19–50.

12 Fergus Kelly, *A Guide to Early Irish Law* (Dublin, 1991 reprint).

13 Ó Cróinín, *Early Medieval Ireland*, p. 196.

Chapter 2

For this period see especially, Art Cosgrove (ed.), *A New History of Ireland*. Vol. II, *Medieval Ireland, 1169–1534* (Oxford, 1987); R. R. Davies, *The First English Empire: Power and Identities in the British Isles 1093–1343* (Oxford, 2002); Brendan Smith (ed.), *Britain and Ireland 900–1300: Insular Responses to Medieval European Change* (Cambridge, 1999); T. B. Barry, *The Archaeology of Medieval Ireland* (London, 1987); J. P. Mallory and T. E. McNeill, *The Archaeology of Ulster* (Belfast, 1991). Brendan Smith, *Colonisation and Conquest in Medieval Ireland: the English in Louth, 1170–1330* (Cambridge, 1999) is an important micro-study. Robin Frame, *Colonial Ireland 1169–1369* (Dublin, 1981) remains a classic.

1 For the wider context see Davies, *The First English Empire* and Robert Bartlett, *The Making of Europe: Conquest, Colonisation and Cultural Change, 950–1350* (London, 1993).
2 Giraldus Cambrensis [Gerald of Wales], *Expugnatio Hibernica: The Conquest of Ireland*, trans. A. B. Scott and F. X. Martin (Dublin, 1978).
3 *Expugnatio*, p. 231; see also Marie-Therese Flanagan, 'Irish and Anglo-Norman warfare in twelfth-century Ireland', in Thomas Bartlett and Keith Jeffery (eds.), *A Military History of Ireland* (Cambridge, 1996), pp. 52–75.
4 *Expugnatio*, p. 247.
5 See F. H. A. Aalen, Kevin Whelan and Matthew Stout (eds.), *Atlas of the Irish Rural Landscape* (Cork, 1997).
6 J. A. Watt, 'Gaelic polity and cultural identity', in *New History of Ireland*, II, p. 325.

Chapter 3

In this chapter I have drawn chiefly on the following outstanding works: T. W. Moody, F. X. Martin and F. J. Byrne, *A New History of Ireland*. Vol. III, *Early Modern Ireland, 1534–1691* (Oxford, 1976); N. P. Canny, *Making Ireland British, 1580–1650* (Oxford, 2001); S. J. Connolly, *Contested Island: Ireland 1460–1630* (Oxford, 2007); S. J. Connolly, *Divided Kingdom: Ireland, 1630–1800* (Oxford, 2008); S. G. Ellis, *Ireland in the Age of the Tudors, 1447–1603* (London, 1998); Colm Lennon, *Sixteenth Century Ireland* (Dublin, 2005); and Mary O'Dowd, *A History of Women in Ireland, 1500–1800* (Harlow, 2005). All of these provide detailed bibliographies for further reading.

1 The classic study of the dissolution in Ireland is Brendan Bradshaw, *The Dissolution of the Religious Orders in Ireland under Henry VIII* (Cambridge, 1974).
2 See Ciaran Brady, *The Chief Governors: the Rise and Fall of Reform Government in Tudor Ireland, 1536–1588* (Cambridge, 1994); D. B. Quinn, *The Elizabethans and the Irish* (Ithaca, New York, 1966).
3 Michael MacCarthy-Morrogh, *The Munster Plantation: English Migration to Southern Ireland, 1583–1641* (Oxford, 1986) remains the authoritative account.
4 On these matters see Allan Macinnes, *The British Revolution, 1629–1660* (Basingstoke, 2005); Padraig Lenihan, *Consolidating Conquest: Ireland, 1603–1727* (Harlow, 2008); David Scott, *Politics and War in the Three Stuart Kingdoms, 1637–49* (Houndsmills, 2004); Raymond Gillespie, *Seventeenth Century Ireland* (Dublin, 2006).

5 See Nicholas Canny, *Making Ireland British, 1580–1650* (Oxford, 2001); M. Percival-Maxwell, *The Outbreak of the Irish Rebellion of 1641* (Dublin, 1994); B. MacCuarta (ed.), *Ulster 1641: Aspects of the Rising* (Belfast, 1991).

6 See Jane H. Ohlmeyer, *Civil War and Restoration in the Three Stuart Kingdoms: the Career of Randal MacDonnell, Marquis of Antrim, 1609–1683* (Cambridge, 1993); M. O Siochrú, *Confederate Ireland, 1642–1649* (Dublin, 1999); T. O hAnnracháin, *Catholic Reformation in Ireland: the Mission of Rinuccini 1645–1649* (Oxford, 2002).

7 See Pádraic Lenihan (ed.), *Conquest and Resistance: War in Seventeenth Century Ireland* (Leiden, 2001); J. Scott Wheeler, *Cromwell in Ireland* (London, 2000).

8 T. C. Barnard, *Cromwellian Ireland: English Government and Reform in Ireland 1649–1660* (Oxford, 1975).

9 S. J. Connolly, *Religion, Law and Power: the Making of Protestant Ireland, 1660–1760* (Oxford, 1992).

10 For the war see especially John Childs, *The Williamite Wars in Ireland, 1688–1691* (London, 2007).

Chapter 4

1 Valuable interpretations of this period are Sean Connolly, *Divided Kingdom, Ireland 1630–1800* (Oxford, 2008); David Dickson, *New Foundations: Ireland 1660–1800* (Dublin, 1987); T. C. Barnard, *A New Anatomy of Ireland: the Irish Protestants, 1649–1770* (New Haven, 2003) and T. W. Moody and W. E. Vaughan, *A New History of Ireland*. Vol. IV, *Eighteenth-Century Ireland* (Oxford, 1986), all of which contain copious bibliographies.

2 See David Hayton, *Ruling Ireland, 1685–1742: Politics, Politicians, and Parties* (London, 2004); David Hayton (ed.), *The Irish Parliament in the Eighteenth Century: the Long Apprenticeship* (Edinburgh, 2001).

3 See Thomas Bartlett, '"A people made rather for copies than originals": the Anglo-Irish 1760–1800', *International History Review*, 12 (1990), pp. 11–25; Thomas Bartlett, *The Fall and Rise of the Irish Nation: the Catholic Question, 1690–1830* (Dublin, 1992); Thomas Bartlett, '"This famous island set in a Virginia sea": Ireland in the British empire, 1690–1801', in P. J. Marshall, *The Oxford History of the British Empire*. Vol. II, *The Eighteenth Century* (Oxford, 1998), pp. 253–75.

4 See Patrick McNally, *Parties, Patriots and Undertakers: Parliamentary Politics in early Hanoverian Ireland* (Dublin, 1997); Eoin Magennis, *The Irish Political System, 1740–1765* (Dublin, 2000).

5 See Thomas Bartlett, 'The origins and progress of the Catholic question, 1690–1800', in Thomas Power and Kevin Whelan (eds.), *Endurance and Emergence: Catholics in Ireland in the Eighteenth Century* (Dublin, 1990), pp. 1–20.

6 In addition to other works cited, see Martyn Powell, *Britain and Ireland in the Eighteenth Century Crisis of Empire* (Manchester, 2003).

7 See in particular, Vincent Morley, *Irish Opinion and the American Revolution, 1760–1783* (Cambridge, 2002).

8 James Kelly, *Prelude to Union: Anglo-Irish politics in the 1780s* (Cork, 1992); A. P. W. Malcomson, *John Foster: the Politics of the Anglo-Irish Ascendancy* (Oxford, 1978).

9 See Nancy Curtin, *The United Irishmen: Popular Politics in Ulster and Dublin, 1791–1798* (Oxford, 1994); Marianne Elliott, *Partners in Revolution: the United Irishmen and France* (New Haven, 1982); D. Dickson, D. Keogh and K. Whelan (eds.), *The United Irishmen: Republicanism, Radicalism and Rebellion* (Dublin, 1993).

10 Daniel Gahan, *The People's Rising, Wexford 1798* (Dublin, 1995); Tom Dunne, *Rebellions: Memoir, Memory, and 1798* (Dublin, 2004); Guy Beiner, *Remembering the Year of the French: Irish Folk History and Social Memory* (Madison, Wis., 2007); T. Bartlett, D. Dickson, D. Keogh and K. Whelan (eds.), *1798: A Bicentenary Perspective* (Dublin, 2003).

11 Patrick Geoghegan, *The Irish Act of Union: a Study in High Politics, 1798–1801* (Dublin, 1999).

12 In this section I have drawn freely on my *Acts of Union, an inaugural lecture delivered at University College Dublin on 24 February 2000* (Dublin, 2000).

13 See Bartlett, *The Fall and Rise of the Irish Nation*, chs. 13 and 14; W. E. Vaughan, *A New History of Ireland*. Vol. v, *Ireland, 1800–1870* (Oxford, 1989) especially chs. 1–4 by Sean Connolly, and the works cited earlier.

14 Samuel Clark and James S. Donnelly Jr. (eds.), *Irish Peasants: Violence and Political Unrest 1780–1914* (Manchester, 1983).

15 Fergus O'Ferrall, *Catholic Emancipation: Daniel O'Connell and the Birth of Irish Democracy* (Dublin, 1985): see also Oliver MacDonagh's two-volume biography, *Daniel O'Connell* (London, 1988–9).

Chapter 5

Important surveys of this period on which I have drawn are Paul Bew, *Ireland: the Politics of Enmity, 1789–2006* (Oxford, 2007); D. George Boyce, *Nineteenth Century Ireland: the Search for Stability* (London, 1990); the same author's *Ireland 1828–1923: from Ascendancy to Democracy* (Oxford, 1992); Oliver MacDonagh, *States of Mind: a Study of Anglo-Irish Conflict 1780–1980* (London, 1983); Alvin Jackson, *Ireland 1798–1998* (Oxford, 1999); the same author's *Home Rule: an Irish History 1800–2000* (London, 2003); K. Theodore Hoppen, *Ireland since 1800: Conflict and Conformity* (London, 1999); Cormac O Gráda, *A New Economic History of Ireland, 1780–1939* (Oxford, 1994); Pauric Travers, *Settlements and Divisions: Ireland, 1870–1922* (Dublin, 1988); W. E. Vaughan (ed.), *A New History of Ireland*. Vol. v: *Ireland under the Union I: 1801–1870* (Oxford, 1989); David Fitzpatrick, *Irish Emigration, 1801–1921* (Dundalk, 1984); F. S. L. Lyons, *Ireland since the Famine* (2nd edn, London, 1973); Maria Luddy, *Prostitution and Irish Society, 1800–1940* (Cambridge, 2007); Caitriona Clear, *Social Change and Everyday Life in Ireland, 1850–1922* (Manchester, 2007).

1 See Richard Davis, *The Young Ireland Movement* (Dublin, 1987); D. G. Boyce, *Nationalism in Ireland* (London, 1991).

2 Peter Gray, *Famine, Land and Politics: British Government and Irish Society 1843–50* (Dublin, 1999); Cathal Póirtéir (ed.), *The Great Irish Famine* (Cork, 1995); James Donnelly Jr, *The Great Irish Potato Famine* (Stroud, Gloucs., 2001); Cormac O Gráda, *The Great Irish Famine* (Dublin, 1989); Timothy Guinnane, *The Vanishing Irish: Households, Migration, and the Rural Economy in Ireland, 1850–1914* (Princeton, 1997).

3 See Philip Bull, *Land, Politics and Nationalism: a Study of the Irish Land Question* (Dublin, 1996).

4 See Owen McGee, *The IRB* (Dublin, 2005); Matthew Kelly, *The Fenian Ideal and Irish Nationalism* (London, 2008); Vincent Comerford, *The Fenians in Context: Irish Politics and Society 1848–82* (Dublin, 1985).

5 In addition to works cited earlier, I have drawn on Síghle Bhreathnach-Lynch, *Ireland's Art, Ireland's History: Representing Ireland, 1845 to Present* (Omaha, Nebr., 2005); Keith Jeffery (ed.), *An Irish Empire? Aspects of Ireland and the British Empire* (Manchester, 1996); Kevin Kenny (ed.), *Ireland and the British Empire* (Oxford, 2004); James H. Murphy, *Abject Loyalty: Nationalism and Monarchy in Ireland during the Reign of Queen Victoria* (Cork, 2001).

6 In this section I have drawn principally on W. E. Vaughan (ed.), *A New History of Ireland*. Vol. VI: *Ireland under the Union II: 1870–1921* (Oxford, 1996); C. Cruise O'Brien, *Parnell and his Party, 1880–1890* (Oxford, 1957); F. S. L. Lyons, *Charles Stewart Parnell* (London, 1977); T. W. Moody, *Davitt and Irish Revolution, 1846–82* (Oxford, 1981); Alvin Jackson, *The Ulster Party: Irish Unionists in the House of Commons, 1884–1911* (Oxford, 1989); Alvin Jackson, *Colonel Edward Saunderson, Land and Loyalty in Victorian Ireland* (Oxford, 1995); Alvin Jackson, *Sir Edward Carson* (Dundalk, 1993); Paul Bew, *John Redmond* (Dundalk, 1996); Paul Bew, *Ideology and the Irish Question: Ulster Unionism and Irish Nationalism, 1912–16* (Oxford, 1994); Paul Bew, *C. S. Parnell* (Dublin, 1980); Tom Garvin, *Nationalist Revolutionaries in Ireland, 1858–1928* (Oxford, 1987); Michael Wheatley, *Nationalism and the Irish Party: Provincial Ireland, 1910–1916* (Oxford, 2005); Senia Paseta, *Before the Revolution: Nationalism, Social Change and Ireland's Catholic Élite, 1879–1922* (Cork, 1999); D. George Boyce (ed.), *The Revolution in Ireland, 1879–1923* (London, 1988); D. George Boyce and Alan O'Day (eds.), *The Ulster Crisis, 1885–1921* (Basingstoke, Hants, 2006); D. George Boyce and Alan O'Day (eds.), *Ireland in Transition, 1867–1921* (London, 2004); Andrew Gailey, *Ireland and the Death of Kindness: Constructive Unionism, 1890–1905* (Cork, 1987); Richard T. Shannon, *Gladstone* (2 vol., London, 1982–99); Margaret O'Callaghan, *British High Politics and Nationalist Ireland: Criminality, Land and Law under Forster and Balfour* (Cork, 1994); Eunan O'Halpin, *The Decline of the Union: British Government in Ireland, 1892–1920* (Dublin, 1987); Rosemary Cullen Owens, *A Social History of Women in Ireland, 1870–1970* (Dublin, 2005).

7 Samuel Clark, *Social Origins of the Irish Land War* (Princeton, 1979); James S. Donnelly Jr, *The Land and People of Nineteenth Century Cork: the Rural Economy and the Land Question* (London, 1975); Charles Townshend, *Political Violence in Ireland: Government and Resistance since 1848* (Oxford, 1983); W. E. Vaughan, *Landlords and Tenants in mid-Victorian Ireland* (Oxford, 1994).

8 See F. L. S. Lyons, *Culture and Anarchy: Ireland 1890–1939* (Oxford, 1979); and especially R. F. Foster, *W. B. Yeats: a Life* (2 vols., Oxford, 1997–2003).

Chapter 6

Valuable surveys of Irish history in the twentieth century on which I have drawn in this and the next chapter include David Fitzpatrick, *The Two Irelands 1912–1939* (Oxford, 1998); Dermot Keogh, *Twentieth Century Ireland: Nation and State* (Dublin, 1994);

John A. Murphy, *Ireland in the Twentieth Century* (new edn, Dublin, 1989); Tom Garvin, *Preventing the Future: Why was Ireland so Poor for so Long?* (Dublin, 2005); Diarmaid Ferriter, *The Transformation of Ireland, 1900–2000* (Dublin, 2004); J. R. Hill (ed.), *A New History of Ireland.* Vol. VII: *Ireland 1921–1984* (Oxford, 2003); J. J. Lee, *Ireland, 1912–1984* (Cambridge, 1987); Terence Brown, *Ireland: a Social and Cultural History, 1922–2002* (London, 2004). The works by Bew, *Ireland: the Politics of Enmity*, and by Jackson, *Ireland, 1798–1998*, both cited earlier, are central.

1 Charles Townshend, *Easter 1916: the Irish Rebellion* (London, 2005); Gabriel Doherty and Dermot Keogh, *1916: the Long Revolution* (Cork, 2007); Michael Laffan, *The Resurrection of Ireland: the Sinn Féin Party 1916–1923* (Cambridge, 1999); K. B. Nowlan (ed.), *The Making of 1916: Studies in the History of the Rising* (Dublin, 1969).

2 John Horne and Alan Kramer, *German Atrocities, 1914: a History of Denial* (New Haven, 2001).

4 I have followed Charles Townshend, *The British Campaign in Ireland 1919–1921* (Oxford, 1975); David Fitzpatrick, *Politics and Irish Life, 1913–1921* (new edn, Cork, 1998); Peter Hart, *The IRA and its Enemies: Violence and Community in Cork, 1916–1923* (Oxford, 1998); Peter Hart, *The IRA at War* (Oxford, 2003); Joost Augusteijn, *From Public Defiance to Guerilla Warfare: the Experience of Ordinary Volunteers in the Irish War of Independence, 1916–1921* (Dublin, 1996); Michael Hopkinson, *Green against Green: the Irish Civil War* (Dublin, 1988); Bill Kissane, *The Politics of the Irish Civil War* (Oxford, 2005); Joost Augusteijn (ed.), *The Irish Revolution 1913–23* (Basingstoke, Hants, 2002); Peter Hart, *Mick, the Real Michael Collins* (London, 2005); Diarmaid Ferriter, *Judging Dev: a Re-assessment of the Life and Legacy of Eamon de Valera* (Dublin, 2007).

4 See Keith Jeffery, *Field Marshal Sir Henry Wilson: a Political Soldier* (Oxford, 2006) for the wider imperial context.

5 Thomas Hennessy, *A History of Northern Ireland 1920–1996* (Dublin, 1997); David Harkness, *Northern Ireland since 1920* (Dublin, 1983); Ronan Fanning, *Independent Ireland* (Dublin, 1983); Marianne Elliott, *The Catholics of Ulster: a History* (London, 2000); Enda Staunton, *The Nationalists of Northern Ireland, 1918–1973* (Dublin, 2001); Eamon Phoenix, *Northern Nationalism: Nationalist Politics, Partition and the Catholic Minority in Northern Ireland, 1890–1940* (Belfast, 1994); Nicholas Mansergh, *The Unresolved Question: the Anglo-Irish Settlement and its Undoing, 1912–72* (New Haven, 1991); John M. Regan, *The Irish Counter-revolution, 1921–36* (Dublin, 1999); Bill Kissane, *Explaining Irish Democracy* (Dublin, 2002).

6 In addition to works cited earlier see Richard Dunphy, *The Making of Fianna Fáil Power in Ireland, 1923–48* (Oxford, 1995).

7 See Fearghal McGarry, *Eoin O'Duffy, a Self-made Hero* (Oxford, 2005).

8 In addition to works cited earlier, I have relied on Dermot Keogh and Andrew McCarthy, *The Making of the Irish Constitution. 1937: Bunreacht na hEireann* (Cork, 2007).

9 Brian Girvin, *The Emergency: Neutral Ireland 1939–45* (London, 2006); Brian Girvin and Geoffrey Roberts (eds.), *Ireland and the Second World War: Politics, Society and Remembrance* (Dublin, 2000); Clair Wills, *That Neutral Island: a Cultural History of Ireland during the Second World War* (London, 2007).

Chapter 7

In addition to the works by Brown, Ferriter, Hennessy, Lee, Garvin, Hill, and Fanning cited in the previous chapter I have drawn on principally: Mary E. Daly, *The Slow Failure; Population Decline and Independent Ireland, 1920–73* (Wisconsin, 2006); Jonathan Powell, *Great Hatred, Little Room: Making Peace in Northern Ireland* (London, 2008); Richard English, *Irish Freedom: a History of Nationalism in Ireland* (London, 2007); Richard English, *Armed Struggle: a History of the IRA* (London, 2005); R. F. Foster, *Luck and the Irish: a Brief History of Change, 1970–2000* (London, 2007); Steve Bruce, *God Save Ulster: the Religion and Politics of Paisleyism* (Oxford, 1989); Gerry Adams, *Falls Memories* (Tralee, 1984); Henry Patterson, *Ireland since 1939* (London, 2006); Don Akenson, *Conor: a Biography of Conor Cruise O'Brien* (Montreal and Kingston, 1994); Garret FitzGerald, *All in a Life: an Autobiography* (Dublin, 1991). Valuable eye-witness accounts of the 'Troubles' can be found in Eamonn McCann's *War in an Irish Town* (London, 1980) and Kevin Myers, *Watching the Door: Drinking up, Getting down, and Cheating death in 1970s Belfast* (Dublin, 2006).

INDEX

31901047469095